W9-BKC-572

NINTH EDITION

accounting principles

C. ROLLIN NISWONGER, PhD, CPA
Professor of Accountancy
Miami University, Oxford, Ohio

PHILIP E. FESS, PhD, CPA
Associate Professor of Accountancy
University of Illinois, Urbana

PUBLISHED BY

SOUTH-WESTERN PUBLISHING COMPANY
Cincinnati • Chicago
Dallas • New Rochelle, N. Y.
Burlingame, Calif.

Library of Congress Catalog Card Number 65-13807

K967 Printed in the United States of America

Preface

This ninth edition of *Accounting Principles* retains the emphasis of earlier editions on basic concepts of accounting and uses of accounting data. It is designed for students who plan to continue with additional courses in the field as well as for those whose needs are limited to an introductory course.

Greater attention has been given in this edition to analyses and reports for the use of management in planning and controlling operations. The increased emphasis on decision-making has been accompanied by a reduction in the time devoted to procedural aspects of accounting. There remains, however, sufficient coverage of the techniques of data processing to provide the foundation for an adequate understanding of the basics of systems design and internal controls.

Some of the subjects in the preceding edition have been omitted, the treatment of others has been condensed or expanded, and entirely new topics have been introduced — all in recognition of modern tendencies and developments in accounting practice. The subject of general manufacturing accounting has been eliminated and the coverage of cost accounting has been expanded to achieve a more logical and sophisticated presentation of theory and procedures. The treatment of standards and budgetary controls has been enlarged, and such topics as direct costing, cost-volume-profit analysis, evaluations of proposed capital expenditures, and differential analysis are also included.

The discussion of partnership accounting has been rewritten and compressed into a single chapter without omitting any of the basic essentials of income distribution, admission or withdrawal of partners, or settlements among partners upon liquidation. Changes in sequence have permitted the inclusion of corporation income taxes and materials on capital gains and losses. The effect of income taxes on business decisions and the importance of considering alternative courses of action are stressed both in the narrative and in many of the questions and problems.

The explanatory and illustrative materials on the funds statement follow an entirely new format. The traditional techniques that teach proficiency in the preparation of funds statement working papers have been completely discarded and replaced by an approach that emphasizes the meaning of funds source and application. Reliance upon memorization of a technique is replaced by understanding of basic principles. New materials on cash flow analysis and on consolidated statements have been added. As in the case of the funds statement, an entirely new approach to consolidated statements has been employed, attention being directed to the underlying principles of consolidation rather than to specialized working papers.

An appendix on automated data processing describes modern methods of processing accounting data by the use of mechanical and electronic devices. Applications of wide usage are illustrated. The discussion concludes with a description of an integrated system.

Accounting Principles, the pioneer in multicolor printing, continues in this edition the judicious use of color in directing attention to important relationships, emphasizing data that might otherwise be overlooked, and identifying principal headings.

The number of questions, exercises, and problems has been substantially increased to provide greater flexibility in demonstrating applications of the concepts presented. Problems for use in alternate sections of the course, for use in alternate years, or for review purposes are provided in an appendix. The problem materials reproduced in the correlating working papers have been markedly increased, with a consequent saving of time for the student.

Four short practice sets, each containing transactions for a single month, may be used in developing greater student proficiency or for review purposes. Each set is briefly described in the table of contents of this volume. Workbooks of study guides, transparencies, and other teaching aids are also available.

We are greatly indebted to many teachers who have given suggestions based on their use of earlier editions. Space limitations prohibit a listing of all who have made significant contributions over the years. Special recognition is due, however, to a number of persons who submitted detailed recommendations based upon a review of the eighth edition or of manuscript for this ninth edition. We acknowledge with thanks the contributions made by Professors Edwin Cohen, DePaul University; John E. Field, University of Auckland; Emerson O. Henke, Baylor University; Harold Q. Langenderfer, University of North Carolina; Vern E. Odmark, San Diego State College; Harry R. Price and J. Everett Royer, University of Miami; Franklyn H. Sweet, Kent State University; and Silvan A. Tesoriere, Fordham University.

We are also grateful to the American Institute of Certified Public Accountants for permission to use materials from their copyrighted publications and to the corporations whose financial statements are reproduced in Appendix C.

C. Rollin Niswonger

Philip E. Fess

Contents

PAGE

PART ONE

Basic structure of accounting

1. Fundamental accounting relationships

Need for accounting

Accounting is often characterized as "the language of business." It is the "language" employed to communicate financial information. There are a variety of reasons why such information is sought. Owners and prospective owners of a business need to know about the financial status of the enterprise and the outlook for the future. Before granting credit to a business organization, bankers and suppliers of commodities and services appraise its financial soundness and the risks involved. Government agencies are concerned with the financial activities of business organizations for purposes of taxation and regulation. Employees are also vitally interested in the stability and the profitability of the organization that employs them.

It is through accounting that the manager is kept informed about the operations of an enterprise. The manager of a small business may be thoroughly familiar with all operating and financial details and hence require relatively little accounting information. As the size of a business unit increases, however, the manager becomes farther and farther removed from direct contact with day-to-day transactions. He must be supplied with timely information about various aspects of the business. Much of the needed information is financial in nature. The growth of large business units and of the importance of accounting in such organizations has given rise to the expression that accounting provides the "eyes and ears of management."

The accountant has the responsibility of keeping track of the essential dollars-and-cents information affecting the organization, of interpreting the information in terms of relative success or failure, and of helping to plan the course of future action.

Relationship to other fields

Individuals engaged in such areas of business as finance, production, marketing, personnel, and general management need not be expert accountants, but their usefulness is enhanced and their advancement is more assured if they have a good understanding of accounting principles. Everyone engaged in business activity, from the youngest employee to the manager and owner, comes into contact with accounting. The higher the level of authority and responsibility, the greater is the need for an understanding of accounting concepts and terminology.

Many other persons with specialized training in nonbusiness areas who are employed by business organizations also make use of accounting data and need to understand accounting principles. For example, an engineer responsible for selecting the most desirable solution to a technical manufacturing problem may consider cost accounting data to be the decisive factor. Lawyers use accounting data in tax cases and in lawsuits involving property ownership and damages from breach of contract. Governmental agencies rely on accounting data in evaluating the efficiency of government operations and for appraising the desirability of proposed revenue and expenditure programs. Also, every adult engages in business transactions and must necessarily be concerned with the financial aspects of his own life, and perhaps of others. Accounting plays an important role in modern society and, broadly speaking, it can be said that all citizens are affected by accounting. The closer the contact with financial activity, of course, the greater the need for an understanding of accounting concepts and terminology.

Profession of accountancy

Accountancy is a profession with stature comparable to that of law or engineering. The tremendous development of accounting theory and technique during the current century has been accompanied by an ever-increasing number of professionally trained accountants. Among the factors contributing to this growth have been the increase in number, size, and complexity of business corporations; the imposition of new and more complex taxes, especially since the adoption of the Federal Income Tax Amendment in 1913; and the restrictions imposed on business operations by governmental regulations.

Accountants who render accounting services on a fee basis, and staff accountants employed by them, are said to be engaged in *public accounting*. Accountants employed by a particular business firm, perhaps as chief accountant or controller, are said to be engaged in *private accounting*.

Recognizing the need for reliable professional accounting service, all the states have enacted laws providing for the licensing of certified public accountants, commonly called CPA's. Only those individuals who have met the qualifications and received a license may designate themselves as CPA's.

The qualifications required for the CPA certificate differ in the various states. All states require a specified level of education, often the completion of a collegiate course of study in accounting. In most states the applicant must have had from one to three years' experience in public accounting or in accounting work considered equivalent. In all states candidates must successfully pass a uniform examination prepared by the American Institute of Certified Public Accountants, the national organization of CPA's. The examination covers the subjects of auditing, commercial law, theory of accounts, and accounting practice. A few states also require candidates to pass an examination in an additional subject, such as business economics, governmental accounting, or taxation.

Although all states provide for the licensing of CPA's, many of them do not restrict the practice of public accounting to those so licensed. In the absence of express prohibition, any person may style himself as a public accountant, or P.A. Details regarding the requirements of any specific state can be obtained from the state board of accountancy or other agency charged with administering the law.

The scope of activities and responsibilities of private accountants varies quite widely. Private accountants are concerned with the financial records of a particular business enterprise or nonprofit organization. They are frequently referred to as administrative or executive accountants, or, if they are employed by a manufacturing concern, as industrial accountants. Various branches of federal, state, and local governments also employ accountants in increasing numbers. Many CPA's are engaged in private accounting. The accounting division of business enterprises has long been recognized as a training ground for business executives, and many high positions in industry and government are held by professional accountants.

Specialized accounting fields

As in many other areas of human activity in the twentieth century, accountants have developed a number of specialized fields. This tendency toward specialization has been caused in large measure by growth in size of business units, mounting taxes, and increasing regulation of business by law and by governmental agencies. These influences, together with rapid technological advances and accelerated economic growth, have created the need for a high degree of expertness in various specialties.

The term *general accounting* or *financial accounting* applies to the overall accounting for an economic unit. It is concerned with the recording of transactions for a business or other economic unit and the periodic preparation of statements from these records. The various general purpose and special purpose reports and statements prepared from the accounting records are used to impart useful information to managers, owners, creditors, governmental agencies, and the general public. The accounting principles and techniques that will be developed in this book are in large part included in general accounting.

Auditing represents a field of accounting activity that independently reviews general accounting. Auditing was the first service rendered by public accountants and is still one of their principal activities. These accountants examine records and statements and express an opinion regarding their fairness and accuracy. Large corporations with widely dispersed operations frequently employ their own staffs of *internal auditors.* One of the most important duties of internal auditors is to determine whether the various operating divisions observe the policies and procedures prescribed by management.

Cost accounting emphasizes the determination and the control of costs, particularly the costs of manufacturing processes and of manufactured products. It deals with actual costs to be reported on financial statements. In addition, one of the principal functions of the cost accountant is to assemble and interpret cost data, both actual and prospective, for the use of management in controlling current manufacturing operations and in planning for the future.

Management accounting employs both historical and estimated data in assisting management with day-to-day problems and planning for the future. It deals with specific problems that confront enterprise managers at various organizational levels and functional fields. The management accountant is frequently concerned with locating alternative courses of action and then helping to select the best one. For example, he may assist the company treasurer in preparing plans for future financing, or he may develop data for the use of the sales manager in determining the selling price to be placed on a new product. In recent years, public accounting firms have come to realize that their training and experience uniquely qualify them to advise management on policies and administration, even in matters that on the surface seem to have little relationship to accounting. This rapidly growing field of specialization by CPA's is frequently called *management services.*

Tax accounting includes the preparation of tax returns and the consideration of the tax consequences of proposed business transactions. Accountants specializing in this field must be familiar with the tax statutes affecting their employer or clients and also must keep up to date on administrative regulations and court decisions.

Accounting systems is the special field concerned with the creation of accounting and office procedures for the accumulation and the reporting of financial data. The systems accountant may select or design the forms to be used by the enterprise. He must also be familiar with the uses and the relative merits of available mechanical and electronic data processing equipment.

Budgetary accounting presents the plan of financial operations for a period and, through accounts and summaries, provides comparisons of actual operations with the predetermined plan. It is a combination of planning, coordination, and control of future operations.

Governmental accounting specializes in the transactions of political units, such as states and municipalities. It seeks to provide useful accounting information with regard to the business aspect of public administration, and it helps to control the expenditure of public funds according to law or legislative dictates.

Accounting instruction is perhaps the most obvious field of specialization. In addition to teaching, many accounting professors engage in auditing, tax accounting, or other areas of accounting on a part-time or consulting basis.

There is some overlapping among the various specialties, and leaders in any particular field are likely to be well versed in related fields. There is also some specialization within the specialized fields. For example, within the field of auditing one may become an expert in a particular classification such as department stores or public utilities; in tax accounting one may specialize in the problems of oil and gas producing companies; or in systems one may become an expert in electronic data processing equipment.

Principles and practice

In accounting, as in the physical and biological sciences, experimentation, development, and change are never-ending. Capable scholars devote their lives and their intellectual energies to analyzing accounting phenomena. Experienced professional accountants contribute their best thinking to the solution of problems forever confronting their clients or employers. The several professional accounting associations regard research as a major activity. It is from such research that accounting principles evolve to form the underlying basis for accounting practice.

This book is devoted both to explanations of accounting principles and to demonstrations of related practices or procedures. It is through this duality of emphasis on the "why" of accounting as well as on the "how" that the full significance of accounting is learned.

Accounting defined

In a general way, the purpose of accounting may be said to be to provide information concerning property and the rights to property, and to show how property and the rights to it have been affected by business operations. More specifically, accounting has been described as:

> ...the art of recording, classifying, and summarizing in a significant manner and in terms of money, transactions and events which are, in part at least, of a financial character, and interpreting the results thereof.[1]

Recording commits the transactions and events to writing. The recording may be in the form of pen or pencil markings made by hand or it may be accomplished by various mechanical and electronic devices. Hence, "writing" is meant to include information recorded in various media such as magnetic impressions or holes in cards or tapes.

Classifying involves sorting the many transactions in an orderly and systematic manner. Special forms and procedures are devised to facilitate this process. A mass of isolated transactions conveys little meaning when considered individually; the data become useful only when sorted according to predetermined classes. Transactions must be understood before they can be classified. It is therefore of paramount importance that the student of accounting gain a thorough understanding of the effect of all types of transactions upon property and property rights.

Summarizing brings the accounting data together in a form that further enhances their usefulness. It is not the single business act but the sum of all the operations of a day, a week, a month, or a year that has the greatest significance. Therefore, summaries of operations and their effect on property and rights to property are prepared at intervals. These reports are made to the managers of the enterprise and to others who need the information. Some reports must be made frequently; others, only at longer intervals. For example, it may be desirable to have a daily summary of transactions affecting cash, while an annual report of transactions affecting buildings may be satisfactory.

Interpreting the results of operations, as summarized in the various reports, is an essential part of accounting. Interpretation frequently takes the form of percentage analyses and ratios. Comparisons between different dates and periods of time may reveal important trends. From these

---

[1]*Accounting Research and Terminology Bulletins, Final Edition,* "No. 1, Review and Resume," 1961 (New York: American Institute of Certified Public Accountants), p. 9.

ratios and trends, the most significant developments in the affairs of a business may be explained, emphasized, and guided.

Bookkeeping and accounting

There is some confusion over the distinction between "bookkeeping" and "accounting." This is due in part to the fact that the two are related and that there is no universally accepted line of demarcation between them.

In general, *bookkeeping* is the recording of business data in a prescribed manner. A bookkeeper may be responsible for keeping all of the records of a business or only a small segment, such as a portion of the customers' accounts in a department store. Much of the work of the bookkeeper is clerical in nature.

Accounting is primarily concerned with the design of the system of records, the preparation of reports based on the recorded data, and the interpretation of the reports. Accountants often direct and review the work of bookkeepers. The larger the firm, the greater is the number of gradations in responsibility and authority. The work of accountants at the beginning levels may include some bookkeeping. In any event, it is apparent that the accountant must possess a much higher level of knowledge and analytical skill than is required of the bookkeeper.

Accounting entity

Accounting always applies to an economic organization or unit in society. Economic units include profit-making businesses; governmental units, such as states, cities, and school districts; consumers, such as families and individuals; and social organizations, such as churches, hospitals, and clubs. Each economic unit has business transactions that must be recorded, classified, summarized, and interpreted. The accounting must therefore apply to each unit. For example, it is each particular automobile manufacturer, not the automobile industry as a whole, that has business transactions.

The *accounting entity* concept does not mean, however, that accounting data for a particular unit cannot be combined with data for other similar units to obtain an overall picture. For example, accounting data accumulated by each airline in the country may be assembled to provide financial information about the entire airline industry. Similarly, figures for national income and for the combined state and federal debt may be developed from the accounting records of many separate economic units.

Although accounting principles and techniques have been developed for all types of economic units, this textbook emphasizes those applicable to profit-making business enterprises. Such enterprises may be organized in a variety of ways. The principal forms of organization are sole proprietorship, partnership, and corporation. A *sole proprietorship* is a business that is owned entirely by one individual. A *partnership* is an enterprise owned by two or more individuals in accordance with a contractual arrangement among them. A *corporation* is a separate legal entity, organized in accordance with state or federal statutes, in which ownership is divided into shares of stock. The principal difference among the three types of organization, from the standpoint of accounting, lies in the nature of the ownership and in the legal rights and responsibilities related to it.

The accounting principles developed in the early chapters of this textbook are based on the sole proprietorship form of organization. It is the simplest type of business organization and by far the most common. Later chapters will be devoted to variations in accounting related to the other two forms of organization.

Basic business operations

The use of property is essential to the conduct of business. A place for the business must be provided in a building that is owned or rented; equipment adapted to the activities of the business must be owned or leased; if goods are sold, they must be purchased or manufactured and kept in stock prior to sale; if services are rendered, the equipment and the supplies needed to render the services must be available for use. Wherever there is business, property is found.

Through the sale of commodities or services at a profit, business operations usually produce funds that may be used to purchase additional property as the business expands. These funds constitute an important element in the total property of the business. If a business is conducted in such a way that its total ownership increases, the business is said to be successful. In contrast, if its operations result in a decrease in its ownership, the business is considered to be unsuccessful.

The primary purpose of business enterprise, then, is to make a profit. Those who invest in business firms do so with the expectation that they will receive benefits in the form of income. They also incur the risk of losing part or all of their investment.

Business transactions and business records

A *business transaction* is the occurrence of an event or of a condition that must be recorded. For example, the payment of a monthly telephone bill of $25, the purchase of $500 of merchandise on credit, and the acquisition of land and a store building for $100,000 are illustrative of the variety of business transactions.

The first two transactions are relatively simple, being a payment of money in exchange for a service and a promise to pay within a short time in exchange for commodities. The purchase of a building and the land on which it is situated is usually a more complex transaction. The total price agreed upon must be allocated between the land and the building, and the agreement usually provides for spreading the payment of a substantial part of the price over a period of years and for the payment of interest on the unpaid balance. There may be other special provisions designed to safeguard the seller until the full price has been paid.

It can readily be seen that a particular business transaction may lead to an event or a condition that constitutes another transaction. For example, the purchase of merchandise on credit referred to above will be followed by payment to the creditor, which is another transaction; and each time a portion of the merchandise is sold, another transaction occurs. Each of these events needs to be recorded. Each payment to the seller of the land and the building is a transaction, as is the payment of interest. The fact that the building will not last forever must also be given recognition in the records.

The wearing-out of the building is not an exchange of goods or services between the business and an outsider, but it is nevertheless a significant event that must be recorded. Transactions of this type, as well as others not directly related to outsiders, are sometimes referred to as *internal* transactions.

The system of records begins with the recording of each transaction. There are many different methods of recording transactions. For example, a sale of a service for cash may be recorded by a handwritten sales ticket, or it may be recorded by merely depressing the appropriate keys of a cash register. Regardless of the recording system used, the historical data thus accumulated provide the basis for the preparation of various summarizing reports. In addition, the supporting documents and other forms of evidence furnish a basis for subsequent review and verification by internal auditors, independent CPA's, and government auditors. Throughout this textbook a variety of supporting documents will be discussed and illustrated.

Role of accounting in business decisions

Knowledge of the past performance of an enterprise is of additional value beyond its historical aspects; it is useful in planning future operations. By comparing summaries of the most recent month with the preceding month and with the comparable month of the preceding year, trends become apparent. Further study and analysis may develop the contributory causes of the trends and point the way to accelerating those that are favorable and to halting those that are undesirable. For example, an increase in the volume of services or merchandise sold is a favorable indication. If the increase is accompanied by increases in costs and expenses of such magnitude that net income is decreased, the end result is, of course, unfavorable. Questions such as the following should be answered: Was the increased volume of sales attributable to excessive reductions in selling price? Did the cost of the merchandise increase without a comparable adjustment in selling price? Which expenses increased and what were the causes of the increases? Which increases were unavoidable and which ones can be reduced in the future without adverse effects?

A business that is contemplating expansion needs to give careful consideration to the probable effect of the added facilities on future volume of business and expenses. Will the return on the additional investment justify the expansion? There may also be problems of financing. If money is to be borrowed, when can it be repaid? These are illustrations of the many problems that constantly confront business managers in planning future operations. Business records do not supply all of the answers, nor do they take the place of good judgment. The data obtainable from the records are essential, however, as a partial basis for making decisions.

There are many other needs of a more routine nature served by records. For example, it is necessary to know the amount owed to each creditor and by each customer and the date each payment is due. Records of property are necessary in determining the amount and type of insurance that should be carried and in ascertaining the amount of any insured loss that may occur. Knowing when to place orders for merchandise and supplies, granting credit to customers, anticipating the amount of cash required at any particular time — these and many other essential items of information can be obtained in a timely and orderly fashion only if adequate records are maintained.

In addition to managers and owners, there are others who must be supplied with reports based on the business records. Banks customarily require periodic statements from businesses from which they have loans outstanding. It is customary to submit annual reports to credit-rating companies. Many branches of federal, state, and local governments require reports, particularly in connection with income, property, sales, social security, and other taxes. One of the prerequisites to the issuance of securities by corporations is the filing of detailed reports on business operations and financial position with governmental agencies. Stock exchanges also require periodic reports from corporations whose stocks are listed. The foregoing reasons for preparing accounting reports for outsiders are merely illustrative; there are many others.

Thus far attention has been focused on business enterprises. Records are also needed by those engaged in professional pursuits and even by persons who have retired from active participation in a business or profession. Governmental units need records of their transactions; they are required to report to other units at a higher level of authority and also to the citizenry. In addition, performance in the past serves as a basis for future planning. Lodges, clubs, churches, educational institutions, labor unions, and other organizations need to maintain records and report on their financial transactions.

Business transactions and monetary amounts

When properties or services are purchased by a business, the amount at which they are recorded is the price agreed upon in the business transaction. For example, if a business building is purchased for $50,000, that amount is used in the buyer's accounting records. The seller may have been asking $60,000 for the building up to the time of sale; the buyer may have initially offered $40,000 for it; the building may have been assessed at $35,000 for property tax purposes and insured for $45,000; and the buyer may have received an offer of $75,000 for the building the day after he acquired it. These latter amounts have no effect on the accounting records because they do not originate from an exchange transaction. The transaction price, or cost, of $50,000 determines the basis at which the building is recorded. Cost results from the actions of an informed buyer and an informed seller who are each attempting to obtain the most favorable price. It is an objective fact that can be verified from the evidence created by an exchange transaction; it is not a mere subjective opinion.

The offer of $75,000 for the building is an indication that it was a bargain at $50,000; but to record the building at $75,000 would give recognition to a fictitious profit of $25,000. If the purchaser should accept the offer of $75,000 and sell the building, there would then be a new accounting amount for the new owner. The building would be entered on the accounting records of the new owner at his cost of $75,000 and, of course, the seller would realize a profit of $25,000 on the sale.

Accounting is fundamentally a process of accounting for costs and revenues; it is not a process of valuation. Only the amount agreed upon between buyer and seller in a transaction is sufficiently objective for accounting purposes. If upward and downward adjustments to properties were made on the basis of mere offers, appraisals, and opinions, accounting records would soon become so unstable and unreliable as to be meaningless.

Assets, liabilities, and capital

The use of property in the operation of a business has been emphasized. It has also been pointed out that accounting deals with property and rights to property. For every business enterprise, the sum of the properties owned is equal to the sum of the rights to the properties.

The properties owned by a business are called *assets*. The rights to the properties are called *equities*. The relationship between assets and equities may therefore be stated in the equation:

Assets = Equities

Equities may be subdivided into two principal types: the rights of creditors and the rights of owners. The equities of creditors represent *debts* of the business and are called *liabilities*. The equity of the owner is called *capital*, *proprietorship*, or *owner's equity*. Expansion of the equation to give recognition to the two basic types of equities yields the following, which is known as the *accounting equation*:

Assets = Liabilities + Capital

It is customary to place "Liabilities" before "Capital" in the accounting equation because creditors have preferential rights to the assets. The residual claim of the owner or owners may be given greater emphasis by transposing liabilities to the other side of the equation to yield:

Assets − Liabilities = Capital

All business transactions, regardless of their complexity, can be stated in terms of their effect on the three basic elements of the accounting equation.

Transactions and the accounting equation

The effect of changes in assets, liabilities, and capital on the accounting equation can be demonstrated by studying some typical transactions. As the basis of the illustration we will assume that Roy Ward establishes a new business under the name of Ward Taxi. Each transaction or group of similar transactions during the first month of operations will be described and the effect on the accounting equation shown.

(a) Ward's first transaction is to deposit $9,000 in a bank account in the name of Ward Taxi. The effect of this transaction is to increase the asset cash by $9,000 and to increase capital, on the other side of the equation, by the same amount. After the transaction the equation for Ward Taxi will appear as follows:

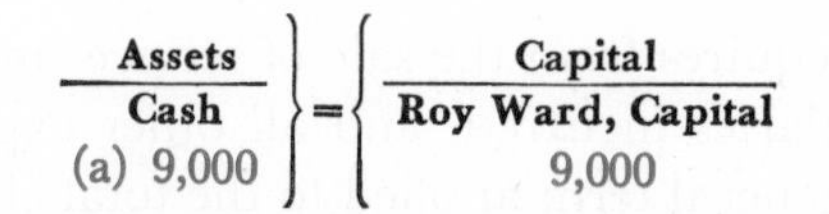

Assets	=	Capital
Cash		Roy Ward, Capital
(a) 9,000		9,000

It should be noted that the equation applies only to the business enterprise. Ward's personal assets, such as his home and his personal bank account, and his personal liabilities are excluded from consideration. Accounting is concerned only with the business as a separate entity.

(b) Ward's next transaction in establishing his business is to purchase automobiles and other equipment, for which he pays $7,400 in cash. This transaction changes the composition of the assets but does not change the total. The items in the equation prior to this transaction, this transaction, and the new balances after the transaction are as follows:

	Assets			=	Capital
	Cash	+	Equipment		Roy Ward, Capital
Bal.	9,000				9,000
(b)	−7,400		+7,400		
Bal.	1,600		7,400		9,000

(c) During the month Ward purchases $650 of gasoline, oil, and other supplies from various businesses, agreeing to pay in the near future. This type of transaction is called a purchase *on account* and the liability created is termed an *account payable.* In actual practice each transaction would be recorded as it occurred and a separate record would be maintained for each creditor. The effect of this group of transactions is to increase assets and liabilities by $650, as indicated below:

	Assets					=	Liabilities	+	Capital
	Cash	+	Supplies	+	Equipment		Accounts Payable	+	Roy Ward, Capital
Bal.	1,600				7,400				9,000
(c)			+650				+650		
Bal.	1,600		650		7,400		650		9,000

(d) During the month Ward pays $300 to his creditors on account, thereby reducing both assets and liabilities. The effect on the equation is as follows:

	Assets					=	Liabilities	+	Capital
	Cash	+	Supplies	+	Equipment		Accounts Payable	+	Roy Ward, Capital
Bal.	1,600		650		7,400		650		9,000
(d)	− 300						−300		
Bal.	1,300		650		7,400		350		9,000

The principal objective of the owner of a business enterprise is to increase his capital by earning a net income. For Roy Ward this means that the assets he acquires from the sale of services must exceed the cost of supplies used, salaries incurred, and all other expenses of operating the business. The general term applied to the total charges to customers for goods or services sold is *revenue.*[2] Other more specific terms may be used for particular types of revenue, such as *sales* for the sale of merchandise or business services, *fees earned* for charges by a physician to his patient, *rent earned* for the use of real estate or other property, and *fares earned* for Ward's business.

The excess of the revenue over the expenses incurred in earning the revenue is called *net income.* If the expenses of the enterprise exceed the revenue, the excess is a *net loss.* As it is ordinarily impossible to determine the exact amount of expense incurred in connection with each revenue transaction, it is considered satisfactory to determine the net income or the net loss for a specified period of time, such as a month or a year, rather than for each sale or small group of sales.

(e) Continuing with the illustration of transactions completed by Roy Ward, his records indicate that during the first month of operations he earned taxi fares of $2,000, for which he received cash. The total effect of these transactions is to increase cash by $2,000 and to yield revenue in the same amount. Although the revenue of $2,000 is not wholly an increase in capital, it is customary to treat it as such. When expenses are incurred, they are treated as offsets against revenue and hence as reductions in capital. In terms of the accounting equation, the effect of the receipt of cash for services performed is as follows:

	Assets			=	Liabilities +	Capital	
	Cash +	Supplies +	Equipment		Accounts Payable +	Roy Ward, Capital	
Bal.	1,300	650	7,400		350	9,000	
(e)	+2,000					+ 2,000	Fares earned
Bal.	3,300	650	7,400		350	11,000	

Instead of requiring the payment of cash at the time goods or services are sold, a business may make sales *on account,* allowing the customer to pay later. In such cases the firm acquires an asset called *accounts receivable* and realizes revenue in exactly the same manner as though cash had been received. When the money is collected from the customer later, the asset cash increases and the asset accounts receivable decreases.

(f) Various business expenses incurred and paid during the month were as follows: wages, $550; rent, $50; utilities, $25; miscellaneous, $75. The effect of this group of transactions is to reduce cash and to reduce capital, as indicated in the following equation:

[2] *Accounting Research and Terminology Bulletins, Final Edition,* "No. 2, Proceeds, Revenue, Income, Profit, and Earnings," 1961 (New York: American Institute of Certified Public Accountants), p. 34.

	Assets				Liabilities +	Capital	
	Cash +	Supplies +	Equipment		Accounts Payable +	Roy Ward, Capital	
Bal.	3,300	650	7,400	=	350	11,000	
(f)	− 700					− 550	Wages exp.
						− 50	Rent expense
						− 25	Utilities exp.
						− 75	Misc. expense
Bal.	2,600	650	7,400		350	10,300	

(g) At the end of the month Ward determines that the cost of the supplies on hand is $250, the remainder ($650 − $250) having been used in the operations of the business. This reduction of $400 in supplies and capital may be shown as follows:

	Assets				Liabilities +	Capital	
	Cash +	Supplies +	Equipment		Accounts Payable +	Roy Ward, Capital	
Bal.	2,600	650	7,400	=	350	10,300	
(g)		−400				− 400	Supplies exp.
Bal.	2,600	250	7,400		350	9,900	

(h) Although Ward has used the automobile and other equipment throughout the month, there is no apparent reduction in the amount on hand as was the case with the supplies. It is obvious, however, that the equipment does gradually lose its usefulness with the passage of time. The expiration of usefulness represents a business expense, which is called *depreciation.* It has the effect of decreasing both assets and capital. For reasons that will become apparent in a later chapter, it is customary to keep a cumulative record of the recognized depreciation rather than to deduct it directly from the equipment. The effect on the equation of the estimated depreciation expense of $200 is as follows:

	Assets					Liabilities +	Capital	
	Cash +	Supplies +	Equipment −	Accumulated Depreciation		Accounts Payable +	Roy Ward, Capital	
Bal.	2,600	250	7,400		=	350	9,900	
(h)				+200			− 200	Depr. exp.
Bal.	2,600	250	7,400	200		350	9,700	

Although the balance of $7,400 shown for equipment is unchanged, the remaining cost of the asset is clearly only $7,200, shown as follows:

Equipment	$7,400	
Less accumulated depreciation	200	$7,200

It should be noted that the addition of $200 to accumulated depreciation on the left side of the equation represents a decrease in assets and that it is matched by the $200 decrease in capital on the right side of the equation.

(i) The final transaction to be considered is the withdrawal of $500 cash by Ward for personal use. This transaction has the same effect on the equation as the payment of expenses in transaction (f). It is different in one important particular, however; it is not a business expense and is therefore not considered in determining the net income from operations of the business. The balances in the equation, the withdrawal of $500, and the new balances are as follows:

	Assets				=	Liabilities +	Capital	
	Cash +	Supplies +	Equipment −	Accumulated Depreciation	=	Accounts Payable +	Roy Ward, Capital	
Bal.	2,600	250	7,400	200		350	9,700	
(i)	− 500						− 500	Drawing
Bal.	2,100	250	7,400	200		350	9,200	

Summary of illustration

The business transactions of Roy Ward are summarized in tabular form below. The transactions are identified by letter, and the balance of each item is shown after each transaction. Note the following:

(1) For all business enterprises, the effect of every transaction can be stated in terms of increases and/or decreases in one or more of the elements of the accounting equation.

(2) For all business enterprises, the two sides of the accounting equation are always equal.

	Assets				=	Liabilities +	Capital	
	Cash +	Supplies +	Equipment −	Accumulated Depreciation	=	Accounts Payable +	Roy Ward, Capital	
(a)	+9,000						+ 9,000	
(b)	−7,400		+7,400					
	1,600		7,400				9,000	
(c)		+650				+650		
	1,600	650	7,400			650	9,000	
(d)	− 300					−300		
	1,300	650	7,400			350	9,000	
(e)	+2,000						+ 2,000	Fares earned
	3,300	650	7,400			350	11,000	
(f)	− 700						− 550	Wages exp.
							− 50	Rent expense
							− 25	Utilities exp.
							− 75	Misc. expense
	2,600	650	7,400			350	10,300	
(g)		−400					− 400	Supplies exp.
	2,600	250	7,400			350	9,900	
(h)				+200			− 200	Depr. expense
	2,600	250	7,400	200		350	9,700	
(i)	− 500						− 500	Drawing
	2,100	250	7,400	200		350	9,200	

Accounting statements

The principal accounting statements are the *balance sheet* and the *income statement.* They are usually accompanied by a less important, but nevertheless useful, statement called the *capital statement.* The three statements may be described in general terms as follows:

Balance sheet
A list of the assets, liabilities, and capital of a business entity as of a specific date, usually at the close of the last day of a month.

Income statement
A summary of the revenue and the expenses of a business entity for a specific period of time, such as a month or a year.

Capital statement
A summary of the changes in capital of a business entity that have occurred during a specific period of time, such as a month or a year.

The basic features of the three statements and their interrelationships are illustrated on page 18. The data for the statements were taken from the summary of transactions of Ward Taxi presented in the preceding section.

All financial statements should be identified by the name of the business, the title of the statement, and the date or period of time. The data presented in the balance sheet are for a specific date; the data presented in the income statement and the capital statement are for a period of time.

The use of indentions, captions, dollar signs, and rulings in the financial statements should be noted. They are employed to accentuate the several distinct sections of the various statements.

Balance sheet. The amounts of Ward Taxi's assets, liabilities, and capital at the end of the first month of operations appear on the last line of the summary on page 16. Minor rearrangements of these data and the addition of a heading yield the balance sheet illustrated on page 18. This form of balance sheet, with the liability and capital sections presented below the asset section, is called the *report form.* Another arrangement in common use lists the assets on the left and the liabilities and capital on the right. Because of its similarity to the account, a basic accounting device described in the next chapter, it is referred to as the *account form* of balance sheet.

It is customary to begin the asset section with cash, which is followed by receivables, supplies, and other assets, such as prepaid expenses, that will be converted into cash or consumed in the near future. The assets of a relatively permanent nature, such as equipment, buildings, and land, follow in that order.

Ward Taxi
Balance Sheet
August 31, 1965

Assets		
Cash		$2100 00
Supplies		250 00
Equipment	$7400 00	
Less accumulated depreciation	200 00	7200 00
Total assets		$9550 00
Liabilities		
Accounts payable		$350 00
Capital		
Roy Ward, capital		9200 00
Total liabilities and capital		$9550 00

Balance sheet — report form

Ward Taxi
Income Statement
For Month Ended August 31, 1965

Fares earned		$2000 00
Operating expenses:		
Wages expense	$550 00	
Supplies expense	400 00	
Depreciation expense	200 00	
Rent expense	50 00	
Utilities expense	25 00	
Miscellaneous expense	75 00	
Total operating expenses		1300 00
Net income from operations		$700 00

Income statement

Ward Taxi
Capital Statement
For Month Ended August 31, 1965

Capital, August 1, 1965		$9000 00
Net income for the month	$700 00	
Less withdrawals	500 00	
Increase in capital		200 00
Capital, August 31, 1965		$9200 00

Capital statement

In the liabilities and capital section of the balance sheet, it is customary to present the liabilities first, followed by capital. In the illustration on page 18 the liabilities are composed entirely of accounts payable. When there are two or more categories of liabilities, each should be listed and the total amount of liabilities shown, as in the following illustration:

Liabilities		
Notes payable	$ 600	
Accounts payable	1,500	
Salaries payable	100	
Total liabilities		$ 2,200
Capital		
Thomas R. Norton, capital		14,700
Total liabilities and capital		$16,900

Income statement. Ward's revenue and expenses during the month were recorded in the equation as changes in capital. The details, together with net income in the amount of $700, are reported in the income statement on page 18.

The order in which the operating expenses are presented in the income statement varies among businesses. One of the arrangements commonly followed is to list them approximately in the order of size, beginning with the larger items. Miscellaneous expense is usually shown as the last item regardless of amount.

Capital statement. Comparison of the original investment of $9,000 at the beginning of the month with the $9,200 of capital reported in the balance sheet at the end of the month reveals an increase in capital of $200. This net increase is composed of two significant changes in capital that occurred during the period: net income of $700 and withdrawals of $500 by the owner. This information is presented in the capital statement on page 18, which serves as a connecting link between the two principal statements.

Accounting periods

The interval of time between accounting statements varies among businesses. The maximum length of the accounting period is ordinarily one year, which includes a complete cycle of the seasons and of business activities. Income and property taxes are also based on yearly periods and thus require that annual reckonings be made.

The shortest accounting period is customarily one month. Many businesses prepare financial statements at the end of each month. In addition to the balance sheet as of the last day of the month and an income statement for the month, it is common practice to prepare an income statement for the entire period since the beginning of the year. The accompanying capital statements could report details either for the year to date or for the most recent month only. If the former alternative is adopted, the statements that would be prepared for the first three months of a business year beginning on January 1 would be as follows:

At the end of January
Balance sheet as of January 31
Income statement for January 1–31
Capital statement for January 1–31

At the end of February
Balance sheet as of February 28
Income statement for February 1–28
Income statement for January 1–February 28
Capital statement for January 1–February 28

At the end of March
Balance sheet as of March 31
Income statement for March 1–31
Income statement for January 1–March 31
Capital statement for January 1–March 31

The annual accounting period adopted by an enterprise is known as its *fiscal year.* Fiscal years ordinarily begin with the first day of any particular month and end on the last day of the twelfth month hence. The period most commonly adopted is the calendar year, beginning on January 1 and ending on December 31, but other periods are not infrequently elected, particularly by incorporated businesses.

The long-term financial history of a business enterprise may be depicted by a succession of balance sheets prepared at yearly intervals. The history of operations for the intervening periods is presented in a series of income statements. Serving as a connecting link between these two principal statements is the capital statement. If the life of a business enterprise is represented by a line moving toward the right, accounting statements may be diagrammed as follows:

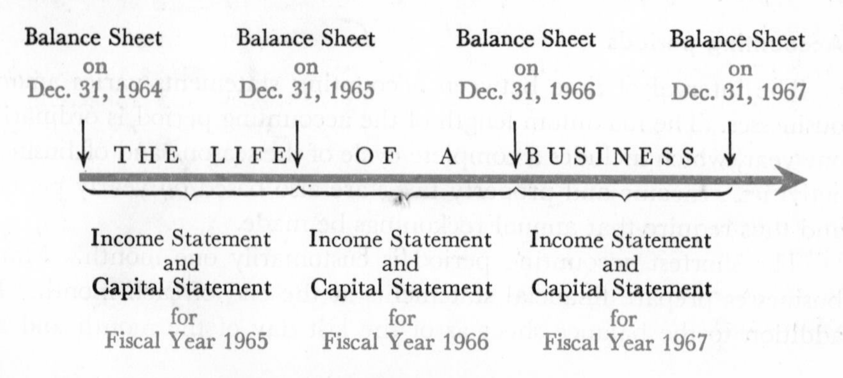

QUESTIONS

1. Why is a knowledge of accounting concepts and terminology useful to all individuals engaged in business activities?

2. Distinguish between public accounting and private accounting.

3. Describe in general terms the requirements that an individual must meet to become a CPA.

4. Explain briefly the recording, classifying, summarizing, and interpreting phases of accounting.

5. What is meant by the *accounting entity* concept?

6. What are the three principal forms of profit-making business organizations and in what principal respect do they differ, so far as accounting is concerned?

7. Is the meaning of "business transaction" restricted solely to an exchange or a contract between an enterprise and outsiders? Discuss.

8. In what way are accounting reports of past performance useful to the owner or manager in making plans for the future?

9. Distinguish between *cost* and *value* and explain their relative significance in accounting.

10. Two years ago Thomas Booth acquired for $30,000 land that had an assessed value for tax purposes of $19,000. Today the assessed valuation is $26,000 and he has an opportunity to sell the land for $40,000. (a) At what amount should the land have been recorded by Booth at the time of acquisition? (b) What recognition should be given in the accounting records to today's values? Discuss.

11. (a) If the liabilities and the capital of an enterprise amount to $10,000 and $20,000 respectively, what is the total amount of the assets owned?
(b) If the assets and the capital of an enterprise amount to $30,000 and $18,000 respectively, what is the total amount owed to creditors?
(c) If the assets and the liabilities of an enterprise amount to $40,000 and $15,000 respectively, what is the amount of the owner's capital?

12. State the possible effects on the three elements in the accounting equation of a transaction that (a) decreases an asset and (b) decreases a liability.

13. John Burton sold for $6,000 a vacant lot that he had originally purchased for $4,000 and had not yet paid for. How did this transaction affect the total amount of his (a) assets, (b) liabilities, and (c) capital?

14. Service sales for an enterprise during a month totaled $8,000, of which $5,000 were for cash and the remainder were on account. Expenses incurred during the same month totaled $6,000, of which $5,000 were paid in cash and the remainder were on account. What was the amount of the enterprise's (a) revenue, (b) total expenses, and (c) net income from operations?

15. Indicate for each of the following whether it is for a particular date or for a period of time: (a) income statement, (b) balance sheet, (c) capital statement.

16. What is (a) the report form of balance sheet? (b) the account form of balance sheet?

17. What item, for a service business, appears on (a) both the income statement and the capital statement, and (b) both the balance sheet and the capital statement?

18. The following facts relate to the operations of Westvale Company for the fiscal year just ended: net income, $26,000; withdrawals by owner during year, $12,000 (no additional investments); increase in total assets at end of year as compared with beginning of year, $8,000. What was the amount and the direction of the year's change in (a) capital and (b) total liabilities?

19. David Green's income statement for the month of October indicates a net income of $1,200. During the same period he withdrew $1,400 in cash from the business for personal use. Would it be correct to say that Green incurred a *net loss* of $200 during the month?

EXERCISES

1. The following selected transactions were completed by the M. & H. Laundry during the month of September:

(a) Purchased supplies on account, $160.
(b) Paid rent for September, $100.
(c) Purchased laundry equipment for cash, $600.
(d) Paid miscellaneous expenses, $60.
(e) Paid creditors on account, $110.
(f) Charged customers for services sold on account, $170.
(g) Received $350 from cash customers.
(h) Received $120 from customers on account.
(i) Withdrew $150 in cash for personal use.
(j) Determined by taking an inventory that $130 of supplies had been used during the month.

Copy the following description of transactions and list after each the identifying letter of each of the above transactions that fits the description:

(1) Increase in one asset, decrease in another asset.
(2) Increase in an asset, increase in a liability.
(3) Increase in an asset, increase in capital.
(4) Decrease in an asset, decrease in a liability.
(5) Decrease in an asset, decrease in capital.

2. A list of transactions for the J. L. Davis Company is presented below. Indicate the increase or the decrease (+ or −) in assets, liabilities, and capital resulting from each transaction. Tabulate your answers, using Assets, Liabilities, and Capital as column headings.

(a) Paid a liability.
(b) Rendered services on account.
(c) The owner, J. L. Davis, invested additional cash in the business.
(d) Paid advertising expense.
(e) Purchased equipment on account.
(f) The owner, J. L. Davis, withdrew cash.
(g) Returned defective equipment originally purchased on account and not yet paid for.
(h) Purchased a car on account for personal use of the owner, J. L. Davis.

3. Summary financial data of Bluefield Enterprises (a service business) for November are presented in the following equation. Each line designated by a letter indicates the effect of a transaction on the equation. Only transactions (c), (e), (f), and (g) affect revenue and expenses.

(1) Describe each transaction.
(2) What is the amount of increase in cash for the month?
(3) What is the amount of the net income for the month?
(4) How much of the net income was retained in the business?

	Cash +	Supplies +	Equipment −	Accumulated Depreciation =	Liabilities +	Capital
	2,000	3,000	8,000	2,000	1,000	10,000
(a)	− 200				− 200	
	1,800	3,000	8,000	2,000	800	10,000
(b)	− 300		+ 300			
	1,500	3,000	8,300	2,000	800	10,000
(c)	+ 2,600					+ 2,600
	4,100	3,000	8,300	2,000	800	12,600
(d)		+ 100			+ 100	
	4,100	3,100	8,300	2,000	900	12,600
(e)	− 800					− 800
	3,300	3,100	8,300	2,000	900	11,800
(f)		− 600				− 600
	3,300	2,500	8,300	2,000	900	11,200
(g)				+ 100		− 100
	3,300	2,500	8,300	2,100	900	11,100
(h)	− 500					− 500
	2,800	2,500	8,300	2,100	900	10,600

4. The total assets and the total liabilities of a business at the beginning and the end of a year were as follows:

	Assets	*Liabilities*
Beginning of year..........................	$30,000	$10,000
End of year..............................	45,000	15,000

Determine the net income from operations for the year under each of the following assumptions:

(a) There had been no additional investments and no withdrawals by the owner during the year.
(b) The owner had withdrawn $8,000 during the year.
(c) The owner had made no withdrawals but had made an additional investment of $3,000 during the year.
(d) The owner had withdrawn $6,000 and had made an additional investment of $20,000 during the year.

5. Fielding Co. manufactures a product at a unit cost of 50 cents and sells it at a unit price of 95 cents. Annual sales have averaged 1,000,000 units and total annual operating expenses have been approximately $220,000. On the basis of a study of markets, costs, and expenses it is concluded that (1) reduction of the selling price to 85 cents would result in a 50% increase in the number of units sold, (2) a 50% increase in production would result in a cost reduction of 5 cents a unit, (3) a 50% increase in volume would be accompanied by a 25% increase in operating expenses, and (4) the increased volume would not require the investment of additional funds in the business.

Assuming the correctness of the study, determine whether the reduction in price would increase or decrease net income from operations, and the amount.

PROBLEMS

1-1. On August 1 of the current year James Benton established an enterprise under the name Benton Realty. Transactions completed during the month were as follows:

(a) Opened a business bank account with a deposit of $1,000.
(b) Purchased equipment (desk, chairs, filing cabinet, etc.) for $1,200, paying cash of $500 with the balance on account.
(c) Purchased supplies (stationery, stamps, pencils, ink, etc.) for cash, $50.
(d) Paid office rent for the month, $200.
(e) Earned sales commissions, receiving cash, $900.
(f) Paid creditor on account, $300.
(g) Paid automobile expenses (including rental charge) for month, $110, and miscellaneous expenses, $60.
(h) Withdrew cash from the bank account for personal use, $300.
(i) Determined by taking an inventory that the cost of supplies used was $5.
(j) Estimated depreciation on the equipment to be $20.

Instructions: (1) Record the transactions and the balances after each transaction, using the following tabular headings:

Assets					Liabilities		Capital
			Accumulated	=	Accounts	+	James Benton,
Cash +	Supplies +	Equipment −	Depreciation		Payable		Capital

Indicate the nature of each increase and decrease in capital subsequent to the initial investment by appropriate notations at the right of each change.

(2) Prepare an income statement for August, a capital statement for August, and a balance sheet as of the end of August.

1-2. On January 1 of the current year the amount of Henry Sherman's capital in Sherman Co. was $29,870. During the year he made weekly cash withdrawals of $300 (total of $15,600). The amounts of the enterprise's assets and liabilities at December 31 of the current year and of its revenue and expense for the year ended on that date are listed below.

Accounts payable	$ 3,740
Accounts receivable	7,550
Advertising expense	3,340
Building	36,300
Accumulated depreciation — building	17,900
Cash	6,320
Depreciation expense — building	960
Depreciation expense — equipment	1,310
Equipment	14,640
Accumulated depreciation — equipment	8,410
Insurance expense	840
Land	2,100
Miscellaneous expense	1,480
Prepaid insurance	1,640
Sales	61,630
Salaries payable	170
Salary expense	21,750
Supplies	1,980

Supplies expense	$1,820
Taxes expense	2,630
Taxes payable	610
Utilities expense	2,070

Instructions: (1) Prepare an income statement for the current fiscal year ending December 31, exercising care to include each item of expense listed.
(2) Prepare a capital statement for the current fiscal year.
(3) Prepare a balance sheet as of December 31 of the current fiscal year.

1-3. H. J. Barker operates a business known as Gem Dry Cleaners. The actual work of dry cleaning is done by another company at wholesale rates. The assets and the liabilities of the business on June 1 of the current year are as follows: Cash, $1,000; Accounts Receivable, $300; Supplies, $80; Equipment, $4,600; Accumulated Depreciation, $1,100; Accounts Payable, $640. His business transactions during June are summarized below.

(a) Paid rent for June, $150.
(b) Paid creditors on account, $520.
(c) Purchased supplies on account, $60.
(d) Received $1,100 from cash customers for dry cleaning sales.
(e) Charged customers for dry cleaning sales on account, $550.
(f) Received monthly invoice of $800 for dry cleaning expense (to be paid by July 10).
(g) Received $520 from customers on account.
(h) Reimbursed a customer $22 for a garment lost by the cleaning company, which agreed to deduct the amount from the invoice received in transaction (f).
(i) Paid the following: wages expense, $120; truck expense, $55; utilities expense, $20; miscellaneous expense, $25.
(j) Purchased an item of equipment on account, $30.
(k) Paid personal expenses by checks drawn on the business, $360, and withdrew $50 in cash for personal use.
(l) Determined by taking an inventory that $15 of supplies had been used during the month.
(m) Estimated depreciation of equipment (including truck) for the month at $75.

Instructions: (1) State the assets, liabilities, and capital as of June 1 in equation form similar to that shown in this chapter.
(2) Record the transactions in tabular form, determining the new balances after each transaction. Identify increases and decreases in capital by appropriate notations.
(3) Prepare an income statement, a capital statement, and a balance sheet.

1-4. On October 1 of the current year John Lee established a business enterprise. The transactions of the business for the three months ending on December 31 are summarized below.

(a) Deposited cash in a business bank account	$12,000

(b) Purchased a going business operating under the name of Superior Parcel Delivery.

Assets acquired:		
Accounts receivable	$ 2,800	
Automobile supplies	650	
Office supplies	50	
Trucks	12,500	$16,000
Liabilities assumed:		
Accounts payable		1,000
Terms of payment to be made:		
Cash	$ 9,000	
Four non-interest-bearing notes payable of $1,500 each, due at three-month intervals	6,000	$15,000

(c) Charged delivery service sales to customers on account	$11,000
(d) Purchased automobile supplies on account	1,300
(e) Purchased office supplies on account	70
(f) Received cash from customers on account	10,000
(g) Paid creditors on account	1,600
(h) Paid first of the four notes payable	1,500
(i) Paid license taxes in advance	420
(j) Paid insurance premiums in advance	1,280
(k) Purchased automobile supplies for cash	130
(l) Paid drivers' wages	3,800
(m) Paid rent expense	360
(n) Paid utilities expense	90
(o) Paid repairs expense	210
(p) Paid miscellaneous expenses	80
(q) Paid to Lee as personal withdrawals	1,350
(r) Automobile supplies used	1,400
(s) Office supplies used	20
(t) Depreciation of trucks	720
(u) Insurance expired	300
(v) Taxes expired	100

Instructions: (1) List the following captions in a single line at the top of a sheet turned sideways.

Cash + **Accounts Receivable** + **Automobile Supplies** + **Office Supplies** + **Prepaid Insurance** + **Prepaid Taxes** + **Trucks**

− **Accumulated Depreciation** = **Notes Payable** + **Accounts Payable** + **John Lee, Capital** **Capital Notations**

(2) Record Lee's original investment and the remaining transactions in the appropriate columns, identifying each by letter. Indicate increases by + and decreases by −. *Do not determine the new balances of the items after each transaction.* In the space for capital notations, identify each revenue and expense item and withdrawals by the owner.

(3) Insert the final balances in each column and determine that the equation is in balance at December 31, the end of the period.

(4) Prepare the following: (a) income statement for the three months, (b) capital statement for the three months, and (c) balance sheet as of December 31. (The name of the business was not changed.)

2.

Ledger and trial balance

Recording transactions

The transactions completed by a business during any fiscal period effect many changes in the various asset, liability, and capital items. In order to prepare periodic financial statements, it is necessary that the results of each transaction be recorded in a systematic manner. It is the purpose of this chapter to describe and illustrate the ledger, which is a basic record in the system known as double-entry accounting.

The effect of each transaction could be shown by the use of the accounting equation, as was done in Chapter 1, or the financial statements could be revised after each transaction. It is not necessary, however, that the owner or the manager be informed of the effect of each individual transaction. Information about the effects of groups of similar transactions is usually sufficient for his purpose. Consequently, a separate record is maintained for each item that is to appear on the financial statements. At periodic intervals the individual records are summarized and the data thus obtained are presented in the balance sheet, the income statement, and the capital statement.

The form of record used for each individual item is called an *account*, and a group of related accounts is called a *ledger*. For example, an enterprise might have thirty accounts, each one being a record of a particular asset, liability, capital, revenue, or expense item. The thirty accounts would be referred to collectively as the ledger.

Nature of an account

The simplest form of an account has three parts: (1) a title, which is the name of the item recorded in the account; (2) a space for recording increases in the amount of the item, in terms of money; and (3) a space for recording decreases in the amount of the item, also in monetary terms. This form of an account, illustrated below, is known as a *T account* because of its similarity to the letter T. Other account forms that provide spaces for recording additional information are illustrated later. Regardless of form, however, the three basic parts of an account are a title, a section for increases, and a section for decreases.

TITLE	
Left or *debit* side	Right or *credit* side

T account

The left side of the account is called the *debit* side and the right side is called the *credit* side. The word *charge* is frequently used as a synonym for debit. Amounts entered on the left side of an account, regardless of the account title, are called *debits* or *charges* to the account, and the account is said to be *debited* or *charged.* Amounts entered on the right side of an account are called *credits,* and the account is said to be *credited.*

CASH		
	3,000	500
	2,500	1,000
	4,000	2,500
4,300	9,500	300
		900
		5,200

In the illustration at the left, receipts of cash during a period of time have been listed in vertical order on the debit side of the cash account. The cash payments for the same period have been listed in similar fashion on the credit side of the account. This arrangement for recording the increases and the decreases in cash facilitates the determination of the totals of each. The total of the cash receipts, $9,500, is shown in small pencil figures to distinguish it from debits to the account. The total of the cash payments, $5,200, is also shown in small pencil figures so that it will not be confused with the credits to the account. (The process of adding a formal column of figures and recording the temporary total is called *pencil footing.*) Finally, by subtracting $5,200, the sum of the credits, from $9,500, the sum of the debits, the difference of $4,300 is obtained. The difference between the total debits and the total credits in an account is termed the *balance.* In this case the cash account has a debit balance of $4,300. This temporary balance is placed on the debit side of the account beside the pencil footing. If a balance sheet were to be prepared at this time, the amount of cash to be reported thereon would be $4,300.

Accounts and the balance sheet

The relationship of accounts to the balance sheet can be observed from a study of the following illustrations.

(a) On September 1, 1965, T. J. Scott deposited $2,600 cash in a bank account for use in a business venture to be known as Scott TV Service. Immediately after the money was deposited, the balance sheet for the business, in account form, would appear as follows:

Scott TV Service
Balance Sheet
September 1, 1965

Assets		*Capital*	
Cash.	$2,600	T. J. Scott, Capital.	$2,600

The transaction could be recorded in accounts by debiting Cash and crediting T. J. Scott, Capital as follows:

CASH

(a)	2,600		

T. J. SCOTT, CAPITAL

		(a)	2,600

Note that the title of each account is written above the horizontal line. The title is descriptive of the data to be recorded in the account. It is not necessary to label the two sides of the accounts, inasmuch as the left side is *always* the debit side and the right side is *always* the credit side.

The amount of the asset Cash, which is on the left side of the account form of balance sheet, was recorded on the left or debit side of the cash account. The amount of the capital, which is on the right side of the balance sheet, was recorded on the right or credit side of the account T. J. Scott, Capital. Similarly, all other assets are entered on the left or debit side of appropriate accounts; all other capital increases and all liabilities are entered on the right or credit side of appropriate accounts. The balances of all of the accounts can then be conveniently assembled to form a balance sheet, with the assets on the left and the liabilities and the capital on the right.

(b) Scott TV Service purchased supplies for $700 in cash. This transaction resulted in the acquisition of a new asset, Supplies. The cost of this new asset, like that of any other asset, was recorded on the left or debit side of an account. The transaction also resulted in a decrease in the asset Cash. This decrease was entered on the right or credit side of the cash account. After this transaction was recorded, the ledger appeared as follows:

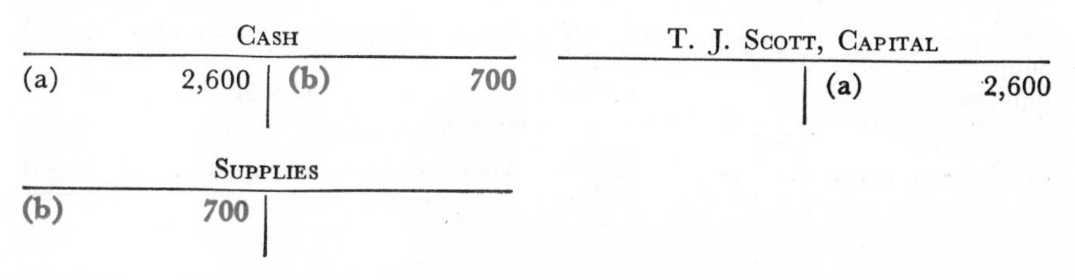

CASH

(a)	2,600	(b)	700

T. J. SCOTT, CAPITAL

		(a)	2,600

SUPPLIES

(b)	700		

(c) Scott TV Service wished to purchase equipment from White & Co. for $2,400, but reference to the cash account revealed that payment of the entire amount was not possible at that time. The business therefore arranged with White & Co. to pay $1,500 in cash and the balance in 90 days. The effect of this transaction was to increase the asset Equipment by $2,400, to reduce the asset Cash by $1,500, and to increase the liability Accounts Payable by $900.

Liability accounts appear on the right side of the account form of balance sheet; similarly, increases in liabilities are recorded on the right or credit side of appropriate accounts. This transaction was therefore recorded as follows: Equipment was debited for $2,400 to record the cost of this new asset; Cash was credited for $1,500 to record the decrease in this asset; and Accounts Payable was credited for $900 to record this new liability. The ledger of Scott TV Service then appeared as follows:

CASH

(a)	2,600	(b)	700
		(c)	1,500

ACCOUNTS PAYABLE

		(c)	900

SUPPLIES

(b)	700		

T. J. SCOTT, CAPITAL

		(a)	2,600

EQUIPMENT

(c)	2,400		

When there is more than one account payable, it is necessary to maintain a separate record for each creditor. The method of accounting for each individual account payable will be presented in Chapter 6.

At this time the following balance sheet, in account form, could be prepared from the accounts of Scott TV Service:

Scott TV Service
Balance Sheet
September 1, 1965

Assets		*Liabilities*	
Cash	$ 400	Accounts payable	$ 900
Supplies	700		
Equipment	2,400	*Capital*	
		T. J. Scott, capital	2,600
Total assets	$3,500	Total liabilities and capital	$3,500

Classification of accounts

Before a further analysis of transactions in terms of debit and credit is presented, the customary subdivisions of assets, liabilities, capital, revenue, and expenses will be described and the nature and composition of the most common accounts will be explained.

Assets. Any physical thing (tangible) or right (intangible) owned that has a money value is an asset. Assets are frequently presented on the balance sheet as two distinct groups: (1) *current assets* and (2) *plant assets*. These two categories and the most common individual accounts in each are discussed in the paragraphs that follow.

Current assets. Cash and other assets that may reasonably be expected to be realized in cash or sold or consumed usually within a year or less through the normal operations of the business are called *current assets*. In addition to cash, the assets in this group usually owned by a service business are notes receivable and accounts receivable, and supplies and other prepaid expenses.

Cash is any medium of exchange that a bank will accept at face value; it includes bank deposits, currency, checks, bank drafts, and money orders. *Notes receivable* are claims against debtors evidenced by a written promise to pay a certain sum in money at a definite time to the order of a specified person or to bearer. *Accounts receivable* are claims against debtors, less formal than notes, that arise from sales of services or merchandise on account. *Prepaid expenses* include supplies on hand and advance payments of expenses such as insurance and property taxes.

Plant assets. Tangible assets used in the business that are of a relatively fixed or permanent nature are called *plant assets* or *fixed assets*. Such assets, with the exception of land, wear out or *depreciate* with the passage of time. The amount of *depreciation* for an accounting period cannot be determined with the same degree of certainty that applies to the expiration of insurance or of other prepaid expenses; consequently the cost of the plant assets is recorded in one account and the accumulated depreciation is recorded in another account.

Typical titles of plant asset accounts are Equipment, Buildings, and Land. Equipment may be classified by functions, with separate accounts entitled Delivery Equipment, Store Equipment, and Office Equipment.

Liabilities. Liabilities are amounts owed to outsiders (creditors) and are customarily described in the balance sheet by titles that include the word *payable*. They are divided into two principal classes: (1) *current liabilities* and (2) *long-term liabilities*.

Current liabilities. Liabilities that will be due within a short time (usually one year or less) and that are to be paid out of current assets are called *current liabilities.* The most common liabilities in the group are *notes payable* and *accounts payable,* which are exactly like their receivable counterparts except that the debtor-creditor relationship is reversed. Other current liability accounts commonly found in the ledger are Salaries Payable, Interest Payable, and Taxes Payable.

Long-term liabilities. Liabilities that will not be due for a comparatively long time (usually more than one year) are called *long-term liabilities* or *fixed liabilities.* As they come within the one-year range and are to be paid, such liabilities become current. If the obligation is to be renewed rather than paid at maturity, however, it would continue to be classed as long-term. When payment of a long-term debt is to be spread over a number of years, the installment due within one year from a balance sheet date is classed as a current liability.

Long-term liabilities are usually evidenced by *notes payable.* When notes are accompanied by security in the form of a mortgage, the obligation may be referred to as *mortgage notes payable* or *mortgage payable.*

CAPITAL. *Capital* is the term applied to the owner's equity in the business. It is a residual claim against the assets of the business after the total liabilities are deducted. Other commonly used terms for capital are *owner's equity, proprietorship,* and *net worth.*

REVENUE. *Revenue* is the gross increase in capital attributable to business activities. It results from the sale of merchandise, the performance of services for a customer or a client, the rental of property, the lending of money, and other business and professional activities entered into for the purpose of earning income. More specific terms employed to identify the source of revenue include *sales, fees, commissions revenue, fares earned,* and *interest income.* If an enterprise has several different types of revenue, a separate account should be maintained for each.

EXPENSES. Costs that have been consumed in the process of producing revenue are *expired* costs or *expenses.* The number of expense categories and individual expense accounts maintained in the ledger varies with the nature and the size of an enterprise. A large business with authority and responsibility spread among many employees may use an elaborate classification and hundreds of accounts as an aid in controlling expenses. For a small service business of the type that has been used here for illustrative purposes, a modest number of expense accounts is satisfactory.

Debit and credit

Balance sheet accounts. In an earlier section of this chapter it was observed that the left side of asset accounts is used for recording increases and the right side is used for recording decreases. It was also observed that the system for liability and capital accounts is exactly the opposite, with the right side being used to record increases and the left side to record decreases. The left side of all accounts, whether asset, liability, or capital, is called *debit* and the right side is called *credit.* Consequently, a debit may signify either an increase or a decrease, depending on the nature of the account, and a credit may likewise signify either increase or decrease. The rules of debit and credit may therefore be stated as follows:

DEBIT **signifies:**	CREDIT **signifies:**
Increase in asset accounts	**Decrease in asset accounts**
Decrease in liability accounts	**Increase in liability accounts**
Decrease in capital accounts	**Increase in capital accounts**

The effect of transactions is ordinarily stated in terms of debit and credit rather than in terms of left and right or of increase and decrease. For example, the effect of the purchase of $700 of supplies for cash is stated as follows: debit Supplies for $700 and credit Cash for $700.

The rules of debit and credit may also be stated in relationship to the accounting equation and the account form of balance sheet as in the following diagram:

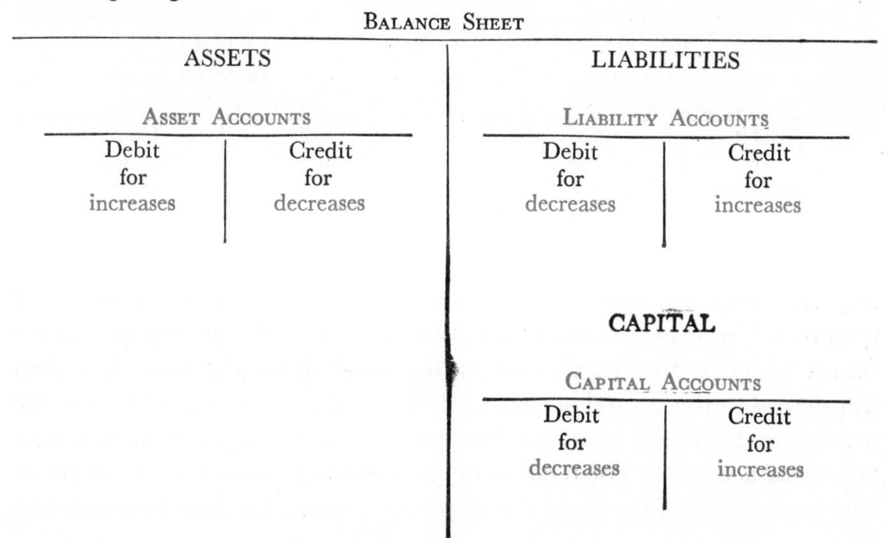

A business transaction always affects at least two accounts. If only two accounts are affected, one of them must be debited and the other must be credited for a like amount. If more than two accounts are affected, the sum of the debits is always equal to the sum of the credits. This equality of debit and credit for each transaction is inherent in the fundamental equation. It naturally follows that the sum of all the debit entries in the ledger equals the sum of all the credit entries.

Income statement accounts. The theory of debit and credit in its application to revenue and expense accounts is based on the relationship of these accounts to capital. The net income or the net loss for a period, as revealed by the income statement, is the net increase or decrease in capital resulting from operations. In order to collect efficiently the data that are needed to prepare the income statement, accounts are maintained in the ledger for each type of revenue and expense.

Revenue increases capital; hence increases in revenues during an accounting period are recorded as credits to appropriately titled revenue accounts.

Expenses have the effect of decreasing capital and are therefore recorded as debits to the various expense accounts, such as Rent Expense, Delivery Expense, and Advertising Expense. Although debits to expense accounts signify *decreases in capital*, they may also be referred to as *increases in expense*. The usual practice is to consider debits to expense accounts in the positive sense (increases in expense) rather than in the negative sense (decreases in capital). The rules of debit and credit as applied to revenue and expense accounts are shown in the diagram below.

Capital Accounts

DEBIT ***Decreases***		CREDIT ***Increases***	
Expense Accounts		Revenue Accounts	
Debit for increases	Credit for decreases	Debit for decreases	Credit for increases

At the close of the fiscal period, the balances of the revenue and expense accounts are reported in the income statement. Their balances are then transferred to a summary account. The balance of the summary account, which is the net income or the net loss for the period, is then transferred to the capital account. Because of this periodic closing of the revenue and expense accounts, they are sometimes called *temporary capital* or *nominal* accounts. The balance of each asset and each liability account and the balance of the capital account are carried forward to succeeding fiscal periods. They are more permanent in nature and are sometimes referred to as *real* accounts.

Drawing account. The owner of a sole proprietorship customarily makes periodic withdrawals of cash from his business. This is particularly true if he devotes full time to managing the business or if it is his principal source of income. Such withdrawals reduce the capital of the business and could be recorded as debits to the capital account. It is preferable to record them in a separate *drawing* or *personal* account, however, in order that total withdrawals may more readily be determined at the end of the accounting period.

Debits to the drawing account may be considered either as decreases in capital or as increases in drawings. In this respect they are similar to debits to expense accounts, which record decreases in capital but increases in expense. Drawings differ from expenses, however, in that they do not represent expired costs allocable against revenue. Ordinarily the periodic withdrawals of the owner are made in anticipation that the enterprise will operate at a profit.

Normal balances. The account serves as a mathematical device for recording increases and decreases in monetary terms. Increases are placed on one side of the account and decreases are placed on the opposite side. The total of the increases can easily be found by adding all the items on the increase side; the total of the decreases can be similarly determined.

The sum of the increases in an account will customarily be equal to or greater than the sum of the decreases; consequently the normal balances of all accounts are positive rather than negative. When the balance of an account is to be determined, the smaller of the two totals is subtracted from the larger. For example, the total debits (increases) in an asset account will ordinarily be greater than the total credits (decreases); thus, asset accounts normally have debit balances. It is entirely possible, of course, for the debits and the credits in an account to be equal, in which case the account is said to be *in balance.*

The rules of debit and credit, and the normal balances of the various types of accounts, are summarized below. Note that drawing and expense accounts are considered in the positive sense. Increases in both types of accounts, which represent decreases in capital, are recorded as debits.

Type of Account	*Increase*	*Decrease*	*Normal Balance*
Asset	Debit	Credit	Debit
Liability	Credit	Debit	Credit
Capital			
Capital	Credit	Debit	Credit
Drawing	Debit	Credit	Debit
Revenue	Credit	Debit	Credit
Expense	Debit	Credit	Debit

When an account that normally has a debit balance actually has a credit balance, or vice versa, it is an indication of an error in recording or of an unusual transaction. A credit balance in the office equipment account, for example, could result only from an error in recording. On the other hand, a debit balance in an account payable account could result from paying an amount greater than that owed.

Arrangement of accounts in the ledger

In practice, ledgers ordinarily have removable bindings, and each account appears on a separate sheet. Such procedures make it possible to insert additional accounts that may be needed, to remove accounts that may be discontinued, and to substitute new pages when old ones are filled. It is customary to arrange accounts in the ledger in the order in which the items are presented in the balance sheet and the income statement. Current assets are first, followed by accounts for plant assets, current liabilities, long-term liabilities, capital, and drawing. The income statement accounts begin with sales or other operating revenue accounts and are followed by the various operating expense accounts, approximately in order of magnitude, to complete the ledger.

Illustration of a complete ledger

The application of the rules of debit and credit will be illustrated by recording the transactions of an enterprise for the month of October. In the illustration, the accounts are arranged to conform to the account form of the balance sheet; that is, asset accounts are presented on the left side of the page and liability and capital accounts, including revenue and expenses, are presented on the right. The increase and decrease sides of each account are indicated by + and − signs, and the letter used to identify each transaction is recorded in the accounts to facilitate cross-referencing.

(a) James B. Hill, CPA, in opening a public accounting practice, invested $4,000 in cash, office equipment costing $500, and a library costing $800.

Analysis: The three asset accounts, Cash, Office Equipment, and Library, increased by the amounts indicated and were debited for $4,000, $500, and $800 respectively. Hill's claim against these assets was equal to the total of the three amounts; hence his capital account was credited for $5,300.

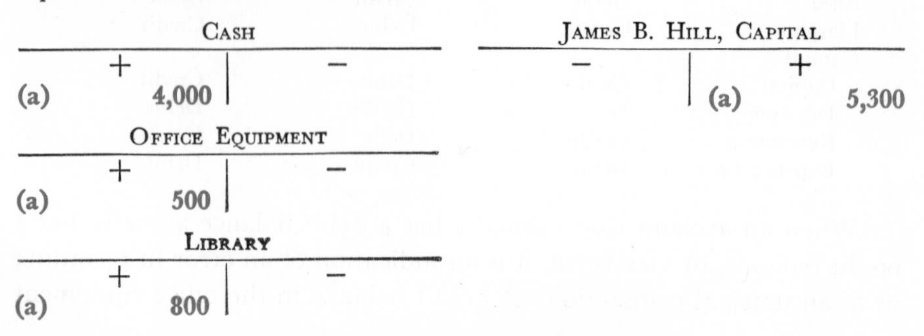

(b) Hill paid office rent for the month, $200.

Analysis: Rent is usually paid at the beginning of the month and is therefore an asset at the time of payment. But if the payment is made for one month only, at the end of the month it will be an expense. It is customary, therefore, to treat it as an expense at the time of payment. Expense accounts are subdivisions of capital. Increases in expense are decreases in capital; hence the expense account Rent Expense was debited for $200. The asset Cash was reduced by the transaction; therefore that account was credited for $200.

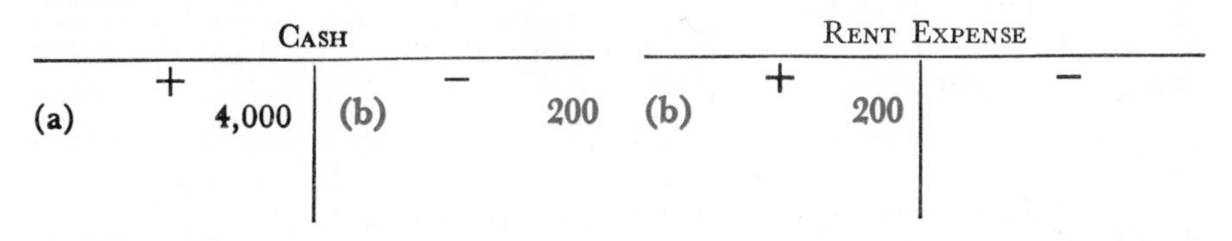

(c) Purchased on account from Barton Equipment Co. additional office equipment for $600.

Analysis: The asset Office Equipment increased and was therefore debited for $600. The liability Accounts Payable increased and was credited for $600.

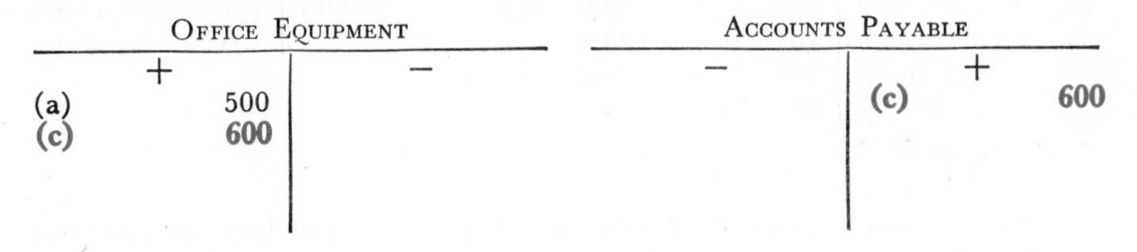

(d) Purchased an automobile for business use from Alden Motors Corp., $2,800, paying $1,000 in cash and agreeing to pay the remainder in twelve monthly installments of $150 each.

Analysis: The asset Automobile increased as a result of the transaction and was debited for $2,800. Another asset, Cash, decreased by $1,000 and was credited for that amount. Alden Motors Corp. acquired a claim of $1,800 against the business; hence Accounts Payable, a liability account, increased by $1,800 and was credited. The recording of the transaction may be expressed as follows: debit Automobile, $2,800; credit Cash, $1,000, and credit Accounts Payable, $1,800. Note that the one debit of $2,800 was equal to the two credits totaling $2,800.

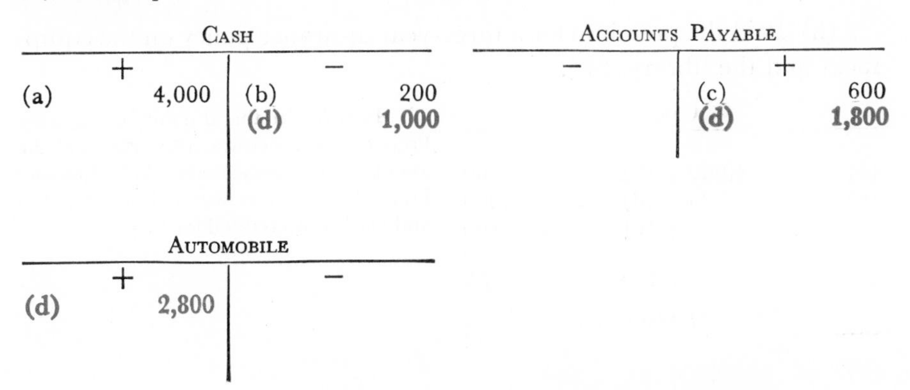

(e) Purchased office supplies for cash, $100.

CASH

	+		−
(a)	4,000	(b)	200
		(d)	1,000
		(e)	**100**

OFFICE SUPPLIES

	+		−
(e)	**100**		

Analysis: This transaction represented the exchange of one asset, Cash, for another asset, Office Supplies. The office supplies account was debited for $100 to record the increase, and Cash was credited for $100 to record the decrease. Although the supplies will become an expense as they are used, it is proper to record them as an asset at the time of purchase.

(f) Paid Barton Equipment Co. $300 on account.

Analysis: This payment reduced the liability account Accounts Payable, and that account was debited for $300. It also reduced the asset account Cash, which was credited for $300.

CASH

	+		−
(a)	4,000	(b)	200
		(d)	1,000
		(e)	100
		(f)	**300**

ACCOUNTS PAYABLE

	−		+
(f)	**300**	(c)	600
		(d)	1,800

(g) Received $225 in payment of professional fees for services rendered a client.

Analysis: Cash was increased and was debited for $225. The revenue account Professional Fees, which is a subdivision of capital, was increased and was credited for $225.

CASH

	+		−
(a)	4,000	(b)	200
(g)	**225**	(d)	1,000
		(e)	100
		(f)	300

PROFESSIONAL FEES

	−		+
		(g)	**225**

(h) Paid the premium for a three-year insurance policy on the equipment and the library, $75.

CASH

	+		−
(a)	4,000	(b)	200
(g)	225	(d)	1,000
		(e)	100
		(f)	300
		(h)	**75**

PREPAID INSURANCE

	+		−
(h)	**75**		

Analysis: In this transaction the asset Prepaid Insurance was increased and the asset Cash was decreased by $75; therefore Prepaid Insurance was debited for $75 and Cash was credited for $75.

(i) Paid biweekly salaries, $600.

Analysis: This transaction resulted in an increase in expense (decrease in capital) and a decrease in cash; therefore Salary Expense was debited for $600 and Cash was credited for $600.

Cash

+		−	
(a)	4,000	(b)	200
(g)	225	(d)	1,000
		(e)	100
		(f)	300
		(h)	75
		(i)	600

Salary Expense

+		−
(i)	600	

Transactions (j) through (p) are similar to those that have been analyzed and recorded above. Although each is not illustrated separately, the effect of all is shown in the accounts on page 41.

(j) Received $400 for professional services. [See transaction (g).]

Analysis: Debit Cash, $400; credit Professional Fees, $400.

(k) Paid a one-year insurance premium on the automobile, $90. [See transaction (h).]

Analysis: Debit Prepaid Insurance, $90; credit Cash, $90.

(l) Received a $150 fee for services. [See transaction (g).]

Analysis: Debit Cash, $150; credit Professional Fees, $150.

(m) Paid telephone and other miscellaneous expense bills, $290. [See transaction (b).]

Analysis: Debit Miscellaneous Expense, $290; credit Cash, $290.

(n) Paid biweekly salaries, $600. [See transaction (i).]

Analysis: Debit Salary Expense, $600; credit Cash, $600.

(o) Received a $300 fee for services. [See transaction (g).]

Analysis: Debit Cash, $300; credit Professional Fees, $300.

(p) Paid automobile expenses, $80. [See transaction (b).]

Analysis: Debit Automobile Expense, $80; credit Cash, $80.

(q) Hill withdrew $450 cash for personal use.

Analysis: This transaction resulted in a decrease in capital and a decrease in cash. The decrease in capital could be recorded as a debit to the capital account, but the more usual practice is to debit it to the owner's *drawing* account. The transaction was recorded by a debit of $450 to James B. Hill, Drawing, and a credit of $450 to Cash.

Cash			
+		−	
(a)	4,000	(b)	200
(g)	225	(d)	1,000
(j)	400	(e)	100
(l)	150	(f)	300
(o)	300	(h)	75
		(i)	600
		(k)	90
		(m)	290
		(n)	600
		(p)	80
		(q)	450

James B. Hill, Drawing			
+		−	
(q)	450		

(r) Sent invoices to clients for services rendered during the month, $1,400.

Analysis: The revenue of $1,400 had been earned but not received in cash during the month. The claims against the clients were recorded by a debit to the asset Accounts Receivable, and the revenue was recorded by a credit to the revenue account Professional Fees. (At the time cash is received in payment of an account, Cash will be debited and Accounts Receivable will be credited.)

Accounts Receivable			
+		−	
(r)	1,400		

Professional Fees			
−		+	
		(g)	225
		(j)	400
		(l)	150
		(o)	300
		(r)	1,400

Hill's ledger, after all transactions for October have been recorded, appears on page 41. In order to recognize more easily the nature of each account, the accounts are grouped under the three major classifications of the fundamental accounting equation, with the drawing, revenue, and expense accounts appearing as subdivisions of capital. In order to obtain the maximum benefit from the illustration, the statement of each transaction should be reviewed and the entries should be traced to the ledger.

The small italicized figures appearing in the accounts represent pencil footings and balances. Note that they are inserted only when they serve a purpose. For example, a pencil footing in accounts with a single debit or credit, such as Accounts Receivable and James B. Hill, Capital, would be superfluous. Similarly, the pencil footing below the two debits in Prepaid Insurance is sufficient to indicate the balance of the account, as there are no credits.

Trial balance

The debits resulting from each transaction should equal the credits from each transaction. This equality of debits and credits has been ob-

Assets = Liabilities + Capital

Assets

Cash

(a)	4,000	(b)	200
(g)	225	(d)	1,000
(j)	400	(e)	100
(l)	150	(f)	300
(o)	300	(h)	75
1,290	*5,075*	(i)	600
		(k)	90
		(m)	290
		(n)	600
		(p)	80
		(q)	450
			3,785

Accounts Receivable

(r)	1,400		

Office Supplies

(e)	100		

Prepaid Insurance

(h)	75		
(k)	90		
	165		

Automobile

(d)	2,800		

Office Equipment

(a)	500		
(c)	600		
	1,100		

Library

(a)	800		

Liabilities

Accounts Payable

(f)	300	(c)	600
		(d)	1,800
		2,100	*2,400*

Capital

James B. Hill, Capital

		(a)	5,300

James B. Hill, Drawing

(q)	450		

Revenue

Professional Fees

		(g)	225
		(j)	400
		(l)	150
		(o)	300
		(r)	1,400
			2,475

Expenses

Salary Expense

(i)	600		
(n)	600		
	1,200		

Rent Expense

(b)	200		

Automobile Expense

(p)	80		

Miscellaneous Expense

(m)	290		

served in recording the transactions in the preceding illustration; consequently, the sum of all the debits in the ledger should be equal to the sum of all the credits. A test of this equality is made at intervals, usually at the end of each month. Such a test is known as a *trial balance.*

The trial balance also serves as a summary of the ledger and provides much of the information needed to prepare the balance sheet and the income statement.

A trial balance of totals could be taken by listing in parallel columns the total of the debits and the total of the credits of each account in the ledger and then adding the two columns. If the equality of debits and credits had been maintained for each transaction and there were no arithmetical errors, the sum of the column of debit totals would equal the sum of the column of credit totals.

In preparing financial statements, however, it is the balance of each account that is needed rather than the total debits and the total credits of each account. Referring to the cash account in the ledger of James B. Hill, for example, it is the balance of $1,290 that will appear on the balance sheet, not the total debits of $5,075 and the total credits of $3,785. Therefore, a trial balance of balances is usually preferable to a trial balance of totals. If the sum of the debit balances equals the sum of the credit balances, it is evident that the debits and the credits in the ledger are equal. The trial balance of Hill's ledger, prepared according to the latter method, is illustrated on page 43.

Proof provided by the trial balance

The trial balance does not provide complete proof of the accuracy of the ledger. It indicates only that the *debits* and the *credits* are *equal.* This proof is of value, however, because errors frequently affect the equality of debits and credits. If the two totals of a trial balance are not equal, it is probably due to one or more of the following types of errors:

(1) Error in preparing the trial balance.
  (a) One of the columns of the trial balance was incorrectly added.
  (b) The amount of an account balance was incorrectly recorded on the trial balance.
  (c) A debit balance was recorded on the trial balance as a credit, or vice versa, or a balance was omitted entirely.

(2) Error in determining the account balances.
  (a) A balance was incorrectly computed.
  (b) A balance was entered on the wrong side of an account.
  (c) One side of an account was incorrectly computed.

(3) Error in recording a transaction in the ledger.
  (a) An erroneous amount was recorded as a debit or as a credit in an account.
  (b) A debit entry was recorded as a credit, or vice versa.
  (c) A debit or a credit entry was omitted.

James B. Hill, CPA
Trial Balance
October 31, 1965

Cash	1290 00	
Accounts Receivable	1400 00	
Office Supplies	100 00	
Prepaid Insurance	165 00	
Automobile	2800 00	
Office Equipment	1100 00	
Library	800 00	
Accounts Payable		2100 00
James B. Hill, Capital		5300 00
James B. Hill, Drawing	450 00	
Professional Fees		2475 00
Salary Expense	1200 00	
Rent Expense	200 00	
Automobile Expense	80 00	
Miscellaneous Expense	290 00	
	9875 00	9875 00

Trial balance

Among the types of errors that will not cause an inequality in the trial balance totals are the following:

(1) Failure to record a transaction.
(2) Recording the same erroneous amount for both the debit and the credit parts of a transaction.
(3) Recording the same transaction more than once.
(4) Recording one part of a transaction in the wrong account.

It is readily apparent that in entering transactions in the ledger, care should be exercised in recording correct figures in the appropriate accounts. The desirability of accuracy in determining account balances and reporting them on the trial balance is equally obvious.

QUESTIONS

1. What is a ledger?

2. Name the three parts ot an account.

3. Do the terms *debit* and *credit* signify increase or decrease, or may they signify either? Explain.

4. What are current assets?

5. Marathon Company acquired plant assets at a total cost of $40,000, paying $10,000 cash and giving a mortgage note for the remainder. The agreement provided that the debt be paid in monthly installments of $500 each. How should this liability be classified on the balance sheet on December 31 of the current year, at which time the amount still owed is $20,000?

6. What is the effect of: (1) credits to revenue accounts (a) on revenue, (b) on capital; (2) debits to expense accounts (a) on capital, (b) on expenses?

7. Distinguish between real and nominal accounts.

8. (a) Why are withdrawals of cash or other assets by the owner recorded in a drawing account instead of in the capital account? (b) Are they recorded as debits or credits? Why?

9. Identify each of the following accounts as asset, liability, capital, revenue, or expense, and state in each case whether the normal balance is a debit or a credit: (a) Accounts Receivable, (b) Advertising Expense, (c) C. R. Cooper, Capital, (d) Cash, (e) C. R. Cooper, Drawing, (f) Equipment, (g) Interest Income, (h) Notes Payable, (i) Supplies.

10. Assuming that during the month a business has a substantial number of transactions affecting each of the accounts listed below, state for each account whether it is likely to have (1) debit entries only, (2) credit entries only, or (3) both debit and credit entries.

(a) Cash
(b) David Ford, Drawing
(c) Accounts Receivable
(d) Professional Fees Earned
(e) Accounts Payable
(f) Miscellaneous Expense

11. Arvada Laundry deposits all cash receipts in a bank account and makes all payments by check. The cash account at the end of the current fiscal period has a credit balance of $210 and there is no undeposited cash on hand. (a) Assuming that there were no errors in recording, what is the explanation of this unusual balance? (b) At this particular time is the cash account an asset, a liability, capital, a revenue, or an expense?

12. Explain how it would be possible for an account with a customer to have a credit balance. In such a case does the balance represent an asset, a liability, capital, a revenue, or an expense?

13. A business enterprise renders services to a customer for $500 in one fiscal period and receives payment from the customer in the following period. What accounts should be debited and credited in the period in which (a) the service was rendered and (b) the cash was received?

14. At the beginning of the fiscal period the account H. B. Carter, Capital had a credit balance of $7,000. During the period the owner's withdrawals totaled $6,000 and the business incurred a net loss of $2,500; there were no additional investments in the business. Assuming that there have been no recording errors, will the balance sheet prepared at this time balance? Explain.

15. During the month Banner Service Station received $9,300 in cash and paid out $8,100 in cash. (a) How were the receipts and the disbursements entered in the cash account? (b) Do these data indicate that there was a net income of $1,200 for the month? Explain.

16. What is a trial balance and what does it prove?

17. Indicate which of the following errors, each considered individually, would cause the trial balance totals to be unequal:

(a) A fee of $200 due from a client was not charged to Accounts Receivable or credited to a revenue account because the cash had not been received.

(b) A receipt of $75 from an account receivable was recorded as a debit of $75 to Cash and a credit of $75 to Sales.
(c) A withdrawal of $200 by the owner was recorded as a debit of $20 to Salary Expense and a credit of $20 to Cash.
(d) A payment of $120 for supplies was recorded as a debit of $100 to Supplies and a credit of $120 to Cash.
(e) A payment of $140 to a creditor was recorded as a credit of $140 to Accounts Payable and a credit of $140 to Cash.

18. In recording a receipt of $160 of cash from a customer on account, the cash account is erroneously credited instead of being debited. (Accounts Receivable is credited for the correct amount.) Assuming no other errors and that the total of the debit column of the trial balance at the end of the month is $9,600, what is the total of the credit column?

EXERCISES

1. Record the following transactions in T accounts, identifying each debit and credit by the letter designating the transaction, and prepare a trial balance as of June 30. Accounts needed are: Cash; Supplies; Equipment; Accounts Payable; H. L. Adams, Capital; H. L. Adams, Drawing; Service Income; Salary Expense; Rent Expense.

(a) On June 1, H. L. Adams invested $600 in cash and $1,200 in equipment in an enterprise to be known as Adams Shoe Repairs.
(b) Paid rent for June, $90.
(c) Purchased additional equipment on account, $1,000.
(d) Purchased supplies for cash, $200.
(e) Received cash for services rendered during the month, $800.
(f) Paid $250 on account for the equipment purchased.
(g) Withdrew $300 for personal use.
(h) Paid assistant's salary for the month, $350.

2. Arrange the following accounts and their balances (all normal) in proper sequence in the form of a trial balance, supplying the missing figure for Cash.

Accounts Payable	1,600	Miscellaneous Expense	1,600
Accounts Receivable	3,100	Mortgage Payable (due 1970)	5,000
Advertising Expense	600	Prepaid Insurance	1,600
Buildings	12,000	Salary Expense	6,000
Cash	X	Supplies	1,000
Equipment	30,000	Utilities Expense	800
Fees Earned	30,000	B. T. Winters, Capital	38,700
Land	5,000	B. T. Winters, Drawing	12,000

3. Eight transactions are recorded in the T accounts shown at the top of page 46. Indicate for each debit and each credit: (1) the type of account affected (asset, liability, capital, revenue, or expense) and (2) whether the account was increased (+) or decreased (−). Answers may be presented in the following form, transaction (a) being given as an example;

	Account Debited		*Account Credited*	
Transaction	*Type*	*Effect*	*Type*	*Effect*
(a)	asset	+	capital	+

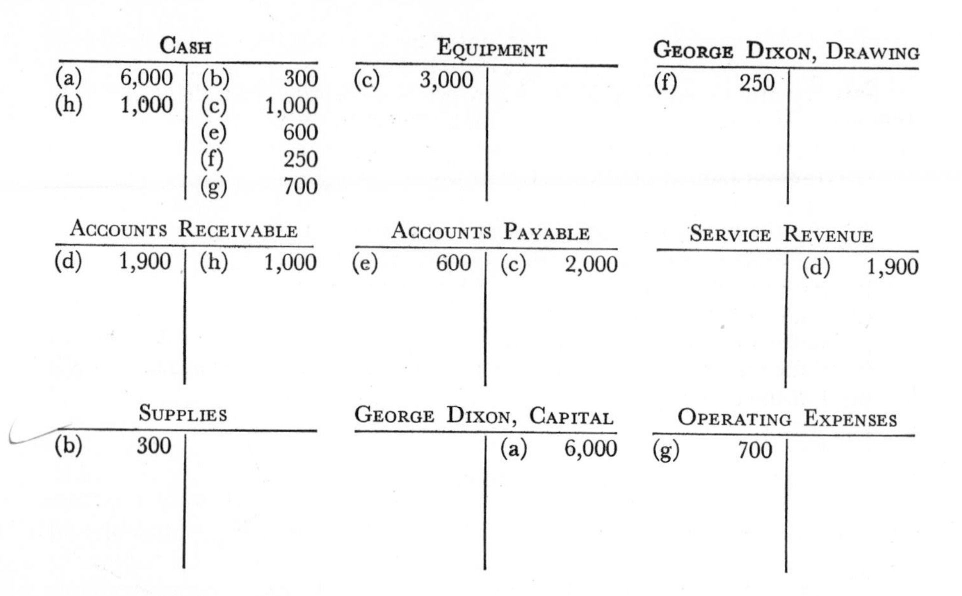

Cash

	Debit		Credit
(a)	6,000	(b)	300
(h)	1,000	(c)	1,000
		(e)	600
		(f)	250
		(g)	700

Equipment

	Debit		Credit
(c)	3,000		

George Dixon, Drawing

	Debit		Credit
(f)	250		

Accounts Receivable

	Debit		Credit
(d)	1,900	(h)	1,000

Accounts Payable

	Debit		Credit
(e)	600	(c)	2,000

Service Revenue

	Debit		Credit
		(d)	1,900

Supplies

	Debit		Credit
(b)	300		

George Dixon, Capital

	Debit		Credit
		(a)	6,000

Operating Expenses

	Debit		Credit
(g)	700		

4. List the following accounts in the order in which they would appear in the ledger of Howard Green:

(a) Accounts Payable
(b) Accounts Receivable
(c) Howard Green, Capital
(d) Cash
(e) Howard Green, Drawing
(f) Miscellaneous Expense
(g) Prepaid Insurance
(h) Salaries Payable
(i) Salary Expense
(j) Sales

5. The trial balance of Bancroft Company presented below does not balance. In reviewing the ledger and other records you discover the following: (a) the debits and the credits in the cash account total $14,640 and $11,340, respectively; (b) a payment of $800 to a creditor on account was not recorded in the cash account; (c) a receipt of $500 from a customer on account was not credited to the accounts receivable account; (d) the balance of the equipment account was $5,200; (e) each account had a normal balance. Prepare a corrected trial balance.

Bancroft Company
Trial Balance
November 30, 19—

Account	Debit	Credit
Cash	3,200	
Accounts Receivable	2,200	
Prepaid Insurance		800
Equipment	2,500	
Accounts Payable		2,100
Salaries Payable	400	
W. T. Bancroft, Capital		4,600
Service Revenue		7,000
Salary Expense	2,600	
Advertising Expense		900
Miscellaneous Expense	400	
	11,300	15,400

PROBLEMS

2-1. Gordon L. Tracy, architect, opened an office on October 1 of the current year. During the month he completed the following transactions connected with his professional practice:

(a) Transferred cash from a personal bank account to an account to be used for the business, $3,500.
(b) Purchased used automobile for $1,800, paying $1,000 cash and giving a non-interest-bearing note for the remainder.
(c) Paid October rent for office and workroom, $300.
(d) Paid cash for supplies, $225.
(e) Purchased office and drafting room equipment on account, $2,200.
(f) Paid cash for insurance policies on automobile and equipment, $192.
(g) Received cash from a client for plans delivered, $525.
(h) Paid cash to creditors on account, $1,100.
(i) Paid cash for miscellaneous expenses, $40.
(j) Received invoice for blueprint service, due in following month, $35.
(k) Recorded fee earned on plans delivered, payment to be made in following month, $910.
(l) Paid salary of assistant, $500.
(m) Paid cash for miscellaneous expenses, $38.
(n) Paid installment due on note payable, $100.
(o) Paid gas, oil, and repairs on automobile for October, $70.

Instructions: (1) Record the foregoing transactions in the following T accounts: Cash; Accounts Receivable; Supplies; Prepaid Insurance; Automobile; Equipment; Notes Payable; Accounts Payable; Gordon L. Tracy, Capital; Professional Fees; Salary Expense; Rent Expense; Automobile Expense; Blueprint Expense; Miscellaneous Expense. Record the letter identifying the transaction at the left of each debit and each credit in the accounts.

(2) Prepare a trial balance as of October 31 of the current year.

2-2. The accounts in the ledger of Edward R. Sanders, M.D., are listed below, together with their balances as of August 1 of the current year: Cash, $4,200; Accounts Receivable, $6,100; Supplies, $250; Prepaid Insurance, $325; Equipment, $12,000; Accounts Payable, $500; Edward R. Sanders, Capital, $22,375; Edward R. Sanders, Drawing; Professional Fees; Salary Expense; Rent Expense; Laboratory Expense; Utilities Expense; Miscellaneous Expense.

Transactions completed during August were as follows:

(a) Paid office rent for August, $600.
(b) Purchased equipment on account, $1,600.
(c) Received cash on account from patients, $2,900.
(d) Purchased supplies on account, $80.
(e) Returned part of equipment purchased in (b), $50.
(f) Paid cash for renewal of property insurance policy, $180.
(g) Sold X-ray film to another doctor at cost, as an accommodation, receiving cash, $20.
(h) Paid cash to creditors on account, $1,500.
(i) Received cash in payment of services rendered to patients during August, $2,700.
(j) Paid salaries of receptionist and nurses, $1,400.
(k) Paid gas and electricity expense, $136.
(l) Paid water expense, $21.

(m) Paid invoice for laboratory analyses, $135.
(n) Recorded fees charged to customers on account for services rendered in August, $1,850.
(o) Paid cash from business bank account for personal expenses, $950.
(p) Discovered that a fee of $40 was erroneously charged to a patient in (n).
(q) Paid telephone expense, $39.
(r) Paid miscellaneous expenses, $85.

Instructions: (1) Set up a ledger of T accounts and record the balances as of August 1. Identify the balances by writing "Bal." to the left of the amount.

(2) Record the transactions for August. Identify each debit and each credit by the letter designating the transaction.

(3) Prepare a trial balance as of August 31 of the current year.

(4) Assuming that the total of supplies expense, insurance expense, and depreciation expense for the month of August is determined to be $270:

(a) What is the amount of the net income for the month?
(b) What is the capital as of August 31?

2-3. The following trial balance for Ward Services as of September 30 of the current year does not balance because of a number of errors.

Cash	5,060	
Accounts Receivable	2,210	
Supplies	415	
Prepaid Insurance	238	
Equipment	8,920	
Notes Payable		2,300
Accounts Payable		1,850
L. G. Ward, Capital		8,609
L. G. Ward, Drawing	100	
Sales		6,910
Salary Expense	1,600	
Advertising Expense	42	
Gas, Electricity, & Water Expense	115	
Miscellaneous Expense	236	
	18,936	19,669

In the process of comparing the amounts in the trial balance with the ledger, recomputing the balances of the accounts, and comparing the entries with the original evidences of the transactions, the following errors were discovered:

(a) The pencil footing of the credits to Cash in the ledger was understated by $1,000.
(b) A cash receipt of $140 was recorded as a debit to Cash of $410.
(c) A debit of $200 to Accounts Receivable was not recorded.
(d) An insurance policy acquired at a cost of $90 was recorded as a credit to Prepaid Insurance.
(e) A debit of $100 in Notes Payable was overlooked when determining the balance of the account.
(f) The pencil footings of $1,970 debit and $3,720 credit in Accounts Payable were correct but the balance was computed incorrectly.
(g) A debit of $200 for a withdrawal by the owner was recorded as a credit to the capital account.

(h) The balance of the sales account should have been $6,800.
(i) The balance of $420 in Advertising Expense was entered as $42 in the trial balance.
(j) Rent Expense, with a balance of $310, was omitted from the trial balance.
(k) A return of $25 of defective supplies was erroneously recorded as a $250 credit to Supplies.

Instructions: Prepare a corrected trial balance as of September 30 of the current year.

2-4. The following transactions were completed by John T. Collins during June of the current year:

(a) Deposited $16,000 cash in a bank account for use in acquiring and operating Midway Drive-In Theatre.
(b) Purchased the Midway Drive-In Theatre for $24,000, allocated as follows: equipment, $6,000; buildings, $10,000; land, $8,000. Paid $10,000 in cash and gave a mortgage note for the remainder.
(c) Paid premiums for property and casualty insurance policies, $1,248.
(d) Paid for June billboard and newspaper advertising, $400.
(e) Purchased supplies, $250, and equipment, $800, on account.
(f) Cash receipts from admissions for the week, $2,100.
(g) Paid miscellaneous expense, $65.
(h) Cash receipts from admissions for the week, $1,960.
(i) Paid semimonthly wages, $1,600.
(j) Returned portion of equipment purchased in (e) to the supplier, receiving full credit for its cost, $150.
(k) Paid miscellaneous expenses, $39.
(l) Entered into a contract for the operation of the refreshment stand at a rental of 10% of the concessionaire's sales, with a minimum of $250 a month, payable in advance. Received cash of $125 as the advance payment for the period June 16, the effective date of the contract, to June 30.
(m) Cash receipts from admissions for the week, $1,890.
(n) Paid cash to creditors on account, $500.
(o) Purchased supplies for cash, $21.
(p) Paid for advertising leaflets for June, $30.
(q) Paid semimonthly wages, $1,650.
(r) Cash receipts from admissions for remainder of the month, $2,420.
(s) Paid electricity and water bills, $265.
(t) Paid creditors on account, $120.
(u) Withdrew cash for personal use, $700.
(v) Recorded invoice of $1,700 for rental of film for June. Payment is due on July 10.
(w) Recorded amount due from concessionaire, based on his report of sales of $1,800 for the second half of June. Payment is due on July 5.

Instructions: (1) Record the transactions in the following T accounts, identifying each debit and credit by letter: Cash; Accounts Receivable; Prepaid Insurance; Supplies; Equipment; Buildings; Land; Accounts Payable; Mortgage Note Payable; John T. Collins, Capital; John T. Collins, Drawing; Admissions Income; Concession Income; Wages Expense; Film Rental Expense; Advertising Expense; Electricity & Water Expense; Miscellaneous Expense.
(2) Prepare a trial balance as of June 30 of the current year.

PART TWO

Accounting cycle for a service enterprise

3. Journals and posting to accounts

Need for journals

The ledger is the basic record in which the effects of business transactions are classified and summarized. In the preceding chapter the debits and the credits were recorded in appropriate accounts directly from informal descriptions of transactions. In actual practice, an initial record of each transaction, or of a group of similar transactions, is customarily evidenced by a business document such as a sales ticket, a check stub, or a cash register tape. On the basis of the evidence provided by the business documents, the transactions are first entered in chronological order in a record called a *journal* or *book of original entry*. All entries in the journal are subsequently transferred to the ledger. The sequence of events leading to entries in the ledger may be diagrammed as follows:

Business Transaction occurs ⟶ Business Document prepared ⟶ Entry recorded in Journal ⟶ Entry transferred to Ledger

The record provided by a journal is useful in several ways. Each transaction is recorded in its entirety in one place, whereas in the ledger a portion of a transaction is recorded in one account and the remaining portion is recorded in one or more other accounts. It is therefore easier to determine from a journal the correctness of the analysis of a transaction and the equality of the debits and the credits being recorded. There is also more space in a journal for recording details or explanations of complex transactions.

The journal is a permanent chronological record of the debits and the credits resulting from transactions, together with all necessary explanations of the transactions. From time to time the debits and the credits are transferred to the accounts in the ledger, which in turn supply the cumulative data for financial statements and other reports for owners and managers.

Both journals and ledger accounts play indispensable roles in the recording of business transactions. Journals furnish the chronological record of the effect of individual transactions on the accounting equation. Ledger accounts provide for the classification and the summarization of the cumulative effects of all transactions on assets, liabilities, capital, revenue, and expense.

Two-column journal

There are various kinds of journals. The number and the type used in a particular business will depend upon the size of the business and the nature of its operations. The simplest form of journal has only two amount columns and may be used for recording all transactions of the business in chronological order.

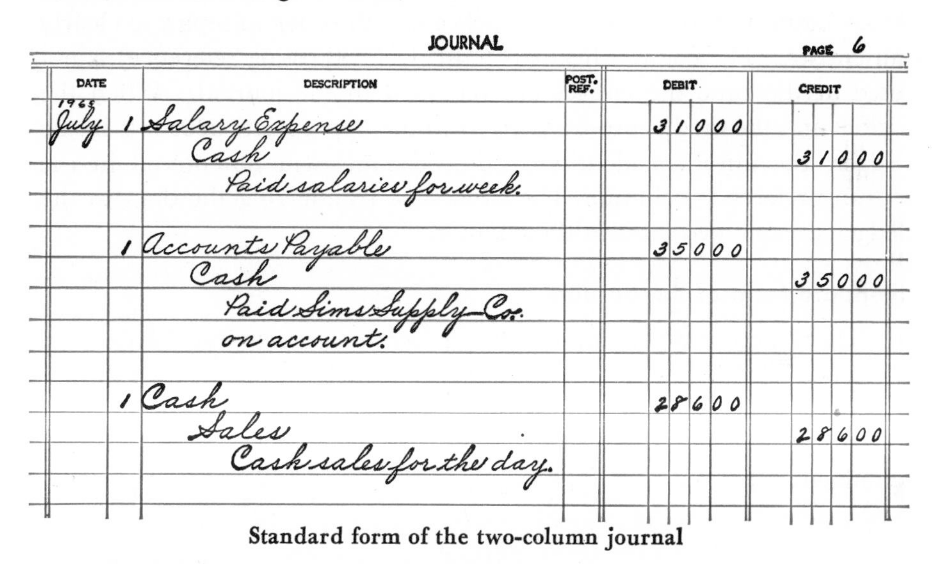

JOURNAL PAGE 6

DATE		DESCRIPTION	POST. REF.	DEBIT	CREDIT
1965 July	1	Salary Expense		310 00	
		Cash			310 00
		Paid salaries for week.			
	1	Accounts Payable		350 00	
		Cash			350 00
		Paid Sims Supply Co.			
		on account.			
	1	Cash		286 00	
		Sales			286 00
		Cash sales for the day.			

Standard form of the two-column journal

The process of recording a transaction in a journal is called *journalizing*. The procedures followed in journalizing are as follows:

(1) The year is written in small figures at the top of the first column. It is not written again on a page unless the year changes.

(2) The month of the first transaction is written on the first line in the first column. The name of the month is entered again only at the top of a new page or at the beginning of a new month.

(3) The day of each transaction is written in the second column on the first line used by each transaction. It is repeated for each transaction regardless of the number of transactions completed on the same day.

(4) The title of the account to be debited is written at the extreme left of the Description column, and the amount of the debit is entered in the left-hand or Debit amount column.

(5) The title of the account to be credited is written on the following line, indented about one-half inch, and the amount of the credit is entered in the right-hand or Credit amount column.

(6) The explanation is written on the next line, with an additional indention of about one-half inch. The explanation, while not necessarily limited to one line, should be as brief as possible without omitting essential information not readily apparent from reading the entry.

It should be noted that all transactions are recorded in terms of debits and credits to specific accounts in accordance with the rules of debit and credit discussed in the preceding chapter. The titles used in the entries should correspond to the titles of the accounts in the ledger. For example, a desk purchased for use in the office should be debited to Office Equipment, not to "desks purchased," and cash received should be debited to Cash, not to "cash received."

A blank line is left between each entry in order to separate clearly all entries. The column headed "Post. Ref." (posting reference) is not used at the time the entries are recorded in the journal. When the debits and the credits are transferred to the appropriate accounts in the ledger, the numbers identifying the accounts will be entered in the posting reference column. The process of transferring the data to the ledger is explained later in the chapter.

Standard form of the account

The T accounts used in Chapter 2 were constructed in the simplest form possible. While such a form provides the basic elements of the account, it is used primarily for illustrative purposes. By adding special rulings to the basic T account form, the following standard form is obtained:

Cash — ACCOUNT NO. 11

DATE		ITEMS	POST. REF.	DEBIT	DATE		ITEMS	POST. REF.	CREDIT
1965					1965				
July	1	Balance	✓	2115 00	July	1		6	310 00
	1		6	286 00		1		6	350 00
	3		6	319 00		3		6	110 00
	3		6	260 00		3		6	19 00
						3		7	125 00

Standard form of the account

Both sides of the account are identical except that the left side is used for debits and the right side is used for credits. The columns on each side provide for: (1) the date; (2) a brief explanation of the entry, if it is desired; (3) the page reference to the journal in which the transaction was recorded; and (4) the amount.

Journal and ledger paper are also available without the "Date," "Items," and other column headings shown in the illustrations.

Posting

The process by which the entries in the journal are transferred to accounts in the ledger is called *posting*. It consists in transferring each amount in the Debit column of the journal to the debit side of an account and in transferring each amount in the Credit column of the journal to the credit side of an account. The account to which each item is to be posted is determined from the account title stated in the journal. The debits and the credits may be posted in sequence as they appear in the journal or, if a considerable amount of posting is to be done at one time, all of the debits may be posted first, followed by the credits. The use of the latter procedure reduces the likelihood of posting items to the wrong side of accounts.

In some accounting systems much of the posting is done by machines designed for the purpose. However, when the posting is done manually, each debit and each credit is posted in the following manner:

(1) The date and the amount in the journal entry are entered in the corresponding *account*. If the item appears as a debit in the journal, the posting will be to the debit side of the account; if it appears as a credit, the posting will be to the credit side of the account. The system of entering dates (year, month, and day) is similar to that employed in the journal.

(2) The number of the journal page from which the posting is made is entered in the posting reference column of the *account*.

(3) The number of the account to which the posting has been made is entered in the posting reference column of the *journal*. This procedure serves two purposes: first, it indicates that the item has been posted; and second, it completes the cross reference between the journal and the ledger.

The foregoing procedures are illustrated in the diagrams that appear on page 54.

Chart of accounts

The number of accounts maintained by a particular business is affected by the nature of its operations, its volume of business, and the extent to which details are desired. For example, one particular enterprise may have separate accounts for Executive Salaries, Office Salaries,

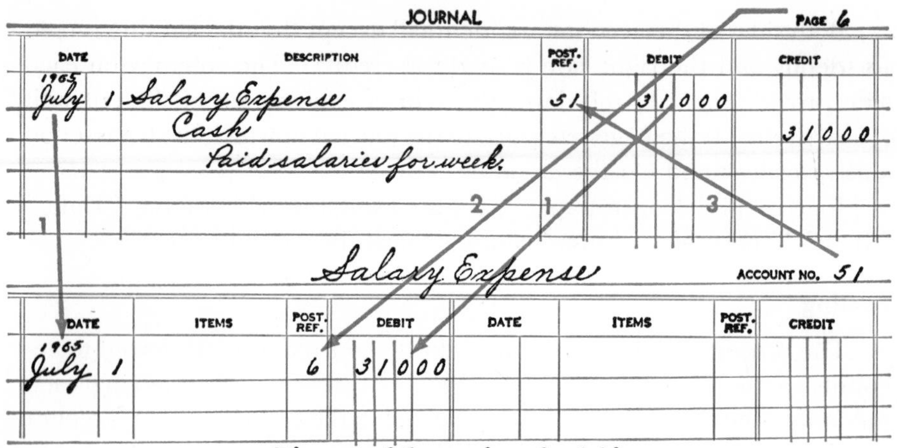

Diagram of the posting of a debit

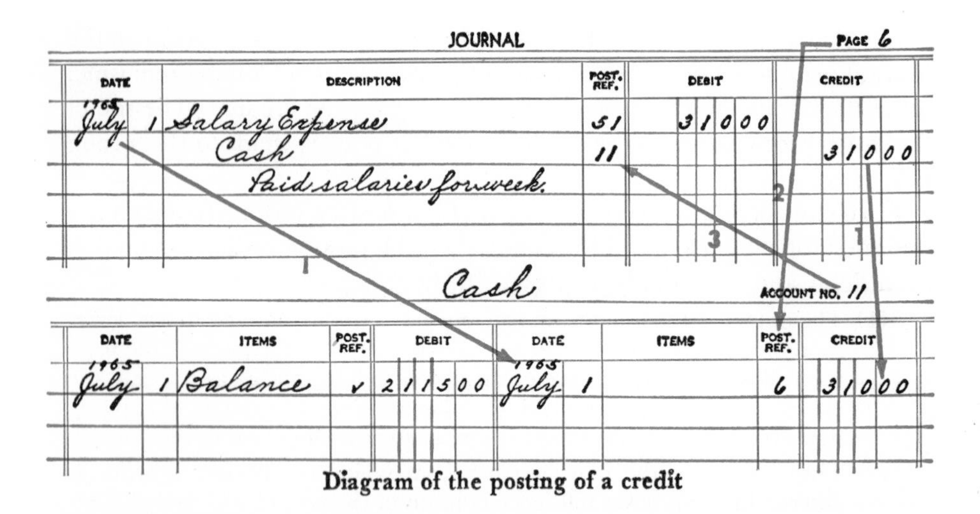

Diagram of the posting of a credit

and Sales Salaries, while another may find it satisfactory to record all types of salaries in a single account entitled Salary Expense.

Insofar as possible, the order of the accounts in the ledger should agree with the order of the items in the balance sheet and the income statement. The accounts are numbered to permit indexing and also for use as posting references in the journal.

Accounts may be numbered consecutively like the pages of a book, or a flexible system of indexing may be used. In the chart of accounts illustrated on page 55, all account numbers have two digits. The first digit indicates the major division of the ledger in which the account is placed. Accounts beginning with 1 represent assets; 2, liabilities; 3, capital; 4, revenue; and 5, expenses. The second digit indicates the position of the account within its division. A numbering system of this type has the advantage of permitting the later insertion of new accounts in their proper sequence without disturbing the other account numbers. For a large enterprise with a number of departments or branches, it is not unusual for each account number to have four or more digits.

Balance Sheet Accounts	Income Statement Accounts
1. *Assets*	4. *Revenue*
11. Cash	41. Sales
12. Accounts Receivable	
14. Supplies	5. *Expenses*
15. Prepaid Rent	
18. Printing Equipment	51. Salary Expense
19. Accumulated Depreciation	52. Supplies Expense
	53. Rent Expense
2. *Liabilities*	54. Depreciation Expense
	59. Miscellaneous Expense
21. Accounts Payable	
22. Salaries Payable	
3. *Capital*	
31. David Hull, Capital	
32. David Hull, Drawing	
33. Expense and Revenue Summary	

Chart of accounts for Hull Print Shop

Illustrations of the journal and the ledger

David Hull operated a printing business in his home workshop on a part-time basis. He decided to move to rented quarters as of October 1 and to devote full time to the business, which was to be known as Hull Print Shop. The following assets were invested in the enterprise: cash, \$900; accounts receivable, \$600; supplies, \$400; and printing equipment, \$3,200. This investment could have been recorded in the journal by four separate entries, each debiting one asset account for the amount of the asset and crediting David Hull, Capital for the same amount. The preferred method, however, is to journalize the entire transaction in a single entry, debiting the four asset accounts and crediting the capital account for the total, as illustrated on page 56. An entry composed of three or more items is called a *compound entry*.

If there had been any creditors' claims against the assets, such as accounts payable, the appropriate account title and amount would have been included in the opening entry as a credit. The amount of the credit to David Hull, Capital would have been correspondingly reduced.

JOURNAL PAGE 1

DATE		DESCRIPTION	POST. REF.	DEBIT	CREDIT
1965 Oct.	2	Cash		900 00	
		Accounts Receivable		600 00	
		Supplies		400 00	
		Printing Equipment		3200 00	
		David Hull, Capital			5100 00
		Invested assets in Hull			
		Print Shop.			

Compound journal entry

The transactions completed by Hull Print Shop during the month of October are described below. In order to limit the length of the illustration and avoid repetition, some of the transactions are stated as a summary. For example, sales for cash are given only at the middle of the month and at the end of the month. In actual practice they would be recorded each day. Similarly, all sales on account during the month are summarized in one entry; in practice each sale would be recorded separately.

Oct. 2. Paid $600 cash on a lease rental contract, the payment representing three months' rental. (As only a part of this payment was an expense of October, the asset account Prepaid Rent was debited.)
3. Purchased additional printing equipment on account from Blake Equipment Co. for $1,800.
4. Received $525 from customers in payment of their accounts.
6. Paid $40 for a newspaper advertisement.
10. Paid $400 cash to Blake Equipment Co. to apply on the $1,800 owed them.
13. Paid part-time assistants $240 for two weeks' salaries.
16. Received $920 cash from sales for the first half of October.
20. Paid $350 for additional supplies.
27. Paid part-time assistants $240 for two weeks' salaries.
31. Paid $20 for telephone bill for the month.
31. Paid $45 for electric bill for the month.
31. Received $850 cash from sales for the second half of October.
31. Sales on account totaled $510 for the month.
31. Withdrew $500 cash for personal use.

The foregoing transactions are recorded in the journal that appears on pages 57 and 58. Each entry should be studied in connection with the narrative of the transaction. The account numbers appearing in the posting reference column were not placed there at the time the entry

JOURNAL PAGE 1

Date		Description	Post. Ref.	Debit	Credit
1965 Oct.	2	Cash	11	900 00	
		Accounts Receivable	12	600 00	
		Supplies	14	400 00	
		Printing Equipment	18	3200 00	
		David Hull, Capital	31		5100 00
		Invested assets in Hull Print Shop.			
	2	Prepaid Rent	15	600 00	
		Cash	11		600 00
		Paid three months' rent.			
	3	Printing Equipment	18	1800 00	
		Accounts Payable	21		1800 00
		On account from Blake Equipment Co.			
	4	Cash	11	525 00	
		Accounts Receivable	12		525 00
		Received cash on account.			
	6	Miscellaneous Expense	59	40 00	
		Cash	11		40 00
		Newspaper advertisement.			
	10	Accounts Payable	21	400 00	
		Cash	11		400 00
		Blake Equipment Co.			
	13	Salary Expense	51	240 00	
		Cash	11		240 00
		Biweekly salaries.			
	16	Cash	11	920 00	
		Sales	41		920 00
		Cash sales for first half of month.			
	20	Supplies	14	350 00	
		Cash	11		350 00
		Cash purchase of supplies.			

Journal — Hull Print Shop

JOURNAL PAGE 2

DATE		DESCRIPTION	POST. REF.	DEBIT	CREDIT
1965 Oct.	27	Salary Expense	51	240 00	
		Cash	11		240 00
		Biweekly salaries.			
	31	Miscellaneous Expense	59	20 00	
		Cash	11		20 00
		October telephone bill.			
	31	Miscellaneous Expense	59	45 00	
		Cash	11		45 00
		October electric bill.			
	31	Cash	11	850 00	
		Sales	41		850 00
		Cash sales for second half of month.			
	31	Accounts Receivable	12	510 00	
		Sales	41		510 00
		Charge sales for month.			
	31	David Hull, Drawing	32	500 00	
		Cash	11		500 00
		Withdrew cash.			

Journal — Hull Print Shop (concluded)

was made; they were recorded in the journal as the final step in posting each item to the ledger.

After all of the entries for the month have been posted, the ledger will appear as shown on pages 59 and 60. Tracing each entry from the journal to the accounts in the ledger will give a clear understanding of the posting process.

Each account is on a separate page in the ledger. The accounts are numbered in accordance with the chart of accounts shown on page 55. Six accounts listed in the chart do not appear in the illustration of the ledger. They will be required in completing the work of the accounting cycle, which will be discussed in the next chapter.

Cash — ACCOUNT NO. 11

DATE	ITEMS	POST. REF.	DEBIT	DATE	ITEMS	POST. REF.	CREDIT
1965				1965			
Oct. 2		1	900 00	Oct. 2		1	600 00
4		1	525 00	6		1	40 00
16		1	920 00	10		1	400 00
31	760.00	2	850 00	13		1	240 00
			3195 00	20		1	350 00
				27		2	240 00
				31		2	20 00
				31		2	45 00
				31		2	500 00
							2435 00

Accounts Receivable — ACCOUNT NO. 12

DATE	ITEMS	POST. REF.	DEBIT	DATE	ITEMS	POST. REF.	CREDIT
1965				1965			
Oct. 2		1	600 00	Oct. 4		1	525 00
31	585.00	2	510 00				
			1110 00				

Supplies — ACCOUNT NO. 14

DATE	ITEMS	POST. REF.	DEBIT	DATE	ITEMS	POST. REF.	CREDIT
1965							
Oct. 2		1	400 00				
20		1	350 00				
			750 00				

Prepaid Rent — ACCOUNT NO. 15

DATE	ITEMS	POST. REF.	DEBIT	DATE	ITEMS	POST. REF.	CREDIT
1965							
Oct. 2		1	600 00				

Printing Equipment — ACCOUNT NO. 18

DATE	ITEMS	POST. REF.	DEBIT	DATE	ITEMS	POST. REF.	CREDIT
1965							
Oct. 2		1	3200 00				
3		1	1800 00				
			5000 00				

Accounts Payable — ACCOUNT NO. 21

DATE	ITEMS	POST. REF.	DEBIT	DATE	ITEMS	POST. REF.	CREDIT
1965				1965			
Oct. 10		1	400 00	Oct. 3	1400.00	1	1800 00

Ledger — Hull Print Shop

David Hull, Capital — ACCOUNT NO. 31

DATE		ITEMS	POST. REF.	DEBIT	DATE		ITEMS	POST. REF.	CREDIT
					1965 Oct.	2		1	5100 00

David Hull, Drawing — ACCOUNT NO. 32

DATE		ITEMS	POST. REF.	DEBIT	DATE		ITEMS	POST. REF.	CREDIT
1965 Oct.	31		2	500 00					

Sales — ACCOUNT NO. 41

DATE		ITEMS	POST. REF.	DEBIT	DATE		ITEMS	POST. REF.	CREDIT
					1965 Oct.	16		1	920 00
						31		2	850 00
						31		2	510 00

Salary Expense — ACCOUNT NO. 51

DATE		ITEMS	POST. REF.	DEBIT	DATE		ITEMS	POST. REF.	CREDIT
1965 Oct.	13		1	240 00					
	27		2	240 00					

Miscellaneous Expense — ACCOUNT NO. 59

DATE		ITEMS	POST. REF.	DEBIT	DATE		ITEMS	POST. REF.	CREDIT
1965 Oct.	6		1	40 00					
	31		2	20 00					
	31		2	45 00					

Ledger — Hull Print Shop (concluded)

Trial balance procedures

As the first step in preparing the trial balance, the accounts having two or more debits or credits were footed. For accounts having both debits and credits, the balance was also entered. These procedures are illustrated by the cash account appearing on page 59. The total debits and the total credits were entered in small pencil figures immediately below the last entry in each column so that they would not be mistaken for an entry nor interfere with a later posting on the following line. The balance of $760 was then entered in small pencil figures in the Items column of the debit side of the cash account on the same line as the footing.

The supplies, printing equipment, sales, salary expense, and miscellaneous expense accounts are also footed, but the balances are not entered in the Items columns as each account contains entries on one side of the account only and therefore the total is also the balance. Accounts having only one debit and one credit, such as the accounts payable account on page 59, are not footed, but the balance is entered in the Items column. Accounts that contain only one entry, such as the prepaid rent account, are not footed, and the balance is not entered in the Items column because the amount of the entry is the amount of the balance.

The trial balance taken from the ledger of Hull Print Shop on October 31 is shown below.

Hull Print Shop
Trial Balance
October 31, 1965

Cash	760 00	
Accounts Receivable	585 00	
Supplies	750 00	
Prepaid Rent	600 00	
Printing Equipment	5000 00	
Accounts Payable		1400 00
David Hull, Capital		5100 00
David Hull, Drawing	500 00	
Sales		2280 00
Salary Expense	480 00	
Miscellaneous Expense	105 00	
	8780 00	8780 00

Trial balance — Hull Print Shop

Other journal forms

The two-column journal provides for a chronological record of transactions. Its use also eliminates, for the most part, any need for explanations in the ledger accounts. It does increase the amount of work, however, as each debit and credit is recorded twice, first in the journal and then in the ledger. Some of the detail in the journal and the ledger is unnecessary and can be eliminated by adding special columns to the journal. In any particular case, the number of columns to be added and the manner of their use depend upon the frequency of occurrence of different types of transactions.

For example, examination of the journal on pages 57 and 58 discloses that out of a total of fifteen transactions recorded during the month, thirteen included a receipt or a payment of cash. It was necessary to write "Cash" in the journal thirteen times, and it was also necessary to make thirteen postings to the cash account. The necessity of writing "Cash" in the journal can be avoided by adding special "Cash Debit" and "Cash Credit" columns, and the many individual postings to the cash account in the ledger can be avoided by posting only the columnar totals at the end of each month. A four-column journal with special cash columns is illustrated below.

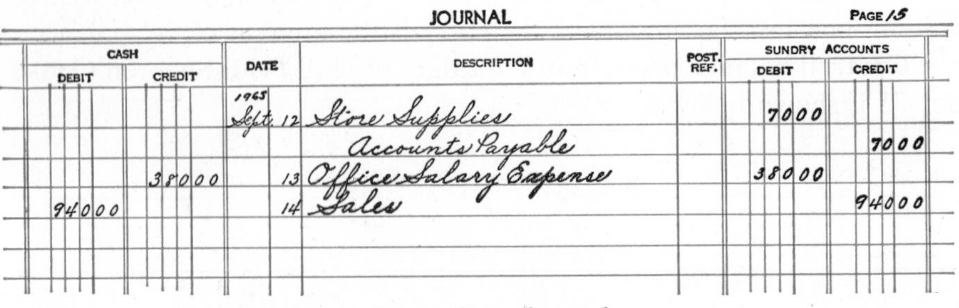

JOURNAL PAGE 15

Cash Debit	Cash Credit	Date	Description	Post. Ref.	Sundry Accounts Debit	Sundry Accounts Credit
		1965				
		Sept. 12	Store Supplies		70 00	
			Accounts Payable			70 00
	380 00	13	Office Salary Expense		380 00	
940 00		14	Sales			940 00

Four-column journal

The two amount columns on the left side of the journal are used exclusively for debits and credits to Cash; the two amount columns on the right side, captioned "Sundry Accounts," are used for debits and credits to all other accounts. The Description column is used for the titles of accounts that are debited or credited in the sundry columns.

The procedure for recording a transaction that does not affect Cash is the same as that followed in the two-column journal. The title of the account to be debited is written at the extreme left of the Description column and the title of the account to be credited is written on the next line, indented about one-half inch. The amounts are entered in the Sundry Accounts Debit and Credit columns in the usual manner.

Each transaction affecting Cash and one other account is recorded on one line. The amount of the debit or the credit to Cash is entered in the proper column at the left. The title of the other account affected is written in the Description column, and the amount is entered in the Sundry Accounts Debit or Credit column at the right. The account title may be written at the extreme left of the Description column, regardless of whether the account is being debited or credited.

It is usually unnecessary to insert explanations of routine transactions in multicolumn journals. The possible advantage of having an explanation after each entry is outweighed by the extra bookkeeping expense. In the relatively rare cases in which it becomes necessary to refer back to the explanation of a transaction, the details can be found in the supporting document that gave rise to the entry. For example, all disbursements of cash are supported by check stubs, paid-out slips, receipt forms, or other written evidence; and purchases of supplies, equipment, and other assets are supported by invoices. If in any case an explanation is desired in the columnar journal, it can be written in the Description column immediately below the entry.

It should be noted at this point that even though the four-column journal illustrated may be suitable for a specific business, it is merely one example. Many other applications of the multicolumn technique are used in practice. The number and the arrangement of the columns in any particular case depend upon the specific needs of the business.

Four-column journal illustrated

In order to illustrate more fully the use of the journal with special columns for cash, it will be assumed that David Hull adopts it as of January 1 of the following year. The journal for the month is illustrated on page 64. It has been totaled and all postings have been made. The procedure for posting the items in the Sundry Accounts Debit and Sundry Accounts Credit columns is exactly the same as in the case of the two-column journal illustrated earlier. The procedures for totaling and proving the amount columns and posting to the cash account are as follows:

(1) A single line is drawn across the money columns on the line below the last entry for the month.

(2) All four columns are added and the totals are entered below the ruled line.

(3) The equality of debits and credits is proved. This may be done on an adding machine tape or by a listing similar to the following:

	DEBIT	CREDIT
Cash columns	2,188.00	1,462.00
Sundry Accounts columns . . .	2,033.00	2,759.00
Total.	4,221.00	4,221.00

The totals of debits and credits have no significance in the accounting process other than to serve as a proof of the debit-credit equality of the entries in the journal.

(4) Below the totals, double lines are drawn across all columns except the Description column.

JOURNAL PAGE 9

CASH DEBIT	CASH CREDIT	DATE	DESCRIPTION	POST. REF.	SUNDRY ACCOUNTS DEBIT	SUNDRY ACCOUNTS CREDIT
		1966 Jan. 2	Printing Equipment	18	265 00	
			Accounts Payable	21		265 00
	30 00	2	Supplies	14	30 00	
290 00		5	Accounts Receivable	12		290 00
	240 00	9	Salary Expense	51	240 00	
		10	Accounts Receivable	12	250 00	
			Sales	41		250 00
	320 00	12	Accounts Payable	21	320 00	
	25 00	13	Miscellaneous Expense	59	25 00	
630 00		15	Sales	41		630 00
	150 00	16	David Hull, Drawing	32	150 00	
340 00		19	Accounts Receivable	12		340 00
	240 00	23	Salary Expense	51	240 00	
		26	Supplies	14	56 00	
			Accounts Payable	21		56 00
	93 00	29	Accounts Payable	21	93 00	
	22 00	31	Miscellaneous Expense	59	22 00	
	42 00	31	Miscellaneous Expense	59	42 00	
	300 00	31	David Hull, Drawing	32	300 00	
928 00		31	Sales	41		928 00
2,188 00	1,462 00				2,033 00	2,759 00
(11)	(11)				(✓)	(✓)

Four-column journal — Hull Print Shop

Cash ACCOUNT NO. 11

DATE	ITEMS	POST. REF.	DEBIT	DATE	ITEMS	POST. REF.	CREDIT
1966 Jan. 1	Balance	✓	1,038 61	1966 Jan. 31		9	1,462 00
31		9	2,188 00				

Cash account

(5) A check mark is placed in parentheses below the Sundry Accounts Debit and Sundry Accounts Credit totals. The check mark indicates that these totals are not to be posted because the individual items in the columns are posted separately.

(6) The total of the Cash Debit column is posted to the cash account and the number of the cash account is recorded in parentheses below the total. The same routine is followed in posting the total of the Cash Credit column.

The use of the four-column journal does not alter the postings to any of the accounts except Cash. The saving in time required in posting to the cash account may be observed by tracing the posting of the cash columns in the illustrative four-column journal to the cash account, which is reproduced immediately below the journal. If the January transactions of Hull Print Shop had been recorded in a two-column journal, there would have been four debit postings and ten credit postings to Cash instead of only one debit and one credit.

The foregoing presentation of a four-column journal is suggestive of the flexibility in the form of records of original entry. Additional forms of specialized journals will be discussed in later chapters.

Discovery of errors

The existence of errors in the accounts may be ascertained in a variety of ways: through audit procedures, through chance discovery, or through the medium of the trial balance. As was emphasized in Chapter 2, there are some types of errors that are not disclosed by the trial balance. If the debit and the credit totals of the trial balance are unequal, however, the reason for the discrepancy must be found and the error must be corrected.

The amount of the difference between the two totals of the trial balance sometimes gives a clue to the type or the location of the error. For example, a difference of 10, 100, or 1,000 in two totals is frequently the result of an error in addition. A difference between totals can also be due to the omission of a debit or a credit posting or, if it is divisible evenly by 2, to the posting of a debit as a credit, or vice versa. For example, if the debit and the credit totals of a trial balance are $20,640 and $20,236 respectively, the difference of $404 may indicate that a credit posting of that amount was omitted or that a credit of $202 was erroneously posted as a debit.

Two other common types of errors are known as *transpositions* and *slides*. A transposition is the erroneous rearrangement of digits, such as writing $542 as $452 or $524. In a slide the entire number is erroneously moved one or more spaces to the right or the left, such as writing $542.00 as $54.20 or $5,420.00. If a single error of either type has occurred, the discrepancy between the trial balance totals will be evenly divisible by 9.

A preliminary examination along the lines suggested by the preceding paragraphs will frequently disclose the error. If it does not, the general procedure is to retrace the various steps in the accounting process, beginning with the last step and working back to the original entries in the journal. While there are no rigid rules governing this check or audit, the following plan is suggested:

(1) Double check the totals that were obtained for the trial balance by re-adding the columns.

(2) Compare the listings in the trial balance with the balances shown in the ledger, making certain that no accounts have been omitted.
(3) Verify the accuracy of the account footings and balances by recomputing them.
(4) Trace the postings in the ledger back to the journal, placing a small check mark by the item in the ledger and also in the journal. If the error is not found, scrutinize each account to see if there is an entry without a check mark; do the same with the entries in the journal.
(5) Verify the equality of the debits and the credits in the journal.

Ordinarily, errors that affect the trial balance will be revealed before the foregoing procedures have been completed.

Correction of errors

It is inevitable that errors will occasionally be made in recording transactions in the journal and in posting to the accounts. Such errors should not be corrected by erasures, as erasures may arouse suspicions of dishonesty. The procedure for correcting errors varies with the nature of the error and the time of its discovery. If an incorrect account title or amount in a journal is discovered before the item has been posted, the correction is made by drawing a line through the error and by writing the correct title or amount immediately above. An incorrect amount posted to an account may be corrected in the same manner, by crossing out the incorrect amount and by inserting the correct figure immediately above.

The person responsible may initial the correction, as shown in the illustration below, if there is any likelihood of questions arising later.

Miscellaneous Expense ACCOUNT NO. *59*

DATE	ITEMS	POST. REF.	DEBIT	DATE	ITEMS	POST. REF.	CREDIT
1965 *Oct. 6*	*DC*	*1*	*440 00* ~~*400 00*~~				

Account with corrected posting

If an erroneous account title is entered in the journal and the posting has been completed, it is preferable to correct the error by means of an additional journal entry. For example, if at the end of the month it is discovered that a disbursement of $500 for office equipment on March 5 had been incorrectly journalized and posted as a debit to Office Supplies, a correcting entry should be made. Before attempting to record a correcting entry, it is helpful to set forth clearly (1) the erroneous entry and (2) the entry that should have been made. This may be done by the use of T accounts as in the example on the following page.

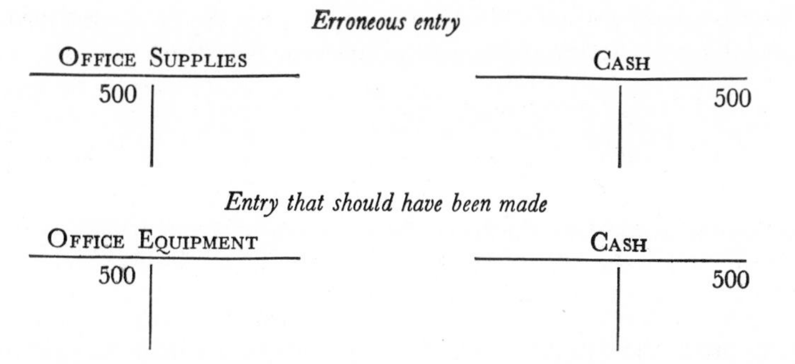

Comparison of the two sets of T accounts reveals that the erroneous debit of $500 to Office Supplies may be corrected by a $500 credit to that account and that Office Equipment should be debited for the same amount. The correcting entry is then journalized as follows:

Mar.	31	Office Equipment		500 00	
		Office Supplies			500 00
		To correct erroneous charge			
		to Office Supplies on March 5.			
		See invoice from Travis Supply			
		Company. CRN			

Correcting entry

Although there is some latitude in the methods employed to correct errors, the explanations should be sufficiently clear to be readily understood by anyone examining the records.

QUESTIONS

1. Rearrange the following in proper sequence: (a) business document prepared, (b) entry transferred to ledger, (c) entry recorded in journal, (d) business transaction occurs.

2. What is the synonym frequently used for journal?

3. To which record, the two-column journal or the ledger, should one refer to determine the following: (a) details of a specific transaction, (b) amount of the cash balance on the last day of the preceding month, (c) amount of service sales for a preceding month, (d) amount of cash paid in connection with a trade-in of equipment that occurred the preceding day.

4. When is it necessary to analyze transactions in terms of debit and credit: when journalizing? when posting? or at both times?

5. (a) When are account numbers recorded in the posting reference column of the journal? (b) What two things does the presence of a number in the posting reference column of the journal indicate?

6. What is the general sequence of accounts in the ledger?

7. Describe the three steps involved in posting the credit portion of the following journal entry (Accounts Payable is Account No. 21):

JOURNAL PAGE 16

19— Nov.	15	Equipment..........................		2,000	
		Accounts Payable..................			2,000

8. An invoice is received for $600 of equipment and $20 of supplies purchased on account. Give the compound journal entry to record the transaction.

9. Is it necessary to add the columns of a two-column journal at the end of the month to prove the equality of debits and credits? Explain.

10. Does the amount listed for Cash in the trial balance represent (a) the cash at the beginning of the period, (b) the receipts during the period, (c) the disbursements during the period, (d) the receipts minus the disbursements during the period, or (e) the balance of cash on the trial balance date?

11. At the end of September it is determined that cash of $94 received from David Alden on account was credited to Sales rather than to Accounts Receivable. (a) What effect would this error have on the trial balance totals? (b) When would such an error usually be discovered?

12. Give an example of (a) a transposition and (b) a slide.

13. In journalizing a purchase of supplies of $146.75 for cash, both amounts were recorded and posted as $164.75. (a) Would this error cause the trial balance to be out of balance? (b) Would the answer be the same if the entry had been journalized correctly but the credit to Cash had been posted as $164.75?

14. Are the totals of the Sundry Accounts Debit and Credit columns of a four-column journal posted to the ledger? Explain.

15. Would it be feasible to include enough special columns in a multicolumn journal to make Sundry Accounts Debit and Credit columns unnecessary? Explain.

EXERCISES

1. The Secretarial Employment Service has the following accounts in its ledger: Cash; Accounts Receivable; Supplies; Office Equipment; Accounts Payable; Helen Bowers, Capital; Helen Bowers, Drawing; Commissions Earned; Rent Expense; Advertising Expense; Utilities Expense; Miscellaneous Expense.

Record the following transactions completed during the month of July of the current year in a two-column journal:

July 1. Paid rent for the month, $150.
5. Paid cash for supplies, $25.
10. Purchased office equipment on account, $340.
14. Collected accounts receivable, $210.
21. Paid advertising expense, $30.
26. Paid creditor on account, $105.
29. Withdrew cash for personal use, $250.
31. Commissions earned and billed for month, $680.
31. Paid telephone and electricity bills for the month, $38.

2. (a) Record the transactions given in Exercise 1 in a four-column journal similar to the one on page 64.
(b) Total and rule the journal.
(c) Prove the equality of debits and credits, reporting the details as a part of your solution.

3. A number of errors in posting from a two-column journal are described below. Assuming in each case that no other errors had occurred during the month, you are to indicate: (1) whether the trial balance at the end of the month would be out of balance; (2) if answer to (1) is "yes", the amount by which the trial balance totals would differ; and (3) which column of the trial balance would have the larger total. Use a tabular form for your answers, employing the following headings:

Error	(1) Out of Balance (yes or no)	(2) Difference (amount)	(3) Larger Total (Dr. or Cr.)

(a) A credit of $200 to Accounts Receivable was posted to Sales.
(b) A debit of $300 to Equipment was posted twice.
(c) A debit of $738 to Supplies was posted as $378.
(d) A credit of $100 to Accounts Payable was not posted.
(e) An entry debiting Miscellaneous Expense and crediting Cash for $20 was not posted.
(f) A credit of $120 to Cash was posted as $1,200.
(g) A debit of $50 to Accounts Receivable was posted as a credit.

4. A number of errors in recording transactions are described below. Present the necessary correcting entries in a two-column journal.

(a) A $200 payment for advertising expense was charged to Supplies.
(b) A cash withdrawal of $300 was recorded as a debit to H. B. Morris, Capital and a credit to Cash.
(c) Cash of $340 received from a customer on account was recorded as a debit to Cash and a credit to Accounts Receivable for $430.
(d) Equipment of $2,000 purchased for cash was recorded as a debit to Buildings and a credit to Accounts Payable.
(e) Rent of $150 for the current month was recorded as a debit to Prepaid Insurance and a credit to Cash.

PROBLEMS

3-1. The ledger of Judson Decorators includes the following accounts: Cash, 11; Accounts Receivable, 12; Supplies, 13; Prepaid Insurance, 14; Truck, 16; Equipment, 18; Notes Payable, 21; Accounts Payable, 22; B. T. Judson, Capital, 31; B. T. Judson, Drawing, 32; Sales, 41; Wages Expense, 51; Rent Expense, 53; Truck Expense, 54; Miscellaneous Expense, 59.

The enterprise completed the following transactions during October of the current year:

Oct. 16. The owner invested cash, $2,000, and equipment, $300, in the business.
16. Purchased supplies for cash, $70.
16. Purchased a truck for $3,400, paying $1,000 cash and giving a note payable for the remainder.

Oct. 17. Purchased additional equipment on account, $150.
18. Paid rent for period of October 16 to end of month, $75.
19. Received cash for job completed, $120.
22. Purchased supplies on account, $260.
23. Paid wages of employees, $410.
25. Paid premiums on property and casualty insurance, $296.
26. Paid creditors on account, $240.
27. Recorded sales on account and sent invoices to customers, $1,920.
28. Received cash for job completed, $140. This sale had not been recorded previously.
29. Received an invoice for truck expenses, to be paid in November, $41.
29. Paid miscellaneous expenses, $33.
30. Received cash from customers on account, $1,400.
31. Paid wages of employees, $430.
31. Withdrew cash for personal use, $300.

Instructions: (1) Open the accounts listed above.
(2) Record the transactions for October in a two-column journal.
(3) Post from the journal to the ledger.
(4) Take a trial balance of the ledger.

3-2. The ledger of Starr TV Service includes the accounts listed below. The amounts shown for the asset, liability, and capital accounts are the balances as of January 1 of the current year.

Acct. No.	*Account Title*	*Balance*	*Acct. No.*	*Account Title*	*Balance*
11	Cash	$1,637.70	22	Accounts Payable	$ 379.30
12	Supplies	964.00	31	H. W. Starr, Capital	5,217.80
13	Prepaid Insurance	86.80	32	H. W. Starr, Drawing	——
14	Prepaid Rent	——	41	Service Sales	——
16	Equipment	4,724.60	51	Wages Expense	——
17	Accumulated Depr.	1,816.00	52	Utilities Expense	——
21	Notes Payable	——	53	Advertising Expense	——
			58	Miscellaneous Exp.	——

The transactions completed by the business during January were as follows:

Jan. 2. Paid rent for three months, beginning January 1, $450.
2. Paid cash for advertising, $20.
4. Purchased equipment for $1,000, paying $400 cash and giving a note payable for the balance.
5. Purchased supplies on account, $77.60.
6. Recorded cash sales for the week, $397.70.
9. Paid premium on property insurance, $36.
10. Paid creditors on account, $247.20.
13. Paid biweekly wages, $460.
13. Recorded cash sales for the week, $415.60.
15. Paid cash for repairs to equipment, $17.40.
16. Owner withdrew cash for personal use, $225.
19. Purchased supplies on account, $122.60.
20. Recorded cash sales for the week, $462.20.
22. Returned supplies purchased on the 19th for credit, $11.40.
25. Paid miscellaneous expenses, $21.40.

Jan. 27. Recorded cash sales for the week, $375.60.
27. Paid biweekly wages, $440.
30. Owner withdrew cash for personal use, $250.
31. Paid electricity and gas expenses for the month, $37.60.
31. Recorded cash sales for the remainder of the month, $176.10.
31. Paid water expense for the month, $9.30.

Instructions: (1) Open all accounts listed above.

(2) Record the balances in the accounts under the date of Jan. 1, write "Balance" in the Items column, and place a check mark in the posting reference column.

(3) Record the transactions for January in a four-column journal similar to the one illustrated on page 64.

(4) Total and rule the journal. Prove the equality of debits and credits.

(5) Post to the ledger.

(6) Take a trial balance of the ledger.

(7) How many additional postings would have been required if a two-column journal had been used instead of a four-column journal?

3-3. The selected transactions and errors described below relate to the accounts of Melody Heights Co. during the current fiscal year:

June 16. J. D. Boone established the business with the investment of $5,000 in cash and $600 in equipment, on which there was an unpaid balance of $250. The account payable is to be recorded on the books of the enterprise.

July 7. Discovered that $30 of supplies returned to the supplier for credit had been journalized and posted as a debit to Accounts Receivable and a credit to Equipment.

Aug. 12. Received $408 as payment on a note receivable ($400) and interest income ($8).

Aug. 25. Discovered that cash of $420, received from a customer on account, had been journalized and posted as a debit to Cash and a credit to Commissions Earned.

Sept. 10. Acquired land and a building to be used as an office at a contract price of $20,000, of which $2,000 was allocated to the land. The property was encumbered by a mortgage of $11,000. Paid the seller $9,000 in cash and agreed to assume the responsibility for paying the mortgage note.

Oct. 20. Discovered that a cash payment of $52 for supplies had been journalized and posted as a debit to Miscellaneous Expense of $25 and a credit to Cash of $25.

Nov. 5. Discovered that a withdrawal of $600 by the owner had been charged to Salary Expense.

Dec. 9. Paid the installment due on the mortgage note, $500, and interest expense, $165.

Instructions: Journalize the transactions and the corrections in a two-column journal. When there are more than two items in an entry, present the entry in compound form.

3-4. Robert Conlon owns and manages Conlon Realty, which acts as an agent in buying, selling, renting, and managing real estate. The account balances at the end of April and the transactions for May of the current year are presented on the following page.

		Dr.	Cr.
11	Cash	1,742	
12	Accounts Receivable	4,624	
13	Prepaid Insurance	297	
14	Office Supplies	85	
16	Automobile	4,800	
17	Accumulated Depreciation — Automobile		2,700
18	Office Equipment	3,160	
19	Accumulated Depreciation — Office Equipment		965
21	Accounts Payable		148
31	Robert Conlon, Capital		5,607
32	Robert Conlon, Drawing	4,000	
41	Revenue from Fees		24,912
51	Salary and Commission Expense	13,200	
52	Rent Expense	1,200	
53	Advertising Expense	765	
54	Automobile Expense	283	
59	Miscellaneous Expense	176	

May 1. Paid rent for month, $300.
2. Purchased office supplies on account, $72.
4. Purchased office equipment on account, $420.
10. Received cash from clients on account, $2,415.
12. Paid premium on automobile insurance, $223.
15. Paid salaries and commissions, $1,620.
15. Recorded revenue earned and billed to clients during first half of month, $2,514.
16. Discovered that the $72 amount stated and journalized for the transaction of May 2 should have been $27.
18. Paid creditors on account, $595.
20. Received cash from clients on account, $3,130.
23. Paid advertising expense, $162.
24. Returned for credit an item of office equipment purchased on May 4, $41.
28. Paid automobile expenses, $74.
29. Paid miscellaneous expenses, $53.
30. Conlon withdrew cash for personal use, $1,000.
31. Recorded revenue earned and billed to clients during second half of month, $2,274.
31. Paid salaries and commissions, $1,565.

Instructions: (1) Open an account in the ledger for each item for which an account balance is given.

(2) Record the balance in each account under the date of May 1, write the word "Balance" in the Items column, and place a check mark in the posting reference column.

(3) Record the transactions for May in a two-column journal.

(4) Post to the ledger.

(5) An error is discovered in billing the fees for the second half of the month. The correct amount is $2,247 instead of $2,274. Journalize the correcting entry and post.

(6) Take a trial balance of the ledger.

(7) What is the nature of the balance in Accounts Payable? Asset -

4.

Completion of the accounting cycle

Trial balance and accounting statements

The trial balance prepared at the close of an accounting period provides much, but not all, of the information needed in preparing the financial statements. During the period all transactions between the enterprise and other companies or individuals were journalized and posted to the ledger. Barring errors, it might seem reasonable to assume that the account balances listed in the trial balance are the correct amounts for use in preparing the balance sheet, the income statement, and the capital statement. The assumption of correctness is valid for some accounts but not for others. For example, the balance of the cash account represents the amount of cash available on the last day of the period. On the other hand, the balance of the supplies account represents the cost of the supplies in stock at the beginning of the period plus the cost of those acquired during the period. Some of these supplies have been used during the period and consequently the balance of the account is greater than the cost of the supplies on hand at the end of the period.

Similarly, the balances in the prepaid insurance account and the other prepaid expense accounts will be greater than the cost of the unexpired assets remaining at the end of the period. Transactions between the enterprise and outsiders that affected these accounts were recorded as they occurred, but the day-by-day expirations of the assets have not been recorded.

Data in the trial balance may also be incomplete because of unrecorded revenue or expense of the period that will not be collected or paid until some later date. For example, salaries incurred between the last payday and the end of the fiscal period would not be recorded in the accounts because salaries are customarily recorded only when they are paid. They are an expense of the period, however, because the services were rendered during the period, and they are a liability as of the last day of the period because they are owed to the employees.

The foregoing examples of unrecorded transactions of an internal nature evidence the need for additional accounting procedures that will provide correct data for the financial statements.

Mixed accounts and business operations

An account with a balance that is partly a balance sheet amount and partly an income statement amount is called a *mixed account*. For example, the balance of the supplies account, as listed on the trial balance, represents the cost of all supplies on hand at the beginning of the period plus those purchased during the period. At the end of the period it is known that some of the supplies have been used. Therefore, the trial balance amount is composed of two elements, the supplies on hand at the end of the period, which is an unexpired cost or asset, and the supplies used during the period, which is an expired cost or expense. Before financial statements are prepared, it is necessary to determine the amount allocable to the asset and the amount allocable to the expense.

The amount of the asset can be determined by counting the quantity of each of the various commodities, multiplying each quantity by the unit cost of that particular commodity, and totaling the dollar amounts thus obtained. The resulting figure represents the amount of the supplies inventory (asset). The cost of the supplies consumed (expense) is then determined by deducting the amount of the inventory from the balance of the supplies account. On the basis of this information, the cost of the supplies used can be transferred from the asset account to the supplies expense account.

An alternative to initially recording the cost of supplies and other prepaid expenses as assets is to record them as expenses. When this procedure is adopted, Supplies Expense and other expense accounts would be mixed accounts at the end of the period and it would be necessary to transfer the unexpired cost from the expense accounts to appropriate asset accounts. Further consideration will be given to this alternative procedure in Chapter 9. In the meantime all expenditures that include prepayments of expense for future periods will be initially recorded as assets. It is important to note that, before preparing financial statements, it is always necessary to determine the portions of mixed accounts allocable to assets and expenses, regardless of the recording procedure employed.

Advance payments applicable solely to a particular accounting period are sometimes made at the beginning of that particular period. When this is the case, the expenditure is usually debited directly to an expense account. The expense account will be mixed during the period, but it will be wholly expense at the end of the period. For example, if rent for March is paid on March 1, it is almost entirely an asset at the time of payment. The asset expires gradually from day to day, and at the end of the month the entire amount has become an expense. Therefore, if the expenditure is initially recorded as a debit to Rent Expense, no additional entry will be required at the close of the period.

Adjusting process

The entries required at the end of a fiscal period to record internal transactions are called *adjusting entries*. In a broad sense they may be said to be corrections to the ledger. But the necessity for bringing the ledger up to date is a planned part of the accounting procedure; it is not caused by errors. The term "adjusting entries" is therefore more appropriate than "correcting entries."

The illustrations of adjusting entries that follow are based on the ledger of Hull Print Shop. T accounts are used in place of the standard form of accounts and the adjusting entries are shown in bold face type to differentiate them from the entries recorded during the month.

Prepaid expenses. According to Hull's trial balance appearing on page 61, the balance in the supplies account on October 31 is $750. Some of these supplies (paper, ink, etc.) have been used during the past month and some are still in stock. If the amount of either is known, the other can be readily determined. It is more economical to determine the cost of the supplies on hand at the end of the month and to assume that the remainder have been used than it is to keep a record of those used from day to day. Assuming that the inventory of supplies on October 31 is determined to be $230, the amount to be transferred from the asset account to the expense account is computed as follows:

Supplies available (balance of account)	$750
Supplies on hand (inventory)	230
Supplies used (amount of adjustment)	$520

Increases in expense accounts are recorded as debits and decreases in asset accounts are recorded as credits. Hence the adjusting entry required is a debit to Supplies Expense and a credit to Supplies of $520. After the $520 has been transferred to Supplies Expense, the asset account has a debit balance of $230 and the expense account has a debit balance of $520.

Supplies					Supplies Expense		
Oct. 2	400	Oct. 31	520	→	Oct. 31	520	
20	350						
	750						

Prepaid Rent is another mixed account that requires adjustment at the end of the accounting period. The debit balance in this account represents in part an expense of the current period and in part a prepayment of expense of future periods. The portion that is expense should be transferred to the expense account, Rent Expense.

The debit of $600 in the prepaid rent account represents payment of rent for three months, October, November, and December. At the end of October, the rent expense account should be increased (debited) and the prepaid rent account should be decreased (credited) for $200, the rental for one month. The two accounts appear as follows after the adjusting entry has been recorded:

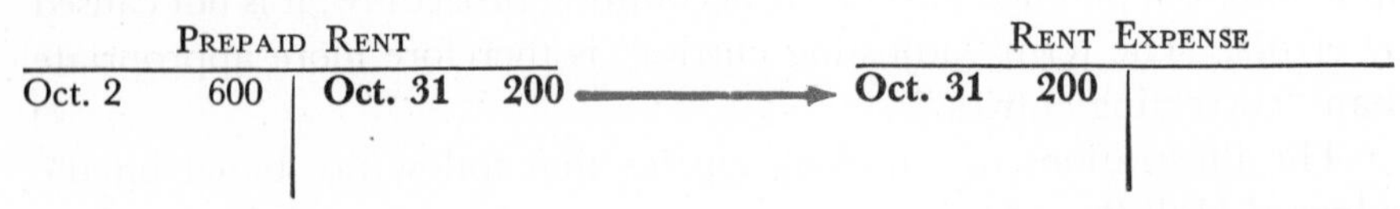

Prepaid Rent					Rent Expense		
Oct. 2	600	Oct. 31	200	→	Oct. 31	200	

The prepaid rent account now has a debit balance of $400, which is an asset; the rent expense account has a debit balance of $200, which is an expense.

If adjustments for these prepayments were not made, assets and capital would be overstated on the balance sheet for October 31 and net income would be overstated on the income statement for the month of October.

Plant assets. As was explained in earlier chapters, all plant assets except land depreciate. The adjusting entry to record depreciation is similar to those illustrated in the preceding section in that there is a transfer from an asset account to an expense account. The amount to be transferred to expense, however, must be based on estimate rather than on verifiable facts, as in the case of expiration of rent and other prepaid expenses. Because of this and the desire to present both the original cost and the accumulated depreciation on the balance sheet, the reduction of the asset is credited to an account entitled "Accumulated Depreciation."

The adjusting entry to record depreciation for October is illustrated in the T accounts below. The estimated amount of depreciation[1] for the month is $40.

---

[1]Methods of estimating depreciation will be presented in a later chapter.

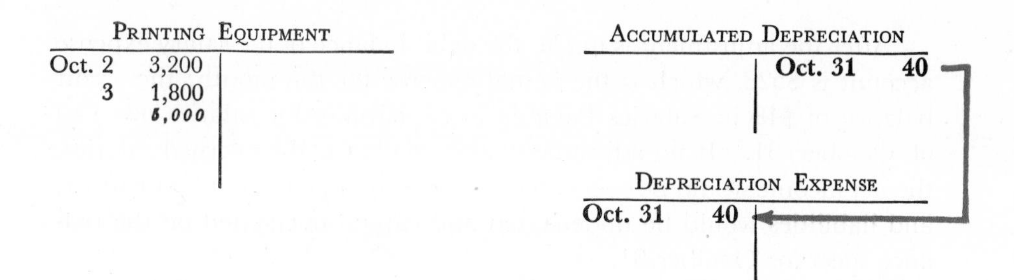

The accumulated depreciation account is called a *contra asset* account. The $40 increase in the account represents a subtraction from the corresponding asset account. The relationship of the two accounts is perhaps indicated best by the manner in which they are presented on the balance sheet, which is as follows:

Plant assets:		
Printing equipment	$5,000	
Less accumulated depreciation	40	$4,960

The difference between cost and accumulated depreciation represents the unexpired cost of the plant asset and is customarily referred to as *book value*.

Accrued expenses (liabilities). It is customary to pay for some types of services and commodities, such as insurance and supplies, in advance of their use. It is also customary to receive other services and commodities for which payment is not made until after they have been consumed. One of the most common examples is salaries. The expense accrues day by day and payment is made on a weekly, biweekly, or other regular basis. If the last day of a pay period does not coincide with the last day of the fiscal period, there is an expense and a liability that must be recorded in the accounts by an adjusting entry.

The data in the T accounts below were taken from the ledger of Hull Print Shop. The debits of $240 on October 13 and 27 in the salary expense account were biweekly payments on alternate Fridays for the payroll periods ended on those days. The salaries earned on Monday and Tuesday, October 30 and 31, amount to $48. This amount is an additional expense of October and it is therefore debited to the salary expense account. It is also a liability as of October 31 and it is therefore credited to Salaries Payable.

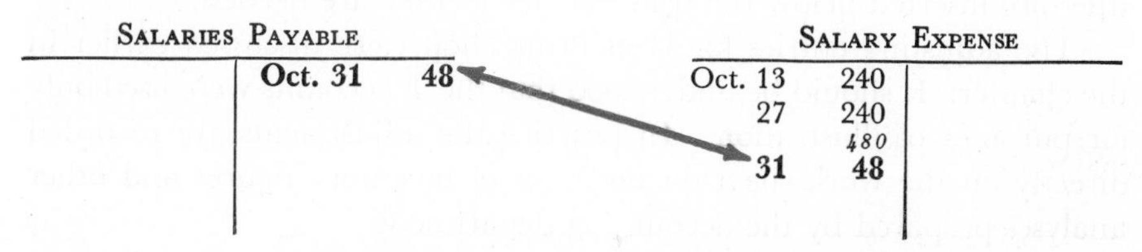

After the adjustment is made, the debit balance of the salary expense account is $528, which is the actual expense for the month; the credit balance of $48 in Salaries Payable is the liability for salaries owed as of October 31. If no adjustment were made for the accrued salaries, the net income would be overstated on the income statement for October, and liabilities would be understated and capital overstated on the balance sheet for October 31.

Work sheet

Adjustments such as those just discussed must be considered in preparing the income statement and the balance sheet. But before the adjustments are actually recorded in the journal and posted to the ledger, a form known as a *work sheet* may be prepared. Its use lessens the chance of overlooking an adjustment, provides a check on the accuracy of the work, and arranges data in a logical form for the preparation of the statements.

The work sheet for Hull Print Shop is presented on page 79. Note that there are three parts to the heading: (1) the name of the enterprise, (2) the title "Work Sheet," and (3) the period of time covered. It has a column for account titles and ten money columns, arranged in five pairs of debit and credit columns. The principal headings of the five sets of money columns are as follows:

1. Trial Balance
2. Adjustments
3. Adjusted Trial Balance
4. Income Statement
5. Balance Sheet

Trial Balance columns. The first step in the preparation of the work sheet is the trial balance. The trial balance may be prepared on another sheet first and then copied on the work sheet, or it may be prepared directly on the work sheet.

Adjustments columns. The adjustments required at the end of the period are recorded in the Adjustments columns. Inasmuch as the debit and the credit portions of an adjustment are usually widely separated on the work sheet, it is customary to cross-reference them by inserting a letter at the left of each item. Some of the accounts requiring adjustment do not appear in the trial balance. In such cases the appropriate account titles are inserted below the trial balance as they are needed.

The adjusting entries for Hull Print Shop were discussed earlier in the chapter. It should be understood that the T accounts were used only for purposes of illustration. In practice the adjustments are recorded directly on the work sheet on the basis of inventory figures and other analyses prepared by the accounting department.

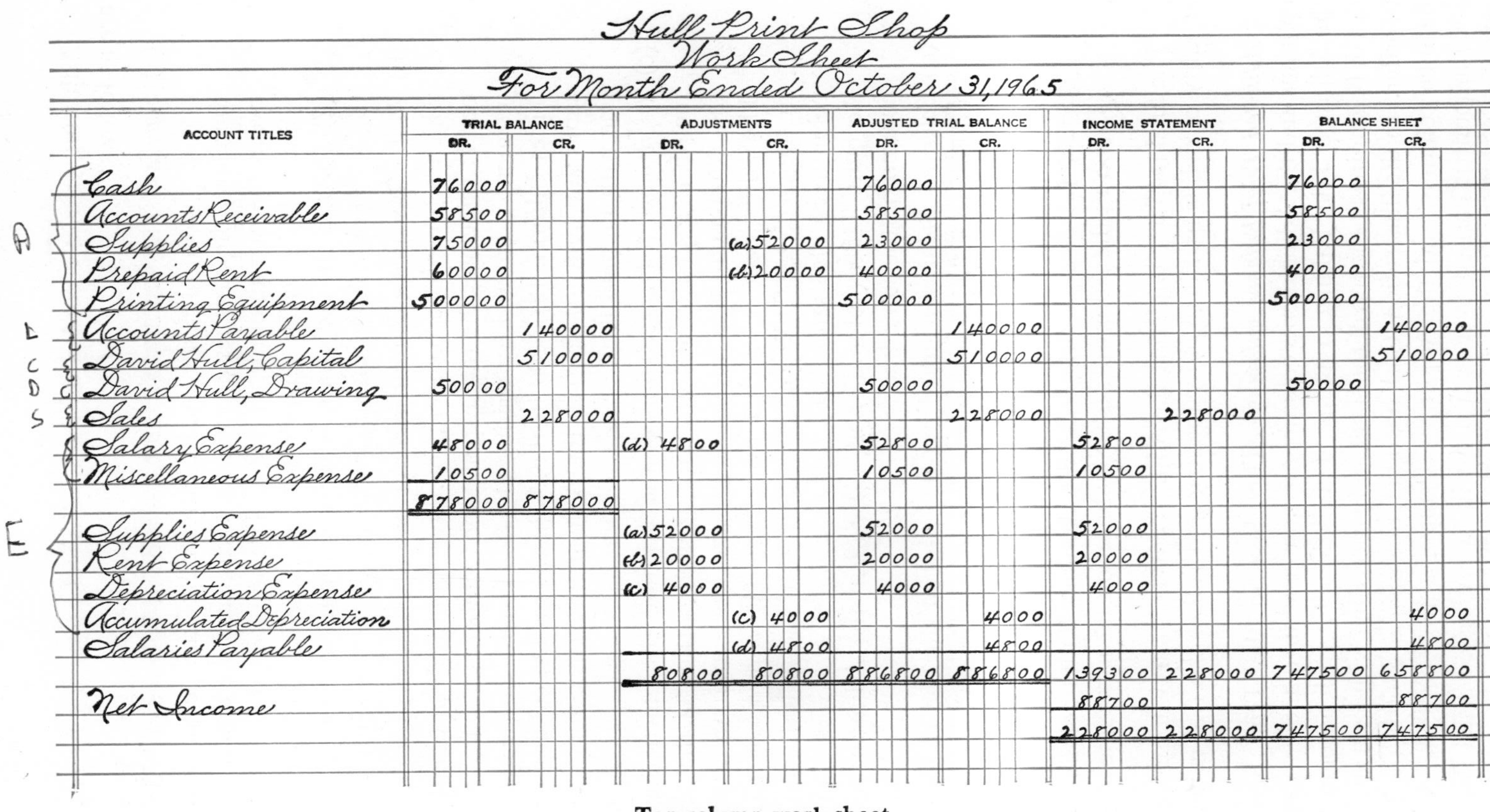

Hull Print Shop
Work Sheet
For Month Ended October 31, 1965

ACCOUNT TITLES	TRIAL BALANCE		ADJUSTMENTS		ADJUSTED TRIAL BALANCE		INCOME STATEMENT		BALANCE SHEET	
	DR.	CR.	DR.	CR.	DR.	CR.	DR.	CR.	DR.	CR.
Cash	76000				76000				76000	
Accounts Receivable	58500				58500				58500	
Supplies	75000			(a) 52000	23000				23000	
Prepaid Rent	60000			(b) 20000	40000				40000	
Printing Equipment	500000				500000				500000	
Accounts Payable		140000				140000				140000
David Hull, Capital		510000				510000				510000
David Hull, Drawing	50000				50000				50000	
Sales		228000				228000		228000		
Salary Expense	48000		(d) 4800		52800		52800			
Miscellaneous Expense	10500				10500		10500			
	878000	878000								
Supplies Expense			(a) 52000		52000		52000			
Rent Expense			(b) 20000		20000		20000			
Depreciation Expense			(c) 4000		4000		4000			
Accumulated Depreciation				(c) 4000		4000				4000
Salaries Payable				(d) 4800		4800				4800
			80800	80800	886800	886800	139300	228000	747500	658800
Net Income							88700			88700
							228000	228000	747500	747500

Ten-column work sheet

Adjusting entries recorded on the work sheet appearing on page 79 are as follows:

(a) *Supplies.* The supplies account has a debit balance of $750; the cost of the supplies on hand at the end of the period is $230; therefore, the supplies expense for October is the difference between the two amounts, or $520. The adjustment is entered by writing (1) *Supplies Expense* in the Account Titles column, (2) *$520* in the Adjustments Dr. column on the same line, and (3) *$520* in the Adjustments Cr. column on the line with Supplies.

(b) *Rent.* The prepaid rent account has a debit balance of $600, which represents a payment for three months beginning October 1; therefore, the rent expense for October is $200. The adjustment is entered by writing (1) *Rent Expense* in the Account Titles column, (2) *$200* in the Adjustments Dr. column on the same line, and (3) *$200* in the Adjustments Cr. column on the line with Prepaid Rent.

(c) *Depreciation.* Depreciation of the printing equipment for the month is estimated at $40. This expired portion of the cost of the equipment is a reduction in the asset and an expense. The adjustment is entered by writing (1) *Depreciation Expense* in the Account Titles column, (2) *$40* in the Adjustments Dr. column on the same line, (3) *Accumulated Depreciation* in the Account Titles column, and (4) *$40* in the Adjustments Cr. column on the same line.

(d) *Salaries.* Salaries accrued but not paid at the end of October amount to $48. This is an increase in expense and an increase in liabilities. The adjustment is entered by writing (1) *$48* in the Adjustments Dr. column on the same line with Salary Expense, (2) *Salaries Payable* in the Account Titles column, and (3) *$48* in the Adjustments Cr. column on the same line.

The final step in completing the Adjustments columns is to prove the equality of debits and credits by totaling and ruling the two columns.

Adjusted Trial Balance columns. The data in the Trial Balance columns and the Adjustments columns are now combined and entered in the Adjusted Trial Balance columns. This is done for each account title listed, beginning at the top of the sheet and proceeding with each account in order. In the illustration, Cash has a debit balance of $760 in the Trial Balance columns, and the Adjustments columns are blank; hence the $760 amount is carried over as a debit in the Adjusted Trial Balance columns. Similarly, the balance in Accounts Receivable is carried over.

Supplies has a debit balance of $750 and a credit adjustment of $520, which yields an adjusted debit balance of $230.

This procedure is continued until all account balances, with or without adjustment as the case may be, have been entered in the Adjusted Trial Balance columns. Note that for accounts listed below the trial balance totals, the amount of the adjustment becomes the adjusted balance of the account. For example, Supplies Expense has an initial balance of zero and a debit adjustment of $520, yielding an adjusted debit balance of $520.

The Adjusted Trial Balance columns are completed by totaling and ruling the two columns to prove that the equality of debits and credits has been maintained.

Income Statement and Balance Sheet columns. Each amount entered in the Adjusted Trial Balance columns is extended to one of the remaining four columns. Asset, liability, and capital items are extended to the Balance Sheet columns, and revenue and expense items are extended to the Income Statement columns. All debit balances in the Adjusted Trial Balance columns will then appear in either the Balance Sheet Dr. column or the Income Statement Dr. column, and all credit balances will likewise appear in the appropriate credit columns.

After all of the balances have been extended, the four columns are totaled. The amount of the net income or the net loss for the period is then determined by ascertaining the amount of the difference between the totals of the two Income Statement columns. If the credit column total is greater than the debit column total, the excess is the net income. For the work sheet presented on page 79, the computation of net income is as follows:

Total of credit column (revenue)	$2,280.00
Total of debit column (expenses)	1,393.00
Net income (excess of revenue over expenses)	$ 887.00

The income statement accounts are temporary accounts that are used to accumulate revenues and expenses during the fiscal period. At the end of the fiscal period, the net balance of all of these accounts is transferred to capital. In this case, the net credit balance of $887 is transferred to the credit side of the capital account. The transfer is shown on the work sheet by a debit entry in the Income Statement Dr. column and a credit entry in the Balance Sheet Cr. column. The words "Net Income" are written in the Account Titles column as an explanation of this transfer.

The columns are then totaled and ruled in the manner shown on page 82. The totals of the two Income Statement columns are equal

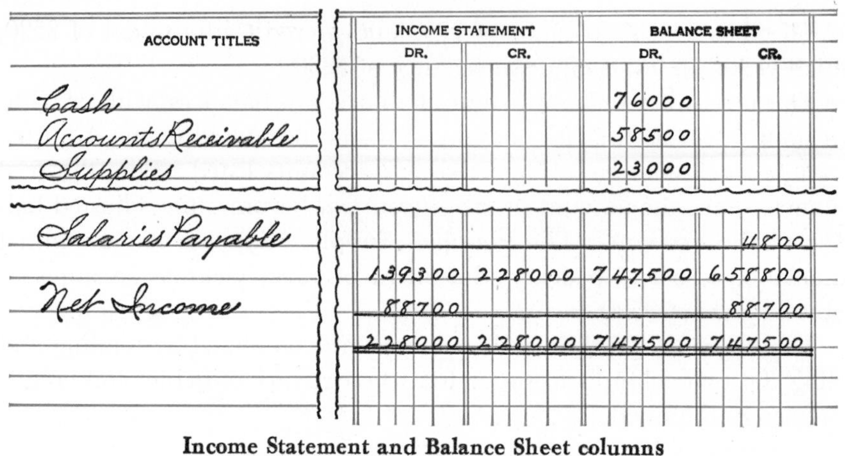

ACCOUNT TITLES	INCOME STATEMENT DR.	INCOME STATEMENT CR.	BALANCE SHEET DR.	BALANCE SHEET CR.
Cash			76000	
Accounts Receivable			58500	
Supplies			23000	
Salaries Payable				4800
	139300	228000	747500	658800
Net Income	88700			88700
	228000	228000	747500	747500

Income Statement and Balance Sheet columns of the work sheet totaled and ruled

because the net income, $887, was obtained as the difference between the original totals of these columns. The totals of the Balance Sheet columns are also equal because, after the net income has been transferred to the capital account, Assets = Liabilities + Capital.

If total expenses of the period should exceed total revenue, the subtotal of the Income Statement Dr. column would be greater than the subtotal of the credit column. The difference between the two amounts would be the net loss for the period. Losses decrease capital; therefore the net loss would be entered in the Income Statement Cr. column and would be transferred to the Balance Sheet Dr. column as a decrease in capital.

The work sheet is a device employed by the accountant as the basis for completing the work at the end of the fiscal period. It is not a formal statement and does not take the place of the formal balance sheet and income statement. Since the work sheet is not presented to the owner, manager, or others interested in the business, it is customarily prepared in pencil.

Financial statements

The income statement, balance sheet, and capital statement prepared from the work sheet of Hull Print Shop appear on pages 83 and 84. With the exception of the balance sheet, the form of the statements corresponds to those presented in Chapter 1.

The asset and liability sections of the balance sheet are expanded by the addition of subcaptions for current assets, plant assets, and current liabilities. The form may be varied slightly by deducting the sum of the liabilities from the sum of the assets to yield capital. This emphasizes the accounting equation in the form A − L = C. Additional variations in the form of the balance sheet will be presented in later chapters. There are also a number of variations in the title given to the statement, such as *statement of financial condition* and *statement of financial position.*

Hull Print Shop
Income Statement
For Month Ended October 31, 1965

Sales		$2,280.00
Operating expenses:		
Salary expense	$ 528.00	
Supplies expense	520.00	
Rent expense	200.00	
Depreciation expense	40.00	
Miscellaneous expense.	105.00	
Total operating expenses. . . .		1,393.00
Net income from operations.		$ 887.00

Income statement

Hull Print Shop
Balance Sheet
October 31, 1965

Assets		
Current assets:		
Cash	$ 760.00	
Accounts receivable.	585.00	
Supplies	230.00	
Prepaid rent	400.00	
Total current assets.		$1,975.00
Plant assets:		
Printing equipment	$5,000.00	
Less accumulated depreciation .	40.00	4,960.00
Total assets.		$6,935.00
Liabilities		
Current liabilities:		
Accounts payable	$1,400.00	
Salaries payable	48.00	
Total liabilities		$1,448.00
Capital		
David Hull, capital		5,487.00
Total liabilities and capital		$6,935.00

Balance sheet

Hull Print Shop
Capital Statement
For Month Ended October 31, 1965

Capital, October 2, 1965.		$5,100.00
Net income for the month.	$ 887.00	
Less withdrawals.	500.00	
Increase in capital		387.00
Capital, October 31, 1965		$5,487.00

Capital statement

All the accounting information for the income statement and the balance sheet is taken from the last four columns of the work sheet. In preparing the capital statement it is necessary to refer to the capital account in the ledger to determine the balance at the beginning of the period and the amount of any additional investments that may have been made during the period. In the illustration, the balance in the capital account remained unchanged during the period. The amounts of net income and withdrawals for the period are taken from the Balance Sheet columns of the work sheet, and the balance of capital at the end of the period is determined arithmetically.

The form of the capital statement can be modified to meet the circumstances of any particular case. In the preceding illustration the amount withdrawn by the owner was less than the net income. If the withdrawals had exceeded the net income, the order of the two items would have been reversed and the difference between the two items, captioned "Decrease in capital," would have been deducted from the beginning capital.

Other occurrences, such as additional investments by the owner or a net loss for the period, also necessitate modifications in form, as:

Capital, January 1.	$35,000.00	
Additional investment, July 1.	6,000.00	
Total.		$41,000.00
Net loss for the year.	$ 8,000.00	
Withdrawals.	3,600.00	
Decrease in capital.		11,600.00
Capital, December 31.		$29,400.00

The capital statement that accompanies the balance sheet of a partnership is basically the same as those illustrated above except that the changes in each individual partner's capital are shown. For a corporation a report called a *retained earnings statement* serves somewhat the same purpose. It summarizes the changes during the period in the accumulated net income of a corporation.

Journalizing and posting adjusting entries

At the end of the fiscal period, the adjusting entries are recorded in the journal and are then posted to the ledger. The data in the accounts are then in agreement with the financial statements.

The adjusting entries may be copied directly from the Adjustments columns of the work sheet, using the next available space in the journal. The adjusting entries are dated as of the last day of the accounting period, even though they are actually recorded at a later date. Each entry may be supported by an explanation, or the group may be identified by writing "Adjusting Entries" above the first entry in the series. The work sheet and the supporting documents on adjustment data should be kept on file for future reference.

The adjusting entries in the journal of Hull Print Shop appear below. The accounts to which the adjusting entries have been posted appear in the ledger beginning on page 89. All adjusting entries are identified in the Items columns of the accounts as an aid to the student. It is not necessary that this be done in actual practice.

JOURNAL PAGE 2

DATE		DESCRIPTION	POST. REF.	DEBIT	CREDIT
		Adjusting Entries			
	31	Supplies Expense	52	520 00	
		Supplies	14		520 00
	31	Rent Expense	53	200 00	
		Prepaid Rent	15		200 00
	31	Depreciation Expense	54	40 00	
		Accumulated Depreciation	19		40 00
	31	Salary Expense	51	48 00	
		Salaries Payable	22		48 00

Adjusting entries

Closing entries

As was explained earlier, the revenue, expense, and drawing accounts are temporary accounts employed in classifying and summarizing changes in capital during the accounting period. At the end of the period the net effect of these accounts must be recorded in the permanent capital account so that its balance will agree with the amount of capital shown on the balance sheet. The balances in the temporary accounts must also be reduced to zero so that they can be used to record data for the ensuing accounting period. Both objectives are accomplished by a series of entries known as *closing entries.*

An account titled *Expense and Revenue Summary* is used for summarizing the data in the revenue and expense accounts. It is employed only at the end of the accounting period and is both opened and closed during the closing process. Various other titles are used for the account, including *Profit and Loss Summary*, *Income and Expense Summary*, and *Income Summary*.

The entries required to close the temporary accounts at the end of the period are as follows:

(1) Each revenue account is debited for the amount of its balance, and Expense and Revenue Summary is credited for the total revenue.
(2) Each expense account is credited for the amount of its balance, and Expense and Revenue Summary is debited for the total expense.
(3) Expense and Revenue Summary is debited for the amount of its balance (net income), and the capital account is credited for the same amount. (Debit and credit will be reversed for a net loss.)
(4) The drawing account is credited for the amount of its balance, and the capital account is debited for the same amount.

After the foregoing series of entries are journalized and posted to the ledger, the balance in the capital account will agree with the amount shown on the balance sheet and the revenue, expense, and drawing accounts will be closed (zero balances). The closing entries for Hull Print Shop are illustrated in T accounts on page 87. The arrows indicate the direction of the flow of figures.

The account titles and amounts needed in journalizing the closing entries may be obtained from the work sheet, from the income and capital statements, or directly from the accounts in the ledger. An advantage of using the work sheet as the source is that all of the data appear on one sheet. The amounts appearing in the Income Statement columns correspond to the balances of the revenue and expense accounts in the ledger and are used for the first two closing entries. The amount of net income or net loss appears at the bottom of the Income Statement and Balance Sheet columns and is used for the third closing entry. Finally, reference

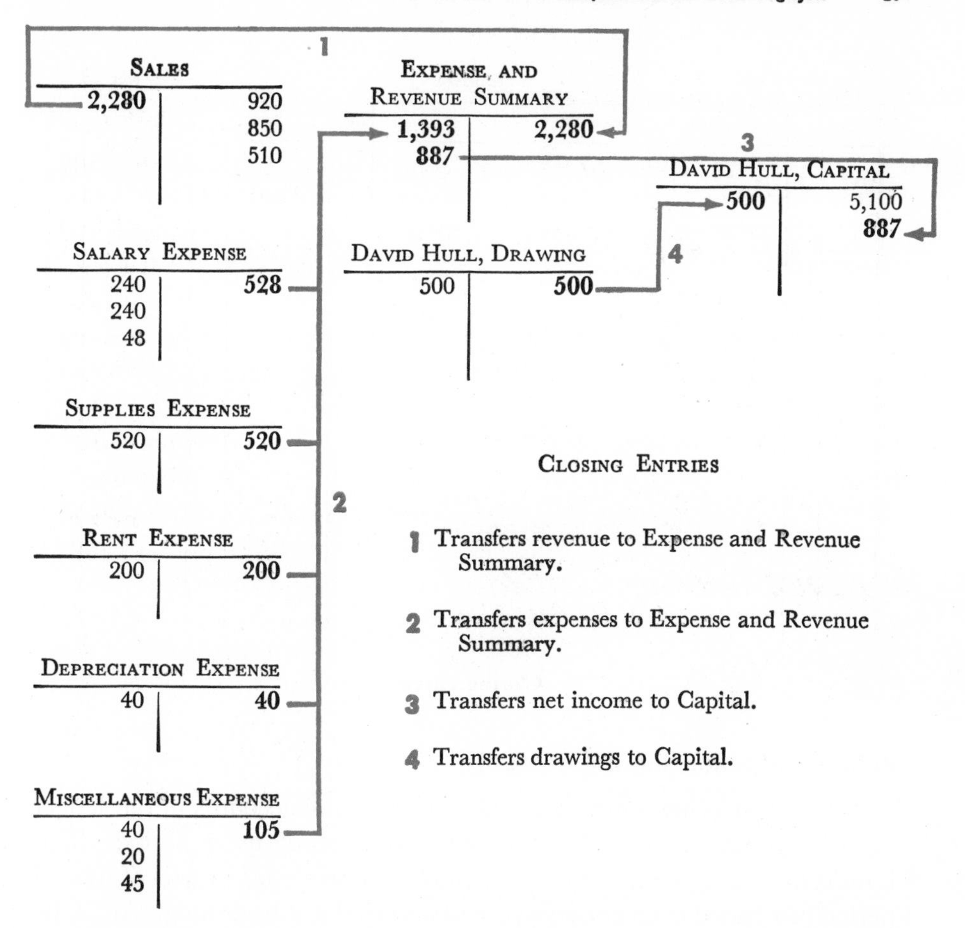

to the balance of the drawing account appearing in the Balance Sheet Dr. column supplies the information needed for the fourth closing entry.

The data for the closing entries appearing in the journal on page 88 are taken from the work sheet for Hull Print Shop on page 79. Each journal entry may be supported by an explanation, or the group may be identified by writing "Closing Entries" above the first entry in the series. The entries are dated as of the last day of the accounting period, even though they are actually recorded at a later date.

The accounts to which these closing entries are posted are shown in the ledger of Hull Print Shop beginning on page 89. All closing entries are identified in the Items columns of the accounts as an aid to the student. It is not necessary that this be done in actual practice.

A frequently used variant of the third closing entry is to close Expense and Revenue Summary to the drawing account instead of the capital account. The net increase or the net decrease in capital for the period (exclusive of any additional investments by the owner) is then transferred from the drawing account to the capital account.

JOURNAL PAGE 3

DATE		DESCRIPTION	POST. REF.	DEBIT	CREDIT
		Closing Entries			
1965 Oct.	31	Sales	41	2280 00	
		Expense and Revenue Summary	33		2280 00
	31	Expense and Revenue Summary	33	1393 00	
		Salary Expense	51		528 00
		Miscellaneous Expense	59		105 00
		Supplies Expense	52		520 00
		Rent Expense	53		200 00
		Depreciation Expense	54		40 00
	31	Expense and Revenue Summary	33	887 00	
		David Hull, Capital	31		887 00
	31	David Hull, Capital	31	500 00	
		David Hull, Drawing	32		500 00

Closing entries

Ruling and balancing the accounts

After the closing entries have been posted, the accounts in the ledger must be prepared to receive entries for the ensuing fiscal period. This is done by ruling them in such a manner as to segregate entries of the old period just ended from entries of the new period just beginning. All of the procedures are illustrated in the ledger of Hull Print Shop beginning on page 89. As each procedure is explained, reference will be made to one of the accounts in the ledger that illustrates the procedure.

Temporary capital accounts. After the revenue, expense, and drawing accounts have been closed, the debits in each account are equal to the credits in each account. To avoid the possibility of erroneously combining any of these entries with entries of the ensuing period, it is necessary to proceed as follows (see Sales):

(1) A single ruling is drawn across the amount columns immediately below the last figure in the longer of the two columns and on the same line of the shorter column.
(2) The total of each column is written below the single rulings.
(3) Double rulings are drawn below the totals and across all columns except the Items columns.

If an account has only one debit and one credit (see Supplies Expense), there is no need to repeat the same figures as totals; the double rulings are drawn immediately below the entries.

Cash — Account No. 11

Date		Items	Post. Ref.	Debit	Date		Items	Post. Ref.	Credit
1965 Oct.	2		1	900 00	1965 Oct.	2		1	600 00
	4		1	525 00		6		1	40 00
	16		1	920 00		10		1	400 00
	31		2	850 00		13		1	240 00
		760.00		3 195 00		20		1	350 00
						27		2	240 00
						31		2	20 00
						31		2	45 00
						31		2	500 00
									2 435 00
						31	Balance	✓	760 00
				3 195 00					3 195 00
Nov.	1	Balance	✓	760 00					

Accounts Receivable — Account No. 12

Date		Items	Post. Ref.	Debit	Date		Items	Post. Ref.	Credit
1965 Oct.	2		1	600 00	1965 Oct.	4		1	525 00
	31		2	510 00		31	Balance	✓	585 00
		585.00		1 110 00					
				1 110 00					1 110 00
Nov.	1	Balance	✓	585 00					

Supplies — Account No. 14

Date		Items	Post. Ref.	Debit	Date		Items	Post. Ref.	Credit
1965 Oct.	2		1	400 00	1965 Oct.	31	Adjusting	2	520 00
	20		1	350 00		31	Balance	✓	230 00
				750 00					
				750 00					750 00
Nov.	1	Balance	✓	230 00					

Prepaid Rent — Account No. 15

Date		Items	Post. Ref.	Debit	Date		Items	Post. Ref.	Credit
1965 Oct.	2		1	600 00	1965 Oct.	31	Adjusting	2	200 00
						31	Balance	✓	400 00
				600 00					600 00
Nov.	1	Balance	✓	400 00					

Printing Equipment — Account No. 18

Date		Items	Post. Ref.	Debit	Date		Items	Post. Ref.	Credit
1965 Oct.	2		1	3 200 00	1965 Oct.	31	Balance	✓	5 000 00
	3		1	1 800 00					
				5 000 00					
				5 000 00					5 000 00
Nov.	1	Balance	✓	5 000 00					

Ledger after the accounts have been adjusted, closed, ruled, and balanced

Accumulated Depreciation ACCOUNT NO. 19

DATE	ITEMS	POST. REF.	DEBIT	DATE	ITEMS	POST. REF.	CREDIT
				1965 Oct. 31	Adjusting	2	40 00

Accounts Payable ACCOUNT NO. 21

DATE	ITEMS	POST. REF.	DEBIT	DATE	ITEMS	POST. REF.	CREDIT
1965 Oct. 10		1	400 00	1965 Oct. 3	1400.00	1	1800 00
31	Balance	✓	1400 00				
			1800 00				1800 00
				Nov. 1	Balance	✓	1400 00

Salaries Payable ACCOUNT NO. 22

DATE	ITEMS	POST. REF.	DEBIT	DATE	ITEMS	POST. REF.	CREDIT
				1965 Oct. 31	Adjusting	2	48 00

David Hull, Capital ACCOUNT NO. 31

DATE	ITEMS	POST. REF.	DEBIT	DATE	ITEMS	POST. REF.	CREDIT
1965 Oct. 31	Closing	3	500 00	1965 Oct. 2		1	5100 00
31	Balance	✓	5487 00	31	Closing	3	887 00
			5987 00				5987 00
				Nov. 1	Balance	✓	5487 00

David Hull, Drawing ACCOUNT NO. 32

DATE	ITEMS	POST. REF.	DEBIT	DATE	ITEMS	POST. REF.	CREDIT
1965 Oct. 31		2	500 00	1965 Oct. 31	Closing	3	500 00

Expense and Revenue Summary ACCOUNT NO. 33

DATE	ITEMS	POST. REF.	DEBIT	DATE	ITEMS	POST. REF.	CREDIT
1965 Oct. 31	Closing	3	1393 00	1965 Oct. 31	Closing	3	2280 00
31	Closing	3	887 00				
			2280 00				2280 00

Ledger after the accounts have been adjusted, closed, ruled, and balanced — continued

Sales — ACCOUNT NO. 41

DATE		ITEMS	POST. REF.	DEBIT	DATE		ITEMS	POST. REF.	CREDIT
1965 Oct.	31	Closing	3	2,280 00	1965 Oct.	16		1	920 00
						31		2	850 00
						31		2	510 00
				2,280 00					2 2 8 0 0 0 2,280 00

Salary Expense — ACCOUNT NO. 51

DATE		ITEMS	POST. REF.	DEBIT	DATE		ITEMS	POST. REF.	CREDIT
1965 Oct.	13		1	240 00	1965 Oct.	31	Closing	3	528 00
	27		2	240 00					
	31	Adjusting	2	4 8 0 0 0 48 00					
				528 00					528 00

Supplies Expense — ACCOUNT NO. 52

DATE		ITEMS	POST. REF.	DEBIT	DATE		ITEMS	POST. REF.	CREDIT
1965 Oct.	31	Adjusting	2	520 00	1965 Oct.	31	Closing	3	520 00

Rent Expense — ACCOUNT NO. 53

DATE		ITEMS	POST. REF.	DEBIT	DATE		ITEMS	POST. REF.	CREDIT
1965 Oct.	31	Adjusting	2	200 00	1965 Oct.	31	Closing	3	200 00

Depreciation Expense — ACCOUNT NO. 54

DATE		ITEMS	POST. REF.	DEBIT	DATE		ITEMS	POST. REF.	CREDIT
1965 Oct.	31	Adjusting	2	40 00	1965 Oct.	31	Closing	3	40 00

Miscellaneous Expense — ACCOUNT NO. 59

DATE		ITEMS	POST. REF.	DEBIT	DATE		ITEMS	POST. REF.	CREDIT
1965 Oct.	6		1	40 00	1965 Oct.	31	Closing	3	105 00
	31		2	20 00					
	31		2	45 00					
				1 0 5 0 0 105 00					105 00

Ledger after the accounts have been adjusted, closed, ruled, and balanced — concluded

Assets, liabilities, and capital. The entries in each asset, liability, and capital account are summarized and the balance is recorded in the account as the first item for the new period. The procedure for balancing and ruling the accounts is as follows (see Cash):

(1) The balance of the account is written in the amount column of the first available line of the smaller of the two sides. "Balance" is written in the Items column, a check mark is placed in the Posting Reference column to differentiate it from posted entries, and the last day of the period is written in the Date column.

(2) A single ruling is drawn across the amount columns immediately below the last figure in the longer of the two columns and on the same line of the shorter column.

(3) The total of each column is written below the single rulings.

(4) Double rulings are drawn below the totals and across all columns except the Items columns.

(5) The balance is written in the amount column of the side that was originally the larger, "Balance" is written in the Items column, a check mark is placed in the Posting Reference column, and the first day of the new period is written in the Date column.

Post-closing trial balance

The final procedure of the accounting cycle is the preparation of a post-closing trial balance. Its purpose is to assure that debit-credit equality has been maintained in the ledger throughout the adjusting, closing, and balancing processes. All accounts and amounts appearing on the post-closing trial balance should correspond exactly with those shown on the balance sheet.

The post-closing trial balance for Hull Print Shop is shown at the top of page 93. A common practice is to proceed directly from the balances in the ledger to the preparation of adding machine listings, omitting the more formalized procedure. The adding machine tapes then become, in effect, the post-closing trial balance.

Accounting cycle

The principal accounting procedures of a fiscal period have been presented in this and the preceding chapter. The sequence of procedures is frequently called the *accounting cycle*. It begins with the analysis and the journalizing of transactions and ends with the post-closing trial balance. Although there are many possible variations in sequence and other details, the basic outline of the cycle is fundamental to accounting practice.

An understanding of all phases of the accounting cycle is essential as a foundation for further study of accounting principles and the uses of

Hull Print Shop
Post-Closing Trial Balance
October 31, 1965

Account	Debit	Credit
Cash	760 00	
Accounts Receivable	585 00	
Supplies	230 00	
Prepaid Rent	400 00	
Printing Equipment	5000 00	
Accumulated Depreciation		40 00
Accounts Payable		1400 00
Salaries Payable		48 00
David Hull, Capital		5487 00
	6975 00	6975 00

Post-closing trial balance

accounting data by management. The following outline summarizes the basic steps of the cycle:

(1) The transactions are analyzed.
(2) The transactions are journalized.
(3) The journal entries are posted to the ledger.
(4) A trial balance is prepared.
(5) The data needed to adjust the accounts are assembled.
(6) A work sheet is prepared.
(7) The financial statements are prepared.
(8) The adjusting entries are journalized and posted.
(9) The closing entries are journalized and posted.
(10) The ledger accounts are ruled and balanced.
(11) A post-closing trial balance is prepared.

Interim statements

In the illustrative case of Hull Print Shop the accounting cycle was completed in one month. Most business enterprises close the temporary capital accounts only at the end of the fiscal year rather than at the end of each month. Regardless of the length of the period, the closing procedures are the same. In order to restrict the number of transactions and the physical space requirements, a period of one month was used in the illustration.

When the books are closed annually, only Steps 1 through 4 of the accounting cycle need to be repeated monthly. The completion of posting and the preparation of a trial balance at the end of each month is customary regardless of when the books are closed. If interim financial statements are to be prepared monthly, Steps 5 through 7 of the accounting cycle, ending with the financial statements, must also be completed monthly.

When the books are not closed each time the statements are prepared, the revenue and expense data for the interim income statements will be cumulative. For example, assuming a fiscal year that begins on January 1, the amounts in the income statement columns of the February work sheet will be the cumulative totals for January and February; the revenue and expenses on the March work sheet will be the cumulative totals for January, February, and March; and so on. An income statement for each individual month may be prepared, however, by subtracting from the current cumulative amount of each revenue and expense the amount of the corresponding items on the preceding cumulative statement. Thus the sales figure reported on the cumulative statement for January 1 to March 31 minus the sales figure reported on the cumulative statement for January 1 to February 28 will be the sales figure for the month of March, and so on.

QUESTIONS

1. What is the nature of the balance in the supplies account at the end of the accounting period (a) before adjustment? (b) after adjustment?

2. What is the term usually employed in referring to (a) unexpired costs? (b) expired costs?

3. State whether each of the following assets and services is customarily paid for in advance of its use or after it has been consumed: (a) rent, (b) supplies, (c) services of office employees, (d) property insurance, (e) office equipment, (f) electric power, (g) water.

4. If an adjusting entry has the effect of decreasing the balance of an asset account, will it also decrease the balance of a liability account, decrease the balance of an expense account, or increase the balance of an expense account?

5. Does every adjusting entry have an effect on the determination of the amount of net income for a period? Explain.

6. On October 1, H. G. Barnes Co. pays the October rent on the building that it uses. (a) Do the rights acquired at the time of the payment represent an asset or an expense? (b) What is the justification for debiting Rent Expense at the time of payment?

7. (a) Explain the purpose of the depreciation expense account and the accumulated depreciation account. (b) What is the normal balance of each account? (c) Is it customary for the balances of the two accounts to be equal in amount? (d) In what financial statements, if any, will each of the accounts appear?

8. What is meant by "book value" of a plant asset?

9. At the end of January, the first month of the fiscal year, the usual adjusting entry transferring expired insurance to an expense account is inadvertently omitted. What is the effect of the omission on (a) the amount of net income reported for January and (b) the balance sheet as of January 31?

10. Accrued salaries of $700 owed on December 31, the end of the fiscal year, are not taken into consideration in preparing the statements for the year. What is the effect of this error on (a) the amount of net income reported for the year and (b) the balance sheet as of December 31?

11. Assuming that the error in Question 10 is not corrected and that payment for the salaries accrued on December 31 is included in the first salary payment in January, what will be the effect on (a) the net income reported for January and (b) the balance sheet as of January 31?

12. Does the work sheet take the place of financial statements? Discuss.

13. What is the purpose of the expense and revenue summary account?

14. Identify the accounts in the following list that should be closed to Expense and Revenue Summary at the end of the fiscal year: (a) Accounts Payable, (b) Accumulated Depreciation, (c) B. Bourne, Drawing, (d) Cash, (e) Delivery Expense, (f) Depreciation Expense, (g) Office Equipment, (h) Prepaid Taxes, (i) Service Sales, (j) Taxes Expense.

15. Are adjusting and closing entries in the journal dated as of the last day of the fiscal period or as of the day the entries are actually made? Explain.

16. Which of the following accounts in the ledger will ordinarily appear in the post-closing trial balance: (a) Accounts Receivable, (b) Accumulated Depreciation, (c) Building, (d) C. L. Carter, Capital, (e) Cash, (f) C. L. Carter, Drawing, (g) Depreciation Expense, (h) Prepaid Insurance, (i) Sales, (j) Taxes Expense.

17. How frequently are the books customarily closed?

18. Warren Co. closes its books annually on September 30, the end of its fiscal year. What period will be covered by the income statement prepared from the work sheet as of June 30?

EXERCISES

1. A business enterprise pays weekly sales salaries of $4,500 on Friday for a five-day week ending on Friday. Journalize the necessary adjusting entry at the end of the fiscal period, assuming that the fiscal period ends (a) on Tuesday, (b) on Wednesday.

2. On January 2 a business enterprise pays $420 to the city for license fees for the calendar year. During January the same enterprise incurs an additional tax expense of $120 applicable to January that need not be paid to the state until May. (a) Journalize the two adjusting entries required to bring the accounts up to date as of January 31. (b) What is the amount of tax expense for January?

3. The balance in the prepaid insurance account at the end of the year is $1,680. Journalize the adjusting entry required under each of the following assumptions: (a) the insurance expired during the year was $415; (b) the unexpired insurance applicable to future periods is $1,120.

4. After all revenues and expenses have been closed at the end of the fiscal year, Expense and Revenue Summary has a debit of $70,000 and a credit of $88,000. As of the same date T. M. Booth, Capital has a credit balance of $35,000 and T. M. Booth, Drawing has a debit balance of $12,000. (a) Journalize the entries required to complete the closing of the books. (b) State the amount of Booth's capital at the end of the period.

5. Selected accounts from a ledger are presented below. (a) Journalize the adjusting entries that have been posted to the accounts. (b) Journalize the closing entries that have been posted to the accounts. (c) List any open accounts that should have been closed.

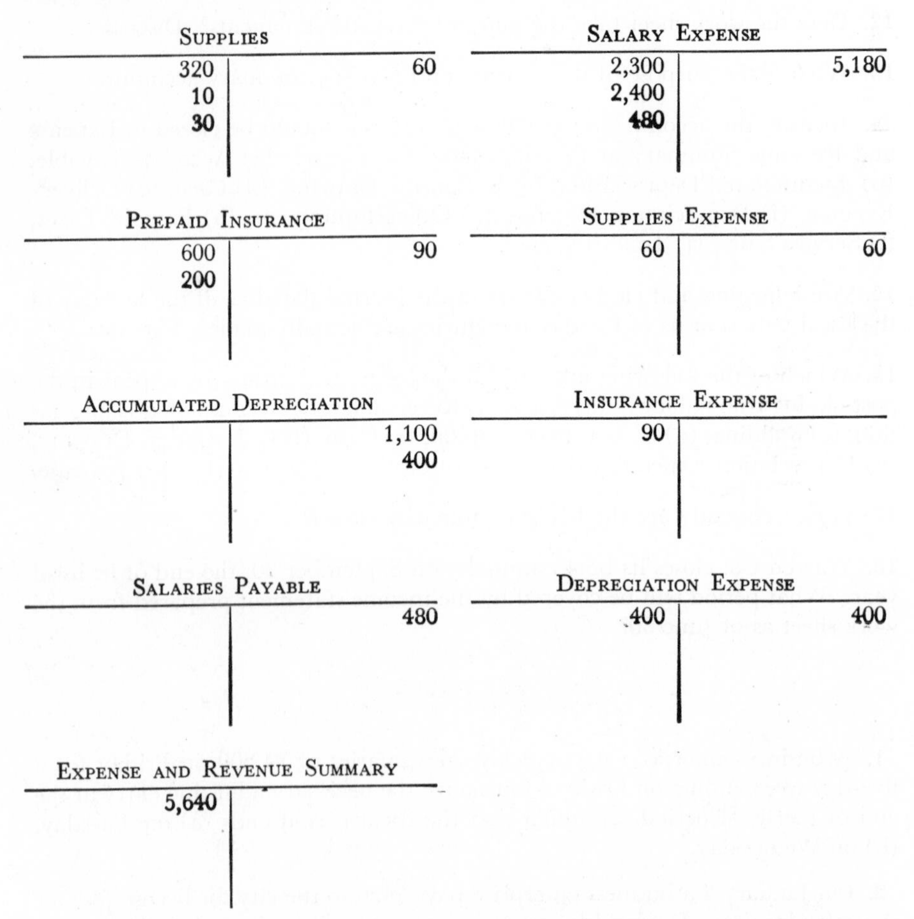

6. The capital, drawing, and expense and revenue summary accounts of Coleman & Co. for the current year ended December 31 are given on the following page. Prepare a capital statement for the year.

Robert Coleman, Capital

Dec. 31	6,000	Jan. 1	25,000
		Dec. 31	4,000

Robert Coleman, Drawing

June 30	2,000	Dec. 31	6,000
Sept. 30	2,000		
Dec. 31	2,000		

Expense and Revenue Summary

Dec. 31	78,000	Dec. 31	82,000
31	4,000		

PROBLEMS

4-1. The trial balance of Glendale Laundromat at December 31, the end of the current fiscal year, and data needed for year-end adjustments are presented below.

Glendale Laundromat
Trial Balance
December 31, 19—

Cash	1,420	
Laundry Supplies	1,960	
Prepaid Insurance	472	
Laundry Equipment	18,700	
Accumulated Depreciation		6,400
Accounts Payable		265
Helen Neal, Capital		9,042
Helen Neal, Drawing	6,000	
Laundry Revenue		19,910
Wages Expense	4,640	
Rent Expense	1,200	
Utilities Expense	760	
Miscellaneous Expense	465	
	35,617	35,617

Adjustment data:

(a) Laundry supplies on hand at December 31	$ 310
(b) Insurance expired during the year	210
(c) Depreciation for the year	1,530
(d) Wages accrued at December 31	43

Instructions: (1) Record the trial balance on a ten-column work sheet.

(2) Complete the work sheet.

(3) Prepare an income statement, a capital statement (no additional investments were made during the year), and a balance sheet in report form.

(4) Record the adjusting entries in a two-column journal.

(5) Record the closing entries in a two-column journal.

(6) Compute the following:

(a) Percent of net income to sales.

(b) Percent of net income to the capital balance at the beginning of the year.

4-2. As of June 30, the end of the current fiscal year, the accountant for Collins Company prepared a trial balance, journalized and posted the adjusting entries, prepared an adjusted trial balance, prepared the statements, and completed the other procedures required at the end of the accounting cycle. The two trial balances as of June 30, one before adjustments and the other after adjustments, are presented below.

Collins Company
Trial Balance
June 30, 19—

	Unadjusted		Adjusted	
Cash	1,845		1,845	
Supplies	2,130		430	
Prepaid Rent	3,150		1,050	
Prepaid Insurance	465		325	
Automobile	4,500		4,500	
Accumulated Depreciation — Automobile		1,000		2,000
Equipment	3,200		3,200	
Accumulated Depreciation — Equipment		320		640
Accounts Payable		385		470
Salaries Payable		—		110
Taxes Payable		—		20
John Collins, Capital		5,075		5,075
John Collins, Drawing	6,600		6,600	
Service Fees Earned		27,400		27,400
Salaries Expense	11,200		11,310	
Rent Expense	—		2,100	
Supplies Expense	—		1,700	
Depreciation Expense — Automobile	—		1,000	
Utilities Expense	640		725	
Depreciation Expense — Equipment	—		320	
Taxes Expense	140		160	
Insurance Expense	—		140	
Miscellaneous Expense	310		310	
	34,180	34,180	35,715	35,715

Instructions: (1) Present the eight journal entries that were required to adjust the accounts at June 30. None of the accounts was affected by more than one adjusting entry.

(2) Present the journal entries that were required to close the books at June 30.

(3) Prepare a capital statement for the fiscal year ended June 30. There were no additional investments during the year.

*If the working papers correlating with this textbook are not used, omit **Problem 4-3.***

4-3. The ledger of Quality Home Repairs as of October 31, the end of the first month of its current fiscal year, is presented in the working papers. The books had been closed on September 30.

Instructions: (1) Prepare a trial balance of the ledger, listing only the accounts with balances, on a ten-column work sheet.

(2) Complete the ten-column work sheet. Data for the adjustments are as follows:

Supplies on hand at October 31	$314.00
Insurance expired during the month	32.45
Truck depreciation for the month	140.00
Equipment depreciation for the month	65.00
Salaries accrued at October 31	139.00

(3) Prepare an income statement, a capital statement, and a balance sheet.
(4) Record the adjusting entries in a two-column journal and post.
(5) Record the closing entries in a two-column journal and post.
(6) Rule the closed accounts and balance and rule the remaining accounts that contain more than one entry.
(7) Prepare a post-closing trial balance.

4-4. Central Bowling Lanes prepares interim statements at the end of each month and closes its books annually as of December 31. The trial balance at April 30 of the current year, the adjustment data needed at April 30, and the income statement for the three months ended March 31 of the current year are presented below.

Central Bowling Lanes
Trial Balance
April 30, 19—

Cash	3,460	
Prepaid Insurance	976	
Supplies	1,320	
Equipment	80,400	
Accumulated Depreciation — Equipment		14,600
Building	48,000	
Accumulated Depreciation — Building		3,400
Land	12,000	
Accounts Payable		3,230
Mortgage Note Payable (Due 1972)		50,000
Gordon Davis, Capital		67,109
Gordon Davis, Drawing	2,000	
Bowling Fees Earned		16,739
Salaries and Wages Expense	3,500	
Advertising Expense	1,216	
Repairs Expense	840	
Utilities Expense	765	
Miscellaneous Expense	601	
	155,078	155,078

Adjustment data at April 30 are:

(a) Insurance expired for the period January 1–April 30	$ 133
(b) Inventory of supplies	954
(c) Depreciation of equipment for the period January 1–April 30	2,200
(d) Depreciation of building for the period January 1–April 30	640
(e) Accrued wages and salaries	110

Central Bowling Lanes
Income Statement
For Three Months Ended March 31, 19—

Bowling fees earned		$12,747
Operating expenses:		
Salaries and wages expense	$ 2,690	
Depreciation expense — equipment	1,650	
Advertising expense	902	
Repairs expense	610	
Utilities expense	590	
Depreciation expense — building	480	
Supplies expense	270	
Insurance expense	101	
Miscellaneous expense	360	
Total operating expenses		7,653
Net income from operations		$ 5,094

Instructions: (1) Record the trial balance on a ten-column work sheet.
(2) Complete the work sheet.
(3) Prepare an interim income statement for the four months ended April 30 and a balance sheet as of April 30.
(4) Prepare an income statement for April.
(5) Compute the percent of net income to revenue for:
(a) The three-month period ended March 31.
(b) The four-month period ended April 30.
(c) The month of April.

PART THREE

Accounting cycle for a merchandising enterprise

5. Sales and cash receipts

Need for special journals

Although every transaction of an enterprise may be recorded in a single two-column journal, a considerable saving of time may be effected by expanding the journal to include special columns. This was demonstrated in Chapter 3 by adding a column for recording debits to Cash and a column for recording credits to Cash. The journalizing and posting process may be facilitated further by the addition of other special columns, such as Accounts Receivable Debit, Accounts Receivable Credit, and Sales Credit. An all-purpose multicolumn journal is often satisfactory for a business employing only one bookkeeper; but when the volume of transactions is such that additional bookkeepers are required, it is not practicable for all of them to use a single journal.

The customary practice in medium-size and large businesses is to employ a number of special journals, each of which is designed to record a particular type of transaction. Obviously, special journals are needed only for transactions that occur frequently. For example, most accounting systems employ a special journal for recording cash receipts and a special journal for recording cash payments because in most businesses there are many transactions of both types. A business that extends credit might advantageously use a special journal to record sales of merchandise or services on account. On the other hand, a business that does not extend credit would have no need for such a journal.

In addition to variations in the number of special journals used by different types of businesses, there are also many possible variations in the design of any particular journal. For example, the sources of revenue of a financial institution, such as a bank, are quite different from those of a merchandising business. Both would use a special journal for cash receipts, but their journals would be unlike in many respects.

Merchandising

Special journals suitable for a merchandising business with numerous sales and purchases transactions will be described and illustrated in this and the succeeding chapter. The accounting procedures applicable to an enterprise engaged in buying and selling commodities are different in some respects from those employed by a service type of business, but there are also many similarities. Therefore much of the discussion will apply equally to both types of business activity.

Merchandising activities may ordinarily be classified as *wholesale* or *retail*. Manufacturers, producers, and importers usually sell their goods to wholesalers, to brokers, or directly to retailers. Wholesale merchants sell to retailers and sometimes to large consumers, such as schools and hospitals. Retail merchants sell to consumers.

The number, purpose, and design of the special journals used in merchandising will of necessity vary, depending upon the needs of the particular enterprise. In the typical firm of moderate size the transactions that occur most frequently and the special journals in which they are recorded are as follows:

Transactions		*Special Journals*
Sales of merchandise on account	*recorded in*	Sales journal
Receipts of cash from various sources	*recorded in*	Cash receipts journal
Purchases of merchandise and other items on account	*recorded in*	Purchases journal
Payments of cash for various purposes	*recorded in*	Cash payments journal

Although most of the transactions of a typical business may be recorded in the foregoing special journals, every business has some transactions that are neither sales or purchases on account, nor receipts or payments of cash. The journal used for recording these miscellaneous transactions is known as a *general journal*. The most common form of the general journal is the two-column journal that was illustrated in Chapter 3.

Frequency of sales transactions

The principal source of revenue of a business appears as the first item on the income statement. For a merchandising business this item is sales of merchandise, which is usually shortened to *Sales*. The number of individual sales transactions to be recorded is usually large in relationship to other transactions and often ranks second only to cash transactions in order of frequency.

Some merchandising businesses sell goods only for cash, others sell largely on credit, and still others have many transactions of both types. *Cash sales* result in both a receipt of cash and a sale of merchandise, and it is customary to record them in the *cash receipts journal*. Sales of merchandise *on account*, and only such sales, are recorded in the *sales journal*.

Trade discounts

Manufacturers and wholesalers of certain types of commodities frequently grant substantial reductions from the *list price* quoted in their catalogs. Such reductions in price are called *trade discounts*. Trade discounts are a convenient method of making revisions in prices without the necessity of reprinting catalogs. As prices fluctuate, new schedules of discounts may be issued. Trade discounts may also be used to make price differentials among different classes of customers. For example, the schedule of discounts issued by a manufacturer to wholesalers may differ from that issued to retailers.

Trade discounts are not recorded in the books of account. They are used only as a means of arriving at the selling price. For accounting purposes it is the contract price, that is, the list price minus the trade discount, that is significant. For example, the seller of an article listed at $100 with a trade discount of $40 would record the transaction as a sale of $60. Similarly, the buyer would record the cost as $60. Since trade discounts are not recorded in the books of account, they are mentioned here merely to distinguish between them and the cash discounts discussed in later paragraphs.

Sales procedures

Every sale is made in response to an order received from a customer. An order given a retail store is usually oral; an order given a manufacturing, a wholesale, or a mail-order business is ordinarily written. There are many methods of handling orders and of recording sales, the routines varying with the type and the size of the business.

In a retail business a *sales ticket* is usually prepared for a sale on account. This sales ticket is made in duplicate or triplicate. One copy is given to the customer, one copy is sent to the accounting department for use as the basis of an entry in the sales journal, and one copy may be used as the salesman's personal record of his sales or for such other purposes as the organization of the business requires.

In a manufacturing, a wholesale, or a mail-order business a written order is received from a customer or from the salesman who obtained the order from the customer. After the order has been approved by the credit department, it is sent to the billing department, where the invoice is prepared. At least two copies of a *sales invoice* are made by the billing department. The original is sent to the customer, and the carbon copy is sent to the accounting department for use as the basis of an entry in the sales journal. Sometimes additional copies of the invoice are made for the use of different departments of the business. For example, the credit department may desire a copy for use in following up the payment of the invoice, or the shipping department may need a copy as authorization to pack and ship the goods.

One of the sales invoices used by Bennett Electrical Supplies is illustrated below.

BENNETT ELECTRICAL SUPPLIES No. 615

813 Hamilton St. Allentown, Pa. 18100

Sold to E. A. Albertson
321 Dauphin St.
Philadelphia, Pa. 19120

Date October 2, 1965
Terms 2/10,n/30
Shipped Via Express Collect

6	Transformers, Model 392 E	40.00	240.00
12	Switches, Model 719 J	5.00	60.00
50	Resistors, Model 420 K	1.00	50.00
			350.00

Sales invoice

Controlling accounts and subsidiary ledgers

In earlier chapters of this book, amounts debited and credited to customers on account have been recorded only in a single accounts receivable account. Consideration will now be given to the procedure for recording the amounts owed the business by each individual customer.

Although it is possible to eliminate the accounts receivable account from the ledger and to substitute the individual customers' accounts, such a solution is not satisfactory when there is a substantial number of customers. The inclusion of a large number of accounts with customers would delay the preparation of the trial balance, make the ledger cumbersome, complicate posting, and make errors more difficult to find.

When a business has a large number of accounts that have a common characteristic, it is customary to segregate them in a special ledger called a *subsidiary ledger*. In order to differentiate between ledgers, the principal ledger that contains all of the balance sheet and income statement accounts is then referred to as the *general ledger*. A single account summarizing the many accounts in a subsidiary ledger must be maintained in the general ledger. This summarizing account is called a *controlling account* and may be said to *control* the related subsidiary ledger.

The *controlling account* for customers to whom sales are made on account is *Accounts Receivable;* it is located in the *general ledger*. The individual accounts with such customers comprise a *subsidiary ledger*, in this case called the *accounts receivable ledger* or *customers' ledger*.

The special journals in which numerous transactions affecting customers are to be recorded are designed in such a way as to facilitate the posting of monthly totals to the controlling account, Accounts Receivable, and the posting of the individual transactions to the customers' ledger. The basic techniques of posting a sales journal are depicted in the following flow chart.

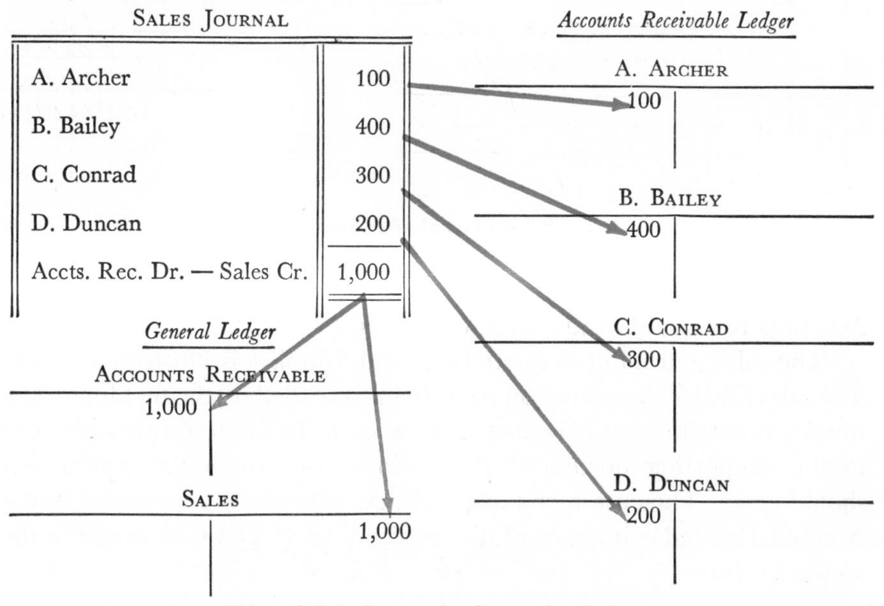

Flow of data from sales journal to ledgers

The total of the sales journal, $1,000, is posted as a credit to Sales and a debit to Accounts Receivable in the general ledger. In addition, the debits to Archer, Bailey, Conrad, and Duncan recorded in the sales journal are posted to their respective accounts in the accounts receivable ledger. It is evident that the sum of the debits to the four accounts in the subsidiary ledger is equal to the single debit to the controlling account in the general ledger.

Sales journal

The sales journal is used solely for recording *sales of merchandise on account.* Sales of merchandise for cash are recorded in the cash receipts journal. Sales of plant assets or other assets not a part of the stock in trade are recorded in either the cash receipts journal or the general journal. The restriction of the sales journal to sales of merchandise on

SALES JOURNAL PAGE 35

DATE		INVOICE NO.	ACCOUNT DEBITED	POST. REF.	ACCTS. REC. DR. SALES CR.
1965 Oct.	2	615	E. A. Albertson	✓	350 00
	3	616	Quaker Supply	✓	604 00
	5	617	James Owen	✓	305 00
	9	618	E. A. Albertson	✓	1 396 00
	10	619	Acme Co.	✓	750 00
	17	620	R. E. Holt	✓	865 00
	23	621	G. L. Bates	✓	502 00
	26	622	Howard Strauss	✓	260 00
	27	623	Quaker Supply	✓	908 00
	31				5 940 00
					(113) (411)

Sales journal after posting

account is necessary because the journal total is posted as a debit to Accounts Receivable and a credit to Sales.

The sales journal of Bennett Electrical Supplies is illustrated above. The sales invoice illustrated on page 104 is recorded on the first line. The invoice number (615) is recorded in order to facilitate future reference to the supporting document if questions concerning the transaction should arise. The customer's name (E. A. Albertson) is recorded in the Account Debited column, and the invoice total ($350) is recorded in the amount column.

Posting the sales journal

Each entry in the sales journal is posted as a debit to the appropriate account in the accounts receivable ledger. The postings should be made at frequent intervals, preferably daily, so that the status of all customers' accounts can be readily determined at all times. The posting references inserted in the accounts should identify the sales journal by the letter "S."

It is not customary to assign numbers to customers' accounts. Instead, they are arranged in alphabetical sequence to provide ready availability. New accounts may be inserted and inactive accounts may be removed without disturbing the arrangement. At the time a debit is posted to a customers' account, a check mark (√) is placed in the posting reference column of the sales journal. The check mark has the same significance that an account number would have; it indicates that the item has been posted and requires no further attention.

A customer's account with a single posting is illustrated by the account with Acme Co., which appears below. Instead of the T form presented in earlier chapters, it is a three-column form designed to display the current balance of the account at all times. Inasmuch as the balances in customers' accounts are normally debits, it is not necessary to identify normal balances as debits. When an occasional credit balance does occur, it should be identified by an asterisk, parentheses, or other notation. When a customer's account is in balance, a line may be drawn in the Balance column, as illustrated on page 118.

NAME Acme Co.
ADDRESS 118 James Street, Allentown, Pa. 18100

DATE		ITEMS	POST. REF.	DEBIT	CREDIT	BALANCE
1965 Oct.	10		S35	750 00		750 00

An account in the accounts receivable ledger

At the end of each month the sales journal is totaled and the total is posted as a debit to Accounts Receivable and a credit to Sales. The respective account numbers are then inserted below the total to indicate that the posting has been completed. The procedure is illustrated by the sales journal appearing on page 106 and the two general ledger accounts presented on page 108.

The general ledger account forms illustrated differ from both the three-column form used in the accounts receivable ledger and the T form heretofore used in the general ledger. The traditional T form emphasizes to the greatest possible extent the difference between debit entries and credit entries. It is primarily because of this feature that it is customarily used at the beginning of the introductory course in accounting. In actual practice there has been a tendency for the four-column form to displace the simpler T form, though the latter is still widely used.

Accounts Receivable ACCOUNT NO. 113

DATE		ITEMS	POST. REF.	DEBIT	CREDIT	BALANCE	
						DEBIT	CREDIT
1965 Oct.	1	Balance	✓			4260 00	
	31		S35	5940 00		10200 00	

Sales ACCOUNT NO. 411

DATE		ITEMS	POST. REF.	DEBIT	CREDIT	BALANCE	
						DEBIT	CREDIT
1965 Oct.	1	Balance	✓				98236 00
	31		S35		5940 00		104176 00

Accounts receivable account and sales account in the general ledger after the sales journal has been posted

The principal advantage of the four-column form lies in its provision for clearly displaying the amount and the debit-credit nature of account balances, reducing possible confusion and errors in preparing a trial balance. The single date column and the contiguity of the debit and credit columns also facilitate both the scanning of an account and the careful examination of its details. Finally, the four-column form permits a marked simplification of the periodic ruling and balancing procedures that are employed with the T form. These features will be illustrated in a later chapter.

When posting machines are used with the four-column form, the new balance of an account is automatically computed and printed in the proper column after each posting. The account balance is thus always readily available. The same procedure may be followed when the posting is done manually. An alternative is to postpone the computation of the balance until all postings for the month have been completed. When this is done, only the final month-end balance is inserted in the appropriate balance column, usually at the time the trial balance is being prepared. The exact procedure adopted in a particular situation will depend upon such factors as the accessibility of adding machines and the desirability of having current balances readily available at all times.

Sales returns and allowances

Goods sold on account may be returned by the customer (*sales return*) or, because of defects or for other reasons, the customer may be allowed a reduction from the original price at which the goods were sold (*sales allowance*). In such cases the seller usually issues to the customer a *credit memorandum* indicating the amount for which the customer is to be credited and the reason therefor. A typical credit memorandum is illustrated below.

Credit Memorandum — No. 32

BENNETT ELECTRICAL SUPPLIES
813 Hamilton St.
ALLENTOWN, PA. 18100

October 13, 1965

Acme Co.
118 James St.
Allentown, Pa. 18100

We credit your account as follows:

1 #393 F Transformer returned 25.00

Credit memorandum

The effect of a sales return or allowance is a reduction in sales revenue and a reduction in accounts receivable. If the sales account is debited, however, the balance of the account at the end of the period will represent net sales, and the volume of returns and allowances will not be disclosed. Because of the loss in revenue resulting from allowances, and the various expenses (transportation, unpacking, repairing, etc.) related to returns, it is advisable that management be informed of the magnitude of such transactions. It is therefore preferable to debit an account entitled Sales Returns and Allowances. The remainder of the transaction is recorded by a credit to the accounts receivable (controlling) account in the general ledger and to the customer's account in the accounts receivable (subsidiary) ledger.

Bennett Electrical Supplies issued two credit memorandums during the month. They were recorded in the general journal as shown below.

GENERAL JOURNAL — PAGE 18

DATE		DESCRIPTION	POST. REF.	DEBIT	CREDIT
1965 Oct.	13	Sales Returns and Allowances	412	25 00	
		Accounts Receivable—Acme Co.	113/✓		25 00
		Credit Memo No. 32.			
	28	Sales Returns and Allowances	412	45 00	
		Accounts Receivable—G. L. Bates	113/✓		45 00
		Credit Memo No. 33.			

General journal entries for sales returns

Note that in each transaction both the controlling account and the customer's account are credited. As an indication that the amount must be posted to both the general ledger and the subsidiary ledger, a diagonal line should be placed in the posting reference column *at the time the entry is recorded in the general journal.* When the credit is posted to the customer's account, a check mark is placed to the right of the diagonal line. The number of the accounts receivable controlling account is entered at the left in accordance with the usual routine of posting to that account in the general ledger. After the posting has been completed, the accounts receivable account and the sales returns and allowances account in the general ledger and the customers' accounts in the subsidiary ledger appear as follows:

GENERAL LEDGER

Accounts Receivable — ACCOUNT NO. 113

DATE		ITEMS	POST. REF.	DEBIT	CREDIT	BALANCE DEBIT	BALANCE CREDIT
1965 Oct.	1	Balance	✓			4,260 00	
	13		J18		25 00	4,235 00	
	28		J18		45 00	4,190 00	

Sales Returns and Allowances — ACCOUNT NO. 412

DATE		ITEMS	POST. REF.	DEBIT	CREDIT	BALANCE DEBIT	BALANCE CREDIT
1965 Oct.	1	Balance	✓			2,365 00	
	13		J18	25 00		2,390 00	
	28		J18	45 00		2,435 00	

ACCOUNTS RECEIVABLE LEDGER

NAME Acme Co.
ADDRESS 118 James Street, Allentown, Pa. 18100

DATE		ITEMS	POST. REF.	DEBIT	CREDIT	BALANCE
1965 Oct.	10		S35	750 00		750 00
	13		J18		25 00	725 00

NAME G. L. Bates
ADDRESS 1211 State St., Trenton, N.J. 08603

DATE		ITEMS	POST. REF.	DEBIT	CREDIT	BALANCE
1965 Oct.	23		S35	502 00		502 00
	28		J18		45 00	457 00

Accounts receivable account, sales returns and allowances account, and customers' accounts after the posting of sales returns

If sales returns and allowances are of frequent occurrence, special columns for Sales Returns and Allowances Debit and for Accounts Receivable Credit may be inserted in the general journal, or a special sales returns and allowances journal similar to the one illustrated below may be used. The recording and posting routines for this special journal are the same as those that apply to the sales journal.

SALES RETURNS AND ALLOWANCES JOURNAL — PAGE 2

DATE		CR. MEMO. NO.	ACCOUNT CREDITED	POST. REF.	SALES RET. & ALLOW. DR. ACCTS. REC. CR.
1965					
Nov.	2	12	Ralph Boyer	√	142 00
	6	13	Morrow & Co.	√	150 00
	29	26	J. R. Field Co.	√	13 00
	30				1,762 50
					(412) (113)

Sales returns and allowances journal

It should be noted that in each of the foregoing illustrations the amount of the return or the allowance was credited to Accounts Receivable and a customer's account. If merchandise is returned or an allowance is granted after the customer has made full payment of his account, the seller may make a cash refund instead of crediting the customer's account. In such cases the transaction is recorded in the cash payments journal, which is considered in Chapter 6.

Sales invoices as a sales journal

Many enterprises use the carbon copies of their sales invoices as a sales journal. When this is done, the postings to the customers' accounts are made directly from the duplicate invoices. The total amount of sales for the month is determined from an adding machine listing of the duplicate invoices. The total amount thus obtained provides the basis for an entry in the general journal debiting Accounts Receivable and crediting Sales.

The use of sales invoices as a journal may effect a material savings in bookkeeping expenses, particularly if there is a large volume of sales transactions. Not only is the necessity of copying the name of the customer and other details in the sales journal avoided, but the elimination of this intermediate step also reduces the number of errors and the amount of time devoted to their detection and correction. In addition, posting to customers' accounts can be facilitated by dividing invoices into a number of alphabetical groupings and assigning each segment to a particular posting clerk.

The same system can be employed with equal effectiveness in accounting for returns and allowances, carbon copies of the credit memorandums becoming in effect the sales returns and allowances journal.

Sources of cash receipts

All transactions that increase the amount of cash are recorded in a cash receipts journal. Cash may be received from a variety of sources, such as investments in the business by the owner, receipts from cash sales, collections from customers to whom sales have been made on account, and collections of principal and interest on notes receivable. In a typical merchandising business the most frequent sources of cash receipts are likely to be cash sales and collections from customers on account.

Before describing the form and the use of the cash receipts journal, it is necessary that consideration be given to the nature of the agreement between the business enterprise and its customers.

Credit terms

The arrangements agreed upon by the seller and the buyer as to when payments for goods are to be made are called the *credit terms*. If payment is required immediately upon delivery of the goods, the terms are said to be "cash" or "net cash." Otherwise, the buyer is allowed a period of time, known as the *credit period*, in which to pay.

There is considerable variation in credit periods. Retailers may require that all purchases by customers in one month be paid for by a particular date in the succeeding month. They sometimes stipulate that purchases made after a particular date, such as the 25th, will not be included in the billing for that month but will be carried over to the succeeding month. They may also have special "budget" and "layaway" terms.

Among manufacturers and wholesalers it is usual for the credit period to begin with the date of the sale as evidenced by the date of the invoice. If payment is due within a stated number of days after the date of the invoice, for example 30 days, the terms are said to be "net 30 days," which may be written as "n/30." If payment is due by the end of the month in which the sale was made, it may be expressed as "n/eom."

Cash discounts

As a means of encouraging payment before the expiration of the credit period, a discount may be offered for the early payment of cash. Thus the expression "2/10, n/30" means that, while the credit period is 30 days, the debtor may deduct 2% of the amount of the bill if payment is made in 10 days from the date of the invoice. This deduction is known as a *cash discount*.

For example, assume a sales invoice totaling $500 dated July 6, with credit terms of 2/10, n/30. If the buyer mails his check on or before July 16, he may deduct $10 from the invoice and pay $490. If he wishes to wait the full credit term, payment of the full amount should be made on or before August 5.

From the seller's point of view, cash discounts are known as *sales discounts;* the purchaser refers to them as *purchases discounts.* At one time cash discounts were considered to be similar to interest for the use of money and were accordingly treated as an expense by the seller and as revenue by the buyer. Today, however, when cash discounts are offered by the seller, it is with the expectation that the customer will pay within the discount period. In effect the seller is offering to make the sale for the invoice price reduced by the amount of the cash discount. In accordance with this interpretation, it is customary for the seller to view cash discounts as a reduction in sales revenue and for the buyer to consider them as a deduction from the quoted price of the commodity purchased.

Cash receipts journal

As was demonstrated in Chapter 3, journalizing and posting can be expedited by the use of special columns for accounts frequently debited or credited. Inasmuch as all transactions involving receipts of cash, and only such transactions, are recorded in the cash receipts journal, it should have a special column entitled Cash Dr. Receipts of cash by Bennett Electrical Supplies that occur most frequently are from cash sales and collections from retailers to whom sales have been made on 2/10, n/30 terms. There are also occasional receipts of cash from various other sources. Accordingly, the cash receipts journal illustrated on page 114 has the following columns:

For credits — Sundry Accounts, Sales, Accounts Receivable
For debits — Sales Discount, Cash

The Sundry Accounts Cr. column is used for recording credits to any account for which there is no special column. For example, on October 2 Bennett Electrical Supplies collected $150 on a note receivable. The transaction was recorded by writing the account title "Notes Receivable" in the Account Credited column and $150 in the Sundry Accounts Cr. column and the Cash Dr. column. The posting reference column was left blank until the credit was posted.

The Sales Cr. column is used for recording sales of merchandise for cash. Each individual sale is recorded on a cash register, and the totals thus accumulated are recorded in the cash receipts journal daily, weekly, or at other regular intervals. This is illustrated by the entry of

CASH RECEIPTS JOURNAL PAGE 14

DATE		ACCOUNT CREDITED	POST. REF.	SUNDRY ACCOUNTS CR.	SALES CR.	ACCOUNTS RECEIVABLE CR.	SALES DISCOUNT DR.	CASH DR.
1965								
Oct.	2	Notes Receivable	112	15000				15000
	5	E. A. Albertson	✓			80000	1600	78400
	6	John B. Deatrick	✓			62500	1250	61250
	7	Sales	✓		120000			120000
	10	James Owen	✓			60000	1200	58800
	13	Quaker Supply	✓			60400	1208	59192
	14	Sales	✓		163200			163200
	17	Acme Co.	✓			72500	1450	71050
	19	R. E. Holt	✓			185000		185000
	21	Sales	✓		192030			192030
	23	Purchases Ret. and Allow.	513	3620				3620
	24	O. L. Tanner	✓			20000		20000
	27	R. E. Holt	✓			86500	1730	84770
	28	Sales	✓		158600			158600
	31	Sales	✓		42340			42340
	31			18620	676170	626900	8438	1313252
				(✓)	(411)	(113)	(413)	(111)

Cash receipts journal after posting

October 7 recording weekly sales of $1,200. The account title "Sales" was written in the Account Credited column and $1,200 was entered in the Sales Cr. and Cash Dr. columns. Inasmuch as the total of the Sales Cr. column will be posted at the end of the month, a check mark was inserted in the posting reference column to indicate that the $1,200 item needed no further attention.

Credits to customers' accounts for payments of invoices are recorded in the Accounts Receivable Cr. column. The amount of the cash discount granted, if any, is recorded in the Sales Discount Dr. column and the amount of cash actually received is recorded in the Cash Dr. column. The entry on October 5 illustrates the use of these columns. The title of the account in the subsidiary ledger, E. A. Albertson, was written in the Account Credited column; the amount of the invoice for which payment was received, $800, was entered in the Accounts Receivable Cr. column; the 2% cash discount of $16 was entered in the Sales Discount Dr. column; and the $784 cash received was entered in the Cash Dr. column. The Post. Ref. column was left blank until the credit was posted to the customer's account, at which time a check mark was inserted.

It should be noted that when a debtor has returned merchandise or has been granted an allowance, the discount should be computed on the amount of the invoice reduced by the amount of the credit memorandum. For example, on October 17 a check for $710.50 is received from Acme Co. in settlement of an invoice of $750, less a credit of $25 for merchandise returned. The discount granted is 2% of $725, or $14.50.

Posting the cash receipts journal

Each amount in the Sundry Accounts Cr. column of the cash receipts journal is posted to the appropriate account in the general ledger at any time during the month and the posting is indicated by writing the account number in the posting reference column. At regular intervals the amounts in the Accounts Receivable Cr. column are posted to the customers' accounts in the subsidiary ledger and check marks are placed in the posting reference column to indicate that they have been posted and need no further attention. None of the individual amounts in the remaining three columns of the cash receipts journal is posted.

At the end of the month all the amount columns are footed and ruled as shown in the illustration. To check the accuracy of the footings, the equality of debits and credits should be proved by use of an adding machine or a listing similar to the following:

Debit Totals		Credit Totals	
Sales Discount	$ 84.38	Sundry Accounts	$ 186.20
Cash	13,132.52	Sales	6,761.70
		Accounts Receivable	6,269.00
	$13,216.90		$13,216.90

The total of the Sundry Accounts Cr. column is not posted, as the amounts in this column have been posted individually to general ledger accounts. A check mark may be inserted below this column total to indicate that no further action is necessary. The totals of the other four columns are posted to the appropriate accounts in the general ledger and their account numbers are inserted below the totals to indicate that the posting has been completed.

In terms of posting procedures, there are three distinct types of columns in the cash receipts journal. They may be described as follows:

(1) Individual entries posted to general ledger accounts, column total not posted:

Sundry Accounts Cr. column

(2) Individual entries not posted, column total posted to a general ledger account:

Sales Cr. column
Sales Discount Dr. column
Cash Dr. column

(3) Individual entries posted to subsidiary ledger accounts, column total posted to the corresponding general ledger controlling account:

Accounts Receivable Cr. column

The relationship between the cash receipts journal and the ledgers of Bennett Electrical Supplies is presented in a flow diagram on page 116.

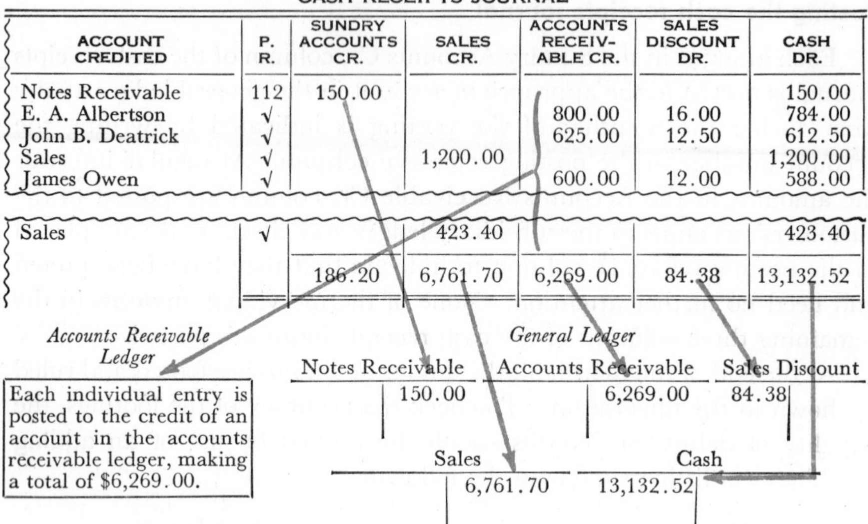

CASH RECEIPTS JOURNAL

ACCOUNT CREDITED	P. R.	SUNDRY ACCOUNTS CR.	SALES CR.	ACCOUNTS RECEIV-ABLE CR.	SALES DISCOUNT DR.	CASH DR.
Notes Receivable	112	150.00				150.00
E. A. Albertson	√			800.00	16.00	784.00
John B. Deatrick	√			625.00	12.50	612.50
Sales	√		1,200.00			1,200.00
James Owen	√			600.00	12.00	588.00
Sales	√		423.40			423.40
		186.20	6,761.70	6,269.00	84.38	13,132.52

Relationship between the cash receipts journal and the ledgers

Accounts receivable control and subsidiary ledger

During October the following postings were made to Accounts Receivable in the general ledger of Bennett Electrical Supplies:

Debits

Oct. 31 (Total sales on account, from sales journal)............ $5,940.00

Credits

Oct. 13 (A sales return, from general journal)................ 25.00
Oct. 28 (A sales return, from general journal)................ 45.00
Oct. 31 (Total credits resulting from cash received on account, from cash receipts journal)........................ 6,269.00

The controlling account with its opening balance, the foregoing postings, and the balances is shown below.

Accounts Receivable ACCOUNT NO. *113*

DATE		ITEMS	POST. REF.	DEBIT	CREDIT	BALANCE DEBIT	BALANCE CREDIT
1965 Oct.	1	Balance	✓			4260 00	
	13		J18		25 00	4235 00	
	28		J18		45 00	4190 00	
	31		S35	5940 00		10130 00	
	31		CR14		6269 00	3861 00	

Accounts receivable account in the general ledger at the end of the month

As was indicated in the discussion of posting the sales journal, postings to the customers' accounts in the subsidiary ledger should be made daily. In order to answer inquiries from customers about the status of their account and in approving sales for additional credit, it is imperative that all customers' accounts be up to date. There is also an obvious advantage in spreading the posting over the month rather than allowing it to accumulate until the end of the month.

The accounts receivable ledger of Bennett Electrical Supplies after the posting of all entries for the month is shown on the following pages.

The sum of the balances of the accounts in the customers' ledger should be compared periodically with the balance of the accounts receivable account in the general ledger. This is customarily done at the end of each month at the same time that the trial balance is prepared. If the subsidiary ledger and the controlling account are not in agreement, the error must be found and corrected. As in the case of the trial balance, however, arithmetic equality is not an absolute guarantee of correctness. For example, the erroneous posting of a credit for cash received from a particular customer as a credit to another customer's account would not be revealed by this comparison.

The balances in the subsidiary ledger accounts may be summarized by use of an adding machine, or a schedule of accounts receivable similar to the one illustrated below may be prepared. Note that the total of the schedule, $3,861, is in agreement with the balance of the accounts receivable account appearing on page 116.

Bennett Electrical Supplies
Schedule of Accounts Receivable
October 31, 1965

E. A. Albertson	$1,746.00
G. L. Bates	457.00
James Owen	305.00
Quaker Supply	908.00
Howard Strauss	260.00
O. L. Tanner	185.00
Total accounts receivable	$3,861.00

Schedule of accounts receivable

Delivery of merchandise sold

The terms of a sales agreement include an implied or expressed provision concerning the cost of delivering the goods to the buyer. If the seller is to assume the cost of transportation, the terms are said to be *FOB* (free on board) *destination;* if the buyer is to absorb the cost, the terms are stated as *FOB shipping point.*

NAME Acme Co.
ADDRESS 118 James Street, Allentown, Pa. 18100

DATE		ITEMS	POST. REF.	DEBIT	CREDIT	BALANCE
1965 Oct.	10		S35	750 00		750 00
	13		J18		25 00	725 00
	17		CR14		725 00	—

NAME E. A. Albertson
ADDRESS 321 Dauphin St., Philadelphia, Pa. 19120

DATE		ITEMS	POST. REF.	DEBIT	CREDIT	BALANCE
1965 Sept.	27		S34	800 00		800 00
Oct.	2		S35	350 00		1,150 00
	5		CR14		800 00	350 00
	9		S35	1,396 00		1,746 00

NAME G. L. Bates
ADDRESS 1211 State St., Trenton, N.J. 08603

DATE		ITEMS	POST. REF.	DEBIT	CREDIT	BALANCE
1965 Oct.	23		S35	502 00		502 00
	28		J18		45 00	457 00

NAME John B. Deatrick
ADDRESS 46 First Ave., Allentown, Pa. 18103

DATE		ITEMS	POST. REF.	DEBIT	CREDIT	BALANCE
1965 Sept.	28		S34	625 00		625 00
Oct.	6		CR14		625 00	—

Accounts receivable ledger at the end of the month

NAME R. E. Holt
ADDRESS 1213 River Road, Easton, Pa. 18042

DATE		ITEMS	POST. REF.	DEBIT	CREDIT	BALANCE
1965						
Sept.	19		S34	1 850 00		1 850 00
Oct.	17		S35	865 00		2 715 00
	19		CR14		1 850 00	865 00
	27		CR14		865 00	—

NAME James Owen
ADDRESS 1619 Washington St., Allentown, Pa. 18112

DATE		ITEMS	POST. REF.	DEBIT	CREDIT	BALANCE
1965						
Sept.	29		S34	600 00		600 00
Oct.	5		S35	305 00		905 00
	10		CR14		600 00	305 00

NAME Quaker Supply
ADDRESS 907 Barr St., Reading, Pa. 19602

DATE		ITEMS	POST. REF.	DEBIT	CREDIT	BALANCE
1965						
Oct.	3		S35	604 00		604 00
	13		CR14		604 00	—
	27		S35	908 00		908 00

NAME Howard Strauss
ADDRESS 192 Ember St., Narberth, Pa. 19072

DATE		ITEMS	POST. REF.	DEBIT	CREDIT	BALANCE
1965						
Oct.	26		S35	260 00		260 00

NAME O. L. Tanner
ADDRESS 1014 Slauson Ave., Reading, Pa. 19603

DATE		ITEMS	POST. REF.	DEBIT	CREDIT	BALANCE
1965						
Aug.	24		S33	385 00		385 00
Oct.	24		CR14		200 00	185 00

Accounts receivable ledger at the end of the month — concluded

If the seller agrees to absorb the costs of delivering the merchandise, the amount paid to railways, trucking companies, etc., is debited to Delivery Expense or Freight-Out, which is classified as a selling expense.

If the buyer agrees to absorb the delivery costs and pays the carrier directly, the seller's responsibility ceases when the merchandise is turned over to the carrier. However, a not infrequent practice is for the seller to pay the carrier even though the terms are FOB shipping point. When shipment is by parcel post, it is not possible to do otherwise. Even when shipment is by other agencies, the seller may prepay the transportation charges as a convenience to the customer. In such cases the postage or other delivery costs are stated as a separate item on the sales invoice and are charged to the customer's account along with the sales price of the commodities sold.

SALES JOURNAL PAGE 43

DATE		INVOICE NO.	ACCOUNT DEBITED	POST. REF.	ACCOUNTS RECEIVABLE DR.	DELIVERY EXPENSE CR.	SALES CR.
1965 Nov.	1	2477	Reed Corp.	√	820 00	20 00	800 00
	30				26,925 00	525 00	26,400 00
					(113)	(615)	(411)

Sales journal designed for charging prepaid transportation costs to customers

A sales journal designed to accommodate such transactions is illustrated above. Each amount recorded in the Accounts Receivable Dr. column and posted to a customer's account is the sum of the sale plus the prepaid delivery charges. Inasmuch as payments of cash to the carrier are separate transactions, and in many cases are made on a weekly or monthly basis, the delivery charges passed on to the customer are credited to Delivery Expense. For example, in the illustration the selling price of the merchandise sold to Reed Corp. was $800, to which was added delivery costs of $20, making a total charge of $820 to the customer. The columnar totals of the sales journal, including the $525 credit to Delivery Expense, are posted at the end of the month.

If in the foregoing illustration it is assumed that delivery charges of $650 were incurred and paid during November, the status of the delivery expense account at the end of the month would be as shown at the left. The debit balance of $125 in the account represents delivery charges borne by the seller, pre-

Delivery Expense

Paid		Charged	
to carriers	650	to customers	525

sumably on shipments made on an FOB destination basis. It is an operating expense of the business.

When delivery costs are prepaid as an accommodation on sales subject to a cash discount, the discount should be computed on the sale price only; it does not apply to the transportation charges advanced by the seller. For example, assuming that the sale to Reed Corp. discussed on the preceding page is subject to a discount of 2%, the discount would amount to $16 (2% of $800) and the amount to be paid would be $804 ($800 − $16 + $20). In order to have the basis for determining the discount readily available, the amount of each transportation charge may be recorded in the Items section of the customers' account when the sales journal is posted.

Automated data processing

Handwritten illustrations are employed in this and other chapters for two principal reasons: (1) manually kept records are commonly used in small business enterprises and to some degree in most types and sizes of economic units, and (2) they serve as a guide for students when preparing solutions to problems.

A thorough understanding of the basic purposes and principles of classifying and summarizing accounting data can best be obtained through the use of manual techniques. In accounting practice, however, various types of mechanical and electronic equipment are commonly used to accelerate the accounting process. For example, automatic equipment may be used to record all of the essential data of each sale at the time an invoice is prepared. All of the postings to the customers' accounts and to the general ledger, as well as various analyses of sales, can then be accomplished by the equipment with amazing speed.

Further attention will be given to automated data processing in later chapters and particularly in Appendix A.

QUESTIONS

1. Benson Hardware Co., which records its sales on account in a two-column general journal, is considering the use of a sales journal. State the approximate reduction in the work of (a) recording and (b) posting 400 charge sales monthly that would result from the change.

2. Differentiate between trade discounts and cash discounts.

3. Describe the two related transactions recorded in the T accounts below.

Cash		Accounts Receivable		Sales		Sales Discount	
(b) 1,960		(a) 2,000	(b) 2,000		(a) 2,000	(b) 40	

4. The following errors were made in recording transactions in a single-column sales journal or in posting therefrom. How will each error be discovered other than by chance?

(a) A sale of $200 to John B. Lee was recorded and posted as a sale to John R. Lee.
(b) A sale of $25 to L. J. Marsh was recorded and posted as $52.
(c) A sale of $40 to Taylor Corp. was recorded correctly in the sales journal but was posted to the customer's account as $4.
(d) The sales journal for the month was overfooted by $1,000.

5. Assuming the use of the sales journal and the cash receipts journal described in this chapter and a two-column general journal, indicate the journal in which each of the following should be recorded:

(a) Investment of additional cash in the business by the owner.
(b) Sale of merchandise for cash.
(c) Sale of office supplies on account, at cost, to a competitor as an accommodation.
(d) Receipt of cash refund for an overcharge on an insurance premium.
(e) Issuance of a credit memorandum to a customer.
(f) Adjustment of Prepaid Rent at the end of the year.
(g) Sale of merchandise on account.
(h) Closing of the owner's drawing account at the end of the year.

6. Why is it advisable to maintain an account for sales returns and allowances when the same net result may be obtained by debiting them directly to the sales account?

7. After receiving full payment for a sale of merchandise on account, the buyer returns a portion of the shipment for credit and the seller credits the buyer's account. What is the nature of the credit balance in the customer's account?

8. The Sutter Equipment Co. maintains a subsidiary ledger for accounts receivable. In posting the journal entry given below, the bookkeeper failed to post the credit to the controlling account. (a) How will this error be discovered? (b) Describe the technique that is designed to prevent oversights of this kind.

Oct. 10	Sales Returns and Allowances	412	150	
	Accounts Receivable — R. T. Borden	✓		150

9. What is the meaning of (a) 2/10, n/30; (b) n/eom?

10. What is the term applied to cash discounts by (a) the seller, (b) the buyer?

11. What is the amount of the cash discount allowable on a sale of $1,100, terms 2/10, n/30, on which a credit memo for $100 was issued prior to payment?

12. (a) What is the normal balance of Sales Discount? (b) Is it an asset, expense, or contra revenue account?

13. After receiving payment from a customer, within the discount period, of the amount due on a sale of $500, terms 2/10, n/30, the seller consents to the return of the entire shipment. (a) What is the amount of the refund owed to the customer? (b) State the entry in general journal form to record the return and the refund.

14. Who bears the transportation costs when the terms of sale are (a) FOB destination, (b) FOB shipping point?

15. Is the buyer entitled to a discount on prepaid freight, assuming that the terms are FOB shipping point and that he pays the invoice within the discount period? Give a reason for your answer.

16. What is the amount of the cash discount allowable on a sale of $1,200, terms 2/10, n/30, FOB shipping point, on which the seller prepays the freight of $30.

17. Bancroft Co. makes sales to wholesalers on an FOB destination basis and to consumers on an FOB shipping point basis. Bancroft Co. prepays the delivery charges in all cases. What will be the normal balance of the delivery expense account after posting is completed at the end of the month, and what does it represent?

EXERCISES

1. For each of the following sales determine (a) the amount to be recorded for the sale, and (b) the amount of the cash to be paid.

	Invoice Date	List Price	Trade Discount	Credit Terms	Date Paid
(1)	August 4	$ 500	40%	2/10, n/30	August 14
(2)	August 12	800	50%	n/eom	August 31
(3)	August 17	1,000	—	2/10, n/30	August 31
(4)	August 20	1,200	25%	2/10, 1/20, n/30	September 9

2. R. M. Teller Co. uses carbon copies of its sales invoices and credit memorandums in place of a sales journal and a sales returns and allowances journal, respectively. For November the total of the 1,320 invoices was $139,600 and the total of the 34 credit memorandums was $536. (a) Present the general journal entries required to record the foregoing data at the end of November. (b) What is the source for posting debits to the customers' ledger?

3. Determine for each of the sales described below, all of which are subject to terms of 2/10, n/30, (a) the amount of the cash discount and (b) the amount of cash required to pay the account within the discount period. Assume that all credit memorandums were issued prior to payment.

	Amount of Sale	Transportation Terms	Prepaid Transportation	Credit Memorandum
(1)	$ 700	FOB destination	$25	$ 50
(2)	1,000	FOB shipping point	45	—
(3)	1,200	FOB shipping point	—	100
(4)	1,500	FOB shipping point	60	200

4. Stephens Co. sells merchandise to Hammond Corp. on September 15 for $900, terms FOB shipping point, 1/10, n/30. Stephens Co. prepays delivery expense of $40. On September 20, Stephens Co. issues a credit memorandum for $70 for goods returned, and on September 25 the company receives a check for the amount due on the invoice. Present the entries, in general journal form, to record (a) the sale, (b) the issuance of the credit memorandum, and (c) the receipt of cash.

5. A two-column general journal is to be expanded by the addition of special columns to record credit memorandums issued to customers. List the exact caption to be used for each of the four amount columns (without regard to sequence) in the expanded general journal.

6. Present the general journal entries necessary to correct each of the errors described below. Assume that the incorrect entries had been posted and that the errors are discovered in the same fiscal period in which they occurred.

(a) Cash of $15 received as repayment for an overcharge on a purchase of equipment was recorded as a sale of merchandise for cash.
(b) A cash sale of $60 was recorded as a sale to Ralph Grant on account.
(c) A $400 sale to Henry Ballard on account, FOB shipping point, with prepaid delivery expense of $25, was recorded as a $425 debit to Ballard (and Accounts Receivable) and a $425 credit to Sales.
(d) A cash receipt of $588 ($600 less 2% discount) from Blair & Co. was recorded as a $588 debit to Cash and a $588 credit to Blair & Co. (and Accounts Receivable).

PROBLEMS

5-1. Turner Trading Co. was established in July of the current year. Its sales of merchandise on account and related returns and allowances during the remainder of the month are described below. Terms of all sales were n/30, FOB shipping point.

July 14. Sold merchandise on account to Neal Corporation, Invoice No. 1, $460.
15. Sold merchandise on account to Jacobs & Keller, Invoice No. 2, $520.
17. Sold merchandise on account to Sarver & Co., Invoice No. 3, $750.
18. Sold merchandise on account to A. J. Cross Co., Invoice No. 4, $1,130.
19. Issued Credit Memorandum No. 1 for $60 to Jacobs & Keller for merchandise returned.
22. Sold merchandise on account to Sarver & Co., Invoice No. 5, $480.
23. Issued Credit Memorandum No. 2 for $40 to Neal Corporation for merchandise returned.
24. Sold merchandise on account to John Young Corp., Invoice No. 6, $310.
25. Sold merchandise on account to Robert Gordon, Inc., Invoice No. 7, $640.
26. Sold merchandise on account to Jacobs & Keller, Invoice No. 8, $190.
29. Issued Credit Memorandum No. 3 for $20 to John Young Corp. for damages to merchandise caused by faulty packing.
31. Sold merchandise on account to A. J. Cross Co., Invoice No. 9, $270.

Instructions: (1) Open the following accounts in the general ledger, using the account numbers indicated: Accounts Receivable, 113; Sales, 411; Sales Returns and Allowances, 412.

(2) Open the following accounts in the accounts receivable ledger: A. J. Cross Co.; Robert Gordon, Inc.; Jacobs & Keller; Neal Corporation; Sarver & Co.; John Young Corp.

(3) Record the transactions for July, posting to the customers' accounts in the accounts receivable ledger immediately after recording each entry. Use a sales journal similar to the one illustrated on page 106 and a two-column general journal.

(4) Post (a) the general journal and (b) the sales journal to the accounts opened in the general ledger, inserting the balances only after the last postings.

(5) (a) What is the sum of the balances of the subsidiary accounts? (b) What is the balance of the controlling account?

If the working papers correlating with the textbook are not used, omit Problem 5-2.

5-2. Three journals, the accounts receivable ledger, and portions of the general ledger of Sloan Company are presented in the working papers. Sales invoices and credit memorandums were entered in the journals by an assistant. Terms of sales on account are 2/10, n/30, FOB shipping point. Transactions in which cash was received during May of the current year are as follows:

May 1. Received cash for a note receivable due today, $1,800.
2. Received cash from Evans & Ford, Inc. in payment of April 22 invoice, less discount, $931.
Post transactions of May 2, 3, and 4 to customers' accounts.
8. Received cash from Henry R. Wilson in payment of April 28 invoice, less discount, $588.
9. Received cash from J. K. McDonald Corp. in payment of April 9 invoice, $1,400; no discount.
Post transactions of May 8, 9, 10, 12, and 15 to customers' accounts.
16. Cash sales for first half of May, $8,415.
17. Received cash refund for return of defective equipment purchased for cash in April, $500.
19. Received cash from Evans & Ford, Inc. in payment of balance due on May 10 invoice, less discount, $1,029.
22. Received cash from J. K. McDonald Corp. in payment of May 12 invoice, less discount, $539.
Post transactions of May 18, 19, 22, 23, 24, 25 and 26 to customers' accounts.
29. Received cash for sale of store supplies at cost, as an accommodation, $12.
30. Received cash from Paul Black & Co. in partial payment of May 3 invoice, $400; no discount.
31. Cash sales for second half of May, $6,273.
Post transaction of May 30 to the customer's account.

Instructions: (1) Record the cash receipts for May and post all three journals to the customers' accounts, in date sequence, at the points indicated in the narrative of transactions.

(2) Post the appropriate individual transactions to the general ledger.

(3) Add the columns of the sales journal and the cash receipts journal and post the appropriate totals to the general ledger. Insert the balance of each account after the last posting.

(4) Prepare a schedule of accounts receivable and compare the total with the balance of the controlling account.

5-3. Transactions related to sales and cash receipts completed by B. J. Price Co. during June of the current year are described below. The terms of all sales on account are 2/10, n/30, FOB destination.

June 1. Sold merchandise on account to Martin & Martin, Inc., Invoice No. 314, $1,974.
7. Sold merchandise on account to Draper Corp., Invoice No. 315, $1,281.
8. Additional cash investment made by the owner, B. J. Price, $1,500.
9. Issued to Draper Corp. a credit memorandum for merchandise damaged in shipment, $31.
12. Sold merchandise on account to S. T. Wheeler Co., Invoice No. 316, $2,217.

June 13. Received cash refund for a premium overcharge on property insurance, $28.
14. Sold merchandise on account to Draper Corp., Invoice No. 317, $700.
15. Cash sales for June 1 to 15, $6,482.
16. Received cash from Draper Corp. in payment of the balance due on the June 7 invoice, less discount.
17. Issued to S. T. Wheeler Co. a credit memorandum for merchandise returned, $67.
19. Sold merchandise on account to S. T. Wheeler Co., Invoice No. 318, $1,875.
22. Received cash from S. T. Wheeler Co. in payment of the balance due on the June 12 invoice, less discount.
23. Received cash from Draper Corp. in payment of the June 14 invoice, less discount.
27. Sold merchandise on account to Draper Corp., Invoice No. 319, $2,590.
29. Received cash for a note receivable due today, $600.
30. Received cash from Martin & Martin, Inc. in payment of the June 1 invoice; no discount.
30. Cash sales for June 16 to 30, $7,831.

Instructions: (1) Open the following accounts in the general ledger:

111 Cash
112 Notes Receivable
113 Accounts Receivable
117 Prepaid Insurance
311 B. J. Price, Capital
411 Sales
412 Sales Returns and Allowances
413 Sales Discount

(2) Open the following accounts in the accounts receivable ledger: Draper Corp.; Martin & Martin, Inc.; S. T. Wheeler Co.

(3) Record the transactions for the month in a sales journal similar to the one illustrated on page 106, a cash receipts journal similar to the one illustrated on page 114, and a two-column general journal. All postings to the *accounts receivable ledger* should be made immediately after journalizing each entry affecting a customer's account.

(4) Post the appropriate individual transactions to the *general ledger*.

(5) Add the columns of the sales journal and the cash receipts journal and post the appropriate totals to the general ledger. The balances of the accounts need not be determined except for Accounts Receivable.

(6) Determine whether the subsidiary ledger is in agreement with the controlling account.

5-4. Transactions related to sales and cash receipts completed by Todd Company during January of the current year are described below. The terms of all sales on account are 2/10, n/30, FOB shipping point. All delivery charges are prepaid and charged to the customer.

Jan. 2. Received cash from Arden Co. for the balance due on its account, less discount.
3. Issued Invoice No. 766 to H. T. Vance Co., $1,550; delivery, $36; total, $1,586.
5. Issued Invoice No. 767 to Arden Co., $690; delivery, $20; total, $710.
6. Received cash from Zimmer & Tobin for the balance due on their account, less discount.

Post all journals to the accounts receivable ledger.

Jan. 8. Issued Invoice No. 768 to J. M. Jacobs, $830; delivery, $23; total, $853.
10. Issued Credit Memo No. 33 to Arden Co., $40.
11. Issued Invoice No. 769 to H. T. Vance Co., $1,800; delivery, $39; total, $1,839.
12. Received cash refund for return of office supplies, $21.
13. Received cash from H. T. Vance Co. for invoice of January 3, less discount.

Post all journals to the accounts receivable ledger.

15. Received cash from Arden Co. for balance due on invoice of January 5, less discount.
16. Recorded cash sales for first half of the month, $4,860.
17. Received cash from J. M. Jacobs for the balance owed on January 1; no discount.
17. Issued Invoice No. 770 to Zimmer & Tobin, $2,182; delivery, $41; total, $2,223.
21. Received cash from H. T. Vance Co. for invoice of January 11, less discount.
24. Issued Credit Memo No. 34 to Zimmer & Tobin, $32.

Post all journals to the accounts receivable ledger.

24. Issued Invoice No. 771 to H. T. Vance Co., $1,360; delivery, $27; total $1,387.
26. Received cash in payment of a note receivable, $1,600.
27. Received cash from Zimmer & Tobin for the balance due on invoice of January 17, less discount.
29. Issued Invoice No. 772 to Arden Co., $2,000; delivery, $43; total, $2,043.
31. Recorded cash sales for the second half of the month, $5,420.
31. Issued Credit Memo No. 35 to Arden Co., $55.

Post all journals to the accounts receivable ledger.

Instructions: (1) Open the following accounts in the general ledger, inserting the balances indicated, as of January 1:

111 Cash	$2,964	411 Sales	———
112 Notes Receivable	2,400	412 Sales Returns and Allowances	———
113 Accounts Receivable	3,557	413 Sales Discount	———
115 Office Supplies	195	615 Delivery Expense	———

(2) Open the following accounts in the accounts receivable ledger, inserting the balances indicated, as of January 1: Arden Co., $982, including a delivery charge of $32; J. M. Jacobs, $1,845, including a delivery charge of $45; H. T. Vance Co.; Zimmer & Tobin, $730, including a delivery charge of $30. Make a notation of the amount of the delivery charges in the Items column of each account.

(3) Record the transactions for the month in a sales journal similar to the one illustrated on page 120, a sales returns and allowances journal similar to the one illustrated on page 111, and a cash receipts journal similar to the one illustrated on page 114. Post to the accounts receivable ledger at the points indicated in the narrative of transactions.

(4) Add the columns of the journals and post the individual entries and totals to the general ledger. Insert the account balances after the last posting.

(5) Determine that the subsidiary ledger agrees with the controlling account.

6. Purchases and cash payments

Purchasing procedures

The procedures followed in purchasing activities vary considerably among business firms. In a small retail store the proprietor may do all of the buying, in many cases placing orders with salesmen or by telephone. Larger enterprises may maintain a purchasing department that is responsible for determining best sources of supply, investigating quality, knowing current market prices and their trends, placing orders, and doing all other things necessary to assure the efficient operation of all buying activities.

To avoid misunderstanding, all orders for merchandise, equipment, supplies, or other assets should be in writing. An order may be written on a form supplied by the vendor, or the buyer may use his own forms. The original of the purchase order is sent to the supplier; it is his authorization to deliver the items listed at the prices specified. A duplicate copy of the order should be retained as evidence of what was ordered and of the other terms stipulated.

The seller usually mails an invoice to the buyer at about the time the goods are shipped. From the viewpoint of the seller, the invoice is a sales invoice; the buyer refers to it as a purchase invoice. An invoice should contain the names and the addresses of both the buyer and the seller; the date of the transaction; the terms; the method of shipment; and the quantities, descriptions, and prices of the goods. An invoice from Allied Electronics Supply in response to a purchase order of Bennett Electrical Supplies is shown on the following page.

The invoice form illustrated is a standard form recommended by the National Association of Purchasing Agents. It is divided into three distinct sections: (1) upper left section for miscellaneous details of the terms of the transaction; (2) lower section for quantity, description, unit price, and amount; and (3) upper right section for use by the purchaser as a record that various comparisons and verifications have been made.

ALLIED ELECTRONICS SUPPLY
405 Murray Street
CHICAGO, ILLINOIS 60615

Customer's Order No. & Date 412
Refer to Invoice No. 106-8
Requisition No.
Contract No.
Invoice Date Oct. 11, 1965
Vendor's Nos.

SOLD TO Bennett Electrical Supplies
813 Hamilton Street
Allentown, Pennsylvania 18100

Shipped to and Destination Same
Date Shipped Oct. 11, 1965 From Chicago
Prepaid or Collect? Prepaid
Car Initials and No. F. O. B. Allentown
How Shipped and Route Eastern Trucking Co.
Terms 2/10,n/30
Made in U. S. A.

FOR CUSTOMER'S USE ONLY
Register No. Voucher No.
F. O. B. Checked
Terms Approved
Price Approved W.K.
Calculations Checked C. R. S.
Transportation
Freight Bill No. Amount
Material Received 10/13 19 65 M.A.S. Rec. Cl.
Date Signature Title
Satisfactory and Approved
Adjustments
Accounting Distribution
Audited J.H.C.
Final Approval K.C.

QUANTITY	DESCRIPTION	UNIT PRICE	AMOUNT
10✓	392E Transformers	30.00✓	300.00✓
50✓	719J Switches	2.50✓	125.00✓
20✓	406P Capacitors	4.00✓	80.00✓
5✓	215J Reactors	10.00✓	50.00✓
			555.00✓

Invoice

The invoice usually arrives in advance of the goods, and it is sometimes recorded in the journal before the shipment is received. Terms, quantities, prices, and other details on the invoice should be compared with the corresponding items on the copy of the purchase order. When the goods arrive, they should be counted and inspected. This work is ordinarily done by the receiving department, which may check the quantities received against those indicated on the invoice or may make an independent report to the purchasing department of quantities received. In the latter case the purchasing department will compare the receiving report with the invoice, thus affording better internal check over the receiving operations of the business. Before a purchase invoice is approved for payment, the following verifications should be made: (1) that the billing is in accordance with the provisions of the purchase order, (2) that all of the commodities purchased have been received in good condition, and (3) that all arithmetic details (such as price extensions) have been checked.

Purchases journal

A wide variety of assets may be purchased by a business enterprise. Property most frequently purchased on account by a trading concern is of the following types: (1) merchandise for resale to customers, (2) supplies for use in conducting the business, and (3) plant assets. Because of the variety of assets acquired on credit terms, the purchases journal should be designed to accommodate the recording of everything purchased on account. The number and the purpose of the special columns provided in the journal depend upon the nature of the business and the frequency of purchases of the various assets. The form of purchases journal used by Bennett Electrical Supplies is illustrated below and on page 131.

For each transaction recorded in the purchases journal, the credit is entered in the Accounts Payable Cr. column. The next three columns are used in accumulating debits to the particular accounts most frequently affected.

PAGE 19 PURCHASES JOURNAL

	DATE		ACCOUNT CREDITED	POST. REF.	ACCOUNTS PAYABLE CR.	
1	1965 Oct.	2	United Parts Wholesalers	✓	619 00	1
2		3	Queen Electronics	✓	406 00	2
3		7	Reed Supplies, Inc.	✓	57 00	3
4		9	Queen Electronics	✓	208 00	4
5		11	Black Electric Corp.	✓	623 00	5
6		13	Allied Electronics Supply	✓	555 00	6
7		14	Wilson Manufacturing Co.	✓	910 00	7
8		16	Office Equipment Distributors	✓	570 00	8
9		19	State Distributors	✓	1000 00	9
10		21	Wilson Manufacturing Co.	✓	165 00	10
11		25	Reed Supplies, Inc.	✓	32 00	11
12		27	Black Electric Corp.	✓	375 00	12
13		31			5520 00	13
14					(211)	14
15						15
16						16
17						17
18						18
19						19
20						20
21						21

Purchases journal, left page

The Purchases Dr. column is for merchandise bought for resale. A more exact title for the column and the account to which the total is posted would be "Merchandise Purchases." It is customary, however, to refer to merchandise bought for resale as just "Purchases." The purpose of the Store Supplies Dr. and Office Supplies Dr. columns is readily apparent. If supplies of these two categories were bought only infrequently, the two columns could be omitted from the journal.

The final set of columns, under the principal heading Sundry Accounts Debit, is used to record purchases on account of items not provided for in the special debit columns. The title of the particular account in the general ledger is entered in the Account column and the amount of the debit is recorded in the Amount column; the number of the account is written in the Post. Ref. column at the time of posting.

Controlling account and subsidiary ledger

The necessity for maintaining a separate account for each creditor is evident. Although it would be possible to keep these accounts in the general ledger, it is ordinarily preferable to segregate them in a subsidiary ledger. The account in the general ledger that summarizes the debits and the credits to the individual accounts in the subsidiary ledger is entitled

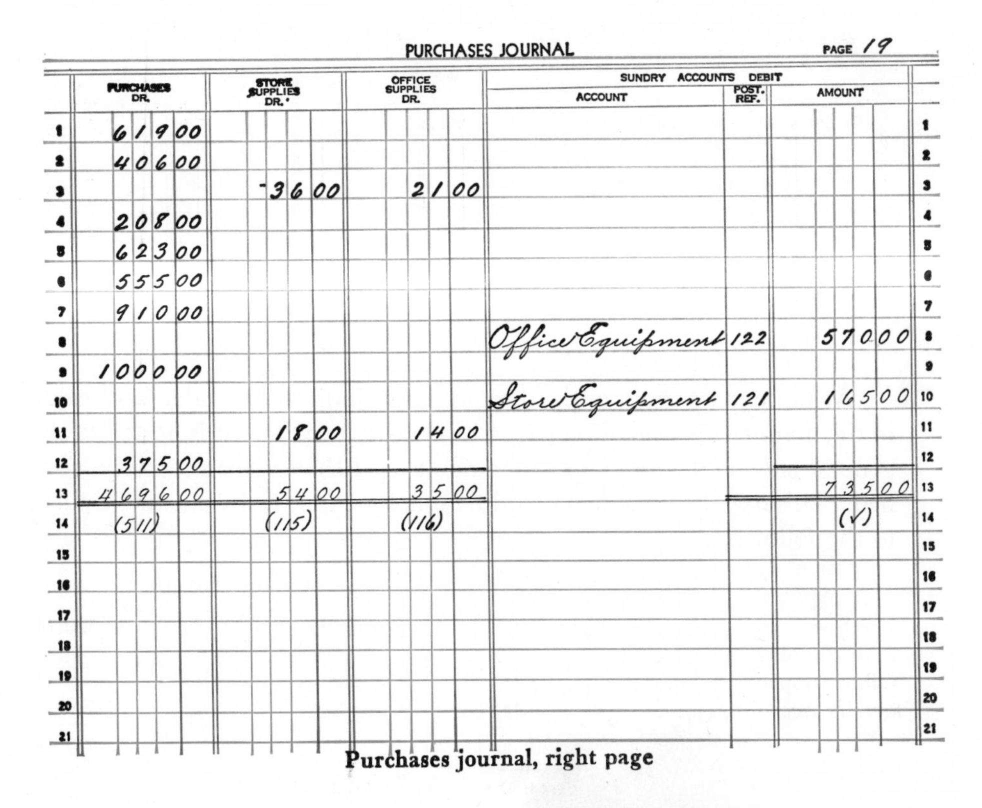

PURCHASES JOURNAL — PAGE 19

	Purchases Dr.	Store Supplies Dr.	Office Supplies Dr.	Sundry Accounts Debit: Account	Post. Ref.	Amount	
1	619 00						1
2	406 00						2
3		36 00	21 00				3
4	208 00						4
5	623 00						5
6	555 00						6
7	910 00						7
8				Office Equipment	122	570 00	8
9	1000 00						9
10				Store Equipment	121	165 00	10
11		18 00	14 00				11
12	375 00						12
13	4696 00	54 00	35 00			735 00	13
14	(511)	(115)	(116)			(✓)	14
15							15
16							16
17							17
18							18
19							19
20							20
21							21

Purchases journal, right page

Accounts Payable. It is a *controlling account.* The subsidiary ledger may be referred to as the *accounts payable ledger* or the *creditors' ledger.*

Posting the purchases journal

At frequent intervals, usually daily, throughout the month the amounts in the Accounts Payable Cr. column are posted to the creditors' accounts in the subsidiary ledger. As each posting is completed, a check mark is placed in the posting reference column of the purchases journal at the left of the amount posted.

The three-column account form ordinarily used for the accounts payable ledger is designed to show at all times the balance owed each creditor. The accounts are arranged alphabetically so as to permit easy access. A loose-leaf binder is used to facilitate the insertion of new accounts and the withdrawal of pages that have been completely filled.

As each item is posted to a creditor's account, the source of the entry is recorded in the posting reference column of the account by the letter "P" and the page number of the purchases journal. The account with Allied Electronics Supply, taken from the accounts payable ledger of Bennett Electrical Supplies, is presented below as an example.

NAME Allied Electronics Supply

ADDRESS 405 Murray St., Chicago, Ill. 60615

DATE		ITEMS	POST. REF.	DEBIT	CREDIT	BALANCE
1965						
Oct.	13		P19		555 00	555 00

An account in the accounts payable ledger

At the end of the month, the purchases journal is totaled and ruled in the manner illustrated on pages 130 and 131. Before it is posted to the general ledger, the equality of the debits and the credits should be verified. This may be done on an adding machine tape or by a listing similar to the following:

Debit Totals		Credit Totals	
Purchases	$4,696.00	Accounts Payable	$5,520.00
Store Supplies	54.00		
Office Supplies	35.00		
Sundry Accounts	735.00		
	$5,520.00		$5,520.00

The total of the Accounts Payable Cr. column is posted to the accounts payable account in the general ledger and the posting reference is indicated below the column total. The totals of the Purchases Dr., Store Supplies Dr., and Office Supplies Dr. columns are posted in a similar manner. Each individual amount in the Sundry Accounts Debit section is posted to the appropriate account in the general ledger, the posting reference being entered at the left of the amount. The total of the column is not posted. A check mark is therefore placed below the $735 total to indicate that no action is required.

Postings were made to six accounts in the general ledger of Bennett Electrical Supplies. Three of the accounts are presented below. The debit of $570 to Office Equipment was posted from the Sundry Accounts Dr. column of the purchases journal; the credit of $5,520 to Accounts Payable and the debit of $4,696 to Purchases were posted as totals from the Accounts Payable Cr. and Purchases Dr. columns, respectively.

Office Equipment — ACCOUNT NO. 122

DATE		ITEMS	POST. REF.	DEBIT	CREDIT	BALANCE	
						DEBIT	CREDIT
1965 Oct.	1	Balance	✓			4600 00	
	16		P19	570 00		5170 00	

Accounts Payable — ACCOUNT NO. 211

DATE		ITEMS	POST. REF.	DEBIT	CREDIT	BALANCE	
						DEBIT	CREDIT
1965 Oct.	1	Balance	✓				6275 00
	31		P19		5520 00		11795 00

Purchases — ACCOUNT NO. 511

DATE		ITEMS	POST. REF.	DEBIT	CREDIT	BALANCE	
						DEBIT	CREDIT
1965 Oct.	1	Balance	✓			49218 00	
	31		P19	4696 00		53914 00	

General ledger accounts after posting from purchases journal

The relationship between the purchases journal and the ledgers of Bennett Electrical Supplies is shown in a flow diagram on the following page.

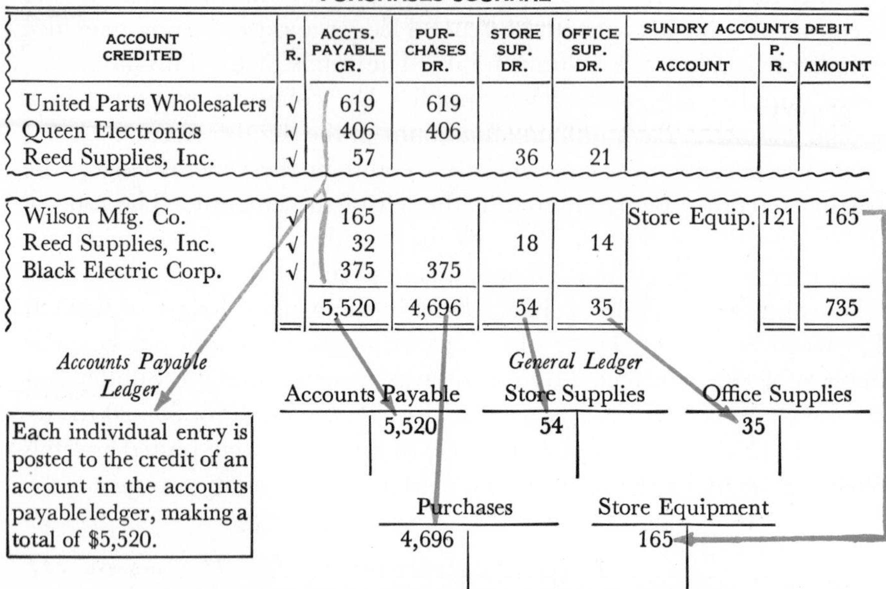

PURCHASES JOURNAL

ACCOUNT CREDITED	P. R.	ACCTS. PAYABLE CR.	PUR-CHASES DR.	STORE SUP. DR.	OFFICE SUP. DR.	SUNDRY ACCOUNTS DEBIT		
						ACCOUNT	P. R.	AMOUNT
United Parts Wholesalers	√	619	619					
Queen Electronics	√	406	406					
Reed Supplies, Inc.	√	57		36	21			
Wilson Mfg. Co.	√	165				Store Equip.	121	165
Reed Supplies, Inc.	√	32		18	14			
Black Electric Corp.	√	375	375					
		5,520	4,696	54	35			735

Relationship between the purchases journal and the ledgers

Two points in particular should be noted: (1) the purchases journal is the source of postings to both the accounts payable ledger and the general ledger, and (2) the sum of the *individual* postings to creditors' accounts in the subsidiary ledger is equal to the *columnar total* posted to Accounts Payable in the general ledger.

Purchases returns and allowances

When merchandise or other commodities purchased on account are returned or a price adjustment is requested, the purchaser usually communicates with the seller in writing. The details may be stated in a letter or the debtor may use his own *debit memorandum* form. This form, illustrated on page 135, is a convenient medium for informing the creditor of the amount to be debited to his account on the buyer's books and the reasons therefor.

The debtor may use a copy of his own debit memorandum as the basis for an entry or he may await confirmation from the creditor, which is usually in the form of a *credit memorandum.* In either event, both the creditor's account and the controlling account must be debited and the account to which the commodities were originally charged must be credited. Thus, if the return or the allowance relates to office equipment, the amount of the reduction is credited to Office Equipment. If the reduction is in the cost of merchandise purchased for resale, the credit is made to Purchases. If management wishes to know both the total dollar

Debit Memorandum **No. 18**

BENNETT ELECTRICAL SUPPLIES
813 Hamilton St.
ALLENTOWN, PA. 18100

October 20, 1965

Allied Electronics Supply
405 Murray Street
Chicago, Illinois 60615

We debit your account as follows:

3 719J Switches, your Invoice No. 106-8, are being returned via parcel post, switches badly damaged	2.50	7.50

Debit memorandum

amount of merchandise purchases and the total dollar amount of merchandise returns and allowances, the credit may be made to a separate account entitled Purchases Returns and Allowances. If the balance of this account becomes large in relation to the balance of Purchases, the reason therefor should be investigated. It may be an indication that purchasing procedures are faulty and that remedial action should be taken by management.

On October 20 Bennett Electrical Supplies issued a debit memorandum to Allied Electronics Supply for merchandise returned. The entry may be recorded in a two-column general journal as follows:

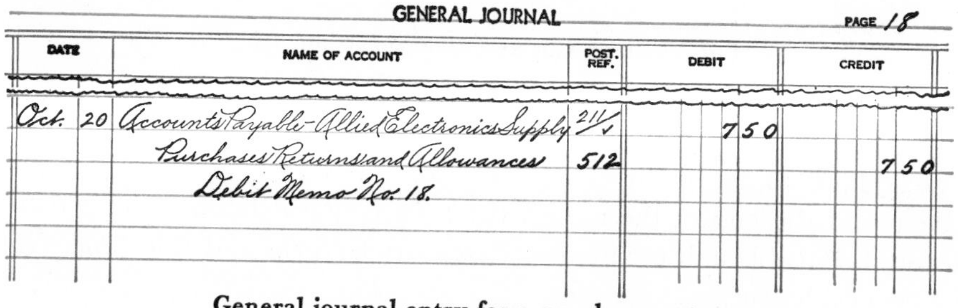

GENERAL JOURNAL PAGE 18

Date		Name of Account	Post. Ref.	Debit	Credit
Oct.	20	Accounts Payable—Allied Electronics Supply	211/✓	7 50	
		Purchases Returns and Allowances	512		7 50
		Debit Memo No. 18.			

General journal entry for a purchases return

Note that the debit is posted to the accounts payable account, which is Account No. 211 in the general ledger, and also to the creditor's account in the subsidiary ledger. The necessity for posting this item to two different accounts is indicated by placing the diagonal line in the posting reference column when the transaction is recorded; the account number and the check mark are written in when the respective postings are made. When this general journal posting has been completed, the accounts payable ledger account for Allied Electronics Supply will appear as follows:

NAME Allied Electronics Supply
ADDRESS 405 Murray St., Chicago, Ill. 60615

DATE		ITEMS	POST. REF.	DEBIT	CREDIT	BALANCE
1965 Oct.	13		P19		555 00	555 00
	30		J18	7 50		547 50

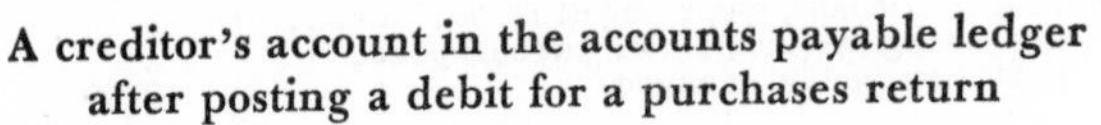

A creditor's account in the accounts payable ledger after posting a debit for a purchases return

If merchandise purchases returns and allowances are of frequent occurrence, special columns for Accounts Payable Debit and Purchases Credit or Purchases Returns and Allowances Credit may be inserted in the general journal. Another alternative is to employ a special purchases returns and allowances journal similar to the one illustrated below.

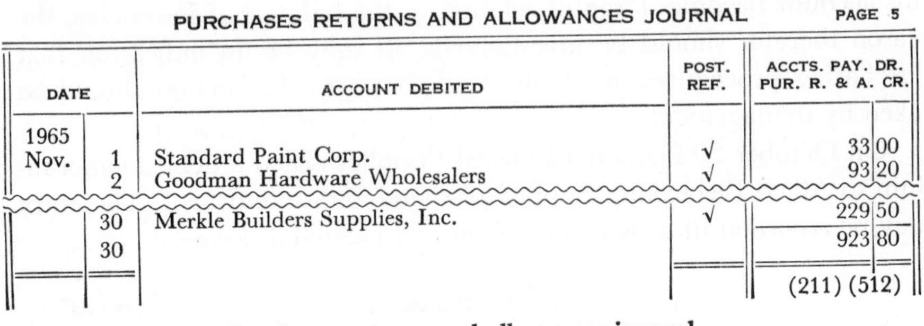

PURCHASES RETURNS AND ALLOWANCES JOURNAL PAGE 5

DATE		ACCOUNT DEBITED	POST. REF.	ACCTS. PAY. DR. PUR. R. & A. CR.
1965 Nov.	1	Standard Paint Corp.	√	33 00
	2	Goodman Hardware Wholesalers	√	93 20
	30	Merkle Builders Supplies, Inc.	√	229 50
	30			923 80
				(211) (512)

Purchases returns and allowances journal

During the month the individual items in the amount column are posted daily to the debit of the creditors' accounts in the subsidiary ledger. At the end of the month the total of the column is debited to Accounts Payable and credited to Purchases Returns and Allowances in the general ledger.

In all of the foregoing examples the creditor's account was debited. When the return or the allowance is granted after the invoice has been paid, the settlement may be made in cash. In such cases the transaction is recorded in the cash receipts journal as a debit to Cash and a credit to Purchases Returns and Allowances.

Purchases invoices as a journal

Many business enterprises dispense with a formal purchases journal, replacing it with the invoices themselves. When this system is used, the original invoices become the basis for posting credits to the individual accounts in the subsidiary ledger. As each credit is posted, an appropriate notation of the fact is stamped or written on the invoice. At the end of each month, the data on all invoices received during that month are summarized and an entry is made in the *general journal* debiting the appropriate general ledger accounts and crediting the accounts payable account. For example, if the summary lists purchases of merchandise, $8,612, office supplies, $340, store supplies, $218, and office equipment, $670, the general journal entry would be as follows:

Nov.	30	Purchases		8,612	
		Office Supplies		340	
		Store Supplies		218	
		Office Equipment		670	
		Accounts Payable			9,840

Credit terms and cash discounts

Credit terms vary among sellers. Some may sell on a net cash basis and others may grant credit for varying periods of time. The payment of accounts as they become due is an important factor in maintaining a good credit rating. It is also important that advantage be taken of all available cash discounts, even though it may be necessary to borrow money to do so. For example, assume a purchase invoice for $800, with terms of 2/10, n/30. The obligation could be discharged within 10 days by payment of $784, representing a savings of $16. In contrast, the interest expense incurred by borrowing $784 for the remaining 20 days of the credit period would be $2.61, assuming an interest rate of 6%. The net savings accruing to the purchaser would thus be the difference between the cash discount of $16 and the interest expense of $2.61, or $13.39.

There are various systems designed to assure payment within the discount period or on the last day of the credit period. A simple but effective method is to file unpaid invoices according to the dates when payment should be considered. The file is composed of a group of folders numbered from 1 to 31, the numbers representing dates. Each invoice is first filed by its discount date. For example, a purchase invoice dated October 10, with terms of 2/10, n/30, should be considered for payment on October 20, the last day of the discount period. It is therefore placed in the folder numbered "20." On October 20 this invoice, together with all other invoices requiring consideration on that date, will be taken from the folder by the treasurer or other person responsible for making disbursements. Each invoice in the folder will then either be paid or be refiled in the appropriate folder. For example, if the October 10 invoice is not paid on October 20, it should be considered again on November 9, the last day of the credit period, and it should accordingly be refiled in the "9" folder.

Cash payments journal

The criteria for determining the special columns to be provided in the cash payments journal are the same as for other journals illustrated earlier, namely, the nature of the transactions to be recorded and the frequency of their occurrence. It is necessary, of course, to have a Cash Cr. column. Payments to creditors on account are usually sufficiently frequent to require columns for Accounts Payable Dr. and Purchases Discount Cr. The cash payments journal illustrated below has these three columns and an additional column for Sundry Accounts Dr. If payments for one or more specific operating expenses were sufficiently numerous, other special columns could be added to the journal.

All payments by Bennett Electrical Supplies are made by check and the check stubs serve as the written evidence of the transactions. As

CASH PAYMENTS JOURNAL PAGE 16

DATE		CHK. NO.	ACCOUNT DEBITED	POST. REF.	SUNDRY ACCOUNTS DR.	ACCOUNTS PAYABLE DR.	PURCHASES DISCOUNT CR.	CASH CR.
1968 Oct.	2	312	Purchases	511	195 00			195 00
	4	313	Office Equipment	122	270 00			270 00
	12	314	Queen Electronics	✓		406 00	4 06	401 94
	12	315	Sales Salaries	611	380 00			380 00
	12	316	Office Salaries	711	160 00			160 00
	14	317	Misc. General Expense	715	26 40			26 40
	16	318	Prepaid Insurance	117	84 00			84 00
	18	319	Queen Electronics	✓		208 00	2 08	205 92
	20	320	Moore Wholesalers	✓		1850 00		1850 00
	21	321	Sales Returns and Allow.	412	62 00			62 00
	23	322	United Parts Wholesalers	✓		1600 00		1600 00
	23	323	Purchases	511	89 20			89 20
	24	324	State Distributors	✓		2300 00		2300 00
	24	325	Wilson Manufacturing Co.	✓		525 00		525 00
	26	326	Sales Salaries	611	380 00			380 00
	26	327	Office Salaries	711	160 00			160 00
	26	328	Allied Electronics Supply	✓		547 50	10 95	536 55
	26	329	Advertising Expense	613	86 00			86 00
	27	330	Misc. Selling Expense	617	41 50			41 50
	28	331	John Bennett, Drawing	312	500 00			500 00
	31				2434 10	7436 50	17 09	9853 51
					(✓)	(211)	(513)	(111)

Cash payments journal after posting

each transaction is recorded in the cash payments journal, the related check number is entered in the column at the right of the Date column. The check numbers facilitate the control of cash payments, since a review of this column will indicate whether all checks have been recorded.

The Sundry Accounts Dr. column is used to record debits to any account for which there is no special column. For example, on October 2 Bennett Electrical Supplies paid $195 for a cash purchase of merchandise. The transaction was recorded by writing the account title "Purchases" in the space provided and $195 in the Sundry Accounts Dr. and the Cash Cr. columns. The posting reference was inserted later, at the time the debit was posted.

Debits to creditors' accounts for invoices paid are recorded in the Accounts Payable Dr. column. If there is no cash discount, the amount recorded in the Cash Cr. column will be the same as the debit to the creditor. If a discount is allowed, the credit to Cash will be correspondingly less. Cash discounts taken on merchandise purchased for resale are recorded in the Purchases Discount Cr. column. For example, the payment to Queen Electronics on October 12 was recorded as a debit to Accounts Payable of $406, a credit to Purchases Discount of $4.06, and a credit to Cash of $401.94.

At frequent intervals during the month, the amounts entered in the Accounts Payable Dr. column are posted to the creditors' accounts in the accounts payable ledger. The source of the entries is indicated by inserting "CP" and the appropriate journal page number in the posting reference column of the accounts. Check marks are placed in the posting reference column of the cash payments journal to indicate that the amounts have been posted. The items in the Sundry Accounts Dr. column are also posted to the appropriate accounts in the general ledger at frequent intervals and the posting is indicated by writing the account numbers in the posting reference column of the cash payments journal.

At the end of the month the cash payments journal is ruled, each of the money columns is footed, and the equality of debits and credits is determined as follows:

Debit Totals		Credit Totals	
Sundry Accounts........	$2,434.10	Purchases Discount.......	$ 17.09
Accounts Payable........	7,436.50	Cash..................	9,853.51
	$9,870.60		$9,870.60

A check mark is placed below the total of the Sundry Accounts Dr. column to indicate that it is not posted. As each of the totals of the other three columns is posted to a general ledger account, the appropriate posting references are inserted below the column totals.

Accounts payable control and subsidiary ledger

During October the following postings were made to Accounts Payable in the general ledger of Bennett Electrical Supplies:

CREDITS

Oct. 31 (Total purchases on account, from purchases journal).... $5,520.00

DEBITS

Oct. 20 (A purchases return, from general journal)............. 7.50
31 (Total debits resulting from payments on account, from cash payments journal).......................... 7,436.50

The controlling account with its opening balance, the foregoing postings, and the resulting balances is shown below.

Accounts Payable — ACCOUNT NO. 211

DATE		ITEMS	POST. REF.	DEBIT	CREDIT	BALANCE DEBIT	BALANCE CREDIT
1965 Oct.	1	Balance	✓				6275 00
	20		J18	7 50			6267 50
	31		P19		5520 00		11787 50
	31		CP16	7436 50			4351 00

Accounts payable account in the general ledger at the end of the month

The accounts payable ledger of Bennett Electrical Supplies, after posting all entries for the month, is shown on this and the following page.

NAME Allied Electronics Supply
ADDRESS 405 Murray St., Chicago, Ill. 60615

DATE		ITEMS	POST. REF.	DEBIT	CREDIT	BALANCE
1965 Oct.	13		P19		555 00	555 00
	20		J18	7 50		547 50
	26		CP16	547 50		—

NAME Black Electric Corp.
ADDRESS 42-46 N. Randolph, Pittsburgh, Pa. 15204

DATE		ITEMS	POST. REF.	DEBIT	CREDIT	BALANCE
1965 Oct.	11		P19		623 00	623 00
	27		P19		375 00	998 00

NAME Moore Wholesalers
ADDRESS 370 Third St., Trenton, N.J. 08605

DATE		ITEMS	POST. REF.	DEBIT	CREDIT	BALANCE
1965 Sept.	21		P18		1850 00	1850 00
Oct.	20		CP16	1850 00		—

Accounts payable ledger at the end of the month

NAME Office Equipment Distributors
ADDRESS 2113 Elwood St., Cincinnati, Ohio 45202

DATE		ITEMS	POST. REF.	DEBIT	CREDIT	BALANCE
1965 Oct.	16		P19		570 00	570 00

NAME Queen Electronics
ADDRESS 1215 College St., Cleveland, Ohio 44105

DATE		ITEMS	POST. REF.	DEBIT	CREDIT	BALANCE
1965 Oct.	3		P19		406 00	406 00
	9		P19		208 00	614 00
	12		CP16	406 00		208 00
	18		CP16	208 00		—

NAME Reed Supplies, Inc.
ADDRESS 2811 N. High St., Reading, Pa. 19602

DATE		ITEMS	POST. REF.	DEBIT	CREDIT	BALANCE
1965 Oct.	7		P19		57 00	57 00
	25		P19		32 00	89 00

NAME State Distributors
ADDRESS 10231 Fortieth St., Pittsburgh, Pa. 15212

DATE		ITEMS	POST. REF.	DEBIT	CREDIT	BALANCE
1965 Sept.	26		P18		2300 00	2300 00
Oct.	19		P19		1000 00	3300 00
	24		CP16	2300 00		1000 00

NAME United Parts Wholesalers
ADDRESS 1319 Hyde Place, Chicago, Ill. 60609

DATE		ITEMS	POST. REF.	DEBIT	CREDIT	BALANCE
1965 Sept.	25		P18		1600 00	1600 00
Oct.	2		P19		619 00	2219 00
	23		CP16	1600 00		619 00

NAME Wilson Manufacturing Co.
ADDRESS 3636 Chestnut St., Philadelphia, Pa. 19106

DATE		ITEMS	POST. REF.	DEBIT	CREDIT	BALANCE
1965 Sept.	28		P18		525 00	525 00
Oct.	14		P19		910 00	1435 00
	21		P19		165 00	1600 00
	24		CP16	525 00		1075 00

Accounts payable ledger at the end of the month — concluded

After all posting has been completed for the month, the sum of the balances in the creditors' ledger should be compared with the balance of the accounts payable account in the general ledger. If the controlling account and the subsidiary ledger are not in agreement, the error or errors must be located and corrected. The balances of the individual creditors' accounts may be summarized on an adding machine tape, or a schedule like the one below may be prepared. The total of the schedule, \$4,351, agrees with the balance of the accounts payable account shown on page 140.

Bennett Electrical Supplies
Schedule of Accounts Payable
October 31, 1965

Black Electric Corp.	\$ 998.00
Office Equipment Distributors.	570.00
Reed Supplies, Inc.	89.00
State Distributors	1,000.00
United Parts Wholesalers	619.00
Wilson Manufacturing Co.	1,075.00
Total accounts payable.	\$4,351.00

Schedule of accounts payable

Transportation on incoming shipments

The cost of merchandise acquired for resale includes the transportation charges for delivery of the goods. Similarly, the cost of plant assets, supplies, and other items purchased includes transportation costs. This is true, in a general sense, regardless of whether the seller or the buyer agrees to bear the cost of transporting the goods from the shipping point to the destination. Businesses that quote prices FOB destination must, of necessity, take transportation costs into consideration when they establish their prices.

When assets are purchased on an FOB shipping point basis, the related freight, express, postage, or other transportation costs should be charged to the same account to which the commodities are charged. Thus, transportation charges on merchandise purchased for resale should be debited to Purchases, transportation charges on store equipment should be debited to Store Equipment, etc. If the buyer pays the transportation agency, the debit is recorded when the bill is paid. If the shipper pays the delivery costs and adds them to the invoice, the entire amount of the invoice, including transportation, is debited to the appropriate account.

Some enterprises maintain an account entitled "Freight-In" or "Transportation-In" for accumulating all separately charged delivery costs on merchandise purchased for resale. If all merchandise is invariably purchased on an FOB shipping point basis, the information thus obtained may be useful in determining the amount of transportation costs to be allocated to the merchandise on hand at the end of a period. If this is not the case, however, the relative size of the balances of the freight-in and purchases accounts at the end of a period is not likely to be significant.

When a separate account is maintained for transportation-in, the amount is sometimes presented on the income statement as an addition to Purchases. Such information is of little significance to the reader; the important matter is that every reasonable effort be made to buy at the lowest possible delivered price. This can be accomplished only through efficient management of the purchasing department. Each time a purchase order is to be issued, consideration must be given not only to the quoted price but also to transportation and discount terms.

QUESTIONS

1. (a) Name two commonly used business forms described in this chapter that are the basis for accounting entries. (b) Name a business form that facilitates but does not represent a completed business transaction.

2. How can an invoice be both a "purchase invoice" and a "sales invoice"?

3. What is the title of the account to which each of the purchases on account described below should be charged by a men's clothing store:

(a) Six dozen neckties.
(b) Pads of sales tickets.
(c) One gross of shirts.
(d) New adding machine for the office.
(e) Fire insurance policy on merchandise for three years.
(f) Fifteen ski jackets.

4. Three related transactions are recorded in the T accounts below. (a) Describe each transaction. (b) What is the rate of the cash discount and on what amount was it computed? (c) Give an alternative method for recording transaction (y).

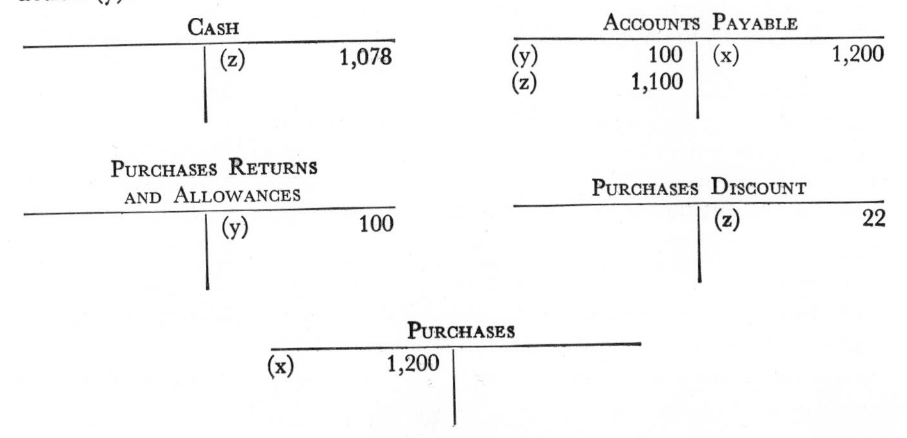

5. Comment on the relative merits of the two systems described below of reporting the receipt of commodities.

(a) The purchase invoice is sent to the receiving department. The receiving department indicates quantities received by inserting a check mark or actual quantities opposite each item on the invoice.
(b) A carbon copy of the purchase order, on which quantities and prices do not appear, is sent to the receiving department. The receiving department inserts the actual quantities received opposite each description on the purchase order.

6. (a) Which are more likely to cause the greater amount of expense to be incurred, sales returns or purchases returns? Comment. (b) Would it be illogical or improper to accumulate sales returns and allowances in a separate account but to credit purchases returns and allowances directly to Purchases?

7. The following errors were made in recording transactions in the purchases journal or in posting therefrom. How will each error come to the attention of the bookkeeper other than by chance discovery?

(a) An invoice for merchandise of $250 from Timmer Co. was recorded as having been received from Timmons Co., another supplier.
(b) A credit of $400 to M. J. Carter, Inc. was posted as $40.
(c) The accounts payable column was underadded by $100.
(d) An invoice for store equipment of $100 was recorded as $10.

8. The accounts payable and cash columns in the cash payments journal were unknowingly underadded by $1,000 at the end of the month. (a) Assuming no other errors in recording or posting, will the error cause the trial balance totals to be unequal? (b) Will the creditors' ledger agree with the accounts payable account?

9. (a) Under what circumstances is a diagonal line inserted in the posting reference column opposite an entry in a two-column general journal? (b) Should the diagonal line be inserted when the entry is recorded in the general journal or at the time the entry is posted?

10. Supplier A offers 100 units of a particular commodity at $10 a unit, FOB shipping point, 2/10, n/30. Transportation costs will amount to $50. Supplier B offers the identical commodity in hundred-unit lots at $10.40 a unit, FOB destination, n/30. Which of the two prices is the lower? Discuss.

11. Name the accounts that would be credited in recording the following returns of commodities purchased on account assuming (a) that there is an account in the ledger for purchases returns and allowances and (b) that there is not such an account in the ledger: (1) Merchandise purchased for resale. (2) Equipment purchased for use in the business.

12. Is the normal balance of Purchases Discount a debit or a credit?

13. In recording a cash payment the bookkeeper enters the correct amount of $700 in the Accounts Payable Dr. column and the correct amount of $693 in the Cash Cr. column but omits the entry for Purchases Discount. How will this error come to his attention other than by chance discovery?

14. Apex Appliance Co. purchases 20 automatic dryers for $125 each, FOB shipping point, 2/10, n/30. The transportation charges on the shipment amount to $80. Assuming that the invoice is paid within the discount period, what is the net unit cost of the dryers?

EXERCISES

1. Determine the amount to be paid in full settlement of each of the following invoices, assuming that credit for returns and allowances was received prior to payment and that all invoices were paid within the discount period.

	Purchase Invoice			Returns and
	Merchandise	Transportation	Terms	Allowances
(a)	$2,000	—	FOB shipping point, 2/10, n/30	$ 50
(b)	1,800	$70	FOB shipping point, 1/10, n/30	—
(c)	700	—	FOB destination, n/30	100
(d)	1,400	30	FOB shipping point, 2/10, n/30	40
(e)	300	—	FOB destination, 1/10, n/30	60

2. Jackson Co. uses its purchases invoices as its purchases journal. Summarization of the invoices for June yields the following totals for the various categories of commodities purchased on account: merchandise for resale, $49,362; store supplies, $620; office supplies, $65; office equipment, $390. Prepare the general journal entry that should be made on the basis of this information.

3. Reed Co. purchases $800 of merchandise from Miller Corp., FOB shipping point, 2/10, n/30. Miller Corp. adds transportation charges of $30 to the invoice. Reed Co. returns merchandise, receiving a credit memorandum for $40, and then pays the amount due within the discount period. Present Reed Co.'s entries, in general journal form, to record (a) the purchase, (b) the merchandise return, and (c) the payment. (Reed Co. maintains a separate account for recording purchases returns and allowances).

4. Present entries in general journal form for the following related transactions of Horton Decorator Co., recording merchandise purchases returns and allowances in the purchases account:

(a) Purchased $700 of fabrics from Taylor Mills on account, terms 2/10, n/30.
(b) Paid the amount owed on the invoice within the discount period.
(c) Discovered that most of the fabrics were not color fast and returned items with an invoice price of $500, receiving credit.
(d) Purchased $300 of fabrics from Taylor Mills on account, terms 2/10, n/30.
(e) Received a check for the balance owed from the return in (c), after deducting for the purchase in (d).

5. Present the general journal entries necessary to correct each of the errors described below, assuming that the incorrect entries had been posted and that the corrections are recorded in the same fiscal period in which the errors occurred.

(a) A $50 cash purchase of merchandise from Hanson & Co. was recorded as a purchase on account.

(b) The $140 cost of faulty equipment (for use in the business) returned to the supplier was credited to Purchases Returns and Allowances.
(c) The payment of a $1,000 invoice for merchandise, less 2% discount, to A. C. Barker Co. was recorded as a $980 debit to A. C. Barker Co. (and Accounts Payable) and a $980 credit to Cash.
(d) Transportation costs of $35 incurred on equipment purchased for use in the business were charged to Purchases.

PROBLEMS

6-1. Purchases on account and related returns and allowances completed by Wayside Book Shop during September of the current year are described below.

Sept. 2. Purchased merchandise on account from Banner Greetings Co., $116.30.
5. Purchased merchandise on account from Herald Press, Inc., $735.
7. Received a credit memorandum from Banner Greetings Co. for merchandise returned, $12.10.
10. Purchased office supplies on account from Nolan Supply Co., $29.80.
14. Purchased office equipment on account from Linton Equipment Co., $426.30.
15. Purchased merchandise on account from Banner Greetings Co., $263.70.
17. Purchased merchandise on account from Vinton Publishing Co., $384.90.
18. Received a credit memorandum from Nolan Supply Co. for office supplies returned, $3.70.
21. Purchased merchandise on account from Tudor Publishers, $436.
23. Received a credit memorandum from Herald Press, Inc. as an allowance for damaged merchandise, $75.
24. Purchased store supplies on account from Nolan Supply Co., $36.70.
25. Purchased merchandise on account from Vinton Publishing Co., $537.90.
29. Purchased office supplies on account from Nolan Supply Co., $16.50.

Instructions: (1) Open the following accounts in the general ledger and enter the balances as of September 1:

114 Store Supplies........	$ 197.50	211 Accounts Payable....	$ 1,379.10
115 Office Supplies.......	86.30	511 Purchases...........	26,862.70
122 Office Equipment....	2,490.00		

(2) Open the following accounts in the accounts payable ledger and enter the balances in the balance columns as of September 1: Banner Greetings Co., $275.20; Herald Press, Inc., $461.00; Linton Equipment Co.; Nolan Supply Co.; Tudor Publishers; Vinton Publishing Co., $642.90.

(3) Record the transactions for September, posting to the creditors' accounts in the accounts payable ledger immediately after each entry. Use a purchases journal similar to the one illustrated on pages 130 and 131 and a two-column general journal.

(4) Post the general journal and the purchases journal to the accounts in the general ledger.

(5) (a) What is the sum of the balances in the subsidiary ledger?
(b) What is the balance of the controlling account?

6-2. Oakwood Men's Wear was established in August of the current year. Transactions related to purchases, returns and allowances, and cash payments during the remainder of the month are described below.

Aug. 16. Purchased store equipment on account from Taylor Supply Co., $6,200.
16. Purchased merchandise on account from Worthmore Clothes, Inc., $2,850.
17. Issued Check No. 1 in payment of rent for August, $300.
17. Issued Check No. 2 in payment of office supplies, $48, and store supplies, $33.
18. Purchased merchandise on account from Lee & Co., $1,875.
19. Purchased merchandise on account from Barron Clothing Co., $1,050.
20. Received a credit memorandum from Lee & Co. for returned merchandise, $75.

Post the journals to the accounts payable ledger.

24. Issued Check No. 3 to Worthmore Clothes, Inc., in payment of invoice of $2,850, less 2% discount.
25. Issued Check No. 4 to Taylor Supply Co. in payment of invoice of $6,200.
25. Received a credit memorandum from Barron Clothing Co. for defective merchandise, $56.
26. Issued Check No. 5 to a cash customer for merchandise returned, $18.
26. Issued Check No. 6 to Lee & Co. in payment of the balance owed, less 2% discount.
27. Purchased merchandise on account from Barron Clothing Co., $2,400.

Post the journals to the accounts payable ledger.

30. Purchased the following from Taylor Supply Co. on account: store supplies, $37; office supplies, $38; office equipment, $900.
30. Issued Check No. 7 to Barron Clothing Co. in payment of the invoice of $1,050 less the credit of $56.
30. Purchased merchandise on account from Worthmore Clothes, Inc., $1,950.
31. Issued Check No. 8 in payment of transportation charges on merchandise purchased, $144.
31. Issued Check No. 9 in payment of sales salaries, $880.

Post the journals to the accounts payable ledger.

Instructions: (1) Open the following accounts in the general ledger, using the account numbers indicated.

111 Cash
116 Store Supplies
117 Office Supplies
121 Store Equipment
122 Office Equipment
211 Accounts Payable
412 Sales Returns and Allowances
511 Purchases
512 Purchases Returns and Allowances
513 Purchases Discount
611 Sales Salaries
712 Rent Expense

(2) Open the following accounts in the accounts payable ledger: Barron Clothing Co.; Lee & Co.; Taylor Supply Co.; Worthmore Clothes, Inc.

(3) Record the transactions for August, using a purchases journal similar to the one illustrated on pages 130 and 131, a purchases returns and allowances

journal similar to the one illustrated on page 136, and a cash payments journal similar to the one illustrated on page 138. Post to the *accounts payable ledger* at the points indicated in the narrative of transactions.

(4) Post the appropriate individual entries to the *general ledger*.

(5) Add the columns of the purchases journal, the purchases returns and allowances journal, and the cash payments journal, and post the appropriate totals to the general ledger.

(6) Prepare a schedule of accounts payable.

If the working papers correlating with the textbook are not used, omit Problem 6-3.

6-3. Marathon Specialty Co. uses carbon copies of its sales invoices as a sales journal, posting to the accounts receivable ledger directly from the invoices. At the end of the month the invoices are totaled and the appropriate entry is recorded in the general journal. Purchases on account are handled in a similar manner, the invoices being used as a purchases journal. Sales and purchases on account during March of the current year were as follows:

Sales

Mar.	4. No. 719 John Payne Corp.	$1,900
	6. No. 720 Wilson & Young	1,450
	10. No. 721 Lewis Abbott & Co.	1,150
	16. No. 722 Frank Gordon	525
	17. No. 723 Lewis Abbott & Co.	3,117
	22. No. 724 Wilson & Young	653

Purchases

Mar.	2. Eaton & Co.: store supplies, $120; office supplies, $32	$ 152
	3. Martin Corp., merchandise	2,675
	11. Hill-Burns, Inc., merchandise	1,800
	18. E. V. Richards, Inc., store equipment	1,250
	19. Trenton Manufacturing Co., merchandise	918
	29. Eaton & Co., store supplies	39
	31. Hill-Burns, Inc., merchandise	1,016

Other transactions completed during the month were recorded in a 4-column general journal, a cash receipts journal, and a cash payments journal, all of which are presented in the working papers. The subsidiary ledgers and the general ledger accounts affected by transactions of the month are also presented in the working papers.

Instructions: (1) Summarize the sales invoices and the purchases invoices listed above and record the appropriate entries in the 4-column general journal.

(2) Post all items affecting the *subsidiary* ledgers, in the following order: sales invoices, purchases invoices, general journal, cash receipts journal, cash payments journal. When postings are made daily, which is the usual practice, the entries in customers' and creditors' accounts will appear in chronological order. The fact that in this problem postings to some of the accounts will not be in perfect date sequence is immaterial.

(3) Post all items recorded in the Sundry Accounts Dr. and Sundry Accounts Cr. columns of the journals, in the following order: general journal, cash receipts journal, cash payments journal.

(4) Add the columns of the general journal and post the appropriate columnar totals of each journal, following the same sequence as in instruction (3).
(5) Prepare a trial balance.
(6) (a) What is the sum of the balances in the accounts receivable ledger?
(b) What is the sum of the balances in the accounts payable ledger?

6-4. The transactions completed by Kent's during June, the first month of the current fiscal year, were as follows:

June 1. Issued Check No. 593 for June rent, $450.
2. Purchased merchandise on account from Price-Spencer Corp., $2,240.
3. Purchased equipment on account from Collins Supply Co., $1,650.
3. Issued Invoice No. 815 to Sanders Corp., $850.
5. Received check for $1,568 from Bryant & Ross in payment of $1,600 invoice, less discount.
5. Issued Check No. 594 in payment of miscellaneous selling expense, $130.
5. Received credit memorandum from Price-Spencer Corp. for merchandise returned to them, $90.
8. Issued Invoice No. 816 to Zeller & Co., $1,500.
9. Issued Check No. 595 for $3,038 to Allen Manufacturing Co. in payment of $3,100 balance less 2% discount.
9. Received check for $833 from Norman Corp. in payment of $850 invoice, less discount.
10. Issued Check No. 596 to G. W. Ludlow & Co. in payment of invoice of $810; no discount.

Post all journals to the accounts receivable ledger and the accounts payable ledger.

10. Issued Invoice No. 817 to Bryant & Ross, $2,460.
11. Issued Check No. 597 to Wade Co. in payment of account, $1,450; no discount.
12. Received check from Sanders Corp. on account, $690; no discount.
14. Issued credit memorandum to Bryant & Ross for damaged merchandise, $110.
15. Issued Check No. 598 for $2,107 to Price-Spencer Corp. in payment of $2,150 balance less 2% discount.
15. Issued Check No. 599 for $595 for cash purchase of merchandise.
15. Cash sales for June 1–15, $4,995.
17. Purchased merchandise on account from G. W. Ludlow & Co., $2,160.
18. Received check for return of merchandise that was originally purchased for cash, $24.
18. Issued Check No. 600 in payment of miscellaneous general expense, $183.
22. Purchased the following on account from Collins Supply Co.: store supplies, $38; office supplies, $32.
22. Issued Check No. 601 in payment of advertising expense, $330.

Post all journals to the accounts receivable ledger and the accounts payable ledger.

23. Issued Invoice No. 818 to Norman Corp., $1,066.
24. Purchased the following on account from Allen Manufacturing Co.: merchandise, $960; store supplies, $17.

June 25. Issued Invoice No. 819 to Zeller & Co., $1,360.
25. Received check for $2,303 from Bryant & Ross in payment of $2,350 balance less discount.
26. Issued Check No. 602 to Collins Supply Co. in payment of account, $1,650; no discount.
29. Issued Check No. 603 to Roy Kent as a personal withdrawal, $725.
30. Issued Check No. 604 for monthly salaries as follows: sales salaries, $900; office salaries, $300.
30. Cash sales for June 16-30, $4,492.
30. Issued Check No. 605 for transportation on commodities purchased during the month as follows: merchandise, $93; equipment, $32.

Post all journals to the accounts receivable ledger and the accounts payable ledger.

Instructions: (1) Open the following accounts in the general ledger, entering the balances indicated as of June 1:

111	Cash	$ 7,240	411	Sales
113	Accounts Receivable	3,140	412	Sales Returns and Allow.
114	Merchandise Inventory	23,220	413	Sales Discount
115	Store Supplies	390	511	Purchases
116	Office Supplies	188	512	Purchases Discount
117	Prepaid Insurance	577	611	Sales Salaries
121	Equipment	14,718	612	Advertising Expense
121.1	Accumulated Depreciation	7,139	619	Miscellaneous Selling Exp.
211	Accounts Payable	5,360	711	Office Salaries
311	Roy Kent, Capital	36,974	712	Rent Expense
312	Roy Kent, Drawing		719	Miscellaneous General Exp.

(2) Open the following accounts in the accounts receivable ledger, entering the balances as of June 1 in the balance columns: Bryant & Ross, $1,600; Norman Corp., $850; Sanders Corp., $690; Zeller & Co.

(3) Open the following accounts in the accounts payable ledger, entering the balances as of June 1 in the balance columns: Allen Manufacturing Co., $3,100; Collins Supply Co.; G. W. Ludlow & Co., $810; Price-Spencer Corp.; Wade Co., $1,450.

(4) Record the transactions for June, using a sales journal (as on page 106), a purchases journal (as on pages 130 and 131), a cash receipts journal (as on page 114), a cash payments journal (as on page 138), and a 2-column general journal. The terms of all sales on account are FOB shipping point, 2/15, n/60. Post to the subsidiary ledgers at the points indicated in the narrative of transactions.

(5) Post the appropriate individual entries to the *general ledger*.

(6) Add the columns of the special journals and post the appropriate totals to the general ledger.

(7) Prepare a trial balance.

(8) Prepare a schedule of accounts receivable and a schedule of accounts payable.

7.

Periodic summary

Outline of the periodic summary

Twelve months is the standard maximum length of the fiscal period. At yearly intervals throughout the life of a business enterprise it is necessary to summarize and report the operating and financial data for owners, creditors, and other interested persons. It is also necessary to prepare the ledger for entries of the ensuing year. Regardless of whether interim statements may have been prepared at the end of each month, it is necessary to record adjusting and closing entries at the end of the year.

Although it is possible to vary the sequence of procedures to a limited extent, the accounting department of a business firm must perform the following year-end tasks:

1. Prepare a trial balance of the general ledger.
2. Determine that each subsidiary ledger is in agreement with the related controlling account in the general ledger.
3. Review the accounts to determine which ones should be adjusted, and compile the data necessary for making the adjustments.
4. Prepare a work sheet from the trial balance and the data for the adjustments.
5. Prepare financial statements from the data in the work sheet.
6. Record the adjusting entries in the general journal.
7. Record the closing entries in the general journal.
8. Post the adjusting and closing entries.
9. Prepare a post-closing trial balance of the general ledger.
10. Record the reversing entries necessary to facilitate the recording of transactions in the following year.
11. Post the reversing entries.

The foregoing outline is similar to the outline presented in Chapter 4. There are two additional procedures, however: (1) comparing controlling account balances with related subsidiary ledgers, and (2) recording and posting reversing entries. It is also assumed that general ledger account forms with balance columns are employed, which eliminates the necessity for the formalized ruling and balancing procedures associated with the T form.

In the illustration of the periodic summary, to which this chapter is devoted, two additional adjusting entries will also be considered. Both are related to merchandise inventory and the determination of the cost of merchandise sold.

Adjustment of merchandise inventory

It would be possible to record merchandise transactions in the same manner as transactions with supplies. The debit balance in the merchandise account at the beginning of the fiscal period would represent the cost of the merchandise on hand, and purchases during the period would be debited to the same account. At the end of the period the cost of merchandise sold would, like the cost of supplies used, be the difference between the balance of the account and the inventory at the end of the period.

Because of the greater importance of merchandise transactions, it is customary to collect more detailed information about the cost of merchandise sold than about supplies used. Such details are often presented on the income statement in the following manner:

Cost of merchandise sold:				
Merchandise inventory, January 1, 1965			$ 16,600	
Purchases		$103,920		
Less: Purchases returns and allowances	$2,640			
Purchases discount	1,857	4,497		
Net purchases			99,423	
Merchandise available for sale			$116,023	
Less merchandise inventory, December 31, 1965			18,200	
Cost of merchandise sold				$97,823

The most efficient way to collect the foregoing data is to provide separate accounts in the ledger. Accordingly, an asset account entitled Merchandise Inventory is used for recording the cost of the inventory at the beginning of the fiscal period. As was explained in the preceding chapter, purchases and purchases discounts during the period are recorded in separate accounts, and, if desired, accounts may also be maintained for transportation-in and for purchases returns and allowances.

At the end of the period it is necessary to replace, in the merchandise inventory account, the amount of inventory at the beginning of the period with the amount of inventory at the end of the period. This is accomplished by two adjusting entries. The first entry transfers the beginning inventory to Expense and Revenue Summary. Inasmuch as this beginning inventory is part of the cost of merchandise sold, it is debited to Expense and Revenue Summary. It is also a subtraction from the asset account Merchandise Inventory and hence is credited to that account. The first adjusting entry is as follows:

Dec.	31	Expense and Revenue Summary....	16,600	
		Merchandise Inventory..........		16,600

The second of the two adjusting entries records the cost of the merchandise inventory at the end of the fiscal period. The amount is debited to Merchandise Inventory to record the asset. It is credited to Expense and Revenue Summary because, as shown on the partial income statement on page 152, it is a deduction from the merchandise available for sale. The second adjusting entry is as follows:

Dec.	31	Merchandise Inventory...........	18,200	
		Expense and Revenue Summary..		18,200

The accounts affected by the foregoing adjustments are presented below, in T-account form:

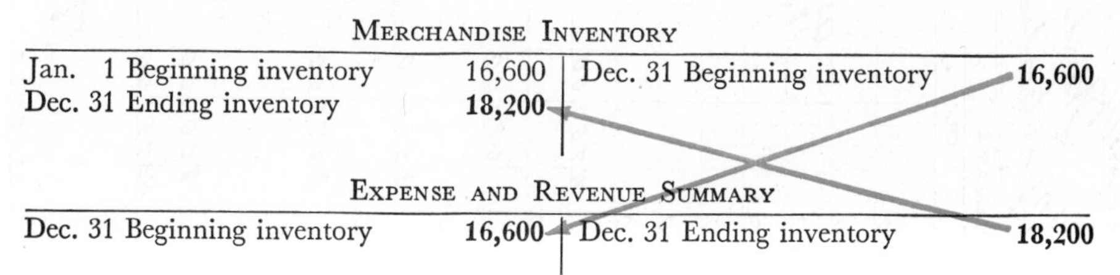
MERCHANDISE INVENTORY

Jan. 1 Beginning inventory	16,600	Dec. 31 Beginning inventory	**16,600**
Dec. 31 Ending inventory	**18,200**		

EXPENSE AND REVENUE SUMMARY

Dec. 31 Beginning inventory	**16,600**	Dec. 31 Ending inventory	**18,200**

Merchandise Inventory now has a debit balance of $18,200, which is the amount of the inventory at the end of the period. Expense and Revenue Summary has a debit for the beginning inventory of $16,600, which is a part of the cost of merchandise available for sale, and it also has a credit for the ending inventory of $18,200, which is a deduction from the cost of merchandise available for sale.

Trial balance, adjustments, and work sheet

After the recording and the posting of transactions for the year has been completed, a trial balance is prepared on work sheet paper. The balances of the accounts in each subsidiary ledger are also added together and the total is compared with the controlling account balance. Any discrepancies should be corrected before the work sheet is finished.

Bennett Electrical Supplies
Work Sheet
For Year Ended December 31, 1965

ACCOUNT TITLES	TRIAL BALANCE		ADJUSTMENTS		INCOME STATEMENT		BALANCE SHEET	
	DR.	CR.	DR.	CR.	DR.	CR.	DR.	CR.
Cash	9675.00						9675.00	
Accounts Receivable	8900.00						8900.00	
Merchandise Inventory	16600.00		(b) 18200.00	(a) 16600.00			18200.00	
Store Supplies	1270.00			(c) 580.00			690.00	
Office Supplies	580.00			(d) 240.00			340.00	
Prepaid Insurance	1520.00			(e) 716.00			804.00	
Store Equipment	12000.00						12000.00	
Accumulated Depr.-Store Equip.		4700.00		(f) 1000.00				5700.00
Office Equipment	3400.00						3400.00	
Accumulated Depr.-Office Equip.		680.00		(g) 340.00				1020.00
Building	28000.00						28000.00	
Accumulated Depr.-Building		3500.00		(h) 700.00				4200.00
Land	3000.00						3000.00	
Accounts Payable		9270.00						9270.00
Commissions Payable				(i) 564.00				564.00
Salaries Payable				(j) 212.00				212.00
Mortgage Payable		8000.00						8000.00
John Bennett, Capital		43751.00						43751.00
John Bennett, Drawing	12000.00						12000.00	
Expense and Revenue Summary			(a) 16600.00	(b) 18200.00	16600.00	18200.00		
Sales		163574.00				163574.00		
Sales Returns and Allowances	3150.00				3150.00			

Sales Discount	1314 00				1314 00			
Purchases	103920 00				103920 00			
Purchases Returns and Allow.		2640 00				2640 00		
Purchases Discount		1857 00				1857 00		
Sales Salaries	14510 00		(j) 152 00		14662 00			
Sales Commissions	6867 00		(i) 564 00		7431 00			
Advertising Expense	2580 00				2580 00			
Depreciation Expense Store Equip.			(f) 1000 00		1000 00			
Delivery Expense	963 00				963 00			
Store Supplies Expense			(c) 580 00		580 00			
Insurance Expense Selling			(e) 420 00		420 00			
Miscellaneous Selling Expense	724 00				724 00			
Office Salaries	5064 00		(j) 60 00		5124 00			
Taxes Expense	1762 00				1762 00			
Depreciation Expense Office Equip.			(g) 340 00		340 00			
Depreciation Expense Building			(h) 700 00		700 00			
Office Supplies Expense			(d) 240 00		240 00			
Insurance Expense General			(e) 296 00		296 00			
Miscellaneous General Expense	693 00				693 00			
Rent Income		1000 00				1000 00		
Interest Expense	480 00				480 00			
	238972 00	238972 00	3915 00	3915 00	162979 00	187271 00	97009 00	72717 00
Net Income					24292 00			24292 00
					187271 00	187271 00	97009 00	97009 00

Work sheet

The trial balance for Bennett Electrical Supplies as of December 31, 1965, appears on the work sheet presented on pages 154 and 155. It differs from those illustrated in earlier chapters in one respect — all ledger accounts are listed in sequence, including titles of accounts that have no balances. This method has the minor advantage of listing accounts in the order in which they will be used when the statements are prepared. If additional accounts are needed in making the necessary adjustments, their titles can be inserted below the trial balance totals, as illustrated in Chapter 4.

The data needed for adjusting the accounts of Bennett Electrical Supplies are presented in summary form as follows:

Merchandise inventory as of December 31, 1965		$18,200
Inventories of supplies as of December 31, 1965:		
Store supplies		690
Office supplies		340
Insurance expired during 1965:		
On merchandise and store equipment	$420	
On office equipment and building	296	716
Depreciation during 1965:		
On store equipment		1,000
On office equipment		340
On building		700
Commissions and salaries accrued on December 31, 1965:		
Sales commissions		564
Sales salaries	$152	
Office salaries	60	212

Explanations of the adjusting entries in the work sheet appearing on pages 154 and 155 are given in the paragraphs that follow.

Merchandise inventory. The $16,600 balance of merchandise inventory appearing in the trial balance represents the amount of the inventory at the beginning of the current year (end of the preceding year). It is a part of the merchandise available for sale during the year and is hence transferred to Expense and Revenue Summary, where it will be combined with the cost of merchandise purchased during the year. (Entry (a) on the work sheet.)

The merchandise on hand at the end of the current year, as determined by a physical inventory, amounts to $18,200. It is an asset and must be debited to the asset account Merchandise Inventory. It must also be deducted from the cost of merchandise available for sale (beginning inventory plus net purchases) to yield the cost of the merchandise sold. These objectives are accomplished by debiting Merchandise Inventory and crediting Expense and Revenue Summary. (Entry (b) on the work sheet.)

Supplies. The $1,270 balance of the store supplies account in the trial balance is the sum of the inventory on hand at the beginning of the current year and net purchases of store supplies during the current year. The physical inventory at the end of the year indicates store supplies on hand totaling $690. The difference of $580 ($1,270 – $690) is therefore the amount of store supplies consumed. The accounts are adjusted by debiting Store Supplies Expense and crediting Store Supplies for $580. (Entry (c) on the work sheet.) The adjustment for office supplies consumed is determined in the same manner. (Entry (d) on the work sheet.)

Prepaid insurance. The adjustment for insurance expired is similar to the adjustment for supplies consumed. The balance in Prepaid Insurance is the sum of the amount prepaid at the beginning of the year and additional premiums paid during the year. Analysis of the various insurance policies reveals that a total of $716 in premiums have expired, of which $420 is applicable to merchandise and store equipment and $296 is applicable to office equipment and building. Insurance Expense — Selling is debited for $420, Insurance Expense — General is debited for $296, and Prepaid Insurance is credited for $716. (Entry (e) on the work sheet.)

Depreciation of plant assets. The expired cost of plant assets is debited to a depreciation expense account and credited to an accumulated depreciation account. A separate account for the expense and for the accumulation is maintained for each plant asset account. Thus, the adjustment for depreciation of the store equipment is recorded by a debit to Depreciation Expense — Store Equipment and a credit to Accumulated Depreciation — Store Equipment for $1,000. The adjustments for depreciation of the office equipment and the building are recorded in a similar manner. (Entries (f), (g), and (h) on the work sheet.)

Commissions and salaries payable. The liability for the commissions earned by employees but not yet paid is recorded by a credit of $564 to the liability account Commissions Payable and a debit to the expense account Sales Commissions. (Entry (i) on the work sheet.) Similarly, salaries earned but not paid are recorded by a credit of $212 to Salaries Payable and debits to Sales Salaries and Office Salaries for $152 and $60, respectively. (Entry (j) on the work sheet.)

Completing the work sheet

After all necessary adjustments are entered on the work sheet, the two Adjustments columns are totaled to prove the equality of debits and credits.

The amounts in the Trial Balance section are then combined with those in the Adjustments section. In the work sheet illustrated in Chapter 4 the amounts were extended to the appropriate columns of the Adjusted Trial Balance section and the arithmetical accuracy of the computations was verified by totaling the columns. Many accountants prefer to omit this intermediate step and to extend the trial balance amounts, after adjustment, directly to the Income Statement and Balance Sheet sections. This latter plan is followed in the illustration on pages 154 and 155.

The most efficient procedure for extending the amounts to the statement sections is to begin at the top of the work sheet and dispose of each item in sequential order.

Both of the adjustments to Expense and Revenue Summary for merchandise inventory are extended to the Income Statement sections of the work sheet. The debit adjustment of $16,600 for the beginning inventory is entered in the debit column of the Income Statement section and the credit adjustment of $18,200 for the ending inventory is entered in the credit column of the Income Statement section. The same net result could be obtained by extending the difference between the two amounts, here a $1,600 credit ($18,200 credit – $16,600 debit). When both inventory amounts are extended, however, all of the data needed for the preparation of the income statement appears in the Income Statement section of the work sheet.[1]

After all of the items have been extended into the statement sections of the work sheet, the four columns are totaled and the net income or loss is determined. In the illustration the difference between the credit and the debit columns of the Income Statement section is $24,292, the amount of the net income. The difference between the debit and the credit columns of the Balance Sheet section is also $24,292, the increase in capital resulting from net income. Agreement between the two balancing amounts is evidence of debit-credit equality and arithmetical accuracy.

Preparation of statements and supporting schedules

The income statement, the capital statement, and the balance sheet are now prepared from the data in the statement sections of the work sheet. For the capital statement it is also necessary to refer to the capital account in the general ledger to determine whether there have been investments or reductions during the year.

Formal schedules of accounts receivable and accounts payable are sometimes prepared from the respective subsidiary ledgers. They may be

---

[1]An alternative method of recording merchandise inventories on the work sheet is presented in Appendix B.

useful to management in reviewing customer accounts for credit purposes and in preparing statements for credit-rating agencies.

When there are several statements and supporting schedules included in a financial report, each may be designated by a letter, or a number, or a combination of the two, as is illustrated by the statements for Bennett Electrical Supplies.

Income statement

Income statements for a merchandising business are likely to be somewhat more complicated than such statements for a service enterprise. The accompanying income statement for Bennett Electrical Supplies, a merchandising business, differs in other respects also from those illustrated in earlier chapters. Because of its numerous subsections and intermediate summary figures, it is sometimes called the *multiple-step* form. The *single-step* form, in which the total of all expired costs is deducted as a single figure from the total of all revenues, is illustrated in a later chapter.

In practice, there is considerable variation in the amount of detail presented in income statements. For example, instead of reporting separately gross sales and the related returns, allowances, and discounts, the statement may begin with net sales. Similarly, the supporting data for the determination of the cost of merchandise sold may be omitted from the statement. The various sections of a conventional multiple-step income statement for a mercantile enterprise are discussed briefly in the paragraphs that follow.

Revenue from sales. Total charges to customers for merchandise sold are reported in this section, from which sales returns and allowances and sales discounts are deducted to yield the net sales.

Cost of merchandise sold. The determination of this important figure was explained and illustrated earlier in the chapter. Other descriptive terms frequently employed are *cost of goods sold* and *cost of sales.*

Gross profit on sales. The excess of the net revenue from sales over the cost of merchandise sold is called *gross profit on sales.* It is termed *gross* because all other expenses for the period must be deducted to obtain the *net* profit or *net* income of the business.

Operating expenses. The operating expenses of a business may be classified under any desired number of headings and subheadings. In a small retail business of the kind that has been used for illustrative purposes, it is usually satisfactory to classify operating expenses as either *selling* or *general.*

Expenses that are incurred directly and entirely in connection with the sale of merchandise are known as *selling expenses.* They include such expenses as salaries of the sales force, store supplies used, depreciation of store equipment, and advertising.

Expenses incurred in the general operations of the business are known as *general expenses* or *administrative expenses.* Examples of these expenses are office salaries, depreciation of office equipment, and office supplies used. Expenses that are partly connected with selling and partly connected with the general operations of the business may be divided between the two categories. In a small business, however, mixed expenses such as rent, insurance, and taxes are commonly reported as general expenses.

Expenses of relatively small amount that cannot be identified with the principal accounts are usually accumulated in accounts entitled "Miscellaneous Selling Expense" and "Miscellaneous General Expense."

Net income from operations. The excess of gross profit on sales over total operating expenses is called *net income from operations.* The amount of the net operating income and its relationship to capital investment and to net sales are important factors in judging the efficiency of management and the degree of profitability of an enterprise. If operating expenses should exceed gross profit, the excess is designated *net loss from operations.*

Other income. Minor sources of revenue are classified as *other income,* or *nonoperating income.* In a merchandising business this category often includes income from interest, rent, dividends, and gains resulting from the sale of plant assets.

Other expense. Expenses that cannot be associated definitely with operations are identified as *other expense,* or *nonoperating expense.* Interest expense that results from financing activities and losses incurred in the disposal of plant assets are examples of items reported in this section.

The two categories of nonoperating items are offset against each other on the income statement. If the total of other income exceeds the total of other expense, the excess is added to net income from operations; if the reverse is true, the difference is subtracted from net income from operations.

Net income. The final figure on the income statement of an unincorporated enterprise is labeled *net income* (or *net loss*). It is the net increase in capital resulting from profit-making activities.

Balance sheet and capital statement

The form of the balance sheet for a merchandising business is basically the same as that for a service enterprise illustrated in Chapter 4. There may be a larger number of both assets and liabilities to report, as in the accompanying balance sheet for Bennett Electrical Supplies. The manner in which the mortgage payable is reported should be noted. The $8,000 balance of this account in the ledger is divided between the $1,000

Bennett Electrical Supplies
Income Statement
For Year Ended December 31, 1965

Exhibit A

Revenue from sales:				
Sales			$163,574	
Less: Sales returns and allowances.		$ 3,150		
Sales discount.		1,314	4,464	
Net sales				$159,110
Cost of merchandise sold:				
Merchandise inventory, January 1, 1965. .			$ 16,600	
Purchases		$103,920		
Less: Purchases returns and allow.	$2,640			
Purchases discount.	1,857	4,497		
Net purchases			99,423	
Merchandise available for sale.			$116,023	
Less merchandise inventory, Dec. 31, 1965			18,200	
Cost of merchandise sold.				97,823
Gross profit on sales				$ 61,287
Operating expenses:				
Selling expenses:				
Sales salaries.		$ 14,662		
Sales commissions		7,431		
Advertising expense		2,580		
Depreciation expense--store equipment .		1,000		
Delivery expense.		963		
Store supplies expense.		580		
Insurance expense--selling.		420		
Miscellaneous selling expense		724		
Total selling expenses.			$ 28,360	
General expenses:				
Office salaries		$ 5,124		
Taxes expense		1,762		
Depreciation expense--office equipment.		340		
Depreciation expense--building.		700		
Office supplies expense		240		
Insurance expense--general.		296		
Miscellaneous general expense		693		
Total general expenses.			9,155	
Total operating expenses.				37,515
Net income from operations.				$ 23,772
Other income:				
Rent income			$ 1,000	
Other expense:				
Interest expense.			480	520
Net income.				$ 24,292

Income statement

Bennett Electrical Supplies
Balance Sheet
December 31, 1965

Exhibit B

Assets			
Current assets:			
Cash		$ 9,675	
Accounts receivable - Schedule 1		8,900	
Merchandise inventory		18,200	
Store supplies		690	
Office supplies		340	
Prepaid insurance		804	
Total current assets			$38,609
Plant assets:			
Store equipment	$12,000		
Less accumulated depreciation	5,700	$ 6,300	
Office equipment	$ 3,400		
Less accumulated depreciation	1,020	2,380	
Building	$28,000		
Less accumulated depreciation	4,200	23,800	
Land		3,000	
Total plant assets			35,480
Total assets			$74,089
Liabilities			
Current liabilities:			
Accounts payable - Schedule 2		$ 9,270	
Mortgage payable (current portion)		1,000	
Commissions payable		564	
Salaries payable		212	
Total current liabilities			$11,046
Long-term liabilities:			
Mortgage payable (final maturity in 1973)			7,000
Total liabilities			$18,046
Capital			
John Bennett, capital - Exhibit C			56,043
Total liabilities and capital			$74,089

Balance sheet

installment due within a year, which is classified as a current liability, and the remaining $7,000, which is classified as a long-term liability.

The form of the capital statement is not affected by the nature of the business operations. As was explained in Chapter 4, the statement summarizes the changes in the owner's capital during the fiscal period and serves as a connecting link between the income statement and the balance sheet. The net income of $24,292, reported on the accompanying income statement, is also reported on the capital statement where it is combined with the withdrawals to yield a capital increase of $12,292. This sum is then added to the capital balance at the beginning of the year to yield a capital balance of $56,043 at the end of the year, which is the amount reported as capital on the balance sheet.

Bennett Electrical Supplies — Exhibit C
Capital Statement
For Year Ended December 31, 1965

Capital, January 1, 1965		$43,751
Net income for the year - Exhibit A	$24,292	
Less withdrawals	12,000	
Increase in capital		12,292
Capital, December 31, 1965		$56,043

Capital statement

Bennett Electrical Supplies — Exhibit B, Schedule 1
Schedule of Accounts Receivable
December 31, 1965

Acme Co.	$ 460
E. A. Albertson	1,890
G. L. Bates	716
John B. Deatrick	602
R. E. Holt	1,140
James Owen	865
Quaker Supply	146
Howard Strauss	1,383
O. L. Tanner	750
Otto Wright	948
Total accounts receivable	$8,900

Schedule of accounts receivable

Bennett Electrical Supplies — Exhibit B, Schedule 2
Schedule of Accounts Payable
December 31, 1965

Allied Electronics Supply	$2,419
Black Electric Corporation	1,298
Office Equipment Distributors	415
Queen Electronics	1,132
Reed Supplies, Inc.	89
State Distributors	1,677
Wilson Manufacturing Company	2,240
Total accounts payable	$9,270

Schedule of accounts payable

Adjusting entries

The analyses required to formulate the adjustments were completed in preparing the work sheet; hence no further consideration need be given to the supporting data when the adjusting entries are journalized and posted. After the posting is completed, the ledger accounts will agree with the details reported in the financial statements. The adjusting entries for Bennett Electrical Supplies are presented below.

GENERAL JOURNAL PAGE 28

DATE	NAME OF ACCOUNT	POST. REF.	DEBIT	CREDIT
	Adjusting Entries			
31	Expense and Revenue Summary	313	16600 00	
	Merchandise Inventory	114		16600 00
31	Merchandise Inventory	114	18200 00	
	Expense and Revenue Summary	313		18200 00
31	Store Supplies Expense	616	580 00	
	Store Supplies	115		580 00
31	Office Supplies Expense	715	240 00	
	Office Supplies	116		240 00
31	Insurance Expense—Selling	617	420 00	
	Insurance Expense—General	716	296 00	
	Prepaid Insurance	117		716 00
31	Depreciation Expense—Store Equip.	614	1000 00	
	Accumulated Depreciation—Store Equip.	122		1000 00
31	Depreciation Expense—Office Equip.	713	340 00	
	Accumulated Depreciation—Office Equip.	124		340 00
31	Depreciation Expense—Building	714	700 00	
	Accumulated Depreciation—Building	126		700 00
31	Sales Commissions	612	564 00	
	Commissions Payable	212		564 00
31	Sales Salaries	611	152 00	
	Office Salaries	711	60 00	
	Salaries Payable	213		212 00

Adjusting entries

Closing entries

The closing entries are recorded in the general journal immediately following the adjusting entries. The effect of the closing entries is to reduce the balances of all temporary capital accounts to zero and to show in the capital account the present capital of the owner. The four closing entries for Bennett Electrical Supplies are illustrated below.

GENERAL JOURNAL PAGE 29

DATE		NAME OF ACCOUNT	POST. REF.	DEBIT	CREDIT
		Closing Entries			
1965 Dec.	31	Sales	411	163574 00	
		Purchases Returns and Allowances	512	2640 00	
		Purchases Discount	513	1857 00	
		Rent Income	812	1000 00	
		Expense and Revenue Summary	313		169071 00
	31	Expense and Revenue Summary	313	146379 00	
		Sales Returns and Allowances	412		3150 00
		Sales Discount	413		1314 00
		Purchases	511		103920 00
		Sales Salaries	611		14662 00
		Sales Commissions	612		7431 00
		Advertising Expense	613		2580 00
		Depreciation Expense—Store Equip.	614		1000 00
		Delivery Expense	615		963 00
		Store Supplies Expense	616		580 00
		Insurance Expense—Selling	617		420 00
		Miscellaneous Selling Expense	618		724 00
		Office Salaries	711		5124 00
		Taxes Expense	712		1762 00
		Depreciation Expense—Office Equip.	713		340 00
		Depreciation Expense—Building	714		700 00
		Office Supplies Expense	715		240 00
		Insurance Expense—General	716		296 00
		Miscellaneous General Expense	717		693 00
		Interest Expense	911		480 00
	31	Expense and Revenue Summary	313	24292 00	
		John Bennett, Capital	311		24292 00
	31	John Bennett, Capital	311	12000 00	
		John Bennett, Drawing	312		12000 00

Closing entries

The closing entries may be described as follows:

(1) The first entry closes all income statement accounts with *credit* balances by transferring the total to the *credit* side of Expense and Revenue Summary.
(2) The second entry closes all income statement accounts with *debit* balances by transferring the total to the *debit* side of Expense and Revenue Summary.
(3) The third entry closes Expense and Revenue Summary by transferring its balance to John Bennett, Capital.
(4) The fourth entry closes John Bennett, Drawing by transferring its balance to John Bennett, Capital.

After the foregoing closing entries have been posted, the expense and revenue summary account will have three debits and two credits. The first debit and the first credit in the account, which is reproduced below, were posted from the two entries adjusting the merchandise inventory account.

Expense and Revenue Summary — ACCOUNT NO. 313

DATE		ITEMS	POST. REF.	DEBIT	CREDIT	BALANCE DEBIT	BALANCE CREDIT
1965 Dec.	31		J28	16600 00		16600 00	
	31		J28		18200 00		1600 00
	31		J29		169071 00		170671 00
	31		J29	146379 00			24292 00
	31		J29	24292 00		—	—

Expense and revenue summary account

After the adjusting entries and the closing entries have been posted to Bennett's ledger, only accounts for assets, contra assets, liabilities, and owner's capital remain open. The balances of these accounts correspond exactly to the amounts on the balance sheet on page 162.

Post-closing trial balance

At the end of a fiscal period the equality of the debits and the credits in the ledger is determined by means of a trial balance. The adjusting and the closing entries are then made. If these entries are recorded and posted correctly, the equality of the debits and the credits in the ledger is not disturbed because the entries consist of equal debits and credits. A post-closing trial balance is therefore taken to determine whether the debit-credit equality has been maintained. The trial balance may be composed of an adding machine listing of the debit balances in the ledger and another of the credit balances, or the details may be recorded in more formal fashion, as illustrated at the top of the following page.

Bennett Electrical Supplies
Post-Closing Trial Balance
December 31, 1965

Account	Debit	Credit
Cash	967500	
Accounts Receivable	890000	
Merchandise Inventory	1820000	
Store Supplies	69000	
Office Supplies	34000	
Prepaid Insurance	80400	
Store Equipment	1200000	
Accumulated Depreciation-Store Equip		570000
Office Equipment	340000	
Accumulated Depreciation-Office Equip		102000
Building	2800000	
Accumulated Depreciation-Building		420000
Land	300000	
Accounts Payable		927000
Commissions Payable		56400
Salaries Payable		21200
Mortgage Payable		800000
John Bennett, Capital		5604300
	8500900	8500900

Post-closing trial balance

Reversing entries

Some adjusting entries recorded at the close of the fiscal period affect the recording of otherwise routine transactions in the following period. A typical example of such a situation is the adjusting entry for salaries accrued at the end of the period. Ordinarily the payment of salaries is recorded by a debit to Salary Expense (or various salary expense accounts) and a credit to Cash. If salaries are paid weekly, this type of transaction would occur 52 or 53 times during the year. When there are accrued salaries at the end of the year, however, the amount owed will be included in the first payment of salaries in the following year. Unless some special provision is made, it will be necessary to debit Salaries Payable for the amount owed for the earlier year and Salary Expense for the portion of the payroll that represents expense for the later year.

In order to illustrate the situation, the following facts will be assumed for an enterprise that pays salaries weekly and closes its books on December 31:

(1) Salaries are paid on Friday for the five-day week ending on Friday.
(2) The balance in Salary Expense as of Friday, December 27, is $62,500.
(3) Salaries accrued for Monday and Tuesday, December 30 and 31, total $500.
(4) Salaries paid on Friday, January 3, of the ensuing year total $1,200.

The foregoing facts are presented in diagrammatic form as follows:

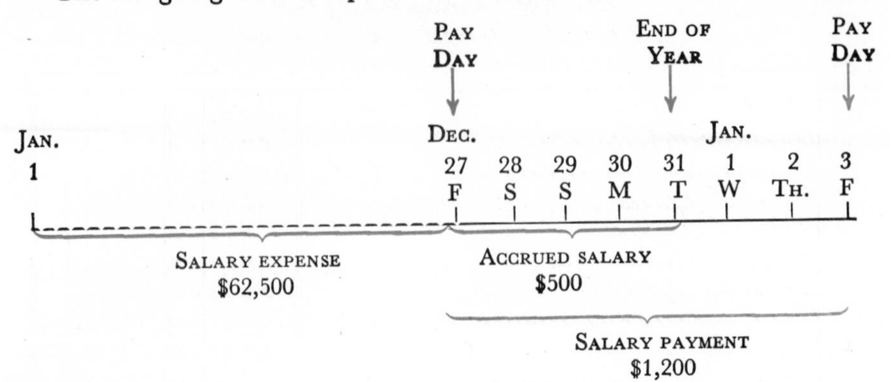

The entry to adjust the salary expense account and the salaries payable account is as follows:

Dec.	31	Salary Expense	611	500	
		Salaries Payable	213		500

After the adjusting entry for accrued salaries has been posted, Salary Expense will have a debit balance of $63,000 ($62,500 + $500) and Salaries Payable will have a credit balance of $500. After Salary Expense is closed, it will have a zero balance, but Salaries Payable will still have a credit balance of $500. As matters now stand it will be necessary to record the $1,200 payroll on January 3 as a debit of $500 to Salaries Payable and a debit of $700 to Salary Expense. This means that the employee who records payroll entries must record this particular payroll in a different manner from the other payrolls for the year, and also that he must refer to the adjusting entries in the journal or to ledger accounts to determine how much of the $1,200 to debit to each of the two accounts.

The necessity of referring back to earlier entries and splitting the debit between two accounts when recording the first payroll of the fiscal period may be avoided by a simple technique known as a *reversing* or *readjusting* entry. As the terms imply, such an entry is the exact reverse of the adjusting entry; the same account titles and amounts are used, but the debits and the credits are reversed. Reversing entries are dated as of the first day of the new fiscal period. For the example above, the reversing entry would be as follows:

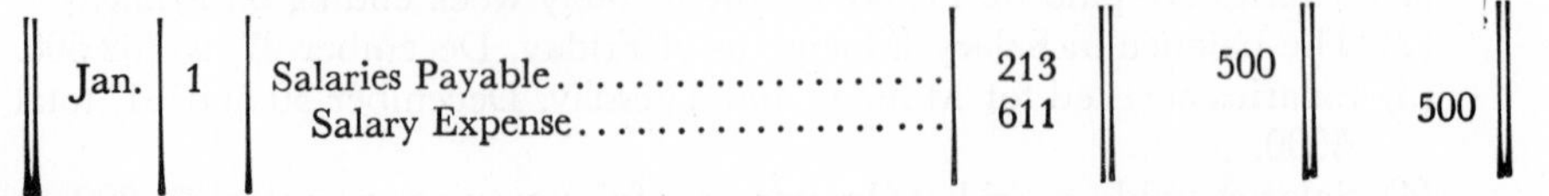

Jan.	1	Salaries Payable	213	500	
		Salary Expense	611		500

The effect of this entry is to transfer the liability from the salaries payable account to the credit side of the salary expense account. When the payroll is paid on January 3, the usual entry would be made debiting Salary Expense and crediting Cash for $1,200. After the entry is posted, the salary expense account will then have a debit balance of $700, which is the amount of the expense for the first three days of January. The entries are also illustrated in the accounts below.

SALARY EXPENSE — ACCOUNT No. 611

Date		Items	Post. Ref.	Debit	Credit	Balance Debit	Balance Credit
1965							
Jan.	5		CP36	1,240		1,240	
Dec.	6		CP80	1,300		58,440	
	13		CP81	1,450		59,890	
	20		CP83	1,260		61,150	
	27		CP84	1,350		62,500	
	31	Adjusting	J8	500		63,000	
	31	Closing	J9		63,000	——	——
1966							
Jan.	1	Reversing	J9		500		500
	3		CP85	1,200		700	

SALARIES PAYABLE — ACCOUNT No. 213

Date		Items	Post. Ref.	Debit	Credit	Balance Debit	Balance Credit
1965							
Dec.	31	Adjusting	J8		500		500
1966							
Jan.	1	Reversing	J9	500		——	——

The adjusting entries for salaries and commissions recorded on the books of Bennett Electrical Supplies are reversed as of January 1 so that at the time of payment the entire amounts may be charged to the appropriate expense accounts. The reversing entries are as follows:

GENERAL JOURNAL — PAGE 29

Date		Name of Account	Post. Ref.	Debit	Credit
		Reversing Entries			
1966					
Jan.	1	Commissions Payable	212	564 00	
		Sales Commissions	612		564 00
	1	Salaries Payable	213	212 00	
		Sales Salaries	611		152 00
		Office Salaries	711		60 00

Reversing entries

After the two reversing entries have been posted, the accounts Salaries Payable and Commissions Payable will have a balance of zero. The liability for salaries and commissions will now appear as credits in the respective accounts. As salaries and commissions are paid in the new period, *the entire amount paid* will be debited to the appropriate expense accounts. The balances of the expense accounts will then automatically represent the expense of the new period.

Errors of past periods

Various procedures for correcting errors in journal and ledger entries were described in Chapter 3. In all of the situations considered, the errors were discovered and corrected in the same period in which they had occurred. The manner in which an error is corrected is affected in some cases by the closing of the books in the interim between the occurrence of the error and its discovery. In other cases, such as errors affecting only asset or liability accounts, the entry to correct the error will be the same regardless of the time of discovery. For example, if the cost of a delivery truck was recorded as a debit to Office Equipment, the correction would be a debit to Delivery Equipment and a credit to Office Equipment regardless of when the error was discovered.

Errors resulting in a misstatement in the amount of net income of a period for which the books have been closed cannot be corrected by an entry in a revenue or expense account of a later period. The effect of the error in the earlier period has already been transferred to the capital account. For example, assume that at the close of the preceding period the following adjustment was recorded:

Dec.	31	Insurance Expense..................	716	425	
		Prepaid Insurance...............	116		425

Early in the current year it is discovered that the amount of insurance expired was $625 instead of $425. The $200 understatement of expenses of the preceding period resulted in an overstatement of $200 in the amount of net income transferred to the capital account. The correcting entry would therefore be as follows:

Jan.	21	Robert Keller, Capital..............	311	200	
		Prepaid Insurance...............	116		200
		To correct error in adjusting entry of Dec. 31.			

All corrections to the capital account should be presented in the capital statement, as otherwise the effect of the errors on the net income previously reported will not be disclosed. Assuming that in addition to the error in insurance expense there had been a $750 overstatement of repairs expense in the preceding year, the corrections would be presented on the capital statement in the following manner:

Keller Sports Center
Capital Statement
For Year Ended December 31, 1965

Capital, January 1, 1965		$52,000
Corrections applicable to past period:		
Add — Overstatement of repair expense in 1964	$ 750	
Deduct — Understatement of insurance expense in 1964	200	550
Capital, January 1, 1965, as corrected		$52,550
Net income for the year	$22,600	
Less withdrawals	15,000	
Increase in capital		7,600
Capital, December 31, 1965		$60,150

There are differences of opinion among accountants as to whether a currently discovered misstatement of net income of an earlier year should be corrected through the capital account or whether the correction should be shown on the current income statement. Until the pros and the cons of these two points of view are discussed in Chapter 18, all corrections of income of prior years will be made directly to the capital account and will be reported on the capital statement.

QUESTIONS

1. Before adjustments are recorded at the end of the fiscal year ended December 31, the balance in the merchandise inventory account is $30,000. (a) What is the nature of this account? (b) When the adjusting entries are recorded, what account will be debited and what account will be credited for the $30,000?

2. (a) What is the effect of the debit entry in the adjustment for the ending merchandise inventory? (b) What is the effect of the credit entry?

3. The merchandise inventory at the beginning of the year was $20,000 and at the end of the year it is $15,000. (a) To which of the two figures will net purchases be added in determining the cost of merchandise available for sale? (b) In determining cost of merchandise sold, which of the two figures will be deducted from merchandise available for sale? (c) Which of the two figures will appear in the current assets section of the balance sheet prepared at the end of the year?

4. In the work sheet illustrated on page 154, two amounts, $16,600 and $18,200, are extended into the Income Statement columns opposite Expense and Revenue Summary. Which of the two amounts (a) is combined with other items in determining merchandise available for sale and (b) is deducted from merchandise available for sale in determining cost of merchandise sold?

5. How does the omission of the Adjusted Trial Balance columns in the work sheet illustrated in this chapter affect the use of the work sheet?

6. Explain the purpose of (a) adjusting entries, (b) closing entries, and (c) reversing entries.

7. Salary Expense before adjustment at the end of the fiscal year has a balance of $110,000. The amount accrued is $900. Give the required (a) adjusting entry, (b) closing entry, and (c) reversing entry.

8. Assume that the first payment of salaries in the following year (Question 7) amounts to $1,400. (a) Give the entry to record the payment. (b) What is the balance of Salary Expense immediately after the entry?

9. At the end of the current fiscal year Summerfield Company owes $19,200 on a mortgage on its building. The debt is required to be paid in monthly installments of $400. How should the liability be classified on the balance sheet at the end of the current year?

10. Classify the following as selling expense or general expense:
(a) Fire insurance on store equipment.
(b) Gas and electricity (for heat and light).
(c) Salary of the secretary to the general manager.
(d) Depreciation of office equipment.
(e) Gasoline used by delivery truck.
(f) Rental of billboard.
(g) Property taxes on building.

11. On what two financial statements are each of the following items reported: (a) net income for the period and (b) capital balance at the end of the period?

12. After the closing entries have been posted, it is discovered that an expenditure of $75 for gas and electricity had been erroneously debited to Advertising Expense. Should a correcting entry be made to correct this error or would presentation of the correct amounts of the two expense items in the income statement be sufficient? Discuss.

13. Immediately after the work of the periodic summary has been completed at the end of the year, Commissions Expense has a *credit* balance of $1,240. Assuming that there have been no errors, what is the nature of this balance?

14. Accrued taxes of $770 not yet due at the end of fiscal Year A were overlooked and no adjusting entry was made. Early in the following Year B, the tax bill of $840, which included the accrual of $770 from Year A, was paid and charged to Taxes Expense. (There were no other errors in either year.) Indicate the amount of the error and whether the error caused an overstatement or an understatement in each of the following items:
(a) Net income for Year A.
(b) Net income for Year B.
(c) Assets, liabilities, or capital at end of Year A.
(d) Assets, liabilities, or capital at end of Year B.

15. After the books have been closed for the past year, it is discovered that a cash refund of $100, representing an overcharge on the purchase of equipment used in the business, was erroneously credited to Miscellaneous Income. What accounts should be debited and credited to correct the mistake?

EXERCISES

1. On the basis of the following data, journalize the necessary adjusting entries at December 31, the close of the current fiscal year.

(a) Merchandise inventory: January 1, $16,460; December 31, $13,150.
(b) The prepaid insurance account before adjustments on December 31 has a balance of $1,120. An analysis of the policies indicates that $405 has expired during the year.
(c) Sales salaries are uniformly $1,500 for a five-day work week, ending on Friday. The last payday of the year was Friday, December 28.
(d) Office supplies physical inventory, December 31, $61; office supplies account balance before adjustment, $175.

2. At the beginning of the year the merchandise inventory was $40,000; during the year net purchases of merchandise amounted to $132,600; the physical inventory of merchandise at the end of the year is $37,500. Determine the following:

(a) Merchandise available for sale.
(b) Cost of merchandise sold.

3. Two or more items are omitted in each of the following tabulations of income statement data. Determine the amounts of the missing items, identifying them by letter.

Sales	*Sales Returns*	*Net Sales*	*Beginning Inventory*	*Net Purchases*	*Ending Inventory*	*Cost of Merchandise Sold*	*Gross Profit on Sales*
$41,000	(a)	$38,000	$ 7,000	$35,000	(b)	$30,000	$ 8,000
(c)	$3,000	45,000	(d)	45,000	$25,000	35,000	10,000
73,000	5,000	68,000	20,000	(e)	15,000	(f)	11,000
50,000	3,000	(g)	12,000	40,000	(h)	38,000	(i)
80,000	(j)	80,000	(k)	65,000	12,000	(l)	12,000

4. The accounts listed alphabetically below were selected from the Income Statement and Balance Sheet columns of the N. W. Nippert Co. work sheet for the current fiscal year ended June 30.

Account	Amount	Account	Amount
Accumulated Depreciation—Building	$ 16,200	Purchases	$137,500
General Expenses (total)	16,400	Purchases Discount	2,100
Merchandise Inventory 7/1	45,000	Rent Income	1,200
Merchandise Inventory 6/30	52,300	Salaries Payable	900
N. W. Nippert, Capital	61,700	Sales	200,000
N. W. Nippert, Drawing	12,000	Sales Discount	1,000
Prepaid Insurance	750	Sales Returns and Allow.	1,600
		Selling Expenses (total)	32,300

(a) Prepare an income statement for the year.
(b) Journalize the entries to adjust the merchandise inventory.
(c) Journalize the closing entries, assuming that there is only one account for selling expenses and one account for general expenses.

5. A portion of the salary expense account of an enterprise is presented in T-account form below. (a) Describe the nature of the transaction or entry that resulted in each of the postings identified by letter. (b) Present in general journal form the entry from which each of the items identified by letter was posted.

Salary Expense

19—					19—				
Jan.	6		CP15	1,700	Dec.	31	(D)	J11	87,400
	27	(A)	CP35	2,000					
	31	(B)	J10	700					
				87,400					87,400
19—					19—				
Jan.	3	(C)	CP36	1,800	Jan.	1	(E)	J11	700

6. The fiscal year of Carter Markets, owned by L. B. Carter, ends on December 31. The errors described below, applicable to the past year, were discovered in February of the current year. Present the general journal entries (with explanations) required to correct the errors.

(a) Merchandise inventory taken on December 31 was understated by $3,700.

(b) No adjustment was made for office supplies consumed. The office supplies account had a balance of $420 but the inventory of office supplies at December 31 was $140.

(c) A receipt of cash of $120 on account from Spear & Co. was erroneously credited to R. J. Spear Corp.

(d) Prepayment of $1,500 of rent applicable to the current year had been charged to Rent Expense.

7. At the beginning of the current year the balance of the owner's capital account on the books of Carter Markets in Exercise 6 was $59,600 (before giving effect to the correcting entries). The net income for the current year is $31,000 and the withdrawals total $20,000. Prepare a capital statement for the current year.

PROBLEMS

7-1. The accounts in the ledger of the Cooper Company, with the balances on December 31, the end of the current fiscal year, are as follows:

Cash	$ 4,400	Sales	$143,000
Accounts Receivable	8,700	Purchases	92,000
Merchandise Inventory	24,800	Sales Salaries	16,000
Store Supplies	650	Advertising Expense	1,560
Prepaid Insurance	2,200	Delivery Expense	1,300
Store Equipment	12,400	Depreciation Expense — Store Equipment	—
Accum. Depreciation — Store Equipment	2,500	Store Supplies Expense	—
Accounts Payable	6,200	Rent Expense	6,000
Salaries Payable	—	Insurance Expense	—
John Cooper, Capital	29,540	Misc. General Expense	2,100
John Cooper, Drawing	9,000	Loss on Disposal of Equipment	130
Expense and Revenue Summary	—		

The data needed for year-end adjustments on December 31 are as follows:

Merchandise inventory on December 31	$26,300
Store supplies inventory on December 31	350
Insurance expired during the year	600
Depreciation for the current year	1,000
Accrued salaries on December 31	160

Instructions: (1) Prepare an eight-column work sheet for the fiscal year ended December 31, listing all of the accounts in the order given.

(2) Prepare an income statement (Exhibit A).

(3) Prepare a capital statement (Exhibit C). There were no additional investments during the year.

(4) Prepare a balance sheet (Exhibit B).

(5) Compute the following:

(a) Percent of net income from operations to net sales.
(b) Percent of net income to the capital balance at the beginning of the year.

If the working papers correlating with this textbook are not used, omit Problem 7-2.

7-2. R. D. Scott owns and operates Scott Appliances. The general ledger balances at the beginning of the twelfth month and the journals for the twelfth month of the current fiscal year are presented in the working papers.

Instructions: (1) Post the appropriate individual items and the totals of the journals to the general ledger accounts. The balances need not be determined until the posting is completed. An assistant has posted entries to the subsidiary ledgers.

(2) Take a trial balance at December 31 on an eight-column work sheet, listing all of the accounts in the ledger.

(3) Complete the work sheet. Adjustment data are:

Merchandise inventory at December 31	$14,160.00
Insurance expired during the year	272.00
Supplies on hand at December 31	132.50
Depreciation for the current year on:	
Store equipment	640.00
Office equipment	165.00
Accrued taxes at December 31	178.50

(4) Prepare an income statement, a capital statement, and a balance sheet. There were no additional investments of capital by the owner during the year.

(5) Journalize the adjusting entries and post to the ledger.

(6) Journalize the closing entries and post to the ledger, indicating closed accounts by inserting a line in both balance columns.

(7) Prepare a post-closing trial balance.

(8) Journalize the reversing entry or entries as of January 1 and post to the ledger.

7-3. A portion of the work sheet of Bancroft & Co. for the current year ending December 31 is presented below.

Account Titles	Income Statement		Balance Sheet	
	Dr.	Cr.	Dr.	Cr.
Cash			28,800	
Accounts Receivable			40,100	
Merchandise Inventory			51,000	
Supplies			1,660	
Prepaid Rent			400	
Prepaid Insurance			1,200	
Store Equipment			12,400	
Accumulated Depr. — Store Equip.				4,800
Office Equipment			4,000	
Accumulated Depr. — Office Equip.				1,600
Accounts Payable				28,700
Sales Salaries Payable				800
Mortgage Payable				15,000
John Bancroft, Capital				70,500
John Bancroft, Drawing			9,000	
Expense and Revenue Summary	48,200	51,000		
Sales		290,800		
Sales Returns and Allowances	8,600			
Purchases	208,300			
Purchases Discount		2,600		
Sales Salaries	16,900			
Delivery Expense	11,900			
Supplies Expense	2,240			
Depreciation Expense — Store Equip.	1,200			
Miscellaneous Selling Expense	400			
Office Salaries	11,700			
Rent Expense	4,800			
Insurance Expense	2,400			
Depreciation Expense — Office Equip.	400			
Miscellaneous General Expense	300			
Interest Income		100		
	317,340	344,500	148,560	121,400

Instructions: (1) Journalize the adjusting entries to be recorded on the books of Bancroft & Co., based on the partial work sheet presented above. The only accounts affected by more than one adjusting entry were Merchandise Inventory and Expense and Revenue Summary. The balance in Prepaid Rent after adjustment represents the remainder of the prepayment of thirteen months' rent in January of the year just ended.

(2) Determine:

(a) The amount of net income for the year.

(b) The amount of the owner's capital at the end of the year.

7-4. During the past fiscal year ending on December 31, the errors described below were made in the accounts of Summit Hardware Co., owned by Howard Conrad. Appropriate correcting entries were made from time to time as the errors were discovered during the current fiscal year.

The balance in the capital account on January 1 of the current fiscal year was $26,400. Charges to the drawing account during the year totaled $7,200, and net income closed from Expense and Revenue Summary to the capital account at the end of the current year was $13,860.

(a) Prepaid Rent at December 31 of the past year was overstated $800.

(b) The amount of expired insurance for the past year was overstated $500.

(c) Accrued sales commissions payable on December 31 of the past year were understated $450.

(d) Miscellaneous Office Expense for the past year included a $400 debit for the cost of a calculator, purchased on July 1, that should have been debited to Office Equipment.

(e) Depreciation expense was understated $20 because of the error in recording the calculator. (See item (d).)

(f) Miscellaneous selling expenses of $378 incurred during the past year were erroneously charged to Miscellaneous General Expense.

(g) Merchandise inventory at December 31 of the past year was understated $3,000.

Instructions: (1) Present the correcting entries made during the current year, using the identifying letters in place of dates.

(2) On the basis of the facts given above and the correcting entries recorded during the year, prepare a capital statement for the current year.

7-5. The accounts and their balances in the ledger of Parker Novelty Co. on June 30 of the current year are as follows:

Account	Balance	Account	Balance
Cash	$ 18,900	Purchases	$230,300
Accounts Receivable	30,200	Purchases Returns and Allowances	7,800
Merchandise Inventory	38,400	Purchases Discount	3,160
Store Supplies	1,600	Sales Salaries	24,600
Office Supplies	570	Delivery Expense	6,800
Prepaid Insurance	2,500	Rent Expense — Selling	4,800
Store Equipment	17,000	Depreciation Exp. — Store Equipment	——
Accum. Depreciation — Store Equipment	4,500	Insurance Exp. — Selling	——
Office Equipment	5,200	Store Supplies Expense	——
Accum. Depreciation — Office Equipment	1,600	Misc. Selling Expense	1,250
Accounts Payable	30,900	Office Salaries	13,600
Salaries Payable	——	Rent Exp. — General	1,200
Mortgage Note Payable (due 1971)	6,000	Depreciation Exp. — Office Equipment	——
Ray S. Parker, Capital	44,700	Office Supplies Exp.	——
Ray S. Parker, Drawing	12,000	Insurance Exp. — General	——
Expense and Revenue Summary	——	Misc. General Expense	1,360
Sales	317,600	Gain on Disposal of Plant Assets	720
Sales Ret. and Allow.	6,400	Interest Expense	300

The data for year-end adjustments on June 30 are as follows:

Merchandise inventory on June 30		$41,600
Inventory of supplies on June 30:		
Store supplies		900
Office supplies		220
Insurance expired during year:		
Allocable as selling expense	$970	
Allocable as general expense	260	1,230
Depreciation:		
Store equipment		1,750
Office equipment		500
Salaries payable on June 30:		
Sales salaries		460
Office salaries		210

Instructions: (1) Prepare an eight-column work sheet for the fiscal year ended June 30, listing all accounts in the order given.

(2) Prepare an income statement (Exhibit A).

(3) Prepare a capital statement (Exhibit C). There were no additional investments during the year.

(4) Prepare a balance sheet (Exhibit B).

(5) Record the adjusting entries in a general journal.

(6) Record the closing entries in a general journal.

(7) Record the reversing entries as of July 1 in a general journal.

7-6. On February 15 of the current fiscal year the following errors were discovered in the books of Reed's Market, owned and operated by Joseph B. Reed:

(a) Sales returns and allowances totaling $620 in December of the preceding year were erroneously recorded as debits to Purchases.

(b) The adjusting entry for store supplies at the end of the preceding year transferred $620 to the expense account. The amount should have been $260.

(c) Merchandise inventory at the end of the preceding year was overstated $3,000.

(d) No provision was made at the end of the preceding year for accrued sales salaries payable, $520.

(e) Land acquired for $12,000 last year for use as a site for a new building was erroneously debited to Building. As a result, the building depreciation for the year was overstated by $300.

(f) Equipment purchased for $600 in December for use in Reed's home was charged to Store Equipment.

Instructions: (1) Journalize the necessary correcting entries.

(2) Open a general ledger account for Joseph B. Reed, Capital, and enter a balance of $23,700 as of January 1 of the current year in the account. Post the applicable portions of the correcting entries to the account.

(3) As of December 31 of the current year, journalize the entries to close the expense and revenue summary account (credit balance, $15,900) and the drawing account (debit balance, $8,400).

(4) Post the closing entries to the capital account; extend the balance after the last posting.

(5) Prepare a capital statement for the current year.

PART FOUR

Notes, deferrals, and accruals

8. Notes and interest

Use of credit instruments in business

The extension of credit plays an important role in the operations of many business enterprises. Credit may be granted on open account or on the basis of a formal instrument of credit such as a *promissory note*. The use of the latter is customary for credit periods in excess of 60 days, as in sales of equipment on the installment plan, and for transactions of relatively large dollar amounts. Credit instruments may also be used in settlement of an open account and in borrowing or lending money.

From the point of view of the creditor, a claim evidenced by a credit instrument has some advantages over a claim in the form of an account receivable. By signing a note, the debtor acknowledges the debt and agrees to pay it in accordance with the terms specified. It is therefore a stronger legal claim in the event of court action. It is also more liquid than an open account because the holder may transfer it to one of his creditors in settlement of a debt or to a bank in exchange for cash.

A promissory note, frequently referred to simply as a *note*, is a written promise to pay a certain sum of money at a fixed or determinable future time. As in the case of a check, it must be payable to the order of a particular person or firm, or to bearer. It must also be signed by the person or firm that makes the promise. The one to whose order the note is payable is called the *payee*, and the one making the promise is called the *maker*. In the illustration at the top of the following page, James Otis is the payee and Frank Long is the maker.

The person or firm owning a note refers to it as a *note receivable* and records it at its face amount in the asset account Notes Receivable. The maker of a note refers to it as a *note payable* and records it at its face amount in the liability account Notes Payable. Thus, the note in the

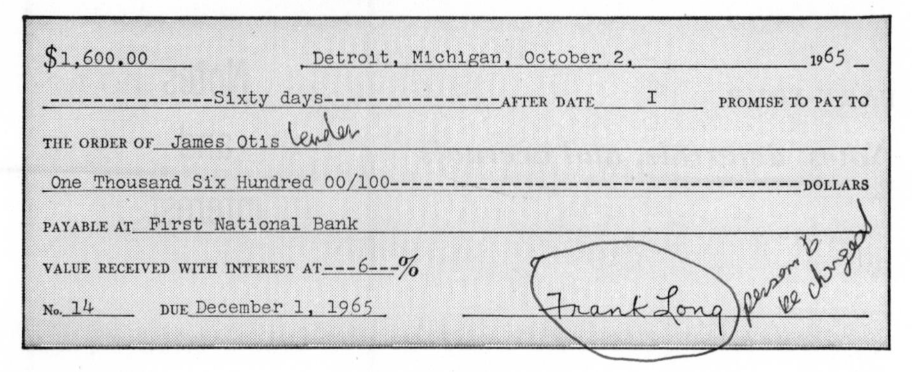

$1,600.00 Detroit, Michigan, October 2, 1965

---------------Sixty days--------------- AFTER DATE I PROMISE TO PAY TO

THE ORDER OF James Otis lender

One Thousand Six Hundred 00/100---------------------------------- DOLLARS

PAYABLE AT First National Bank

VALUE RECEIVED WITH INTEREST AT ---6---%

No. 14 DUE December 1, 1965 Frank Long person to be charged

Interest-bearing note

illustration would appear in Otis' notes receivable account at $1,600 and in Long's notes payable account at $1,600.

A note that provides for the payment of interest for the period between the issuance date and the due date is called an *interest-bearing note*. If a note makes no provision for interest, it is said to be *non-interest-bearing*. In such cases, however, interest may be charged at the legal rate for any time that the note remains unpaid after it is due. The interest that a business is obliged to pay is an expense and is called *interest expense*. The interest that a business is entitled to receive is income and is called *interest income*.

Determining interest

Rates of interest are usually stated in terms of a period of one year. Thus, the interest on a $1,500, 1-year, 6% note would amount to 6% of $1,500, or $90. If, instead of one year, the term of the note was six months, interest at the rate of 6% would amount to one half of $90, or $45.

Notes covering a period of time longer than a year ordinarily provide that the interest be paid annually, semiannually, or at some other stated interval. The time involved in commercial credit transactions is usually less than a year, and the interest provided for by the note is payable at the time the note is paid. In computing interest for a period of less than a year, agencies of the federal government use the actual number of days in the year; for example, 90 days is considered to be 90/365 of a year. The usual commercial practice is to use 360 as the denominator of the fraction; thus 90 days is considered to be 90/360 of a year. The commercial practice will be followed in this book.

The basic formula for computing interest is as follows:

$$\text{Principal} \times \text{Rate} \times \text{Time} = \text{Interest}$$

To illustrate the application of the formula, assume a note for $800, payable 15 days from date, with interest at 6%. The interest would be $2, computed as follows:

$$\$800 \times \frac{6}{100} \times \frac{15}{360} = \$2 \text{ interest}$$

There are a number of shortcut methods of computing interest. One that is commonly used is called the 60-day, 6% method. This method is based on the fact that interest for 60 days (1/6 of a year) at the rate of 6% per year is equal to 1% (1/6 of 6%). The interest on any amount for 60 days at 6% can be determined, therefore, by moving the decimal point in the principal two places to the left. Thus for 60 days, the interest at 6% on $1,342 is $13.42; on $264, the interest is $2.64; and on $982.73, the interest is $9.83.

The interest on $800 for 66 days at 6% may be determined as follows:

$800 for 60 days (1% of $800)	$8.00
$800 for 6 days (1/10 of $8.00)	.80
Interest for 66 days at 6%	$8.80

It is often necessary to determine the interest for a particular period at a rate greater or smaller than 6%. The shortcut method may still be used by first computing the interest at the rate of 6%. The proper amount to be added to or subtracted from this amount is then computed, and the interest at the given rate is thus ascertained. For example, the interest on $924 for 81 days at 4% may be calculated as follows:

$924 for 60 days at 6%	$ 9.24
$924 for 15 days at 6% (1/4 of $9.24)	2.31
$924 for 6 days at 6% (1/10 of $9.24)	.92
Interest for 81 days at 6%	$12.47
$924 for 81 days at 2% (1/3 of $12.47)	4.16
Interest for 81 days at 4%	$ 8.31

The particular method used in computing interest is a matter of individual preference. In the illustration above, for example, solving by the basic formula might require less time and afford less opportunity of arithmetic error.

When the term of a note is expressed in months, each month may be considered as being 1/12 of a year, or, alternatively, the actual number of days in the term may be counted. For example, the interest on a 3-month note dated June 1 could be computed on the basis of 3/12 of a year or on the basis of 92/360 of a year. It is the usual commercial practice to employ the first method, while banks usually charge interest for the exact number of days. For the sake of uniformity, the commercial practice will be followed here.

Determining due date

The period of time between the issuance date and the maturity date of a short-term note may be expressed in either days or months. When the term of a note is expressed in days, the due date is the specified number of days after the issuance date of the note. The due date may be determined in the following manner:

(1) Subtract the date of the note from the number of days in the month in which it is dated.
(2) Add as many full months as possible without exceeding the number of days in the note, counting the full number of days in these months.
(3) Subtract the sum of the days obtained in (1) and (2) from the number of days in the note.

Assuming a 90-day note dated March 16, the due date is determined as follows:

Term of the note			90
March (days)	31		
Date of note	16		
Remainder		15	
April (days)		30	
May (days)		31	
Total			76
Due date, June			14

When the term of a note is expressed as a specified number of months after the issuance date, the due date is determined by counting the number of months from the issuance date. Thus, a 3-month note dated June 5 would be due on September 5. In those cases in which there is no date in the month of maturity that corresponds to the issuance date, the due date becomes the last day of the month. For example, a 2-month note dated July 31 would be due on September 30.

Notes payable

Notes payable are ordinarily issued to a relatively small number of creditors; consequently, all notes may be recorded in a single account in the general ledger. A subsidiary ledger for notes payable may be employed if desired, but it is usually not necessary. If a carbon copy is prepared when a note is issued, the details of each note will always be readily available.

When a note is issued to a creditor in payment of an account, the liability Accounts Payable is decreased and the liability Notes Payable is increased. These facts are recorded by debiting the accounts payable account and the account of the creditor to whom the note was issued, and by crediting the notes payable account.

For example, if a business requests an extension of time for payment of an invoice, the creditor may require that the debtor issue a note for the period involved. Assume that on June 6 George Burke gives a 30-day, non-interest-bearing note for $900 to F. B. Murray on account. The transaction is recorded in Burke's general journal as follows:

June	6	Accounts Payable — F. B. Murray..........	213/√	900 00	
		Notes Payable..........................	211		900 00
		Issued a 30-day, non-interest-bearing note.			

The payee may hold the note until July 6, the due date, or he may transfer it by endorsement to one of his creditors or to his bank. Regardless of who holds the note at maturity, when the maker pays the note his liability Notes Payable decreases and his asset Cash decreases. The payment of the note is recorded in the cash payments journal in the following manner:

CASH PAYMENTS JOURNAL PAGE 16

DATE		CHECK NO.	ACCOUNT DEBITED	POST. REF.	SUNDRY ACCTS. DR.	ACCTS. PAY. DR.	PUR. DISC. CR.	CASH CR.
1965 July	6	318	Notes Payable	211	900 00			900 00

Recording interest expense

Expense incurred for money borrowed or for an extension of credit is recorded as a debit to Interest Expense. For example, on October 5 George Burke gave a creditor, John Davis, a note for $600, due in 60 days and bearing interest at the rate of 6%. On December 4 Burke gave Davis a check for $606 in payment of the note and the interest. The issuance of the note was recorded in Burke's general journal and the payment of the note and the interest was recorded in his cash payments journal as follows:

Oct.	5	Accounts Payable — John Davis............	213/√	600 00	
		Notes Payable..........................	211		600 00
		Issued a 60-day, 6% note.			

CASH PAYMENTS JOURNAL PAGE 20

DATE		CHECK NO.	ACCOUNT DEBITED	POST. REF.	SUNDRY ACCTS. DR.	ACCTS. PAY. DR.	PUR. DISC. CR.	CASH CR.
1965 Dec.	4	421	Notes Payable	211	600 00			606 00
			Interest Expense	911	6 00			

All of the examples considered thus far have involved notes issued to a creditor on account. A business may also issue notes in borrowing money from a bank. For example, on September 19 George Burke borrows $4,000 from the First National Bank, the loan being evidenced by a note due in 90 days, with interest at the rate of 6%. The entry to record the receipt of the money and the issuance of the note is as follows:

CASH RECEIPTS JOURNAL PAGE 9

DATE		ACCOUNT CREDITED	POST. REF.	SUNDRY ACCTS. CR.	SALES CR.	ACCTS. REC. CR.	SALES DISC. DR.	CASH DR.
1965 Sept.	19	Notes Payable	211	4,000 00				4,000 00

Ninety days later Burke pays the note and the interest, recording the transaction in his cash payments journal as follows:

CASH PAYMENTS JOURNAL PAGE 20

DATE		CHECK NO.	ACCOUNT DEBITED	POST. REF.	SUNDRY ACCTS. DR.	ACCTS. PAY. DR.	PUR. DISC. CR.	CASH CR.
1965 Dec.	18	432	Notes Payable	211	4,000 00			4,060 00
			Interest Expense	911	60 00			

Mortgage notes

When relatively large sums are borrowed for an appreciable period of time, the borrower may be required to furnish some type of security. The same practice is followed when payments for substantial purchases of land, buildings, or equipment are to be spread over a number of years. One of the most frequently employed types of security is a mortgage, which gives the creditor a lien, or claim, on property owned by the debtor.

In the event that the debtor (mortgagor) defaults on his obligation, the creditor (mortgagee) may, under certain conditions, take possession of the property or force its sale to satisfy his claim. When a note secured by a mortgage is fully paid, the lien is canceled.

Although the mortgage contract does not take the place of the promissory note or other written evidence of the obligation, the liability is usually recorded in an account entitled "Mortgage Payable" or "Mortgage Notes Payable." Mortgage notes may be payable on a specified date or in periodic installments. They are presented on the balance sheet as long-term liabilities, except for the amount due within one year of the balance sheet date, which should be classified as a current liability.

Notes receivable

The typical retail enterprise makes most of its sales for cash or on account. If the account of a customer becomes delinquent, the creditor may insist that the account be converted into a note. In this way the debtor may be given an extension of time, and if the creditor needs additional funds he may endorse and transfer the note to his bank. Notes may also be received by retail firms that sell merchandise on long-term credit. For example, a dealer in household appliances may require a down payment at the time of sale and accept a note or a series of notes for the remainder. Such arrangements usually provide for monthly payments. Wholesale firms and manufacturers are likely to receive notes more frequently than retailers, although here, too, much depends upon the nature of the product and the length of the credit period.

When a note is received from a customer to apply on his account, the asset Notes Receivable is increased and the asset Accounts Receivable is decreased. These facts are recorded by debiting the notes receivable account and by crediting the accounts receivable account and the account of the customer from whom the note is received. It is not necessary to maintain a subsidiary ledger for notes receivable because the notes themselves provide detailed information. The amount due from each customer on a note can be ascertained by examining the notes on hand. The due date, the interest terms, and other details can be determined in the same manner. However, if numerous notes are received, the details of each one may be set forth in a supplementary record.

For example, assume that the account of T. J. Cole on the books of George Burke has a debit balance of $300. The account is past due. On October 19 Burke receives Cole's note for $300, dated October 18 and due 20 days after the date of issue, bearing interest at the rate of 6%. The receipt of the note is recorded in Burke's general journal as follows:

Oct.	19	Notes Receivable........................	113	300 00	
		Accounts Receivable — T. J. Cole.........	115/√		300 00
		Received a 20-day, 6% note dated October 18.			

The debit entry is posted to the notes receivable account in the general ledger. The credit entry is posted to the accounts receivable controlling account in the general ledger and to the account of T. J. Cole in the subsidiary ledger.

If many notes are received, the time consumed in recording and posting such transactions can be reduced by inserting special columns for Notes Receivable Dr. and Accounts Receivable Cr. in the general journal.

Recording interest income

Revenue earned for money loaned or credit granted to others is recorded as a credit to Interest Income. To illustrate the recording of the collection of the principal and the interest on a note receivable, assume that George Burke received payment from T. J. Cole for the $300, 20-day,

6% note dated October 18. The transaction is recorded in the cash receipts journal as follows:

CASH RECEIPTS JOURNAL PAGE 12

DATE		ACCOUNT CREDITED	POST. REF.	SUNDRY ACCTS. CR.	SALES CR.	ACCTS. REC. CR.	SALES DISC. DR.	CASH DR.
1965								
Nov.	7	Notes Receivable	113	300 00				301 00
		Interest Income	811	1 00				

Discounting notes

A note that makes no provision for the payment of interest for the period from the date of issuance to the date of maturity is called a non-interest-bearing note. It does not necessarily follow that there can be no interest charge at the time of issuing or transferring such a note. In making loans to their depositors, banks sometimes prefer to receive non-interest-bearing notes. They deduct the interest charge from the face of the note and pay cash or credit the depositor's account for the remainder. This procedure is referred to as *discounting a note*. The rate used in computing the interest is sometimes called the *discount rate*, the deduction made for interest is referred to as the *discount*, and the net amount available to the customer is called the *proceeds*.

Discount on a note is computed in the same manner as interest is computed on an interest-bearing note except that the discount rate is always applied to the maturity value of the note. For a non-interest-bearing note, the maturity value is the same as the face value. The significant difference between *interest* and *discount* is that discount is deducted in advance.

Notes payable. To illustrate the discounting of a note payable, assume that on September 11 George Burke issues a $3,000, 60-day, non-interest-bearing note to the First National Bank. The bank charges a discount rate of 5%, making the discount $25 and the proceeds $2,975. The transaction with the bank is recorded in the cash receipts journal as follows:

CASH RECEIPTS JOURNAL PAGE 9

DATE		ACCOUNT CREDITED	POST. REF.	SUNDRY ACCTS. CR.	SALES CR.	ACCTS. REC. CR.	SALES DISC. DR.	CASH DR.
1965								
Sept.	11	Notes Payable	211	3,000 00				2,975 00
		Interest Expense	911	(25 00)				

The interest expense is recorded in the Sundry Accounts Credit Column and is circled to identify it as a debit. A circled or red-ink entry in any journal identifies the item as being the opposite of the debit or the credit designation at the top of the column.

An additional sundry accounts column may be inserted in any special journal to provide greater flexibility. The foregoing transaction recorded in a cash receipts journal with a Sundry Accounts Dr. column is illustrated below.

CASH RECEIPTS JOURNAL — PAGE 9

DATE		ACCOUNT	POST. REF.	SUNDRY ACCOUNTS DR.	SUNDRY ACCOUNTS CR.	SALES CR.	ACCTS. REC. CR.	SALES DISC. DR.	CASH DR.
1965									
Sept.	11	Notes Payable	211		3,000 00				2,975 00
		Interest Expense	911	25 00					

It should be observed that the note payable is recorded at the face amount of $3,000 and the discount of $25 is debited to Interest Expense. The adjusting entry that may be required for prepaid interest at the close of the fiscal period is considered in Chapter 9.

On November 10 Burke pays the bank $3,000, the maturity value of the note. The transaction is recorded as follows:

CASH PAYMENTS JOURNAL — PAGE 19

DATE		CHECK NO.	ACCOUNT DEBITED	POST. REF.	SUNDRY ACCTS. DR.	ACCTS. PAY. DR.	PUR. DISC. CR.	CASH CR.
1965								
Nov.	10	391	Notes Payable	211	3,000 00			3,000 00

Non-interest-bearing notes receivable. One of the advantages of a note receivable over an account receivable is that a note may be readily converted into cash at any time. Instead of holding notes until maturity, the owner may transfer them to a bank by endorsement. The bank discounts the note from its due date to the date of the transfer. The discount is computed on the maturity value of the note, and the remainder, or proceeds, is paid by the bank.

For example, on August 21 George Burke receives from a customer, R. L. Haley, the latter's 90-day, non-interest-bearing note for $1,340 to apply on his account. This transaction is recorded as follows:

Aug.	21	Notes Receivable.	113	1,340 00	
		Accounts Receivable — R. L. Haley	115/✓		1,340 00
		Received a 90-day, non-interest-bearing note.			

Thirty days later, on September 20, Burke needs additional cash and therefore discounts this note at his bank. From the bank's standpoint, the note is not worth $1,340, inasmuch as that amount could not be collected from the maker of the note until 60 days later; consequently it deducts discount, or interest, on $1,340 for 60 days. The bank rate of discount is 6% and the amount of the discount is $13.40. Burke therefore receives proceeds of $1,326.60 ($1,340 – $13.40). The transaction with the bank is recorded in the cash receipts journal as follows:

CASH RECEIPTS JOURNAL PAGE 9

DATE		ACCOUNT	POST. REF.	SUNDRY ACCOUNTS DR.	SUNDRY ACCOUNTS CR.	SALES CR.	ACCTS. REC. CR.	SALES DISC. DR.	CASH DR.
1965 Sept.	20	Notes Receivable	113		1,340 00				1,326 60
		Interest Expense	911	13 40					

Interest-bearing notes receivable. The note in the preceding illustration was non-interest-bearing and therefore its maturity value and its face value were the same. When an interest-bearing note receivable is discounted, its maturity value must be computed before the amount of the discount and the proceeds can be determined. To illustrate, assume that on November 8 Burke received from John Mason a 90-day note for $1,800 bearing interest at 5%. The transaction is recorded in the general journal as follows:

Nov.	8	Notes Receivable	113	1,800 00	
		Accounts Receivable — John Mason	115/✓		1,800 00
		Received a 90-day, 5% note.			

Ten days later, on November 18, the note is discounted at the bank at a discount rate of 6%. The amount that the maker of the note promises to pay in 90 days is the face amount, $1,800, plus interest of $22.50, or a total of $1,822.50. The bank therefore uses $1,822.50, the maturity value, as the basis for computing the discount. Inasmuch as the bank must wait for 80 days to collect the principal and the interest, the maturity value of $1,822.50 is discounted for 80 days at the bank discount rate of 6%, yielding a discount of $24.30. This amount, $24.30, is subtracted from the maturity value, $1,822.50, to determine the proceeds of $1,798.20. These computations may be tabulated as follows:

Face value of note	$1,800.00
Interest on note — 90 days at 5%	22.50
Maturity value of note	$1,822.50
Discount on maturity value — 80 days at 6%	24.30
Proceeds of note	$1,798.20

The same information is presented graphically below. In reading the data, follow the direction of the arrows.

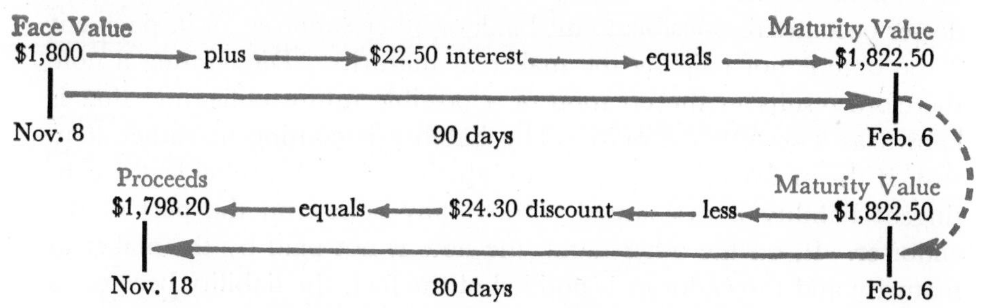

The note that Burke discounts has been recorded on his books at $1,800, its face value. The proceeds of the note amount to $1,798.20. The difference between these two amounts, $1.80, is interest expense. The transaction is recorded in the cash receipts journal as follows:

CASH RECEIPTS JOURNAL PAGE 12

DATE		ACCOUNT	POST. REF.	SUNDRY ACCOUNTS DR.	SUNDRY ACCOUNTS CR.	SALES CR.	ACCTS. REC. CR.	SALES DISC. DR.	CASH DR.
1965									
Nov.	18	Notes Receivable	113		1,800 00				1,798 20
		Interest Expense	911	1 80					

In the foregoing example the proceeds of the discounted interest-bearing note were less than the face value, resulting in interest expense. But the proceeds received from discounting a customer's interest-bearing note are not necessarily less than the face value of the note. For example, if a note receivable bearing interest at the rate of 7% is discounted at the rate of 6%, the proceeds will always be greater than the face value, regardless of how short a period of time it has been held. Another determining factor is the length of the period between the issuance date and the discount date in comparison with the length of the period between the discount date and the maturity date.

For example, if Burke had discounted Mason's note 40 days instead of 80 days prior to maturity, the discount would have amounted to $12.15 and he would have received proceeds of $1,810.35. The $10.35 excess of the proceeds over the face of the note would have been interest income and the entry in the cash receipts journal would have been:

CASH RECEIPTS JOURNAL PAGE 12

DATE		ACCOUNT	POST. REF.	SUNDRY ACCOUNTS DR.	SUNDRY ACCOUNTS CR.	SALES CR.	ACCTS. REC. CR.	SALES DISC. DR.	CASH DR.
1965									
Dec.	28	Notes Receivable	113		1,800 00				1,810 35
		Interest Income	811		10 35				

Contingent liability. When a note receivable is discounted, it is necessary for the owner to endorse the note. By endorsing the note, the endorser becomes responsible to the bank or other endorsee for its payment if the note is not paid by the maker at maturity. Discounting a note therefore results in the creation of a possible future obligation that is known as a *contingent liability*. The liability is contingent rather than real. If the maker pays the note at maturity, which is probable, the contingent liability is discharged without any action on the part of the endorser. If, on the other hand, the note is not paid by the maker at maturity and the endorser is notified of the fact, the liability becomes a real one.

In preparing a balance sheet, the total amount of discounted notes receivable that are not yet due at the balance sheet date should be disclosed. Disclosure may be made by a note in the liability section or at the bottom of the balance sheet, somewhat along the following lines: "The company is contingently liable for notes receivable discounted in the amount of $16,420." The amount of the contingent liability can be determined from a memorandum record of amounts, due dates, and disposition of all notes receivable.

An alternative procedure recommended in some textbooks is to maintain a current record of the contingent liability in the ledger. This is done by crediting Notes Receivable Discounted at the time the note is discounted. As each discounted note matures, it is then necessary to debit Notes Receivable Discounted and to credit Notes Receivable. The amount of notes receivable on hand at any time is the excess of the debit balance in Notes Receivable over the credit balance in Notes Receivable Discounted. The procedure is seldom used in practice because of the many additional entries required and the ease of obtaining the same information from supplementary records.

It should be noted that it is only the amount of the unmatured discounted notes on the balance sheet date that is significant. The number of notes for which there is a contingent liability at the end of the fiscal year is usually only a small fraction of the total number of short-term notes that were discounted during the year.

Dishonored notes receivable

A note that is not paid when it becomes due is said to be *dishonored*. When a note receivable held by a business is dishonored, the note is no longer negotiable. For this reason the amount due should ordinarily be transferred to the accounts receivable account. For example, if the $300, 20-day, 6% note received and recorded on October 19 (page 185) had been dishonored at maturity, the entry to charge the note back to the customer's account would have been as follows:

Nov.	7	Accounts Receivable — T. J. Cole..........	115/✓	301 00	
		Notes Receivable..........................	113		300 00
		Interest Income...........................	811		1 00
		Dishonored note and interest.			

If there had been some assurance that Cole would pay the note within a few days after maturity, the foregoing entry could have been omitted. In extending credit to the customer in the future, however, it is desirable that his account disclose the fact that the note was dishonored.

In the event that a customer's note that has been discounted is dishonored, the bank will notify the endorser. The latter will then have to pay the note and any interest accrued. For example, if the note that was discounted on November 18 (page 188) is dishonored, Burke, the endorser, will have to pay the bank the face of the note, $1,800, plus interest of $22.50. The entire amount of the payment would be charged to the maker's account, as shown in the following entry:

CASH PAYMENTS JOURNAL PAGE 23

DATE		CHECK NO.	ACCOUNT DEBITED	POST. REF.	SUNDRY ACCTS. DR.	ACCTS. PAY. DR.	PUR. DISC. CR.	CASH CR.
1966 Feb.	6	572	Accts. Rec. — John Mason	115/ √	1,822 50			1,822 50

In some cases the bank submits to the endorser a notarized statement of the facts of the dishonor. The fee for this statement, known as a *protest fee*, is charged to the endorser, who in turn charges it to the maker of the note. For example, if there had been a protest fee of $2 in connection with the dishonor and the payment recorded above, the debit to the maker's account and the credit to Cash would have been $1,824.50.

QUESTIONS

1. Name and identify the two parties to a promissory note.

2. What are the titles of the accounts used for recording notes?

3. Why are claims evidenced by credit instruments more liquid than accounts receivable?

4. Is the interest rate stated on an interest-bearing note the annual rate or is it the rate to be paid for the term of the note?

5. What is the basic formula for computing interest?

6. The questions below relate to a 90-day, 6% note for $1,000.
(a) What is the face value of the note?
(b) What is the interest on the note?
(c) The interest is what percent of $1,000?
(d) What is the maturity value of the note?

7. What general ledger accounts should be debited and credited (a) to record the issuance of a 60-day, 6% note for $500 to a creditor on account and (b) to record payment of the note at maturity?

8. What is the meaning of (a) discounting a note, (b) discount rate, (c) discount period, (d) proceeds, (e) dishonored note?

9. Does the maker of a note incur a contingent liability when he discounts his own note payable?

10. The payee of a $2,000, 90-day, 6% note receivable discounts the note at his bank. The note is dishonored and the payee pays the bank the face amount, $30 for interest, and $2 for the protest fee. To what account or accounts should the $2,032 be charged? Explain.

11. During the year Dayton Furniture Co. discounted $60,000 of notes receivable. At December 31, the end of the fiscal year, discounted notes in the amount of $16,000 have not matured. (a) What is the amount of the contingent liability? (b) How should the contingent liability be disclosed on the financial statements?

12. The series of six transactions recorded in the following T accounts were incident to a sale to a customer. Describe each transaction briefly.

Cash

	Debit		Credit
(d)	602.97	(e)	606.00
(f)	609.03		

Notes Receivable

	Debit		Credit
(c)	600.00	(d)	600.00

Accounts Receivable

	Debit		Credit
(a)	620.00	(b)	20.00
(e)	606.00	(c)	600.00
		(f)	606.00

Sales

	Debit		Credit
(b)	20.00	(a)	620.00

Interest Income

	Debit		Credit
		(d)	2.97
		(f)	3.03

EXERCISES

1. Determine the interest on the following notes, using the 60-day, 6% method:

Amount of Note	Days	Interest Rate
(a) $ 182.65	83 days	5%
(b) 1,875.50	36 days	6%
(c) 936.10	67 days	5½%
(d) 2,184.00	39 days	7%
(e) 1,115.48	59 days	4%

2. Harold J. Hunter issued to Robert T. Lambert on account the note illustrated below.
(a) What is the due date of the note?
(b) What is the amount of interest to be paid on the note at maturity?

(c) Present entries, in general journal form, to record the following:
(1) Issuance of the note by the maker.
(2) Receipt of the note by the payee.
(3) Payment of the note at maturity.
(4) Receipt of payment of the note at maturity.

$900.00 Boulder, Colorado, March 18, 1965
---------------Ninety days--------------- AFTER DATE I PROMISE TO PAY TO
THE ORDER OF Robert T. Lambert
Nine hundred 00/100-- DOLLARS
PAYABLE AT City Bank and Trust Company
VALUE RECEIVED WITH INTEREST AT --6--- %
No. 18 Harold J. Hunter

3. In negotiating a 90-day loan, Tru-Valu Markets has the option of either (1) issuing a $20,000, non-interest-bearing note that will be discounted at the rate of 6%, or (2) issuing a $20,000 note bearing interest at the rate of 6% that will be accepted at face value. (a) What would be the amount of the interest expense in each case? (b) What would be the amount of the proceeds in each case? (c) Which of the two alternatives is more favorable to the borrower? (d) Assuming that the first alternative is adopted, give the entry, in general journal form, at the time the note is issued and at the time the note is paid.

4. On July 1 Business Office Plaza purchases land for $40,000 and a building for $500,000, paying $90,000 in cash and issuing a 5% note, secured by a mortgage on the property, for the remainder. The terms of the note provide for eighteen semiannual payments of $25,000 on the principal plus accrued interest. Give the entry, in general journal form, to record (a) the transaction on July 1, (b) payment of the first installment on December 31, and (c) payment of the second installment the following June 30.

5. Hamilton Co. holds a 60-day, 5% note for $1,200, dated August 5, that was received from a customer on account. On September 4 the note is discounted at First National Bank at the rate of 6%. (a) What is the maturity value of the note? (b) How many days are there in the discount period? (c) What is the amount of the discount? (d) What is the amount of the proceeds? (e) Give the entry, in general journal form, to record the discounting of the note on September 4.

6. Record the following transactions, each in general journal form, on the books of T. D. Carroll Company:

Apr. 1. Received a $1,600, 90-day, 5% note dated April 1 from Carl Bryant on account.
May 1. Discounted the note at Citizens State Bank, discount rate 6%.
June 30. The note is dishonored; paid the bank the amount due on the note plus a protest fee of $2.
July 30. Received amount due on the dishonored note plus interest at 6% on the amount outstanding since June 30.

PROBLEMS

8-1. The following were selected from among the transactions completed by Patterson Co. during the current year:

Jan. 15. Purchased merchandise on account from J. M. Carter Co., $700.
25. Paid J. M. Carter Co. for the invoice of January 15, less 2% discount.
Feb. 6. Purchased merchandise on account from Jordan & Co., $950.
Mar. 8. Issued a 30-day, 6% note for $950 to Jordan & Co. on account.
Apr. 7. Paid Jordan & Co. the amount owed on the note of March 8, $954.75.
May 18. Issued a 60-day, non-interest-bearing note for $4,000 to Citizens National Bank, receiving proceeds of $3,960.
July 17. Paid Citizens National Bank the amount due on the note of May 18.
Aug. 20. Borrowed $3,000 from Merchants National Bank, issuing a 60-day, 6% note for that amount.
Oct. 19. Paid Merchants National Bank the $30 interest due on the note of August 20 and renewed the loan by issuing a new 30-day, 6% note for $3,000.
Nov. 18. Paid Merchants National Bank the amount due on the note of October 19, $3,015.
Nov. 29. Purchased office equipment from Sullivan Co. for $4,800, paying $800 in cash and issuing a series of eight 6% notes for $500 each, coming due at 30-day intervals.
Dec. 29. Paid the amount due Sullivan Co. on the first note in the series issued on November 29, $502.50.

Instructions: Record the transactions in general journal form, using a two-column general journal.

8-2. The following were selected from among the transactions completed by Richmond & Co. during the current year:

Jan. 8. Sold merchandise on account to Black & Harris, $650.
18. Accepted a 30-day, 7% note for $650 from Black & Harris on account.
Feb. 17. Received from Black & Harris the amount due on the note of January 18, $653.79.
Mar. 10. Sold merchandise on account to Kline Co., $900, charging an additional $15 for prepaid transportation costs.
Mar. 20. Received from Kline Co. the amount due on the invoice of March 10, less 2% discount.
Apr. 4. Loaned $300 cash to Henry Wells, receiving a 30-day, 6% note.
May 4. Received interest of $1.50 from Henry Wells and a new 30-day, 6% note as a renewal of the loan.
June 3. Received from Henry Wells the amount due on his note, $301.50.
Aug. 6. Sold merchandise on account to S. T. Sarver, Inc., $1,200.
Oct. 5. Accepted a 60-day, 8% note for $1,200 from S. T. Sarver, Inc. on account.
25. Discounted the note from S. T. Sarver, Inc. at the Bank of Boulder at 6%, receiving proceeds of $1,207.89.
Dec. 4. Received notice from Bank of Boulder that S. T. Sarver, Inc. had dishonored its note. Paid the bank the amount of the face of the note, $1,200, interest of $16, and a protest fee of $3.
24. Received from S. T. Sarver, Inc. the amount owed on the dishonored note, plus additional interest of $5.42.

Instructions: Record the transactions in general journal form, using a two-column general journal.

8-3. The following were selected from among the transactions completed by Superior Co. during the current fiscal year:

Apr. 10. Purchased merchandise on account from Beckett & Co., $600.
17. Sold merchandise on account to H. R. Lindsey, Invoice No. 365, $450.
25. Discounted a 90-day, non-interest-bearing note payable for $3,000 at First National Bank; discount rate 6%.
27. Received cash from H. R. Lindsey for the invoice of Apr. 17, less 2% discount.

May 5. Sold merchandise on account to A. T. Grant, Invoice No. 398, $750.
10. Issued a 90-day, 7% note for $600 to Beckett & Co. on account.
11. Sold merchandise on account to Halstead & Co., Invoice No. 413, $1,100.
15. Purchased merchandise on account from Walker & Son, $900.
25. Issued Check No. 614 to Walker & Son for the amount due on the purchase of May 15, less 2% discount.

June 4. Received from A. T. Grant on account a 60-day, 6% note for $750, dated June 4.
9. Sold merchandise on account to Martin's, Inc., Invoice No. 521, $800.
10. Received from Halstead & Co. on account a 1-month, 6% note for $1,100, dated June 10.
24. Discounted A. T. Grant's $750 note, dated June 4, at Security National Bank; discount rate 6%.

July 6. Received from Martin's, Inc. on account a 30-day, 6% note for $800, dated July 6.
10. Received cash from Halstead & Co. for the amount owed on the note dated June 10.
24. Issued Check No. 678 to First National Bank for the amount due on the note dated April 25.

Aug. 3. Received notice from Security National Bank that A. T. Grant had dishonored his note dated June 4. Issued Check No. 697 in payment of the amount due; no protest fee.
5. Martin's, Inc. dishonored its note dated July 6. Charged the dishonored note to its account.
8. Issued Check No. 703 to Beckett & Co. in payment of the note dated May 10.
13. Received cash from A. T. Grant for the principal and the interest on his dishonored note, plus additional interest at 8% on the total amount from August 3.

Instructions: Record the transactions, using the following journals: sales journal (as illustrated on page 106); purchases journal (with only one money column, headed Purchases Dr. and Accts. Pay. Cr.); cash receipts journal (as illustrated on page 184); cash payments journal (as illustrated on page 184); two-column general journal.

8-4. The following transactions were completed by Valley Industries Co. during the current fiscal year:

Jan. 7. Received from Tri-State Metal Co. a 90-day, non-interest-bearing note for $5,000, dated January 6, on account.
21. Issued to Preston & Son a 2-month, 7% note for $4,000, on account.

Feb. 20. Discounted at Manufacturers Trust Co. at 6% the note received from Tri-State Metal Co., dated January 6.

Mar. 21. Issued Check No. 464 to Preston & Son in payment of the note issued on January 21.

Apr. 14. Discounted a 60-day, non-interest-bearing note payable for $8,000 at Manufacturers Trust Co.; discount rate, 6%.

May 6. Received from General Supply Co. a 90-day, 5% note for $1,000, dated May 4, on account.

18. Purchased land for a building site from Modern Development Co. for $35,000, issuing Check No. 503 for $5,000 and a 5% mortgage note for the balance. The contract provides for payments of $3,000 of principal plus accrued interest at intervals of six months.

June 13. Issued Check No. 531 to Manufacturers Trust Co. for the amount due on the note payable issued on April 14.

20. Discounted at the Manufacturers Trust Co. at 6% the note received from General Supply Co., dated May 4.

Aug. 3. Received notice from the Manufacturers Trust Co. that General Supply Co. had dishonored the note due on August 2. Issued Check No. 610 for the amount due on the note, plus a protest fee of $3.

Sept. 21. Received from Campus Plaza a 90-day, 5% note for $800, dated September 20, on account.

Oct. 2. Received from General Supply Co. the amount due on the note dishonored on August 2, including interest at 6% from August 2 to October 1 on the maturity value of the note plus protest fee.

Nov. 18. Issued Check No. 749 for principal and interest due on mortgage note.

Dec. 19. Campus Plaza dishonored its note dated September 20. Charged the dishonored note to its account.

Instructions: Record the transactions, using the following journals: cash receipts journal (as illustrated on page 187); cash payments journal (as illustrated on page 187, except for an additional column for Sundry Accounts Cr.); two-column general journal.

8-5. The Bradshaw Contracting Co. received the notes described below during the last three months of the current fiscal year. Notes (1), (2), (3), and (4) were discounted at Peoples State Bank on the dates indicated; discount rate 6%.

Date	Face Amount	Term	Interest Rate	Date Discounted
(1) Oct. 3	$2,000	60 days	6%	Oct. 9
(2) Oct. 21	1,000	30 days	—	Nov. 3
(3) Nov. 10	960	90 days	7%	Dec. 2
(4) Nov. 20	1,400	30 days	5%	Dec. 10
(5) Dec. 10	1,800	60 days	6%	—
(6) Dec. 15	3,000	60 days	5%	—

Instructions: (1) Determine for each note (a) the due date and (b) the amount of interest due at maturity, identifying each note by number.

(2) Determine for each of the first four notes (a) the maturity value, (b) the discount period, (c) the discount, (d) the proceeds, and (e) the interest income or interest expense, identifying each note by number.

(3) Present, in general journal form, the entries to record the discounting of Notes (1) and (2).

(4) Assuming that Notes (5) and (6) are held until maturity, determine for each the amount of interest earned (a) during the fiscal year in which the notes were received, and (b) during the following fiscal year.

9. Deferrals and accruals

Accounting and periodic reports

The allocation of revenues and expenses to the proper periods of time in the life of business enterprises engages much of the attention of accountants. When cash is exchanged at the instant a revenue is earned or the benefit of an expenditure is received, the effects on net income of the period are readily evident. It is when there are time differentials between either the earning of revenues or the occurrence of expenses and the recognition of their related effect on assets and liabilities that accounting problems arise. Such problems are made more acute by the need for periodic reports on financial position and operating results. The maximum interval of time between these periodic financial statements is one year. As was indicated earlier, it is also customary to prepare interim income statements and balance sheets at quarterly or monthly intervals.

The basic principles and procedures related to the preparation of financial statements have been described in earlier chapters. The necessity for recording deferrals and accruals has been emphasized as an important part of the periodic summary. There are many situations in which adjusting entries are required to bring the accounts into as close as possible agreement with the true state of affairs. Some of them have been described and illustrated in earlier chapters. This chapter is devoted to further consideration of procedures that are employed in effecting proper recognition of deferrals and accruals. Their underlying purpose is to assure a fair statement of all revenues and expenses for the period and a fair statement of all assets and equities as of the last day of the period.

Classification and terminology

There are many kinds of revenues and expenses that may require deferral or accrual in particular circumstances. A *deferral* is a postponement of the recognition of a revenue already collected or of an expense already paid. An *accrual* is a gradual accumulation of a revenue or an expense that has not yet been recorded. Deferrals and accruals are recorded as adjusting entries on the work sheet used in preparing financial statements. If the work sheet is for the fiscal year, the adjustments are also recorded in the general journal and posted to the ledger. For interim statements, the adjustments may appear only on the work sheet.

One basic characteristic of all adjusting entries, regardless of whether or not they are recorded in the accounts, should be noted. Each adjustment affects one or more balance sheet accounts and one or more income statement accounts. For example, if one effect of an adjustment is to increase a liability account (a credit), the other effect will be to increase an expense account (a debit) or decrease a revenue account (a debit). In no case will the student encounter an adjustment that will require changes only in an asset account and a liability account, or an adjustment that will require changes only in an expense account and a revenue account.

The types of adjustments to be discussed and illustrated in this chapter are classified below.

DEFERRALS

Prepaid expense (an asset); also called *prepayment* or *deferred charge.*
Unearned revenue (a liability); also called *income received in advance* or *deferred credit.*

ACCRUALS

Accrued liability (a liability); also called *accrued payable.*
Accrued asset (an asset); also called *accrued receivable.*

Prepaid expenses

Prepaid expenses are commodities and services that have been purchased for consumption but that are unconsumed at the end of the accounting period. The portion of the asset that has been used during the period has become an expense; the remainder will become an expense in the future. It is because of this deferral of benefits to the future that prepaid expenses are sometimes termed *deferred charges*. Prepaid expenses include such items as prepaid insurance, prepaid rent, prepaid advertising, prepaid interest, and various types of supplies.

Two methods of accounting for prepaid expenses will be explained. Prepaid insurance will be used to illustrate the first method, and prepaid interest will be used to illustrate the second method. It should be understood that either of the alternative methods may be employed in any particular case.

Prepaid expenses recorded initially as assets. When prepaid insurance or other consumable services or supplies are purchased, they may be debited to an asset account. Although it is known at the time of purchase that some portion of the services or the supplies will be used during the accounting period, the amount actually consumed is not determined until financial statements are to be prepared.

The expired insurance may be analyzed according to the various types of property insured so that the amount allocable to selling expense and the amount allocable to general expense can be determined. For example, expired insurance on merchandise and store equipment is considered a selling expense; that on office equipment and building, a general expense.

To illustrate, assume that the prepaid insurance account has a balance of $814 at the close of the year. This amount represents the unexpired insurance at the beginning of the year plus the total of premiums paid during the year. It is ascertained that $506 of insurance has expired during the year, of which $426 represents selling expense and $80 represents general expense. The adjusting entry to record the expired insurance appears as follows:

Dec.	31	Insurance Expense — Selling	615	426	
		Insurance Expense — General	716	80	
		Prepaid Insurance	118		506

After this entry has been posted, the three accounts affected appear as follows:

PREPAID INSURANCE ACCT. No. 118

DATE		ITEMS	POST. REF.	DEBIT	CREDIT	BALANCE	
						DEBIT	CREDIT
1965							
Jan.	1	Balance	√			430	
Mar.	18		CP6	110		540	
Aug.	26		CP16	180		720	
Nov.	11		CP21	94		814	
Dec.	31	Adjusting	J17		506	308	

INSURANCE EXPENSE — SELLING — ACCT. NO. 615

DATE		ITEMS	POST. REF.	DEBIT	CREDIT	BALANCE	
						DEBIT	CREDIT
1965							
Dec.	31	Adjusting	J17		426	426	

INSURANCE EXPENSE — GENERAL — ACCT. NO. 716

DATE		ITEMS	POST. REF.	DEBIT	CREDIT	BALANCE	
						DEBIT	CREDIT
1965							
Dec.	31	Adjusting	J17		80	80	

After $506 of expired insurance is transferred to the expense accounts, the balance of $308 remaining in Prepaid Insurance represents the premiums on various policies that apply to future periods. It is listed as a current asset in the balance sheet. The amounts transferred to the two expense accounts appear in the income statement.

Prepaid expenses recorded initially as expenses. In the foregoing illustration the prepaid expenses were originally debited to the asset account. An alternative is to charge them directly to the appropriate expense account as they are acquired. This method is frequently used in recording the discount on notes issued to banks, which are ordinarily for a period of from 30 to 90 days. If the prepaid interest is charged to Interest Expense at the time the funds are borrowed and if the notes are paid by the end of the fiscal year, no adjusting entry is necessary. When one or more discounted notes are still outstanding on the last day of the year, however, the portion of the interest applicable to the following period should be deducted from the expense account and transferred to the asset account in an adjusting entry.

To illustrate this alternative method, assume that during the year four non-interest-bearing notes payable were discounted and that in each case the discount was debited to Interest Expense. Three of the notes became due and were paid during the year. The fourth, a $12,000, 90-day note, had been issued on December 1 at a discount of $180.

As of the last day of the fiscal year, only 30 days of the 90-day term of the $12,000 note have elapsed. Therefore only $60 (1/3 of $180) of the discount is an expense of the year; the remaining $120 (2/3 of $180) is a prepayment that will become an expense during the first 60 days of the following year. The adjusting entry to transfer the $120 to the asset account is as follows:

Dec.	31	Prepaid Interest	117	120	
		Interest Expense	911		120

After this entry has been posted, the asset account and the expense account appear as follows:

PREPAID INTEREST — ACCT. NO. 117

DATE		ITEMS	POST. REF.	DEBIT	CREDIT	BALANCE	
						DEBIT	CREDIT
1965							
Dec.	31	Adjusting	J17	120		120	

INTEREST EXPENSE — ACCT. NO. 911

DATE		ITEMS	POST. REF.	DEBIT	CREDIT	BALANCE	
						DEBIT	CREDIT
1965							
Feb.	5		CR3	50		50	
May	15		CR8	144		194	
June	10		CR10	105		299	
Dec.	1		CR20	180		479	
	31	Adjusting	J17		120	359	

The remaining balance of $359 in Interest Expense is the amount of expense for the year. It is reported in the income statement and will be transferred to Expense and Revenue Summary in the process of closing the books. The balance of $120 in Prepaid Interest is reported in the balance sheet as a current asset.

During the first 60 days of the following year, the prepaid interest on the loan becomes interest expense at the rate of $2 a day ($120 ÷ 60). It would be possible, though obviously unnecessary, to record a $2 transfer from the asset account to the expense account on each of the 60 days. Another possibility would be to wait until the 60 days had elapsed and then transfer the entire $120 from the asset account to the expense account. If there were additional notes on which interest was prepaid, a similar transfer would be required each time a note became due.

The alternative, which is least time-consuming and least likely to invite errors, is to incorporate *reversing entries* as a part of the periodic summary procedures. The effect is to transfer the entire balance of the asset account to the expense account immediately after the books have been closed. The reversing entry for the prepaid interest, which is the exact reverse of the adjusting entry, is as follows:

Jan.	1	Interest Expense	911	120	
		Prepaid Interest	117		120

After the reversing entry has been posted, the prepaid interest account and the interest expense account appear as follows:

PREPAID INTEREST — ACCT. No. 117

DATE		ITEMS	POST. REF.	DEBIT	CREDIT	BALANCE DEBIT	BALANCE CREDIT
1965							
Dec.	31	Adjusting	J17	120		120	
1966							
Jan.	1	Reversing	J18		120	—	—

INTEREST EXPENSE — ACCT. No. 911

DATE		ITEMS	POST. REF.	DEBIT	CREDIT	BALANCE DEBIT	BALANCE CREDIT
1965							
Feb.	5		CR3	50		50	
May	15		CR8	144		194	
June	10		CR10	105		299	
Dec.	1		CR20	180		479	
	31	Adjusting	J17		120	359	
	31	Closing	J17		359	—	—
1966							
Jan.	1	Reversing	J18	120		120	

At the beginning of the new fiscal year there is a debit balance of $120 in Interest Expense. Although the balance is in reality an asset at this time, the $120 will need no further attention because it will become expense before the close of the year. Whenever an expense account needs adjustment for a prepayment at the end of a period, the adjusting entry should be reversed after the books have been closed.

Comparison of the two methods. The two methods of recording prepaid expenses and the related entries at the end of an accounting period may be summarized as follows:

Prepaid expense recorded initially as an *asset*.

Adjusting entry: Transfer amount *used* to appropriate *expense* account.
Closing entry: Transfer balance of expense account to expense and revenue summary account.
Reversing entry: None.
Balance of prepaid expense, beginning of new period: In *asset* account.

Prepaid expense recorded initially as an *expense*.

Adjusting entry: Transfer amount *unused* to appropriate *asset* account.
Closing entry: Transfer balance of expense account to expense and revenue summary account.
Reversing entry: Transfer amount *unused* back to *expense* account.
Balance of prepaid expense, beginning of new period: In *expense* account.

Some accountants prefer to use the first method, others prefer the second method, and still others use the first method for prepayments of certain types of expenses and the second method for other types. For example, the first method appears to be particularly logical for prepayments of insurance because they are usually for periods of from one to five years and an adjustment will always be necessary at the end of the year. On the other hand, interest charges on notes payable are usually for short periods, some charges may be recorded when a note is issued (as in the illustration), other charges may be recorded when a note is paid, and few, if any, of the debits for interest may require adjustment at the end of the period. It therefore seems logical to debit all interest charges to the expense account rather than to the asset account.

Regardless of which method is employed in any particular case, the amount that is reported as expense in the income statement will be the same. Similarly, the amount that will be listed as an asset in the balance sheet will not be affected by the method used. To avoid confusion and waste of time, the method adopted for each particular type of prepaid expense should be consistently followed from year to year.

Unearned revenue

Revenue received during a particular period may be only partly earned by the end of the period. Items of revenue that are received in advance represent a liability that may be termed *unearned revenue.* The portion of the liability that is discharged during the period through delivery of commodities or services has been earned; the remainder will be earned in the future. It is because of this deferment that unearned revenues are frequently called *deferred credits.* For example, magazine publishers ordinarily receive advance payment for subscriptions extending for periods ranging from a few months to a number of years. At the end of an accounting period, the portion of the receipts applicable to future periods has not been earned and should appear in the balance sheet as a liability.

Other examples of unearned revenue are rent received in advance on property owned, interest deducted in advance on notes receivable, premiums received in advance by an insurance company, tuition received in advance by a school, an annual retainer fee received in advance by an attorney, and amounts received in advance by an advertising firm for advertising services to be rendered in the future.

By accepting payment for the commodity or the service in advance, a business renders itself liable to furnish the commodity or the service at some future time. At the end of the accounting period, if some portion of the commodity or the service has been furnished, part of the revenue has been earned. The earned portion appears in the income statement. The unearned portion represents a liability of the business to furnish the commodity or the service in a future period and is reported in the balance sheet as a liability.

As in the case of prepaid expenses, two methods of accounting for items of unearned revenue will be described. Unearned rent will be used in illustrating both methods.

Unearned revenue recorded initially as a liability. When revenue is received in advance, it may be credited to a liability account. For example, assume that on October 1 a business rents a portion of its building for a period of one year, receiving $3,600 in payment for the entire term of the lease. The transaction was originally recorded by a debit to Cash and a credit to Unearned Rent. On December 31, the end of the fiscal year, one fourth of the amount has been earned and three fourths of the amount remains a liability. The adjusting entry to record the revenue and reduce the liability appears as follows:

Dec.	31	Unearned Rent....................	218	900	
		Rent Income....................	812		900

After this entry has been posted, the unearned rent account and the rent income account appear as follows:

UNEARNED RENT — ACCT. NO. 218

DATE		ITEMS	POST. REF.	DEBIT	CREDIT	BALANCE DEBIT	BALANCE CREDIT
1965							
Oct.	1		CR8		3,600		3,600
Dec.	31	Adjusting	J17	900			2,700

RENT INCOME — ACCT. NO. 812

DATE		ITEMS	POST. REF.	DEBIT	CREDIT	BALANCE DEBIT	BALANCE CREDIT
1965							
Dec.	31	Adjusting	J17		900		900

After the amount earned, $900, is transferred to Rent Income, the balance of $2,700 remaining in Unearned Rent is a liability to render a service in the future and it therefore appears as a current liability in the balance sheet. Rent Income appears in the Other Income section of the income statement; the account is closed to the expense and revenue summary account along with other revenue accounts.

Unearned revenue recorded initially as revenue. Instead of being credited to a liability account, unearned revenue may be credited to a revenue account as it is received. For example, assume the same facts as in the preceding illustration, except that the transaction was originally recorded on October 1 by a debit to Cash and a credit to Rent Income. On December 31, the end of the fiscal year, three fourths of the balance in Rent Income is still unearned and the remaining one fourth has been earned. The adjusting entry to record the transfer to the liability account appears as follows:

Dec.	31	Rent Income........................	812	2,700	
		Unearned Rent..................	218		2,700

After this entry has been posted, the unearned rent account and the rent income appear as follows:

UNEARNED RENT — ACCT. NO. 218

DATE		ITEMS	POST. REF.	DEBIT	CREDIT	BALANCE DEBIT	BALANCE CREDIT
1965							
Dec.	31	Adjusting	J17		2,700		2,700

RENT INCOME — ACCT. NO. 812

DATE		ITEMS	POST. REF.	DEBIT	CREDIT	BALANCE DEBIT	BALANCE CREDIT
1965							
Oct.	1		CR8		3,600		3,600
Dec.	31	Adjusting	J17	2,700			900

The unearned rent of $2,700 is listed as a current liability in the balance sheet, and the rent income of $900 is reported in the income statement. In the process of closing the books, the balance of the rent income account is closed to the expense and revenue summary account.

The $2,700 of unearned rent at the end of the year will be earned during the following year. If it is transferred to the income account by a *reversing* entry immediately after the books are closed, no further action will be needed either month by month or at the end of the nine-month period. Furthermore, since the $3,600 rent was credited initially to the income account, all such payments received in the following year will presumably be treated in a similar fashion. If a reversing entry is not made, there may be balances in both the liability account and the income account at the end of the following year, necessitating analysis of both accounts and causing possible confusion. The reversing entry for the unearned rent, which is the exact reverse of the adjusting entry, is as follows:

Jan.	1	Unearned Rent	218	2,700	
		Rent Income	812		2,700

After this entry has been posted, the unearned rent account and the rent income account appear as follows:

UNEARNED RENT — Acct. No. 218

Date		Items	Post. Ref.	Debit	Credit	Balance Debit	Balance Credit
1965							
Dec.	31	Adjusting	J17		2,700		2,700
1966							
Jan.	1	Reversing	J18	2,700		—	—

RENT INCOME — Acct. No. 812

Date		Items	Post. Ref.	Debit	Credit	Balance Debit	Balance Credit
1965							
Oct.	1		CR8		3,600		3,600
Dec.	31	Adjusting	J17	2,700			900
	31	Closing	J17	900		—	—
1966							
Jan.	1	Reversing	J18		2,700		2,700

At the beginning of the new fiscal year there is a credit balance of $2,700 in Rent Income. Although the balance is in reality a liability at this time, it will become revenue before the close of the year. Whenever a revenue account needs adjustment for an unearned amount at the end of a period, the adjusting entry should be reversed after the books have been closed.

Comparison of the two methods. The two methods of recording unearned revenue and the related entries at the end of the accounting period may be summarized as follows:

Unearned revenue recorded initially as a *liability*.

Adjusting entry: Transfer amount *earned* to appropriate *revenue* account.
Closing entry: Transfer balance of revenue account to expense and revenue summary account.
Reversing entry: None.
Balance of unearned revenue, beginning of new period: In *liability* account.

Unearned revenue recorded initially as *revenue*.

Adjusting entry: Transfer amount *unearned* to appropriate *liability* account.
Closing entry: Transfer balance of revenue account to expense and revenue summary account.
Reversing entry: Transfer amount *unearned* back to *revenue* account.
Balance of unearned revenue, beginning of new period: In *revenue* account.

When unearned revenue is credited to a liability account as it is received (first method), the amount unearned is in the liability account after the work of the periodic summary has been completed. When unearned revenue is credited to the revenue account as it is received (second method), the amount unearned is in the revenue account after the work of the periodic summary has been completed.

As was explained in connection with prepaid expenses, the results obtained are the same under both methods. The method adopted for each particular kind of unearned revenue should be consistently followed from year to year.

Accrued liabilities

Some expenses accrue from day to day but are ordinarily recorded only when they are paid. Examples are salaries and interest expense on interest-bearing obligations. The amounts of such items accrued but unpaid at the end of the fiscal period are both an expense and a liability. It is for this reason that the accrual may be referred to as an *accrued liability*, an *accrued payable*, or an *accrued expense*.

To illustrate the adjusting entry for an accrued liability, assume that on December 31, the end of the fiscal year, the salary expense account has a debit balance of $32,500. During the year salaries have been paid each Friday for the five-day week then ended. For this particular fiscal year, December 31 falls on Wednesday. Reference to the records of the business reveals that the salary accrued for these last three days of the year amounts to $375. The adjusting entry to record the additional expense and the liability is:

Dec.	31	Salary Expense	611	375	
		Salaries Payable	214		375

After this entry has been posted, the salaries payable account and the salary expense account appear as follows:

SALARIES PAYABLE — ACCT. No. 214

DATE		ITEMS	POST. REF.	DEBIT	CREDIT	BALANCE DEBIT	BALANCE CREDIT
1965							
Dec.	31	Adjusting	J17		375		375

SALARY EXPENSE — ACCT. No. 611

DATE		ITEMS	POST. REF.	DEBIT	CREDIT	BALANCE DEBIT	BALANCE CREDIT
1965							
Dec.	31	Balance	√			32,500	
	31	Adjusting	J17	375		32,875	

The accrued salaries of $375 recorded in Salaries Payable will appear in the balance sheet of December 31 as a current liability. The salary expense of $32,875 now recorded in Salary Expense will appear in the income statement for the year ended December 31. The salary expense account will be closed to the expense and revenue summary account in the usual manner.

When the weekly salaries are paid on January 2 of the following year, part of the payment will discharge the liability of $375 and the remainder will represent salary expense of the first two days of January. In order to avoid the necessity of analyzing the payment, a reversing entry is made at the beginning of the new year. The effect of the entry is to transfer the credit balance in the salaries payable account to the credit side of the salary expense account. This entry appears as follows:

Jan.	1	Salaries Payable....................	214	375	
		Salary Expense....................	611		375

After this entry has been posted, the salaries payable account and the salary expense account appear as follows:

SALARIES PAYABLE — ACCT. No. 214

DATE		ITEMS	POST. REF.	DEBIT	CREDIT	BALANCE DEBIT	BALANCE CREDIT
1965							
Dec.	31	Adjusting	J17		375		375
1966							
Jan.	1	Reversing	J18	375		—	—

SALARY EXPENSE — ACCT. No. 611

DATE		ITEMS	POST. REF.	DEBIT	CREDIT	BALANCE	
						DEBIT	CREDIT
1965							
Dec.	31	Balance	√			32,500	
	31	Adjusting	J17	375		32,875	
	31	Closing	J18		32,875	—	—
1966							
Jan.	1	Reversing	J18		375		375

The liability for salaries on December 31 now appears as a credit in Salary Expense. Assuming that the salaries paid on Friday, January 2, amount to $550, the debit to Salary Expense will automatically record the discharge of the liability of $375 and the expense of $175 ($550 − $375).

The discussion of the treatment of accrued salary expense is illustrative of the method of handling accrued liabilities in general. If, in addition to accrued salaries, there are other accrued liabilities at the end of a fiscal period, separate liability accounts may be set up for each type. When these liability items are numerous, however, one liability account, termed Accrued Payables or Accrued Liabilities, may be used. All accrued liabilities may be recorded as credits to this account instead of to separate accounts.

Because of peculiarities in the timing of their accrual and payment, the adjusting process applicable to property taxes is frequently more complicated than it is for salaries and interest. Accounting for property taxes is described and illustrated later in this chapter.

Accrued assets

All assets belonging to the business at the end of an accounting period and all revenue earned during the period should be recorded in the ledger. But, during a fiscal period, it is the customary practice to record some types of revenue only as the cash is received; consequently, at the end of the period there may be items of revenue that have not been recorded. In such cases it is necessary to record the amount of the accrued revenue by debiting an asset account and crediting a revenue account. Because of the dual nature of such accruals, they are referred to as *accrued assets*, *accrued receivables*, or *accrued revenues*.

To illustrate the adjusting entry for an accrued asset, assume that on December 31, the end of the fiscal year, the interest income account has a credit balance of $384. Assume further that on the same date the business owns three short-term, interest-bearing notes accepted from customers. The three notes are for varying amounts and have varying due dates in January and February of the succeeding year. The interest accrued on each note from its date of issuance to December 31 is determined, and the three amounts total $67. The adjusting entry to record this claim against debtors and the additional revenue earned is as follows:

Dec.	31	Interest Receivable..................	114	67	
		Interest Income..................	811		67

After this entry has been posted, the interest receivable account and the interest income account appear as follows:

INTEREST RECEIVABLE — Acct. No. 114

Date		Items	Post. Ref.	Debit	Credit	Balance Debit	Balance Credit
1965							
Dec.	31	Adjusting	J17	67		67	

INTEREST INCOME — Acct. No. 811

Date		Items	Post. Ref.	Debit	Credit	Balance Debit	Balance Credit
1965							
Dec.	31	Balance	√				384
	31	Adjusting	J17		67		451

The accrued interest of $67 recorded in Interest Receivable will appear in the balance sheet of December 31 as a current asset. The credit balance of $451 now recorded in Interest Income will appear in the Other Income section of the income statement for the year ended December 31. The interest income account will be closed to the expense and revenue summary account in the usual manner.

When the amount due on each of the three notes is collected in the succeeding year, part of the interest received will be applied to reduction of the interest receivable and the remainder will represent revenue for the new year. To avoid the inconvenience of analyzing each receipt of interest in the new year, a reversing entry is made immediately after the books are closed. The effect of the entry is to transfer the debit balance in the interest receivable account to the debit side of the interest income account. This entry is shown at the top of the following page.

Jan.	1	Interest Income	811	67	
		Interest Receivable	114		67

After this entry has been posted, the interest receivable account and the interest income account appear as follows:

INTEREST RECEIVABLE ACCT. No. 114

DATE		ITEMS	POST. REF.	DEBIT	CREDIT	BALANCE DEBIT	BALANCE CREDIT
1965							
Dec.	31	Adjusting	J17	67		67	
1966							
Jan.	1	Reversing	J18		67	—	—

INTEREST INCOME ACCT. No. 811

DATE		ITEMS	POST. REF.	DEBIT	CREDIT	BALANCE DEBIT	BALANCE CREDIT
1965							
Dec.	31	Balance	√				384
	31	Adjusting	J17		67		451
	31	Closing	J17	451		—	—
1966							
Jan.	1	Reversing	J18	67		67	

The interest receivable on December 31 now appears as a debit in Interest Income. When cash is received for the principal and the interest on each note, the transaction will be recorded in the usual manner; that is, the entire amount of the interest will be credited to Interest Income. The excess of the total credits over the debit balance of $67 in the Interest Income account will be the amount of interest earned on these notes in the new year.

The treatment of interest accrued on notes receivable illustrates the method of handling accrued assets in general. If, in addition to accrued interest, there are other accrued assets at the end of a fiscal period, separate accounts may be set up. Each of these accounts will be of the same nature as the account with interest receivable. When such items are numerous, one asset account, termed Accrued Receivables or Accrued Assets, may be opened. All accrued assets may be recorded as debits to this account instead of to separate accounts.

Property taxes

Various types of taxes are levied on businesses by federal, state, and local governments. The total tax expense incurred by an enterprise each year frequently amounts to a substantial portion of its revenues. It is usually the responsibility of the accounting department to prepare the required tax reports, to design the procedure for recording taxes in the accounts, and to prescribe the manner of reporting taxes in the financial statements. The remainder of this chapter is devoted to a discussion of property taxes, with particular emphasis on their deferral or accrual.

Types of property. In law, all property is either real property or personal property. *Real property*, also called *realty* or *real estate*, includes land and anything permanently attached to the land. Buildings, trees, fences, water lines, sidewalks, and other improvements to land come within the definition of real property.

All property not classified as realty is termed *personal property*, or *personalty*. Such property is subdivided into two major categories, *tangible* and *intangible*. Tangible personalty includes equipment, merchandise, supplies, and other physical assets. Intangible personalty includes investments in stocks and bonds, accounts and notes receivable, prepaid insurance, bank deposits, and other assets having no physical existence.

Tax base. The method of determining the value of property for tax purposes varies among taxing jurisdictions and for different types of property. The value assigned to real estate is frequently determined by the tax assessor without reference to cost, book value, or other evidence provided in the accounts and records of the owner. In general, the assessed value tends to be lower than the fair market value of the property. Personal property may also be appraised by an assessor, or the owner may be required to declare the value of his property. In the latter case the cost of the property is usually the starting point in determining value for tax purposes. Methods of determining the amount of depreciation to be deducted from cost in arriving at the tax base are usually prescribed by statute or administrative regulations.

Tax rates. A governmental unit determines its tax rate each year by dividing the total revenue to be raised from the tax by the total assessed value of the property within its jurisdiction. For example, if the budgeted revenue requirements of a county for the year amount to $2,000,000 and the value of all taxable property in the county is $100,000,000, the county tax rate will be set at 20 mills (2 cents) per $1 of assessed value ($2,000,000 ÷ $100,000,000). A person whose property is assessed at $30,000 will be required to pay a tax of $600 for the year (.02 x $30,000). In some cases the tax rate on tangible personal property is lower than the tax rate on real property.

Payment of taxes. The time specified for payment of property taxes varies greatly among governmental units. Real estate taxes and personal property taxes may be billed together or they may be billed separately and at different times. Frequently the law provides for payment in two installments. If taxes are not paid on time, they become *delinquent* and the property owner may be charged with an additional sum as a penalty. If the taxes and the penalties are not paid within a specified period of time, the property may be seized by the government and sold. Property taxes become a *lien* against the property, usually from the date of assessment until they are paid. A purchaser of property on which the taxes have not been paid acquires it subject to the lien of the government.

Accounting for property taxes

The liability for annual property taxes is usually incurred on a particular day of the year specified by the laws of the taxing jurisdiction. The period covered by the tax may be the year just ended, the year just begun, or some other twelve-month period, depending upon the tax laws applicable. Inasmuch as the governmental services to which the tax relates are spread over an entire year, it is logical to allocate the expense equitably over that period.

The selection of the particular twelve-month period for allocation is complicated by the fact that the exact amount of the tax assessment may not be known until several months after the liability attaches to the property. A difference between the fiscal year of the taxpayer and the fiscal year of the taxing authority may also complicate the problem. Various methods of accounting for property taxes are acceptable, provided the method selected is followed consistently from year to year.

The method to be described here provides for monthly allocation over the fiscal year of the taxing authority for which the tax is levied.[1] Two alternative procedural patterns may be followed: (1) interim monthly adjustments may be recorded solely on working papers, with any required year-end adjustments being recorded in the accounts, or (2) monthly adjustments may be recorded in the accounts. Because of the cumulative nature of the adjustments for property taxes, the second alternative is frequently used. It will be used in the illustration that follows. The allocations reported in the interim and year-end financial statements will be the same regardless of which procedure is adopted. The illustration is based on the following assumed facts:

---

[1]Recommended by *Accounting Research and Terminology Bulletins, Final Edition,* "No. 43 Restatement and Revision of Accounting Research Bulletins," 1961 (New York: American Institute of Certified Public Accountants), pp. 81–85.

Fiscal year of the business enterprise: January 1, 1965, to December 31, 1965.
Fiscal year of the taxing authority: July 1, 1965, to June 30, 1966.
Tax statement received: October 15, 1965.
Tax paid in equal installments on November 10, 1965, and May 10, 1966.

The adjustments data and related transactions are described below, followed by the related entries, in each case in general journal form.

At the end of July the taxpayer estimates that the property tax assessment for the 1965–66 fiscal year of the taxing authority will be $3,240. The amount to be accrued as of July 31, 1965, is therefore $270 ($3,240 ÷ 12) and the entry to record the accrual on the taxpayer's books is as follows:

July	31	Property Tax Expense	270	
		Property Tax Payable		270

An entry for the same amount is recorded as of the last day of August and again on September 30, by which time there is a balance of $810 (3 × $270) in the property tax payable account.

On October 15 a tax statement for $3,480 is received, half of which is payable on November 10. The correct amount of the accrual apportionable to each of the past three months is therefore $290 ($3,480 ÷ 12) instead of $270. Ordinarily the difference between the actual and the estimated monthly expense is not material and the underestimate or overestimate is corrected in the adjusting entry for the month in which the actual amount of the tax becomes known. The amount of the accrual to be recorded at the end of October is therefore determined as follows:

Amount of tax allocable to July, Aug., Sept. and Oct., 4×$290	$1,160
Amount of tax allocated to July, Aug. and Sept., 3×$270	810
Tax allocation for October	$ 350

The $350 allocation for October may also be computed by adding the $60 deficiency (3 × $20) for the first three months to the regular October monthly allocation of $290. The adjusting entry as of October 31 is as follows:

Oct.	31	Property Tax Expense	350	
		Property Tax Payable		350

One half of the tax bill, $1,740, is paid on November 10. Of this amount, $1,160 is in payment of the accrual and $580 represents a deferral. The entry to record the payment is as follows, in general journal form:

Nov.	10	Property Tax Payable	1,160	
		Prepaid Property Tax	580	
		Cash		1,740

At the end of November, and again at the end of December, the following adjusting entry is made:

Nov.	30	Property Tax Expense	290	
		Prepaid Property Tax		290

At December 31, the end of the fiscal year for the business enterprise, one half of the 1965–66 property tax has been charged to expense and there is neither a tax accrual nor a tax deferral recorded in the accounts. The legal obligation for the entire tax of 1965–66 was created in 1965, but the usual accounting treatment is to spread the cost ratably over the period to which the tax relates. If it were considered necessary to report the accrual of the second half of the tax bill as a liability on the balance sheet at December 31, 1965, it would also be necessary to report a deferral of equal amount as an asset.

The adjusting entries and the entry for payment of the second half of the tax bill during January through June of the following year would be similar to those presented for the period July through December. There would, however, be no need to estimate the property tax assessment; the monthly charges to expense would be uniformly $290.

QUESTIONS

1. What is meant by (a) a deferral and (b) an accrual?

2. Give one or more common terms used to describe (a) a deferral of an expense, (b) an accrual of an expense, (c) a deferral of a revenue, and (d) an accrual of a revenue.

3. Classify the following items as (1) prepaid expense, (2) unearned revenue, (3) accrued asset, or (4) accrued liability.

(a) Property taxes paid in advance.
(b) Interest owed but not yet due.
(c) A three-year premium paid on a fire insurance policy.
(d) Supplies on hand.
(e) Taxes owed but payable in the following period.
(f) Interest paid in advance at the time a note was discounted at the bank.
(g) Receipts from sale of meal tickets by a restaurant.
(h) Salary owed but not yet due.
(i) Rent received in advance on property owned.
(j) Interest earned but not received.
(k) Receipts from sale of season tickets for a series of concerts.
(l) Subscriptions collected in advance by a publisher.
(m) Portion of fee earned by CPA but not due until completion of audit.
(n) Life insurance premiums received by an insurance company.

4. Each of the following debits and credits represents one half of an adjusting entry. Name the title of the account affected by the remaining half of the entry.

(a) Prepaid Insurance is credited.
(b) Unearned Rent is debited.

(c) Interest Payable is credited.
(d) Interest Income is debited.
(e) Supplies is credited.
(f) Prepaid Interest is debited.

5. Georgian Company prepares financial statements at the end of each month and closes its books annually on December 31. It pays its employees weekly. (a) What entry should be made on the work sheet for January to recognize accrued salary expense of $1,300 at the end of January? (b) Should the adjusting entry be journalized and posted to the ledger? (c) The first payment of salaries in February, which includes the accrual on January 31, totals $3,400. What is the entry to record the payment? (d) What entry should be made on the work sheet for the two-month period, January-February, to recognize accrued salary expense of $1,400 at the end of February?

6. The interest accrued on a $10,000 note payable at the end of the year is $60. In the following year the note is paid, including interest of $100. What is the entry for the payment of the note and interest at maturity, assuming (a) that the adjusting entry for $60 had been reversed and (b) that the adjusting entry had not been reversed?

7. The accountant for a real estate brokerage and management company adheres to the following uniform procedures in recording certain transactions:
(1) Supplies purchased are debited to Supplies Expense.
(2) Premiums on fire insurance are debited to Prepaid Insurance.
(3) Management fees, which are collected for one year in advance, are credited to Management Fees when received.

At the end of the fiscal year an adjusting entry is required for each of the foregoing. (a) What accounts should be debited and credited in each of the adjustments? (b) Which of the adjusting entries should be reversed as of the beginning of the following year?

8. Assuming that the appropriate accounts require adjustment in each of the following cases at the end of the year, indicate those that should be reversed at the beginning of the following year.
(a) Revenue received in advance is credited to a liability account.
(b) Revenue received in advance is credited to an income account.
(c) Prepayment of an expense is debited to an asset account.
(d) Prepayment of an expense is debited to an expense account.

9. Does the reversing of adjustments for accrued assets and accrued liabilities facilitate the recording of transactions? Explain.

10. (a) Is it almost a certainty that a business enterprise will always have prepaid insurance at the end of each fiscal year? Explain.

(b) Is it almost a certainty that a business enterprise that occasionally discounts short-term notes payable at its bank will always have prepaid interest at the end of each fiscal year? Explain.

(c) Would it be logical to record prepayments of type (a) as assets and prepayments of type (b) as expenses? Discuss.

11. The real estate tax rate in a certain county is $36.40 per thousand dollars of valuation. (a) What is the tax rate per dollar of valuation? (b) What is the tax rate stated as a percent?

12. Identify the following as realty, tangible personalty, or intangible personalty: (a) shares of stock, (b) typewriter, (c) heating pipes installed in a building, (d) office desk, (e) notes receivable, (f) metal fence around parking lot, (g) building, (h) accounts receivable, (i) cash in bank.

13. At the end of the first month of the year, the Meadowbrook Company estimates its property taxes at $2,400 for such year. Give the adjusting entry to be recorded on the books of Meadowbrook Company.

14. During the first three months of the year, J. D. Barker & Co. records accruals of estimated property tax of $400 a month. The tax statement received in the fourth month is for $4,200, which means that the actual tax accrual is $350 a month. Give the adjusting entry to be recorded at the end of the fourth month.

15. After closing and reversing entries have been posted and before any time has elapsed, balances in certain accounts are as follows:

(a) Unearned Rent, credit of $900.
(b) Interest Income, debit of $210.
(c) Prepaid Insurance, debit of $630.
(d) Salary Expense, credit of $1,100.

Identify each of the foregoing items as (1) asset or (2) liability.

16. Is it possible to determine by examination of the unadjusted trial balance whether a particular type of prepaid expense has been recorded as an asset or as an expense? Explain.

17. There are balances in each of the following accounts after adjustments have been made at the end of the fiscal year. Identify each as (1) asset, (2) liability, (3) revenue, or (4) expense.

(a) Prepaid Interest
(b) Insurance Expense
(c) Interest Payable
(d) Supplies
(e) Interest Income
(f) Unearned Rent
(g) Salary Expense
(h) Interest Receivable
(i) Prepaid Insurance
(j) Interest Expense
(k) Rent Income
(l) Rent Expense

EXERCISES

1. The office supplies inventory of the Peerless Company at the beginning of the fiscal year is $225, purchases of office supplies during the year total $595, and the inventory at the end of the year is $260.

(a) Assuming that the accountant initially records office supplies as an asset, set up T accounts for Office Supplies and Office Supplies Expense, and record the following directly in the two accounts, identifying each entry by number: (1) opening balance; (2) purchases for the period; (3) adjusting entry at end of the period; (4) closing entry; (5) reversing entry, if appropriate.

(b) Assuming that the accountant initially records office supplies as an expense, set up T accounts for Office Supplies and Office Supplies Expense and follow the remaining instructions in (a) above.

2. (a) Set up T accounts for Salary Expense, Expense and Revenue Summary, and Salaries Payable, and enter a balance of $64,850 in Salary Expense as of December 26.
   (b) Record the following entries directly in the T accounts:
      (1) Record accrued salaries of $1,100 as of December 31, the end of the fiscal year.
      (2) Close the salary expense account as of December 31.
      (3) Reverse the adjusting entry as of January 1.
      (4) Record the debit for salaries of $1,350 paid on January 2.
   (c) Answer the following questions:
      (1) Is the balance of the salary expense account on January 1 an asset, a liability, a revenue, or an expense?
      (2) What is the balance of the salary expense account on January 2?
      (3) Of the $1,350 salary payment on January 2, how much is expense of January?
      (4) If there had been no reversing entry on January 1, how should the debit for the salary payment of January 2 have been recorded?

3. In their first year of operations the Crown Publishing Co. receives $215,000 from advertising contracts and $142,000 from magazine subscriptions, crediting the two amounts to Advertising Income and Circulation Income, respectively. At the end of the year the deferral of advertising revenue amounts to $65,000 and the deferral of circulation revenue amounts to $48,000. (a) If no adjustments are made at the end of the year, will income for the year be overstated or understated, and by what amount? (b) Present the adjusting entries that should be made at the end of the year. (c) Present the entries to close the two revenue accounts. (d) Present the reversing entries, if appropriate.

4. (a) Present entries, in general journal form, for the following:
   Nov. 21. Issued to J. T. Walker, Inc., on account, an $8,000, 60-day, 6% note dated November 21.
   Dec. 31. Recorded an adjusting entry for accrued interest on the note of November 21.
   31. Closed the interest expense account. The only entry in this account originated from the above adjustment.
   Jan. 1. Recorded a reversing entry for accrued interest.
   20. Paid J. T. Walker, Inc. $8,080 on the note due today.
   (b) Set up T accounts for Interest Payable and Interest Expense and post the foregoing entries.
   (c) What is the balance in Interest Expense after the entry of January 20?
   (d) How many days' interest on $8,000 at 6% does the amount reported in (c) represent?

5. Included among the accounts on an unadjusted trial balance at the end of the year are Prepaid Insurance, with a debit balance of $670, and Insurance Expense, with a debit balance of $960. The amount of insurance premiums applicable to future periods is determined to be $1,030.
   (a) Assuming that in the future insurance is to be recorded as an expense, present journal entries for: (1) adjusting the accounts; (2) closing the appropriate account; and (3) reversing the adjustment, if appropriate.
   (b) Assuming that in the future insurance is to be recorded as an asset, present journal entries for: (1) adjusting the accounts; (2) closing the appropriate account; and (3) reversing the adjustment, if appropriate.

6. The entries in the following account that are identified by letters are related to the work of the periodic summary. (1) Identify each entry as adjusting, closing, or reversing and (2) present the title of the account to which the offsetting debit or credit was posted.

INTEREST INCOME

Date		Items	Debit	Credit	Balance Debit	Balance Credit
Jan.	1	(a)	50		50	
	1	(b)		65		15
Jan. to Dec.	1 31	Transactions during the year		530		545
	31	(c)		45		590
	31	(d)	25			565
	31	(e)	565		—	—
Jan.	1	(f)	45		45	
	1	(g)		25	20	

7. The real estate tax rate for Richmond is $37.29 per thousand dollars of valuation. Equipment used in business is subject to tax at one half the real estate rate. On tax listing day, the total cost of all equipment recorded in the accounts of Barton Co. is $63,500; accumulated depreciation determined in accordance with the regulations of the taxing authority totals $21,400. Determine the property tax on the equipment.

PROBLEMS

9-1. The accounts listed below appear in the ledger of Sunset Realty at December 31, the end of the current fiscal year. None of the year-end adjustments has been recorded.

113	Interest Receivable	$ —	411	Rental Income	$83,800
114	Supplies	460	511	Salary and Commissions Expense	18,200
115	Prepaid Insurance	1,200	513	Advertising Expense	2,900
116	Prepaid Advertising	—	514	Insurance Expense	—
117	Prepaid Interest	—	515	Supplies Expense	—
213	Salaries and Commissions Payable	—	611	Interest Income	380
215	Unearned Rent	—	711	Interest Expense	520
313	Expense and Revenue Summary	—			

The following information relating to adjustments at December 31 was obtained from physical inventories, supplementary records, and other sources:

(a) Interest accrued on notes receivable at December 31, $72.
(b) Inventory of supplies at December 31, $130.
(c) The insurance record indicates that $390 of insurance has expired during the year.
(d) Of a prepayment of $800 for advertising space in a local newspaper, 30% has been used and the remainder will be used in the following year.

(e) A short-term non-interest-bearing note payable was discounted at a bank in December. The amount of the total discount of $150 applicable to December is $60.
(f) Salaries and commissions accrued at December 31, $1,460.
(g) Rent collected in advance that will not be earned until the following year, $4,740.

Instructions: (1) Open the accounts listed and record the balances as of December 31.

(2) Journalize the adjusting entries and post to the appropriate accounts after each entry. Identify the postings by writing "Adjusting" in the items columns.

(3) Prepare a compound journal entry to close the revenue accounts and another compound entry to close the expense accounts.

(4) Post the closing entries. Identify the postings by writing "Closing" in the items columns.

(5) Prepare the reversing journal entries that should be made on January 1 and post to the appropriate accounts after each entry. Write "Reversing" in the items columns.

9-2. Sands Co. closes its books annually on December 31. All relevant data regarding notes payable and interest from November 1 through February 14 of the following year are presented below. (All notes are dated as of the day they are issued.)

Nov. 11. Issued a $6,000, 6%, 90-day note on account.
Dec. 1. Issued a $4,000, 6%, 60-day note on account.
16. Borrowed $8,000 from Citizens National Bank, issuing a 6%, 60-day note.
20. Paid principal, $3,500, and interest, $70, on note payable due today.
31. Recorded an adjusting entry for the interest accrued on the notes dated November 11, December 1, and December 16. There are no other notes outstanding on this date.
31. Recorded the entry to close the interest expense account.
Jan. 1. Recorded a reversing entry for the accrued interest.
12. Issued a $7,000, 6%, 30-day note on account.
30. Paid $4,040 on the note issued on December 1.
Feb. 9. Paid $6,090 on the note issued on November 11.
11. Paid $7,035 on the note issued on January 12.
14. Paid $8,080 on the note issued on December 16.

Instructions: (1) Open accounts for Interest Payable (Acct. No. 214) and Interest Expense (Acct. No. 711), and record a debit balance of $463 in the latter account as of November 1 of the current year.

(2) Present entries, in general journal form, to record the transactions and other data described above, posting to the two accounts after each entry affecting them.

(3) If the reversing entry were not made as of January 1, how would the four interest payments subsequent to that date be recorded? Arrange your answers in this form:

Note (face amount)	Dr. Interest Payable	Dr. Interest Expense

9-3. The following information was obtained from a review of the ledger and other records of Carson Company at the close of the current fiscal year ended December 31:

(a) Office Supplies Expense has a debit balance of $290 at December 31. The inventory of supplies on hand at that date totals $160.

(b) Prepaid Advertising has a debit balance of $2,340 at December 31, which represents the advance payment on October 1 of a yearly contract for a uniform amount of space in 52 consecutive issues of a weekly publication. As of December 31, advertisements had appeared in 13 issues of the publication.

(c) Prepaid Insurance has a debit balance of $1,473 at December 31. Details of the premiums expired during the past year are as follows:

Policy No.	Monthly Premium Expiration	Expiration Applicable To Past Year
1487	$ 9	12 months
3642X	17	10 months
8326AB	13	7 months
6173	11	5 months

(d) Notes Receivable has a debit balance of $7,000 at December 31. The two notes on hand, both of which were accepted at face value, are as follows:

Date	Face	Term	Interest Rate
Nov. 16	$4,000	60 days	6%
Dec. 11	3,000	90 days	6%

(e) Rent Expense has a debit balance of $5,200 on December 31, which includes rent of $400 for January for the following year, paid on December 31.

(f) Mortgage Payable has a credit balance of $30,000 at December 31. Interest at the rate of 5% is payable semiannually on March 31 and September 30. No entry has been made for the interest accrued since September 30.

(g) Unearned Rent has a credit balance of $1,200, composed of the following: (1) January 1 balance of $240, representing rent prepaid for January through April, and (2) a credit of $960 representing payment for annual rent at $80 a month, beginning May 1.

Instructions: (1) Journalize the adjusting entries as of December 31 of the current fiscal year.

(2) Journalize the reversing entries that should be made as of January 1 of the succeeding fiscal year.

If the working papers correlating with the textbook are not used, omit Problem 9-4.

9-4. The J. T. Parker Company prepares interim financial statements at the end of each month and closes its books annually on December 31. Its income statement for the two-month period, January and February of the current year, is presented in the working papers. In addition, the trial balance of the ledger as of one month later is presented on an eight-column work sheet in the working papers. Data needed for adjusting entries at March 31, the end of the three-month period, are as follows:

(a) Estimated merchandise inventory at March 31, $81,460.
(b) Insurance expired during the three-month period:
 Allocable as selling expense, $190.
 Allocable as general expense, $75.
(c) Estimated inventory of store supplies at March 31, $280.
(d) Included in notes payable is a $10,000, 90-day, non-interest-bearing note discounted at Merchants Bank and Trust Co. on March 1. The $150 discount was debited to Interest Expense.
(e) Depreciation for the three-month period:
 Store equipment, $400.
 Office equipment, $100.
(f) Estimated property tax of $120 a month was accrued for January and February. The tax statement, which was received in March, indicates a liability of $1,680 for the calendar year.
(g) Salaries accrued at March 31:
 Sales salaries, $250.
 Office salaries, $55.
(h) Included in notes payable is a $2,000, 6%, 6-month note dated December 1 of the preceding year. (Accrue interest for 4 months.)

Instructions: (1) Complete the eight-column work sheet for the three-month period ended March 31 of the current year.

(2) Prepare an income statement for the three-month period, using the last three-column group of the nine-column form in the working papers.

(3) Prepare an income statement for the month of March, using the middle three-column group of the nine-column form in the working papers.

(4) Prepare a capital statement for the three-month period. There were no additional investments during the period.

(5) Prepare a balance sheet as of March 31.

9-5. The Buckeye Co. prepares interim statements at the end of each month and closes its books annually on December 31. Property taxes are assessed for fiscal years beginning on July 1 and ending on June 30. Selected transactions and property tax allocations for the period July 1 to December 31 of one year and of January 1 to June 30 of the following year are presented below.

July 31. Property tax allocation for July based on estimated property tax of $6,000 for the taxing authority's fiscal year beginning July 1.
Sept. 30. Property tax allocation for September, based on tax statement dated September 20 indicating a tax assessment of $6,504.
Oct. 15. Paid first half of tax assessment, $3,252.
 31. Property tax allocation for October.
Dec. 31. Property tax allocation for December.
Jan. 31. Property tax allocation for January.
May 15. Paid second half of tax assessment, $3,252.
 31. Property tax allocation for May.
June 30. Property tax allocation for June.

Instructions: Present, in general journal form, the entries to record the selected tax allocations and payments, assuming in all cases that appropriate entries have been recorded in the books for all intervening months.

9-6. Transaction and adjustment data related to a prepaid expense and an unearned income are summarized below.

(a) Balance of prepaid advertising at January 1, the beginning of the fiscal year, $800 (for two months beginning on January 1).
Additional advertising paid, $3,600 (for one year beginning on May 1).

(b) Balance of unearned rent at January 1, $4,200.
Additional rentals collected during the year, $97,000.
Unearned rent at the end of the fiscal year, $5,800.

Instructions: (1) Open accounts for Prepaid Advertising, Advertising Expense, Unearned Rent, and Rent Income. Record the following directly in the accounts: (a) opening balances, (b) summary transactions for the year, (c) adjusting entries at December 31, (d) closing entries at December 31, and (e) reversing entries at January 1, if appropriate. Employ the system of initially recording prepaid expense as an asset and unearned revenue as a liability, and identify the nature of the entries in the items columns.

(2) Open a duplicate set of accounts and follow the remaining instructions in Instruction (1) except to employ the system of initially recording prepaid expense as expense and unearned revenue as revenue.

(3) Determine the amounts that would appear in the balance sheet at December 31 as asset and liability respectively, and in the income statement for the year as expense and revenue respectively, according to the method employed in Instruction (1) and the method employed in Instruction (2). Present your answers in the following form:

Method	Asset	Expense	Liability	Revenue
Instruction (1)	$	$	$	$
Instruction (2)				

9-7. Selected accounts from the ledger of Greenbrier Co., with the account balances before and after adjustment, at the close of the fiscal year are:

	Unadjusted Balance	Adjusted Balance		Unadjusted Balance	Adjusted Balance
Interest Receivable . . .	$ —	$ 70	Rent Income.	$ 9,100	$ 8,400
Supplies.	1,250	590	Wages Expense.	24,650	24,825
Prepaid Insurance. . . .	1,410	970	Depreciation Expense—Equipment.	—	500
Prepaid Property Tax.	100	—	Supplies Expense. . . .	—	660
Prepaid Interest.	—	60	Property Tax Expense	1,300	1,400
Accumulated Depreciation—Equipment.	2,700	3,200	Insurance Expense. . .	—	440
Wages Payable.	—	175	Interest Income.	460	530
Interest Payable.	—	40	Interest Expense.	300	280
Unearned Rent.	—	700			

Instructions: (1) Journalize the adjusting entries that were posted to the ledger at the close of the fiscal year.

(2) Insert the letter "R" in the date column opposite each adjusting entry that should be reversed as of the first day of the following fiscal year.

PART FIVE

Receivables, inventory, and plant assets

10. Receivables and merchandise inventory

Classification of receivables

The term *receivables* includes all money claims against individuals, organizations, or other debtors. They are acquired by a business enterprise in various types of transactions, the most common being the sale of merchandise or services on a credit basis. Accounts and notes receivable originating from sales transactions are sometimes referred to as *trade receivables*. In the absence of other descriptive words or phrases, accounts and notes receivable may be assumed to have originated from sales in the usual course of the business.

Other receivables of not infrequent occurrence include interest receivable, loans to officers or employees, and loans to affiliated companies. Separate accounts should be maintained in the general ledger for each type of receivable.

All receivables that are expected to be realized in cash within a year are shown in the current assets section of the balance sheet. Those that are not currently collectible, such as long-term loans, should be listed under the caption "Investments" below the current assets section.

The importance of accounts and notes receivable to a particular enterprise varies with the volume of charge sales and the length of the credit period. For many businesses the revenue from sales on account is the largest factor influencing the amount of net income or loss. Claims against customers may also represent a major portion of current assets.

Uncollectible accounts

When merchandise or services are sold without the immediate receipt of cash, a portion of the claims against customers ordinarily proves to be uncollectible. This is usually the case regardless of the care used in granting credit and the efficacy of the collection procedures employed. The operating expense incurred because of the failure to collect receivables is variously termed an expense or a loss from *uncollectible accounts*, *doubtful accounts*, or *bad debts*.

There is no single general rule for determining when an account or a note becomes uncollectible. Bankruptcy of the debtor is one of the most positive indications of partial or complete worthlessness of a receivable. Other evidence includes discontinuance of the debtor's business, disappearance of the debtor, failure of repeated attempts to collect, and the barring of collection by the statute of limitations.

There are two generally accepted methods of accounting for receivables thought to be uncollectible: (1) the *direct write-off* method and (2) the *allowance* or *reserve* method. These two methods are discussed in the following paragraphs. Both conform to acceptable accounting practice when used in appropriate circumstances. Both are also permissible in determining net income for purposes of federal income tax. Whichever method is adopted should be used consistently from year to year unless changed circumstances indicate the desirability of a change of method.

Direct write-off of uncollectible accounts

If an enterprise sells most of its merchandise or services on a cash basis, the amount of its expense from uncollectible accounts is ordinarily minor in relation to its revenue. The amount of its receivables at any time is also likely to represent a relatively small portion of its total current assets. These observations are based on the assumption that the credit period is short, which would be usual if sales are preponderantly on a cash basis, and that credit policies and collection procedures are adequate. The nature of the service or the product sold and the type of clientele may also have an important bearing on collection experience. For example, an enterprise that sells most of its output on account to a small number of companies, all of which are financially strong, will incur little, if any, expense from inability to collect its accounts.

In such situations, as well as in many small business and professional enterprises, it is satisfactory to defer recognition of uncollectibility until the period in which an account is actually written off. The entry to write off an account believed to be uncollectible is as follows:

May	10	Uncollectible Accounts Expense	717	42	
		Accounts Receivable — D. L. Ross	114/ √		42
		To write off uncollectible account.			

The expense is reported on the income statement as either selling expense or general expense, depending upon the department responsible. Credits and collections may be the responsibility of the sales department or of an independent department within the general administrative framework.

Accounts that have been written off are sometimes collected later. If the recovery is in the same fiscal year as the write-off, the earlier entry should be reversed to reinstate the account. The receipt of cash and the credit to the receivable account are then recorded in the usual manner. To illustrate, assume that the account of D. L. Ross that was written off above is collected in November of the same fiscal year. The entry to reinstate the account would be as follows:

Nov.	21	Accounts Receivable — D. L. Ross	114/ √	42	
		Uncollectible Accounts Expense	717		42
		To reinstate account written off earlier in the year.			

The receipt of cash in payment of the reinstated account would be recorded in the cash receipts journal.

It is evident that the reinstatement entry and the cash entry could be combined into a single entry debiting Cash and crediting Uncollectible Accounts Expense. It is usually considered preferable to record the recovery in the customer's account, however, so that the information will be available for credit purposes in the future.

When an account that has been written off is collected in a subsequent fiscal year, it may be reinstated by an entry like that illustrated above. An alternative is to credit some other appropriately titled account, such as Recovery of Uncollectible Accounts Written Off. The credit balance in such an account at the end of the year may then be reported on the income statement as a deduction from Uncollectible Accounts Expense, or the net expense only may be reported. Such amounts are likely to be relatively minor and to have little effect on net income.

Advance provision for uncollectible accounts

In most large business enterprises it is customary to provide currently for the expense that will result from the future write-off of uncollectible trade receivables acquired in the current period. The allowance method provides for: (1) allocation of the uncollectible accounts expense to the period in which the revenue from the related sales was recognized, and (2) reduction of the receivables to the amount of cash expected to be realized from their collection.

The estimated expense from uncollectible accounts is recorded as an adjusting entry either on a monthly basis or at the end of the fiscal year. For purposes of illustration, a new enterprise is assumed to have accounts receivable of $80,000 on the date selected for the close of its fiscal year. None of the accounts receivable can be identified as wholly or partly worthless at this time, but it is estimated that of the total amount $3,000 will be uncollectible. The amount of uncollectible accounts expense to be allocated to the period just ended is therefore $3,000 and the amount expected to be realized eventually from the accounts receivable is $77,000 ($80,000 – $3,000). The $3,000 reduction in the accounts receivable cannot be allocated among the individual accounts in the subsidiary ledger and should therefore not be credited to the controlling account in the general ledger. The customary practice is to employ a *contra asset* account entitled Allowance for Doubtful Accounts. The adjusting entry to record the expense and the reduction in the asset is as follows:

Dec.	31	Uncollectible Accounts Expense	717	3,000	
		Allowance for Doubtful Accounts	114.1		3,000

In the process of closing the books as of December 31, the balance of $3,000 in Uncollectible Accounts Expense is transferred to Expense and Revenue Summary along with all other expenses. After the adjusting and closing entries have been posted, the asset account, the contra asset account, and the expense account will appear as follows:

ACCOUNTS RECEIVABLE — ACCT. No. 114

Date		Items	Post. Ref.	Debit	Credit	Balance Debit	Balance Credit
1965							
Aug.	31		S3	20,000		20,000	
Sept.	30		S6	25,000		45,000	
	30		CR4		15,000	30,000	
Oct.	31		S10	40,000		70,000	
	31		CR7		25,000	45,000	
Nov.	30		S13	38,000		83,000	
	30		CR10		23,000	60,000	
Dec.	31		S16	50,000		110,000	
	31		CR13		30,000	80,000	

ALLOWANCE FOR DOUBTFUL ACCOUNTS — ACCT. No. 114.1

Date		Items	Post. Ref.	Debit	Credit	Balance Debit	Balance Credit
1965							
Dec.	31	Adjusting	J4		3,000		3,000

UNCOLLECTIBLE ACCOUNTS EXPENSE — ACCT. No. 717

DATE		ITEMS	POST. REF.	DEBIT	CREDIT	BALANCE	
						DEBIT	CREDIT
1965							
Dec.	31	Adjusting	J4	3,000		3,000	
	31	Closing	J4		3,000	—	—

The debit balance of $80,000 in Accounts Receivable is the face amount of the total claims against customers on open account, and the credit balance of $3,000 in Allowance for Doubtful Accounts is the amount to be deducted from Accounts Receivable to determine their expected realizable value. The $3,000 reduction in the asset has been transferred to an expense account and from thence to the expense and revenue summary account where it is combined with other expenses as a deduction from revenues.

The accounts receivable may be listed on the balance sheet at the net amount ($77,000) with a parenthetical notation disclosing the amount of the allowance, or the details may be presented in the following manner:

Winthrop Company
Balance Sheet
December 31, 1965

Assets

Current assets:		
Cash		$ 19,400
Accounts receivable	$80,000	
Less allowance for doubtful accounts	3,000	77,000

When the allowance includes provision for doubtful notes as well as accounts, the allowance should be deducted from the total of Notes Receivable and Accounts Receivable.

Charging doubtful accounts to the allowance account

When the allowance method is employed, the individual accounts thought to be uncollectible are written off against the allowance account in the following manner:

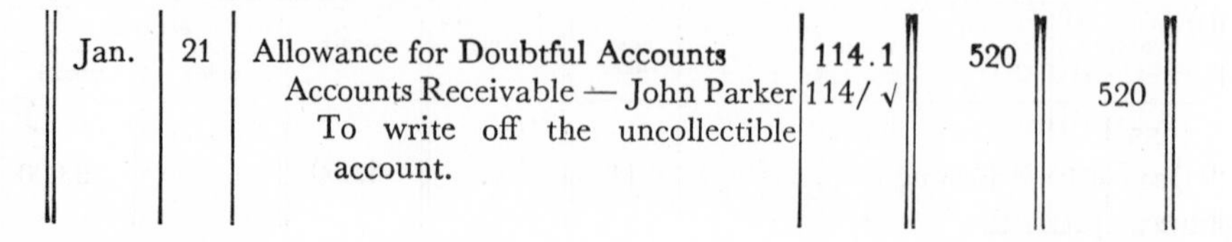

Jan.	21	Allowance for Doubtful Accounts	114.1	520	
		Accounts Receivable — John Parker	114/ √		520
		To write off the uncollectible account.			

It should be noted that the debit is to the contra asset account rather than to the expense account. The reason is that the expense is recorded by the adjusting entry debiting the expense account and crediting the contra asset account. The effect of the write-off is to reduce the asset account and the contra asset account by the same amount. That it has no effect on the amount of cash expected to be realized from the accounts receivable is demonstrated below.

	Accounts Receivable	−	Allowance for Doubtful Accounts	=	Realizable Amount
Balance before write-off...	$80,000		$3,000		$77,000
Less write-off...........	520		520		—
Balance after write-off....	$79,480		$2,480		$77,000

As additional accounts are determined to be worthless during the year, the amounts are written off against Allowance for Doubtful Accounts. If a portion of an account is collected and the balance is uncollectible because of bankruptcy or other reasons, the amount collected is recorded in the cash receipts journal in the usual manner and the remainder is written off by a general journal entry.

Instructions for write-offs should originate with the credit manager or other designated official. The authorizations, which should always be written, serve as objective evidence in support of the accounting entry.

Naturally enough, the sum of the receivables written off is rarely in exact agreement with the amount provided in the allowance account. If the adjusting entry debiting the expense account and crediting the allowance account is not made until the end of the year, the allowance account may have either a credit balance or a debit balance immediately before the annual adjustment. The existence of a debit balance does not necessarily indicate that the allowance was inadequate. It may have resulted from write-offs of receivables acquired in the current year. Provision for receivables acquired in the current year, including those already written off, will be made in the year-end adjusting entry. After the adjusting entry is recorded, the allowance account will of course have a credit balance.

When an account that has been charged to the allowance account is subsequently collected, the account should be reinstated by an entry that is just the reverse of the write-off entry. As was pointed out earlier, the purpose of the reinstatement is to provide information that will be useful in re-establishing the customer's credit.

Assuming that John Parker, whose account of $520 was written off on January 21, pays in full on June 10, the following entry is made in the general journal:

June	10	Accounts Receivable — John Parker..	114/ √	520	
		Allowance for Doubtful Accounts..	114.1		520
		To reinstate account written off earlier in the year.			

The receipt of $520 from John Parker would be recorded in the cash receipts journal in the usual manner.

Estimating uncollectible accounts expense

The estimate of uncollectible accounts expense at the end of the fiscal period is based on past experience modified by forecasts of future business activity. When the trend of general sales volume is upward and there is relatively full employment, the magnitude of the expense should ordinarily be less than when the trend is in the opposite direction. The estimate is customarily based on either (1) the amount of sales for the period or (2) the amount and the age of trade receivables on hand at the end of the fiscal period.

Estimate based on sales. Accounts receivable are acquired as a result of sales on account. The volume of such sales during the year may therefore be used as an indication of the probable amount of the accounts that will be uncollectible. For example, if it is known from past experience that about 1% of charge sales will be uncollectible and the charge sales for a particular year amount to $600,000, the adjusting entry for uncollectible accounts at the end of the year is as follows:

Dec.	31	Uncollectible Accounts Expense.....	717	6,000	
		Allowance for Doubtful Accounts.	114.1		6,000

Instead of charge sales, total sales (including those made for cash) may be used in developing the percentage. The total sales figure is obtainable from the ledger without the necessity for the analysis that may be required to determine charge sales. If the ratio of sales on account to cash sales does not change materially from year to year, the results obtained will be equally satisfactory. For example, if in the example above the balance of the sales account at the end of the year is assumed to be $800,000, the application of ¾ of 1% to that amount would also yield an estimate of $6,000.

If it becomes apparent over a period of time that the amount of the write-offs is consistently greater or less than the amount provided by the adjusting entry, the percentage applied to sales data should be revised accordingly. A newly established business enterprise, having no record of credit experience, may obtain data on the probable amount of the expense from trade association journals and other publications containing information on credit and collections.

Estimate based on analysis of trade receivables. Instead of using sales data, many business enterprises base their estimate on an analysis of the trade receivable accounts at the end of the period. The process of analyzing the accounts is called *aging the receivables.*

The balance of each receivable is classified according to the age of the claim. For example, the age intervals used might be as follows: not due; 0–30 days past due; 31–60 days past due; 61 days–6 months past due; and over 6 months past due. After the amounts in each age group are totaled, a sliding scale of percentages is applied to obtain the estimated uncollectibles in each group, and the group estimates are totaled. The figure thus obtained is the desired balance of the allowance account after adjustment. The excess of this figure over the balance of the allowance account before adjustment is the amount of the current provision to be made for uncollectible accounts expense.

To illustrate the foregoing, assume an analysis of the customers' ledger indicates doubtful accounts of $6,900; also assume that Allowance for Doubtful Accounts before adjustment has a credit balance of $1,100. The amount of the adjustment is therefore $5,800 ($6,900 – $1,100) and the entry is as follows:

Dec.	31	Uncollectible Accounts Expense.....	717	5,800	
		Allowance for Doubtful Accounts.	114.1		5,800

After the adjusting entry is posted, the balance in the allowance account will be $6,900, which is the desired amount. If the balance of the allowance account before adjustment had been a debit of $300, the amount of the adjustment would have been $7,200 ($6,900 + $300).

The use of the analysis of receivables method of determining the uncollectible accounts expense yields a more reasoned estimate of the current realizable value of the receivables and is frequently preferred over the percent of sales method. An inadequate or excessive provision in one period automatically influences the amount of the adjustment for the succeeding period. The percent of sales method lacks this relatively automatic device for keeping the amount of the estimated expense close to the actual net write-offs.

Importance of inventories

The term *inventories* is used to designate merchandise held for sale in the normal course of business and also materials in the process of production or held for such use. The remainder of this chapter is devoted to problems arising in the determination of the inventory of merchandise purchased for resale, commonly called *merchandise inventory.* Consideration will be given in a later chapter to inventories of raw materials and partially processed materials of a manufacturing enterprise.

Merchandise is one of the most active elements in the operation of wholesale and retail businesses, being continuously purchased and sold. The sale of merchandise at more than its cost provides the principal source of revenue for such enterprises. In determining net income, the cost of merchandise sold is the largest deduction from sales; in fact, it is customarily larger than all other deductions combined. In addition, a substantial portion of a merchandising firm's resources is invested in inventory; it is usually the largest of the current assets.

Inventory determination plays an important role in matching costs with revenues of the period. The effect of inventories on the computation of the cost of merchandise sold was illustrated in Chapter 7. An error in the inventory figure will cause a misstatement of net income of equal amount, and in the balance sheet both assets and capital will be incorrectly reported.

Inventory systems

There are two principal systems of inventory accounting, *periodic* and *perpetual.* When the periodic system is employed, only the revenue from sales is recorded each time a sale is made; no entries are made to credit the inventory account or the purchases account for the cost of the merchandise that has been sold. Consequently, it is only by a detailed listing of the merchandise on hand (called a *physical inventory*) at the close of an accounting period that the cost of the inventory can be determined. It is ordinarily feasible to make such a determination, or "take the inventory," only at the end of the fiscal year. When the merchandise inventory can be determined only by a physical measurement at specified intervals, the system can be characterized as *periodic.*

In contrast to the periodic system, the perpetual inventory system employs accounting records that continuously disclose the amount of the inventory. A separate account for each type of merchandise is maintained in a subsidiary ledger. Increases in inventory items are recorded as debits to the appropriate accounts, and decreases are recorded as credits; the balances of the accounts are called the *book* inventories of the items on hand. A physical inventory of each type of goods should be taken at least once a year to determine the accuracy of the perpetual records. The book inventory is then brought into agreement with the physical inventory.

Periodic inventory procedures are ordinarily used by retail enterprises that sell a great variety of low unit cost merchandise, such as groceries, hardware, and drugs. The expense of maintaining perpetual inventory records is likely to be prohibitive in such cases. Firms selling a relatively small number of high unit cost items, such as office equipment, automobiles, or fur garments, are more likely to employ the perpetual system. Most large manufacturing enterprises, as well as many smaller organizations, also use the perpetual system. Periodic procedures will be discussed in the remaining pages of this chapter; perpetual inventory procedures will be given further consideration in later chapters.

Determining quantities in the inventory

The first stage in the process of "taking" an inventory is the determination of the quantity of each type of merchandise owned by the enterprise. Where the periodic system is used, the counting, weighing, and measuring should be done at the end of the accounting period. In order to accomplish this, the inventory crew may work during the night, or business operations may be suspended until the count is completed.

The details of the specific procedures for determining quantities and assembling the data vary considerably among companies. A common practice is to employ two-man teams; one person counts or otherwise determines quantity, and the other lists the description and the quantity on inventory sheets. The count of major items should be verified by a third person at some time during the inventory-taking period.

All of the merchandise owned by the business on the inventory date, and only such merchandise, should be included in the inventory. It may be necessary to examine sales and purchase invoices of the last few days of the accounting period and the first few days of the ensuing period to determine legal title to merchandise in transit on the inventory date. When goods are purchased or sold FOB shipping point, title ordinarily passes to the buyer when the goods are shipped. When the terms are FOB destination, title usually does not pass to the buyer until the goods are delivered. For example, if goods purchased FOB shipping point are shipped on December 31, the last day of the buyer's accounting period, the merchandise will probably not be received until early in January. The purchase should be recorded as of December 31, however, and the goods should be included in the inventory count.

Merchandise may also be transferred to a retailer on a consignment basis, in which case the consignor retains title until the commodities are sold by the retailer. Such merchandise should be included in the consignor's inventory even though he does not have physical possession. The consignee should not, of course, include consigned goods in his inventory.

Determining the cost of inventory

The cost of inventory includes all expenditures incurred in acquiring the merchandise, including purchasing costs, transportation, customs duties, insurance, and storage. Some of these costs may be readily traceable to specific items in the inventory, and others may be prorated over all merchandise on the basis of cost or by some other means. Minor costs that are difficult to allocate may be excluded entirely from inventory cost and treated as operating expenses of the period.

If purchases discounts are treated as a deduction from the invoice price of merchandise purchased, they should also be deducted in assigning costs to items in the inventory. If it is not feasible to determine the exact amount of discount applicable to each item in the inventory, a pro rata amount of the total discount for the period may be deducted from the inventory. For example, if net purchases and purchases discount for the period amount to \$200,000 and \$3,000 respectively, the discount represents 1½% of purchases. If the inventory cost, before considering cash discount, is \$30,000, the amount may be reduced by 1½%, or \$450, to yield an inventory cost of \$29,550.

One of the most significant problems encountered in determining the cost of merchandise on hand is related to the fact that identical units of a commodity may have been acquired at different cost prices during the period. The nature of the problem and its effect on income determination and inventory valuation may be introduced by means of a simple illustration.

Three identical units of a particular commodity have been available for sale during the year. Details of their acquisition and the cost of each are as follows:

Inventory, beginning of year	1 unit	\$ 9
Purchased in March	1 unit	13
Purchased in October	1 unit	14
Total	3 units	\$36
Average cost per unit		\$12

At the end of the year there is one unit of the commodity in the inventory, the other two having been sold. If the unit remaining in the inventory can be specifically identified, the appropriate cost figure can be deducted from the total of \$36 to obtain the cost of the units sold. If identification is not possible, it is necessary to adopt a method of determining the *flow of costs.* Alternative methods of transferring the cost of merchandise to cost of merchandise sold are as follows: (1) in the order in which the expenditures were made, (2) in accordance with the average of the expenditures, and (3) in the reverse of the order in which the expenditures were made. The cost of merchandise sold and the cost of the inventory obtained by each of the methods are presented below.

Assumed Cost Flow	Cost of 3 Units Available		Cost of 2 Units Sold		Cost of 1 Unit Remaining
In order of expenditures	$36	–	$22 ($ 9 + $13)	=	$14
In accordance with average expenditures	36	–	24 ($12 + $12)	=	12
In reverse order of expenditures	36	–	27 ($14 + $13)	=	9

The application of the three methods produces widely disparate amounts for the cost of merchandise sold and the inventory cost. These differences would continue on through the determination of gross profit on sales and net income.

In actual practice it may be possible to identify units with specific invoices if both the variety of merchandise carried in stock and the volume of sales are relatively small. Ordinarily, however, specific identification procedures are too laborious and costly to justify their use. It is customary, therefore, to employ a system based on an assumed flow of costs rather than to attempt specific identification.

First-in, first-out method. The first-in, first-out (*fifo*) method of costing inventory is based on the assumption that costs should be charged against revenue in the order in which they were incurred. Hence the inventory remaining is assumed to be composed of the most recent costs. The illustration of the application of this method is based on the following data for a particular commodity:

Jan. 1	Inventory	200 units at $ 9	$ 1,800
Mar. 10	Purchase	300 units at 10	3,000
Sept. 21	Purchase	400 units at 11	4,400
Nov. 18	Purchase	100 units at 12	1,200
Available for sale during year		1,000	$10,400

The physical count on December 31 indicates that 300 units of the commodity are on hand. In accordance with the assumption that the inventory is composed of the most recent costs, the cost of the 300 units is determined as follows:

Most recent costs, Nov. 18	100 units at $12	$1,200
Next most recent costs, Sept. 21	200 units at 11	2,200
Inventory, Dec. 31	300	$3,400

Deduction of the inventory ($3,400) from merchandise available for sale ($10,400) yields $7,000 as the cost of merchandise sold, which represents the earliest costs incurred for this particular commodity.

In most businesses there is a tendency to dispose of commodities in the order of their acquisition. This would be particularly true of perishable merchandise and other goods in which style or model changes are frequent. Thus the fifo method is generally in harmony with the physical movement of merchandise in an enterprise. To the extent that this is the case, the fifo method approximates the results that would be obtained by specific identification of costs.

Last-in, first-out method. The last-in, first-out (*lifo*) method is based on the assumption that the most recent costs incurred should be charged against revenue. Hence the inventory remaining is assumed to be composed of the earliest costs. Based on the illustrative data presented in the preceding section, the cost of the inventory is determined in the following manner:

Earliest costs, Jan. 1	200 units at $ 9	$1,800
Next earliest costs, Mar. 10	100 units at 10	1,000
Inventory, Dec. 31	300	$2,800

Deduction of the inventory ($2,800) from merchandise available for sale ($10,400) yields $7,600 as the cost of merchandise sold, which represents the most recent costs incurred for this particular commodity.

The use of the lifo method was originally confined to the relatively rare situations in which the units sold were taken from the most recently acquired stock. Its use has greatly increased during the past two decades and it is now employed without regard to the actual physical flow of commodities.

Weighted average method. The weighted average method is based on the assumption that costs should be charged against revenue on the basis of an average, taking into consideration the number of units acquired at each price. The same average unit cost is employed in computing the cost of the merchandise remaining in the inventory. The weighted average is determined by dividing the total costs of a commodity available for sale by the total number of units of that commodity available for sale. Assuming the same cost data as in the preceding illustrations, the weighted average cost of the 1,000 units and the cost of the inventory are determined as follows:

Weighted average cost	$10,400 ÷ 1,000 = $10.40 per unit	
Inventory, Dec. 31	300 units at $10.40	$3,120

Deduction of the inventory ($3,120) from merchandise available for sale ($10,400) yields $7,280 as the cost of merchandise sold, which represents the average of the costs incurred for this particular commodity.

For businesses in which various purchases of identical units of a commodity are mingled, the weighted average method has some relationship to the physical flow of inventory.

Comparison of inventory costing methods. Each of the three alternative methods of costing inventories under the periodic system is based on a different assumption as to the flow of costs. If the cost of commodities and the prices at which they were sold remained perfectly stable, all three methods would yield the same results. Prices do not remain stable, however, and as a consequence the three methods will ordinarily yield different amounts for both (1) the inventory at the end of the period and (2) the cost of the merchandise sold during the period. The examples presented in the preceding sections illustrated the effect of rising prices. They may be summarized as follows:

	First-in, First-out	Last-in, First-out	Weighted Average
Merchandise available for sale	$10,400	$10,400	$10,400
Merchandise inventory, December 31	3,400	2,800	3,120
Cost of merchandise sold	$ 7,000	$ 7,600	$ 7,280

In comparing and evaluating the results obtained in the illustration, it should be borne in mind that both the amount reported as net income and the amount reported as inventory are affected. The method that yields the lowest figure for the cost of merchandise sold will yield the highest figure for gross profit and net income reported on the income statement; it will also yield the highest figure for inventory reported on the balance sheet. Conversely, the method that yields the highest figure for the cost of merchandise sold will yield the lowest figure for gross profit and net income and the lowest figure for inventory.

During periods of consistently rising prices the use of first-in, first-out yields the highest possible amount of net income. The reason for this effect is that business enterprises increase their selling prices in accordance with market trends, regardless of the fact that merchandise in stock was acquired before the price increase. In periods of declining prices the effect is reversed and the fifo method yields the lowest possible net income. The principal criticism of the fifo method is this tendency to accentuate the effect of inflationary and deflationary trends on reported income. On the other hand, the amount reported for inventory on the balance sheet will closely approximate its current replacement cost, which is advantageous.

During periods of consistently rising prices the use of last-in, first-out yields the lowest possible amount of net income. The reason for this effect is that the cost of the most recently acquired units most nearly approximates the expenditure required to replace the units sold. In periods of declining prices the effect is reversed and the lifo method yields the highest possible net income. The principal justification for lifo is this tendency to minimize the effect of price trends on reported net income. A criticism of the general use of lifo is its complete lack of relationship to the physical flow of merchandise in most enterprises. The amount reported for inventory on the balance sheet may also be quite far removed from current replacement cost, which is undesirable. If there is little change in the physical composition of the inventory from year to year, the inventory cost reported remains nearly constant, regardless of extreme changes in price levels.

The weighted average method of inventory costing is, in a sense, a compromise between fifo and lifo. The effect of price trends is averaged, both in the determination of net income and the determination of inventory cost. For any given series of acquisitions, the weighted average cost will be the same regardless of the direction of price trends. For example, a complete reversal of the sequence of acquisitions and unit costs presented in the illustration on page 235 would not affect the reported net income or the inventory cost. The time required to assemble the data is likely to be greater for the weighted average method than for the other two methods. The additional expense incurred could be significant if there are numerous purchases of a wide variety of merchandise items.

All three methods of inventory costing are acceptable in determining income subject to the federal income tax.

The foregoing comparisons are indicative of the many factors that management should consider in selecting the inventory costing method. The method selected must be consistently employed from year to year. A change may be made only if there are sufficient reasons, but frequent changes in method are not justifiable.

Valuation at cost or market, whichever is lower

An alternative to stating the inventory at cost is to compare cost with market price and to value the inventory at the lower of the two. It should be borne in mind throughout the following discussion that in any case it is necessary first to determine the cost of the inventory. "Market," as used in the phrase *cost or market, whichever is lower*, is interpreted to mean the replacement cost of the merchandise on the inventory date. To the extent practicable, the market or replacement price should be based on quantities typically purchased from the usual source of supply. A decline in the market price is ordinarily accompanied by a reduction in the selling price. Recognition of the inventory decline charges the loss to the period in which it was incurred. For example, assume that the cost assigned to the inventory by one of the methods described in the preceding section is $50,000 and that because of a market decline in some of the items the inventory could be replaced for $46,000. If the inventory is valued at the lower figure, the reported cost of merchandise sold will be increased by $4,000 and the gross profit and the net income for the period will be reduced by the same amount.

The lower of cost or market rule may be applied to (1) individual items in the inventory, (2) independent categories or departments, or (3) the inventory as a whole. The three methods are illustrated in the tabulation below.

			Cost or Market, Whichever Is Lower		
	Cost	Market	Each Item	Each Dept.	Inventory Total
Dept. 1					
Commodity A.........	$ 5,950	$ 6,000	$ 5,950		
Commodity B.........	6,470	6,230	6,230		
	$12,420	$12,230		$12,230	
Dept. 2					
Commodity C.........	$ 4,300	$ 3,900	3,900		
Commodity D.........	5,600	6,300	5,600		
	$ 9,900	$10,200		9,900	
Total..................	$22,320	$22,430			$22,320
Inventory valuation......			$21,680	$22,130	$22,320

The lower of cost or market rule is customarily applied to each individual item in determining the inventory valuation. It usually yields the most conservative valuation, as in the illustration above. In any event, the total obtained by application to each item will never exceed the total obtained by either of the other two methods of applying the rule.

As with the method selected for determining the cost of the inventory, valuation at either (1) cost or (2) cost or market, whichever is lower, must be followed consistently from year to year. Both methods are acceptable for determining income for federal income tax purposes, except that when the last-in, first-out procedure is employed in determining cost, the inventory must be stated at cost. Another income tax rule that may be noted is that if cost or market, whichever is lower, is elected, the procedure must be applied to each item in the inventory.

Retail method of inventory costing

An additional method of inventory costing that is widely used by retail businesses, particularly department stores, is called the *retail inventory method.* It is employed in connection with the periodic system of inventories and is based on the relationship of the cost of merchandise available for sale to the retail price of the same merchandise. The retail prices of all merchandise acquired are accumulated in supplementary records, and the inventory at retail is determined by deducting sales for the period from the retail price of the goods that were available for sale during the period. The inventory at retail is then converted to cost on the basis of the ratio of the cost of the merchandise available for sale to the selling price of the merchandise available for sale.

Determination of the inventory by the retail method is illustrated as follows:

	COST	RETAIL
Merchandise inventory, January 1	$19,400	$ 36,000
Purchases in January (net)	42,600	64,000
Merchandise available for sale	$62,000	$100,000
Ratio of cost to retail price: $\frac{\$62,000}{\$100,000} = 62\%$		
Sales for January (net)		70,000
Merchandise inventory, January 31, at retail price		$ 30,000
Merchandise inventory, January 31, at estimated cost price ($30,000 × 62%)		$ 18,600

There is an inherent assumption in the retail method that the composition or "mix" of the goods in the ending inventory, in terms of percent of cost to selling price, is comparable to the entire stock of merchandise available for sale. For example, in the illustration above it is unlikely that the retail price of every item was composed of exactly 62% cost and 38% gross profit margin. It is assumed, however, that the weighted average of the cost percentages of the merchandise in the inventory ($30,000) is the same as in the merchandise available for sale ($100,000). Where the inventory is composed of different classes of merchandise with significantly different gross profit rates, the cost percentages and the inventory should be developed separately for each section or department.

The use of the retail method does not eliminate the necessity for taking a physical inventory at the end of the year. The items are recorded on the inventory sheets at their selling prices instead of their cost prices, however. The physical inventory at selling price is then converted to cost by applying the ratio of the cost of merchandise available for sale to the selling price of the same merchandise. To illustrate, assume that the data presented in the example above are for an entire fiscal year rather than for the first month of the year only. If the physical inventory taken on

December 31, priced at retail, totaled $29,000, it would be this amount rather than the $30,000 in the illustration that would be converted to cost. Accordingly, the inventory at cost would be $17,980 ($29,000 × 62%) instead of $18,600 ($30,000 × 62%).

The advantages of the retail method of inventory costing are as follows:

(1) Inventories for use in preparing interim statements may be obtained without the necessity of a physical count.
(2) Elimination of the necessity of determining unit costs when taking the physical inventory results in a saving of time and expense.
(3) Comparison of the physical inventory at retail with the computed inventory at retail provides management with a check on inventory shortages.

Presentation of merchandise inventory on the balance sheet

Merchandise inventory is customarily presented on the balance sheet immediately below receivables. Both the method of determining the cost of the inventory (lifo, fifo, or average) and the method of valuing the inventory (cost, or lower of cost or market) should be disclosed. Both are significant to the reader. The details may be disclosed by a parenthetical notation or a footnote. The use of a parenthetical notation is illustrated by the following partial balance sheet:

Winthrop Company
Balance Sheet
December 31, 1965

Assets		
Current assets:		
Cash		$19,400
Accounts receivable	$80,000	
Less allowance for doubtful accounts	3,000	77,000
Merchandise inventory — at lower of cost (first-in, first-out method) or market		$216,300

It is not unusual for manufacturers and other large enterprises with diversified activities to use different costing and pricing methods for different segments of their inventories. The following note from the balance sheet of a merchandising chain is illustrative: "Merchandise inventories in stores are stated at the lower of cost or market, as calculated by the retail method of inventory. Merchandise in warehouses and in transit and food products inventories in restaurants are stated at cost."

Gross profit method of estimating inventories

When perpetual inventories are maintained or when the retail inventory method is used, the inventory on hand may be closely approximated at any time without the necessity of a physical count. In the absence of these devices the inventory may be estimated by the *gross profit method*, which utilizes an estimate of the gross profit realized on sales during the period.

If the rate of gross profit on sales is known, the dollar amount of sales for a period can be divided into its two components: (1) gross profit and (2) cost of merchandise sold. The latter may then be deducted from the cost of merchandise available for sale to yield the inventory of merchandise on hand.

To illustrate this method, assume that the inventory on January 1 is $17,000, that net purchases during the month amount to $9,000, that net sales during the month amount to $15,000, and finally that gross profit is *estimated* to be 30% of net sales. The inventory on January 31 may be estimated as follows:

Merchandise inventory, January 1		$17,000
Purchases in January (net)		9,000
Merchandise available for sale		$26,000
Sales in January (net)	$15,000	
Less estimated gross profit ($15,000 × 30%)	4,500	
Estimated cost of merchandise sold		10,500
Estimated merchandise inventory, January 31		$15,500

The estimate of the rate of gross profit may be based on the actual rate for the preceding year, adjusted for any known changes in markups during the current period. Inventories estimated in this manner are useful in preparing interim statements. The method may also be employed in establishing an estimate of the cost of merchandise destroyed by fire.

QUESTIONS

1. Under what caption should a five-year loan to an employee be listed on the balance sheet?

2. Under what circumstances is the direct write-off method of accounting for uncollectible accounts satisfactory?

3. Which of the two methods of accounting for uncollectible accounts provides for recognition of the expense at the earlier date?

4. Why should an account receivable that has been written off be reinstated when it is subsequently collected?

5. Is the normal balance of Allowance for Doubtful Accounts a debit or a credit after the account has been adjusted at the end of the year?

6. The balance of $400 in the account of Johnson & Co. is to be written off because it is considered to be uncollectible. (a) What general ledger account should be credited? (b) What general ledger account should be debited, assuming that: (1) the direct write-off method is used and (2) the allowance method is used?

7. Near the end of the year Allowance for Doubtful Accounts has a credit balance of $400. Doubtful accounts totaling $700 are to be written off. To what account should the $700 be debited?

8. Immediately before writing off an uncollectible account receivable of $500, Accounts Receivable and Allowance for Doubtful Accounts have normal balances of $50,000 and $2,000, respectively. What is the expected realizable value of the accounts receivable (1) before writing off the account and (2) after writing off the account?

9. Merchandise with an inventory value of $6,000 was inadvertently omitted from the physical inventory at the end of the year. (a) Did the error cause a $6,000 overstatement or understatement of the net income for the year? (b) Which items on the balance sheet at the end of the year were overstated or understated by $6,000 as a result of the error?

10. Assume that the error in Question 9 was not discovered and that the inventory at the end of the following year is correctly stated. (a) Will the earlier error cause a $6,000 overstatement or understatement of the net income for the following year? (b) Which items on the balance sheet at the end of the following year will be overstated or understated by $6,000 as a result of the error in the earlier year?

11. When does title to merchandise ordinarily pass from the seller to the buyer when terms of shipment are (a) FOB destination and (b) FOB shipping point?

12. (a) Differentiate between the periodic system and the perpetual system of inventory determination. (b) Which system ordinarily entails the greater amount of operating expense?

13. In which of the following types of businesses would a perpetual inventory system be practicable: (a) retail hardware store, (b) wholesale grocer, (c) sheet steel manufacturer, (d) retail druggist, (e) restaurant, and (f) safe and vault manufacturer?

14. Under which, if any, of the following systems or methods of inventory determination is a periodic physical inventory unnecessary: (a) retail inventory method, (b) perpetual inventory system, (c) gross profit method, (d) periodic inventory system?

15. Does "first-in" in the fifo inventory method refer to identification of the inventory or to the flow of costs? Explain.

16. Under which method of cost flow are (a) the most recent costs assigned to inventory, (b) the earliest costs assigned to inventory, and (c) average costs assigned to inventory?

17. The balances in Purchases and Purchases Discounts at the end of the year are $200,000 and $3,200, respectively. The inventory at the end of the year, at cost without regard to cash discounts, is $50,000. What amount should be deducted from the $50,000 to recognize the effect of the cash discounts?

18. The cost of a particular inventory item is $50, the current replacement cost is $45, and the selling price is $60. At what amount should the item be included in the inventory according to the rule of cost or market, whichever is lower?

19. In the "cost or market, whichever is lower" method of inventory pricing, what is meant by "market"?

20. The unit costs of three lots of Commodity A available for sale during the year are $5, $5.50, and $6, respectively. If the weighted average method of costing is employed, will the unit cost of the lots on hand at the end of the period be $5.50? Explain.

21. Assuming a consistently rising price level, which of the three methods of inventory costing, fifo, lifo, or weighted average, will yield (a) the highest gross profit, (b) the lowest gross profit, (c) the highest inventory cost, and (d) the lowest inventory cost?

22. Which of the three methods of inventory costing, fifo, lifo, or weighted average, will in general yield an inventory cost most nearly approximating current replacement cost?

EXERCISES

1. At the end of the current year the accounts receivable account has a debit balance of $100,000 and net sales for the year total $1,200,000. Determine the amount of the adjusting entry to record the provision for doubtful accounts under each of the following assumptions:

(a) The allowance account before adjustment has a credit balance of $1,300.
   (1) Uncollectible accounts expense is estimated at 1% of net sales.
   (2) Analysis of the accounts in the customers' ledger indicates doubtful accounts of $11,400.

(b) The allowance account before adjustment has a debit balance of $400.
   (1) Uncollectible accounts expense is estimated at ¾ of 1% of net sales.
   (2) Analysis of the accounts in the customers' ledger indicates doubtful accounts of $9,100.

2. The beginning inventory and the purchases of Commodity A for the year are presented below:

	Commodity A
Inventory	20 units at $19.50
Purchase	30 units at $21.00
Purchase	16 units at 20.50
Purchase	14 units at 22.00

Assuming that there are 21 units on hand at the end of the year, determine (a) the cost of the inventory and (b) the cost of merchandise sold by each of the following methods: (1) fifo, (2) lifo, and (3) weighted average.

3. From the following data determine the inventory by applying the rule of cost or market, whichever is lower, (a) to each item in the inventory and (b) to the total inventory.

Commodity	Quantity	Unit Cost	Unit Market
A	100	$1.05	$1.10
B	300	2.20	2.00
C	200	3.50	2.90
D	400	2.10	2.60

4. The cost of four categories of merchandise purchased during the month and the markup are given below. Determine the following for each category: (a) selling price, (b) amount of gross profit, (c) percent of gross profit to selling price, and (d) percent of cost to selling price.

Class	Cost	Markup on Cost
W	$20,000	25%
X	18,000	33 ⅓%
Y	10,000	50%
Z	5,000	100%

5. From the following information determine the estimated cost of the inventory on January 31, presenting the details of the computation:

		Cost	Retail
Jan. 1	Merchandise inventory	$84,200	$130,000
Jan. 1–31	Purchases (net)	46,600	70,000
Jan. 1–31	Sales (net)		60,000

6. The merchandise inventory of Parker's Variety Store was destroyed by fire on April 10. The following data were obtained from the accounting records:

Jan. 1	Merchandise inventory	$28,000
Jan. 1–April 10	Purchases	26,400
	Purchases returns and allowances	1,300
	Sales	51,000
	Sales returns and allowances	200
	Estimated gross profit rate	41%

Estimate the cost of the merchandise destroyed.

PROBLEMS

10-1. The following transactions, adjusting entries, and closing entries related to doubtful accounts were completed during the current fiscal year ending December 31:

Mar. 8. Wrote off the account of H. Harmon, Inc., $290.
May 16. Received $150 from J. B. Sutton in payment of his account, which was written off in the preceding year.

June 24. Received 5% of the $900 balance owed by Blair & Co., a bankrupt, and wrote off the remainder as uncollectible.

Sept. 9. Received $80 from Paul S. Moore in payment of his account, which was written off in the preceding year.

Dec. 30. Wrote off the following accounts as uncollectible (compound entry): Edward Arlen, $410; Dodd & Cromer, $825; I. T. Null Corp., $632; Ray B. Young, $527.

Dec. 31. On the basis of an analysis of the accounts receivable, Allowance for Doubtful Accounts is to be adjusted to a balance of $3,200.

Dec. 31. Recorded the entry to close the appropriate account to Expense and Revenue Summary.

Instructions: (1) Open the following accounts, recording the credit balance indicated as of January 1:

114.1	Allowance for Doubtful Accounts	$2,900
313	Expense and Revenue Summary	—
718	Uncollectible Accounts Expense	—

(2) Record in general journal form the transactions, adjusting entries, and closing entries described above, and post to the three accounts, extending the balance after each entry.

(3) The accounts receivable account has a debit balance of $117,520 at December 31. What is the expected realizable value of the accounts receivable at that date?

(4) Assuming that, instead of basing the provision for uncollectible accounts on an analysis of receivables, the adjusting entry on December 31 had been based on an estimated loss of 1% of net sales for the year of $340,000, determine the following:

(a) Uncollectible accounts expense for the year.

(b) Balance in Allowance for Doubtful Accounts after the adjustment of December 31.

(c) Expected realizable value of the accounts receivable on December 31.

10-2. Details regarding the inventory at January 1, purchases during the year, and the inventory count at December 31 for Bellevue Television are as follows:

Model	Inventory Jan. 1	1st Purchase	2nd Purchase	3rd Purchase	Inventory Count Dec. 31
101	4 at $ 66	8 at $ 69	4 at $ 72	——	3
104	2 at 91	9 at 97	4 at 97	4 at $100	7
315	5 at 150	6 at 150	7 at 159	5 at 165	4
317	——	9 at 225	6 at 240	3 at 249	6
525	7 at 250	6 at 250	5 at 259	7 at 265	8
530	2 at 168	4 at 174	6 at 178	——	4
999	6 at 325	5 at 331	4 at 340	6 at 345	3

Instructions: (1) Determine the cost of the inventory on December 31 by the first-in, first-out method. Present data in columnar form, using the columnar headings indicated below. If more than one unit cost is applied to the inventory of a particular model, use a separate line for each.

Model	Quantity	Unit Cost	Total Cost

(2) Determine the cost of the inventory on December 31 by the last-in, first-out method, following the same procedures prescribed in instruction (1).

(3) Determine the cost of the inventory on December 31 by the weighted average method, using the same columnar headings as in instruction (1).

10-3. Data needed to estimate the merchandise inventory by the retail method and the gross profit method are presented below.

	Cost	Retail
(a) Retail method:		
Merchandise inventory, January 1	$228,300	$353,500
Transactions during January:		
Purchases	103,200	155,500
Purchases discounts	650	
Sales		226,000
Sales returns and allowances		2,900
(b) Gross profit method:		
Merchandise inventory, July 1	$301,400	
Transactions during July and August:		
Purchases	366,400	
Purchases discounts	5,800	
Sales		$508,500
Sales returns and allowances		10,700
Estimated gross profit rate		36%

Instructions: (1) Determine the estimated cost of the inventory on January 31 in (a), presenting details of the computation.

(2) Determine the estimated cost of the inventory on August 31 in (b), presenting details of the computation.

If the working papers correlating with the textbook are not used, omit Problem 10-4.

10-4. Data on the physical inventory of Ward & Co. as of December 31 of the current year are presented in the working papers. The quantity of each commodity on hand has been determined and recorded on the inventory sheet; unit prices obtained from current price quotations and other sources have also been recorded on the sheet. The inventory is to be priced at the lower of cost or market, with cost being determined by the first-in, first-out method. The quantity of each commodity purchased and the unit cost for the last two purchases are summarized on the following page.

	Most recent purchase		Next most recent purchase	
Description	Quantity	Unit Cost	Quantity	Unit Cost
1821A	8	$ 48	20	$ 47
326LM	100	29	100	28
1931M	50	93	35	90
WD190	60	14	150	13
SL911	300	9	300	10
942VW	40	42	70	40
1839B	75	17	50	16
XXX86	250	5	100	5
555FS	175	9	75	8
FC566	60	74	120	74
CS999	96	20	144	19
OPL14	25	210	25	200
E3B1Y	240	15	480	14
JG796	12	250	24	240
MJ630	300	5	600	5
BC042	360	5	120	4
AAA40	48	50	96	47
653ND	500	8	350	6

Instructions: Record the relevant unit cost data on the inventory sheet and complete the pricing of the inventory. When there are two different unit costs applicable to a commodity, rule out the quantity shown on the inventory sheet and substitute the number to which the most recent cost applies. Record the quantity and the unit cost of the remaining portion of the inventory on the following line.

10-5. The following preliminary income statement was prepared before the books were adjusted or closed at the end of the year:

Bradshaw & Co.
Income Statement
For Year Ended September 30, 19--

Sales (net)		$242,000
Cost of merchandise sold:		
Merchandise inventory, October 1, 19--	$ 48,720	
Purchases (net)	173,840	
Merchandise available for sale	$222,560	
Less: Merchandise inventory, September 30, 19--	52,390	
Cost of merchandise sold		170,170
Gross profit on sales		$ 71,830
Operating expenses		51,418
Net income		$ 20,412

The following errors were discovered by the independent accountant retained to conduct the annual audit:

(a) A number of errors were discovered in pricing inventory items, in extending amounts, and in footing inventory sheets. The net effect of the corrections, exclusive of those described below, was to increase by $3,200 the amount stated as the ending inventory on the income statement.
(b) An invoice for merchandise of $400, dated September 28, had been correctly recorded but the merchandise was in transit on September 30 and had not been included in the ending inventory. Title had passed to Bradshaw & Co.
(c) An invoice for merchandise of $1,350, dated September 28, was not received until after September 30 and had not been recorded. The merchandise had arrived, however, and was properly included in the ending inventory.
(d) A sales order for $1,200, dated September 30, had been recorded as a sale but the merchandise was not shipped until October 4. The cost of the merchandise ($900) was not included in the ending inventory.
(e) An item of equipment, received on September 30, was included in the ending merchandise inventory at its cost, $650. The invoice had been recorded correctly.
(f) A sales invoice for $1,100, dated September 30, had not been recorded. The merchandise was shipped on September 30, FOB shipping point, and its cost, $750, was not included in the ending inventory.

Instructions: (1) Journalize any entries necessary to correct accounts in the general ledger, inserting the identifying letters in the date column. All purchases and sales were made on account. (An assistant will make the necessary corrections to the subsidiary ledgers.)

(2) Enter the reported ending inventory of $52,390 in a T account and record the necessary corrections based on the audit, identifying each item by letter.

(3) Prepare a revised income statement.

10-6. The unadjusted trial balance of Italia Importers, distributor of imported motor scooters, as of the end of the current fiscal year, is as follows:

Italia Importers
Trial Balance
June 30, 19--

Cash	13,640	
Notes Receivable	10,000	
Accounts Receivable	15,620	
Allowance for Doubtful Receivables		425
Merchandise Inventory	48,900	
Notes Payable		19,000
Accounts Payable		15,050
R. T. Ranallo, Capital		32,585
R. T. Ranallo, Drawing	12,600	
Sales		232,000
Purchases	149,800	
Operating Expenses (control account)	48,000	
Interest Income		600
Interest Expense	1,100	
	299,660	299,660

Data needed for adjustments at June 30:

(a) The cost of the merchandise inventory is determined by the first-in, first-out method and the rule of the lower of cost or market is applied to each item on hand. The inventory of repair parts and accessories on June 30, determined in accordance with the foregoing, is $6,350. Details regarding the inventory of motor scooters are as follows:

Description	Quantity	Unit Cost	Unit Market
Sport	210	$ 90	$ 95
Continental	120	170	160
Imperial	70	240	230

(b) Expense from the doubtful collectibility of receivables is estimated at ½ of 1% of sales.

(c) Prepaid interest on notes payable, $218.

(d) Interest accrued on notes receivable, $110.

Instructions: (1) Determine the merchandise inventory at June 30.

(2) Journalize the necessary adjusting entries.

(3) Prepare (a) an income statement, (b) a capital statement, and (c) a balance sheet in report form, without the use of a conventional work sheet.

10-7. Universal Sales Co. has just completed its fourth year of operations. The direct write-off method of recording uncollectible accounts expense has been employed during the entire period. The manager of the firm is considering the possibility of changing to the allowance method. Information is requested as to the effect that an annual provision of 1% of sales would have had on the amount of uncollectible accounts expense reported for each of the past four years. It is also considered desirable to know what the balance of Allowance for Doubtful Accounts would have been at the end of each year. The following data have been obtained from the accounts:

			Year in Which Uncollectible Accounts Written Off Were Acquired			
Year	Sales	Uncollectible Accounts Written Off	1st	2nd	3rd	4th
1st	$600,000	$ 600	$ 600			
2nd	700,000	5,500	5,000	$ 500		
3rd	800,000	7,200	500	6,000	$ 700	
4th	900,000	7,700		400	6,500	$ 800

Instructions: (1) Assemble the desired information, using the following columnar captions:

	Uncollectible Accounts Expense			
Year	Expense Actually Reported	Expense Based on 1% of Sales	Increase in Amount of Expense	Balance of Allowance Account, End of Year

(2) Does it appear that the estimate of 1% of sales is reasonably close to the actual experience with uncollectible accounts? Give reasons for your answer.

11.

Plant assets—depreciation

Nature of plant assets

Plant assets may be described as tangible assets of a relatively fixed or permanent nature that are used in the operations of a business. A characteristic that may be inferred from the description is that such assets are not held for sale. Each of the qualities essential for classification as a plant asset is briefly discussed in the paragraphs that follow.

Tangible. Equipment, furniture, buildings, and land are tangible in nature and qualify as plant assets. Intangible properties, such as patents, that possess some of the characteristics of plant assets will be discussed in a later chapter.

Long-lived. Assets that are capable of repeated use and that have a life of at least several years qualify as plant assets. Although there is no standard criterion as to the minimum length of life, assets that are consumed in the process of a single use or over a relatively short period of time are not considered to be long-lived.

Used in the business. Frequent or continuous use of an asset is not essential to classification as a plant asset. For example, standby equipment for use in the event of breakdown of regular equipment or for use during periods of greater than normal business activity is included in plant assets.

Not held for sale. Assets acquired for purposes of resale in the normal course of business are not classified as plant assets regardless of their durability. Land or other long-lived tangible assets acquired as a speculation should not be classified as plant assets. When a plant asset is removed from use and held for sale, it ceases to be a plant asset.

Because of their relative permanency, plant assets are often called *fixed assets.* Other descriptive titles frequently employed are *property, plant,* and *equipment,* used either singly or in various combinations.

Initial costs

The initial cost of a plant asset includes all expenditures necessary to get it in place and ready for use. Unnecessary expenditures resulting from carelessness, vandalism, or other abnormal causes should be excluded. Such items do not add to the utility of the asset and should be charged to operating expenses. For example, if a plant asset is damaged while it is being unloaded or readied for use, the expenditures required to repair the asset should be charged as an expense of the period.

Expenditures incurred for sales taxes, transportation, insurance in transit, installation, or other necessary items should be charged to the plant asset to which they relate. When a secondhand asset is purchased, the initial costs of getting it ready for use, such as expenditures for new parts, repairs, and painting, are properly chargeable to the asset account.

The cost of land includes not only the negotiated price but broker's commissions, title fees, surveying fees, and other expenditures connected with securing title. If delinquent real estate taxes are assumed by the buyer, they also are chargeable to the land account. If buildings are located on land acquired for a plant site, the cost of their razing or removal, less any salvage recovered, is properly chargeable to the land account. The cost of leveling or otherwise permanently changing the contour is also an additional cost of the land.

Other expenditures for improvements to the land, whether paid directly or to a taxing authority as special assessments, are sometimes charged to the land account and at other times to the building account. The controlling factors are the degree of permanency and responsibility for future replacement. For example, if the property owner bears only the initial cost of paving the public street bordering his land, with future repairs and replacements to be borne by the taxing authority, the paving may be considered to be as permanent as the land. On the other hand, the cost of constructing sidewalks leading to a building might well be charged to the building account and depreciated along with the building if both are expected to have the same life span.

When expenditures for improvements are significant in amount, temporary in nature, and of varying life spans, it is preferable to charge them to the account Land Improvements. They can then be depreciated as a distinct category and in all other respects treated as a specific type of plant asset. Some of the more common items included are sewers, underground water systems, paved surfaces, fences, and shrubbery.

The cost of constructing a building includes the fees paid to architects and engineers for plans and supervision, insurance during construction, and all other necessary expenditures applicable to the project. Interest incurred during the construction period on money borrowed to finance a building project should be treated as an expense. It is a payment for the use of funds rather than an essential cost of the building.

Nature of depreciation

All plant assets except land lose their usefulness with the passage of time. The several factors that contribute in varying degrees to this decline in utility are wear, the action of the elements, inadequacy, and obsolescence. Accordingly, the cost of such assets should be charged to expense in a systematic manner during their useful life. This cost expiration that is periodically matched against revenue is called *depreciation.*

The factors contributing to decline in utility may be divided into two categories, *physical* depreciation, which includes wear and deterioration, and *functional* depreciation, which includes inadequacy and obsolescence. A plant asset is said to be inadequate if its capacity is insufficient to meet the needs of the owner. For example, if the capacity of a newspaper press is insufficient to fulfill the demands of increased circulation, it is inadequate regardless of the fact that it is still operating efficiently. A plant asset is obsolete if the product that it produces is no longer in demand or if a newer machine can produce the product at considerably less cost or can produce a product of superior quality. The continued acceleration of technological progress during this century has made obsolescence an increasingly important component of depreciation. Although individual factors comprising depreciation can be defined, it is not feasible to identify them when recording depreciation expense.

The meaning of the term "depreciation" as used in accounting is frequently misunderstood because the same term is also commonly used in business to connote a decline in the market value of an asset. Any similarity between the amount of unexpired cost of plant assets reported in the balance sheet and the amount that could be realized from sale is merely coincidental. Plant assets are held for use rather than for sale, and their market values are irrelevant. It is assumed that the enterprise will continue indefinitely as a going concern. Consequently the decision to dispose of a plant asset is based primarily on its utility to the enterprise rather than the amount that could be realized from its sale.

Another common misconception is that depreciation accounting provides a fund of cash for the replacement of plant assets. Expired portions of the cost of the assets are periodically transferred to expense by debits to depreciation expense accounts and credits to accumulated depreciation accounts. The cash account is not affected by such entries. The confusion originates from the fact that depreciation expense, unlike most expenses, does not require an equivalent outlay of cash in the period in which the expense is recorded.

Recording depreciation

The entry to record depreciation allocates a portion of the cost of plant assets to operating expenses of the period. The portion of the entry that records the decrease in the asset is credited to a *contra asset* account rather than to the plant asset account. The use of a contra asset account, which may be entitled *Accumulated Depreciation, Allowance for Depreciation*, or *Reserve for Depreciation*, permits the original cost to remain undisturbed in the plant asset account. Retaining the original cost in the plant asset accounts serves a number of purposes. It facilitates the computation of periodic depreciation, the listing of plant assets and accumulated depreciation on the balance sheet, and the reporting required for property tax and income tax purposes.

Periodic adjusting entries for depreciation may be recorded on the books monthly or they may be postponed until the close of the year. When the latter alternative is adopted, current depreciation must nevertheless be taken into account when interim statements are prepared. It is also advisable to record the current depreciation on plant assets immediately prior to their disposal, regardless of when such disposal occurs. As will be illustrated later in the chapter, the amount of the accrued depreciation for the year affects the recording of the disposal of the asset. Another reason for recording the depreciation at the time the accounts are relieved of the asset is to eliminate the risk of its being overlooked at the end of the year.

Depreciation methods

The factors to be considered in computing the periodic depreciation of an asset are its (1) cost, (2) estimated residual value, and (3) estimated period of usefulness. The various expenditures that comprise the initial cost of a depreciable asset have already been discussed.

The estimated residual value of a depreciable asset, which is the amount expected to be realized upon its eventual disposition, is frequently termed *scrap*, *salvage*, or *trade-in* value. The excess of cost over the estimated residual value is the amount that is to be charged to depreciation expense during the asset's life. The quantitative relationship between the residual value and the cost of an asset varies considerably among types of assets and among enterprises. For example, the trade-in value of salesmen's automobiles will represent a larger percentage of cost than the scrap value of highly specialized factory machinery. Also, the ratio of trade-in value to cost of salesmen's automobiles will be higher for an enterprise that replaces them annually than for a business that keeps them for three years. When residual value is expected to be insignificant in amount, which is frequently true of buildings, it may be ignored.

The period of usefulness of a depreciable asset must also be estimated. The life of any particular type of plant asset is not necessarily uniform for all enterprises. Climate, frequency of use, maintenance policies, minimum standards of efficiency, and other considerations will affect the estimate. Suggested life estimates for various assets are available in trade association and other publications.

Two publications of the Internal Revenue Service contain life estimates for many kinds of assets used by a wide variety of industries. Bulletin "F," which was last revised in 1942, lists for more than 100 industries the useful lives of both individual assets and also, where practicable, of composite groups. For example, adding machines are estimated to be useful for 10 years, safes for 50 years, and office equipment as a group for 15 years. Revenue Procedure 62-21, which was issued in 1962, contains guidelines for depreciation classified by the following types of enterprises: (1) business in general, (2) manufacturing, (3) transportation, communications, and public utilities, and (4) other nonmanufacturing. The guideline lives are appreciably shorter than those in the earlier publication and they apply to about 75 broad classes of assets rather than to explicitly detailed items of depreciable property. For example, the guideline life for equipment used by a soap manufacturer is 11 years as contrasted with life estimates ranging from 5 years to 40 years on about 180 specific items listed for soap manufacturers in Bulletin "F."

The method of determining depreciation adopted by the management of an enterprise should provide for a reasonable and systematic allocation of asset cost to the periods benefited. It is not necessary that the same method be applied to all classes of depreciable assets. The methods employed in determining the amount of depreciation to be recorded in the accounts may also differ from those used in determining income taxes and property taxes. The depreciation methods most commonly used are (1) straight-line, (2) units-of-production, (3) declining-balance, and (4) sum-of-the-years-digits.

In order to simplify the illustrations that follow, each depreciation method will be applied to a particular item of equipment rather than to a group or class. In such cases a calendar month is commonly the smallest unit of time employed. Thus, an asset placed in service or taken out of service during the first half of a month would be treated as if it had been received or disposed of on the first day of that month. Similarly, additions or reductions during the second half of a month would be considered to have happened on the first day of the following month.

Straight-line method. The straight-line method of determining depreciation provides for equal periodic charges to expense over the estimated life of the asset. To illustrate this method, assume the cost of a depreciable asset to be $15,000, its estimated residual value to be $3,000, and its estimated life to be 10 years. The annual depreciation is computed as follows:

$$\frac{\$15{,}000 - \$3{,}000}{10 \text{ years}} = \$1{,}200 \text{ annual depreciation}$$

The annual depreciation of $1,200 would be prorated for the first and the last partial years of use. Assuming a fiscal year ending on December 31 and first use on September 10, the pro rata depreciation from that date to the end of the year would be $400 (4 months). If usage began on September 19, the pro rata depreciation would be $300 (3 months).

The relationship of the annual depreciation to the total amount to be depreciated is sometimes stated as a percent of the cost of the asset. Thus, in the example, the depreciation rate could be stated as 8% of cost ($1,200 ÷ $15,000). When nominal residual values are excluded from consideration in determining depreciation, the estimated life may be converted directly to a depreciation rate. For example, a life of 40 years is equivalent to a rate of 2½%, a life of 10 years is equivalent to a rate of 10%, and a life of 8 years is equivalent to a rate of 12½%.

The straight-line method is widely used. In addition to its simplicity, it provides a reasonable allocation of costs to periodic revenue when usage is relatively uniform from period to period.

Units-of-production method. The units-of-production method relates depreciation to the estimated productive capacity of the asset. Depreciation is first computed for an appropriate unit of production, such as hours, miles, or number of operations. The depreciation for each period is then determined by multiplication of the unit depreciation by the number of units used during the period. For example, assume that a machine with a cost of $21,000 and estimated residual value of $1,000 is expected to have an estimated life of 40,000 hours. The depreciation for a unit of one hour is computed as follows:

$$\frac{\$21{,}000 - \$1{,}000}{40{,}000 \text{ hours}} = \$.50 \text{ an hour depreciation}$$

Assuming that the machine was in operation for 2,000 hours during a particular year, the depreciation for that year would be $1,000 ($.50 × 2,000).

When the amount of usage of a plant asset varies considerably from period to period, the units-of-production method is preferable to the straight-line method. The necessity of maintaining a record of the amount of usage is a disadvantage, however.

Declining-balance method. The declining-balance method provides a steadily declining periodic depreciation charge over the estimated life of the asset. Of several variants in technique, the one customarily used applies twice the straight-line depreciation rate (without regard to residual value) to the declining book value of the asset. For example, if the estimated life of an asset is 5 years, the depreciation rate is 40% (20% × 2). For the first year the rate is applied to the cost of the asset; in succeeding years it is applied to the declining book value (cost minus accumulated depreciation). The method is illustrated by the following tabulation:

Year	Cost	Accumulated Depreciation at Beginning of Year	Book Value at Beginning of Year	Rate	Depreciation for Year
1	$10,000	—	$10,000	40%	$4,000.00
2	10,000	$4,000	6,000	40%	2,400.00
3	10,000	6,400	3,600	40%	1,440.00
4	10,000	7,840	2,160	40%	864.00
5	10,000	8,704	1,296	40%	518.40

It should be noted that estimated residual value is not considered in determining the depreciation rate. It is also ignored in computing periodic depreciation, except that the asset should not be depreciated below the estimated residual value. In the foregoing example it was assumed that the book value of $777.60 ($1,296.00 − $518.40) at the end of the fifth year approximates the estimated trade-in value. If the estimated residual value had been $1,000, the depreciation for the fifth year would have been $296 instead of $518.40.

The declining-balance method may be applied to all types of depreciable assets. Its use is most appropriate, however, in cases in which the decline in productivity or earning power of the asset is proportionately greater in the early years of its use than in later years. Further justification for its use is based on the tendency of repairs to increase with the age of an asset. The reduced amounts of depreciation in later years are therefore offset to some extent by increased maintenance expenses.

In the foregoing example there was an implicit assumption that the first use of the asset coincided with the beginning of a fiscal year. This is not ordinarily the case, however. The slight variation in the computation may be illustrated by assuming that the above asset was placed in service after 3 months of the fiscal year had elapsed. A pro rata portion of the first full year's depreciation would be taken for the first fiscal year, and for succeeding years the amount would be determined by applying the rate to the declining book value. In terms of the example, the depreciation charged for the first fiscal year would be 9/12 of (40% × $10,000), or $3,000, and for the second fiscal year the depreciation would be 40% × ($10,000 − $3,000), or $2,800.

Sum-of-the-years-digits method. The sum-of-the-years-digits method also provides a steadily declining periodic depreciation charge over the estimated life of the asset. This is accomplished by applying a successively smaller fraction each year to cost less residual value. The numerator of the changing fraction is the number of remaining years of life and the denominator is the sum of the digits representing the years of life. Assuming an estimated life of 5 years, the denominator[1] of the fraction is 15 (5 + 4 + 3 + 2 + 1); for the first year the numerator is 5, for the second year 4, and so on. For a $16,000 asset with an estimated life of 5 years and residual value of $1,000, the schedule of depreciation is:

Year	Cost Less Residual Value	Rate	Depreciation for Year	Accumulated Depreciation at End of Year	Book Value at End of Year
1	$15,000	5/15	$5,000	$ 5,000	$11,000
2	15,000	4/15	4,000	9,000	7,000
3	15,000	3/15	3,000	12,000	4,000
4	15,000	2/15	2,000	14,000	2,000
5	15,000	1/15	1,000	15,000	1,000

When the first use of the asset does not coincide with the beginning of a fiscal year, it is necessary to allocate each full year's depreciation between the two fiscal years benefited. Assuming that the asset in the example was placed in service after 3 months of the fiscal year had elapsed, the depreciation for that fiscal year would be 9/12 of (5/15 × $15,000), or $3,750. The depreciation for the second year would be $4,250, computed as follows:

3/12 of (5/15×$15,000)	$1,250
9/12 of (4/15×$15,000)	3,000
Total, second fiscal year	$4,250

The sum-of-the-years-digits method may be applied to all types of depreciable assets and yields periodic charges similar to those provided by the declining-balance method.

The recent popularity of the accelerated methods of depreciation has been due in large part to the income tax advantage of rapid write-offs. The greater depreciation deductions in the earlier years of the life

[1]The denominator can also be determined from the following formula where S = sum of the digits and N = number of years of estimated life:

$$S = N\left(\frac{N+1}{2}\right)$$

of a plant asset reduce the income tax for those years and correspondingly increase the amount of funds available to pay for the asset or for addition to working capital.

Capital and revenue expenditures

In addition to the initial cost of acquiring a plant asset, other costs related to its efficiency or capacity are incurred from time to time during its service life. It is often difficult to differentiate between expenditures that add to the utility of the asset for more than one accounting period and those that constitute an expense of the period in which they are incurred. Costs that are chargeable to an asset account or its related accumulated depreciation account are termed *capital expenditures;* those that are chargeable to current operations are referred to as *revenue expenditures.*

Expenditures for an addition to a plant asset would clearly constitute capital expenditures. For example, the cost of installing an air conditioning unit in an automobile or of adding a wing to a building should be charged to the respective asset accounts. It is equally clear that expenditures for maintenance and repairs of a recurring nature should be classified as revenue expenditures. Thus, the cost of replacing spark plugs in an automobile or of repainting a building should be charged to expense. In less obvious situations, several criteria may be considered in classifying the expenditures.

Expenditures that increase operating efficiency or capacity for the remaining useful life of an asset should be capitalized. For example, if the power unit attached to a machine is replaced by one of greater capacity, the cost and the accumulated depreciation applicable to the old motor should be removed from the accounts and the cost of the new one should be charged to the asset account.

Expenditures that increase the useful life of an asset beyond the original estimate are also capital expenditures. They should be debited to the accumulated depreciation account, however, rather than to the asset account. To illustrate, assume that a machine with an estimated life of 10 years is completely overhauled at the end of its seventh year of use. It is expected that the extraordinary repairs will extend the life of the machine an additional 3 years beyond the original estimate. The expenditures restore or "make good" a portion of the depreciation recorded in prior years, and it is therefore appropriate that they be debited to the accumulated depreciation account.

When the cost of improvements or extraordinary repairs is substantial or when there is a material change in estimated life, the depreciation charge for future periods should be recomputed on the basis of the new book value of the asset and the new estimate of the remaining useful life.

Expenditures that are minor in amount are usually treated as repair expense even though they may have the characteristics of capital expenditures. The consequent saving in time and accounting expenses justifies the sacrifice of a small degree of accuracy. Some businesses establish a minimum amount for classifying an item as a capital expenditure.

Disposal of plant assets

Plant assets that are no longer useful may be discarded, sold, or applied toward the purchase of other plant assets. The details of the entry to record the disposal will vary, but in all cases it is necessary to remove the book value of the asset from the accounts. This is accomplished by debiting the appropriate accumulated depreciation account for the total depreciation to the date of disposal and crediting the asset account for the cost of the asset.

Discarding of plant assets. When plant assets that are no longer useful cannot be sold, they are discarded. For example, if fully depreciated equipment acquired at a cost of $1,000 is discarded as worthless, the following entry is made:

Apr.	1	Accumulated Depreciation—Equipment	121.1	1,000	
		Equipment	121		1,000
		To write off equipment discarded.			

If the equipment had not been fully depreciated, it would have been necessary to record a loss at the time of its disposal. To illustrate, assume that the balance in the accumulated depreciation account as of the preceding December 31, the end of the fiscal year, is $800 and that the equipment is depreciated at the rate of 10%. The entry to record the depreciation for the 3 months of the current year is as follows:

Apr.	1	Depreciation Expense — Equipment	714	25	
		Accumulated Depreciation — Equipment	121.1		25
		To record 3 months' depreciation on equipment discarded.			

The equipment is then removed from the accounts and the loss is recorded by the following entry:

Apr.	1	Accumulated Depreciation—Equipment	121.1	825	
		Loss on Disposal of Plant Assets	912	175	
		Equipment	121		1,000
		To write off equipment discarded.			

Losses and gains on the disposal of plant assets are nonoperating items and may be reported in the Other Expense and Other Income sections, respectively, of the income statement.

A plant asset that has been depreciated for the full period of its estimated life but that is still useful to the enterprise should not be removed from the accounts. This is true even though the asset has no residual value and the accumulated depreciation is exactly equal to the cost. Otherwise the accounts would contain no evidence of the continued existence of useful plant assets and the control function of the ledger would be impaired. In addition, the cost and the accumulated depreciation data on such assets are frequently needed in reporting for property tax and income tax purposes.

Sale of plant assets. The entry to record the sale of a plant asset is similar to the entries illustrated in the preceding section except that the cash or other asset received must also be recorded. If the selling price is in excess of the book value of the asset, the transaction results in a gain; if the selling price is less than the book value, there is a loss. To illustrate various possibilities, assume that equipment acquired at a cost of $1,000 and depreciated at the rate of 10% is sold on October 1 of the seventh year of its use. The accumulated depreciation in the account as of the preceding December 31 is $600. The entry to record the depreciation for the 9 months of the current year is as follows:

Oct.	1	Depreciation Expense — Equipment....	714	75	
		Accumulated Depreciation — Equipment..........................	121.1		75
		To record 9 months' depreciation on equipment sold.			

Three different assumptions as to the price at which the equipment is sold and the related entry, in general journal form, are:

(1) Selling price $325, which is exactly equal to the book value of the asset:

Oct. 1	Cash..	325	
	Accumulated Depreciation — Equipment..................	675	
	Equipment..		1,000

(2) Selling price $200, which is $125 less than the book value of the asset:

Oct. 1	Cash..	200	
	Accumulated Depreciation — Equipment..................	675	
	Loss on Disposal of Plant Assets.........................	125	
	Equipment..		1,000

(3) Selling price $425, which is $100 greater than the book value of the asset:

Oct. 1	Cash..	425	
	Accumulated Depreciation — Equipment..................	675	
	Equipment..		1,000
	Gain on Disposal of Plant Assets......................		100

Exchange of plant assets. Old equipment is frequently traded in for new equipment having a similar use. The trade-in allowance granted by the seller is deducted from the price of the new equipment and the balance is paid in cash at the time of the exchange or in accordance with the credit agreement. If the trade-in allowance is greater than the book value of the asset, there is a gain on disposal; if it is less than the book value, there is a loss. According to the Internal Revenue Code, however, gains and losses resulting from the exchange of similar types of plant assets are not recognized for income tax purposes. The nonrecognition affects not only the amount of taxable income in the year of the exchange but also the cost basis of the asset acquired and the amount of deductible depreciation expense in subsequent years. As a matter of expediency, many accountants record exchanges in conformity with the provisions of the Code.

As a basis for illustrating the two methods of recording the exchange, assume the following data:

Cost of old item of equipment traded in	$4,000
Accumulated depreciation on the equipment as of December 31, the close of the preceding fiscal year	$2,800
Depreciation from January 1 to June 30, the date of the exchange	$ 400
Price of the new (similar) equipment	$5,000
Trade-in allowance granted on the old equipment	1,100
Balance paid in cash	$3,900

Depreciation accrued for the current year is recorded as follows:

June	30	Depreciation Expense — Equipment	714	400	
		Accumulated Depreciation — Equipment	121.1		400
		To record 6 months' depreciation on equipment traded in.			

Gain or loss recognized. The amount of the gain realized on the old equipment is determined as follows:

Trade-in allowance on old equipment		$1,100
Book value of old equipment:		
Cost	$4,000	
Accumulated depreciation	3,200	800
Gain on exchange		$ 300

The debits and the credits required to record the exchange, in general journal form, are as follows:

June 30	Accumulated Depreciation — Equipment	3,200	
	Equipment	5,000	
	Equipment		4,000
	Cash		3,900
	Gain on Disposal of Plant Assets		300

Gain or loss not recognized. If the gain or the loss on an exchange transaction is not recognized in the accounts, the amount recorded as the cost of the new asset is the sum of (1) the book value of the old asset and (2) the amount to be paid.

The cost basis of the new equipment, assuming the same transaction data, is determined as follows:

Book value of old equipment	$ 800
Amount to be paid	3,900
Cost of new equipment	$4,700

The effect of the nonrecognition of the gain from the exchange on the cost basis of the new equipment may also be computed as follows:

Price of new equipment	$5,000
Less unrecognized gain on exchange	300
Cost of new equipment (same as above)	$4,700

The debits and the credits required to record the exchange, in general journal form, are as follows:

June 30	Accumulated Depreciation — Equipment	$3,200	
	Equipment	4,700	
	Equipment		4,000
	Cash		3,900

If the exchange had resulted in an unrecognized loss instead of a gain, the loss would have been *added* to the price of the new equipment in the computation above.

It should be noted that the nonrecognition of the gain or the loss at the time of the exchange is in reality a postponement. In the above illustration the periodic depreciation on the new equipment will be based on a cost of $4,700 instead of $5,000. By excluding the unrecognized gain of $300 from the cost basis of the asset, the total amount of depreciation expense over the life of the asset will also be reduced by $300.

Subsidiary ledgers for plant assets

When depreciation is to be computed individually on a substantial number of assets comprising a functional group, it is advisable to maintain a subsidiary ledger. For example, assume that an enterprise owns about 200 individual items of office equipment with an aggregate cost of approximately $100,000. Unless the business is newly organized, the equipment would have been acquired over a number of years. The individual cost, estimated residual value, and estimated life would vary in any case, and the composition of the group will continually change as a result of acquisitions and disposals.

There are many variations in the form of subsidiary records for depreciable assets. Multicolumn analysis sheets may be employed, with details of each asset spread across one line, or a separate ledger account may be maintained for each asset. The form should be designed to provide spaces for recording the acquisition and the disposal of the asset, the depreciation charged each period, the accumulated depreciation to date, and any other pertinent data desired. An example of a subsidiary ledger account for a plant asset appears below.

PLANT ASSET RECORD

ACCOUNT NO. 123-215

ITEM Bookkeeping machine GENERAL LEDGER ACCOUNT Office Equipment

SERIAL NO. AT 47-3926 DESCRIPTION Accounts receivable posting

FROM WHOM PURCHASED Hamilton Office Machines Co., Inc.

ESTIMATED LIFE 10 years ESTIMATED SCRAP OR TRADE-IN VALUE $500 DEPRECIATION PER YEAR $240

DATE			EXPLANATION	ASSET			ACCUMULATED DEPRECIATION			BOOK VALUE
MO.	DAY	YR.		DR.	CR.	BAL.	DR.	CR.	BAL.	
4	8	65		2,900		2,900				2,900
12	31	65						180	180	2,720
12	31	66						240	420	2,480

An account in the office equipment ledger

The number assigned to the account illustrated is composed of the number of the office equipment account in the general ledger (123) followed by the sequential number assigned to each item of office equipment purchased (215). An identification tag or plaque with the corresponding account number is attached to the asset. Depreciation for the year in which the asset was acquired, computed for 9 months on a straight-line basis, is $180; for the following year it is $240. These amounts, together with the corresponding amounts from all other accounts in the subsidiary ledger, provide the figures for the respective year-end adjusting entries debiting the depreciation expense account and crediting the accumulated depreciation account.

The sum of the asset balances and the sum of the accumulated depreciation balances in all of the accounts should be compared periodically with the balances of their respective controlling accounts in the general ledger. When a particular asset is disposed of, the asset section of the subsidiary account is credited and the accumulated depreciation section is debited, reducing the balances of both sections to zero. The account is then removed from the ledger and filed for possible future reference.

Subsidiary ledgers for plant assets are useful to the accounting department in (1) determining the periodic depreciation expense, (2) recording the disposal of individual items, (3) preparing tax returns, and (4) preparing insurance claims in the event of insured losses. The forms may also be expanded to provide spaces for accumulating data on the operating efficiency of the asset. Such information as frequency of breakdowns, length of time out of service, and cost of repairs is useful in comparing similar equipment produced by different manufacturers. When new equipment is being purchased, the experience records aid management in deciding upon size, model, and other specifications and the best source of supply.

Regardless of whether subsidiary equipment ledgers are maintained, plant assets should be inspected periodically in order to ascertain whether they are still in use and their state of repair.

Depreciation based on averages

In all of the preceding illustrations, depreciation has been computed on each individual plant asset and, unless otherwise stated, this procedure will be assumed in the problem materials at the end of the chapter. An alternative procedure is to determine depreciation for entire groups of assets by use of a single rate. The basis for grouping may be similarity in life estimates or other common characteristics, or it may be broadened to include all assets within a functional class, such as office equipment.

When depreciation is computed on the basis of a composite group of assets of differing life spans, it is necessary to develop a rate based on averages. This may be done by computing the annual depreciation for each item in the group and dividing the total depreciation for the group by the total cost of the assets. The procedure is illustrated below.

Item No.	Cost	Residual Value	Estimated Life	Annual Depreciation
101	$ 20,000	$4,000	10 years	$ 1,600
102	15,600	1,500	15 years	940
147	41,000	1,000	8 years	5,000
	$473,400			$49,707

Composite rate: $49,707 ÷ $473,400 = 10.5%

As new assets are added to the group and old assets are retired, it is assumed that the "mix" remains relatively unchanged. No gain or loss should be recognized on the retirement of items within the group. Instead, the asset account is credited for the cost of the asset and the accumulated depreciation account is debited for the excess of cost over the amount realized from the disposal. Any deficiency in the amount of depreciation recorded on the shorter-lived assets is presumed to be balanced by excessive depreciation on the longer-lived assets.

When composite rates are used, they may be applied against total asset cost on a monthly basis, or some reasonable assumption may be made regarding the timing of increases and decreases in the group. A common practice is to assume that all additions and retirements have occurred uniformly throughout the year; the composite rate is then applied to the average of the beginning and the ending balances of the account. Another acceptable averaging technique is to assume that all additions and retirements during the first half of the year occurred as of the first day of the year, and that all additions and retirements during the second half occurred on the first day of the following year.

Regardless of whether depreciation is computed for each individual unit or for composite groups, the periodic depreciation charge is based on estimates. The effect of obsolescence and inadequacy on the life of plant assets is particularly difficult to forecast. Any system that provides for the allocation of depreciation in a systematic and rational manner fulfills the requirements of good accounting.

Reporting plant assets in the financial statements

There are many variations in the manner of presenting plant assets in the financial statements. The balance of each asset account, together with the balance of the related account for accumulated depreciation, may be presented in the manner illustrated in earlier chapters. The same data may also be arranged in a more compact fashion, as follows:

Urban Custom Crafts
Balance Sheet
December 31, 1965

Assets

	Cost	Accumulated Depreciation	Book Value	
Total current assets				$262,500
Plant assets:				
Office equipment	$ 20,000	$ 3,000	$ 17,000	
Factory equipment	250,000	92,000	158,000	
Buildings	100,000	26,000	74,000	
Land	10,000	—	10,000	
Total plant assets	$380,000	$121,000		259,000

When there are too many classes of plant assets to list each separately on the balance sheet, or if maximum condensation is desired, a single figure may be presented as the total book value of all plant assets. Details may then be set forth in a supporting schedule.

QUESTIONS

1. What are the four characteristics of plant assets?

2. Indicate which of the following expenditures incurred in connection with the acquisition of a printing press should be charged to the asset account: (a) freight charges, (b) insurance while in transit, (c) interest on funds borrowed to make the purchase, (d) new parts to replace those damaged in unloading, (e) cost of special foundation, (f) fee paid to factory representative for assembling and adjusting.

3. In order to increase the size of its customer parking area, the Baseline Supermarket buys an adjoining lot and an old building for $12,000. The net expense incurred in razing the building and leveling the land, after deducting the amounts received from the sale of salvaged building materials, is $1,300. To what account should the $1,300 be charged?

4. (a) Discuss the nature of depreciation as the term is used in accounting. (b) Does the recognition of depreciation in the accounts provide a special cash fund for the replacement of plant assets?

5. Do the amounts at which plant assets are reported on the balance sheet purport to be their approximate market values?

6. What are the four factors that are included in the broad definition of depreciation?

7. (a) What is the nature of the account Accumulated Depreciation? (b) What is its normal balance? (c) Do credits to this account increase or decrease the amount of the account balance? (d) What effect do credits to this account have on the book value of the related plant assets?

8. Convert each of the following life estimates to a depreciation rate, stated as a percent, assuming that residual value of the plant asset is to be ignored: (a) 4 years, (b) 6 years, (c) 10 years, (d) 25 years, (e) 33⅓ years, (f) 40 years.

9. A plant asset with a cost of $100,000 has an estimated trade-in value of $5,000 and an estimated life of 10 years. (a) What is the annual depreciation, computed by the straight-line method? (b) The annual depreciation is what percent of the cost of the asset?

10. What percent of the cost of a plant asset, acquired at the beginning of the year, with a life estimate of 5 years, is written off in the first year by the declining-balance method, using twice the straight-line rate?

11. An asset with an estimated life of 5 years is to be depreciated by the sum-of-the-years-digits method. (a) What is the denominator of the depreciation fraction? (b) What is the numerator of the fraction for the second year?

12. When should the cost and the accumulated depreciation of a fully depreciated plant asset be removed from the accounts?

13. In what sections of the income statement are gains and losses from the disposal of plant assets presented?

14. A plant asset with a book value of $3,000 is traded for a similar asset with a price of $30,000. The trade-in allowance is $1,000. (a) What is the amount of cash to be paid? (b) What is the gain or the loss on the disposal? (c) If the gain or the loss is not recognized in the accounts, at what amount will the new asset be recorded? (d) If the gain or the loss is not recognized in the accounts at the time of the exchange, how will it be recognized in the future?

15. Differentiate between capital expenditures and revenue expenditures.

16. Immediately after a used truck is acquired, a new motor is installed and the tires are replaced at a total cost of $530. Is this a capital expenditure or a revenue expenditure?

17. A building that cost $400,000 has no estimated residual value and an estimated life of 40 years. (a) What is the amount of the annual depreciation by the straight-line method? (b) What is the amount of accumulated depreciation at the end of 30 years? (c) At the beginning of the thirty-first year, the roof is replaced at a cost of $10,000, with the expectation that the useful life of the building will be extended 10 years beyond the original estimate. To what account should this expenditure be charged? (d) What is the amount of the depreciation for the thirty-first year (straight-line)?

18. If the cost of a composite group of equipment is $200,000 and the total annual depreciation, computed on the individual items, totals $25,000, what is the composite rate?

EXERCISES

1. A building acquired on January 12 at a cost of $200,000 has an estimated life of 40 years. Assuming that it will have no residual value, determine the depreciation for each of the first two years (a) by the straight-line method and (b) by the declining-balance method, using twice the straight-line rate.

2. A diesel-powered electric generator with a cost of $35,000 and estimated salvage value of $2,000 is expected to have a useful operating life of 150,000 hours. During October the generator was operated 500 hours. Determine the depreciation for the month.

3. Balances in the accounts Trucks and Accumulated Depreciation—Trucks at the end of the year prior to adjustment are $38,550 and $23,450, respectively. Details of the subsidiary ledger are presented below. (a) Determine the amount to be credited to the accumulated depreciation section of each of the subsidiary accounts for the current year. (b) Present the general journal entry to record depreciation for the year.

Truck No.	Cost	Residual Value	Useful Life in Miles	Accumulated Depreciation at Beginning of Year	Miles Operated During Year
1	$ 6,500	$ 500	120,000	$5,200	12,000
2	5,000	400	100,000	2,500	8,000
3	12,050	1,200	175,000	9,750	20,000
4	15,000	2,000	200,000	6,000	25,000

4. A plant asset acquired at the beginning of the fiscal year at a cost of $24,825 has an estimated trade-in value of $2,000 and an estimated useful life of 10 years. Determine the following: (a) the annual depreciation charge by the straight-line method, (b) the amount of depreciation for the second year computed by the declining-balance method (at twice the straight-line rate), (c) the amount of depreciation for the second year computed by the sum-of-the-years-digits method.

5. On September 8 Bryson Stores acquired a new bookkeeping machine with a list price of $2,600, receiving a trade-in allowance of $200 on an old bookkeeping machine and giving a note for the remainder. The following information about the old equipment is obtained from the account in the office equipment ledger: cost, $1,600; accumulated depreciation on December 31, the close of the preceding fiscal year, $1,050; annual depreciation, $150. Present entries, in general journal form, to record the following: (a) current depreciation accrued on the old equipment to date of trade-in; (b) the transaction on September 8, assuming that gain or loss is to be recognized; (c) the transaction on September 8, assuming that gain or loss is not to be recognized.

6. On the first day of the fiscal year a delivery truck with a list price of $6,200 was acquired in an exchange transaction in which there was a loss of $800. The truck is to be depreciated over 4 years by the straight-line method, assuming a trade-in value of $600. Determine the following: (a) annual depreciation expense, assuming that the loss was recognized; (b) annual depreciation expense, assuming that the loss was not recognized; (c) the amount of the exchange loss included in the annual depreciation expense determined in (b).

7. An item of equipment acquired at a cost of $9,990 has an estimated residual value of $1,170 and an estimated life of 6 years. It was placed in service on May 5 of the current fiscal year, which ends on December 31. Determine the depreciation for the current fiscal year and for the following fiscal year (a) by the declining-balance method (at twice the straight-line rate) and (b) by the sum-of-the-years-digits method.

8. Details of a plant asset account are presented below. A composite depreciation rate of 11% is applied annually to the account. Determine the depreciation for the year according to each of the following assumptions: (a) that all additions and retirements have occurred uniformly throughout the year and (b) that additions and retirements during the first half of the year occurred on the first day of the year and those during the second half occurred on the first day of the following year.

Factory Machines

Jan. 1 Balance	146,200	Mar. 7	1,800
Mar. 10	5,800	Apr. 18	2,600
May 15	10,700	Aug. 4	12,000
July 22	3,600		
Nov. 6	2,100		

PROBLEMS

11-1. The following expenditures and receipts are related to land, land improvements, and buildings acquired for use in a business enterprise. The receipts are identified by an asterisk.

(a)	Cost of real estate acquired as a plant site: Land	$ 35,000
	Building	20,000
(b)	Delinquent real estate taxes on property, assumed by purchaser	1,800
(c)	Cost of razing and removing the building	2,000
(d)	Fee paid to attorney for title search	350
(e)	Architect's fee for plans and supervision	25,000
(f)	Premium on 1-year insurance policy during construction	4,000
(g)	Cost of land fill and grading	1,300
(h)	Paid to building contractor for new building	500,000
(i)	Cost of paving parking lot to be used by customers	1,100
(j)	Cost of trees and shrubbery	600
(k)	Cost of repairing windstorm damage during construction	3,100
(l)	Cost of sidewalks	750
(m)	Real estate taxes accrued during construction	1,700
(n)	Interest accrued on building loan during construction	20,000
(o)	Special assessment for installation of sewers, paid to city	650
(p)	Proceeds from sale of salvage materials from old building	500*
(q)	Money borrowed to pay building contractor	300,000*
(r)	Proceeds from insurance company for windstorm damage	2,900*
(s)	Refund of premium on insurance policy (f) canceled after 11 months	250*
		$313,700

Instructions: (a) Assign each expenditure and receipt (indicate receipts by an asterisk) to Land, Land Improvements, Building, or "Other Accounts." Identify each item by letter and list the amounts in columnar form, as follows:

Item	Land	Land Improvements	Building	Other Accounts

(b) Total the amount columns.

11-2. An item of new equipment acquired at a cost of $50,000 at the beginning of a fiscal year has an estimated life of 5 years and an estimated trade-in value of $5,000. The manager requested information (details given in Instruction 1) regarding the effect of alternative methods on the amount of the annual depreciation expense.

Upon the basis of the data presented to the manager in accordance with Instruction 1, the sum-of-the-years-digits method was elected. At the beginning of the fourth year the equipment was traded in for similar equipment priced at $60,000. The trade-in allowance on the old equipment was $10,000 and a note payable was issued for the balance.

Instructions: (1) Determine the annual depreciation for each of the estimated 5 years of use and the book value of the equipment at the end of each year by (a) the straight-line method, (b) the declining-balance method (at twice the straight-line rate), and (c) the sum-of-the-years-digits method. The following columnar headings are suggested for each schedule:

Year	Depreciation Expense	Book Value End of Year

(2) Present the debits and the credits required to record the trade-in transaction at the beginning of the fourth year, (a) recognizing gain or loss on the disposal and (b) postponing recognition of gain or loss on the disposal.

If the working papers correlating with the textbook are not used, omit Problem 11-3.

11-3. Peerless Printing Co. maintains a subsidiary equipment ledger for the printing equipment and accumulated depreciation accounts in the general ledger. A small portion of the subsidiary ledger, the two controlling accounts, and a general journal are presented in the working papers. The company computes depreciation on each individual item of equipment. Transactions and adjusting entries affecting the printing equipment are described below.

1965

Oct. 7. Purchased a power cutter (Challenger Model, Serial No. 58432) from Marion Typograph Co. on account for $4,512. The estimated life of the asset is 8 years, it is expected to have no residual value, and the straight-line method of depreciation is to be used. (This is the only transaction of the year that directly affected the printing equipment account.)

Dec. 31. Entered depreciation for the year in subsidiary accounts 125-64 to 66, and inserted the new balances. (It is assumed that an assistant enters the depreciation and the new balances in accounts 125-1 to 63.)

31. Recorded the annual depreciation on printing equipment. The depreciation for the year entered in subsidiary accounts 125-1 to 63 totals $18,732, to which must be added the depreciation entered in accounts 125-64 to 66.

1966

Mar. 24. Purchased a Model A10 rotary press from Grossman Press, Inc., priced at $23,725, giving the Model 21 flatbed press (Acct. No. 125-64) in exchange plus $5,000 cash and a series of twelve $1,000 notes payable, maturing at 6-month intervals. (Record depreciation to date in 1966 on item traded in; gain or loss on the disposal is not to be recognized.)

Instructions: (1) Record the transaction of October 7 in general journal form. Post to the printing equipment account in the general ledger and to Account 125-66 in the subsidiary ledger.

(2) Make the entries required on December 31 and post to the accumulated depreciation — printing equipment account in the general ledger.

(3) Make the entries in general journal form required by the purchase of printing equipment on March 24. Post to the printing equipment account and to the accumulated depreciation — printing equipment account.

(4) Assuming that the rotary press purchased on March 24 has an estimated residual value of $3,000 and an estimated life of 10 years, determine the depreciation on this press by the declining-balance method, at twice the straight-line rate, for the fiscal years ending December 31, (a) 1966 and (b) 1967.

11-4. The following transactions, adjusting entries, and closing entries were completed by Modern Furniture Co. during a three-year period. All are related to the use of delivery equipment.

1965
Mar. 10. Purchased a used delivery truck for $2,800, paying cash.
15. Paid garage $190 for tires and $214 for repairs to the truck.
Sept. 16. Paid garage $37 for miscellaneous repairs to the motor.
Dec. 31. Recorded depreciation on the truck for the fiscal year. The estimated life of the truck is 2 years, with a trade-in value of $300. The straight-line method of depreciation is used.
Dec. 31. Closed the appropriate accounts to Expense and Revenue Summary.

1966
Aug. 28. Traded in the used truck on a new truck priced at $5,194, receiving a trade-in allowance of $700 and paying the balance in cash. (Record depreciation to date in 1966; gain or loss on exchange is not to be recognized.)
Nov. 19. Paid garage $49 for repairs to the truck.
Dec. 31. Recorded depreciation on the truck. It has an estimated trade-in value of $800 and an estimated life of 4 years. The declining-balance method (twice the straight-line rate) of depreciation is used.
31. Closed the appropriate accounts to Expense and Revenue Summary.

1967
June 23. Purchased a new truck for $4,900, paying cash.
Oct. 10. Sold the truck purchased in 1966 for $2,400 cash. (Record depreciation).
Dec. 31. Recorded depreciation on the remaining truck. It has an estimated trade-in value of $600 and an estimated life of 4 years. The declining-balance method (twice the straight-line rate) of depreciation is used.
31. Closed the appropriate accounts to Expense and Revenue Summary.

Instructions: (1) Open the following accounts in the ledger:

121 Delivery Equipment
121.1 Accumulated Depreciation — Delivery Equipment
614 Depreciation Expense — Delivery Equipment
615 Truck Repair Expense
912 Loss on Disposal of Plant Assets

(2) Record the transactions and the adjusting and closing entries in general journal form. Post to the accounts and extend the balances after each entry.

11-5. A number of errors in recording transactions are described below.

(a) The $500 cost of a major motor overhaul expected to prolong the life of a truck beyond the original estimate was charged to Delivery Equipment. The truck was acquired new 2 years earlier.
(b) The $1,800 cost of repainting the interior of a building that has been owned for 7 years was charged to Building.
(c) The sale of a copying machine for $500 was recorded by a $500 credit to Office Equipment. The original cost of the machine was $2,500 and

the related balance in Accumulated Depreciation at the end of the year preceding the year of sale was $1,600. Depreciation of $150 accrued during the year of sale had not been recorded.

(d) Incoming transportation charges of $120 on an item of factory equipment were debited to Purchases.

(e) The $225 cost of repairing factory equipment damaged in the process of installation was charged to Factory Equipment.

(f) The cost of a razed building, $8,000, was charged to Loss on Disposal of Plant Assets. The building and the land on which it was located had been acquired at a total cost of $24,000 ($16,000 debited to Land, $8,000 debited to Building) as a site for a discount store.

(g) The fee of $1,000 paid to the wrecking contractor to raze the building in (f) was debited to Miscellaneous Expense.

(h) Cash of $375 received from the sale of materials salvaged in razing the building in (g) was credited to Miscellaneous Income.

Instructions: Journalize the necessary correcting entries, assuming that they are recorded in the same fiscal year in which the errors occurred. Identify each entry by letter.

11-6. The trial balance of Jewel Markets at the end of the current fiscal year, before adjustments, is as follows:

Jewel Markets
Trial Balance
December 31, 19—

Cash	29,650	
Merchandise Inventory	116,830	
Prepaid Expenses	7,340	
Delivery Equipment	18,620	
Accumulated Depreciation — Delivery Equipment		7,145
Store Equipment	32,930	
Accumulated Depreciation — Store Equipment		17,238
Office Equipment	5,410	
Accumulated Depreciation — Office Equipment		3,124
Buildings	86,200	
Accumulated Depreciation — Buildings		32,690
Land	6,500	
Notes Payable (short term)		23,000
Accounts Payable		36,110
L. J. Harper, Capital		150,177
L. J. Harper, Drawing	12,000	
Sales (net)		876,460
Purchases (net)	732,660	
Operating Expenses (control account)	97,334	
Gain on Disposal of Plant Assets		315
Interest Expense	610	
Loss on Disposal of Plant Assets	175	
	1,146,259	1,146,259

Data needed for year-end adjustments:

(a) Merchandise inventory at December 31, $123,740.

(b) Insurance and other prepaid operating expenses expired during the year, $2,260.

(c) Depreciation is computed on the average of the beginning and the ending balances of the plant asset accounts. The beginning balances and the composite rates are as follows:
Delivery equipment, $14,260, 25%. Office equipment, $6,130, 10%.
Store equipment, $30,670, 10½%. Buildings, $86,200, 2½%.

(d) Accrued liabilities at the end of the year, $1,940, of which $630 is for interest on the notes and $1,310 is for wages and other operating expenses.

Instructions: (1) Prepare an income statement for the current year.

(2) Prepare a balance sheet in report form, presenting the plant assets in the manner illustrated in this chapter.

11-7. In each of the following selected transactions it is assumed that subsidiary equipment ledgers are maintained and that the fiscal year ends on December 31. Depreciation is recorded only at the end of each year, except for depreciation on items disposed of during the year.

(a) Jan. 11. Paid $4,500 for replacing the roof on a building. It is estimated that the new roof will extend the life of the building from an original estimate of 25 years to a total life of 30 years. Details from the subsidiary ledger are as follows: cost, $120,000; accumulated depreciation on preceding December 31, $72,000; age of building, 15 years.

(b) Apr. 10. Discarded store equipment, realizing no salvage. Details from the subsidiary ledger are as follows: cost, $600; accumulated depreciation on preceding December 31, $516; annual depreciation, $48.

(c) May 24. Sold 10 desks (office equipment) for cash, $100. The desks were identical and had been acquired at the same time. Details from the subsidiary ledger are as follows: total cost, $1,300; total accumulated depreciation on preceding December 31, $1,025; total annual depreciation, $120.

(d) June 8. Traded in an old delivery truck for a new one priced at $4,800, receiving a trade-in allowance of $600 and paying the balance in cash. Data on the old truck are as follows: cost, $3,200; accumulated depreciation on preceding December 31, $2,600; annual depreciation, $660. Gain or loss is to be recognized.

(e) July 16. Discarded a duplicating machine (office equipment), realizing no salvage. Details from the subsidiary ledger are as follows: cost, $240; accumulated depreciation, $240.

(f) Oct. 21. Traded in an old refrigerated display case (store equipment) for a new one priced at $1,600, receiving a trade-in allowance of $400 and giving a note for the balance. Data on the old equipment are as follows: cost, $1,000; accumulated depreciation on preceding December 31, $685; annual depreciation, $90. Gain or loss is not to be recognized.

Instructions: (1) Present entries, all in general journal form, to record the transactions and, where appropriate, to accrue the depreciation for the partial year preceding the transaction. Identify each entry by letter.

(2) Determine the depreciation on the building affected by entry (a) for the year in which the roof was replaced, using the straight-line method and assuming no residual value.

(3) Determine the depreciation on the new store equipment recorded in entry (f), using the declining-balance method (twice the straight-line rate) for (a) the remainder of the year and (b) the following year. The expected useful life of the display case is 8 years.

PART SIX
Accounting systems and concepts

12. Systems and controls

Accounting systems

One of the areas of specialization in accounting described in Chapter 1 is the design and installation of accounting systems. In developing principles of accounting in the intervening chapters, attention has been focused to a large extent on analysis and recording of accounting data, preparation of financial statements, and uses of accounting data by management. Consideration has also been given, however, to some aspects of accounting systems, such as special journals, charts of accounts, subsidiary ledgers, and documentary evidence of transactions.

There are an infinite number of variations in the details of accounting systems. But all systems provide for channeling of the documents evidencing transactions, such as invoices and checks, into the written accounting records, which include journals, ledgers, and financial statements. In each particular case the system must be designed to fit the nature of the enterprise, the volume of transactions of various types, and the number and the capacities of the personnel.

A properly designed accounting system provides for: (1) efficient accumulation, recording, and reporting of data; (2) measurement of all phases of a firm's operations; (3) assignment of authority and responsibility; and (4) prevention of errors and fraud.

Internal control

In a small business it is possible for the owner-manager to instruct and supervise the employees personally. As the number of employees and the complexities of an enterprise increase, it becomes increasingly difficult for management to maintain contact with all phases of operations. It is necessary to delegate authority and to rely on reports and other forms of accounting data rather than on personal observation.

Plans and procedures designed to meet the need for controlling operations are called *internal control.* It comprises the plan of organization and the related methods and procedures adopted within a company to (1) safeguard its assets, (2) produce accurate accounting data, (3) contribute to efficient operation, and (4) encourage adherence to management policies. In a broad sense, internal control also includes such activities as motion and time study, quality control, and statistical analysis. The portion of internal control related to the accounting system is sometimes referred to as *internal check.*

Some degree of internal control is needed in all businesses. For example, the requirement that each cash sale be recorded by depressing the appropriate keys on a cash register is a fundamental part of internal control. The use of sales tickets, sales invoices, and other documentary evidences of transactions is also a part of internal control. The details of a system of internal control will of necessity vary with the nature and the size of a firm. There are, however, a number of broad principles that should be considered.

Responsibility for a sequence of related transactions should be divided among different persons. Complete control by one individual over a sequence of related transactions presents opportunities for inefficiency, errors, and fraud. For example, no single individual should be authorized to order merchandise, verify the receipt of the goods, and pay the supplier. To do so would invite such abuses as placing orders on the basis of friendship with a supplier rather than on price, quality, and other objective factors; perfunctory verification of the quantity and the quality of goods received; conversion of goods to the personal use of the employee; carelessness in verifying the validity and the accuracy of invoices; and payment of fictitious invoices. When the responsibility for purchasing, receiving, and paying are divided among three persons or departments, the possibilities of such abuses are minimized.

Documentary evidence of the work of each department, including purchase orders, receiving reports, and invoices, is routed to the accounting department for comparison and recording. It should be noted that the "checks and balances" provided by distributing authority among various departments requires no duplication of effort. The work of each department, as evidenced by the business documents that it prepares, must "fit" with those prepared by the other departments.

Responsibility for maintaining records should be separated from the responsibility for operations and custody of assets. If employees who engage in transactions also record the transactions, the control function of the ledger accounts is lost. For example, the person who receives remittances from customers on account should not have access to the journals or the ledgers. Separation of the two functions reduces the possibilities of errors and defalcations.

Proofs and security measures should be utilized to the limits of feasibility. This principle applies to a wide variety of techniques and procedures, such as: the use of controlling accounts and subsidiary ledgers; the use of a bank account and other safekeeping measures for cash, investments, and other valuable documents; and the use of various types of mechanical equipment. Cash registers are widely employed in making the initial record of cash sales. The conditioning of the public to observe the amount recorded as the sale or to accept a printed receipt from the salesclerk increases the machine's effectiveness as a part of internal control. Other devices with a similar feature include gasoline pumps and automatic counters in city buses.

The use of fidelity insurance is also an aid to internal control. It insures against losses caused by fraud on the part of employees who are entrusted with company assets and serves as a psychological deterrent to the misappropriation of assets.

Responsibility should be clearly established. As a prerequisite to determining the proficiency of employees, it is essential that their responsibilities be clearly defined. Again using the cash register as an example, each salesclerk should be assigned a separate cash drawer and register key. By such means, daily proof of the handling of cash can be obtained for each clerk. Similarly, if a number of employees are assigned to posting entries to customers' accounts, each should be assigned to a particular alphabetical section so that errors can be traced to the person responsible for the error.

Control over cash

Because of its high value in relation to bulk and because of other obvious qualities, cash is the asset most often subject to improper diversion and use. In addition, almost every transaction eventually affects the receipt or the payment of cash. It is therefore desirable to provide special controls over cash. The most important of these measures are discussed in the following paragraphs.

Using a bank account

Most businesses deposit all cash receipts in a bank and make all payments by checks drawn against the bank account. The forms used by the depositor in connection with a bank account are signature card, deposit ticket, check, and bank statement.

Signature card. At the time an account is opened, the bank requires that a *signature card* be signed personally by each individual authorized to sign checks drawn on that account. The card is used by the bank to determine the authenticity of the signature on checks presented to it for payment.

Deposit ticket. The details of a deposit are listed by the depositor on a printed form supplied by the bank. *Deposit tickets* are frequently prepared in duplicate. The carbon copy is stamped or initialed by the bank's teller and is given to the depositor as a receipt. When deposits are mailed to the bank or are placed in a night deposit vault, the bank mails the duplicate deposit ticket or other receipt form to the depositor.

Check. A *check* is a written instrument signed by the depositor, ordering the bank to pay a specified sum of money to a designated person or to his order. There are three parties to a check: the *drawer*, the one who signs the check; the *drawee*, the bank on which the check is drawn; and the *payee*, the one to whose order the check is drawn. When checks are issued to pay obligations, they are recorded as credits to Cash even though they are not presented to the drawer's bank until some later time. Conversely, when checks are received from customers, they are recorded as debits to Cash, on the assumption that the customer has sufficient funds on deposit.

Check forms may be obtained in a variety of styles. The name and the address of the depositor may be printed on each check, and the checks may be serially numbered for purposes of internal control. Some banks employ automatic check-sorting and posting machines, in which case the bank's identification number and the depositor's account number are printed on each check in magnetic ink.

A carbon copy of the check may be prepared for use in recording the transaction in the cash payments journal, or the information may be entered on a *stub* such as that illustrated below. The check stub may also be used as a memorandum record of the current bank balance.

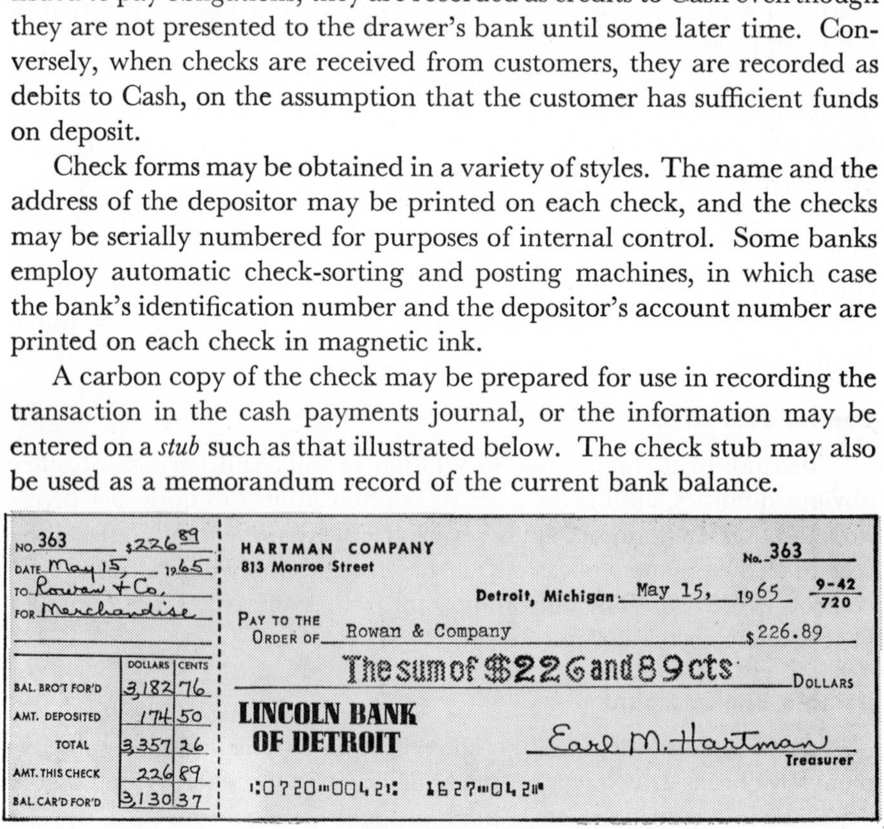

NO. 363 $226.89
DATE May 15, 1965
TO Rowan & Co.
FOR Merchandise

	DOLLARS	CENTS
BAL. BRO'T FOR'D	3,182	76
AMT. DEPOSITED	174	50
TOTAL	3,357	26
AMT. THIS CHECK	226	89
BAL. CAR'D FOR'D	3,130	37

HARTMAN COMPANY
813 Monroe Street
No. 363
Detroit, Michigan May 15, 1965 9-42/720
PAY TO THE ORDER OF Rowan & Company $226.89
The sum of $226 and 89 cts DOLLARS
LINCOLN BANK OF DETROIT
Earl M. Hartman
Treasurer
⑆0720⑈0042⑆ 1627⑈042⑈

Check and stub

A check sent to a creditor for a payment on account is frequently accompanied by a notification of the particular invoice that is being paid. The purpose of such notification, sometimes called a *remittance advice*, is to assure proper credit on the books of the creditor. Misunderstandings are less likely to arise and the possible need for exchanges of correspondence is avoided.

An alternative procedure is to record the invoice number or other identification on the face of the check or on an attachment to it. A check containing remittance information is known as a *voucher check.*

Bank statement

Banks maintain an original and a carbon copy of all checking accounts. The original becomes the statement of account that is mailed to the depositor, usually at the end of each month. Like any account with a customer or a creditor, the bank statement begins with the opening balance, lists debits (deductions by the bank) and credits (additions by the bank), and ends with the balance at the close of the period. Accompanying the bank statement are the depositor's checks received by the bank during the period, arranged in the order of payment. The *paid* or *canceled* checks are perforated or stamped "Paid" together with the date of payment.

Debit or credit memorandums describing other entries on the depositor's account may also be enclosed with the statement. For example, the bank may have debited the depositor's account for service charges or for deposited checks returned because of insufficient funds; or it may have credited the account for receipts from notes receivable left for collection or for bank loans to the depositor. A typical bank statement is illustrated on page 280.

Bank reconciliation

When all cash receipts are deposited in the bank and all payments are made by check, the cash account is often entitled Cash in Bank. This account in the depositor's ledger is the reciprocal of the account with the depositor in the bank's ledger. Cash in Bank in the depositor's ledger is an asset with a debit balance, and the account with the depositor in the bank's ledger is a liability with a credit balance.

It might seem that the two balances should be equal in amount, but on any specific date they are unlikely to be equal because of either or both of the following: (1) delay by either party in recording transactions, and (2) errors by either party in recording transactions.

There is almost always a time lag of one day or more between the date a check is written and the date that it is presented to the bank for pay-

STATEMENT OF
YOUR ACCOUNT

LINCOLN BANK
OF DETROIT

DETROIT, MICHIGAN

1627-042

Hartman Company
813 Monroe Street
Detroit, Michigan 48206

CHECKS AND OTHER DEBITS			DEPOSITS	DATE	BALANCE
		BALANCE BROUGHT FORWARD →		July 1	4,218.60
819.40	122.54		585.75	July 1	3,862.41
369.50	732.26	20.15	421.53	July 2	3,162.03
600.00	190.70	52.50	781.30	July 3	3,100.13
25.93	160.00		662.50	July 5	3,576.70
36.80	181.02		503.18	July 7	3,862.06
32.26	535.09		932.00	July 29	3,397.40
21.10	126.20		705.21	July 30	3,955.31
		SC 3.00	MS 400.00	July 30	4,352.31
26.12	1,615.13		648.72	July 31	3,359.78

EC—Error Correction NSF—Not Sufficient Funds PS—Payment Stopped
MS—Miscellaneous OD —Overdraft SC—Service Charge

The reconcilement of this statement with your records is essential. Any error or exception should be reported immediately.

Bank statement

ment. If the depositor mails deposits to his bank or uses the night depository, a delay by the bank in recording the deposit is also probable. On the other hand, the bank may debit or credit the depositor's account for transactions about which the depositor will not be informed until later. Examples are service or collection fees charged by the bank and the proceeds of notes receivable given to the bank for collection.

In order to discover the reasons for the difference between book and bank balances and to correct any errors that may have been made by the bank or the depositor, the depositor should *reconcile* the bank statement with his own records. The bank reconciliation is divided into two major sections: one section begins with the balance according to the bank statement and ends with the adjusted balance; the other section begins with the balance according to the depositor's books and also ends with the adjusted balance. The form and the content of the two sections is outlined on the opposite page.

The amount of the bank balance according to the depositor's books is the balance of the ledger account Cash in Bank after all receipts and payments for the month have been posted. It is also possible to ascertain the balance from the check stubs. The two amounts designated as the adjusted balance must be in exact agreement. The adjusted balance is the amount of cash the depositor has available for use as of the date of the bank statement.

Bank balance according to bank statement........................		xx
Add: Additions by depositor not on bank statement................	xx	
Bank errors..	xx	xx
		xx
Deduct: Deductions by depositor not on bank statement..............	xx	
Bank errors..	xx	xx
Adjusted balance..		xx
Bank balance according to depositor's books.......................		xx
Add: Additions by bank not recorded in books......................	xx	
Book errors..	xx	xx
		xx
Deduct: Deductions by bank not recorded in books..................	xx	
Book errors..	xx	xx
Adjusted balance..		xx

To achieve a maximum of internal control, the bank reconciliation should be prepared by an employee who does not engage in or record bank transactions. Errors or irregularities discovered should be reported to the chief accountant, controller, or other supervisory official.

The procedures described in the following paragraphs are employed in locating the reconciling items and determining the adjusted balance of Cash in Bank:

(1) Individual deposits listed on the bank statement are compared with unrecorded deposits appearing in the preceding reconciliation and with duplicate deposit slips or other records of deposits. Deposits not recorded by the bank are added to the balance according to the bank statement.

(2) Paid checks returned by the bank are arranged in numerical order and are compared with outstanding checks appearing on the preceding reconciliation and with checks listed in the cash payments journal. Checks issued that have not been returned by the bank are outstanding and are deducted from the balance according to the bank statement.

(3) Bank credit memorandums are traced to the cash receipts journal. If there are any unrecorded additions to the bank account, the amounts are added to the balance according to the books.

(4) Bank debit memorandums are traced to the cash payments journal. If there are any unrecorded deductions from the bank account, the amounts are deducted from the balance according to the books.

(5) Errors discovered during the process of making the foregoing comparisons are listed separately on the reconciliation. For example, if the amount of a cash payment was erroneously recorded, the amount of the error should be added to or deducted from the balance according to the books. Similarly, errors by the bank should be added to or deducted from the balance according to the bank statement.

Illustration. The bank statement appearing on page 280 will be used as the basis for illustration. After the Hartman Company's cash receipts and cash payments journals for July were posted, the balance in the cash in bank account was $2,242.99. According to the bank statement, the balance on July 31 is $3,359.78. Application of the procedures outlined on the preceding page reveals the following reconciling items:

(1) Deposit of July 31 not recorded on bank statement	$ 816.20
(2) Checks outstanding: No. 812, $1,061.00; No. 878, $435.39; No. 883, $48.60	1,544.99
(3) Note collected by bank (credit memorandum) not recorded in cash receipts journal	400.00
(4) Bank service charges (debit memorandum) not recorded in cash payments journal	3.00
(5) Check No. 879 for $732.26 to Belden Co. on account recorded in cash payments journal as $723.26	9.00

The bank reconciliation based on the bank statement and the above reconciling items is as follows:

Hartman Company
Bank Reconciliation
July 31, 1965

Balance per bank statement		$3,359.78
Add: Deposit of July 31, not recorded by bank		816.20
		$4,175.98
Deduct: Outstanding checks		
No. 812	$1,061.00	
No. 878	435.39	
No. 883	48.60	1,544.99
Adjusted balance		$2,630.99
Balance per books		$2,242.99
Add: Note collected by bank		400.00
		$2,642.99
Deduct: Bank service charges	$3.00	
Error in recording Check No. 879	9.00	12.00
Adjusted balance		$2,630.99

Entries based on bank reconciliation

Unrecorded transactions and errors on the depositor's books revealed by the bank reconciliation must be corrected. The necessary entries may be recorded in the appropriate special journals if they have not already been posted for the month, or they may be recorded in the general journal.

The entries for Hartman Company, based on the bank reconciliation in the preceding section, are as follows:

July	31	Cash in Bank	400	
		Notes Receivable		400
		Note collected by bank		
	31	Miscellaneous General Expense	3	
		Accounts Payable — Belden Co.	9	
		Cash in Bank		12
		Bank service charges and error in recording Check No. 879.		

It should be noted that the data necessary for these adjustments are provided by the section of the bank reconciliation that begins with the balance per books.

After the foregoing entries are posted, the cash in bank account will have a debit balance of $2,630.99, which agrees with the adjusted balance shown on the bank reconciliation. If a memorandum record of the bank balance is maintained on the check stubs, the last stub should be revised by adding the net adjustment of $388 ($400 – $12).

Internal control of cash receipts

A bank account is one of the principal devices for maintaining control over cash. To achieve maximum effectiveness, all cash received must be deposited in the bank and all payments must be made by checks drawn on the bank or from special cash funds. When such a system is strictly adhered to, there is a double record of cash, one maintained by the business and the other by the bank.

Department stores and other retail businesses ordinarily receive cash from two principal sources: (1) over the counter from cash customers and (2) by mail from charge customers making payments on account. At the close of the business day each salesclerk counts the cash in his cash drawer and records the amount on a memorandum form. An employee from the cashier's department removes the cash register tapes on which total receipts were recorded for each cash drawer, recounts the cash, and compares the total with the memorandum and the tape, noting any discrepancies. The cash is taken to the cashier's office, where it is combined with the mail receipts and a deposit ticket is prepared. The cash register tapes and memorandum forms are forwarded to the accounting department, where they become the basis for entries in the cash receipts journal.

The employees who open the mail record the amount received from each customer on the upper portion of the statement of account ordinarily enclosed with the payment. When no separate remittance advice accompanies the payment, the employee prepares one on a special form designed for the purpose. All cash received, usually in the form of checks and money orders, is sent to the cashier's department, and all remittance advices are delivered to the accounting department where they become the basis for entries in the cash receipts journal and for posting to the customers' accounts in the subsidiary ledger.

The duplicate deposit ticket or other bank receipt form obtained by the cashier is forwarded to the controller or other financial officer, who compares the amount with that reported by the accounting department as the total debit to Cash in Bank for the period.

Cash short and over

The amount of cash actually received during a day often does not agree with the record of cash receipts. Whenever there is a difference between the record and the actual cash and no error can be found in the record, it must be assumed that the mistake occurred in making change. The cash shortage or overage is recorded in an account entitled Cash Short and Over. A common method for handling such mistakes is to include in the cash receipts journal a Cash Short and Over Debit column into which all cash shortages would be entered, and a Cash Short and Over Credit column into which all cash overages would be entered. For example, if the actual cash received from cash sales is less than the amount shown by the cash register tally, the entry in the cash receipts journal would include a debit to Cash Short and Over. The complete entry in general journal form is as follows:

Cash in Bank	720.10	
Cash Short and Over	1.90	
Sales		722.00

If there is a debit balance in the cash short and over account at the end of the fiscal period, it is an expense and may be included in Miscellaneous General Expense on the income statement. If there is a credit balance, it is revenue and may be listed in the Other Income section. If the balance becomes larger than may be accounted for by minor errors in making change, the management should take corrective measures.

Cash change funds

Retail stores and other businesses that receive cash directly from customers must maintain a fund of currency and coins in order to make change. The fund may be established by drawing a check for the required amount, debiting the account Cash on Hand and crediting Cash in Bank. No additional charges or credits to the cash on hand account are necessary unless the amount of the fund is to be increased or decreased. At the close of each business day the total receipts are deposited and the change fund is retained. The desired composition of the fund is maintained by exchanging bills or coins for those of other denominations at the bank.

Internal control of cash payments

It is common practice for business enterprises to require that every payment of cash be evidenced by a check signed by a designated official. Some firms require two signatures on all checks or on all checks over a certain amount as an additional control. A seeming exception to the system is made for payments of small amounts from a petty cash fund and from other special funds. However, checks are employed in reimbursing such funds so that they too are kept under control. These funds are described later in the chapter.

When the owner of a business has personal knowledge of all goods and services purchased, he may sign checks with the assurance that the creditors have complied with the terms of their contracts and that he is paying the exact amount of the obligation. Such all-embracing knowledge of affairs by disbursing officials is seldom possible, however. In enterprises of even moderate size the responsibility for issuing purchase orders, inspecting commodities received, and verifying contractual and arithmetical details of invoices is divided among the employees of various departments. It is desirable, therefore, to coordinate these related activities and to link them with the ultimate issuance of checks to creditors. One of the most effective systems employed for this purpose is known as the *voucher system.*

Basic features of the voucher system

A voucher system is composed of records, methods, and procedures employed in (1) verifying and recording liabilities and (2) paying and recording cash payments. As in all other sections of systems of accounting and internal control, many variations in detail are possible. The discussion and the illustrations that follow refer to a merchandising enterprise of moderate size with separate departments for purchasing, receiving, accounting, and disbursing.

A voucher system employs (1) vouchers, (2) a voucher register, (3) a file for unpaid vouchers, (4) a check register, and (5) a file for paid vouchers.

Preparation of vouchers. The term *voucher* is widely used in accounting. In a general sense it means any document that serves as evidence of authority to pay cash, such as an invoice approved for payment, or as evidence that cash has been paid, such as a canceled check. The term has

VOUCHER No. 451

JANSEN AUTO SUPPLIES, INC.

Date July 1, 1965

Payee Allied Manufacturing Company

683 Fairmont Road

Chicago, Illinois 60630

Date	Details	Amount
June 28, 1965	Invoice No. 4693-C F.O.B. Chicago, 2/10, n/30	450.00

Attach Supporting Papers

Voucher — face

ACCOUNT DISTRIBUTION		
Debit	Amount	
Purchases	450	00
Store Supplies		
Advertising Exp.		
Delivery Exp.		
Misc. Selling Exp.		
Misc. General Exp.		
Credit Accounts Payable	450	00

Distribution Approved C. B. White

VOUCHER No. 451

Date 7-1-65 Due 7-8-65

Payee

Allied Manufacturing Company

683 Fairmont Road

Chicago, Illinois 60630

Voucher Summary

Amount	450	00
Adjustment		
Discount	9	00
Net	441	00

Approved R. G. Davis Controller

Recorded T. N.

Payment Summary

Date 7-8-65

Amount 441.00

Check No. 863

Approved C. S. Reed Treasurer

Recorded B. W. RM

Voucher — back

a narrower meaning when applied to the voucher system: a voucher is a special form on which is recorded pertinent data about a liability and the particulars of its payment.

A voucher form is illustrated on page 286. The face of the voucher provides space for the name and the address of the creditor, the date and the number of the voucher, and pertinent details of the invoice or other supporting document, such as the vendor's invoice number and the amount and the terms of the invoice. One half of the back of the voucher is devoted to the account distribution and the other half to summaries of the voucher and the details of payment. Spaces are also provided for the signature or initials of various employees.

Vouchers are customarily prepared by the accounting department on the basis of an invoice or a memorandum that serves as evidence of the expenditure. This is usually done only after the following comparisons and verifications have been completed and noted on the invoice:

(1) Comparison with a copy of the purchase order to verify quantities, prices, and terms.
(2) Comparison with the receiving report to determine receipt of the items billed.
(3) Verification of the arithmetical accuracy of the invoice.

After all data except details of payment have been inserted, the invoice or other supporting evidence is attached to the face of the voucher, which is then folded with the account distribution and summaries on the outside. The voucher is then presented to the designated official or officials for final approval.

Voucher register. After approval by the designated official, each voucher is recorded in a journal known as a *voucher register*. It is similar to and replaces the purchases journal described in Chapter 6.

A typical form of a voucher register is illustrated on pages 288 and 289. The vouchers are entered in numerical sequence, each being recorded as a credit to Accounts Payable (sometimes entitled Vouchers Payable) and as a debit to the account or accounts to be charged for the expenditure.

When a voucher is paid, the date of payment and the number of the check are inserted in the appropriate columns in the voucher register. The effect of such notations is to provide a ready means of determining at any time the amount of individual unpaid vouchers. The total amount of the outstanding liability can also be determined at any time by adding the individual amounts of the vouchers indicated by the voucher register as being unpaid.

Unpaid voucher file. An important characteristic of the voucher system is the requirement that a voucher be prepared for each expenditure. In

VOUCHER REGISTER

	DATE		VCHR. NO.	PAYEE	PAID DATE	PAID CHK. NO.	ACCOUNTS PAYABLE CR.	PURCHASES DR.	
	1965								
1	July	1	451	Allied Mfg. Co.	7–8	863	450 00	450 00	1
2		1	452	Adams Realty Co.	7–1	856	600 00		2
3		2	453	Foster Publications	7–2	857	52 50		3
4		3	454	Benson Express Co.	7–3	859	36 80	24 20	4
5		3	455	Office Outfitters			784 20		5
6		3	456	Moore & Co.	7–11	866	1,236 00	1,236 00	6
7		6	457	J. L. Brown Co.	7–6	860	22 50		7
8		6	458	Turner Corp.			395 30	395 30	8
27		31	477	Central Motors			112 20		27
28		31	478	Petty Cash	7–31	883	48 60		28
29		31					15,551 60	11,640 30	29
30							(212)	(511)	30

Voucher register — left page

fact, a check may not be issued except in payment of a properly authorized voucher. Vouchers may be paid immediately after they are prepared or at a later date, depending upon the credit terms.

After a voucher has been prepared and has been recorded in the voucher register, it is filed in an unpaid voucher file, where it remains until it is paid. The amount due on each voucher represents the credit balance of an account payable, and the voucher itself is comparable to an individual account in a subsidiary accounts payable ledger; accordingly, a separate subsidiary ledger is unnecessary.

All voucher systems include some provision for efficiently determining the vouchers to be paid each day. The method of filing invoices by due date described in Chapter 6 is equally acceptable for filing vouchers. It brings to the attention of the disbursing official the vouchers that are to be paid on each day. It also provides management with a convenient means of continuously forecasting the amount of funds needed to meet maturing obligations.

When a voucher is to be paid, it is removed from the unpaid voucher file and a check is issued in payment. The date, the number, and the amount of the check are listed on the back of the voucher for use in recording the payment in the check register. Paid vouchers and the supporting documents are often run through a canceling machine to prevent accidental or intentional reuse.

VOUCHER REGISTER PAGE 11

	STORE SUPPLIES DR.	ADV. EXP. DR.	DEL. EXP. DR.	MISC. SELLING EXP. DR.	MISC. GENERAL EXP. DR.	SUNDRY ACCOUNTS DR. ACCOUNT	POST. REF.	AMOUNT	
1									1
2						Rent Expense	712	600 00	2
3		52 50							3
4			12 60						4
5	34 20					Office Equipment	122	750 00	5
6									6
7					22 50				7
8									8
27			112 20						27
28	4 30		16 20	19 50	8 60				28
29	59 80	176 40	286 10	48 30	64 90			3,275 80	29
30	(116)	(612)	(613)	(618)	(718)			(√)	30

Voucher register — right page

An exception to the general rule that vouchers be prepared for all expenditures may be made for bank charges evidenced by debit memorandums or notations on the bank statement. For example, such items as bank service charges, safe deposit box rentals, and returned NSF (Not Sufficient Funds) checks may be charged to the depositor's account without either a formal voucher or a check. For large expenditures, such as the repayment of a bank loan, a supporting voucher may be prepared, if desired, even though a check is not written. The paid note may then be attached to the voucher as evidence of the obligation. All bank debit memorandums are, of course, the equivalent of checks as evidence of payment.

Check register. The payment of a voucher is recorded in a *check register*, an example of which is illustrated on page 290. The check register is a modified form of the cash payments journal and is so called because it is a complete record of all checks. Check forms are usually prenumbered as an aid in establishing control. It is therefore customary to record all checks in the check register in sequential order, including occasional checks that are voided because of an error in their preparation.

Each check issued is in payment of a voucher that has previously been recorded as an account payable in the voucher register. The effect of each entry in the check register is consequently a debit to Accounts Payable and a credit to Cash in Bank.

CHECK REGISTER

PAGE 11

	DATE		CHK. NO.	PAYEE	VCHR. NO.	ACCOUNTS PAYABLE DR.	PURCHASES DISCOUNT CR.	CASH IN BANK CR.	BANK DEPOSITS	BANK BALANCE	
	1965									8,743 10	
1	July	1	856	Adams Realty Co.	452	600 00		600 00	1,240 30	9,383 40	1
2		2	857	Foster Publications	453	52 50		52 50		9,330 90	2
3		2	858	Hill and Davis	436	1,420 00	14 20	1,405 80	865 70	8,790 80	3
4		3	859	Benson Exp. Co.	454	36 80		36 80	942 20	9,696 20	4
22		30	879	Voided							22
23		30	880	Stone & Co.	460	14 30		14 30		9,521 80	23
24		30	881	Evans Corp.	448	1,015 00		1,015 00	765 50	9,272 30	24
25		31	882	Graham & Co.	469	830 00	16 60	813 40		8,458 90	25
26		31	883	Petty Cash	478	48 60		48 60	938 10	9,348 40	26
27		31				17,322 90	198 20	17,124 70			27
28						(212)	(513)	(111)			28

Check register

The memorandum columns for Bank Deposits and Bank Balance appearing in the illustration of the check register are optional. Their use eliminates the necessity of recording deposits and calculating bank balances on the check stubs and provides a convenient means of determining the cash available at all times.

Paid voucher file. After payment, vouchers are customarily filed in numerical sequence in a paid voucher file. They are then readily available for examination by employees or independent auditors requiring information about a specific expenditure. Eventually the paid vouchers are destroyed in accordance with the firm's policies on the retention of records.

Voucher system and management. The voucher system not only provides effective accounting controls but also aids management in discharging other responsibilities. For example, the voucher system helps assure that only valid obligations are paid. In addition, continuous information is readily available for use in planning for future cash requirements. This in turn enables management to make the maximum use of cash resources. Invoices on which cash discounts are allowed can be paid within the discount period. Other invoices can be paid in accordance with the credit terms, thus minimizing costs and maintaining a favorable credit standing. Seasonal borrowing for working capital purposes can also be planned more accurately, with a consequent saving in interest costs.

Purchases discount

In preceding chapters, purchases of merchandise were recorded at the invoice price, and cash discounts taken were credited to the purchases discount account at the time of payment. There are two views on how such purchases discounts should be reported in the income statement.

The most widely accepted view, which has been followed in this textbook, is that purchases discounts should be reported as a deduction from purchases. For example, the cost of merchandise with an invoice price of $1,000, subject to terms of 2/10, n/30, is recorded initially at $1,000. If payment is made within the discount period, the discount of $20 reduces the cost to $980. If the invoice is not paid within the discount period, the cost of the merchandise remains $1,000. This treatment of purchases discounts may be attacked on the grounds that the date of payment should not affect the cost of a commodity; the additional payment required beyond the discount period adds nothing to the value of the commodities purchased.

The second view reports discounts taken as "other income." In terms of the example above, the cost of the merchandise is considered to be $1,000 regardless of the time of payment. If payment is made within the discount period, revenue of $20 is realized. The objection to this procedure lies in the recognition of revenue from the act of purchasing a commodity. Theoretically, an enterprise might make no sales of merchandise during an accounting period and yet might report as revenue the amount of cash discounts taken.

A major disadvantage of recording purchases at the invoice price and recognizing purchases discounts at the time of payment is that this method is not very helpful in controlling operations. Efficiently managed enterprises maintain sufficient funds to pay all invoices subject to a discount within the discount period and view the failure to take a discount as an inefficiency. From the point of view of controlling operations, it is better to record purchases invoices at the net amount, assuming that all discounts will be taken, and then to record any discounts not taken in an expense account entitled Discounts Lost. This method measures the cost of failing to take discounts and gives management an opportunity to take remedial action. Again assuming the same data, the invoice for $1,000 would be recorded as a debit to Purchases of $980 and a credit to Accounts Payable for the same amount. If the invoice is paid after the discount period has expired, the entry, in general journal form, would be as follows:

Accounts Payable	980	
Discounts Lost	20	
Cash in Bank		1,000

When the voucher system is employed, under this method all vouchers are prepared and recorded at the net amount. Any discount lost would then be noted on the related voucher and would be recorded in a special column in the check register when the voucher is paid.

Another advantage of this method is that all merchandise purchased is recorded initially at the net price and, except for possible returns and allowances, no subsequent adjustments are necessary. A criticism of this method is that the amount reported as accounts payable in the balance sheet may be less than the amount necessary to discharge the liability.

Petty cash

In most businesses there is a frequent need for payments of relatively small amounts, such as to the postman for postage due, to a deliveryman for transportation charges, or to an employee for the purchase of urgently needed supplies at a nearby retail store. It is readily apparent that payment by check in such cases would result in delay, annoyance, and excessive expense of maintaining the records. It is usual, therefore, to maintain a special cash fund that is designated *petty cash.*

In establishing a petty cash fund, the first step is to estimate the amount needed for cash payments during a specified period such as a week or a month. If the voucher system is used, a voucher is then prepared for this amount and it is recorded in the voucher register as a debit to Petty Cash and a credit to Accounts Payable. The check drawn to pay the voucher is recorded in the check register as a debit to Accounts Payable and a credit to Cash in Bank. If the voucher system is not used, only one entry is required, that is, an entry in the cash payments journal debiting Petty Cash and crediting Cash in Bank.

The check itself is cashed and the money is placed in the custody of the employee authorized to disburse the petty cash fund in accordance with stipulated restrictions as to maximum amount and purpose. Each time a disbursement is made from the fund, the employee records the essential details on a petty cash receipt, obtains the signature of the payee as evidence of the payment, and adds his own signature or initials. A typical petty cash receipt is illustrated on the opposite page.

When the amount of money in the petty cash fund is reduced to the predetermined minimum amount, the fund is replenished. If the voucher system is used, the accounts charged on the replenishing voucher are those indicated by a summary of expenditures. The voucher is then recorded in the voucher register as a debit to the various expense and asset accounts and a credit to Accounts Payable. The entry is similar to that on line 28 of the voucher register on pages 288 and 289. The check in payment of the voucher is recorded in the check register in the usual

PETTY CASH RECEIPT NO. 121

DATE Aug. 1, 1965

PAID TO Western Union

AMOUNT 1 | 30

FOR Telegram

CHARGE TO Miscellaneous General Expense

PAYMENT RECEIVED:

S. O. Hall

APPROVED BY NER

Petty cash receipt

manner, as shown on line 26 of the illustration on page 290. If the voucher system is not used, only one entry is required in the cash payments journal. This entry debits the appropriate expense and asset accounts and credits Cash in Bank.

After the petty cash fund has been replenished, the fund will be restored to its original amount. It should be noted that the sole entry in the petty cash account will be the initial debit unless at some later time the amount of the fund is increased or decreased.

Because of the time lag in recording disbursements, petty cash funds and other special funds that operate in a similar manner should always be replenished at the close of an accounting period. The amount of money actually in the fund will then agree with the balance in the related fund account, and the expenses and the assets for which payment has been made will be recorded in the proper period.

Other cash funds

Other funds may be established to meet the special needs of a business. For example, money advanced to a salesman for travel expenses may be accounted for in the same manner as petty cash. A standard amount is advanced; then upon receipt of expense reports from the salesman, the expenses are recorded and the fund is replenished. A similar technique may be used to provide a working fund for a sales office located in another city. The amount of the fund may be deposited in a local bank and the sales representative may be authorized to draw checks for payment of rent, salaries, and other operating expenses. Each month the representative sends the invoices, bank statement, paid checks, bank reconciliation, and other business documents to the home office. The data are audited, the expenditures are recorded, and a reimbursing check is returned for deposit in the local bank.

Control over noncash items

Earlier chapters have discussed the use of subsidiary records for recording and controlling such items as accounts receivable, equipment, and accounts payable. Perpetual inventory records assist in the management and control of inventory. Two other useful devices that represent an elaboration of the accounting system are described in the paragraphs that follow.

Note registers. The notes receivable and notes payable accounts in the general ledger are primarily summarizing devices. They are not designed for recording detailed information about the terms of each note and its disposition. If numerous notes are received from customers or issued to creditors, it is customary to record the details of each note in a notes receivable register or a notes payable register.

The initial recording is made in the register at the time a note is given or received, showing the details of the note, such as name of maker or payee, place of payment, amount, term, interest rate, and due date. Daily reference to the due date section directs attention to which notes, if any, are due for payment or are to be presented for collection.

Insurance registers. An important means of safeguarding a firm's investment in plant assets is through insurance against losses from fire, windstorm, and other catastrophes. Potential losses resulting from injury to customers or employees while on the business premises, from dishonesty of employees, and from business interruptions caused by fire

INSURANCE

DATE OF POLICY		POLICY NO.	INSURER	PROPERTY OR PURPOSE	AMOUNT	TERM	EXPIRATION DATE	UNEXPIRED PREMIUM	
1960									
Mar.	5	24983	Midland Fire	Equipment	15,000	5	3/5/65	8	96
Oct.	28	469AC	National Fire	Building	30,000	5	10/28/65	110	00
1962									
June	4	79481	Acme Fire & Cas.	Merchandise	25,000	3	6/4/65	47	75
1964									
Oct.	1	6947	Columbia Fire & Cas.	Public Liability	100,000	1	10/1/65	94	50
1965									
Mar.	5	37468	Midland Fire	Equipment	15,000	5	3/5/70	270	60
May	26	2694Y	Liberty Auto	Delivery Equip.		1	5/26/66	542	40
June	4	96423	Acme Fire & Cas.	Merchandise	25,000	3	6/4/68	346	32
Oct.	1	11731	Columbia Fire & Cas.	Public Liability	100,000	1	10/1/66	129	00
	28	9847	U.S. Fire	Building	25,000	5	10/28/70	594	00

Insurance register, left page

are only a few of the many other risks that may need to be insured against. The responsibility for appropriate insurance coverage ordinarily rests with the treasurer, controller, or other accounting officer. It is also the responsibility of the accounting department to determine and to record the amount of insurance expense applicable to each accounting period.

The contract between the insurer and the insured is called the *insurance policy*, and the amount paid for the contract is called the *insurance premium*. Insurance policies are written for a definite amount and for a definite period of time, most commonly for one, three, or five years. The amount of insurance that should be carried on a particular asset does not necessarily correspond to its original cost or book value. The reproduction cost of the asset less accumulated depreciation thereon is a better criterion of the appropriate coverage. In any event, the insured cannot recover more than the actual loss incurred.

A large firm may have literally hundreds of insurance policies in effect. For even a small business the number may be considerable. The review of insurance coverage and the determination of periodic insurance expense are facilitated by the use of a multicolumn form termed an *insurance register*.

An insurance register for a small business is illustrated below. The data for the insurance policies in effect at the beginning of the year are taken from the register for the preceding year; policies acquired during the year are recorded in the order of their acquisition. At the end of

REGISTER — 1965

EXPIRED PREMIUM													UNEXPIRED PREMIUM
JAN.	FEB.	MAR.	APR.	MAY	JUNE	JULY	AUG.	SEPT.	OCT.	NOV.	DEC.	TOTAL	
4.48	4.48											8.96	—
11.00	11.00	11.00	11.00	11.00	11.00	11.00	11.00	11.00	11.00			110.00	—
9.55	9.55	9.55	9.55	9.55								47.75	—
10.50	10.50	10.50	10.50	10.50	10.50	10.50	10.50	10.50				94.50	—
		4.51	4.51	4.51	4.51	4.51	4.51	4.51	4.51	4.51	4.51	45.10	225.50
					45.20	45.20	45.20	45.20	45.20	45.20	45.20	316.40	226.00
					9.62	9.62	9.62	9.62	9.62	9.62	9.62	67.34	278.98
									10.75	10.75	10.75	32.25	96.75
										9.90	9.90	19.80	574.20
35.53	35.53	35.56	35.56	35.56	80.83	80.83	80.83	80.83	81.08	79.98			

Insurance register, right page

each month the insurance expense for that month is determined by adding the appropriate column. For example, the November expiration column in the illustration is totaled at the end of that month and an adjusting entry debiting Insurance Expense and crediting Prepaid Insurance for $79.98 is recorded in the general journal.

At the end of the year the Total Expired Premium column and the two unexpired premium columns are added. The total of the first Unexpired Premium column should agree with the total debits to Prepaid Insurance, the Total Expired Premium column should agree with the credits to the account, and the total of the second Unexpired Premium column should agree with the balance of Prepaid Insurance after all adjustments have been posted.

Processing accounting data

Accounting records and reports may be prepared manually or by the use of various machines. In small businesses the processing of accounting data, from the original documents through journalizing, posting, and the preparation of statements, may be done manually. Even in small businesses, however, the use of typewriters, adding machines, and cash registers is not uncommon. Manual operations may also be aided by the use of carbon paper. For example, the sales invoice, the journal record, and the posting to the customer's account may be prepared simultaneously through the use of carbons.

As the volume and the complexity of transactions performed by an enterprise increase, the recording process becomes more involved and greater attention is given to increasing efficiency and reducing costs. Many devices and machines have been developed that can classify, summarize, and tabulate data at far greater speeds than are possible by manual operations. One such development, used primarily by the banking industry, is magnetic ink. This medium was used to record the identification number of the bank and of the depositor on the check illustrated on page 278. Printing the identification number of the drawee bank in magnetic ink makes it possible to process the check through the bank clearinghouse system by use of character sensing machines that read the magnetic ink characters. Some drawee banks, especially the larger ones, type the amount of the check in magnetic ink in the lower right-hand corner of the check after it reaches them. The checks can then be sorted and posted to depositors' accounts by an automatic process using magnetic character sensing machines.

Many enterprises requiring the processing of large volumes of data in a short period of time employ one or more types of automated data processing equipment. The use of such equipment for processing accounting data has increased rapidly in recent years. The original data may be recorded on punch cards, magnetic tape, paper tape, or other similar media. They can then be processed by a computer, which classifies and stores the information. Summaries of the data, as well as any individual details that may be needed, can be obtained within incredibly short periods of time.[1]

QUESTIONS

1. Name four requisites for a properly designed accounting system.

2. (a) What is the meaning of *internal control*? (b) What is *internal check*?

3. Why should the control over a sequence of related transactions be divided among different persons?

4. The bookkeeper of Alston Company pays all obligations by prenumbered checks. What are the strengths and the weaknesses in the internal control over cash disbursements in this situation?

5. Name and identify the three parties to a check.

6. When checks are received from customers, they are recorded as debits to Cash, the assumption being that the customer has sufficient funds on deposit. What does the accountant do if such a check is returned by the bank for lack of sufficient funds (NSF)?

7. What is the purpose of preparing a bank reconciliation?

8. (a) What are bank memorandums? (b) List three examples of items that might be reported by such memorandums.

9. Identify each of the following reconciling items as: (1) an addition to the balance per bank, (2) a deduction from the balance per bank, (3) an addition to the balance per books, or (4) a deduction from the balance per books. (None of the transactions reported by bank debit and credit memorandums has been recorded by depositor.)

(a) Deposit in transit, $420.15.
(b) Outstanding checks, $772.33.
(c) Note collected by the bank, $150.
(d) Check of a customer returned by bank to depositor because of insufficient funds, $40.
(e) Check drawn by depositor for $100 recorded in check register as $10.
(f) Check for $75 charged by bank as $57.
(g) Bank service charge, $4.10.

10. Which of the reconciling items listed in Question 9 will require an entry in the depositor's books?

11. The procedures employed by MacDonald, Inc. for over-the-counter receipts are as follows: Each salesclerk counts the cash in his cash drawer at the

[1] A more complete discussion of the use of automated data processing equipment in the processing of accounting data is given in Appendix A.

close of business. He then removes the cash register tape and prepares the memorandum daily cash form, noting any discrepancies. An employee from the cashier's office recounts the cash, compares the total with the memorandum, and takes the cash to the cashier's office. (a) Indicate the weak link in internal control. (b) How can the weakness be corrected?

12. The procedures employed by Myers Company for mail receipts are as follows: The mail clerk sends all remittances and remittance advices to the cashier. The cashier deposits the cash in the bank and forwards the remittance advices and duplicate deposit slips to the accounting department. (a) Indicate the weak link in internal control. (b) How can the weakness be corrected?

13. What does a credit balance in the account Cash Short and Over indicate?

14. The combined cash count of all cash registers at the close of business is $7.10 less than the cash sales indicated by the cash register tapes. (a) In what account is the cash shortage recorded? (b) Are cash shortages debited or credited to this account?

15. What is meant by the term "voucher" as applied to the voucher system?

16. Before a voucher for the purchase of merchandise is approved for payment, three documents should be compared to verify the accuracy of the liability. Name these three documents.

17. (a) When the voucher system is employed, is the accounts payable account in the general ledger a controlling account? (b) Is there a subsidiary creditor's ledger?

18. What is the nature of the Bank Deposits and Bank Balance columns in the check register and what purpose do they serve?

19. (a) In what order are vouchers ordinarily filed in the unpaid voucher file? Give a reason for your answer. (b) In what order are vouchers ordinarily filed in the paid voucher file? Give a reason for your answer.

20. Merchandise with an invoice price of $8,000 is purchased subject to terms of 1/10, n/30. What is the cost of the merchandise according to each of the following assumptions:

(a) Discounts taken are considered to be adjustments to the invoice price.
  (1) The invoice is paid within the discount period.
  (2) The invoice is paid after the discount period has expired.
(b) Discounts taken are considered to be other income.
  (1) The invoice is paid within the discount period.
  (2) The invoice is paid after the discount period has expired.
(c) Discounts allowable are considered to be adjustments to the invoice price.
  (1) The invoice is paid within the discount period.
  (2) The invoice is paid after the discount period has expired.

21. The petty cash account has a debit balance of $200. At the end of the accounting period there is $50 in the petty cash fund along with petty cash receipts totaling $150. Should the fund be replenished as of the last day of the period? Discuss.

22. What two purposes are served by an insurance register?

EXERCISES

1. The following data are accumulated for use in reconciling the bank account of Carlson Company for June:

(a) Balance per bank statement at June 30, $2,790.15.
(b) Balance per books at June 30, $2,456.45.
(c) Deposit in transit not recorded by bank, $388.50.
(d) Checks outstanding, $717.80.
(e) A check for $156 in payment of a voucher for rent expense was erroneously recorded in the check register as $165.
(f) Bank debit memorandum for service charges, $4.60.

Prepare a bank reconciliation.

2. Using the data presented in Exercise 1, prepare in general journal form the entry or entries that should be made by the depositor.

3. Accompanying a bank statement for Riley, Inc. is a debit memorandum for $510, representing the principal ($500), interest ($7.50), and protest fee ($2.50) on a discounted note that had been dishonored by Landon Co. The depositor had been notified by the bank at the time of the dishonor but had made no entries. Present the necessary entry by the depositor, in general journal form.

4. Record in general journal form the following transactions, indicating above each entry the name of the journal in which it should be recorded. Assume the use of a voucher register similar to that illustrated on pages 288 and 289 and a check register similar to that illustrated on page 290. All invoices are recorded at invoice price.

April 1. Recorded Voucher No. 717 for $2,000, payable to Olson, Inc., for merchandise purchased on terms of 2/10, n/30.
2. Recorded Voucher No. 718 for $250, payable to *Covington Times*, for advertising appearing in yesterday's newspaper.
10. Issued Check No. 951 in payment of Voucher No. 718.
10. Issued Check No. 952 in payment of Voucher No. 717, less discount.
15. Recorded Voucher No. 719 for $76.18 to replenish the petty cash fund for the following disbursements: Office Supplies, $17.20; Store Supplies, $20.00; Miscellaneous Selling Expense, $19.50; and Miscellaneous General Expense, $19.48.
15. Issued Check No. 953 in payment of Voucher No. 719.

5. Record in general journal form the following related transactions, assuming that invoices for commodities purchased are recorded at their net price after deducting the allowable discount:

May 1. Prepared Voucher No. 410 for the purchase of merchandise from Winters Co., $1,500, terms 1/10, n/30.
3. Prepared Voucher No. 411 for the purchase of merchandise from Merchants Supply Co., $5,000, terms 2/10, n/30.
10. Issued Check No. 526, payable to Winters Co., in payment of Voucher No. 410.
30. Issued Check No. 549, payable to Merchants Supply Co., in payment of Voucher No. 411.

6. Assuming the use of a voucher system, prepare in general journal form the entries to record the following:

(a) Voucher No. 339 is prepared to establish a petty cash fund of $100. When the fund is reduced below $25, it should be replenished.
(b) Check No. 345 is issued in payment of Voucher No. 339.
(c) The petty cash fund has been reduced to $24.50. Voucher No. 386 is prepared to replenish the fund, based on the following summary of petty cash receipts: Office Supplies, $25.70; Miscellaneous Selling Expense, $34.40; Miscellaneous General Expense, $15.20.
(d) Check No. 394 is issued by the disbursing officer in payment of Voucher No. 386. The check is cashed and the money is placed in the fund.

PROBLEMS

12-1. The cash in bank account for Harmon Company at December 31 of the current year indicated a balance of $4,967.53 after both the cash receipts journal and the check register for December had been posted. The bank statement indicated a balance of $6,317.48 on December 31. Comparison of the bank statement and the accompanying canceled checks and memorandums with the records revealed the following reconciling items:

(a) Checks outstanding totaled $2,026.87.
(b) A deposit of $890.17 representing receipts of December 31 had been made too late to appear on the bank statement.
(c) A check for $200 drawn by Hamond Company had been erroneously charged by the bank to Harmon Company's account.
(d) A check for $210 returned with the statement had been recorded in the check register as $120. The check was for the payment of an obligation to Busey Company on account for the purchase of office equipment.
(e) The bank had collected for Harmon Company $510 on a note left for collection. The face of the note was $500.
(f) Bank service charges for December amounted to $6.75.

Instructions: (1) Prepare a bank reconciliation.

(2) Journalize the necessary entries. The books have not been closed. The voucher system is used.

12-2. Paulsen Company has the following vouchers in its unpaid voucher file at August 31 of the current year:

Due Date	Voucher No.	Creditor	Date of Invoice	Amount	Terms
Sept. 7	699	Price Co.	Aug. 28	$ 600	2/10, n/30
Sept. 21	690	Hale, Inc.	Aug. 22	1,250	n/30

The vouchers prepared and the checks issued during the month of September are presented on the opposite page.

Instructions: (1) Set up a four-column account for Accounts Payable, Account No. 212, and record the balance of $1,850 as of September 1.

(2) Record the September vouchers in a voucher register similar to the one illustrated in this chapter, with the following amount columns: Accounts Payable Cr., Purchases Dr., Store Supplies Dr., Office Supplies Dr., and Sundry Accounts Dr. Purchases invoices are recorded at the gross amount.

Vouchers

Date	Voucher No.	Payee	Amount	Terms	Distribution
Sept. 1	701	Petty Cash	$ 50		Petty cash
3	702	Russel Co.	1,300	2/10, n/30	Purchases
5	703	K&W Sales	225	cash	Store supplies
7	704	White Bros.	415	n/30	Office equipment
10	705	Dahl Stationers	135	cash	Office supplies
11	706	Lane, Inc.	2,600	1/10, n/30	Purchases
17	707	Busey Federal Bank	2,020		Note payable, $2,000 Interest, $20
19	708	Reed Co.	280	cash	Store supplies
20	709	Tepper Motors	3,900	n/30	Delivery equipment
24	710	Troy News	120	cash	Advertising expense
26	711	Fisher Co.	4,500	2/10, n/30	Purchases
28	712	Tanner Supply	75	cash	Office supplies
29	713	Petty Cash	36		Store supplies, $13 Delivery exp., $5 Misc. sell. exp., $11 Misc. gen. exp., $7

Checks

Date	Check No.	Payee	Voucher Paid	Amount
Sept. 1	910	Petty Cash	701	$ 50
5	911	K&W Sales	703	225
7	912	Price Co.	699	588
10	913	Dahl Stationers	705	135
13	914	Russel Co.	702	1,274
17	915	Busey Federal Bank	707	2,020
19	916	Reed Co.	708	280
21	917	Hale, Inc.	690	1,250
21	918	Lane, Inc	706	2,574
24	919	Troy News	710	120
28	920	Tanner Supply	712	75
29	921	Petty Cash	713	36

(3) Record the September checks in a check register similar to the one illustrated in this chapter, but omit the Bank Deposits and Balance columns. As each check is recorded in the check register, the check number should be inserted in the appropriate place in the Check No. column of the voucher register. Assume that appropriate notations are made in the Paid column of the voucher register when the August vouchers are paid.

(4) Total and rule the registers and post to the accounts payable account.

(5) Prepare a schedule of unpaid vouchers.

If the working papers correlating with the textbook are not used, omit Problem 12-3.

12-3. Portions of the following accounting records of D. L. Mason Co. are presented in the working papers:

Voucher Register
Check Register
General Journal
Insurance Register
Notes Payable Register

General ledger accounts:
Prepaid Insurance
Notes Payable
Accounts Payable

Expenditures, cash disbursements, and other selected transactions completed during the period March 25–31 of the current year are described below.

Mar. 25. Issued Check No. 842 to Osborn Co. in payment of Voucher No. 631 for $4,300, less cash discount of 2%.
25. Recorded Voucher No. 646 payable to Corbin & Co. for merchandise, $3,740. (Purchases invoices are recorded at the gross amount.)
26. Recorded Voucher No. 647 payable to Hamilton Insurance Co. for the following insurance policy, dated today: No. 1462Y, automobile, 1 year, $1,105.20.
26. Issued Check No. 843 in payment of Voucher No. 647.
27. Recorded Voucher No. 648 payable to Merchants State Bank for note payable (No. 34), $10,000.
27. Issued Check No. 844 in payment of Voucher No. 648.
27. Issued a 60-day, 6% note, dated today (No. 36) to Scott & Turner in settlement of Voucher No. 629, $4,500. The note is payable at First National Bank.
28. Recorded Voucher No. 649 payable to Ajax Fire Insurance Co. for the following insurance policy, dated today: No. 947BR, merchandise & equipment, $50,000, 5 years, $1,104.
28. Issued Check No. 845 in payment of Voucher No. 649.
29. Recorded Voucher No. 650 payable to Harris Corp. for merchandise, $2,750.
30. Recorded Voucher No. 651 payable to *Midvale Gazette* for advertising, $320.
30. Recorded Voucher No. 652 payable to R. L. Eaton Co. for note payable (No. 33), $3,000, and interest, $30.
30. Issued Check No. 846 in payment of Voucher No. 652.
31. Issued Check No. 847 to Ferris & Co. in payment of Voucher No. 643 for $2,500 less cash discount of 1%.
31. Recorded Voucher No. 653 payable to Petty Cash for $186.70, distributed as follows: Store Supplies, $37.40; Advertising Expense, $8.50; Delivery Expense, $17.80; Misc. Selling Expense, $69.10; Misc. General Expense, $53.90.
31. Issued Check No. 848 in payment of Voucher No. 653.

After the journals are posted at the end of the month, the cash in bank account has a debit balance of $16,061.20.

The bank statement indicates a March 31 balance of $22,616.70. Comparison of paid checks returned by the bank with the check register reveals that Nos. 845, 846, and 847 are outstanding. Check No. 798 for $105, which appeared on the February reconciliation as outstanding, is still outstanding. A debit memorandum accompanying the bank statement indicates a charge of $158.50 for a check drawn by F. O. Sprague, a customer, which was returned because of insufficient funds.

Instructions: (1) Record the transactions for March 25–31 in the appropriate journals. Immediately after recording a transaction, post individual items, where appropriate, to the three general ledger accounts given.

(2) Enter the necessary notations in the notes payable register and the insurance register, rounding insurance expirations to the nearest month.

(3) Total and rule the voucher register and the check register, and post totals to the accounts payable account.

(4) Complete the schedule of unpaid vouchers. (Compare the total with the balance of the accounts payable account as of March 31.)

(5) Prepare a bank reconciliation and journalize any necessary entries.

(6) Total the Expired Premium column for March in the insurance register, journalize the adjusting entry, and post to the prepaid insurance account. (Determine the balance of prepaid insurance as of March 31 from the columns in the insurance register and compare it with the balance of the prepaid insurance account as of the same date.)

(7) Determine the amount of interest accrued as of March 31 on notes payable (No. 32 and No. 36). (Assume 28 days in February.)

(8) Determine the amount of interest prepaid as of March 31 on notes payable (No. 35). (The non-interest-bearing note was discounted by the bank.)

12-4. Maxey, Inc. has just adopted the policy of depositing all cash receipts in the bank and of making all payments by check in conjunction with the voucher system. The following transactions were selected from those completed in May of the current year:

May 1. Recorded Voucher No. 1 to establish a petty cash fund of $100 and a change fund of $250.
1. Issued Check No. 717 in payment of Voucher No. 1.
6. Recorded Voucher No. 7 to establish an advances to salesmen fund of $1,200.
6. Issued Check No. 720 in payment of Voucher No. 7.
13. The cash sales for the day according to the cash register tapes totaled $992.50. The count of cash on hand totaled $1,240.40.
27. Recorded Voucher No. 60 to replenish the advances to salesmen fund for the following expenditures for travel: Jack Cooley, $410.50; A. J. Polk, $280; John Spencer, $317.80.
28. The cash sales for the day according to the cash register tapes totaled $818.80. The count of cash on hand totaled $1,073.80.
29. Issued Check No. 766 in payment of Voucher No. 60.
31. Recorded Voucher No. 73 to reimburse the petty cash fund for the following disbursements, each evidenced by a petty cash receipt:
   May 3. Store supplies, $9.
   5. Express charges on merchandise purchased, $8.75.
   8. Office supplies, $11.20.
   9. Postage stamps, $10 (Office Supplies).
   17. Repairs to adding machine, $9.50 (Misc. General Expense).
   22. Postage due on special delivery letter, $.35 (Misc. Gen. Exp.).
   25. Telegram charges, $2.70 (Misc. Selling Expense).
   25. Store supplies, $10.
   29. Repair to typewriter, $9.15 (Misc. General Expense).
   30. Office supplies, $12.50.
31. Issued Check No. 779 in payment of Voucher No. 73.

Instructions: Record the above transactions in general journal form.

12-5. Redmon Bros. makes all disbursements by check in conjunction with a voucher system and deposits receipts in a night depository after banking hours each Wednesday and Friday. The data necessary for reconciling the bank statement as of June 30 of the current year are presented below.

Balance in the cash in bank account as of June 1.........	$6,615.87
Total of Cash in Bank Dr. column in cash receipts journal for June..........	6,393.88
Total of Cash in Bank Cr. column in check register for June.	5,819.57

The firm's records indicated the following deposits during June:

Date	Amount	Date	Amount	Date	Amount
June 2	$572.32	June 14	$915.30	June 23	$ 505.37
7	809.17	16	497.15	28	1,010.11
9	605.21	21	816.20	30	663.05

The check register indicated that the following checks were issued during June:

Check No.	Amount	Check No.	Amount	Check No.	Amount
895	$227.15	902	$615.76	909	$901.10
896	535.34	903	419.56	910	Void
897	619.91	904	80.81	911	310.16
898	315.52	905	91.73	912	93.20
899	289.89	906	390.13	913	117.16
900	77.69	907	212.32	914	202.13
901	110.17	908	40.67	915	169.17

Data appearing on the bank statement for June and the memos and checks accompanying the bank statement are as follows:

Balance, June 1 .... $6,519.19

Deposits reported on the bank statement:

Date	Amount	Date	Amount	Date	Amount
June 1	$713.71	June 10	$605.21	June 22	$ 816.20
3	572.32	15	915.30	24	505.37
8	809.17	17	497.15	29	1,010.11

Checks rearranged in numerical order:

Check No.	Amount	Check No	Amount	Check No.	Amount
872	$ 39.40	898	$315.52	906	$390.13
891	172.55	899	289.89	907	212.32
893	87.16	901	110.17	909	901.10
894	317.92	902	651.76	911	310.16
895	227.15	903	419.56	912	93.20
896	535.34	904	80.81	913	117.16
897	619.91	905	91.73		

Bank memorandums:

Date	Description	Amount
June 12	Bank credit memo for note collected:	
	Principal	$500.00
	Interest	7.50
14	Bank debit memo for check returned because of insufficient funds	125.00
30	Bank debit memo for service charges	1.40
30	Bank debit memo for annual safe deposit box rental. .	10.00

Balance, June 30 .... $7,351.89

The bank reconciliation for the preceding month was as follows:

Redmon Bros.
Bank Reconciliation
May 31, 19—

Balance per bank statement		$6,519.19
Add: Deposit of May 31, not recorded by bank		713.71
		$7,232.90
Deduct: Outstanding checks:		
No. 872	$ 39.40	
No. 891	172.55	
No. 893	87.16	
No. 894	317.92	617.03
Adjusted balance		$6,615.87
Balance per books		$6,617.77
Deduct: Service charges		1.90
Adjusted balance		$6,615.87

Instructions: (1) Prepare a bank reconciliation as of June 30. If errors in recording checks are discovered, assume that the errors were made by the company.

(2) Journalize the necessary entries. The books have not been closed.

(3) What is the amount of Cash in Bank that would appear on the balance sheet at June 30?

12-6. Lollar Company was organized on April 1 of the current year. The voucher system is not used. The following transactions are selected from those completed during April:

April 2. Purchased $6,500 of merchandise from Elston Industries, terms 1/10, n/30. Purchases invoices are recorded at the net price after deducting allowable cash discounts.

6. Issued a check to National Insurance Co. in payment of the premiums on the following insurance policies, all dated April 3:

Policy No.	Property	Amount	Term	Premium
7912	Building	$50,000	3 years	$684
7913	Merchandise	20,000	5 years	315
7914	Delivery Equipment		1 year	570

9. Purchased $1,500 of merchandise from Dexter Co., terms 2/10, n/30.

11. Issued a check for $147 to the Northern Guaranty Insurance Co. in payment of the premium on Policy No. 3712A, dated April 9, covering fidelity insurance for one year in the amount of $15,000.

18. Paid the amount due Dexter Co. for invoice of April 9.

26. Issued a check for $174 to the Acme Insurance Company in payment of Policy No. 6619, dated April 24, covering public liability for one year in the amount of $200,000.

29. Paid the amount due Elston Industries for invoice of April 2.

April 30. Issued a check for $100 to Hardenbrook's Garage in payment of the balance due on charges of $450 for repair of a delivery truck damaged in a collision earlier in the month. National Insurance Co. paid $350 of the charge in accordance with the terms of Policy No. 7914, which has a $100 deductible clause on collision damage.

Instructions: (1) Present in general journal form the debits and the credits required to record the transactions.

(2) Record the relevant data in an insurance register for the current year similar to the one illustrated on pages 294 and 295. In allocating insurance expirations, round all expirations to the nearest whole month.

(3) Journalize the insurance adjustment as of April 30.

(4) Considering only those insurance policies included above:

(a) What will be the total amount of insurance expense for the current year ending December 31?

(b) What will be the amount of unexpired insurance that will appear on the balance sheet at December 31 of the current year?

12-7. The bank statement for Coady Industries for March of the current year indicates a balance of $17,715.32 on March 31. The balance according to the check stubs as of the same date is $17,381.51. The balance of Cash in Bank in the ledger as of March 1 is $19,406.59; pencil footings of the cash receipts journal and the check register for March indicate receipts and disbursements for the month of $29,662.40 and $30,711.16, respectively. Comparison of the bank statement and the accompanying checks and memorandums with the records reveals the following reconciling items:

(a) A deposit of $976.32 on March 12 was not recorded on the check stubs. The cash received was recorded properly in the cash receipts journal.

(b) Checks outstanding: No. 1420, $362.50; No. 1472, $79.75; No. 1473, $131.14; No. 1475, $473.00; No. 1476, $990.10.

(c) Proceeds of a bank loan on March 31 were omitted from the cash receipts journal and the check stubs. The note was for $2,500 and was discounted by the bank at 6% for 60 days.

(d) Receipts of $893.20 from cash sales for March 20 were entered in the cash receipts journal and on the check stubs as $892.20. The receipts, all of which were deposited, appeared on the bank statement as $893.20.

(e) Canceled check No. 1440 for $630 was erroneously listed on the bank statement as $680.

(f) A debit memorandum indicated that the bank had deducted the principal of $5,000, the interest of $100, and the protest fee of $5 on a note that had been discounted at the bank by Coady Industries. Prior notice of the failure of A. B. James Co. to pay the note and of the bank's charge had been received by Coady Industries, but no entry had been made nor had a deduction been recorded on the check stubs.

Instructions: (1) Prepare a reconciliation of the bank statement with the cash in bank account after giving effect to the recorded receipts and disbursements.

(2) Determine the net amount of the adjustment to the check stub balance as of March 31, presenting the computations.

(3) Present in general journal form the necessary entries based on the bank reconciliation.

13.

Payroll taxes and sales taxes

Necessity for payroll records

Detailed payroll data must be accumulated by all business enterprises as well as by nonprofit enterprises and governmental agencies. The most obvious use of such information is in determining the amount owed to employees on payday. There are many other reasons why wage and salary information should be readily available; the need and the manner of use vary with the type of activity in which the employee is engaged and the nature of the employer's operations.

Almost all employers are required by federal laws to withhold certain taxes from the earnings of their employees. They are also required to pay, out of their own revenue, federal taxes based upon the amount of their payroll. In addition, each state levies payroll taxes on employers, and many states and cities require employers to collect taxes levied upon the earnings of their employees. It is the collection, payment, and reporting of these taxes to which the major portion of this chapter is devoted, but other matters inextricably related to payrolls will also be considered.

The original development of the practice of withholding earnings from employees is largely attributable to the requirements of federal tax statutes. It has since been greatly expanded to include the withholding of specific sums for many other purposes, including union dues, insurance premiums, charitable contributions, and employee savings.

Payroll records are also required by management in the control of labor costs and the proper allocation of wages and payroll taxes among expense accounts. They may be employed in the negotiation of contracts with labor unions, in settling grievances held by employees, and in determining entitlement to vacations, sick leaves, and retirement pensions.

Types of remuneration

The term *salary* is usually applied to payment for managerial, administrative, or similar services. The rate of salary is ordinarily expressed in terms of a month or a year. Remuneration for manual labor, both skilled and unskilled, is commonly referred to as *wages* and is stated on an hourly, weekly, or piecework basis. In practice, the terms salary and wages may be used interchangeably. The basic salary or wages of an employee may be supplemented by commissions, bonuses, pensions, profit-sharing plans, or cost-of-living adjustments. The form in which remuneration is paid generally has no effect on the manner in which it is treated by either the employer or the employee. Although remuneration is usually paid in money, payment may be made in other media such as notes, stocks, lodging, meals, or other property or services.

Employer-employee relationship

Not all persons who perform services for a business are classified as employees; some are independent contractors. The relationship of employer and employee generally exists when the person for whom the services are performed has the right to control and direct the individual in the performance of his services. Thus a salesclerk in a department store and a receptionist in a physician's office are clearly employees. On the other hand, a public accountant engaged to audit the accounting records of a business chooses his own means of performing his services and is not subject to the control and guidance of his client. He is an independent contractor rather than an employee. Similarly, a lawyer retained to negotiate a contract or defend a lawsuit is an independent contractor. Other examples of independent contractors are architects, physicians, and public stenographers.

Payments to independent contractors for services are usually called *fees* rather than salary or wages. In any event, such payments are not subject to the various payroll taxes and should not be included in the payroll.

Computation of earnings

The earnings of employees may be based on time worked, sales volume, or some other criterion of productivity. The measure most frequently employed is time, and the remuneration is usually stated as a rate per hour, day, week, month, or year.

Timekeeping. When remuneration is based on time, it is necessary to maintain a record of the time worked by each employee. Most enterprises employing a substantial number of people use automatic time clocks or other special equipment to record and summarize such time-keeping information.

Wage rates, overtime. Wage and salary rates are fixed, in general, by agreement between the employer and the employees. Enterprises engaged in interstate commerce must also conform to the requirements of the Federal Fair Labor Standards Act. Employers covered by this legislation, which is commonly known as the "wages and hours law," are required to pay a minimum rate of 1½ times the regular rate for all hours worked in excess of 40 hours per week. Exemptions from the requirements are provided for executive, administrative, and certain supervisory positions. Premium rates for overtime or for working at night or other less desirable times are fairly common, even when not required by law, and the premium rates may be as much as twice the base rate.

The computation of the earnings of an employee is illustrated below. It is assumed that Thomas R. Allen is employed at the rate of $3.10 per hour for the first 40 hours in the weekly pay period and at $4.65 ($3.10 + $1.55) per hour for any additional hours. His time card reveals that he worked 45 hours during the week ended October 7. His earnings for that week are computed as follows:

Earnings at base rate	40 × $3.10	$124.00
Earnings at overtime rate	5 × $4.65	23.25
Total earnings		$147.25

Deductions from earnings

In nearly all cases the amount that the employer pays an employee is less than the amount earned, the reduction being the amount withheld by the employer for taxes assessed against the employee. In addition, other deductions from earnings authorized by the employee may be withheld by the employer.

FICA tax. Most employers are required by the Federal Insurance Contributions Act to withhold a portion of the earnings of each of their employees. The amount withheld is the employees' contribution to the federal program of old-age, survivors, and disability insurance. It is frequently referred to as the FICA (Federal Insurance Contributions Act) tax or the FOAB (Federal Old-Age Benefits) tax, the latter term emphasizing the old-age benefits feature of the law. Unless specifically exempted, every employer is required to withhold from each employee a tax on earnings up to a specified amount paid in the calendar year.[1]

[1]For purposes of illustration in this chapter, a rate of 4% on earnings up to $5,400 will be assumed. Both the tax rates and the maximum amount subject to tax are frequently changed by Congress. Such changes do not affect the general principles or the accounting procedures.

Federal income tax. Except for certain types of employment, all employers are required to withhold a portion of the earnings of their employees for payment of the employees' liability for federal income tax. The amount required to be withheld varies in accordance with the amount of earnings and the number of exemptions. An employee may claim an exemption for himself, for each person who qualifies as a dependent, such as his children, and for his wife unless she is also employed and claims her own exemption. Additional exemptions are allowed to an employee if he or his wife is 65 years of age or older or is blind. Every employee is required by law to file with his employer an employee's withholding exemption certificate in which he reports the number of his exemptions.

FORM W-4 (Rev. July 1964)
U.S. Treasury Department
Internal Revenue Service

EMPLOYEE'S WITHHOLDING EXEMPTION CERTIFICATE

Print full name Thomas R. Allen — Social Security Account Number 259-08-8114

Print home address 1986 Belmont Street — City Lakewood — State Ohio 44112

EMPLOYEE: File this form with your employer. Otherwise, he must withhold U.S. income tax from your wages without exemption.

EMPLOYER: Keep this certificate with your records. If the employee is believed to have claimed too many exemptions, the District Director should be so advised.

HOW TO CLAIM YOUR WITHHOLDING EXEMPTIONS

1. If SINGLE, and you claim your exemption, write "1", if you do not, write "0" . . . . ________
2. If MARRIED, one exemption each is allowable for husband and wife if not claimed on another certificate.
   (a) If you claim both of these exemptions, write "2"
   (b) If you claim one of these exemptions, write "1"
   (c) If you claim neither of these exemptions, write "0" 2
3. Exemptions for age and blindness (applicable only to you and your wife but not to dependents):
   (a) If you or your wife will be 65 years of age or older at the end of the year, and you claim this exemption, write "1"; if both will be 65 or older, and you claim both of these exemptions, write "2" . . . . ________
   (b) If you or your wife are blind, and you claim this exemption, write "1"; if both are blind, and you claim both of these exemptions, write "2" . . . . ________
4. If you claim exemptions for one or more dependents, write the number of such exemptions. (Do not claim exemption for a dependent unless you are qualified under instruction 3 on other side.) 2
5. Add the number of exemptions which you have claimed above and write the total 4
6. Additional withholding per pay period under agreement with employer. *See* Instruction 1 . . . . . $

I CERTIFY that the number of withholding exemptions claimed on this certificate does not exceed the number to which I am entitled.

(Date) July 20, 1964. (Signed) Thomas R. Allen

Withholding exemption certificate

The amount of income tax to be withheld from the earnings of an employee can be individually computed or it can be determined by reference to a withholding table issued by the Internal Revenue Service. Separate tables are available for various payroll periods, such as weekly, biweekly, semimonthly, and monthly. Provision is made for varying amounts of remuneration and number of exemptions claimed. If the minimum amount required to be withheld will be insufficient to pay the employee's entire tax liability, he may authorize additional withholding by the employer.

State and local taxes. Many of the states and cities levying an income tax on individuals require employers to withhold the tax from the earnings of employees. A few states also require employee contributions to their unemployment compensation program, and these contributions are collected through payroll deductions.

Other deductions. Deductions from earnings for payment of taxes are compulsory; neither the employer nor the employee has any choice in the matter. In addition, however, there may be other deductions authorized by employees either individually or as a group. For example, the deduction of union dues and of premiums on group hospitalization, medical, and life insurance may be provided for in the contract between the employer and the union representing the workers. A partial list of purposes for which other deductions may be made follows:

(1) Deductions to accumulate funds to be used to purchase United States Savings Bonds for the employees.
(2) Deductions to pay the premiums on life, health, hospital, medical, or accident insurance for the employees.
(3) Deductions authorized by the employees for a retirement annuity or pension.
(4) Deductions authorized to be paid to a charitable organization (Red Cross, Community Chest, etc.).
(5) Deductions authorized to repay a loan or an advance from the company or a loan from the employees' credit union.
(6) Deductions authorized to pay for purchases of a product or a service of the company.

Regardless of the purpose of deductions, the employer must keep an accurate record of the amounts deducted and must dispose of the funds as directed. Until payment has been made, the amounts withheld represent liabilities of the enterprise.

Computation of net pay

Earnings for a payroll period less the payroll deductions yields the amount to be paid to the employee, which is frequently called the *take-home* or *net* pay. The amount to be paid Thomas R. Allen is $119.26, based on the following summary:

Total earnings for the week		$147.25
Deductions:		
FICA tax	$ 2.99	
Federal income tax	13.50	
U.S. savings bonds	6.50	
Community Chest	5.00	
Total deductions		27.99
Net pay		$119.26

In computing the FICA tax, it may be necessary to consider the cumulative amount of the employee's remuneration for the year to date. Otherwise, the amount withheld may exceed the maximum required by law. For example, Allen's cumulative earnings prior to the current week amounted to $5,325.25. If $5,400 is the maximum remuneration taxable as is assumed in this chapter, the amount of the current week's earnings subject to FICA tax is $74.75 ($5,400 − $5,325.25). There will be no additional FICA tax on his remuneration for the remainder of the year.

The amount of income tax withheld from Allen's remuneration was determined by reference to the withholding table for a weekly payroll period for earnings of $147.25 with 4 exemptions claimed. The deductions for savings bonds and a contribution to the Community Chest are in accordance with Allen's specific authorizations.

It is customary for employers to supply a statement of earnings and deductions with each paycheck or pay envelope. Checks designed specifically for payrolls are commonly used, many of which have a detachable stub for reporting the details.

Payroll register

The term *payroll* is used to refer to the total wages and salaries for a specified period; it is also applied to the form on which details of employees' earnings and other relevant information are assembled. This form is more specifically referred to as the *payroll register*. The arrangement of data in the register may vary considerably, depending upon whether automatic equipment is used and the type of equipment. A manually prepared form suitable for a small number of employees is illustrated below. A payroll system employing automated data processing is described in Appendix A.

Most of the columns in the payroll register are self-explanatory. The two columns under the heading Taxable Earnings are solely for memo-

PAYROLL FOR WEEK ENDED

NAME	TOTAL HOURS	EARNINGS			TAXABLE EARNINGS	
		REGULAR	OVERTIME	TOTAL	UNEMPLOYMENT COMP.	FICA
Allen, Thomas R.	45	124.00	23.25	147.25		74.75
Ballard, Mary	40	86.00		86.00	86.00	86.00
Davis, John T.	41	88.00	3.30	91.30	41.60	91.30
Drake, Paul W.		275.00		275.00		
Williams, Rose V.	40	120.00		120.00		93.00
York, Henry J.		170.00		170.00		
		3,978.15	207.45	4,185.60	763.20	3,362.75

Other Deductions: AR — Accounts Receivable

Payroll register — left page

randum purposes; their totals are used in computing the employer's payroll taxes. Unemployment compensation taxes apply only to the first $3,000 of remuneration per employee, and, as stated earlier, the FICA tax is assumed to apply to the first $5,400. Information regarding each employee's year-to-date earnings is obtained from the *employees' earnings record*, which is described later in the chapter. Of Thomas R. Allen's earnings for the week, none is subject to unemployment compensation tax and $74.75 is subject to FICA tax. Mary Ballard's cumulative earnings to date are less than $3,000; hence the entire remuneration is subject to both taxes. The cumulative earnings of John Davis passed the $3,000 level during the current week, and Paul Drake, a supervisory employee, had exceeded the $5,400 level earlier.

Deductions from the employee's earnings are inserted in the appropriate columns and the total is deducted from the total earnings to yield the amount to be paid. Recording the check numbers on the payroll register as the checks are written eliminates any necessity of maintaining check stubs or other detailed records of the payment.

The last two columns of the payroll register illustrated are used to accumulate the total wages or salaries to be charged to the expense accounts. This process is usually termed *payroll distribution*. If there is an extensive account classification of labor expense, the charges may be analyzed on a separate payroll distribution sheet.

The columns in the payroll register should be added and the totals cross-verified before the payroll checks are issued or the data are journalized. The "other" deductions must also be summarized by account classi-

OCTOBER 7, 19—

DEDUCTIONS					PAID		ACCOUNTS DEBITED	
FICA TAX	FEDERAL INCOME TAX	U.S. SAVINGS BONDS	OTHER	TOTAL	NET AMOUNT	CHECK NO.	SALES SALARY EXPENSE	OFFICE SALARY EXPENSE
2.99	13.50	6.50	CC 5.00	27.99	119.26	901	147.25	
3.44	10.40	3.25	CC 4.00	21.09	64.91	902		86.00
3.65	10.90		AR 16.50	31.05	60.25	903		91.30
	29.50	20.00	CC 25.00	74.50	200.50	904	275.00	
3.72	15.40	5.00		24.12	95.88	934	120.00	
	22.70	10.00	CC 15.00	47.70	122.30	935		170.00
134.51	422.10	197.25	CC 182.00 AR 16.50	952.36	3,233.24		3,657.90	527.70

CC — Community Chest MI — Medical Insurance

Payroll register — right page

fications and a total inserted for each. The method of cross verification is illustrated by the tabulation below. The computations are ordinarily made on an adding machine, taking the figures directly from the columnar totals.

Earnings:		
Regular	$3,978.15	
Overtime	207.45	
Total		$4,185.60
Deductions:		
FICA tax	$ 134.51	
Federal income tax	422.10	
U.S. Savings Bonds	197.25	
Community Chest	182.00	
Accounts receivable	16.50	
Total		952.36
Paid — net amount		$3,233.24
Accounts debited:		
Sales Salary Expense		$3,657.90
Office Salary Expense		527.70
Total (as above)		$4,185.60

Recording the payroll in the accounts

The general journal entry to record the payroll illustrated on the preceding pages is as follows:

Oct.	7	Sales Salary Expense	3,657.90	
		Office Salary Expense	527.70	
		FICA Tax Payable		134.51
		Employees Income Tax Payable		422.10
		Bond Deductions Payable		197.25
		Community Chest Contributions Payable		182.00
		Accounts Receivable — John T. Davis		16.50
		Salaries Payable		3,233.24
		Payroll for week ended October 7		

The total expense incurred for the services of employees is recorded by the debits to the salary accounts. Amounts withheld from employees' earnings have no effect on the debits to the salary expense accounts. Of the six credits in the compound entry, five represent increases in specific liability accounts and one represents a decrease in the accounts receivable account.

An alternative to recording each payroll separately is to make a single compound entry for all pay periods ending within the month. Another possibility is to treat the payroll register as a special journal and to post columnar totals to the appropriate ledger accounts.

Paying the payroll

The procedures for recording payment of the payroll are affected by the method of payment and the accounting system employed for cash payments generally. Employees may be paid (1) by checks drawn on the regular bank account, (2) by the use of currency, or (3) by special payroll checks drawn on a payroll bank account.

Regular checks. If the employees are paid by checks drawn on the regular bank account and the voucher system is not used, the payment is recorded directly in the cash payments journal as a debit to Salaries Payable and a credit to Cash.

When cash disbursements are controlled through use of the voucher system, it is necessary to prepare a voucher for the net amount to be paid the employees. The voucher is then recorded in the voucher register as a debit to Salaries Payable and a credit to Accounts Payable, and payment is recorded in the check register as a debit to Accounts Payable and a credit to Cash in Bank.

In either case the amount paid may be recorded as a single item regardless of the number of checks issued. Details about each check are available in the payroll register for future reference.

Currency. Currency is sometimes used as the medium of payment when the payroll is paid each week or when the business location or the time of payment are such that banking or check-cashing facilities are not readily available to employees. In such cases a single check, payable to Payroll, is drawn for the entire amount to be paid. The check is then cashed at the bank and the money is inserted in individual payroll envelopes. The entries are the same as when payment is made by regular checks.

Payroll checks. Most employers with a large number of employees use a check designed specifically for payroll purposes. A regular check for the entire amount to be paid the employees is drawn to Payroll and is deposited in a special payroll account at the bank. The individual payroll checks are then drawn against the special payroll account, and the numbers of the payroll checks are inserted in the payroll register.

The use of special payroll checks makes it possible to relieve the treasurer or other executives of the task of signing a large number of regular checks each payday. The responsibility for signing payroll checks may be assigned to the paymaster, or mechanical means of signing the checks may be employed. Another advantage of this system is that the task of reconciling the regular bank statement is simplified. The paid payroll checks are returned separately from regular checks and are accompanied by a statement of the special bank account. Any balance shown by the payroll bank statement should always be equal to the sum of the outstanding payroll checks. In this connection it should be noted that the special payroll bank account does not appear in the ledger. The amount of each deposit is exactly equal to the sum of the payments, thus reducing the balance to zero. The entries to record the payment are the same as when regular checks are used.

Employee's earnings record

It is necessary to know the cumulative earnings of each employee at various times throughout the year in order to determine the amounts to withhold from the employee, the amounts of the employer's payroll taxes, and the amounts to report on various quarterly and annual tax

EMPLOYEE'S

NAME Allen, Thomas R.
ADDRESS 1986 Belmont Street
Lakewood, Ohio 44112
PHONE 531-1149

MALE ✓ FEMALE ___ MARRIED ✓ SINGLE ___ NUMBER OF EXEMPTIONS 4 PAY RATE $124.00 PER DAY ___ WEEK ✓ MONTH ___

OCCUPATION Salesman EQUIVALENT HOURLY RATE $3.10

LINE NO.	PERIOD ENDED	TOTAL HOURS	EARNINGS			
			REGULAR	OVERTIME	TOTAL	CUMULATIVE TOTAL
39	Sept. 30	42	124.00	9.30	133.30	5,325.25
THIRD QUARTER			1,612.00	18.60	1,630.60	
40	Oct. 7	45	124.00	23.25	147.25	5,472.50
41	Oct. 14	42	124.00	9.30	133.30	5,605.80
42	Oct. 21	40	124.00		124.00	5,729.80
43	Oct. 28	40	124.00		124.00	5,853.80
51	Dec. 23	45	124.00	23.25	147.25	6,915.55
52	Dec. 30	43	124.00	13.95	137.95	7,053.50
FOURTH QUARTER			1,612.00	116.25	1,728.25	
YEARLY TOTAL			6,448.00	605.50	7,053.50	

Employee's earnings record — left page

forms. Employees' earnings records may also be useful in determining the rights of employees to bonuses, pensions, and vacation leaves and in answering questions in connection with the wages and hours law.

The form of the employee's earnings record varies, but all types contain much the same information. A portion of the earnings record of Thomas R. Allen is presented below.

The upper portion of the form is used to record miscellaneous personal data about the employee, including such information as the employee's address, social security number, and number of withholding exemptions.

In addition to spaces for recording data for each payroll period, there are spaces for quarterly totals and the yearly total. These totals are used

EARNINGS RECORD

SOC. SEC. NO. 259-08-8114 EMPLOYEE NO. 15

DATE EMPLOYEED June 15, 1962

DATE OF BIRTH April 22, 1937

DATE EMPLOYMENT TERMINATED ______

DEDUCTIONS					PAID		LINE NO.
F.I.C.A. TAX	FEDERAL INCOME TAX	U. S. BONDS	OTHER	TOTAL	NET AMOUNT	CHECK NO.	
5.33	11.40	6.50		23.23	110.07	866	39
65.22	131.60	84.50	AR 22.50	303.82	1,326.78		
2.99	13.50	6.50	CC 5.00	27.99	119.26	901	40
	11.40	6.50		17.90	115.40	936	41
	10.00	6.50	CC 5.00	21.50	102.50	972	42
	10.00	6.50		16.50	107.50	1007	43
	13.50	6.50		20.00	127.25	1216	51
	12.10	6.50		18.60	119.35	1252	52
2.99	147.30	84.50	CC 15.00	249.79	1,478.46		
216.00	621.80	338.00	AR 22.50 CC 15.00	1,213.30	5,840.20		

Employee's earnings record — right page

in preparing various tax reports. The entries in the illustration for the week ended October 7 should be compared with the entries on the first line of the payroll register appearing on pages 312 and 313.

Withholding tax statement

Withholding tax statements for the calendar year must be issued to employees by the end of the succeeding January. Gross remuneration paid and amounts withheld are reported for both FICA tax and income tax purposes. The report is made on Form W-2 in quadruplicate, with two copies for the employee, one for the District Director of Internal Revenue, and one for the employer's files. The employee is required to attach one copy of the form to his income tax return. A W-2 form prepared from the earnings record on pages 316 and 317 appears below.

Evans Electrical Supply Co.
24913 Carnegie Boulevard
Lakewood, Ohio 44112 27-0118342

WITHHOLDING TAX STATEMENT
Federal taxes withheld from wages

Type or print EMPLOYER'S identification number, name, and address above. *Copy A—For District Director*

SOCIAL SECURITY INFORMATION		INCOME TAX INFORMATION		
$216.00 F.I.C.A. employee tax withheld, if any	$5,400.00 Total F.I.C.A. wages paid	$621.80 Federal income tax withheld, if any	$7,053.50 Total wages* paid	

259-08-8114

Thomas R. Allen
1986 Belmont Street
Lakewood, Ohio 44112

EMPLOYER: See instructions on other side.

FOR USE OF INTERNAL REVENUE SERVICE
Employee's copy and employer's copy compared . . . .

Type or print EMPLOYEE'S social security account no., name, and address above.

FORM W-2—U.S. Treasury Department, Internal Revenue Service

*Before payroll deductions or "sick pay" exclusion.

Withholding tax statement

Employer's payroll taxes

Thus far the emphasis has been on the withholding of taxes levied against employees. Consideration will now be given to the payroll taxes levied against employers. Such taxes, which are an operating expense, are incurred by most business enterprises.

FICA tax. Employers are required to contribute to the Federal Insurance Contributions Act program for each employee. The tax is computed at the same rate and on the same earnings used in computing the FICA tax on employees.

Federal unemployment compensation tax. Unemployment insurance is a major feature of the national social security program. It provides temporary relief to those who become unemployed as a result of economic forces beyond their control and also tends to encourage full employment.

Types of employment covered by the unemployment insurance program are substantially the same as for the retirement insurance program, except that employers of less than four persons are exempt from the former. All employers covered by the law are required to pay a federal unemployment compensation tax on the first $3,000 paid to each covered employee during a calendar year. There is no tax on employees.

State unemployment compensation tax. The federal tax discussed in the preceding paragraph is distributed among the states for use in administering their unemployment compensation programs. Benefits paid to unemployed persons are financed by taxes levied upon employers by the state governments. A very few states also require employee contributions. The various state laws differ with respect to the types of covered employment and the number of workers an employer must have before the tax is applicable. In no case is the required number of workers greater than four; in a number of states it is one.

In most states the tax is based on the first $3,000 of earnings paid to each employee during the calendar year. In a small number of states the limit is higher. The tax rates vary among the states. In almost every state, however, employers who provide steady employment for their employees may earn a merit rating and thereby obtain a reduction from the maximum rate.

Recording the employer's payroll taxes

The employer's payroll taxes may be determined and recorded at the end of each payroll period or at the end of each month. In either case the basic data needed to compute the taxes are obtained from the payroll register. According to the payroll register illustrated on pages 312 and 313, for the week ended October 7 the amount of remuneration subject to FICA tax was $3,362.75 and the amount subject to state and federal unemployment compensation taxes was $763.20. Multiplication by the respective tax rates assumed to be applicable yields the following amounts:

FICA tax	$134.51
State unemployment compensation tax	20.61
Federal unemployment compensation tax	3.05
Total payroll tax expense	$158.17

There are various alternatives for recording the expense attributed to the several taxes: (1) the entire amount may be combined and debited to Payroll Tax Expense, (2) each tax may be debited to a separate appropriately identified tax expense account, or (3) the tax expenses may be debited to the respective wage or salary accounts to which they are related. In the interests of simplicity, the first alternative will be followed in this book. The credits required to complete the recording are made to liability accounts. Because of the necessity of reporting and paying the several taxes at different times and to different taxing authorities, an account should be maintained for each liability.

The general journal entry to record the payroll tax expense for the week and the liability for the taxes accrued is as follows:

				Debit	Credit
Oct.	7	Payroll Tax Expense		158 17	
		FICA Tax Payable			134 51
		State Unemployment Tax Payable			20 61
		Federal Unemployment Tax Payable			3 05
		Payroll taxes for the week ended October 7.			

Reporting and paying payroll taxes

The reporting requirements and the due dates of the various payroll taxes vary. Details of the federal income tax withheld and the FICA taxes are combined on a single return that must be filed quarterly. A remittance for the taxes due must accompany the return. If the combined taxes for either the first month or the second month of a calendar quarter exceed $100, earlier payment is required for those months.

All of the states require that returns for the state unemployment compensation tax be filed quarterly, accompanied by payment of the amount due. The federal unemployment compensation tax is reported and paid on an annual basis.

Employers are required to use the calendar year for all payroll tax purposes, regardless of the fiscal year they may employ for financial reporting and income tax purposes. The required tax forms and the amount owed are generally due by the last day of the month following the period covered by the return. Payment of the liability for each of the taxes is recorded in the same manner as the payment of other liabilities. When the voucher system is employed, a voucher should be prepared immediately prior to payment rather than at the time the payroll tax expense and the liability are initially recorded.

Accrual of payroll taxes

All of the payroll taxes levied against the employer become a liability when remuneration is *paid* to employees rather than when the services are performed. When wages incurred in a particular fiscal period are paid within the same fiscal period, the payroll tax expense is automatically allocated to the appropriate period. If, however, an enterprise records wage accruals at the end of the calendar year, which is also its fiscal year, there is a problem of expense allocation. Logically the payroll tax expense and the unpaid wages should both be charged to the period that benefited from the services performed by the employees. On the other hand, there is legally no liability for the payroll taxes until the following year, when the wages will be paid. In determining income for federal income tax purposes, the legal point of view applies. The greater convenience of the income tax method is likely to outweigh the minor loss of accuracy.

In order to simplify explanations and avoid confusion over dates, there has been an implicit assumption in the illustrations that payrolls are paid at the close of the last day of the pay period. In many business firms there is a lag of a variable number of days between the end of the payroll period and the payment of the payroll. Such a delay may be necessitated by the time required to complete the records and prepare the checks. For example, an employer who pays his employees on Friday may end the payroll period on Wednesday, the two-day lag between Wednesday and Friday being required to process the payroll.

When the payroll for the last completed payroll period in December will not be paid until January, the problem of payroll tax allocation again arises. The related employer's payroll tax expense would not be accrued if conformity with federal income tax methods is desired. The tax expense should be accrued if it is desired to relate such taxes to the period in which the wages were earned. It should be noted that in computing the tax accruals it is necessary to begin a new cycle of employee earnings subject to tax.

Sales taxes

Although not as universal as payroll taxes, state and city sales taxes affect many business enterprises. Sales taxes may be levied on the sale of commodities only or they may also apply to the sale of specified services such as dry cleaning, shoe repairs, and property rentals. Such taxes are usually imposed only upon retail sales or sales to consumers, with sales of certain commodities exempted from tax. For example, in some jurisdictions there is no tax on the sale of food for consumption off the premises of the seller. Sales of gasoline, cigarettes, and other commodities subject to a special tax by the state may also be exempted from the general sales tax.

Sales taxes are levied as a percent of all sales except those specifically exempted. In some states the tax is levied directly upon the seller. In others the statutes impose the tax upon the purchaser but require the seller to collect the tax. Sales tax returns, accompanied by a remittance for the amount due, are required to be filed monthly, quarterly, or semiannually, depending upon the law of the state or the city.

Sales tax imposed on the purchaser

Most of the sales tax laws impose the tax on the one making the purchase but require the seller to collect the tax and remit to the taxing authority. Liability for the tax is ordinarily incurred at the time the sale is made, regardless of the terms of payment. The seller therefore collects the tax at the time of a cash sale and charges the customer's account for the tax when credit is granted. The sales account should be credited only for the amount of the sale, the tax being credited to Sales Tax Payable. For example, a sale of $100 on account subject to a tax of 3% would be recorded, in general journal form, as follows:

Accounts Receivable	103	
Sales		100
Sales Tax Payable		3

The amount of tax charged on a sale on account should be reported as a separate item on the sales ticket or invoice. If such original evidences are used as a sales journal, separate monthly totals may be obtained for sales and for sales tax payable and an appropriate entry recorded in the general journal. If a separate sales journal is used, a special column should be provided for recording the credit to the sales tax payable account. A column for exempt sales may also be added if necessary. Arrangements for recording decreases in the tax liability account attributable to returns and allowances can be made in a similar manner.

The sales tax collected on a cash sale is ordinarily recorded as a separate item in the cash register. When this is not possible, the money received for the tax may be physically separated until the close of the day and then counted. Special columns for recording the amount of exempt sales and of sales tax collected can be added to the cash receipts journal.

Sales tax imposed on the seller

Sales taxes levied against the seller without any expectation of their being separately charged to the purchaser are sometimes called *gross receipts* taxes. The tax liability can be determined by applying the tax rate to the net taxable sales or other appropriate tax base. If the business enterprise prepares interim statements, the monthly accrual may be recorded by an adjusting entry similar to the following:

Sept.	30	Sales Tax Expense	474 10	
		Sales Tax Payable		474 10

Similar entries are made from month to month. At the time of payment, Sales Tax Payable is debited.

QUESTIONS

1. (a) Identify the federal taxes that most employers are required to withhold from employees. (b) Give the titles of the accounts to which the amounts withheld are credited.

2. What is the purpose of the Withholding Exemption Certificate?

3. The following questions are based on the assumption of a weekly payroll period and the use of a payroll bank account: (a) At what times should deposits be made in the account? (b) How is the amount of the deposit determined? (c) Is it necessary to have an account entitled "Payroll Bank" in the ledger? Explain. (d) The bank statement for the payroll bank account for the month ended October 31 indicates a bank balance of $416.84. Assuming that the bank has made no errors, how do you explain this fact?

4. The following questions are based on the assumption that the employer pays his employees in currency and that the pay envelopes are prepared by an employee rather than by the bank: (a) Why would it be advisable to obtain from the bank the exact amount of money needed for a payroll? (b) How could the exact number of each bill and coin denomination needed be determined efficiently in advance?

5. An employer who pays in currency draws a check for $18,624.10 for the payroll of November 20. After the money is inserted in the envelopes for the 119 employees, there remains $12 in currency. Assuming that the arithmetical accuracy of the payroll register has been determined and that the amounts of net pay stated on the pay envelopes agree with the payroll register, what would you do to locate the error?

6. What records are used in preparing Withholding Tax Statements (Form W-2) at the end of the year?

7. Indicate the principal uses of the employee's earnings record.

8. Identify the payroll taxes borne by the employer.

9. When an employer who uses the voucher system pays his employees every week, a voucher is prepared for each payroll. Should a voucher also be prepared for each tax liability at the same time? Explain.

10. Prior to the last weekly payroll period of the calendar year, the cumulative earnings of employees A and B are $5,300 and $5,400 respectively. Their earnings for the last completed payroll period of the year, which will be paid in January, are $100 each. If the amount of earnings subject to FICA tax is $5,400 and the tax rate is 4%, what will be the employer's FICA tax on the two salary amounts?

11. When should a sales tax imposed on the purchaser be recorded for a sale on account, at the time of the sale or when the cash is received?

12. A consumer paid $53.55 including sales tax of 2% for a commodity purchased. (a) Was the amount of the sales tax $1.07 (.02 × $53.55)? (b) If the answer to (a) is "no," how can the amount of the sales tax on this purchase be determined?

EXERCISES

1. Howard Borden is employed at the rate of $3.40 per hour, with time-and-one-half for all hours in excess of 40 worked during a week. Data to be considered in preparing the payroll register, Borden's paycheck, and his earnings record for the current week ended September 9 are as follows: hours worked, 43; federal income tax withheld, $16.30; cumulative earnings for year prior to current week, $5,305.60; FICA tax withheld prior to current week, $212.22. Compute the following for the week ended September 9: (a) Borden's earnings; (b) FICA tax to be withheld (4% on maximum of $5,400); (c) net amount to be paid.

2. In the following summary of columnar totals of a payroll register, some amounts have been intentionally omitted:

Earnings:		(6) Medical insurance.....	$ 75.50
(1) At regular rate........	—	(7) Total deductions......	534.80
(2) At overtime rate......	$ 197.40	(8) Net amount paid......	2,637.80
(3) Total earnings........	—	Accounts debited:	
Deductions:		(9) Sales Salaries.........	—
(4) FICA tax............	95.30	(10) Office Salaries........	423.90
(5) Income tax withheld...	—		

(a) Determine the totals omitted in lines (1), (3), (5) and (9). (b) Present the general journal entry to record the payroll. (c) Present, in general journal form, the entry to record the voucher for the payroll. (d) Present, in general journal form, the entry to record the payment of the payroll.

3. Total wage and salary expense of P. J. Mason Co. for the year was $100,000, of which $15,000 was not subject to FICA tax and $25,000 was not subject to state and federal unemployment taxes. Determine the employer's payroll tax expense for the year, using the following rates: FICA, 4%; state unemployment, 2.7%; federal unemployment, .4%.

4. According to a summary of the payroll register of Whitlock and Co. for the four weekly payrolls paid in June, the amount of earnings subject to FICA tax is $12,624.50 and the amount subject to unemployment compensation taxes is $10,374.85. Present the general journal entry to record the accrual of payroll taxes for the month, assuming the following rates: FICA, 4%; state unemployment, 1.9%; federal unemployment, .4%.

5. In recording sales during its first three months of operations, Briggs Hardware Co. failed to differentiate between the amount of its sales and the amount of a 3% sales tax charged on all sales. Credits to the sales account and debits to the sales returns and allowances account included the sales tax. Permission is granted by the state tax department to estimate the amount of tax due for the quarter. Balances in the sales account and the sales returns and allowances account are $101,483.89 and $908.32, respectively. (a) Determine the amount of sales tax due. (b) Present the entry, in general journal form, to record payment of the sales tax.

PROBLEMS

13-1. The Discount Barn has nine employees. They are paid on an hourly basis, receiving time-and-one-half pay for all hours worked in excess of 40 a week. The record of time worked for the week ended Saturday, August 31, of the current year, together with other relevant information, is summarized below:

Name	Total Hours	Hourly Rate	Income Tax Withheld	Bond Deductions	Cumulative Earnings, August 24
A	40	$2.20	$10.70	$2.50	$2,908
B	37	2.00	7.30	1.50	2,520
C	43	2.80	11.80	3.25	3,960
D	32	2.40	7.20		3,400
E	40	2.20	8.90	2.00	2,945
F	40	3.40	13.90		5,280
G	44	3.60	15.90	7.50	5,560
H	41	2.10	10.40	1.00	2,965
I	43	2.50	12.20	1.75	3,780

In addition to withholdings for income tax, FICA tax, and bond purchases, $15 is to be withheld from D for partial payment of his account receivable.

B and F are office employees; the others are salesmen. The following tax rates and limitations are assumed: FICA, 4% on maximum of $5,400; state unemployment (employer only), 2.2% on maximum of $3,000; federal unemployment, .4% on maximum of $3,000.

Instructions: (1) Prepare the payroll register for the week, using a form like the one illustrated on pages 312 and 313 of the textbook.

(2) Journalize the entry to record the payroll for the week.

(3) The company uses a voucher system and pays by regular check. Give the necessary entries in *general journal form* to record the payroll voucher and the issuance of the checks.

(4) Complete the payroll register by inserting the check numbers, beginning with No. 732.

(5) Journalize the entry to record the employer's payroll taxes for the week.

13-2. The following accounts, with the balances indicated, appear in the ledger of Modern Products Co. on December 1 of the current year:

214	Salaries Payable	—
215.1	FICA Tax Payable	$ 296.40
215.2	Employees Income Tax Payable	843.70
215.3	State Unemployment Tax Payable	97.64
215.4	Federal Unemployment Tax Payable	223.38
216.1	Bond Deductions Payable	327.50
216.2	Medical Insurance Payable	425.00
611	Sales Salary Expense	86,420.60
711	Officers Salary Expense	31,900.00
712	Office Salary Expense	8,420.40
719	Payroll Tax Expense	4,318.24

The following transactions relating to payroll, payroll deductions, and payroll taxes occurred during December:

Dec. 1. Prepared Voucher No. 518, payable to First National Bank, for $150 to purchase U.S. Savings Bonds for employees.
2. Issued Check No. 625 in payment of Voucher No. 518.
14. Prepared Voucher No. 539, payable to First National Bank, for the amount of employees income tax and FICA tax due on December 15.
14. Issued Check No. 646 in payment of Voucher No. 539.
14. Prepared a general journal entry to record the biweekly payroll for the period ending yesterday. A summary of the payroll record follows:
Deductions: FICA tax, $62.40; income taxes withheld, $491.10; bond deductions, $71.25; medical insurance deductions, $70.
Salary distribution: sales, $3,620; officers, $1,450; office, $460.
Net amount: $4,835.25.
14. Prepared Voucher No. 547, payable to Payroll Bank Account, for the net amount of the biweekly payroll.
14. Issued Check No. 654 in payment of Voucher No. 547.
16. Prepared Voucher No. 550, payable to Atlas Insurance Co., for $425, the semiannual premium on the group medical insurance policy.
17. Issued Check No. 657 in payment of Voucher No. 550.
28. Prepared a general journal entry to record the biweekly payroll for the period ending yesterday. A summary of the payroll record follows:
Deductions: FICA tax, $57.70; income taxes withheld, $497.50; bond deductions, $76.50.
Salary distribution: sales, $3,642; officers, $1,450; office, $460.
Net amount: $4,920.30.
28. Prepared Voucher No. 582, payable to Payroll Bank Account, for the net amount of the biweekly payroll.
28. Issued Check No. 690 in payment of Voucher No. 582.
29. Prepared Voucher No. 583, payable to First National Bank, for $112.50 to purchase U.S. Savings Bonds for employees.
30. Issued Check No. 692 in payment of Voucher No. 583.
31. Prepared a general journal entry to record the employer's payroll taxes on earnings paid in December. Taxable earnings for the two payrolls, according to the payroll records, are as follows: subject to FICA tax, $3,002.50; subject to unemployment compensation tax, $942.40. Assume the following tax rates: FICA, 4%; state unemployment, 2.2%; federal unemployment, .4%.

Instructions: (1) Open the accounts listed and enter the account balances as of December 1.

(2) Record the transactions, using a voucher register, a check register, and a general journal. The only amount columns needed in the voucher register are Accounts Payable Cr. and Sundry Accounts Dr. (subdivided into Account, Post. Ref., and Amount). The only amount columns needed in the check register are Accounts Payable Dr. and Cash in Bank Cr. After each entry, post to the accounts opened in the ledger and extend the new balances to the appropriate balance column.

(3) Journalize the adjusting entry on December 31 to record salaries for the incomplete payroll period. Salaries accrued are as follows: sales salaries, $345; officers salaries, $120; office salaries, $40. Post to the accounts.

(4) Journalize the entry to close the salary expense and payroll tax expense accounts to Expense and Revenue Summary and post to the accounts.

(5) Journalize the entry on January 1 to reverse the adjustment of December 31 and post to the accounts.

13-3. The state statutes require that retailers collect a sales tax of 2% on all sales to consumers except on certain items, such as seeds and fertilizers, and on sales to governmental units, such as public schools, cities, and counties. In the event that the amount collected is less than 2% of taxable sales, the deficiency must be borne by the retailer. Payments for each calendar quarter are payable by the end of the month following the quarter.

The balances in certain accounts of Bayless Markets as of March 31, after adjustments were made for the additional tax liability for the first quarter, and as of June 30 of the current fiscal year are presented below. The company closes its books on December 31.

	March 31	June 30
Sales Tax Payable	$ 2,124.73	$ 2,675.80
Sales	110,972.20	252,684.30
Sales Returns and Allowances	1,615.20	3,974.60
Sales Tax Expense	10.62	10.62

Supplementary records indicate that sales for the period April 1 through June 30 included nontaxable sales of $5,175.90 and that returns and allowances on nontaxable sales for the same period amounted to $319.60.

Instructions: (1) Determine the amount of the liability for sales tax for the second quarter of the year, presenting your figures in good order.

(2) Present the entry as of June 30 to record the additional liability for sales taxes for the second quarter.

(3) Present the entry on July 31, in general journal form, to record payment of the sales tax liability for the second quarter.

(4) On the basis of the ledger information presented above, determine the amount of the net taxable sales for the *first* quarter of the year.

13-4. The following information relative to the payroll for the week ended December 30 of the current year was abstracted from the payroll register and other records of Bancroft Enterprises:

Salaries:

Sales salaries	$34,700
Warehouse salaries	7,300
Office salaries	8,600
	$50,600

Deductions:

Income tax withheld	$4,140
U.S. Savings Bonds	650
Group insurance	200

FICA tax withheld is assumed to total the same amount as the employer's tax.

Tax rates assumed:

FICA, 4%.
State unemployment (employer only), 1.8%.
Federal unemployment, .4%.

Instructions: (1) Assuming that the payroll for the last week of the year is to be paid on December 31, present the following entries:

(a) December 30, to record the payroll. Of the total payroll for the last week of the year, $12,200 is subject to FICA tax and $3,240 is subject to unemployment compensation taxes.

(b) December 30, to record the employer's payroll taxes on the payroll to be paid on December 31.

(2) Assuming that the payroll for the last week of the year is to be paid on January 2 of the following fiscal year, present the following entries:

(a) December 31, to record the payroll.

(b) January 2, to record the employer's payroll taxes on the payroll to be paid on January 2.

13-5. Summary payroll data for Superior Furniture Co. for the week ended July 25 of the current fiscal year are presented below. Employees on an hourly basis are paid time-and-one-half for hours in excess of 40 a week.

Name	Total Hours	Hourly or Weekly Rate	Income Tax Withheld	Cumulative Earnings, July 18	Classifi-cations
Adams, R. J.	44	$ 2.80	$14.30	$2,910	Sales
Bates, Carl	42	2.00	10.40	2,408	Delivery
Clay, Paul M.		160.00	15.90	4,480	Sales
Fox, Ellen	40	2.10	10.10	2,352	Office
Hughes, Fred		140.00	16.40	3,920	Sales
Lee, John L.		200.00	19.00	5,600	Sales
Miller, Herbert		150.00	12.70	4,200	Office
Rush, Mary A.		130.00	16.80	3,640	Sales
Steber, A. C.	43	2.20	6.40	2,682	Delivery
Yost, J. T.		190.00	18.30	5,320	Sales

Assume the following tax rates: FICA, 4% on maximum of $5,400; state unemployment (employer only), 2.4% on maximum of $3,000; federal unemployment, .4% on maximum of $3,000.

Instructions: (1) Prepare a payroll register similar in form to the one on pages 312 and 313, deleting the deduction column not needed and adding another column for payroll distribution.

(2) Journalize the entry to record the payroll for the week.

(3) Assuming the use of a voucher system and payment by regular check, present the entries, in *general journal form*, to record the payroll voucher and the issuance of the checks to employees.

(4) Complete the payroll register by inserting the check numbers, beginning with No. 534.

(5) Journalize the entry to record the employer's payroll taxes for the four payroll periods in July. A summary of relevant information taken from the payroll register follows: taxable earnings subject to FICA tax, $3,980; taxable earnings subject to unemployment compensation tax, $1,470.

(6) Present the entries, in *general journal form*, to record the following transactions selected from those completed by Superior Furniture Co.:

Aug. 14. Prepared a voucher, payable to Citizens National Bank, for employees income taxes, $565.40, and FICA taxes, $318.40, on salaries paid in July.

14. Issued a check to Citizens National Bank in payment of the above voucher.

14. Concepts and principles

Need for concepts and principles

The historical development of accounting principles and practice has been closely related to the economic development of the country. In its earlier stages the primary objective of accounting was to provide financial data of an enterprise in the form of an income statement and a balance sheet. The statements were used primarily by the owners and the creditors of the enterprise as a means of appraising the results of operations and financial position. Business enterprises were ordinarily managed by their owners, and if a substantial amount was owed to a bank or a supplier, the creditor frequently participated in management decisions.

With the increase in the size and the complexity of business enterprises, a greater demarcation developed between "management" and "outsiders." The latter group, which is composed of owners (stockholders), creditors, government, labor unions, customers, and the general public, continues to be interested in the profitability, stability, and financial status of business enterprises. Management is interested, of course, in these same aspects of the enterprise but, in addition, relies upon accounting to provide an important element of internal control and specialized reports for use in guiding operations and planning for the future.

As business organizations grew and the outside parties became more and more removed from operations, the accounting problems involved in the issuance of financial statements became more complex. With these developments came an increasing awareness of the need for a framework of concepts and generally accepted accounting principles.

Development of concepts and principles

Financial statements are most significant to those who clearly understand the underlying principles upon which they have been based. It is equally evident that accountants must be in substantial agreement as to the meaning and the importance of the guides and the standards that, collectively, comprise accounting principles. Responsibility for their development has rested primarily on practicing accountants and accounting teachers, working both independently and as groups under the sponsorship of such organizations as the American Accounting Association and the American Institute of Certified Public Accountants. These principles are also influenced by business practices and customs, ideas and beliefs of the users of the financial statements, governmental agencies such as the Securities and Exchange Commission, and other business groups such as stock exchanges.

Various terms are employed by accountants in referring to a particular accounting standard. In addition to *principle* and *concept*, the terms *axiom*, *assumption*, *postulate*, *convention*, *tenet*, and *doctrine* are frequently encountered in accounting literature. An examination of the similarities and the differences in meaning of these terms is not essential to the understanding of the particular principles that will be discussed in this chapter; they are mentioned only for the sake of completeness.

It should be borne in mind that the word "principle" as used in this context does not have the same authoritativeness as universal principles or natural laws employed in the study of astronomy, physics, or the other physical sciences. Accounting principles have been developed by man to enhance the usefulness of accounting data in an ever-changing society. They represent the best possible guides, based on reason, observation, and experimentation, to the achievement of the desired results. The selection of the best single method, or of several equally good methods, among a number of alternatives, has come about gradually, and in some subject matter areas is still in a state of change. General acceptance among the leaders of the accounting profession is the criterion for determining an accounting principle. These principles are continually re-examined and revised to keep pace with changes in the economic environment.

The remainder of this chapter is devoted to the underlying assumptions, concepts, and principles of the greatest importance and the widest applicability. Some of them have been introduced in earlier chapters.

Business entity

The *business entity* concept assumes that a business enterprise is separate and distinct from the persons who supply the assets it uses. This is true regardless of the legal form of the business organization. The accounting equation, Assets = Equities, or Assets = Liabilities + Capital, is an expression of the entity concept; it is as if the business itself owns the assets and in turn owes the various claimants. Thus, the accounting process is primarily concerned with the enterprise as a productive economic unit and is only secondarily concerned with the investor as a claimant to the assets.

It is important that the student understand the distinction between the business entity concept employed in accounting for a sole proprietorship and the legal concept of a sole proprietorship. The nonbusiness assets, liabilities, revenues, and expenses of a sole proprietor are excluded from the business accounts. If a sole proprietor owns several distinct business enterprises, each may be treated as a separate entity for accounting purposes. On the other hand, a sole proprietor is personally liable for his business debts and may be required to use nonbusiness assets to satisfy the business creditors. Conversely, business assets are not immune from claims of the sole proprietor's personal creditors.

Differences between the business entity concept and the legal nature of other forms of business organization will be considered in later chapters. For accounting purposes, however, revenues and expenses of any enterprise are viewed as affecting the business assets and liabilities, not the owners' assets and liabilities.

Going concern

Only in rare instances is a business organized with the expectation of remaining in existence for only a specified period of time. In most cases there is no means of foretelling the length of life of an enterprise, and so an assumption must be made. The nature of the assumption will affect the manner of recording some of the business transactions, which in turn will affect the data reported in the financial statements.

It is customary to assume that a business entity has a reasonable expectation of continuing in business at a profit for an indefinite period of time. This assumption that an enterprise is a *going concern* provides much of the justification for recording plant assets at acquisition cost and depreciating them in a systematic manner without reference to their current realizable values. It is pointless to report plant assets on the balance sheet at their estimated realizable values if there is no immediate expectation of selling them. This is true regardless of whether the current market value of the plant assets is less than their book value or greater than their book value. If the firm continues to use the assets, the fluctuation in market value causes no gain or loss, nor does it enhance or diminish the usefulness of the assets. Thus, if the going concern assumption is a valid concept, the investment in plant assets will serve the purpose for which it was made. In this sense the investment will be recovered even though the assets may be individually marketable only at a loss.

The going concern assumption similarly supports the treatment of prepaid expenses as assets even though they may be virtually unsalable. To illustrate, assume that on the last day of its fiscal year a wholesale firm receives from a printer a $20,000 order of catalogs. In the absence of the assumption that the firm is to continue in business, the catalogs would be merely scrap paper and the value reported for them on the balance sheet would be negligible.

A less direct effect of the going concern concept is that it helps to focus attention on earnings rather than assets. The earning power of an enterprise is more significant than the market value of its individual assets in judging the overall worth of a business. Because of this emphasis on earnings, the accountant directs his attention to the proper allocation of revenues and expenses to the current period and needs not be concerned with determining the market value of assets that will not be sold.

Objective evidence

Entries in the accounting records and data for financial statements must be based on objectively determined evidence if the confidence of the many users of the financial statements is to be maintained. For example, objective evidence such as invoices and vouchers for purchases, bank statements for the amount of cash in bank, and physical counts for merchandise on hand supports much of accounting. Such evidence is completely objective and is subject to verification.

Evidence is not always conclusively objective, for there are numerous occasions in accounting where judgments, estimates, and other subjective factors must be taken into account. In such situations, the most objective evidence available should be used. For example, the provision for doubtful accounts is an estimate of the losses expected from failure to collect sales made on account. Estimation of this amount should be based on such objective factors as past experience in collecting accounts receivable and reliable forecasts of future business activities. To provide accounting reports that can be accepted with confidence, evidence should be developed that will minimize the possibility of error, bias, and intentional fraud.

Unit of measurement

All business transactions are recorded in terms of money. Other pertinent information of a nonfinancial nature may also be recorded, such as the description of assets acquired, the terms of purchase and sale contracts, and the purpose, amount, and term of insurance policies. But it is only through the record of dollar amounts that the diverse transactions and activities of a business may be measured, reported, and periodically compared. Money is both the common factor of all business transactions and the only practicable unit of measurement that can be employed to achieve homogeneity of financial data.

The use of the monetary unit as the common denominator imposes two major limitations on accounting for and reporting the activities of an enterprise: (1) it restricts the scope of accounting reports and (2) it assumes a stability of the measurement unit.

Scope of accounting reports. Many factors affecting the activities and the future prospects of an enterprise cannot be expressed in monetary terms. In general, accounting does not attempt to report such factors. For example, information regarding the capabilities of the management, the state of repair of the plant assets, the effectiveness of the employee welfare program, the attitude of the labor union, and the relative strength or weakness of the firm's principal competitors cannot be expressed in monetary terms. Although such information is important to investors and creditors, accountancy assumes no responsibility for providing it.

Stability of monetary unit. The dollar is far inferior, as a unit of measurement, to such quantitative standards as the pound, gallon, or yard, which have remained unchanged for centuries. The instability of the purchasing power of the dollar is well known. The disruptive effects of inflation on accounting reports during the past few decades are acknowledged by accountants, but to date recognition has not been given in the accounts and in the conventional financial statements to the declining value of the unit of measurement.

To indicate the nature of the problem, assume that the plant assets acquired by an enterprise for $100,000 twenty years ago are now to be replaced with similar assets which at present price levels will cost $200,000. The original cost was charged to revenue as depreciation expense over the twenty-year period, and, assuming that the enterprise has earned an income or at least broken even during the period, the initial outlay of $100,000 has been recovered. The amount recovered represents only one half of the cost of replacing the assets, however, or stated in another manner, the $100,000 recovered is worth only half as much as the sum that was originally invested. From either point of view, the firm has suffered a loss in purchasing power that, in a sense, is a loss of capital.

Accounting records and reports are based on verifiable objective evidence, and the use of subjective estimates or opinions concerning the effect of price level changes should be avoided. This is the major reason why accounting treats all dollars alike.

Although the use of original cost provides objectivity, the conventional financial statements do not clearly indicate financial position and results of operations in periods during which the purchasing power of the dollar fluctuates. To view the financial statements in proper perspective, it is generally recognized that information regarding the effects of the fluctuating dollar may be presented in supplementary financial schedules.

Accounting period

A complete and accurate picture of the degree of success achieved by an enterprise cannot be obtained until it discontinues operations and converts its assets into cash. Then, and only then, is it possible to determine with finality its net income. But innumerable decisions regarding the business must be made by management and interested outsiders throughout the period of its existence, and it is therefore necessary to prepare periodic reports on operations and financial position.

Reports may be prepared on the basis of the completion of a particular job or project, but the more usual practice is to prepare them at specified time intervals. For a number of reasons, including custom and various legal requirements, the maximum interval between reports is one year. Periodic measurements are always tentative and conditional. In spite of their provisional nature, however, they are essential to management and other interested parties as a basis for decision making.

It is this element of periodicity that creates many of the problems of accountancy. The fundamental problem is the determination of periodic net income. For example, the necessity for adjusting entries discussed in earlier chapters is directly attributable to the division of an enterprise into arbitrary time periods. Problems of inventory costing, of recognizing the uncollectibility of receivables, and of selecting depreciation methods are also directly related to the periodic measurement process. It should be noted that the amounts of the assets and the equities presented on the balance sheet will also be affected by the methods employed in determining net income. For example, regardless of the cost flow assumption employed in determining the cost of merchandise sold during the accounting period, the costs assigned to the remaining inventory will be the residual amount.

The determination of periodic net income is a two-fold problem involving (1) the revenue realized during the period and (2) the expired costs to be allocated to the period. It is thus a problem of matching expired costs and revenues, the residual amount being the provisional net income or loss for the particular period.

Recognition of revenue

Revenue is measured by the amount charged to customers for merchandise delivered or services rendered to them. The problem created by periodicity is one of timing; at what point is the revenue realized? For any particular accounting period, the question is whether revenue items should be recognized and reported as such in the current period or whether their recognition should be postponed to a future period.

Various criteria are acceptable for determining when revenue is realized. In any case the criteria adopted should be reasonably in accord with the terms of the contractual arrangements with the customer and based in so far as possible on objective evidence. The criteria of most frequent applicability are described in the remaining paragraphs of this section.

Point of sale. It is customary to consider revenue from the sale of commodities as being realized at the time title passes to the buyer. It is at this point that the sale price has been agreed upon, the buyer acquires the right of ownership in the commodity, and the seller has an enforceable claim against the buyer. The realization of revenue from the sale of services may be determined in a somewhat similar manner, although there is frequently a time lag between the time of the initial agreement and the completion of the service. For example, assume that a contract provides that certain repair services be performed, either for a specified price or on a time and materials basis. The initial contract to sell the services does not constitute revenue until the work has been performed.

Theoretically, revenue from the production and sale of commodities and services emerges continuously as effort is expended. As a practical matter, however, it is ordinarily not possible to make an objective determination until the sales price is agreed upon and the seller has completed his portion of the contract.

Receipt of payment. The recognition of revenue may be postponed until payment is received. When this criterion is adopted, revenue is considered to be earned at the time the cash is collected, regardless of when the sale was made. The cash basis is widely used by physicians, attorneys, and other enterprises in which professional services are the source of revenue. It has little theoretical justification but has the practical advantage of avoiding the problem of estimating losses from uncollectible accounts. Its acceptability as a fair method of timing the recognition of revenue is influenced somewhat by its simplicity and the fact that it may be used in determining income subject to the federal income tax. It is not an appropriate method of measuring revenue from the sale of commodities.

Installment method. In some businesses, especially in the retail field, it is common to make sales on the installment plan. In the typical installment sale the purchaser makes a down payment and agrees to pay the remainder in specified amounts at stated intervals over a period of time. The seller may retain technical title to the goods or may take other means to facilitate repossession in the event the purchaser defaults on his payments. An installment sale may be treated in the same manner as any other sale on account, in which case the revenue is considered to be realized at the point of sale. The alternative is to consider each receipt of cash to be composed of (1) a partial return of cost and (2) gross profit.

As a basis for illustration, assume that in the first year of operations the installment sales of a dealer in household appliances totaled $300,000, that the cost of the merchandise sold on installments totaled $180,000, and that down payments and installment payments received during the year totaled $140,000. The percent of cost of merchandise sold to sales was 60% (180,000 ÷ 300,000) and the percent of gross profit to sales was 40% (120,000 ÷ 300,000). According to the installment method, the $140,000 of cash receipts in the year of sale are assumed to represent a return of cost in the amount of $84,000 (60% × $140,000) and gross profit of $56,000 (40% × $140,000). Collections in future periods from the year's sales would similarly be treated as a pro rata return of cost (60%) and gross profit (40%).

As in the cash basis of revenue recognition, there is little theoretical justification for the installment method of determining revenue. Although it is generally accepted as an appropriate method, many accountants are inclined to view the sale and the conversion of the receivable into cash as separate and distinct transactions and believe that they should be so treated.

Degree of contract completion. Enterprises engaged in large construction projects may devote several years to the completion of a particular contract. If the point of sale criterion is employed, the revenue from a contract is not recognized until the job is completed. For example, assume that a contractor is engaged in a project that will require 3 years to complete, for which he is to receive $50,000,000. Assume also that the costs incurred on the contract during the 3-year period will total $44,000,000. It is unrealistic to assume that the net income of $6,000,000 will be earned entirely in the year in which the contract is completed.

In such situations as the foregoing it is acceptable to view the revenue as being earned over the entire life of the contract. The amount earned in any particular period is determined on the basis of the percentage of the contract that has been completed during the period. The costs incurred during the period are then matched against the revenue recognized. There is, of course, an element of subjectivity, and hence of possible error, in the determination of the amount of revenue earned. The financial statements may be more useful, however, in spite of estimates, than they would be if none of the revenue were recognized until the completion of the contract.

A situation somewhat comparable to long-term construction contracts arises in connection with revenue from rentals, loans, and other services that are definitely measurable on a time basis. Neither the point of sale, the receipt of payment, or the installment method is an appropriate criterion for determining the emergence of revenue from such sources. Both the amount of total revenue to be earned and the period over which it is to be earned are readily ascertainable. For example, if a building is leased for a period of 3 years at a rental of $36,000, the revenue is realized at the rate of $1,000 a month. It is immaterial whether the rent is received in a lump sum at the beginning of the lease, in installments over the life of the lease, or at its termination. In accordance with the concept of the going concern, it is assumed that the owner will supply the use of the building during the term of the lease and that the lessee will fulfill his part of the contract.

Allocation of costs

Properties and services acquired by an enterprise are generally recorded at cost. By cost is meant that cash or cash equivalent given to acquire the property or the service. If property other than cash is given to acquire properties or services, the cost is the cash equivalent of the property given. When the properties or the services acquired are sold or consumed, the costs are matched with the related revenue to determine the amount of net income or loss. The costs of properties or services acquired that are on hand at any particular time represent assets. Such costs may also be referred to as "unexpired costs." As the assets are sold or consumed, they become "expired costs" or "expenses."

Theoretically, it is possible to assign all costs to each specific product sold or each service rendered. If this were done, the net income of an enterprise could be measured in terms of units of output. In practice, however, it would be difficult and costly to fragmentize cost allocations to such a degree. As stated earlier in this chapter, the matching of expired costs and revenues on a periodic time basis is satisfactory.

The techniques of determining and recording cost expirations have been described and illustrated in earlier chapters. In general, there are two approaches to cost allocations: (1) compute the amount of the expired cost or (2) compute the amount of the unexpired cost. For example, it is customary to determine the portion of plant assets that have expired. After recording the depreciation for the period, the balances of the plant asset accounts minus the balances of the related accumulated depreciation accounts represent the unexpired cost of the assets. The alternative approach must be employed for merchandise and supplies unless perpetual inventory records are maintained. The cost of the merchandise or supplies on hand at the close of the period is ordinarily determined by taking a physical inventory, and the remaining costs in the related accounts are assumed to have expired. It might appear that the first approach emphasizes expired costs and the second emphasizes unexpired costs. This is not the case, however, as the selection of the method is based on convenience or practicability.

Many of the costs allocable to a period are treated as an expense at the time of incurrence because they will be wholly expired at the end of the period. For example, when a monthly rent is paid at the beginning of a month, the cost incurred is unexpired and hence it is an asset; but since the cost incurred will be wholly expired at the end of the month, it is customary to charge the rental directly to the appropriate expense account, thus avoiding the necessity for an additional entry later. The proper allocation of costs among periods is the paramount consideration; any one of a variety of accounting techniques may be employed.

Consistency

A number of accepted alternative principles affecting the determination of net income and asset values have been presented in earlier sections of the text. Recognizing that different methods may be used under varying circumstances, some guide or standard is needed to assure a high degree of comparability of the periodic financial statements of an enterprise. It is common practice to compare the current income statement and balance sheet with the preceding statements.

The amount and the direction of change in income or financial position from period to period is highly significant to the reader and may greatly influence his decisions. Therefore, interested persons should be able to assume that the successive financial statements of an enterprise are based consistently on the same generally accepted accounting principles. If the principles are not applied consistently, the trends indicated could be the result of changes in accounting methods rather than the result of changes in business conditions or managerial effectiveness.

The concept of consistency does not completely prohibit changes in accounting methods. Changes should be made where changing conditions indicate that another method will more fairly state net income and the financial position. For example, an enterprise that initially adopted the first-in, first-out assumption of inventory flow might at some later date decide to change to the last-in, first-out flow assumption. The change in method and its effect should be clearly disclosed in the financial statements for the period in which the change was made.

Adequate disclosure

Financial statements and their accompanying footnotes or other explanatory materials should contain all of the pertinent data believed essential to the reader's understanding. Criteria for standards of disclosure are of necessity nebulous and indefinite. They are often based on value judgments rather than on objective facts.

The usefulness of financial statements is enhanced by the use of headings and subheadings and by merging items in significant categories. For example, detailed information as to the amount of cash in various special and general funds, the amount on deposit in each of several banks, and the amount invested in a variety of marketable government securities is not needed by the reader of financial statements. Such information displayed on the balance sheet would impede rather than aid understanding. On the other hand, if the terms of significant loan agreements provide for a secured claim through a mortgage on an asset, the details should be disclosed. Some of the less obvious situations that accountants agree should be adequately disclosed on financial statements are briefly described in the following paragraphs.

Accounting methods employed. When there are several acceptable alternative methods that have a significant effect on amounts reported on the statements, the particular method adopted should be disclosed. Examples include inventory cost flow assumptions, inventory pricing methods, and criteria of revenue recognition.

Changes in accounting methods. When a significant change is made in accounting methods, that fact should be disclosed in the statements for the year in which the change is made. The usual practice is to disclose the quantitative effect on net income and on balance sheet items.

Contingent liabilities. Contingent liabilities arising from discounted notes receivable, litigation, guarantees of products, possible tax assessments, or other causes should be disclosed.

Events subsequent to date of statements. Events occurring or becoming known after the close of the period that may have a significant effect on the financial statements should be disclosed. For example, if an enterprise should suffer a crippling loss from a fire or other catastrophe between the end of the year and the issuance of the statements, the facts should be disclosed. Similarly, such occurrences as the settlement of pending litigation, the initiation of litigation, or the sale or purchase of plant facilities after the close of the period should be made known if they materially affect the company.

Materiality

In adhering to generally accepted accounting principles, the accountant must consider the relative importance of any event, accounting procedure, or change in procedure that affects items on the financial statements. Absolute accuracy in accounting and full disclosure in reporting are not ends in themselves, and there is no need to exceed the limits of practicability. The determination of what is material and what is unimportant requires the exercise of judgment; precise criteria cannot be applied.

The size of an item and its nature must be considered in relationship to the size and the nature of other items. The erroneous classification of a $10,000 asset on a balance sheet exhibiting total assets of $10,000,000 would probably be immaterial. If the assets totaled only $100,000, however, it would certainly be material. If the $10,000 represented a loan to an officer of the enterprise, it might well be material even in the first assumption. If the amount of the loan was increased to $100,000 between the close of the period and the issuance of the statements, both the nature of the item at the balance sheet date and the subsequent increase in amount would certainly require disclosure.

The principle of materiality may be applied to procedures employed in recording transactions. As was stated in an earlier chapter, minor expenditures for plant assets may be treated as an expense of the period rather than as an asset. The saving in accounting costs is justified if the practice does not materially affect the financial statements. In establishing a dollar amount as the dividing line between a revenue charge and a capital charge, consideration would need to be given to such factors as: (1) amount of total plant assets, (2) amount of plant assets in relationship to other assets, (3) frequency of occurrence of expenditures for plant assets, (4) nature and expected life of plant assets, and (5) probable effect on the amount of periodic net income reported.

Custom also influences criteria of materiality. In recent years most corporation financial statements omit cents, and some statements round figures to the nearest thousand dollars. For large or medium-sized corporations, cents and hundreds of dollars are certainly not material amounts; in fact, they tend to imply a degree of accuracy that does not exist.

A technique known as "whole-dollar" accounting has also been developed in recent years. The elimination from accounting entries of the cents amounts wherever possible and at the earliest practicable point in the accounting sequence may effect savings in office costs and improve productivity. There are some accounts, such as those with customers and creditors, in which it is not feasible to round to the nearest dollar. In many of the asset, revenue, and expense accounts, however, the errors introduced by rounding the amounts of individual entries at the time of recording tend to be compensating in nature, and the amount of the final error is not material.

It should not be inferred from the foregoing that whole-dollar accounting encourages or condones errors. The unrecorded cents are not lost; they are merely reported in a manner that reduces bookkeeping costs without materially affecting the accuracy of accounting data.

Conservatism

Periodic statements are of necessity affected to a considerable degree by the selection of accounting procedures and other value judgments. Historically, accountants have tended to be conservative, and in selecting among alternatives they often favored the method or the procedure that yielded the lesser amount of net income or asset value. This attitude of conservatism was frequently expressed in the admonition to "anticipate no profits and provide for all losses." For example, it is acceptable to price merchandise inventory at lower of cost or market. If market value is higher than cost, the higher value is ignored in the accounts and, if shown in the financial statements, is shown parenthetically. Such an attitude of pessimism has been due in part to the need for an offset to the optimism of business management. It could also be argued that potential future losses to an enterprise from poor management decisions would be lessened if net income and assets were understated.

Current accounting thought has shifted somewhat from this philosophy of conservatism. Conservatism is no longer considered to be a dominant factor in selecting among alternatives. Revenue should be recognized when earned, and expired costs should be matched against revenue in accordance with principles based on reason and logic. The element of conservatism may be considered only when other factors affecting a choice of alternatives are neutral. The concepts of objectivity, consistency, disclosure, and materiality take precedence over conservatism, and the latter should be a factor only where the others do not play a significant role.

QUESTIONS

1. Accounting principles are broad guides to accounting practice. (a) How are principles developed? (b) Who has the responsibility for the development of accounting principles? (c) Of what significance is acceptability in the development of accounting principles?

2. What is the basic assumption of the business entity concept?

3. Would a banker considering a loan to a sole proprietorship have any interest in the amount and the nature of the personal assets and liabilities of the proprietor? Explain.

4. What is the essence of the going concern concept?

5. The total assets reported on the balance sheet of Watson Company are $500,000. (a) Is it possible that the assets might realize considerably more or considerably less than $500,000 if the business were discontinued and the assets were sold separately? (b) Why aren't assets reported on the balance sheet at their estimated market values?

6. (a) Why are the conventional financial statements based on the assumption of a stable monetary unit? (b) How can the effect of the fluctuating dollar on business operations be presented to users of the financial statements?

7. Merchandise costing $150 is sold by a business for $250 in cash. Because the purchasing power of the dollar has declined, it will cost $175 to replace the merchandise. (a) What is the gross profit that should be reported on the income statement? (b) If the owner withdraws the amount of net income from the business, will he have enough cash remaining from the sale to replace the merchandise sold?

8. A machine that had cost $10,000 some time ago will soon need to be replaced by a similar machine that will cost $15,000. (a) At what amount should the machine presently owned be reported on the balance sheet? (b) What amount should management use in planning for the cash required to replace the machine?

9. If it were unnecessary to prepare annual financial statements during the life of a business enterprise, would there be any necessity for recording the annual adjusting entry for depreciation expense?

10. Differentiate between revenue and net income.

11. At which point is revenue from sales of merchandise on account more commonly recognized, time of sale or time of cash receipt?

12. The Windsor Realty Company acquired a tract of land for $100,000 on January 1 of the current year. During the year $25,000 was spent in subdividing the tract and in paving streets. The market value of the land at the end of the year was $135,000. An income statement was prepared for the year showing revenue of $35,000 less expenses of $25,000 and net income of $10,000. Were generally accepted accounting principles followed? Discuss.

13. Merchandise costing $300,000 was sold on the installment plan for $500,000 during the current year. The down payments and the installment payments received during the current year total $150,000. What is the amount of gross profit considered to be realized in the current year under the installment method of accounting for revenues?

14. A contractor has under construction an atomic power plant for which the total contract price is $9,000,000 and the estimated construction costs are $7,500,000. For the current year the costs incurred were $2,500,000. Under the degree of contract completion method of recognizing revenue, what amount of (a) revenue and (b) net income should be recognized for the current year?

15. A firm constructed a warehouse at a cost of $25,000 after a local contractor had submitted a bid of $30,000. The building was recorded at $30,000 and income of $5,000 was recognized. Were these entries correct? Discuss.

16. One accountant charges all expenditures for office supplies to an expense account and records an adjustment for the unconsumed office supplies at the end of the period. Another accountant charges all such expenditures to an asset account and records an adjustment for the office supplies consumed at the end of the period. Are the two accountants applying different principles to the allocation of costs?

17. The Snell Company acquired machinery for $50,000 at the beginning of a fiscal year. The machinery could be sold for $55,000 at the end of the fiscal year. It was proposed that since the machinery was worth more at the end of the year than at the beginning of the year, (a) no depreciation should be recorded for the current year and (b) the gain of $5,000 should be recorded. Discuss the propriety of the proposals.

18. An enterprise has used the straight-line method of computing depreciation for many years. For the current year, the declining-balance method was used and depreciation expense totaled $25,000; net income was $75,000. Depreciation computed on the straight-line method would have been $15,000. (a) What is the quantitative effect of the change in method on the net income for the current year? (b) Is the effect of the change material? (c) Should the effect of the change in method be disclosed in the financial statements?

19. The accountant for a large wholesale firm charged the acquisition of a wastebasket to an expense account even though the asset had an estimated useful life of 10 years. What concept supports this treatment of the expenditure?

20. In 1935 the Champion Corporation acquired a building with a useful life of 40 years, which it depreciated by the sum-of-the-years-digits method. Is this practice conservative (a) for the year 1935 and (b) for the year 1974? Explain.

EXERCISES

1. Indicate for each of the following the amount of revenue that should be reported for the current year and the amount that should be postponed to a future period. Give a reason for your answer.

(a) Leased a building on the first day of the last month of the current year, receiving one year's rent of $4,800.
(b) Received in the current year an order for merchandise for delivery in the following year. The merchandise had a cost of $2,500 and a selling price of $3,400.

(c) Sold season tickets for a series of four concerts for $40,000. One concert was played during the current year.
(d) Merchandise costing $50,000 in the current year is expected to be sold in the following year for $70,000.
(e) Cash of $5,000 was received in the current year on the sale of gift certificates to be redeemed in merchandise in the following year.
(f) A $50,000, 6%, 60-day note receivable was received 30 days before the end of the current year in settlement of an account receivable.
(g) The contract price for building a ship is $7,000,000 and the total costs for construction are estimated at $5,600,000. At the close of the current year the costs incurred totaled $2,240,000. Revenue is to be recognized by the degree of contract completion method.

2. Baxter Company sells most of its products on a cash basis but extends short-term credit to some of its customers. Invoices for sales on account are placed in a file and are not recorded until cash is received, at which time the sale is recorded in the same manner as a cash sale. The net income reported for the first three years of operations was $40,000, $65,000, and $60,000, respectively. The total amount of the uncollected sales invoices in the file at the end of each of the three years was $4,000, $7,000, and $6,000. In each case the entire amount was collected during the first month of the succeeding year. (a) Determine the amount by which net income was overstated or understated for each of the three years. (b) What items on the balance sheet were overstated or understated as of the end of each year?

3. Keck Furniture Company makes all sales on the installment plan. Data related to merchandise sold during the current fiscal year are as follows:

Sales	$300,000
Cash received on the $300,000 of installment contracts	140,000
Merchandise inventory, beginning of year	65,000
Merchandise inventory, end of year	62,000
Purchases	177,000

Determine the amount of gross profit that would be recognized according to (a) the point of sale method and (b) the installment method of recognizing revenue.

4. The cost of the merchandise inventory of the Howard S. Grant Co. at the close of its first fiscal year, according to three different methods, is as follows: fifo, $40,000; average, $38,500; lifo, $37,000. If the average cost method is employed, the net income reported will be $29,000. (a) What will be the amount of net income reported if the fifo method is adopted? (b) What will be the amount of net income reported if the lifo method is adopted? (c) Which of the three methods is the most conservative? (d) Is the particular method adopted of sufficient materiality to require disclosure in the financial statements?

5. Properties and services acquired by an enterprise are generally recorded at cost. For each of the following, determine the cost:

(a) Lahey Sales purchased $250 of materials and supplies and paid a carpenter $325 to build a showcase. A similar showcase would cost $700 if purchased from a manufacturer.

(b) A plant asset was purchased for $1,200 under terms of n/30, f.o.b. shipping point. The freight amounted to $74 and installation costs totaled $98.
(c) A tract of land adjacent to the Hartley Department Store was acquired for $20,000 to provide additional parking for customers. The structures on the land were removed at a cost of $1,200. The salvage from the structures was sold for $500. The cost of grading the land was $300.

6. At the close of three successive years a firm failed to record accrued sales commissions expense as follows: first year, $12,000; second year, $16,000; third year, $9,000. In each case the commissions were paid during the first month of the succeeding year and were charged as an expense of that year. Accrued sales commissions expense was properly recorded at the end of the fourth year. (a) Determine the amount by which net income was overstated or understated for each of the four years. (b) What items on the balance sheet would have been overstated or understated as of the end of each of the four years as a result of the errors?

7. Of the following matters, considered individually, indicate those that are material and that should be disclosed either on the financial statements or in accompanying explanatory notes:

(a) A change in accounting methods of the current year decreased the amount of net income that would otherwise have been reported from $600,000 to $450,000.
(b) Between the end of its fiscal year and the date of publication of the annual reports, a fire destroyed a portion of the plant. The loss is estimated at $10,000. The net income for the year is $3,900,000.
(c) A manufacturing company employs the lower of cost or market method of pricing inventory.
(d) A public utility is facing litigation involving excessive rates charged over the past three years. The rebate of revenues might amount to $2,000,000. Annual net income reported in the past three years has ranged from $5,000,000 to $6,000,000.

8. Each of the following represents a decision made by the accountant. State whether or not you agree with his decision. Support your answer with reference to generally accepted accounting principles that are applicable in the circumstances.

(a) Since net income is expected to be extremely small this year, no depreciation expense on plant assets is recorded.
(b) Land, used as a parking lot, was purchased 20 years ago for $25,000. Since its market value is now $60,000, the land account is debited for $35,000 and a gain account is credited for a like amount. The gain is shown as an "other income" item in the income statement.
(c) Merchandise transferred to other parties on a consignment basis and not sold is included in merchandise inventory.
(d) In preparing the balance sheet, detailed information as to the amount of cash on deposit in each of several banks was omitted. Only the total amount of cash under a caption "Cash in banks" was shown.
(e) All minor expenditures for machinery and equipment are charged to an expense account.

PROBLEMS

14-1. During its first three years of operations, the Lanford Co. determined the cost of the merchandise inventory at the end of the period by the first-in, first-out method, depreciation expense by the straight-line method, and uncollectible accounts expense by the direct write-off method. The amounts of net income reported and the amounts of the foregoing items for each of the three years were as follows:

	First Year	Second Year	Third Year
Net income reported	$ 40,000	$ 60,000	$ 75,000
Ending merchandise inventory	60,000	75,000	90,000
Depreciation expense	10,000	10,500	11,500
Uncollectible accounts expense	500	3,000	4,500

The firm is considering the possibility of changing to the following methods in determining net income for the fourth and subsequent years: last-in, first-out inventory, sum-of-the-years-digits depreciation, and provision for doubtful accounts through the use of an allowance account. In order to consider the probable future effect of these changes on the determination of net income, the management requests that net income of the past three years be recomputed on the basis of the proposed methods. The inventory, depreciation, and uncollectible accounts expense for the past three years, computed in accordance with the proposed methods, are as follows:

	First Year	Second Year	Third Year
Ending merchandise inventory	$ 58,000	$ 65,000	$ 75,000
Depreciation expense	18,000	16,000	14,200
Uncollectible accounts expense	2,600	3,700	4,200

Instructions: Recompute the net income for each of the three years, presenting the figures in an orderly manner.

14-2. All sales of the Appliance Mart are made on the installment basis. Condensed income statements and the amounts collected from customers for each of the first three years of operations are given below.

	First Year	Second Year	Third Year
Sales	$180,000	$240,000	$200,000
Cost of merchandise sold	108,000	139,200	112,000
Gross profit on sales	$ 72,000	$100,800	$ 88,000
Operating expenses	50,000	55,000	54,000
Net income	$ 22,000	$ 45,800	$ 34,000
Collected from sales of first year	$ 75,000	$ 60,000	$ 40,000
Collected from sales of second year		100,000	80,000
Collected from sales of third year			85,000

Instructions: Determine the amount of net income that would have been reported in each of the three years if the installment method of recognizing revenue had been employed, ignoring the possible effects of uncollectible accounts on the computation. Present figures in good order.

14-3. The Hartman Construction Company began the construction of two dams and related structures during 1965. Dam A was completed in 1966 and Dam B in 1967. The contract prices, estimated total costs, and costs incurred are as follows:

	Contract Price	Estimated Costs	1965 Costs	1966 Costs	1967 Costs
Dam A	$3,000,000	$2,400,000	$1,200,000	$1,250,000	—
Dam B	$4,500,000	$3,600,000	$ 600,000	$1,200,000	$1,870,000

Instructions: Determine the amount of revenue and the net income to be recognized for the following years: 1965, 1966, 1967. Assume that the recognition of revenue is to be spread over the life of the contract. Present computations in good order.

14-4. Lewis Television Sales employs the installment method of recognizing gross profit for sales made on the installment plan. Details of a particular installment sale, amounts collected from the purchaser, and the repossession of the television set are presented below.

First year:
Sold for $500 a television set having a cost of $300 and received a down payment of $100.

Second year:
Received twelve monthly payments of $25 each.

Third year:
The purchaser defaulted on the monthly payments, the set was repossessed, and the remaining four installments were canceled. The set was estimated to be worth $90.

Instructions: (1) Determine the gross profit to be recognized in the first year.
(2) Determine the gross profit to be recognized in the second year.
(3) Determine the gain or the loss to be recognized from the repossession of the set.

14-5. The income statement and the balance sheet prepared from the unadjusted accounts of Beyers Gift Center at the close of the first year of operations are presented on this and the following page.

Beyers Gift Center
Income Statement
For Year Ended December 31, 19—

Sales		$70,000
Purchases		61,000
Gross profit on sales		$ 9,000
Operating expenses:		
Salary expense	$9,000	
Rent expense	3,900	
Utilities expense	780	
Miscellaneous expense	2,620	
Total operating expenses		16,300
Net loss		$ 7,300

Beyers Gift Center
Balance Sheet
December 31, 19—

Cash	$2,700
Equipment	6,000
A. R. Beyers, Capital	$8,700

Beyers has maintained the accounting records. The only transactions recorded have been those in which cash was received or disbursed. The books have not been closed for the year. Because of the large net loss reported by the income statement, Beyers is considering discontinuing operations. Before making a decision, he asks you to review the accounting methods employed and, if material errors are found, to prepare revised statements. The following information is elicited during the course of the review:

(a) The business was established on January 2 by an investment of $16,000 in cash by the owner.
(b) The equipment listed on the balance sheet at $6,000 was purchased for cash on January 3. Equipment purchased June 30 for $2,000 in cash was debited to Purchases. Equipment purchased on December 28 for $1,000, for which a 60-day non-interest-bearing note was issued, was not recorded.
(c) Depreciation on equipment has not been recorded. The equipment is estimated to have a useful life of 20 years and a salvage value of 10% of its original cost. (Use straight-line method.)
(d) Accounts receivable from customers at December 31 total $5,500.
(e) Uncollectible accounts are estimated at $450.
(f) A total of $6,000 is owed to merchandise creditors on account at December 31.
(g) The merchandise inventory at December 31, as nearly as can be determined, has a cost of $19,000.
(h) Insurance premiums of $800 were charged to miscellaneous expense during the year. The unexpired portion at December 31 is $370.
(i) Rent Expense includes an advance payment of $300 for the month of January in the subsequent year.
(j) Supplies of $900 purchased during the year were debited to Purchases. An estimated $400 of supplies were on hand at December 31.
(k) Salaries owed but not paid on December 31 total $350.
(l) The classification of expenses as "selling" and "general" is not considered to be sufficiently important to justify the cost of the analysis.
(m) The proprietor made no additional investments or withdrawals during the year.

Instructions: (1) On the basis of the financial statements presented above, prepare an unadjusted trial balance as of December 31 of the current year on an eight-column work sheet.

(2) Record the adjustments and the corrections in the Adjustments columns and complete the work sheet.

(3) Prepare an income statement, a capital statement, and a balance sheet.

(4) On the basis of your financial statements, evaluate the effectiveness of the first year of operations.

PART SEVEN

Partnerships and corporations

15. Partnerships

Partnership organization and operation

The Uniform Partnership Act, which has been adopted by more than three-fourths of the states, defines a partnership as "an association of two or more persons to carry on as co-owners a business for profit." The partnership form of business organization is widely used for comparatively small businesses that wish to take advantage of the combined capital, managerial talent, and experience of two or more persons. In many cases, the alternative to securing the amount of investment required or the various skills needed to operate a business is to adopt the corporate form of organization, which is discussed in later chapters. The corporate form of organization may not be used, however, by certain professions because of restrictions in state statutes or in professional codes of ethics. Hence, a group of physicians, attorneys, or certified public accountants that wishes to band together to practice a profession do so as a partnership.

The partnership characteristics that have accounting implications are described in the following paragraphs.

Limited life. The length of life of a partnership is highly unpredictable. Dissolution of a partnership may result from a variety of causes, including death, bankruptcy, incapacity, or expressed will of one of the partners. In such cases a new partnership must be formed if the operations of the business are to be continued.

Unlimited liability. Each partner is individually liable to creditors for debts incurred by the partnership. Thus, if a partnership becomes insolvent, the creditors may proceed against any one of the partners regardless of the amount of his investment in the partnership.

Co-ownership of property. The property invested in a partnership by a partner becomes the property of all the partners jointly. Upon dissolution of the partnership and distribution of its assets, each member's claim against the assets is measured by the amount of the balance in his capital account.

Participation in income. Net income and net loss are distributed among the partners in accordance with their agreement. In the absence of any agreement, all partners share equally.

Articles of copartnership. A partnership is created by a voluntary contract containing all the elements essential to any other enforceable contract. It is not necessary that this contract be in writing, nor even that its terms be specifically expressed orally. However, good business practice dictates that the contract should be in writing and should clearly express the intentions of the partners. The contract, known as the *articles of copartnership*, should contain provisions regarding such matters as the amount of investment to be made, limitations on withdrawals of funds, and the manner in which net income and net loss are to be divided.

Accounting for partnerships

Most of the day-to-day accounting for a partnership is the same as the accounting for any other form of business organization. The special journals described in earlier chapters may be employed without alteration by a partnership. The chart of accounts, with the exception of drawing and capital accounts for each partner, does not differ from the chart of accounts of a similar business conducted by a single owner. It is in the areas of the formation, income distribution, dissolution, and liquidation of partnerships that transactions peculiar to partnerships arise. The remainder of the chapter is devoted to the special accounting problems in these areas.

Recording investments

A separate entry is made for the investment of each partner in a partnership. The various assets contributed by a partner are debited to the proper asset accounts; if liabilities are assumed by the partnership, the appropriate liability accounts are credited; and the partner's capital account is credited for the net amount.

To illustrate the entry required to record an initial investment, assume that George M. Alden and James D. Barker, who are sole owners of competing hardware stores, agree to combine their enterprises in a partnership. Each is to contribute specified amounts of cash and other business assets. It is also agreed that the partnership is to assume the liabilities of the individual businesses. The entry to record the assets contributed and the liabilities transferred by George M. Alden, in general journal form, is as follows:

Jan. 1	Cash	7,000	
	Accounts Receivable	6,300	
	Merchandise Inventory	18,600	
	Store Equipment	5,400	
	Office Equipment	1,500	
	Allowance for Doubtful Accounts		1,300
	Accounts Payable		2,500
	George M. Alden, Capital		35,000

The amounts at which the noncash assets are stated are those agreed upon by the partners. They are not necessarily the same as the balances appearing in the accounts of the separate businesses before the partnership was organized. For example, the store equipment stated at $5,400 may have appeared on Alden's ledger at an original cost of $10,000 with accumulated depreciation of $6,500, or a book value of $3,500. The original cost of the equipment, its current condition, changes in price levels, and the bargaining ability of the partners are some of the factors that influence the values assigned to the assets invested.

Equipment contributed to the partnership may be recorded at the amount of the original cost to the partner, with a credit to the accumulated depreciation account for the amount necessary to bring the book value into agreement with the value assigned by the partners. For example, the store equipment invested by Alden could have been recorded at $10,000, with an offsetting credit to the accumulated depreciation account for $4,600, effecting a book value of $5,400. But the preferred practice is to record only the net amount agreed upon, as it represents the acquisition cost to the partnership. A similar choice of methods is not available for recording the value ascribed to receivables invested by a partner. It is necessary to debit Accounts Receivable for the face value and to credit Allowance for Doubtful Accounts for the amount estimated to be uncollectible. At the time the accounts are taken over by the partnership, it is not possible to determine which accounts in the subsidiary ledger will become partially or wholly uncollectible.

Division of net income or net loss

As in the case of a sole proprietorship, the net income of a partnership may be said to include a return for the services of the owners, for the capital invested, and for economic or pure profit. A partner is not legally an employee of the partnership, nor is his capital contribution a loan. If service and capital contributions of partners are equal, an equal sharing in partnership income is equitable. But if one partner contributes a larger portion of capital than the other, his greater contribution should be recognized in the agreement for the distribution of income. Or, if the services of one partner are much more valuable to the partnership than those of the other, provision for unequal service contributions should be given consideration.

To illustrate the division of net income and the accounting for this division, two possible divisions are presented. It should be noted that division of the net income or the net loss among the partners in exact accordance with their partnership agreement is of the utmost importance. If the agreement is silent on the matter, the law provides that all partners share equally, regardless of differences in amounts of capital contributed or time devoted to the business. The partners may, however, make any agreement they wish in regard to the division of income and losses.

Income division recognizing services of partners. As a means of recognizing differences in ability and in amount of time devoted to the business, articles of copartnership often provide for the allocation of a portion of net income to the partners in the form of a salary allowance. The articles may also provide for withdrawals of cash by the partners in lieu of salary payments. A clear distinction must therefore be made between payments to the partners, which are charged to their drawing accounts, and the division of net income, which is recorded by closing the expense and revenue summary account to the capital accounts.

To illustrate the division of net income when the agreement provides for salary allowances, assume that J. M. Stone and R. D. Thomas provide for monthly salary allowances of $600 and $500 respectively, with the balance of the net income to be divided equally. A report of the division of net income may be presented as a separate statement accompanying the balance sheet and the income statement, or it may be added at the bottom of the income statement. Assuming that the latter procedure is selected, the lower part of the income statement will be as follows:

Net income			$18,000
Division of net income:	J. M. Stone	R. D. Thomas	Total
Salary allowance	$7,200	$6,000	$13,200
Remaining income	2,400	2,400	4,800
Net income	$9,600	$8,400	$18,000

The division of net income is recorded as one of the closing entries regardless of whether or not the partners actually withdraw the amounts of their salary allowances. The entry for the division of net income is as follows:

Dec.	31	Expense and Revenue Summary	18,000	
		J. M. Stone, Capital		9,600
		R. D. Thomas, Capital		8,400

If Stone and Thomas had withdrawn their salary allowances monthly, the withdrawals would have accumulated as debits in the drawing accounts during the year. At the end of the year, the debit balances of $7,200 and $6,000 in their respective drawing accounts would be transferred to their respective capital accounts.

Income division recognizing services of partners and investment. Partners may agree that the most equitable plan of income-sharing is to allow salaries commensurate with the services rendered and also to allow interest on the capital investments. The remainder is then shared in an arbitrary ratio. To illustrate, assume that Stone and Thomas (1) are allowed monthly salaries of $600 and $500, respectively; (2) are allowed interest at 6% on capital balances at January 1 of the current fiscal year, which totaled $30,000 and $23,000, respectively; and (3) divide the remainder of net income equally. The division of net income for the year would then be reported as follows:

Net income			$18,000
Division of net income:	J. M. Stone	R. D. Thomas	Total
Salary allowance	$7,200	$6,000	$13,200
Interest allowance	1,800	1,380	3,180
Remaining income	810	810	1,620
Net income	$9,810	$8,190	$18,000

On the basis of the information in the foregoing income statement, the entry to close the expense and revenue summary account would be recorded in the general journal as follows:

Dec.	31	Expense and Revenue Summary	18,000	
		J. M. Stone, Capital		9,810
		R. D. Thomas, Capital		8,190

In the illustrations presented thus far, the net income has exceeded the sum of the allowances for salary and interest. It is obvious that this may not always be the case. If the net income is less than the total of the special allowances, the "remaining balance" will be a negative figure that must be divided among the partners as though it were a loss. The effect of this situation may be illustrated by assuming the same salary and interest allowances as in the preceding illustration but changing the amount of net income to $10,000. The salary and interest allowances to Stone total $9,000 and the comparable figure for Thomas is $7,380. The sum of these amounts, $16,380, exceeds the net income of $10,000 by $6,380. It is therefore necessary to deduct $3,190 (½ of

$6,380) from each partner's share to arrive at the net income, as shown below.

Net income			$10,000
Division of net income:	J. M. Stone	R. D. Thomas	Total
Salary allowance	$7,200	$6,000	$13,200
Interest allowance	1,800	1,380	3,180
Total	$9,000	$7,380	$16,380
Excess of allowances over income	3,190	3,190	6,380
Net income	$5,810	$4,190	$10,000

In closing Expense and Revenue Summary at the end of the year, $5,810 would be credited to J. M. Stone, Capital, and $4,190 would be credited to R. D. Thomas, Capital.

Partners' salaries and interest treated as expenses

Although the traditional view among accountants is to treat salary and interest allowances as allocations of net income, as in the foregoing illustrations, some prefer to treat them as expenses of the enterprise. According to this view, the partnership is considered to be a distinct entity and the partners are employees and creditors of the firm. When salaries for partners' services and interest on partners' investments are viewed as expenses of the enterprise, withdrawals of the agreed amount are charged to expense accounts rather than to the partners' drawing accounts. The expense accounts are then closed into the expense and revenue summary account, and the remaining net income is allocated among the partners in the agreed ratio. The amounts considered to be partners' salary and interest expense should be identified as such on the income statement. Regardless of whether salary and interest are treated as expenses or as a division of net income, the total amount allocated to each partner will be the same.

Statements for a partnership

Details of the division of net income should be disclosed in the financial statements prepared at the end of the fiscal period. This may be done by adding a section to the income statement, which has been illustrated in the preceding pages, or the data may be presented in a separate statement.

Details of the changes in partnership capital during the period should also be presented in a capital statement. The purposes of the statement and the data included in it correspond to those of the capital statement of a sole proprietorship. There are a number of variations in form, one of which is illustrated on the following page.

Stone and Thomas
Capital Statement
For Year Ended December 31, 1965

	J. M. Stone	R. D. Thomas	Total
Capital, January 1, 1965	$30,000	$23,000	$53,000
Additional investment		3,000	3,000
	$30,000	$26,000	$56,000
Net income for the year	9,810	8,190	18,000
	$39,810	$34,190	$74,000
Withdrawals	9,200	8,000	17,200
Capital, December 31, 1965	$30,610	$26,190	$56,800

Under the Internal Revenue Code, enterprises organized as partnerships are not distinct entities and are not required to pay federal income taxes. Instead, the individual partners must report their distributive shares of partnership income on their personal tax returns. However, data on the distributive shares of each partner, as well as a summary of revenue and expense and other financial details of partnership operations, must be reported annually on an "information return." If a partnership provides for payment of salaries or interest to partners without regard to the net income of the enterprise, such payments must be reported on the information return as an expense. The partners are required, in turn, to combine the amounts thus received with their distributive shares so that, regardless of method, all of the income is reported for taxation by the partners.

In spite of the foregoing, partnerships may elect to be taxed as a distinct entity if they meet certain specified conditions of the Internal Revenue Code. Partnerships electing this optional treatment pay an income tax in much the same manner as a corporation and the individual partners do not report their distributive shares in their personal returns.

Partnership dissolution

One of the basic characteristics of the partnership form of organization is its limited life. Any change in the personnel of the membership results in the dissolution of the partnership. Thus, death, bankruptcy, or withdrawal of a partner causes dissolution. Similarly, admission of a new partner effects the dissolution of the old firm.

Dissolution of the partnership is not necessarily followed by the winding up of the affairs of the business. For example, if one of three partners in a business withdraws, the remaining partners may continue to operate the business. Or a partnership composed of two partners may admit an additional partner. In all such cases, a new partnership is formed and new articles of copartnership should be prepared.

Admission of a new partner

A new partner may be admitted to a partnership only with the consent of all the old partners. It does not follow, however, that a partner cannot dispose of part or all of his interest in the firm without the consent of the remaining partners. Under common law, if a partner assigned his interest in the partnership to an outside party, the partnership was automatically dissolved. Under the Uniform Partnership Act, a partner can dispose of part or all of his interest in the firm without the consent of the remaining partners. The person who buys the interest acquires the selling partner's rights to share in income and to assets upon liquidation. He does not automatically become a partner, however, and has no voice in partnership affairs unless he is admitted to the firm. In the discussion that follows, the consent of all parties will always be assumed.

A new partner may be admitted to a partnership through either of two procedures:

1. Purchase of an interest from one or more of the old partners.
2. Contribution of assets to the partnership.

Under the first procedure, the capital interest of the new partner is obtained from the old partners, and neither the total assets nor the total capital of the business is affected. When the second procedure is followed, both the total assets and the total capital of the business are increased.

Admission by transfer of capital interest

When a new partner is admitted by the purchase of an interest from the old partners, the price for the interest is paid to the old partners. The amount received is the property of the partners individually rather than of the partnership; and hence, the cash or other consideration paid is not recorded in the accounts of the partnership. The only entry required is the transfer of the appropriate amounts of capital from the capital accounts of the old partners to the capital account established for the new partner.

As an example, assume that partners John Abbott and Henry Beck have capital balances of $30,000 each. On June 1, each of them sells one sixth of his capital interest to Roger Carson for $5,000, for which Carson pays cash. The only entry required in the partnership accounts is as follows:

June	1	John Abbott, Capital	5,000	
		Henry Beck, Capital	5,000	
		Roger Carson, Capital		10,000

The effect of the transaction on the partnership accounts is presented in the following diagram:

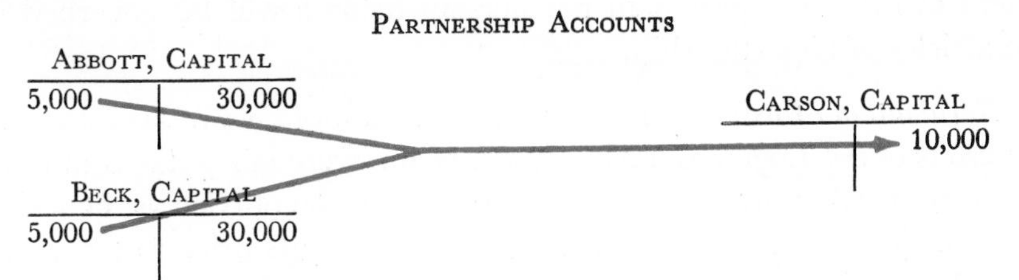

The foregoing entry is made regardless of the amount paid by Carson for the one-sixth interest. If the firm had been earning a high rate of return on the investment and Carson was very eager to obtain the one-sixth interest, he might have paid considerably more than $10,000. Had other circumstances prevailed, he might have acquired the one-sixth interest for considerably less than $10,000. In either event, the journal entry would not be affected.

After the admission of Carson, the total capital of the firm is $60,000, in which he has a one-sixth interest, or $10,000. It does not follow that he will be entitled to a similar share of the partnership net income. Division of net income or loss will be in accordance with the new partnership agreement.

Admission by contribution of assets

Instead of buying an interest from the former partners, the new partner may contribute assets to the partnership. In this case both the assets and the capital of the firm are increased. For example, George Logan and Thomas Macy are partners with capital accounts of $18,000 and $12,000, respectively. On June 1, William Nichols invests $10,000 cash in the business, for which he is to receive an ownership equity of $10,000. The entry to record this transaction, in general journal form, is:

June 1	Cash	10,000	
	William Nichols, Capital		10,000

The essential difference between the circumstances of the admission of Nichols above and of Carson in the preceding example may be observed by comparing the following diagram with the one above.

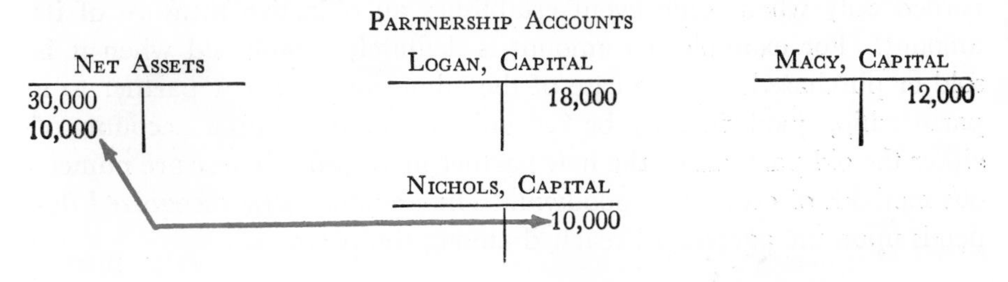

After the admission of Nichols, the total capital of the new partnership is $40,000, of which he has a one-fourth interest, or $10,000. The extent of his participation in partnership income will be governed by the articles of copartnership.

Revaluation of assets. In the preceding example it was assumed that the assets of the Logan and Macy partnership were fairly stated in terms of current market price at the time of the admission of Nichols; hence, no adjustments were made to any of the asset accounts prior to his admission. When the circumstances are otherwise, the book values should be brought into agreement with current prices. The net amount of the revaluation is then allocated to the capital accounts of the old partners in accordance with their income-sharing agreement. For example, if the balance of the merchandise inventory account was $14,000 and the current replacement value was $17,000, the following entry should have been recorded prior to the admission of Nichols, assuming that Logan and Macy share equally in net income:

June	1	Merchandise Inventory	3,000	
		George Logan, Capital		1,500
		Thomas Macy, Capital		1,500

If a number of assets are revalued, the adjustments may be debited or credited to a temporary account entitled Asset Revaluations. After all adjustments are made, the net balance of the account is closed to the capital accounts.

It is important that the assets be stated in terms of current prices at the time of admission of a new partner. Failure to recognize current prices will result in participation by the new partner in gains or losses attributable to the period prior to his admission to the partnership.

Goodwill. In the sense that it is used in business, *goodwill* is an intangible asset that attaches to a business as a result of such favorable factors as location, product superiority, reputation, and managerial ability. Its existence is evidenced by the ability of the business to earn a rate of return on the investment that is in excess of the normal rate for other firms in the same line of business.

Accountants are in general agreement that goodwill should be recorded only when some event establishes an objective measure of its amount. For example, its amount is definitely established when it is sold or purchased. In the case of the admission of a new partner to a partnership, goodwill may be recognized and the capital accounts of either the old partners or the new partner increased. There are numerous methods of estimating goodwill. The amount to be recognized depends upon the agreement reached among the partners.

To illustrate the recognition of goodwill to the old partners, assume that on March 1 the partnership of Joyce and Keller admits Long, who is to contribute cash of $10,000. After the tangible assets of the old partnership have been adjusted to current market prices, the capital balances of Joyce and Keller are $12,000 and $14,000 respectively. The parties agree, however, that the enterprise is worth $30,000. The excess of $30,000 over the capital balances of $26,000 ($12,000 + $14,000) indicates the existence of $4,000 of goodwill, which should be allocated to the capital accounts of the original partners in accordance with their income-sharing agreement.

The entries to record the goodwill and the admission of the new partner, assuming that the original partners share equally in net income, are as follows, in general journal form:

Mar. 1	Goodwill	4,000	
	F. G. Joyce, Capital		2,000
	G. N. Keller, Capital		2,000
1	Cash	10,000	
	W. J. Long, Capital		10,000

If a partnership admits a new partner who is expected to improve the fortunes of the firm, the parties might agree to recognize this high earnings potential. To illustrate, assume that William Ennis is to be admitted to the partnership of Cowen and Dodd for an investment of $30,000. If the parties agree to recognize $5,000 of goodwill attributable to Ennis, the entry to record his admission is as follows, in general journal form:

July 1	Cash	30,000	
	Goodwill	5,000	
	William Ennis, Capital		35,000

Goodwill is classified under *Intangible Assets*, which appears below the plant assets section of the balance sheet.

Withdrawal of a partner

When a partner retires or for some other reason wishes to withdraw from the firm, one or more of the remaining partners may purchase his interest and the business may be continued. In such cases, settlement is made between the partners individually. The only entry required on the books of the partnership is a debit to the capital account of the one withdrawing and a credit to the capital account of the partner or partners acquiring the interest.

If the settlement with the withdrawing partner is made by the partnership, the effect is to reduce the assets and the capital of the firm. In order to determine the ownership equity of the withdrawing partner, the asset accounts should be adjusted to bring them into agreement with current fair prices. The net amount of the adjustment should be allocated among the capital accounts of the partners in accordance with the income ratio. In the event that the cash or the other available assets are insufficient to make complete payment at the time of withdrawal, a liability account should be credited for the balance owed to the withdrawing partner.

Death of a partner

The death of a partner effects the dissolution of the partnership. In the absence of any contrary agreement, the accounts should be closed as of the date of death and the net income for the fractional part of the year should be transferred to the capital accounts. It is not unusual for the partnership agreement to stipulate that the accounts remain open to the end of the fiscal year or until the affairs are wound up, if that should occur earlier. The net income is then prorated to the periods before and after death, or the agreement may provide that the usual income ratio be employed for both.

The balance in the capital account of the deceased partner is then transferred to a liability account with his estate. The surviving partner or partners may continue the business or the affairs may be wound up. If the former course is followed, the procedures for settling with the estate will conform to those outlined earlier for the withdrawal of a partner.

Liquidation of a partnership

When a partnership goes out of business, it ordinarily sells most of the assets, pays the creditors, and distributes the remaining cash or other assets to the partners in accordance with their claims. The winding-up process may be referred to generally as *liquidation.* Although liquidation refers specifically to the payment of liabilities, it is often used in a broader sense to include the entire winding-up process.

When the ordinary business activities are discontinued preparatory to liquidation, the books should be adjusted and closed in accordance with the customary procedures of the periodic summary. The only accounts remaining open will then be the various asset, contra asset, liability, and capital accounts. The sale of the assets is referred to as *realization.* As cash is realized, it is applied first to the payment of the claims of creditors. After all liabilities have been paid, the remaining cash is distributed to the partners in accordance with their ownership equities as indicated by their capital accounts.

If the assets are sold piecemeal, the liquidation process may extend over a considerable period of time. This creates no special problem, however, if the distribution of cash to the partners is postponed until all of the assets have been sold. As a basis for illustration, assume that Alden, Beeler, and Craig, partners, decide to liquidate their partnership. Their income and loss ratio is 5:3:2. After discontinuing the ordinary business operations and closing the books, the following summary of the ledger is prepared:

Cash	$11,000	
All noncash assets	64,000	
All liabilities		$ 9,000
J. Alden, Capital		22,000
B. Beeler, Capital		22,000
H. Craig, Capital		22,000
Total	$75,000	$75,000

Accounting for the liquidation will be illustrated by three examples based on the foregoing statement of facts. In all cases it will be assumed that all noncash assets are disposed of in a single transaction and that all liabilities are paid at one time. This is merely for the sake of brevity. In addition, Assets and Liabilities will be used as account titles in place of the various asset, contra asset, and liability accounts that would be used in recording the transactions in actual practice.

Gain on realization. Alden, Beeler, and Craig sell all noncash assets for $72,000, realizing a gain of $8,000 ($72,000 – $64,000). The gain is divided among the capital accounts in the income-sharing ratio of 5:3:2, the liabilities are paid, and the remaining cash is distributed to the partners according to the balances in their capital accounts. A tabular summary of the transactions follows:

				Capital		
	Cash +	Other Assets =	Liabilities +	J. Alden 50% +	B. Beeler 30% +	H. Craig 20%
Balances before realization	$11,000	$64,000	$ 9,000	$22,000	$22,000	$22,000
Sale of assets and division of gain	+72,000	–64,000		+ 4,000	+ 2,400	+ 1,600
Balances after realization	$83,000		$ 9,000	$26,000	$24,400	$23,600
Payment of liabilities	– 9,000		–9,000			
Balances	$74,000			$26,000	$24,400	$23,600
Distribution of cash to partners	–74,000			–26,000	–24,400	–23,600

The entries to record the several steps in the liquidation procedure are as follows, in general journal form:

Sale of assets

Cash	72,000	
Assets		64,000
Loss and Gain on Realization		8,000

Division of gain

Loss and Gain on Realization	8,000	
J. Alden, Capital		4,000
B. Beeler, Capital		2,400
H. Craig, Capital		1,600

Payment of liabilities

Liabilities	9,000	
Cash		9,000

Distribution of cash to partners

J. Alden, Capital	26,000	
B. Beeler, Capital	24,400	
H. Craig, Capital	23,600	
Cash		74,000

It should be noted that the gain on the sale of the assets of the partnership is divided among the capital accounts in the income-sharing ratio and that the cash is distributed among the partners in accordance with their ownership equities as indicated by the balances in their capital accounts.

Loss on realization; no capital deficiencies. Assume that in the foregoing example Alden, Beeler, and Craig dispose of all noncash assets for $44,000, incurring a loss of $20,000 ($64,000 – $44,000). The various steps in the liquidation of the partnership are summarized as follows:

					Capital	
	Cash +	Other Assets =	Liabilities +	J. Alden 50% +	B. Beeler 30% +	H. Craig 20%
Balances before realization	$11,000	$64,000	$ 9,000	$22,000	$22,000	$ 22,000
Sale of assets and division of loss	+44,000	−64,000		−10,000	− 6,000	− 4,000
Balances after realization	$55,000		$ 9,000	$12,000	$16,000	$18,000
Payment of liabilities	− 9,000		− 9,000			
Balances	$46,000			$12,000	$16,000	$18,000
Distribution of cash to partners	−46,000			−12,000	−16,000	−18,000

The entries required to record the liquidation appear below, in general journal form:

Sale of assets

Cash	44,000	
Loss and Gain on Realization	20,000	
Assets		64,000

Division of loss

J. Alden, Capital	10,000	
B. Beeler, Capital	6,000	
H. Craig, Capital	4,000	
Loss and Gain on Realization		20,000

Payment of liabilities

Liabilities	9,000	
Cash		9,000

Distribution of cash to partners

J. Alden, Capital	12,000	
B. Beeler, Capital	16,000	
H. Craig, Capital	18,000	
Cash		46,000

Loss on realization; capital deficiency. In the preceding illustration the capital account of each partner was more than sufficient to absorb the loss from realization. Each partner shared in the distribution of cash to the extent of the remaining credit balance in his capital account. The share of the loss chargeable to a partner may be such that it exceeds his ownership equity. The resulting debit balance in his capital account, which is referred to as a *deficiency*, is a claim of the partnership against the partner. Pending collection from the deficient partner, the partnership cash will not be sufficient to pay the other partners in full. In such cases the available cash should be distributed in such a manner that, if the claim against the deficient partner cannot be collected, each of the remaining capital balances will be sufficient to absorb the appropriate share of the deficiency.

To illustrate a situation of this type, assume that the partnership sells all of its noncash assets for $10,000, incurring a loss of $54,000 ($64,000 − $10,000). It is readily apparent that the portion of the loss allocable to Alden, which is $27,000 (50% of $54,000) exceeds the $22,000 balance in his capital account. This $5,000 deficiency is a potential loss to Beeler and Craig and must be tentatively divided between them in their income-sharing ratio of 3:2 (30%: 20%). The capital balances remaining represent their claims on the partnership cash. The computations may be summarized in the manner shown at the top of the following page.

Capital	J. Alden 50%	B. Beeler 30%	H. Craig 20%	Total
Balances	$ 22,000	$ 22,000	$ 22,000	$ 66,000
Division of loss on realization	−27,000	−16,200	−10,800	−54,000
Balances	$− 5,000	$ 5,800	$ 11,200	$ 12,000
Division of potential additional loss	5,000	− 3,000	− 2,000	
Claims to partnership cash		$ 2,800	$ 9,200	$ 12,000

The complete summary of the various transactions that have occurred thus far in the liquidation may then be reported, in the form illustrated earlier, as follows:

	Cash +	Other Assets =	Liabilities +	Capital: J. Alden 50% +	Capital: B. Beeler 30% +	Capital: H. Craig 20%
Balances before realization	$11,000	$64,000	$ 9,000	$22,000	$22,000	$22,000
Sale of assets and division of loss	+10,000	−64,000		−27,000	−16,200	−10,800
Balances after realization	$21,000		$ 9,000	*$ 5,000* (Dr.)	$ 5,800	$11,200
Payment of liabilities	− 9,000		− 9,000			
Balances	$12,000			*$ 5,000* (Dr.)	$ 5,800	$11,200
Distribution of cash to partners	−12,000				− 2,800	− 9,200
Balances				*$ 5,000* (Dr.)	$ 3,000	$ 2,000

The entries to record the liquidation to this point, in general journal form, are as follows:

Sale of assets

Cash	10,000	
Loss and Gain on Realization	54,000	
Assets		64,000

Division of loss

J. Alden, Capital	27,000	
B. Beeler, Capital	16,200	
H. Craig, Capital	10,800	
Loss and Gain on Realization		54,000

Payment of liabilities

Liabilities	9,000	
Cash		9,000

Distribution of cash to partners

B. Beeler, Capital	2,800	
H. Craig, Capital	9,200	
Cash		12,000

The affairs of the partnership are not completely wound up until the claims among the partners are settled. Payments to the firm by the deficient partner are credited to his capital account. Any uncollectible deficiency becomes a loss and is written off against the capital balances of the remaining partners. Finally, the cash received from the deficient partner is distributed to the other partners in accordance with their ownership claims.

To continue with the illustration, the capital balances after the cash distribution of $12,000 are as follows: Alden, $5,000 debit; Beeler, $3,000 credit; Craig, $2,000 credit. The entries on the books of the partnership, in general journal form, under three different assumptions as to final settlement are presented below.

If Alden pays all of his deficiency, the final entries will be:

Receipt of deficiency		
Cash	5,000	
J. Alden, Capital		5,000

Distribution of cash to partners		
B. Beeler, Capital	3,000	
H. Craig, Capital	2,000	
Cash		5,000

If Alden pays $3,000 of his deficiency and the remainder is considered to be uncollectible, the final entries will be as follows:

Receipt of part of deficiency		
Cash	3,000	
J. Alden, Capital		3,000

Division of loss		
B. Beeler, Capital	1,200	
H. Craig, Capital	800	
J. Alden, Capital		2,000

Distribution of cash to partners		
B. Beeler, Capital	1,800	
H. Craig, Capital	1,200	
Cash		3,000

If Alden is unable to pay any part of his deficiency, the loss to the other partners will be recorded in the following entry:

Division of loss		
B. Beeler, Capital	3,000	
H. Craig, Capital	2,000	
J. Alden, Capital		5,000

It should be noted that the type of error most likely to occur in the liquidation of a partnership is improper distribution of cash among the partners. Errors of this type result from confusing the distribution of cash with the division of gains and losses on realization. Gains and losses on realization result from the disposal of assets to outsiders; they represent changes in partnership capital and should be divided among the capital accounts in the same manner as net income or loss from operations, namely, in the income-sharing ratio. Distributions of cash (or other assets) to the partners, on the other hand, are entirely different and have no direct relationship to the income-sharing ratio. Withdrawals of assets by the partners upon dissolution of the partnership are just the reverse of contributions of assets by the partners at the time the partnership was organized. A partner is entitled to receive assets to the extent of the credit balance in his capital account after all potential losses have been taken into consideration.

QUESTIONS

1. Is it possible that a partner may lose a greater amount than the amount of his investment in the partnership enterprise? Explain.

2. Downs, Edwards, and Frank are considering the formation of a partnership in which Downs is to invest $25,000 and devote one-fourth time, Edwards is to invest $12,500 and devote one-half time, and Frank is to make no investment and devote full time. (a) In the absence of a specific agreement on the matter, how should the periodic net income or loss be divided? (b) Would Frank be correct in assuming that inasmuch as he is not contributing any assets to the firm he is risking nothing? Explain.

3. As a part of his initial investment, a partner contributes equipment that had cost him $40,000 and on which the accumulated depreciation is $12,000. The partners agree on a valuation of $35,000. How should the equipment be recorded in the accounts of the partnership?

4. It is agreed that accounts receivable of $5,000 invested by a partner will be collectible to the extent of 90%. How should the accounts receivable be recorded in the general ledger of the partnership?

5. (a) What accounts are debited and credited to record a partner's cash withdrawal in lieu of salary? (b) What accounts are debited and credited to record the division of net income among partners at the end of the fiscal year? (c) The articles of copartnership provide for a salary allowance of $700 per month to partner X. If X withdrew only $500 per month, would this affect his share of the partnership net income?

6. (a) What is the purpose of providing for the allocation of a portion of partnership net income to the partners in the form of a salary allowance? (b) What is the ultimate effect on the capital accounts of the partners if salary allowances are treated as expenses rather than as a distribution of net income?

7. Clark, a partner in the firm of Abel, Bell, and Clark, sells his investment (capital balance of $20,000) to Warren. (a) Does the withdrawal of Clark dissolve the partnership? (b) Are Abel and Bell required to admit Warren as a partner?

8. Differentiate between the admission of a new partner to a partnership (a) by purchase of an interest from another partner and (b) by contribution of assets to the partnership.

9. Dean and Edwards are partners who share in net income equally and have capital balances of $10,000 and $15,000 respectively. Edwards, with the consent of Dean, sells one half of his interest to Porter. What entry is required on the partnership books if the sale price is (a) $6,000? (b) $12,000?

10. (a) Define goodwill as the term is used in business. (b) How is goodwill classified on the balance sheet?

11. (a) Differentiate between "dissolution" and "liquidation" of a partnership. (b) When a partnership is being liquidated, what is the process of realization?

12. In the liquidation process, (a) how are losses and gains on realization divided among the partners, and (b) how is cash distributed among the partners?

13. A and B are partners, sharing gains and losses equally. At the time they decide to terminate the partnership, their capital balances are $30,000 and $40,000 respectively. After all noncash assets are sold and all liabilities are paid, there is a cash balance of $60,000. (a) What is the amount of gain or loss on realization? (b) How should the gain or the loss be divided between A and B? (c) How should the cash be divided between A and B?

14. X, Y, and Z share net income and losses equally. After selling all of the assets for cash, dividing the losses on realization, and paying the liabilities, the balances in the capital accounts are as follows: X, $5,000, Cr.; Y, $2,000, Cr.; Z, $2,000, Dr. (a) What is the amount of cash on hand? (b) How should the cash be distributed?

15. C, D, and E are partners sharing income 2:1:1. After distribution of the firm loss from liquidation, E's capital account has a debit balance of $6,000. If E is personally insolvent, how is his capital balance canceled?

EXERCISES

1. Steve Harper and Tom Rose agree to form a partnership by combining the assets of their separate businesses. Harper contributes the following assets to the partnership: cash, $5,500; accounts receivable with a face value of $12,000 and an allowance for doubtful accounts of $800; and equipment with a cost of $7,000 and accumulated depreciation of $3,500. The partners agree that $300 of the accounts receivable are completely worthless and are not to be accepted by the partnership, that $1,100 is a reasonable allowance for the uncollectibility of the remaining accounts, and that the equipment is to be priced at $4,000. Give the entry, in general journal form, to record Harper's investment in the partnership accounts.

2. Boros and Carter form a partnership with investments of $20,000 and $40,000 respectively. Determine their participation in net income of $24,000 for the year under each of the following assumptions: (a) no agreement concerning division of income; (b) income divided in the ratio of their original capital investments; (c) interest at the rate of 5% allowed on original investments and the balance divided in the ratio of 2:1; (d) allowance of interest at the rate of 5% on original investments, salary allowances of $10,000 and $5,000 respectively, and the balance divided equally.

3. Determine the participation of Boros and Carter in a net income of $6,000 for the year according to each of the four assumptions as to income division listed in Exercise 2.

4. The articles of copartnership of R. N. Adams and D. O. Bowers provide for salary allowances to the partners of $800 and $600 a month respectively, with the remaining net income divided equally. After closing all revenue and expense accounts at the end of the year, Expense and Revenue Summary has a credit balance of $22,000. The two drawing accounts have debit balances of $9,600 and $7,500 respectively. (a) Present journal entries to close the expense and revenue summary account and the drawing accounts. (b) What is the amount of the net increase or decrease in each partner's capital account as a result of the entries in (a)?

5. Coleman and Downing, partners, have capital balances of $20,000 and $30,000 respectively. They admit Edwards and Funk to the partnership. Edwards purchases one fourth of Coleman's interest for $6,000 and one third of Downing's interest for $12,000. Funk is admitted to the partnership with an investment of $15,000, for which he is to receive an ownership equity of $15,000. Present the entries in general journal form to record the admission to the partnership of (a) Edwards and (b) Funk. (c) What are the capital balances of each partner after the admission of Edwards and Funk?

6. Charles Bowen is to retire from the partnership of Bowen and Associates as of July 31, the end of the current fiscal year. After closing the books, the capital balances of the partners are as follows: Charles Bowen, $40,000; Roy Carter, $30,000; and Paul Duncan, $25,000. They have shared net income and losses in the ratio of 2:1:1. The partners agree that the merchandise inventory should be increased by $3,500 and that the allowance for doubtful accounts should be reduced by $500. Bowen agrees to accept an interest-bearing note for $25,000 in partial settlement of his ownership equity. The remainder of his claim is to be paid in cash. Carter and Duncan are to share equally in the net income or loss of the new partnership. Present entries in general journal form to record (a) the adjustment of the assets to bring them into agreement with current fair price and (b) the withdrawal of Bowen.

7. Immediately prior to disposing of all assets and winding up partnership affairs, the capital account balances of Simons and Turner are $8,000 and $6,000 respectively. They share income and losses equally. After selling the noncash assets and paying the liabilities, there is $4,000 of cash remaining. How should the cash be distributed?

8. After closing the accounts preparatory to liquidating the partnership, the capital accounts of Roberts, Sutton, and Tepper are $15,000, $12,000, and $10,000 respectively. Cash and noncash assets total $13,000 and $49,000 respectively. Amounts owing to creditors total $25,000. The partners share income and losses in the ratio of 3:3:2. The noncash assets are sold and sufficient cash is available to pay all of the liabilities except one for $3,000. Tepper is personally insolvent, but Roberts and Sutton are able to meet any indebtedness to the firm. Determine how the claim of the creditors should be settled. Present calculations in good form.

9. A, B, and C arrange to import and sell orchid corsages for a university dance. It is agreed that the net income or loss on the venture is to be shared equally. A and B advance $30 and $15 respectively of their own funds to pay for advertising and other expenses. (a) After collecting for all sales and paying creditors, they have $165 in cash. How should the money be distributed? (b) Assuming that they have only $15 instead of $165, how should the money be distributed? (c) Assuming that the money was distributed as determined in (b), does any of the three have claims against another and, if so, how much?

PROBLEMS

15-1. On July 1 of the current year Robert Brown and Jack Collins form a partnership.

Brown is to invest certain business assets at valuations to be agreed upon, is to transfer business liabilities, and is to contribute sufficient cash to bring his total capital to $30,000. Details regarding the book values of the business assets and liabilities, and the agreed valuations, follow:

	Brown's Ledger Balance	Agreed Valuation
Accounts Receivable	$ 9,000	$ 9,000
Allowance for Doubtful Accounts	600	1,000
Merchandise Inventory	16,000	17,500
Store Equipment	4,500	2,200
Accumulated Depreciation — Store Equipment	3,000	
Office Equipment	3,000	800
Accumulated Depreciation — Office Equipment	1,800	
Accounts Payable	8,000	8,000

Collins agrees to invest merchandise inventory priced at $10,000 and $15,000 in cash.

The articles of copartnership include the following provisions regarding the division of net income: interest on original investment at 6%, salary allowances of $6,000 and $9,000 respectively, and the remainder equally.

Instructions: (1) Give the entries, in general journal form, to record the investments of Brown and Collins on the partnership books.

(2) Prepare a balance sheet as of July 1, the date of formation of the partnership.

(3) After adjustments and the closing of revenue and expense accounts at June 30, the end of the first full year of operations, the expense and revenue summary account has a credit balance of $24,300 and the drawing accounts have debit balances of $6,000 (Brown) and $8,250 (Collins). Present the journal

entries to close the expense and revenue summary account and the drawing accounts as of June 30.

15-2. James King and John Long are in the process of forming a partnership. They have agreed that King is to invest $20,000 and that Long is to invest $30,000. King is to devote one half of his time to the business and Long is to devote full time. The following plans for the division of income are under consideration:

(a) Equal division.
(b) In the ratio of original investments.
(c) In the ratio of time devoted to the business.
(d) Interest of 6% on original investments and the remainder equally.
(e) Interest of 6% on original investments, salaries of $5,000 to King and $10,000 to Long, and the remainder equally.
(f) Plan (e), except that Long is also to be allowed a bonus equal to 20% of the amount by which net income exceeds the salary allowances.

Instructions: Determine the division of income under each of the following assumptions: net income of $30,000 and net income of $12,000. Present the data in tabular form, using the following columnar headings:

	$30,000		$12,000	
Plan	King	Long	King	Long

15-3. The capital accounts of C. D. Downs, B. L. Evans, and T. D. Ford, partners, have balances of $30,000, $20,000, and $40,000 respectively on May 1, the beginning of the current fiscal year. Downs invests an additional $5,000 on August 1. Evans withdraws $10,000 during the current fiscal year. Their agreement provides that Evans, the managing partner, be allowed a yearly salary of $10,000; that each partner be allowed 5% on his capital balance at May 1, the beginning of the fiscal year; and that the remaining net income or loss be divided equally. The net income for the year was $17,500.

Instructions: (1) Prepare the income division section of the income statement for the current fiscal year.

(2) Prepare the capital statement for the current fiscal year.

15-4. R. E. Martin and H. N. Nunn have operated a successful firm, sharing income and losses equally. W. E. Kelley is to be admitted to the partnership on July 1 of the current year in accordance with the following agreement:

(a) Assets and liabilities of the old partnership are to be valued at their book values as of June 30, except for the following:
Accounts receivable amounting to $360 are to be written off and the allowance for doubtful accounts is to be increased to 10% of the remaining accounts.
Merchandise inventory is to be priced at $13,750.
Equipment is to be priced at $32,000.
(b) Goodwill of $10,000 is to be recognized as attributable to the firm of Martin and Nunn.
(c) Kelley is to invest $14,000 in cash.
(d) The income-sharing ratio of Martin, Nunn, and Kelley is to be 2:2:1.

The post-closing trial balance of Martin and Nunn as of June 30 follows:

Martin and Nunn
Post-Closing Trial Balance
June 30, 19--

Cash	7,050	
Accounts Receivable	9,860	
Allowance for Doubtful Accounts		300
Merchandise Inventory	14,300	
Prepaid Insurance	690	
Equipment	52,950	
Accumulated Depreciation — Equipment		27,040
Accounts Payable		9,940
Wages Payable		770
R. E. Martin, Capital		22,200
H. N. Nunn, Capital		24,600
	84,850	84,850

Instructions: (1) Present general journal entries as of June 30 to record the revaluations, using a temporary account entitled Asset Revaluations. The balance in the accumulated depreciation account is to be eliminated.

(2) Present the additional entries, in general journal form, to record the remaining transactions related to the formation of the new partnership. Assume that all transactions occur on July 1.

(3) Present a balance sheet for the new partnership as of July 1.

15-5. Holt, Ingle, and Johnson decide to discontinue business operations as of March 31 and to liquidate their enterprise. The firm's post-closing trial balance at that date appears below.

Holt, Ingle, and Johnson
Post-Closing Trial Balance
March 31, 19--

Cash	12,000	
Accounts Receivable	7,700	
Allowance for Doubtful Accounts		1,900
Merchandise Inventory	24,600	
Prepaid Insurance	900	
Supplies	700	
Equipment	6,200	
Accumulated Depreciation — Equipment		3,800
Building	30,000	
Accumulated Depreciation — Building		8,000
Land	4,000	
Accounts Payable		8,600
Mortgage Note Payable		9,000
John Holt, Capital		28,500
Ray Ingle, Capital		16,300
Don Johnson, Capital		10,000
	86,100	86,100

The partners share net income and losses in the ratio 3:2:1. The realization and liquidation transactions are summarized as follows:

(a) Collected $5,175 of accounts receivable; the remainder are worthless.
(b) Sold the merchandise for $20,000 cash.
(c) Realized $700 cash from cancellation of the insurance policies.
(d) Sold the supplies for $450 cash.
(e) Sold the equipment for $3,000 cash.
(f) Sold the land and building for $28,000, purchaser paying $19,000 cash and assuming the mortgage note. The mortgage holder released the partners from further liability.
(g) Paid miscellaneous expenses in connection with the sale of the assets, $525. (Charge to Loss and Gain on Realization.)
(h) Distributed the loss on realization to the partners' capital accounts.
(i) Paid the accounts payable in full.
(j) Distributed remaining cash to the partners.

Instructions: (1) Set up T accounts for Cash, Loss and Gain on Realization, and the capital accounts.

(2) Record the March 31 balances in the T accounts.

(3) Present entries, in general journal form, to record the liquidation; post to the T accounts as appropriate; rule the accounts.

(4) Assuming a net loss on realization of $48,900, prepare a complete summary of the liquidation in the form shown in the chapter. No entries are required.

(5) Assuming a net loss on realization of $51,900, prepare a complete summary of the liquidation in the form shown in the chapter. No entries are required.

15-6. Immediately prior to beginning the process of liquidation, the partners in the firm of Ross, Stone, and Tanner have capital balances of $50,000, $30,000, and $25,000 respectively. The cash balance is $30,000, the book value of noncash assets totals $100,000, and liabilities total $25,000. The partners share income and losses in the ratio of 3:3:2.

Instructions: Present the entries, in general journal form, to record (1) the sale of the assets, (2) the distribution of the loss or gain on realization, (3) the payment of creditors, and (4) the distribution of cash to the partners according to each of the assumptions described below. Use "Assets" as the account title for the noncash assets and "Liabilities" as the account title for creditors' claims. It is suggested that summaries similar to those illustrated in this chapter be prepared as a basis for the entries.

(A) All of the other assets are sold for $108,000 in cash.
(B) All of the other assets are sold for $60,000 in cash.
(C) All of the other assets are sold for $16,000 in cash. After the available cash is paid to the partners:
  (a) The partner with the debit capital balance pays the amount owed to the firm.
  (b) The additional cash is distributed.
(D) All of the other assets are sold for $12,000 in cash. After the available cash is paid to the partners:
  (a) The partner with the debit capital balance pays 50% of his deficiency to the firm.
  (b) The remaining partners absorb the remaining deficiency as a loss.
  (c) The additional cash is distributed.

16.

Corporations—nature and formation

Definition of a corporation

Without doubt the most frequently quoted definition of a corporation is the one formulated in 1819 by Chief Justice Marshall. In the decision on the Dartmouth College case he stated that: "A corporation is an artificial being, invisible, intangible, and existing only in contemplation of the law." The concept underlying this definition has become the foundation for the prevailing legal doctrine that a corporation is an artificial person, created by law and having a distinct existence separate and apart from the natural persons who are responsible for its creation and operation.

Corporations may be classified in a number of ways. For example, the term *public corporation* may refer to a municipality or other political division, and the term *private corporation* may refer to all corporations other than incorporated governmental units. On the other hand, business corporations whose ownership is widely held may be termed *public* or *open corporations*, and those with a relatively small group of owners may be termed *private* or *close corporations*. Corporations may also be classified as profit or nonprofit. *Profit corporations* are organized for the purpose of making a profit. *Nonprofit corporations* include those organized for charitable, educational, or other philanthropic purposes. Regardless of the nature or the purpose of a corporation, it is created in accordance with the statutes and is a separate legal entity.

Almost all large business enterprises in the United States are organized as corporations. Mass production by assembly-line methods requires large investments in inventories, buildings, machinery, and other properties. The large sums needed are usually obtainable only through the pooling of the resources of a number of people in a corporation. The corporate form of organization is also advantageous to individuals who wish to invest savings in business enterprises without incurring responsibilities for management or risking their entire capital.

Characteristics of a corporation

As a legal entity, the corporation has certain characteristics that distinguish it from other types of business organization. The most important of these characteristics will be considered briefly in the following paragraphs.

Separate legal existence. Being a distinct legal entity, the corporation acts under its corporate name. It may obtain, hold, and dispose of property in its corporate capacity. It may borrow funds and assume other obligations. It may enter into contracts with outsiders or with its own stockholders.

Transferable units of ownership. The ownership of a corporation is divided into transferable units known as *shares of stock*. Each share has the same rights and privileges as every other share of the same class. One may own a single share or many thousands of shares. The owners of the corporation, known as *stockholders* or *shareholders*, may sell their stock without interfering with the activities of the corporation. The millions of transactions that occur on stock exchanges are independent transactions between buyers and sellers.

Limited liability of stockholders. Since a corporation is a separate legal entity, it is responsible for its own acts and obligations. Ordinarily the creditors of a corporation may not look beyond the assets of the corporation for satisfaction of their claims. Thus, the loss that a stockholder may suffer is limited to the amount of his investment. The phenomenal growth of the corporate form of business would have been impossible without this feature.

Continuity of existence. The maximum life of a corporation depends upon the terms of its charter; it may be perpetual or it may continue for a specified number of years. In the latter case the term may usually be extended by an application for renewal of the charter. In contrast to a partnership, the life term of the corporation is not affected by the withdrawal, death, or incapacity of one of its owners.

Additional taxes. A corporation is required to pay a fee to the state at the time of its organization and an annual tax thereafter. If it does business in states other than the one in which it is incorporated, it may also be required to pay annual taxes to such states. The earnings of a corporation are subject to the federal income tax. When the remaining earnings are distributed to stockholders as dividends, they are again taxed as income to the individuals receiving them.

Under certain conditions specified in the Internal Revenue Code, corporations with no more than ten stockholders may elect to be treated as a partnership for income tax purposes. The income of corporations electing this optional treatment must be included in the taxable income of the stockholders, regardless of whether or not the income is distributed to the stockholders, and the corporation pays no tax.

Governmental regulation. Being creatures of the state and being owned by stockholders who possess limited liability, corporations are subject to more restrictions and regulations than are sole proprietorships and partnerships. They may not exceed the scope of activities described in their charters. In some states they are restricted as to the amount of real estate that they may own, the amount of their own shares of stock that they may reacquire, and the amount of earnings that they may distribute. Although these and other restrictions do not outweigh the advantages of the corporate form for a large firm, they may represent an important consideration for a small business.

Incorporation

It is customary for incorporators to obtain the services of an attorney to guide them through the various steps in organizing a corporation. The statutory requirements vary among the states, but in general it is necessary: (1) to effect a tentative organization and obtain subscriptions to stock and (2) to obtain a charter or articles of incorporation. The application for a charter is filed with an official of the state government, usually the Secretary of State. Upon approval of the application, the charter is issued. It may be a separate document, or the approved application may become the charter.

The following excerpts from the Ohio statutes are illustrative of the requirements for a charter:

(A) Three or more natural persons, a majority of whom are citizens of the United States, may form a corporation by subscribing and thereafter filing in the office of the Secretary of State articles of incorporation which shall set forth:

(1) The name of the corporation, which shall end with or include "Company," "Co.," "Corporation," "Corp.," "Incorporated," or "Inc.";

(2) The place in this state where the principal office of the corporation is to be located;

(3) The purpose or purposes for which the corporation is formed;

(4) The authorized number and the par value per share of shares with par value, and the authorized number of shares without par value, . . . ; the express terms, if any, of the shares; and, if the shares are classified, the designa-

tion of each class, the authorized number and par value per share, if any, of the shares of each class, and the express terms of the shares of each class;

(5) The amount of stated capital with which the corporation will begin business, which shall not be less than five hundred dollars.

The charter ordinarily contains only the basic rules governing the corporation. Other regulations for the conduct of the internal affairs of the corporation, consistent with the charter and the statutes, are usually adopted as bylaws. Among other things, the bylaws may provide for: (1) time and place of meetings of stockholders, method of notification, and quorum requirements; (2) number of directors, term of office, and manner of fixing remuneration; (3) special committees of the board of directors and their appointment and authority; and (4) titles, qualifications, and duties of officers.

Working organization

Even though the stockholders of a corporation are its owners, they have no direct control over the management of its affairs. They exercise control indirectly by electing a *board of directors*, whose responsibility it is to determine policies and to see that they are carried out by the employees of the corporation.

The board of directors selects the principal executives, to whom it in turn delegates the authority to manage the affairs of the corporation. The extent to which the directors determine policies varies among corporations. They may meet each month, each week, or oftener. A common practice among large corporations is to establish one or more standing committees of the directors, such as an executive committee and a finance committee. The special committees report periodically to the entire board, which confirms or disapproves of their acts and recommendations.

The principal executives of a corporation, consisting of a president, one or more vice-presidents, a secretary, a treasurer, and perhaps others, are responsible to the board of directors. It is not unusual for the president and others among the principal executives also to be members of the board of directors. As the chief executive officer, the president has the responsibility for directing and controlling the activities of the other principal executives.

The chart on the opposite page depicts the flow of authority from the board of directors through intermediate steps down to the rank and file employees. The flow of responsibility is in the reverse direction.

The number of individual stockholders in corporations varies widely, from a very small number to hundreds of thousands. For a large, publicly held corporation, the number of stockholders in attendance at an

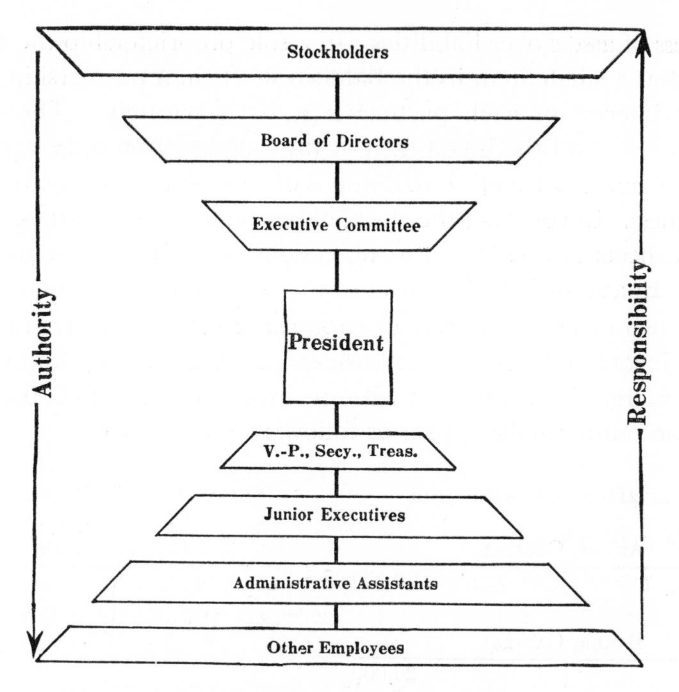

Corporate form of organization

annual meeting is relatively small. Stockholders not expecting to attend the meeting may transfer their voting rights to an agent. This delegation of voting rights is accomplished by the use of a form known as a *proxy.* The management of large corporations customarily mails proxy forms to all stockholders in advance of the annual meeting. The form, or an accompanying statement, discloses the slate of directors proposed by the management and an explanation of any important issues, such as a merger with another corporation, on which the stockholders are to vote.

At the stockholders' meeting, the board of directors, through its chairman or the president of the corporation, generally presents an oral report on past operations and future plans. A printed report is also usually mailed to all stockholders soon after the end of each fiscal year. These reports may be very brief, containing only the condensed financial statements for the year, or they may include supplementary statements, charts, graphs, and explanatory text. Many corporations also issue brief quarterly reports.

Corporate capital

The owners' equity in a corporation is commonly called *stockholders' equity, shareholders' equity, capital,* or *net worth.* As in the case of sole proprietorships and partnerships, the equity of the owners is equivalent to the excess of assets over liabilities. In a sole proprietorship the capital is reported as a single item in the balance sheet; in a partnership the proprietary interest of each partner is stated separately. The amounts reported represent the investment at the balance sheet date, and no distinction is made between contributions of capital and income retained in the business. In contrast, the stockholders' equity section of corporation balance sheets is divided into subsections based on the source of the capital. In addition, the identity of the owners is not disclosed.

The two principal sources of capital are investments by the owners and net income retained in the business. Assuming that Adams, Baker, and Cole organize a business with an investment of $20,000 each, the capital accounts would appear as follows:

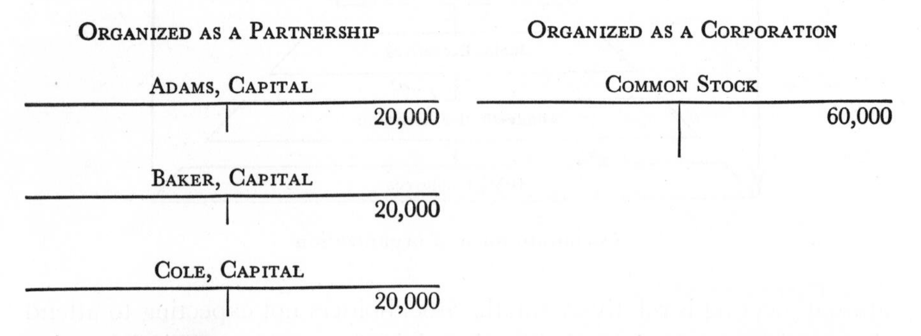

The $60,000 investment of the stockholders, sometimes referred to as the *paid-in capital*, is recorded in a stock account. This represents the legal capital of the corporation. Ordinarily it may not be returned to the stockholders except upon liquidation, and then only after the claims of creditors have been satisfied.

If the new firm earns net income of $9,000 during its first year, the capital accounts would then appear as follows, assuming no distributions of income and equal income sharing by the partners:

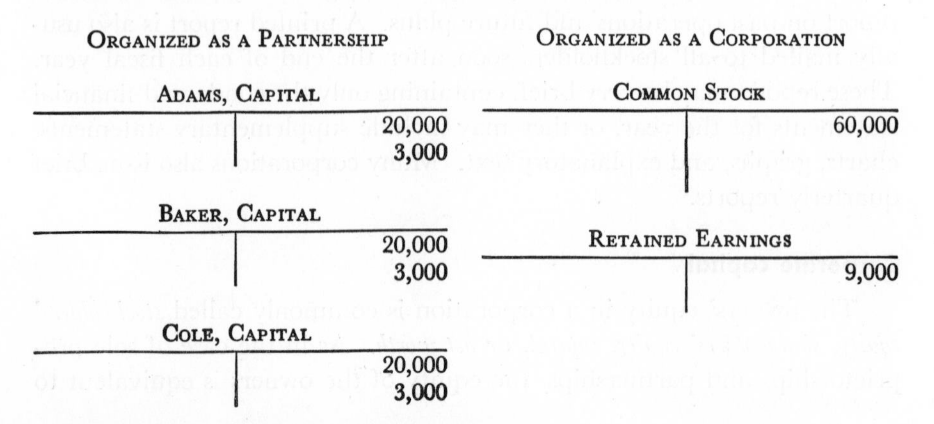

In the partnership form of organization, the net income in Expense and Revenue Summary is transferred to the respective capital accounts of the partners. In the corporate form the net income is transferred to *Retained Earnings,* thus segregating the corporation's retained income from its paid-in capital. Net losses from operations and distributions of income are debited to the retained earnings account.

Until relatively recent years, the term customarily applied to retained earnings was *earned surplus.* The meaning of the older term was often misunderstood by readers of financial statements and has to a great extent been supplanted. Other terminology frequently employed includes *accumulated earnings, earnings retained for use in the business,* and *income reinvested in the business.*

If the retained earnings account has a debit balance, this balance is termed a *deficit.* If in the foregoing illustration the new firm had incurred a net loss of $7,000 in its first year, the retained earnings account would have appeared as shown at the right, and the total capital of the corporation would have been $53,000 ($60,000 – $7,000).

Retained Earnings	
7,000	

Characteristics of stock

The ownership of a corporation is divided into shares that may be referred to as a corporation's *capital stock.* A common practice is to place an arbitrary amount, known as *par,* on the shares. Stock may also be issued without par, in which case it is known as *no-par* stock. Many states provide that no-par stock must be assigned a *stated value* by the board of directors, which in essence makes it similar to par stock. The stated value assigned by the directors may be the minimum fixed by law or some higher arbitrary amount.

Because of the limited liability feature granted the stockholders, the creditors of a corporation have no claim against the personal assets of the stockholders. To afford some protection to the creditors, the law requires that some specific minimum contribution by the stockholders be retained for the protection of the corporate creditors. This amount, called *legal capital,* varies among the states but ordinarily includes the par or stated value of the shares.

Classes of stock. The basic rights that ordinarily accompany ownership of a share of stock include (1) the right to vote, (2) the right to share in earnings, (3) the right to maintain the same fractional interest in the corporation by purchasing a proportionate number of shares of any additional issuances of stock (*pre-emptive right*), and (4) the right to share in assets upon liquidation.

If a corporation has only one class of stock, it is called *common stock* and each share has equal rights. In order to appeal to a broader investment market, a corporation may provide for one or more classes of stock with preferential rights over another class. The preference usually relates to the right to share in earnings. Such stock is called *preferred stock.* The classes of stock that a corporation may issue, together with the contractual preferences and limitations of each class, are set forth in the corporate charter or by-laws.

The authority to distribute earnings to the stockholders rests with the board of directors. Distributions of earnings are called *dividends,* and the directors are said to *declare a dividend.* A corporation can make no guarantee that its operations will be profitable, and hence it cannot guarantee dividends to its stockholders. Furthermore, the directors have wide discretionary powers in determining the extent to which earnings should be retained by the corporation to provide for expansion, to offset possible future losses, or to provide for other contingencies.

A corporation with both preferred and common stock may declare dividends on the common only after it meets the requirements of the stipulated dividend on the preferred. For example, assume that the Apex Corporation has outstanding 1,000 shares of stock with a preference to a $6 dividend and 4,000 shares of common stock. In its first three years of operation it earned $12,000, $25,000 and $60,000 respectively and distributed 60% of the earnings each year. The distribution of the dividends among the two classes of stock is tabulated as follows:

	FIRST YEAR	SECOND YEAR	THIRD YEAR
Net income	$12,000	$25,000	$60,000
Percent to be distributed	60%	60%	60%
Amount of dividend distribution	$ 7,200	$15,000	$36,000
Dividends on preferred ($6 per share)	6,000	6,000	6,000
Balance to common (4,000 shares)	$ 1,200	$ 9,000	$30,000
Dividends per share on common	$ .30	$ 2.25	$ 7.50

Participating and nonparticipating preferred stock. In the foregoing illustration the holders of preferred stock received an annual dividend of $6 per share in each of the three years, in contrast to the common stockholders, whose annual per share dividends were $.30, $2.25, and $7.50. It is apparent from the example that holders of preferred stock have relatively greater assurance of receiving dividends but that holders of common stock have the potentiality of receiving larger dividends. The participation of holders of preferred stock in the earnings of a corporation is ordinarily limited to a stipulated amount. This was assumed to be the case in the example. Stock that is so limited is said to be *non-participating.*

If the contract provides that dividends on preferred stock may exceed the stipulated amount, such stock is known as *participating.* Preferred shares may participate in a variety of ways with common shares, and the contract must be examined to determine the extent of this participation. For example, the contract covering the preferred stock of the Apex Corporation in the preceding illustration may provide that if the earnings to be distributed exceed the regular preferred dividend and a comparable dividend on common, the preferred shall share ratably with the common in the excess earnings. The $36,000 dividend distribution in the third year under such conditions would be allocated as follows:

	To Preferred	To Common	Total
Regular dividend to preferred (1,000 × $6)...	$ 6,000		$ 6,000
Comparable dividend to common (4,000×$6)		$24,000	24,000
Remaining $6,000 to all shares ratably......	1,200	4,800	6,000
Total dividends......................	$ 7,200	$28,800	$36,000
Dividends per share....................	$ 7.20	$ 7.20	

Cumulative and noncumulative preferred stock. As was indicated above, most preferred stock is nonparticipating. Provision is usually made, however, to assure the accumulation of the right to the stipulated dividend if part or all of it is not paid in any particular year. This is accomplished by providing that dividends may not be paid on the common stock if any preferred dividends are in arrears. Such preferred stock is known as *cumulative.* To illustrate, assume that a corporation has outstanding 5,000 shares of cumulative preferred 5% stock of $100 par and that dividends have been *passed* (not paid) for the preceding two years. In the current year it will be necessary to declare preferred dividends of $50,000 for the past two years and $25,000 for the current year before any dividends can be declared on the common stock. Preferred stock that does not have this cumulative right is called *noncumulative.*

Other preferential rights. Thus far the discussion of preferential rights of preferred stock has related to dividend distributions. Preferred stock may also be given a preference over common stock in its claim to assets upon liquidation of the corporation. If the assets remaining after payment of creditors are not sufficient to return the capital contributions of both classes of stock, payment would first be made to the preferred stockholders and any balance remaining would go to the common stockholders. The right may also extend to payment of arrearages in dividends on cumulative preferred stock, even though the amount of retained earnings is less than the amount required for the dividends.

Another usual difference between preferred stock and common stock is that the former may have no voting rights. Some corporations may therefore have more than one class of preferred stock, with differences as to the amount of dividends, priority of claims, and voting rights. In any particular case the rights of a class of stock may be determined by reference to the articles of incorporation, the stock certificate, or some other abstract of the agreement.

Callable preferred stock. It is not uncommon for a corporation issuing preferred stock to reserve the right to redeem it later under specified conditions. Such stock is known as *callable preferred stock.* The *redemption price* is the amount per share that the corporation agrees to pay if it elects to redeem the stock; it is ordinarily somewhat in excess of par.

Book value per share

The total par or stated value of the outstanding stock of a corporation does not necessarily represent the total equity of the stockholders. Some of the stock may have been issued at a price different from par or stated value, and accumulations of earnings or losses are a part of capital. The stockholders' equity per share of stock is termed *book value* or *book equity.* It is the amount that would be paid on each share of stock if the corporation were to liquidate without incurring any losses or gains on the sale of its assets. When there is only one class of stock, the book value per share is determined by dividing total capital by the number of shares outstanding.

To illustrate the computation of book value per share when there is only one class of stock, assume that as of June 30 of the current year the Monarch Corporation has 2,000 shares of $50 par stock outstanding. The balances in the capital accounts at the same date and the computation of the book value per share are shown below.

Common stock	$100,000
Retained earnings (credit balance)	50,000
Total capital	$150,000

$150,000 ÷ 2,000 shares = $75 book value per share

For a corporation with both preferred and common stock, it is necessary first to allocate the total capital between the two classes. The book value per share of each class may then be determined by dividing the allocated capital by the number of shares outstanding. To illustrate, assume that as of December 31 of the current year the Stuart Corporation has outstanding 1,000 shares of $100 par, 6%, cumulative, nonparticipating preferred and 50,000 shares of $10 par common. Assume further that there are no preferred dividends in arrears. The balances in the capital accounts at the same date and the computation of book value per share are as follows:

CAPITAL

Preferred 6% stock, cumulative, $100 par (1,000 shares outstanding)	$100,000
Common stock, $10 par (50,000 shares outstanding)	500,000
Retained earnings	300,000
Total capital	$900,000

ALLOCATION OF TOTAL CAPITAL TO PREFERRED AND COMMON STOCK

Total capital	$900,000
Allocated to preferred stock:	
Par	100,000
Allocated to common stock	$800,000

BOOK VALUE PER SHARE

Preferred stock: $100,000 ÷ 1,000 shares = $100 per share
Common stock: $800,000 ÷ 50,000 shares = $16 per share

Assuming in the foregoing example that preferred dividends were in arrears for two years ($12 per share), retained earnings of $12,000 (1,000 × $12) would be allocated to the preferred and the computations would be as follows:

ALLOCATION OF TOTAL CAPITAL TO PREFERRED AND COMMON STOCK

Total capital		$900,000
Allocated to preferred stock:		
Par	$100,000	
Dividends in arrears	12,000	112,000
Allocated to common stock		$788,000

BOOK VALUE PER SHARE

Preferred stock: $112,000 ÷ 1,000 shares = $112.00 per share
Common stock: $788,000 ÷ 50,000 shares = $15.76 per share

In determining book value per share, it is evident that the various preferential rights of the particular preferred stock must be known. In addition to considering dividends in arrears, it is necessary to recognize dividend participation rights and preference to assets on dissolution.

The book value per share is one of the many factors affecting the *market price*, that is, the price at which a share is bought and sold at a particular moment. A stock may be listed on a national exchange, such as the New York Stock Exchange, or on a local exchange, or it may be available only in the over-the-counter market. Prices of stocks may fluctuate from day to day or hour to hour. Earning capacity, dividend rates, and prospects for the future often affect the market price of stocks to a much greater extent than does book value. For example, the common stock with a book value of $15.76 per share in the illustration above may sell at $7 if earnings, dividends, and future prospects are relatively unfavorable, or its market price may be $40 if these factors are very favorable.

Authorized, issued, and outstanding stock

The number of shares of each class of stock that a corporation is *authorized* to issue to stockholders is set forth in the charter. The exact capital needs of a corporation in its first years of operation may be difficult to determine. It is usually desirable, therefore, to provide for an authorization in excess of the number of shares expected to be issued initially. If a corporation reaches the limit of its authorization and wishes to issue additional shares, it is necessary to apply for an amendment to the charter and pay the requisite state fees.

The term *issued* is applied to the shares issued to the stockholders. A corporation may, under various circumstances discussed in a later chapter, reacquire some of the stock that it has issued. The stock remaining in the hands of the stockholders is then referred to as the stock *outstanding*.

Presentation of stockholders' equity on the balance sheet

The assets and the liabilities of a corporation are reported on the balance sheet in the same manner as the assets and the liabilities of a sole proprietorship or a partnership. The stockholders' equity section is different, however. Two principal subdivisions are paid-in capital and retained or accumulated earnings. The par of the various classes of stock issued, together with the details of dividend preferences and number of shares authorized, appears as illustrated below.

Stockholders' equity

Paid-in capital:		
Preferred 6% stock, cumulative, $50 par (5,000 shares authorized, 3,000 shares issued)	$150,000	
Common, $10 par (50,000 shares authorized and issued)	500,000	
Total paid-in capital	$650,000	
Retained earnings	200,000	
Total stockholders' equity		**$850,000**

The stockholders' equity section appearing below illustrates the reporting of a deficit and some variations in terminology from the foregoing example.

Capital		
Paid-in:		
Preferred 5% stock, $25 par (5,000 shares authorized and issued)	$125,000	
Common, $5 par (100,000 shares authorized, 80,000 shares issued)	400,000	
Total contributions by stockholders	$525,000	
Less deficit	50,000	
Total capital		$475,000

Issuing stock at par for cash or other assets

The entries to record the investment of capital in the corporation are similar to those of other types of business organizations in that cash and other assets received are debited and any liabilities assumed are credited. The credit to capital differs, however, in that there is only one account for each class of stock.[1] To illustrate, assume that the Peerless Corporation, organized on February 15 with an authorization of 10,000 shares of preferred stock of $50 par and 100,000 shares of common stock of $25 par, issues one half of each authorization at par for cash on March 1. The entry to record the stockholders' investment and the receipt of the cash, in general journal form, is as follows:

Mar. 1	Cash	1,500,000	
	Preferred Stock		250,000
	Common Stock		1,250,000

In the foregoing example, the stockholders' contributions to the corporation were in the form of cash, or to state it in another manner, the corporation issued the stock for cash. Stock may be exchanged for assets other than cash, such as land, buildings, or equipment. In such cases the assets should be recorded at a fair market price. The determination of the fair market price valuations is the responsibility of the board of directors. Assuming that on March 10 the Peerless Corporation acquires buildings valued at $260,000 and land valued at $40,000, giving in exchange 1,000 shares of preferred stock and 10,000 shares of common stock, the transaction would be recorded as follows:

Mar. 10	Buildings	260,000	
	Land	40,000	
	Preferred Stock		50,000
	Common Stock		250,000

[1]The maintenance of records for each stockholder is discussed in Chapter 17.

Organization costs

Expenditures incurred in organizing a corporation, such as legal fees, taxes and fees paid to the state, and promotional costs, are charged to an intangible asset account entitled *Organization Costs.* Although such costs have no realizable value upon liquidation, they are as essential as plant and equipment and they benefit the corporation as long as it continues its operations. If the life of a corporation is limited to a definite period of time, the organization costs may well be amortized over the period by annual charges to an expense account. The length of life of most corporations is not determinable in advance, however.

Incorporating a proprietorship or a partnership

A business enterprise operated as a sole proprietorship or as a partnership may incorporate to acquire additional capital or to secure other advantages of the corporate form. In effecting the changes in organization, it is necessary to obtain a corporate charter and to conform with the other statutory requirements of the state. The transfer of the assets and the liabilities to the corporation is comparable to a sale by the sole owner or the partners to the corporation.

The basic accounting procedures involved in incorporating a business are as follows:

On the books of the sole proprietorship or partnership:

(1) Adjust and close the revenue and expense accounts.
(2) Adjust the various asset accounts to the current fair market prices.
(3) Record the transfer of the assets and the liabilities to the corporation.
(4) Record the receipt of the stock from the corporation.
(5) Distribute the stock (also cash or other assets not transferred) to the sole owner or the partners.

On the books of the corporation:

(1) Record the assets and the liabilities acquired from the sole proprietorship or the partnership.
(2) Record the issuance of capital stock in payment for the net assets.

To illustrate the procedures outlined above, assume that Alden and Barker, sharing equally in income and losses, dissolve their partnership and incorporate their business. The post-closing trial balance of the partnership as of May 31, the effective date of the transfer to the corporation, is shown at the top of the following page.

All assets and liabilities are to be transferred to Alden & Barker, Inc., at their book values, except that accounts receivable are to be valued at $58,000 and merchandise inventory is valued at $140,000. In exchange the partnership is to accept, at par, common stock with a par of $50 per share.

Alden and Barker
Post-Closing Trial Balance
May 31, 19-

Cash	20,000	
Accounts Receivable	60,000	
Allowance for Doubtful Accounts		6,000
Merchandise Inventory	150,000	
Store Equipment	12,000	
Accumulated Depreciation — Store Equipment		4,000
Office Equipment	4,000	
Accumulated Depreciation — Office Equipment		2,000
Accounts Payable		14,000
G. M. Alden, Capital		120,000
J. D. Barker, Capital		100,000
	246,000	246,000

The partnership books having already been adjusted and closed for the period ending May 31, the remaining entries are as follows:

Revaluation of assets

Allowance for Doubtful Accounts	4,000	
Asset Revaluations	6,000	
Merchandise Inventory		10,000
G. M. Alden, Capital	3,000	
J. D. Barker, Capital	3,000	
Asset Revaluations		6,000

Transfer of assets and liabilities to the corporation

Receivable from Alden & Barker, Inc.	214,000	
Allowance for Doubtful Accounts	2,000	
Accumulated Depreciation — Store Equipment	4,000	
Accumulated Depreciation — Office Equipment	2,000	
Accounts Payable	14,000	
Cash		20,000
Accounts Receivable		60,000
Merchandise Inventory		140,000
Store Equipment		12,000
Office Equipment		4,000

Receipt of stock from the corporation

Common Stock — Alden & Barker, Inc.	214,000	
Receivable from Alden & Barker, Inc.		214,000

Distribution of stock to the partners

G. M. Alden, Capital	117,000	
J. D. Barker, Capital	97,000	
Common Stock — Alden & Barker, Inc.		214,000

The final entry recording the distribution of the stock to the partners signifies the winding up of the partnership affairs. After the foregoing entries have been posted, all accounts in the ledger will be in balance.

The entries on the books of the corporation are as follows:

Acquisition of assets and liabilities

Cash	20,000	
Accounts Receivable	60,000	
Merchandise Inventory	140,000	
Store Equipment	8,000	
Office Equipment	2,000	
Allowance for Doubtful Accounts		2,000
Accounts Payable		14,000
Payable to Alden and Barker		214,000

Issuance of stock to the partnership

Payable to Alden and Barker	214,000	
Common Stock		214,000

It should be noted that the depreciable assets are entered at their net cost to the corporation; the original cost to the partnership and the accumulated depreciation are not recorded. For accounts receivable, however, both the gross amount and the allowance for doubtful accounts are recorded, as it is not possible to allocate the estimated loss to the accounts of specific debtors.

QUESTIONS

1. Why are most large business enterprises organized as corporations?

2. Brock is a partner in Brock and Myers, in which his capital interest is $40,000. He also owns some stock in The Travis Company acquired at a cost of $10,000. He has other assets worth $80,000. (a) If The Travis Company fails, what is the maximum loss Brock might have to absorb? (b) If Brock and Myers fails, what is the maximum loss Brock might have to absorb? (c) If Brock dies, what effect would his death have on The Travis Company? on the Brock and Myers partnership?

3. Why is it said that the earnings of a corporation are subject to "double taxation"? Discuss.

4. What is meant when it is said that the stockholders of a corporation exercise only indirect control over the management of a corporation's affairs?

5. Name several terms commonly used to describe the owner's equity in a corporation.

6. What are the two principal sources of corporate capital?

7. If the retained earnings account has a debit balance, what is this balance called?

8. The Wagner Company has common stock with a par of $100, while a competitor has common stock with a par of $50. Do the pars give any indication as to which stock is preferable as an investment?

9. What are the basic rights of stockholders?

10. Differentiate between common stock and preferred stock.

11. What is the nature of each of the following features of preferred stock: (a) participating, (b) cumulative, and (c) callable?

12. The Weberg Corporation has a balance of $200,000 in Preferred Stock, representing 2,000 noncumulative, nonparticipating shares. It declares regular quarterly dividends of $2,500 on the preferred stock. (a) What is the par of the stock? (b) What is the annual dividend rate per share in terms of dollars and in terms of percent of par?

13. The par of the common stock of Baxter Chemical Corporation is $50. The current book value and the market price per share are $59.55 and $98.50 respectively. Suggest reasons for the comparatively high market price in relation to par and to book value.

14. The Hart Oil Company has been authorized to issue 50,000 shares of $50 par common stock. On June 1, 1962, it issued 30,000 shares; on May 1, 1964, it issued 10,000 shares; and on August 31, 1966, it reacquired 1,000 shares. What is the number of shares (a) authorized, (b) issued, and (c) outstanding?

15. Describe the type of expenditures charged to the organization costs account. Give examples of such expenditures.

16. Adams and Corley dissolve their partnership and incorporate their business. How should the following assets, which are transferred from the partnership to the corporation at their book values, be recorded on the books of the corporation: (a) accounts receivable of $35,000 with an allowance for doubtful accounts of $2,500; (b) office equipment with a cost of $10,000 and accumulated depreciation of $6,000?

EXERCISES

1. John White is considering purchasing some common stock in Standard Metals, Inc., which is presently quoted at 71½ on the stock exchange. He obtains the following information from the latest published balance sheet: current assets, $300,000; plant assets, $550,000; current liabilities, $100,000; preferred 5% stock, noncumulative, nonparticipating, $100 par, $100,000; common stock, 10,000 shares outstanding, $500,000; retained earnings, $150,000. Determine the following: (a) Par per share of common stock. (b) Book value per share for preferred stock. (c) Book value per share for common stock. (d) Latest market price per share for common stock. (e) Total paid-in capital. (f) Total capital.

2. The capital accounts of the Lawson Corporation are as follows: Preferred 5% Stock ($100 par), $1,000,000; Common Stock ($50 par), $10,000,000; Retained Earnings, $1,000,000. (a) What is the book value per share of each class of stock, assuming that the preferred stock is cumulative and nonparticipating and that one year's dividends are in arrears? (b) Prepare the stockholders' equity section of the balance sheet.

3. Halas Electronics, Inc. has stock outstanding as follows: 10,000 shares of 6%, $100 par, noncumulative, nonparticipating preferred and 20,000 shares of no-par common. The directors' policy is to declare a full or partial dividend on the preferred stock to the extent of current earnings and to distribute 75% of the remainder to common stockholders. Earnings for 1962, 1963, 1964, 1965, and 1966 were $100,000, $20,000, $50,000 loss, $120,000, and $188,000 respectively. Determine the dividends per share for each year on each class of stock.

4. The Michigan Shoe Co. has stock outstanding as follows: 2,000 shares of 5%, $100 par, cumulative, nonparticipating preferred and 10,000 shares of $25 par common. During its first five years of operation the following amounts were distributed as dividends: first year, none; second year, $5,000; third year, $15,000; fourth year, $40,000; fifth year, $60,000. Determine the dividends per share on each class of stock for each of the five years.

5. The outstanding stock of the Dunn Telephone Company is composed of 10,000 shares of participating preferred 6% stock with a par of $50 and 20,000 shares of no-par common stock. The preferred stock is entitled to participate ratably with the common in dividend distributions after allowing a dividend of $3.50 per share on the common. The directors declare dividends of $145,000 for the current year. What is the dividend per share on (a) the preferred stock and (b) the common stock?

6. Tile Specialist, Inc. was organized on June 1 with an authorization of 1,000 shares of cumulative preferred 6% stock, $25 par, and 10,000 shares of $10 par common stock.

(a) Record in general journal form the following selected transactions completed during June:

(1) Issued 500 shares of preferred stock and 5,000 shares of common stock at par for cash.
(2) Issued 100 shares of common stock to an attorney in payment for his legal fees for organizing the corporation.
(3) Paid $250 for state incorporation fees.
(4) Issued 3,000 shares of common stock in exchange for land, buildings, and equipment with fair market prices of $3,000, $20,000, and $7,000 respectively.

(b) Prepare the stockholders' equity section of the balance sheet as of June 30. The net loss for June amounted to $2,100.

PROBLEMS

16-1. The net income or loss of Shelby Corporation for a period of eight years is shown in the table at the top of the following page. During the entire period the corporation had outstanding 1,000 shares of cumulative 5% preferred stock, par $100, and 15,000 shares of common stock, par $20. Each year the board of directors (1) applied earnings to offset any accumulated deficit, (2) declared a partial or full dividend on the preferred stock to the extent of the available current or accumulated earnings, and (3) distributed 70% of any remaining balance of current earnings as a dividend on the common stock.

Year	Net Income or Loss*	Preferred Dividend Declared	Preferred Dividend Total Arrears	Common Dividend Declared	Increase or Decrease* in Retained Earnings	Retained Earnings (Deficit*) Balance
Balance			$5,000			$1,500*
1960	$ 1,000*					
1961	3,500					
1962	15,000					
1963	28,000					
1964	17,000					
1965	1,000*					
1966	19,000					
1967	35,000					

Instructions: (1) Indicate the disposition of the net income or loss for each year by completing the schedule presented above. Use an asterisk to denote deductions and negative items.

(2) Determine the total dividends per share declared on each class of stock.

16-2. The annual dividends declared by Parkhill Motors, Inc. during a six-year period are shown in the table below. During the entire period the outstanding stock of the corporation was composed of 2,000 shares of cumulative, participating, 6% preferred stock, $50 par, and 12,000 shares of common stock, $25 par. The preferred stock contract provides that the preferred stock participates in distributions of additional earnings after allowance of a $2 dividend per share on the common stock, the additional earnings to be divided among common and preferred shares on the basis of the total amount of par stock outstanding.

Year	Total Dividends	Preferred Dividends Total	Preferred Dividends Per Share	Common Dividends Total	Common Dividends Per Share
1962	$12,000				
1963	4,000				
1964	20,000				
1965	38,800				
1966	5,000				
1967	39,000				

Instructions: (1) Determine the total dividends and the per share dividends declared on each class of stock for each of the six years, using the headings shown above. There were no dividends in arrears on January 1, 1962.

(2) Determine the average annual dividend per share for each class of stock for the six-year period.

(3) Assuming that both classes of stock were sold at par at the beginning of the six-year period, determine the percentage return on investment based on the average annual dividend per share (a) for preferred stock and (b) for common stock.

16-3. Selected data from the balance sheets of six corporations, identified by letter, are presented below:

A. Common stock, $50 . . . . $1,500,000
Deficit 90,000

B. Total assets, $1,740,200; total liabilities, $490,400; common stock outstanding, 20,000 shares.

C. Preferred 5% stock, noncumulative, nonparticipating, $100 par $ 500,000
Common stock, $10 par 760,000
Retained earnings 342,760

D. Preferred 6% stock, noncumulative, nonparticipating, $50 par. $ 300,000
Common stock, $50 par 1,100,000
Deficit 195,800
Preferred stock has prior claim to assets upon dissolution.

E. Preferred 6% stock, cumulative, nonparticipating, $100 par . . $ 200,000
Common stock, $25 par 750,000
Retained earnings 30,000
Dividends on preferred stock are in arrears for 3 years. Preferred stock is entitled to unpaid cumulative dividends upon dissolution to the extent of retained earnings.

F. Preferred 5% stock, cumulative, nonparticipating, $50 par . . . $ 500,000
Common stock, $5 par 1,250,000
Retained earnings 42,500
Dividends on preferred stock are in arrears for 4 years. Preferred stock is entitled to unpaid cumulative dividends upon dissolution, regardless of the availability of retained earnings.

Instructions: Determine for each corporation the book value per share of each class of stock, presenting the total capital allocated to the class and the number of shares outstanding.

16-4. The Terminal Transfer and Storage Company was organized by Miller, Reed, and Yates. The charter authorizes 10,000 shares of common stock with a par of $25. The following transactions were completed during October of the current year, the first month of operations:

(a) Sold 1,000 shares of stock at par to Miller for cash.

(b) Purchased land and a building from Yates. The building has a 6%, 18-year mortgage of $15,000 and there is accrued interest of $425 on the mortgage at the time of the purchase. It is agreed that the land is to be priced at $6,000 and the building at $34,000, and that Yates is to accept stock at par for his equity. The corporation agreed to assume responsibility for paying the mortgage and the accrued interest.

(c) Paid Yates $200 cash to reimburse him for the incorporation fees that he had remitted with the charter application.

(d) Purchased equipment from Reed for $27,500. Reed accepted a 6-month non-interest-bearing note for $7,500 and 800 shares of stock for the equipment.

(e) Issued to Reed 100 shares of stock for promotional services connected with organizing the corporation.

(f) Paid an attorney $500 for legal fees connected with organizing the corporation.

(g) Purchased additional land for $3,000 cash.

(h) Paid contractor $5,000 cash for construction of an addition to the building.

(i) Paid advertising expenses of $750.

(j) Paid semiannual interest on the mortgage note.

(k) Received $2,400 for services rendered.

(l) Paid various expenses of $1,250.

(m) Recorded depreciation charges of $50 and $150 on buildings and equipment respectively.

Instructions: (1) Record the corporation's transactions in general journal form.

(2) Assuming that there were no additional transactions and no accruals, prepare a balance sheet for the corporation as of October 31. Omit subcaptions for current assets, current liabilities, etc.

16-5. Dawson & Eisner, partners, and Wilson, a sole proprietor, decided to combine their businesses as a corporation under the name of the Lincoln Office Supply Co. They submitted their application and received a charter with an authorization of 2,000 shares of cumulative 6% preferred stock with a par of $100 and 10,000 shares of common stock with a par of $50.

The post-closing trial balances of the two enterprises as of June 30, the effective date of the transfer to the corporation, are as follows:

	Dawson & Eisner		Wilson	
Cash	37,500		16,700	
Notes Receivable	—		5,000	
Accounts Receivable	60,200		20,300	
Allowance for Doubtful Accounts		2,500		1,100
Merchandise Inventory	155,700		65,000	
Prepaid Insurance	700		300	
Equipment	17,000		8,000	
Accumulated Depreciation — Equipment		6,000		2,700
Building	60,000		—	
Accumulated Depreciation — Building		38,000		—
Land	15,000		—	
Notes Payable		15,000		—
Accounts Payable		30,200		9,400
Mortgage Payable		25,000		—
Peter Dawson, Capital		122,000		—
Robert Eisner, Capital		107,400		
Morris Wilson, Capital		—		102,100
	346,100	346,100	115,300	115,300

The current fair market prices, the agreement as to assets and liabilities to be transferred to the corporation, etc. are as follows:

Dawson & Eisner: (a) Mortgage to be paid with partnership funds; (b) accounts receivable in the amount of $5,000 to be written off as uncollectible, remainder to be valued at $52,300; (c) merchandise inventory to be valued at current market price of $160,000; (d) building to be valued on basis of $100,000 replacement cost new, 60% depreciated; (e) all other assets and liabilities to be transferred at book value as of June 30; (f) 1,000 shares of preferred stock and common stock for the remainder of the net assets to be issued.

Wilson: (a) All notes receivable to be retained by Wilson; (b) accounts receivable to be valued at $18,300; (c) merchandise inventory to be valued at current market price of $64,000; (d) equipment to be valued at $5,800; (e) all other assets and liabilities to be transferred at book value as of June 30; (f) goodwill of $15,000 to be recognized; (g) 500 shares of preferred stock and common stock for the remainder of the net assets to be issued.

Instructions: (1) Prepare entries in general journal form for Dawson & Eisner to record:

(a) The payment of the mortgage.
(b) The revaluation of the assets (income and losses are shared equally.)
(c) The transfer of the assets and the liabilities to the corporation.
(d) The receipt of the stock.
(e) The distribution of the stock (preferred stock is divided equally).

(2) Prepare entries in general journal form for Wilson to record:

(a) The withdrawal of the notes receivable.
(b) The revaluation of the assets, including recognition of the goodwill.
(c) The transfer of the assets and the liabilities to the corporation.
(d) The receipt of the stock.
(e) The transfer of the stock to Wilson.

(3) Prepare entries in general journal form for Lincoln Office Supply Co. to record:

(a) The assets and the liabilities acquired from Dawson & Eisner.
(b) The assets and the liabilities acquired from Wilson.
(c) The issuance of the stock to Dawson & Eisner.
(d) The issuance of the stock to Wilson.

(4) Prepare a balance sheet for the corporation as of June 30.

17.

Corporations—capital stock

Premium and discount on capital stock

In the preceding chapter all issuances of capital stock were assumed to be at par. In practice, however, stock may be issued by a corporation at a price above or below par. When it is issued above par, the excess of the contract price over par is termed a *premium*. When it is issued at a price that is less than par, the excess of par over the contract price is called a *discount*. Thus, if stock with a par of $50 is issued at $60, the amount of the premium is $10; if the same stock is issued at $45, the amount of the discount is $5.

Theoretically, there is no reason for a newly organized corporation to issue stock at a price other than par. As has been demonstrated, the particular par assigned to the stock is arbitrary; it is merely a part of the plan of dividing capital into a number of units of ownership. Hence, a group of persons investing their funds in a new corporation might all be expected to pay par for the shares. The fortunes of an enterprise do not remain static, however, even when it is still in the process of organizing. The changing prospects for its future success may affect the price per share at which the incorporators can secure additional investors.

After a corporation has become established, a need for additional capital may arise. For example, losses during the early period may have depleted working capital, or the operations may have been successful enough to warrant a substantial expansion of plant and equipment. If the funds are to be obtained by the issuance of additional stock, it is apparent that the current price at which the original stock is selling in the market will affect the price that can be obtained for the new shares.

Generally speaking, the price at which stock can be sold by a corporation is influenced by: (1) the financial condition, the earnings record, and the dividend record of the corporation; (2) its potential earning power; (3) the availability of money for investment purposes; and (4) general business and economic conditions and prospects.

Some states do not permit the issuance of stock at a discount; in others, it may be done under specified conditions. When stock is issued at less than its par, it is considered to be fully paid as between the corporation and the stockholder. In some states, however, the stockholders are contingently liable to creditors for the amount of the discount; that is, if the corporation is liquidated and the assets are insufficient to pay creditors in full, the stockholders may be assessed for an additional contribution up to the amount of the discount on their stock.

When capital stock is issued at a premium, cash or other assets are debited for the amount received, the stock account is credited for par, and a premium account is credited for the premium. For example, if the Monroe Corporation issues 1,000 shares of $100 par preferred stock at $104, the entry to record the transaction would be as follows, in general journal form:

Cash	104,000	
Preferred Stock		100,000
Premium on Preferred Stock		4,000

The premium of $4,000 is a part of the investment of the stockholders and is therefore a part of paid-in capital. It is distinguished from the capital stock account because ordinarily it is not a part of legal capital. In many states the premium may be used as a basis for dividends to stockholders. If the premium is later returned to stockholders as a dividend, it should be made quite clear that the dividend is not a distribution of earnings but a return of paid-in capital.

When capital stock is issued at a discount, cash or other assets are debited for the amount received, a discount account is debited for the amount of the discount, and the capital stock account is credited for par. For example, if the Monroe Corporation issues 30,000 shares of $20 par common stock at $19, the entry to record the transaction would be as follows, in general journal form:

Cash	570,000	
Discount on Common Stock	30,000	
Common Stock		600,000

The discount of $30,000 is a contra paid-in capital account and must be offset against Common Stock to arrive at the amount actually invested by the holders of common stock. The discount should not be listed on the balance sheet as an asset, nor should it be amortized against revenue as though it were an expense.

The stockholders' equity section of the balance sheet of the Monroe Corporation, which appears below, illustrates the manner in which discount and premium may be presented on the balance sheet.

Stockholders' equity			
Paid-in capital:			
Preferred 5% stock, cumulative, $100 par (1,000 shares authorized and issued)	$100,000		
Premium on preferred stock	4,000	$104,000	
Common stock, $20 par (50,000 shares authorized, 30,000 shares issued)	$600,000		
Less discount on common stock	30,000	570,000	
Total paid-in capital		$674,000	
Retained earnings		116,000	
Total stockholders' equity			$790,000

When assets other than cash are accepted as payment for capital stock, the assets should be recorded at their fair market price rather than at the total par of the stock issued. For example, assume that 10,000 shares of common stock with a par of $10 are issued in exchange for a building and land. It does not necessarily follow that the property has a value of $100,000 (10,000 × $10 par). If the fair market price of the property is actually $90,000, the stock is being issued at a discount of $10,000 and the transaction should be so recorded. The responsibility for valuation of the assets in such cases rests with the board of directors, and it is not always possible to make an objective determination. If shares of stock are also being issued for cash at about the same time, the price of the stock may provide a good basis for valuation of the property. Assuming in the example above that the stock is currently being issued for cash at $9 a share, a valuation of $90,000 for the property (10,000 × $9 per share) would be indicated.

No-par stock

The issuance of stock without par was first permitted by New York in 1912. At the present time the statutes of almost all of the states authorize the issuance of such stock. The proponents of the idea of no-par stock expected its use to be beneficial in three major respects: (1) the "bargain sale" technique of selling stock below par would not be available and investors would make a more careful investigation before buying stock; (2) stock could be issued at various prices without the difficulty of incurring a contingent liability for discounts; and (3) the use of fair valuations on assets accepted in payment for stock would be encouraged.

The extent to which the expected benefits have materialized is difficult to determine. Over the years questionable practices in the issuance of securities have been eliminated to a considerable degree. Today the rules imposed by organized stock exchanges, federal and state laws, and governmental agencies combine to protect the investor from misrepresentations that in earlier days were not uncommon.

Corporations may issue both preferred and common stock without par. Preferred stock is ordinarily assigned a par, however. When no-par stock is issued, the entire proceeds may be credited to the capital stock account. For example, if the Wheeler Corporation issues 1,000 shares of no-par common stock on February 1 at $19 per share and an additional 1,000 shares on February 20 at $18 per share, the entries would be as follows, in general journal form:

Feb. 1	Cash	19,000	
	Common Stock		19,000
20	Cash	18,000	
	Common Stock		18,000

The laws of some states require that the entire proceeds from the issuance of no-par stock be regarded as legal capital. The entries above are in conformity with this principle, which also conforms to the original concept of no-par stock. In other states no-par stock may be assigned a *stated value* per share and the excess of the proceeds over the stated value may be credited to Paid-in Capital in Excess of Stated Value. Assuming that in the example above the stated value is $5 and the board of directors wishes to credit the common stock for stated value, the transactions would be recorded as follows, in general journal form:

Feb. 1	Cash	19,000	
	Common Stock		5,000
	Paid-in Capital in Excess of Stated Value		14,000
20	Cash	18,000	
	Common Stock		5,000
	Paid-in Capital in Excess of Stated Value		13,000

It is readily apparent that the accounting for no-par stock with a stated value may follow the same pattern as the accounting for par stock.

Subscriptions to capital stock

In the examples thus far it has been assumed that the corporation issued stock directly in exchange for cash or other assets. Ordinarily, investors first enter into an agreement to purchase, that is, they *subscribe* to shares at a specified price per share. The terms may provide for payment in full at some future date or for installment payments over a period of time.

The amount of the subscriptions represents an asset to the corporation. As the subscriptions are received, they are debited to the asset account Stock Subscriptions Receivable and are credited to the capital stock account Stock Subscribed.

Legally, persons subscribing for stock become stockholders at once, but ordinarily they do not acquire all the rights of stockholders until they have made complete payment. The written evidence of the ownership of shares, known as a *stock certificate*, is usually not issued until the entire amount of the subscription has been collected; otherwise the corporation would run the risk of subscribers selling the stock to other persons before the subscribers had completed their payments. Withholding the stock certificates thus operates as security for the amount owed by the subscribers.

If there is more than one class of stock, a subscriptions receivable account and a stock subscribed account should be maintained for each class.

When stock is subscribed for at a price above or below par, the stock subscriptions receivable account is debited for the subscription price rather than par. The stock subscribed account is credited at par, and the difference between the subscription price and par is debited to a discount account or credited to a premium account, as the case may be.

The stock subscriptions receivable account is a controlling account. The individual accounts with each subscriber are maintained in a subsidiary ledger known as a *subscribers ledger*, which is described in more detail later in this chapter. It is used in much the same manner as the accounts receivable ledger.

Issuance of stock certificates

After a subscriber completes his agreed payments, his stock subscriptions receivable account will be in balance. It is at this time that the corporation issues the stock certificate. The stock subscribed account is then debited for the total par of the shares issued, and the capital stock account is credited for the same amount.

The capital stock accounts (Preferred Stock, Common Stock) are controlling accounts. It is necessary to maintain records of the name and the address of each stockholder and the number of shares held in order to issue dividend checks, proxy forms, and financial reports. The accounts with individual stockholders are kept in a subsidiary ledger known as the *stockholders ledger*. It is described later in this chapter.

Subscriptions and stock issuance illustrated

As the basis for illustrating the entries for transactions discussed in the two preceding sections, it will be assumed that the newly organized

Marathon Corporation receives subscriptions, collects cash, and issues stock certificates in accordance with the transactions described below. The required entries, in general journal form, appear after the statement of the transaction.

(1) Received subscriptions to 5,000 shares of $20 par common stock from various subscribers at $21 per share, with a down payment of 50% of the subscription price.

Date	Account	Debit	Credit
April 1	Common Stock Subscriptions Receivable	105,000	
	Common Stock Subscribed		100,000
	Premium on Common Stock		5,000
1	Cash	52,500	
	Common Stock Subscriptions Receivable		52,500

(2) Received 25% of subscription price from all subscribers.

Date	Account	Debit	Credit
May 1	Cash	26,250	
	Common Stock Subscriptions Receivable		26,250

(3) Received final 25% of subscription price from all subscribers and issued the stock certificates.

Date	Account	Debit	Credit
June 1	Cash	26,250	
	Common Stock Subscriptions Receivable		26,250
1	Common Stock Subscribed	100,000	
	Common Stock		100,000

The effect of the foregoing transactions may also be observed in the following T accounts:

Cash

Debit		Credit	
(1)	52,500	Bal.	105,000
(2)	26,250		
(3)	26,250		
	105,000		105,000
Bal.	105,000		

Common Stock Subscriptions Receivable

Debit		Credit	
(1)	105,000	(1)	52,500
		(2)	26,250
		(3)	26,250
	105,000		105,000

Common Stock

Debit		Credit	
		(3)	100,000

Common Stock Subscribed

Debit		Credit	
(3)	100,000	(1)	100,000

Premium on Common Stock

Debit		Credit	
		(1)	5,000

After all collections are made, the subscriptions receivable account is in balance; and after the certificates are issued, the stock subscribed account is in balance. Neither account would be used again unless additional subscriptions were received. It should be noted that the ultimate effect of the series of transactions is a debit to Cash of $105,000 and credits to Common Stock of $100,000 and to Premium on Common Stock of $5,000.

A balance sheet prepared after the transactions of April 1 would show the subscriptions receivable as a current asset and the stock subscribed and the premium as paid-in capital. While it is true that the entire amount has not been "paid-in" in cash, the claim against the subscribers is an asset of equivalent value. The presentation of the items in the balance sheet of the Marathon Corporation as of April 1 is illustrated below.

Marathon Corporation
Balance Sheet
April 1, 19--

Assets		Stockholders' equity	
Current assets:		Paid-in capital:	
Cash....................	$ 52,500	Common stock subscribed..	$100,000
Common stock subscriptions receivable.............	52,500	Premium on common stock.	5,000
Total assets................	$105,000	Total stockholders' equity....	$105,000

Treasury stock

A corporation may reacquire some of its own outstanding stock by purchase or by donation from its stockholders. It may also accept shares of its own stock in payment of a debt owed by a stockholder, which in essence is much the same as acquisition by purchase. The term *treasury stock* may be applied only to: (1) stock of the issuing corporation, (2) that has been issued as fully paid, (3) that has been subsequently reacquired by the corporation, and (4) that has not been canceled or reissued.

Treasury stock is not an asset. A corporation cannot own a part of itself. Treasury stock has no voting rights, nor does it have the preemptive right to participate in additional issuances of stock. When a corporation purchases its own stock, it is returning capital to the stockholders from whom the purchase was made. If stockholders donate stock to the corporation, the total capital of the corporation is not affected; only the number of shares outstanding is reduced.

Corporations sometimes incorrectly list treasury stock on the balance sheet as a current asset if they expect to sell it in the near future. The justification advanced for such treatment is that the stock is a readily available source of cash and is no different from a temporary investment in stock of another corporation. The same argument might well be extended to authorized but unissued stock, which is obviously indefensible. It is generally agreed among accountants that treasury stock should not be reported as an asset.

Purchased treasury stock

Although there are some legal restrictions on the practice, corporations may in general purchase shares of their own stock from stockholders. There are various reasons why a corporation may buy its own stock. For example, it may be to provide shares for resale to employees, for reissuance to employees as a bonus, or to support the market price of the stock. There are several methods of accounting for the purchase and the resale of treasury stock. A commonly used method, known as the *cost basis*, is illustrated in the following paragraphs.

When the stock is purchased, the account Treasury Stock is debited for its cost. The par and the price at which the stock was originally issued are ignored. When the stock is resold, Treasury Stock is credited at the price paid for it, and the difference between the price paid and the selling price is debited or credited to an account entitled Paid-in Capital from Sale of Treasury Stock.

As a basis for illustration, assume that the paid-in capital of the Linden Corporation is composed of:

Common Stock, $50 par (10,000 shares authorized and issued)	$500,000
Premium on Common Stock	50,000

The assumed transactions involving treasury stock and the required entries in general journal form are as follows:

(1) Purchased 800 shares of treasury stock at $65; total $52,000.

Treasury Stock	52,000	
Cash		52,000

(2) Sold 200 shares of treasury stock at $75; total $15,000.

Cash	15,000	
Treasury Stock		13,000
Paid-in Capital from Sale of Treasury Stock		2,000

(3) Sold 200 shares of treasury stock at $63; total $12,600.

Cash	12,600	
Paid-in Capital from Sale of Treasury Stock	400	
Treasury Stock		13,000

The additional capital obtained through the sale of treasury stock is reported in the paid-in capital section of the balance sheet, and the cost of the treasury stock on hand is deducted from the total of the capital accounts. After the three foregoing transactions were completed, the stockholders' equity section of the balance sheet would appear as shown at the top of the following page.

Stockholders' equity

Paid-in capital:			
Common stock, $50 par (10,000 shares authorized and issued)	$500,000		
Premium on common stock	50,000	$550,000	
From sale of treasury stock		1,600	
Total paid-in capital		$551,600	
Retained earnings		100,000	
Total		$651,600	
Deduct treasury stock (400 shares at cost)		26,000	
Total stockholders' equity			$625,600

The stockholders' equity section of the balance sheet indicates that 10,000 shares of stock were issued, of which 400 are held as treasury stock. The number of shares outstanding is therefore 9,600. If dividends were declared at this time, the declaration would apply to 9,600 shares. Similarly, 9,600 shares could be voted at a stockholders' meeting. The computation of book value per share would also be based on the 9,600 shares outstanding.

If treasury stock transactions result in a shrinkage of capital, the net decrease may be reported as a reduction in paid-in capital, or it may be charged to Retained Earnings.

Donated treasury stock

Stockholders occasionally donate shares of stock to the corporation for resale. This generally happens when a corporation that has issued large blocks of stock in exchange for plant and equipment, an invention, mineral rights, or other noncash assets is in need of working capital and encounters difficulty in finding subscribers willing to invest cash equal to the par of the stock. As a means of avoiding the difficulty of selling new stock at a discount, the original stockholders may donate a portion of their stock to the corporation and the corporation may then resell it at any price without the purchaser incurring a contingent liability to creditors. The donating stockholders may actually incur little financial sacrifice by their action.

One of the acceptable methods of accounting for donated stock requires no entry at the time of the donation, except for a memorandum of the number of shares. As the treasury stock is sold, the proceeds are credited to a paid-in capital account entitled Donated Capital.

As a basis for illustration, assume that the Bronson Corporation originally issued 100,000 shares of $10 par common stock at par for oil properties. The stockholders then donate 20,000 shares to the corporation, which the corporation resells for cash. The entries required, in general journal form, and the paid-in capital section of the balance sheet after each entry are as follows:

(1) Issued 100,000 shares of $10 par common stock for oil properties.

Oil Properties	1,000,000	
Common Stock		1,000,000

Paid-in capital:		
Common stock, $10 par (200,000 shares authorized, 100,000 shares issued)		$1,000,000

(2) Received 20,000 shares of stock from stockholders.

(Memo) Received 20,000 shares of stock as a donation.

Paid-in capital:		
Common stock, $10 par (200,000 shares authorized, 100,000 shares issued less 20,000 shares of treasury stock acquired by donation)		$1,000,000

(3) Sold treasury stock at $6 per share for cash.

Cash	120,000	
Donated Capital		120,000

Paid-in capital:		
Common stock, $10 par (200,000 shares authorized, 100,000 shares issued)	$1,000,000	
Donated capital	120,000	
Total paid-in capital		$1,120,000

Redemption of preferred stock

Corporations issuing preferred stock frequently retain the right to redeem the stock. The amount to be paid per share in the event of redemption may be par or a price above par. When stock is redeemed, there is a return of capital to the stockholders, and the accounts related to the stock redeemed must be eliminated from the ledger. If the amount paid to the stockholders is greater than the amount originally received for the shares being redeemed, the excess is considered to be a distribution of earnings and is debited to Retained Earnings. On the other hand, if the amount paid is less than the amount originally received, the difference is a retention of capital and is credited to a paid-in capital account.

To illustrate the entries required upon redemption of stock, assume that the Ferris Corporation issued 1,000 shares of $100 par redeemable preferred stock at $103 per share. The entry to record the sale, in general journal form, is:

Cash	103,000	
Preferred Stock		100,000
Premium on Preferred Stock		3,000

After a number of years of operations, during which the corporation accumulated a substantial amount of income, it is decided to redeem the stock. Assuming a redemption price of $105 per share, the entry would be as follows, in general journal form:

Preferred Stock	100,000	
Premium on Preferred Stock	3,000	
Retained Earnings	2,000	
Cash		105,000

The additional $2,000 over the issuance price paid at redemption is not an expense or a loss. Rather, it is in the nature of a distribution of earnings to the preferred stockholders and is properly chargeable to Retained Earnings.

If a redemption price of $102 per share is assumed, the proper entry would be as follows, in general journal form:

Preferred Stock	100,000	
Premium on Preferred Stock	3,000	
Paid-in Capital from Preferred Stock Redemption		1,000
Cash		102,000

The $1,000 of the original issuance price not returned to the stockholders is not income; it remains a part of paid-in capital and is credited to an appropriate capital account.

Preferred stock that does not have a redemption provision may be purchased on the open market by the issuing corporation and then retired. Stock that has been retired may ordinarily not be reissued. The redemption or the retirement of stock reduces the legal capital of the corporation and hence could have an adverse effect on the creditors and on the remaining stockholders. For this reason, the states have laws and regulations that prescribe the procedures for reducing legal capital.

Special records required by a corporation

For the most part, the accounts in the ledger of a corporation are comparable with those of any other type of business organization. As has been indicated in this and the preceding chapter, the *capital* accounts are different. Several other accounts that are required to record transactions peculiar to corporations will be introduced in later chapters.

The transactions involving purchases, sales, cash receipts, cash payments, and other routine operations are the same for a corporation as for other types of business organizations. The journals illustrated in earlier chapters are equally appropriate for use by a corporation. In designing special journals, the different types of transactions and their frequency must be considered rather than the type of legal organization.

The only distinctive records required by a corporation are those used to record the activities peculiar to the corporate form. The records in most common use are described in the paragraphs that follow.

Minute book. The secretary of the corporation records the proceedings of all meetings of the stockholders and the board of directors in the *minute book*. A copy of the charter and bylaws, with amendments thereto, are often inserted in the minute book so as to bring together in one place a complete and permanent legal record. The decisions and the authorizations recorded in the minute book cover a wide range of subjects, such as results of elections of the board of directors, appointments of officers and their salaries, declarations of dividends, and borrowing of funds. The principal accounting officer and other officers refer to the minute book for authorizations and instructions.

Subscription book. The agreement between the corporation and a purchaser of the corporation's stock is recorded in a subscription contract. The contract specifies the class and number of shares, the price, and details as to payment. Each contract is signed by both parties. These contracts are assembled to form the *subscription book*. They are summarized periodically to provide the basis for the entry debiting the stock subscriptions receivable account, crediting the stock subscribed account, and debiting the discount account or crediting the premium account. Each contract also serves as the basis for posting a debit to the appropriate subscriber's account in the subscribers ledger.

Subscribers ledger. An account in the *subscribers ledger* is opened for each person who agrees to purchase stock. The subscribers ledger is a subsidiary ledger controlled by the stock subscriptions receivable account in the general ledger. As indicated above, the debits to the subsidiary accounts are posted from the contracts in the subscription book. Cash received from subscribers is recorded in the cash receipts journal, to which there may be added a special column for credits to stock subscriptions receivable. The individual items in this column are posted periodically to the accounts in the subscribers ledger, and the total is posted monthly to the controlling account. There is a separate controlling account and subsidiary ledger for each class of stock.

Stock certificate book. The evidence of ownership issued to a stockholder is called a stock certificate. On it are recorded the name of the corporation, the name and the address of the stockholder, the class and the special terms of the stock, the number of shares represented by the certificate, the date of issue, and the certificate number. Blank certificates may be obtained in book form similar to checkbooks. At the time a cer-

Stock certificate

tificate is prepared, the essential details must also be recorded on the stub or on a blank carbon copy of the certificate. The stub or carbon copy is retained by the corporation as its basic record.

An endorsement form is provided on the back of the certificate, which is filled out and signed by the stockholder when he sells the stock. The purchaser or his broker then submits the certificate to the issuing corporation, which cancels the certificate and issues a new one to the new owner.

Stockholders ledger. An account for each stockholder is maintained in a subsidiary ledger called a *stockholders ledger*. There is a ledger for each class of stock, and each ledger is controlled by its related stock issued account in the general ledger. The stockholders ledger differs from other

STOCKHOLDER John L. Mason

ADDRESS 1432 Erie Ave., South Bend, Indiana 46602

DATE			TRANSFERRED FROM OR TO	CERTIFICATE NO.		RECORD OF SHARES		
MO.	DAY	YR.		SURREN'D	ISSUED	SURREN'D	ISSUED	BALANCE
May	4	65	Original issue		393		50	50
Aug.	16	65	R. B. Dalton		561		75	125
June	18	66	Henry E. Thomas	393		50		75

Account in stockholders ledger

ledgers that have been described in that all entries are in terms of number of shares instead of dollars. To illustrate, assume that the Bell Corporation has 10,000 shares of $20 par common stock issued and outstanding. The account Common Stock would have a credit balance of $200,000 and the sum of the balances in the stockholders ledger would be 10,000 shares.

Postings to the accounts in the stockholders ledger may be made directly from the stock certificate stub or the carbon copy of the certificate. It should be noted that transfers of shares from one stockholder to another do not affect the controlling account, as the number of shares outstanding remains unchanged.

QUESTIONS

1. Suggest factors influencing the market price of a corporation's stock.

2. When a corporation issues stock at a premium, does the premium constitute income? Explain.

3. A corporation issues common stock at a discount and also borrows money from a bank by discounting a non-interest-bearing note payable. (a) Differentiate between the two kinds of discount. (b) Classify each discount as an asset, liability, capital, revenue, or expense item.

4. A corporation's balance sheet lists: preferred 7% stock, $800,000; premium on preferred stock, $20,000; common stock, $500,000; discount on common stock, $40,000; and retained earnings, $120,000. (a) What is the amount invested by the stockholders? (b) What is the total stockholders' equity?

5. Property with a fair market value of $55,000 is acquired in return for 500 shares of $100 par 6% preferred stock. At what figure should the property be recorded?

6. (a) Define treasury stock. (b) In what way is treasury stock different from unissued stock? (c) Suggest reasons why a corporation might purchase treasury stock.

7. A corporation purchases 200 shares of its own $100 par common stock for $22,500, recording it at cost. (a) What effect does this transaction have on revenue or expense of the period? (b) What effect does it have on stockholders' equity?

8. The treasury stock in Question 7 is resold for $25,000. (a) What is the effect on revenue of the period? (b) What is the effect on stockholders' equity?

9. Cooley Company issued 40,000 shares of $50 par common stock and subsequently reacquired 1,000 shares. If the board of directors declares a dividend of $3 per share, how much will be paid out as dividends?

10. Stockholders of Howard Corporation donated 2,000 shares of $50 par common stock to the corporation. The corporation resold these shares for cash at $40 per share. What entry is made for (a) the receipt of the stock and (b) the sale of the stock?

11. Preferred stock is redeemed at a price in excess of its issue price. (a) To what account is the excess of the redemption price over the issue price debited? (b) Explain the reason for debiting this account.

12. The liability section and the stockholders' equity section of the balance sheet of the Conrad Corporation list: liabilities, $250,000; 50,000 shares of $20 par common stock outstanding, $1,000,000; and retained earnings, $200,000. The corporation proposes to purchase 10,000 shares from the largest stockholder at $35 a share and to retire the stock. Creditors and other stockholders object to the proposal. Give possible reasons for their objections.

13. Discuss the nature and the purpose of the following special records required by a corporation: (a) subscription book, (b) subscribers ledger, (c) stock certificate book, and (d) stockholders ledger.

14. Carl Watkins, a stockholder of Thompson Company, sells 50 shares of $10 par common stock to James Glasa for $625. What entry does Thompson Company make to record this transfer of stock?

15. (a) What is the normal balance of each of the accounts listed below? (b) Classify each account as asset, liability, capital, revenue, or expense.

(1) Common Stock Subscriptions Receivable
(2) Common Stock Subscribed
(3) Premium on Common Stock
(4) Common Stock
(5) Organization Costs
(6) Preferred Stock
(7) Discount on Preferred Stock
(8) Paid-in Capital from Preferred Stock Redemption
(9) Donated Capital
(10) Treasury Stock
(11) Retained Earnings
(12) Paid-in Capital from Sale of Treasury Stock

EXERCISES

1. On October 10, the Fletcher Corporation issued for cash 1,000 shares of $100 par preferred stock at $105, and on October 30 it issued for cash 5,000 shares of no-par common stock with a stated value of $10 at $22. (a) Give the entries, in general journal form, for October 10 and October 30. (b) What is the amount invested by the stockholders as of October 31?

2. On August 1, the Pearson Co. received subscriptions to 2,000 shares of $50 preferred stock at $55 along with one half of the subscription price. On October 1 the remainder due from all subscribers was received and the stock was issued. (a) Give the entries, in general journal form, for August 1. (b) Give the entries, in general journal form, for October 1. (c) Name two controlling accounts used in the above transactions and the related subsidiary ledger.

3. The stockholders' equity section of the balance sheet on March 31 shows: common stock, $25 par (10,000 shares outstanding), $250,000; discount on common stock, $5,000; retained earnings, $90,000. On April 1, the corporation purchased 1,000 shares of its stock at $29. (a) Determine the book value per share of stock on March 31. (b) Give the entry, in general journal form, to record the purchase of the stock on April 1. (c) Determine the book value per share on April 1.

4. Amalgamated Metals, Inc. issued 100,000 shares of $10 par common stock at $11. It has a deficit of $200,000. All stockholders donate 20% of their stock to the company, and the stock is resold at $5. Determine the following:

(a) Total paid-in capital before the donation.
(b) Total stockholders' equity before the donation.
(c) Book value per share before the donation.
(d) Total book value of 100 shares held by a particular stockholder before the donation.
(e) Total paid-in capital after the donated stock is sold.
(f) Total stockholders' equity after the donated stock is sold.
(g) Book value per share after the donated stock is sold.
(h) Total book value of the 80 shares now held by the stockholder in (d).

5. Safeway Corporation redeems all 1,000 shares of its $100 par preferred stock that had originally been issued at $105. Give the entry, in general journal form, to record the redemption, assuming that the redemption price is (a) $106 and (b) $102.

6. The Crone Company, with an authorization to issue 5,000 shares of preferred stock and 30,000 shares of common stock, completed several transactions involving its capital stock on November 30, the first day of operations. The trial balance at the end of the day follows:

Cash	55,000	
Common Stock Subscriptions Receivable	110,000 NC	
Buildings	105,000	
Land	15,000	
Preferred 5% Stock, $25 par		100,000
Premium on Preferred Stock		20,000
Common Stock, $10 par		50,000
Premium on Common Stock		15,000
Common Stock Subscribed		100,000 NC
	285,000	285,000

Assuming that all shares within each class of stock were sold or subscribed at the same price, that the preferred stock was issued in exchange for the buildings and the land, and that no cash has been received on the common stock subscribed, prepare (a) the entries, in general journal form, to record the stock transactions and (b) the stockholders' equity section of the balance sheet on November 30.

PROBLEMS

17-1. The following accounts and their balances appear in the ledger of the Thoren Corporation on January 1 of the current year:

Common Stock Subscriptions Receivable	—
Preferred 8% Stock, par $50, noncumulative, nonparticipating (10,000 shares authorized and issued)	$ 500,000
Premium on Preferred Stock	20,000
Common Stock, no par (250,000 shares authorized, 160,000 shares issued)	1,760,000
Common Stock Subscribed	—
Retained Earnings	800,000

At a meeting of the board of directors early in the fiscal year, it was decided to issue additional common stock for the purpose of redeeming the preferred stock. To carry out this plan, the following transactions were completed during the year:

Mar. 1. Holders of the common stock were issued rights to subscribe to additional shares at $14 a share, at the rate of 1/4 share for each share held. (No entry.)

May 1. Subscriptions, together with a down payment of 50% of the subscription price, were received for 90% of the shares for which rights were available.

Aug. 1. Collected the remainder due from all subscribers to common stock and issued the stock certificates.

15. Issued 4,000 shares of common stock at $15, receiving cash.

30. In accordance with contract provisions of the preferred stock, the 10,000 shares were redeemed at $54 and retired.

Dec. 31. After closing all revenue and expense accounts for the year, Expense and Revenue Summary has a credit balance of $170,000. Close Expense and Revenue Summary.

Instructions: (1) Set up T accounts for the accounts listed and record the balances as of January 1.

(2) Record the foregoing transactions in general journal form and post to the selected accounts in the ledger.

(3) Prepare the stockholders' equity section of the balance sheet as of December 31.

(4) Determine the book value per share of common stock as of December 31.

17-2. The following accounts and their balances appear in the ledger of the Lambert Corporation on July 1 of the current year:

Preferred 6% Stock, par $100 (5,000 shares authorized, 4,000 shares issued)	$400,000
Premium on Preferred Stock	16,000
Common Stock, par $10 (100,000 shares authorized, 80,000 shares issued)	800,000
Premium on Common Stock	120,000
Retained Earnings (debit balance)	175,000

The company needs $400,000 to modernize its operations and only $150,000 can be borrowed. The stockholders therefore agree to purchase the unissued preferred stock at par and to donate one fourth of their common shares to the corporation for resale. The transactions relating to the plan are as follows:

July 10. Received 20,000 shares of common stock from stockholders.
15. Sold 1,000 shares of preferred stock for cash at par.
24. Sold all of the treasury stock for cash at $8.
31. Borrowed $150,000 from Lincoln Bank, giving a 7% mortgage note.

Instructions: Assuming for the purpose of the problem that no other transactions occurred during July:

(1) Prepare in general journal form the entries to record the foregoing transactions, recording receipt of the treasury stock by a memorandum entry.

(2) Prepare the stockholders' equity section of the balance sheet as of July 10.

(3) Prepare the stockholders' equity section of the balance sheet as of July 31.

17-3. The Bash Construction Co. was organized on February 1 of the current year with an authorization of 2,000 shares of $100 par 7% preferred stock and 25,000 shares of $20 par common stock. Transactions completed during February and March are summarized as follows:

Feb. 3. Received subscriptions to 10,000 shares of common stock at par.
3. Received cash for 50% of the subscription price from all common stock subscribers.
5. Received subscriptions for 500 shares of preferred stock at $102.
5. Received cash for 40% of the subscription price from all preferred stock subscribers.
8. Paid cash for organization costs of $1,500 and issued 200 shares of common stock to the promoters at par in payment for their services.
12. Issued 900 shares of preferred stock for equipment valued at $68,300, a building valued at $19,500, and land valued at $4,000.
19. Purchased construction materials for cash, $55,500.

Mar. 3. Received cash for 50% of the subscription price from February 3 subscribers to 5,000 shares of common stock and issued the certificates.
3. Received cash for 25% of the subscription price from February 3 subscribers to 5,000 shares of common stock.
5. Received balance due from preferred stock subscribers and issued the certificates.
16. Received subscriptions to 5,000 shares of common stock at $24.
16. Received cash for 50% of the subscription price from all March 16 subscribers to common stock.
23. Purchased additional equipment for cash, $20,000.
31. Received the balance due from the February 3 subscribers to 5,000 shares of common stock and issued the certificates.

Instructions: (1) Set up T accounts for the following accounts:

101 Cash
113 Preferred Stock Subscriptions Receivable
114 Common Stock Subscriptions Receivable
122 Construction Materials
133 Equipment
135 Buildings
137 Land
141 Organization Costs
301 Preferred Stock
302 Preferred Stock Subscribed
304 Premium on Preferred Stock
311 Common Stock
312 Common Stock Subscribed
314 Premium on Common Stock

(2) Record the transactions in general journal form and post to the general ledger accounts.

(3) Assuming that no other transactions occurred during the period, prepare a balance sheet as of March 31.

17-4. The capital and related accounts appearing in the ledger of Champion Electronics Manufacturing Corporation on July 1 of the current year are listed below.

Preferred 5% Stock Subscriptions Receivable	$ 505,000
Preferred 6% Stock, par $100 (20,000 shares authorized and issued)	2,000,000
Premium on Preferred 6% Stock	40,000
Preferred 5% Stock, par $100 (50,000 shares authorized and 20,000 shares issued)	2,000,000
Preferred 5% Stock Subscribed (10,000 shares)	1,000,000
Premium on Preferred 5% Stock	30,000
Common Stock, par $10 (1,000,000 shares authorized; 600,000 shares issued)	6,000,000
Premium on Common Stock	600,000
Retained Earnings	4,880,000

During the year the corporation completed a number of transactions affecting the capital structure. They are summarized below.

(a) Received balance due on preferred 5% stock subscribed and issued the certificates.
(b) Issued 100,000 shares of common stock at $11.50, receiving cash.
(c) Called the preferred 6% stock for redemption and retirement, paying the redemption price of $103.
(d) Purchased 20,000 shares of treasury common stock for $240,000.
(e) Received subscriptions to 10,000 shares of preferred 5% stock at $102, collecting 50% of the subscription price.
(f) Sold 10,000 shares of treasury common stock for $130,000.
(g) Received balance due from subscribers to preferred 5% stock and issued the certificates.
(h) Sold 6,000 shares of treasury common stock for $75,000.

Instructions: (1) Prepare entries in general journal form to record the transactions listed above. (Use of T accounts for the capital and related accounts is suggested for accumulating balances needed to record particular transactions and for use in remainder of problem.)

(2) Prepare the stockholders' equity section of the balance sheet as of June 30. Net income for the year amounted to $972,500. Dividends charged to Retained Earnings during the year totaled $570,000.

17-5. The Lawrence Company was organized on April 27 of the current year and prepared its first financial statements as of October 31, the date that had been adopted as the end of the fiscal year. The balance sheet prepared by the bookkeeper as of October 31 is presented at the top of the following page. You are retained by the board of directors to audit the accounts and to prepare a revised balance sheet.

Lawrence Company
Balance Sheet
April 27 to October 31, 19--

Assets		Liabilities	
Cash	$ 40,150	Accounts payable	$ 52,400
Accounts receivable	57,500	Preferred stock	50,000
Merchandise inventory	98,600	Common stock	200,000
Treasury preferred stock	25,000		
Equipment	60,000		
Discount on common stock	15,000		
Retained earnings (deficit)	6,150		
	$302,400		$302,400

The relevant facts developed during the course of your engagement are:

(a) Stock authorized: 5,000 shares of $25 par 7% preferred and 50,000 shares of $5 par common.

(b) Stock issued: 2,000 shares of fully paid preferred at $26 and 30,000 shares of fully paid common at $4.50. The premium on preferred stock was credited to Retained Earnings.

(c) Stock subscribed but not issued: 10,000 shares of common at par, on which all subscribers have paid three fourths of the subscription price. Unpaid subscriptions are included in accounts receivable.

(d) Land costing $10,000, which is to be used as a future building site, was charged to Equipment.

(e) The company reacquired 1,000 shares of the issued preferred stock at $28. The difference between par and the price paid was debited to Retained Earnings. (It is decided that the treasury stock is to be recorded at cost.)

(f) No depreciation has been recognized. The equipment is to be depreciated for one-half year by the declining-balance method, using double the straight-line rate. Estimated life is 10 years.

(g) Organization costs of $1,200 were charged to Advertising Expense. (None of the organization costs is to be amortized.)

(h) All insurance premiums have been charged to expense. The amount prepaid at October 31 is $325.

(i) Included in merchandise inventory is $450 of office supplies.

(j) No dividends have been declared or paid.

(k) In balancing the common stockholders ledger with the common stock control account, it was discovered that the account with John Owens contained a posting for an issuance of 50 shares while the carbon copy of the stock certificate indicated that 500 shares had been issued. The stock certificate was found to be correct.

Instructions: (1) Open T accounts for each item in the balance sheet and record the balances as of October 31.

(2) Prepare general journal entries where necessary to record the corrections. Corrections of net income may be entered in the retained earnings account.

(3) Post to the T accounts, setting up additional accounts as required.

(4) Prepare a balance sheet in report form as of the close of the fiscal period.

18.

Corporations—capital, earnings, and dividends

Classification of corporate capital

The importance of classifying the various elements of corporate capital according to source has been emphasized in preceding chapters. There are two principal subdivisions of capital, namely paid-in capital and retained earnings. The stockholders' equity or capital section of corporate balance sheets of earlier days was frequently not very informative. The preferred and common stock accounts were reported at par, which was clear enough, but the remaining capital was often described merely as "Surplus." In such cases it was not possible for the reader to determine the sources of capital and, in the absence of such information, to form an intelligent opinion about this section of the balance sheet. For example, a "surplus" of $1,000,000 could represent retained earnings of $1,000,000, or it could be the excess of stock premiums (paid-in capital) of $1,200,000 over an accumulated deficit (losses) of $200,000.

The term "capital surplus" has also been employed in the past to describe paid-in capital in excess of par or stated value of the capital stock. The term "surplus," either alone or with such words as "capital," "paid-in," or "earned," as a descriptive caption in financial statements is no longer widely used. It is still encountered, however, particularly in accounting literature and should be understood by students of business.

Paid-in capital

The principal credits to paid-in capital accounts result from the issuance of stock. If par stock is issued at a price above or below par, the difference is recorded in a separate premium or discount account. It is also not uncommon to employ two accounts in recording the issuance of no-par stock, one for the stated value and the other for the excess over stated value. Other accounts for paid-in capital discussed in the preceding chapter were Paid-in Capital from Sale of Treasury Stock and Donated Capital.

There are numerous variations in the arrangement of the paid-in capital section of the balance sheet and also in the terminology employed. A corporation with a large amount of premium on issuance of stock and minor amounts of paid-in capital from miscellaneous sources may combine a number of accounts and report them as a single item in the balance sheet. Some of the variations in arrangement and terminology are illustrated by the three examples that follow.

Capital

Paid-in capital:			
Common stock, $20 par (50,000 shares authorized, 40,000 shares issued)	$800,000		
Premium on common stock	128,000	$928,000	
From stock redemption		30,000	
From sale of treasury stock		10,000	
Total paid-in capital			$968,000

Shareholders' equity

Paid-in capital:			
Common stock, $20 par (50,000 shares authorized, 40,000 shares issued)		$800,000	
Excess of issuance price of stock over par	$128,000		
From retirement of preferred stock	30,000		
From transactions in own stock	10,000	168,000	
Total paid-in capital			$968,000

Stockholders' investment

Contributed capital:		
Common stock, $20 par (50,000 shares authorized, 40,000 shares issued)	$800,000	
Additional paid-in capital	168,000	
Total contributed capital		$968,000

A possible source of paid-in capital is property acquired by gift. A corporation may be given land or land and buildings by a civic organization as an inducement to locate in a particular community. The property so acquired should be recorded in the accounts at its estimated market price, there being no initial cost to the corporation. The entry is completed by a credit to an appropriate account, such as Paid-in Capital from Donation of Land and Buildings, or Donated Capital.

Paid-in capital in excess of par or stated value is ordinarily not a part of legal capital and may in many states be distributed to stockholders as dividends. The statutes of some states require that stockholders be informed of the source of such distributions. Regardless of legal requirements, a corporation using paid-in capital as a basis for dividends should make full disclosure to the stockholders.

Revaluation of assets

After a continuing period of increasing prices, the value of plant assets may be substantially higher than their original cost less accumulated depreciation. At times in the past, particularly during the period 1920–29, many corporations increased the valuation of plant assets to bring them up to their appraised values. Many of these write-ups were followed by write-downs in the following decade.

The offsetting credit resulting from an upward revision of asset values may be described on the balance sheet as "Appraisal capital," "Revaluation capital," "Capital from write-up of plant assets," or various other descriptive phrases. The recognition of appreciation in value in the accounts is now relatively rare. Accountants generally agree that for the financial statements to be of maximum usefulness to the greatest number of users, accounting for plant assets should be based on cost. Any attempts to report current values for plant assets should be restricted to supplementary financial schedules, explanations, or footnotes to the financial statements.[1]

Corporation earnings

The determination of net income or loss for a corporation is comparable, in most respects, to that of other forms of business organization. The particular revenue and expense accounts needed depend upon the nature and the volume of the business operations. Because of its separate legal existence, an individual may be both a stockholder and an employee of a corporation. Payments to such stockholder-employees for services rendered constitute expenses of the corporation. This is in contrast to sole proprietorships, in which all payments to owners are classified as withdrawals rather than expenses.

Corporation income taxes

Sole proprietorships are not entities subject to the federal income tax. The net income of such enterprises is reported by the proprietors in their individual tax returns. Corporations are distinct legal entities and, in general, are subject to the federal income tax. They may also be subject to an income tax levied by a state or a city.

---

[1] *Accounting Research and Terminology Bulletins, Final Edition*, "No. 43, Restatement and Revision of Accounting Research Bulletins," 1961 (New York: American Institute of Certified Public Accountants), pp. 67–69.

The due dates for federal income taxes vary according to the amount of a corporation's tax liability and its fiscal year. The first $100,000 of annual tax liability of all corporations is due in two equal installments within 2½ months and 5½ months, respectively, following the close of the year in which the income is earned. For example, a corporation with a tax liability of $90,000 on income for a fiscal year ended on December 31 must pay two installments of $45,000 each by March 15 and June 15 of the following year.

A pay-as-you-go system of payment for annual taxes in excess of $100,000 was adopted in 1954. Since then there has been a gradual acceleration of payment dates, which is to be completed in 1970. In that year and succeeding years the portion of tax liability estimated to exceed $100,000 is payable in four equal installments during the year in which the income is earned. For a calendar-year corporation the due dates are April 15, June 15, September 15, and December 15. The first $100,000 of income taxes, adjusted for any difference between the estimated tax paid and the actual tax liability, will continue to be due in the following year, as indicated in the preceding paragraph.

The amount of income tax liability determined by a corporation is subject to review and adjustment by the taxing authority. For this reason the liability for income taxes is sometimes described in the current liability section of the balance sheet as "Estimated income tax payable" or "Provision for income tax." The entry to record the charge against net income and the credit to the liability account may be made monthly if interim statements are prepared or if advance payments of the estimated tax are required. To illustrate the recording of income taxes, assume that a corporation's net income for the year ended December 31, before income tax, is $180,000, on which the federal income tax is $79,900. The entry is as follows:

Dec.	31	Income Tax	79,900	
		Income Tax Payable		79,900

The income tax account is closed to Expense and Revenue Summary and the liability account is reduced as payments are made. Because of its nature as a charge against *net income*, it is customary to report the tax in the income statement in the manner illustrated at the top of the following page.

Retained earnings

At the close of each fiscal period the balance in the expense and revenue summary account is closed to Retained Earnings. Net income increases the balance of the account; net losses and distributions of earnings to stockholders decrease the balance of the account. In the

Flagg Corporation
Income Statement
For Year Ended December 31, 19--

Sales	$920,600
~~	~~~
Net income before income tax	$180,000
Income tax	79,900
Net income after income tax	$100,100

absence of changes in the capital structure or adjustments of an unusual nature, the balance of the retained earnings account at any time represents the total earnings from the date of incorporation less the total losses and dividends.

Increases or decreases in capital resulting from issuance of stock at a price other than par or stated value are not income or loss and should not be carried to the retained earnings account. Similarly, transactions in treasury stock and donations of stock or property do not result in income or loss. The changes in capital effected by such occurrences should be reported as a part of paid-in capital.

A portion of retained earnings may be transferred to the capital stock account, thus becoming a part of permanent capital. This is done through the medium of stock dividends, which are discussed later in this chapter.

It is not unusual for corporations to accumulate a substantial amount of earnings in relation to paid-in capital. The board of directors may earmark or appropriate part of the accumulation for a particular purpose, such as expansion of the physical plant. The amount so appropriated is thereafter not available for dividends to stockholders until the directors rescind their action. An appropriation is accomplished by transferring the desired amount from Retained Earnings to a special account designating its purpose, such as Retained Earnings Appropriated for Plant Expansion.

The amount transferred to the special account, which is called an *appropriation* or a *reserve*, remains a part of retained earnings and should be so classified on the balance sheet.

Appropriation of retained earnings

Appropriations of retained earnings may be required by law or contract, or they may be made at the discretion of the directors as illustrated in the preceding section. The laws of many states require that a corporation retain earnings equal to the amount paid for treasury stock. For example, if a corporation with accumulated earnings of $100,000 purchases shares of its own issued stock for $40,000, the corporation would not be permitted to pay more than $60,000 in dividends. The restriction is equal to the $40,000 paid for the treasury stock and assures that legal capital will not be impaired. The entry to record the appropriation would be:

Apr.	24	Retained Earnings	40,000	
		Retained Earnings Appropriated for Treasury Stock		40,000

After the corporation sells the treasury stock, the appropriation is no longer needed and it is therefore transferred back to the retained earnings account by the following entry:

Nov.	10	Retained Earnings Appropriated for Treasury Stock	40,000	
		Retained Earnings		40,000

When a corporation borrows a substantial amount through issuance of bonds or long-term notes, the agreement may provide for restrictions on dividends until the debt is paid. The contract may stipulate that earnings equal to the amount borrowed be restricted during the entire period of the loan, or it may require that the appropriation be built up by annual appropriations. For example, assume that a corporation borrows $500,000 on ten-year bonds. If equal annual appropriations were to be made over the life of the bonds, there would be a series of ten entries, each in the amount of $50,000, debiting Retained Earnings and crediting an appropriation account entitled Retained Earnings Appropriated for Bonded Indebtedness. Even if the bond agreement did not require the restriction on retained earnings, the directors might nevertheless deem it advisable to establish the appropriation. In that case it would be a *discretionary* rather than a *contractual* appropriation. The entries would be exactly the same in either case.

It must be clearly understood that the appropriation account is not directly related to any particular group of asset accounts. Its existence does not imply that there is an equivalent amount of cash or other assets set aside in a special fund. The appropriation serves the purpose of restricting dividends, but it does not assure that the cash that might otherwise be distributed as dividends will not be invested in additional inventories, equipment, or other assets, or used to reduce current liabilities.

Appropriations of earnings may be accompanied by a segregation of equivalent amounts of cash or marketable investments, in which case the appropriation is said to be *funded*. Accumulation of special funds is discussed in the next chapter.

There are other purposes for which the directors may consider appropriations desirable. Expansion of plant facilities was mentioned earlier. Some companies with properties widely scattered geographically may assume their own risk of losses from fire, windstorm, and other casualties rather than obtain protection from insurance companies. In such cases the appropriation account would be entitled Retained Earnings Appropriated for Self-Insurance. An appropriation of this nature is likely to be permanent although its amount may vary as the total value of properties, the extent of fire protection, etc. fluctuates. If a fire loss does occur, it should be debited to a special loss account rather than to the appropriation account, as it is a loss of the particular period and should be disclosed in the financial reports.

A company may also earmark earnings for other specific contingencies, such as inventory price declines or an adverse decision on a pending law suit. A common practice is to establish an appropriation for contingencies to provide for any eventuality.

The details of retained earnings may be presented in the balance sheet in the manner illustrated below. The item designated "Unappropriated" is the balance of the retained earnings account.

Retained earnings:			
Appropriated:			
For plant expansion	$50,000		
For contingencies	10,000	$60,000	
Unappropriated		80,000	
Total retained earnings			$140,000

It is not essential that restrictions on retained earnings be formalized in the ledger by the use of special accounts for appropriations. Compliance with legal requirements and with contractual restrictions is necessary in any case, and the nature and the amount of all restrictions should always be disclosed in the balance sheet. For example, the appropriations data appearing in the foregoing illustration could be presented in the form of a note accompanying the balance sheet. Such an alternative might also be employed as a means of simplifying or condensing the balance sheet even though appropriation accounts are maintained in the ledger.

The alternative presentation, including the note, might appear as follows:

Retained earnings (see note)	$140,000

Note: Retained earnings in the amount of $50,000 are appropriated for expansion of plant facilities and $10,000 are appropriated for contingencies; the remaining $80,000 is unrestricted.

Nature of dividends

A dividend is a distribution by a corporation to its shareholders. It must be on a pro rata basis for all shares of a particular class. In almost all cases, dividends represent distributions of earnings of the corporation. As has been noted earlier, premium on stock and other items of paid-in capital may be distributed to stockholders, but such dividends are unusual. The term *liquidating dividend* is often applied to a distribution out of paid-in capital. Liquidating dividends generally occur when a corporation permanently contracts its operations or winds up its affairs completely. The discussion that follows will be concerned with dividends based on accumulated earnings.

Dividends may be paid in cash, in stock of the paying company, in scrip, or in other property. The discussion in this chapter will be mainly concerned with the two most common types of dividends — *cash dividends* and *stock dividends* (stock of the paying company).

Ordinarily there are three prerequisites to paying a cash dividend: (1) sufficient unappropriated retained earnings, (2) sufficient cash, and (3) formal action by the board of directors. A substantial amount of accumulated earnings does not necessarily indicate that a corporation is able to pay dividends; there must also be sufficient cash over and above working capital needs. The amount of retained earnings is not directly related to cash; the former represents income of past periods retained in the business, but the cash provided by the income may have been used to purchase plant assets, to reduce liabilities, or for other purposes. The directors of a corporation are not compelled by law to declare dividends even when both retained earnings and cash appear to be sufficient. They have broad discretionary powers in the matter. When a dividend has been declared, however, it becomes a liability of the corporation.

Seasoned corporations with a wide distribution of stock usually try to maintain a stable dividend record. They may retain a substantial portion of earnings in good years in order to be able to continue dividend payments in lean years. Dividends may be paid once a year or on a semiannual or quarterly basis. The tendency is to pay quarterly dividends on both common and preferred stock. In particularly good years the directors may declare an "extra" dividend on common stock. It may be paid at one of the usual dividend dates or at some other date. The designation "extra" indicates that the board of directors does not anticipate an increase in the amount of the "regular" dividend.

There are three different dates involved in a dividend declaration: (1) the date of declaration, (2) the date of record, and (3) the date of payment. The first is the date the directors take formal action declaring the dividend, the second is the date as of which ownership of shares is to be determined, and the third is the date payment is to be made. For example, on October 11 the board of directors declares a quarterly dividend to stockholders of record as of the close of business on October 21, payable on November 15. Notices of dividend declarations are usually reported in financial publications and newspapers.

The liability for the dividend is recorded on the declaration date, as it is incurred when the formal action is taken by the directors. No entry is required on the date of record; it merely fixes the date for determining the identity of the stockholders entitled to receive the dividend. The period of time between the record date and the payment date is provided to permit completion of the postings to the stockholders ledger and preparation of the dividend checks. The liability of the corporation is paid by the mailing of the checks.

Dividends on cumulative preferred stock do not become a liability until they are declared. Dividends in arrears at a balance sheet date should be disclosed by a footnote, a parenthetical notation, or a segregation of retained earnings similar to the following:

Retained earnings:		
Required to meet dividends in arrears on preferred stock..	$30,000	
Remainder, unrestricted..........................	16,000	
Total retained earnings..........................		$46,000

Cash dividends

Dividends payable in cash are by far the most usual form of dividend. Dividends on common stock are usually stated in terms of dollars and cents rather than as a percentage of par. In the case of preferred stock, the preference may also be stated as a fixed amount or it may be expressed as a percentage. For example, the annual dividend rate on a particular $100 par preferred stock may be stated as either 5% or $5.

Corporations ordinarily follow a fixed pattern of dividend payment dates, such as January 15, April 15, July 15, and October 15, or March 30, June 30, September 30, and December 30. Assuming a sufficient balance in retained earnings, including estimated net income of the current year, the directors ordinarily consider the following factors in determining whether to pass a dividend or declare a particular amount:

(1) The company's working capital position.
(2) Resources needed for planned expansion or replacement of facilities.
(3) Maturity dates of large liabilities.
(4) Future business prospects of the company and forecasts for the industry and the economy generally.

To illustrate the entries required in the declaration and the payment of cash dividends, assume that on December 1 the board of directors of the Peerless Corporation declares the regular quarterly dividend of $1 on the 5,000 shares of $100 par, 4% preferred stock outstanding ($5,000), and a quarterly dividend of 25¢ on the 100,000 shares of $10 par common stock outstanding ($25,000). Both dividends are to stockholders of record on December 10, and payment checks are to be issued on January 2. The entry to record the declaration of the dividends is as follows:

Dec.	1	Retained Earnings	30,000	
		Cash Dividends Payable		30,000

The cash dividends payable account would be listed as a current liability on the December 31 balance sheet. Payment of the dividends on January 2 would be recorded in the usual manner as a debit to the liability account and a credit to Cash.

Stock dividends

A pro rata distribution of shares of stock to stockholders, accompanied by a transfer of retained earnings to paid-in capital accounts, is called a *stock dividend.* Such distributions are usually in common stock and are issued to holders of common stock. It is possible to issue common stock to preferred stockholders or preferred stock to common stockholders, but such stock dividends are unusual and will not be discussed.

Stock dividends are quite unlike cash dividends in that there is no distribution of cash or other corporate assets to the stockholders. They are ordinarily issued by corporations that "plow back" (retain) earnings for use in acquiring new facilities or otherwise expanding their operations.

The effect of a stock dividend on the capital structure of the issuing corporation is to transfer accumulated earnings to paid-in capital. To illustrate, assume that the balances of the capital accounts of Prescott Corporation on November 30 are as follows:

Common Stock, $10 par (10,000 shares issued)	$100,000
Premium on Common Stock	20,000
Retained Earnings	150,000

The directors declare a 20% stock dividend (2,000 shares) on December 15, to be issued on January 10. The fair market value of the stock to be issued is estimated at $22 per share. According to the recommendation of the Committee on Accounting Procedure of the American Institute of Certified Public Accountants, retained earnings equal to the market value of the shares to be issued should be transferred to paid-in capital accounts.[2] The entry to record the declaration of the stock dividend is as follows:

Dec.	15	Retained Earnings	44,000	
		Stock Dividend Distributable		20,000
		Premium on Common Stock		24,000

[2]*Accounting Research and Terminology Bulletins, Final Edition,* "No. 43, Restatement and Revision of Accounting Research Bulletins," 1961 (New York: American Institute of Certified Public Accountants), p. 51.

The issuance of the stock certificates is recorded by the following entry:

Jan.	10	Stock Dividend Distributable	20,000	
		Common Stock		20,000

The effect of the stock dividend is to transfer $44,000 from the retained earnings account to paid-in capital accounts and to increase by 2,000 the number of shares outstanding. There is no change in the assets, liabilities, or total capital of the corporation.

A stock dividend does not constitute income to the recipient. It does not alter the book value of his total holdings nor his fractional interest in the corporation. The following analysis of the capital accounts of the Prescott Corporation and of the equity of a hypothetical stockholder demonstrates this point. It is assumed that there are no other changes in the capital accounts.

	Before Stock Dividend	After Stock Dividend
Corporation accounts		
Common stock	$100,000	$120,000
Premium on common stock	20,000	44,000
Retained earnings	150,000	106,000
Total stockholders' equity	$270,000	$270,000
Number of shares outstanding	10,000	12,000
Book value per share	$27.00	$22.50
Equity of a hypothetical stockholder		
Number of shares owned	100	120
Book value of total equity	$2,700	$2,700
Portion of corporation owned	1%	1%

The stock dividend distributable account on the books of a corporation is not a liability because it is discharged by the issuance of shares of corporate stock rather than by the disbursement of assets. If a balance sheet is prepared between the date of declaration and the date of issuance, the amount should be presented as a separate item under the common stock heading.

Stock split-up

Corporations sometimes reduce the par or stated value of their common stock and issue a proportionate number of additional shares. Such a procedure is called a *stock split-up*. For example, a corporation with 10,000 shares of $50 par stock outstanding may reduce the par to $25 and increase the number of shares to 20,000. A stockholder who owned 100 shares before the split-up would own 200 shares after the split-up. There are no changes in the balances of any of the corporation's accounts, hence no entry is required.

The primary purpose of a stock split-up is to reduce the selling price of stock when the shares are selling at exceedingly high levels. Such an action will permit more investors to enter the market for this particular security. A stock split-up is seldom employed by small corporations or by corporations whose stock is not listed on the organized stock exchanges.

Dividends and treasury stock

Cash or property dividends are not paid on treasury stock. To do so would place the corporation in the position of earning income through dealing with itself, an obvious fiction. Accordingly, the total amount of a cash (or property) dividend should be based on the number of shares outstanding at the record date. To illustrate, assume that the balances of the capital accounts of Eldora Corporation are as follows:

Common Stock, $10 par (100,000 shares issued)......	$1,000,000 cr.
Retained Earnings..............................	1,600,000 cr.
Treasury Stock (2,000 shares at cost)...............	42,000 dr.

If a cash dividend of $1 a share is declared, the total is computed on the basis of the 98,000 shares outstanding (100,000 – 2,000) and the dividend is $98,000.

The interrelation of stock dividends and treasury stock is less clearcut. Some states do not permit the issuance of stock dividends on treasury stock; others do. If the corporate directors exclude treasury stock from consideration, the total amount of a stock dividend is based on the outstanding stock, which in the above example is 98,000 shares. If the alternative procedure is elected, the total amount of the dividend is based on the number of shares issued, which for Eldora Corporation is 100,000. The accounts affected by the declaration and the issuance of the stock dividend are the same in either case; only the amounts are different. The dollar balance in the treasury stock account is not affected, regardless of which method is used. If the alternative procedure is employed, the number of shares held as treasury stock is increased and the cost basis per share is adjusted accordingly. For example, if Eldora Corporation issues a 5% stock dividend on 98,000 shares, a total of 4,900 shares are issued to stockholders and the number of shares of treasury stock remains at 2,000. On the other hand, if the dividend is based on 100,000 shares, the number of treasury shares is increased by 100 (5% of 2,000) and the per-share cost basis of the treasury stock becomes $20 ($42,000 ÷ 2,100).

The issuance of stock dividends on treasury stock is theoretically sound because the percentage relationship of the treasury stock to the total issuance remains unchanged. In practice, however, either method of determining the total amount of the dividend is satisfactory. In most cases the number of shares held as treasury stock represents a small percent of the number of shares issued and the rate of dividend is also ordinarily small, so that the difference between the end results is usually not material.

There is no legal, theoretical, or practical reason for excluding treasury stock when computing the number of shares to be issued in a stock split-up. The reduction in par or stated value would apply to all shares of the class, including the unissued, issued, and treasury shares. For example, if Eldora Corporation were to reduce the par of its stock from $10 to $5, it would issue certificates for an additional 98,000 shares to stockholders and would increase the number of treasury shares by 2,000.

Quasi-reorganization

A corporation that has incurred operating losses for several years may have a deficit but at the same time may have a potential for successful future operations. For example, such a corporation may have developed new products that might reasonably lead to profitable operations if it could expand to produce and market these new products. The sale of bonds to finance the expansion is not feasible because of the corporation's financial position. Because of the deficit, the payment of dividends is impossible in many states until future operations recover the deficit; consequently the sale of stock at a reasonable price may be difficult. A procedure has been developed for situations such as this where a promising future is impeded by past operations. This procedure, called a *quasi-reorganization*, eliminates the deficit and allows the company to continue operations much as if it had been liquidated and given a fresh start.

A quasi-reorganization restates the assets at current market values and reduces the legal capital to create a reorganization surplus against which the deficit is written off. A new retained earnings account is opened and thereafter, for a period of up to ten years, the beginning date of the account should be disclosed on the balance sheet.[3] Readers are informed in this manner that the balance of retained earnings has accumulated from a specific date subsequent to the date the corporation was organized.

---

[3]*Accounting Research and Terminology Bulletins, Final Edition*, "No. 43, Restatement and Revision of Accounting Research Bulletins," p. 47, and "No. 46, Discontinuance of Dating Earned Surplus," p. 11, 1961 (New York: American Institute of Certified Public Accountants).

Corrections and extraordinary debits and credits

Regardless of the safeguards that may be employed, errors will inevitably occur in recording transactions. When the error is discovered during the same accounting period in which it occurred, a correction may be made and the financial statements will not be affected by the error. The analysis of the effect of an error and the formulation of the correction is facilitated by observing the following procedures: (1) determine the entry that was incorrectly made, (2) formulate the entry that should have been made, and (3) formulate the correcting entry.

To illustrate, assume that new equipment purchased by Douglas Corporation on January 10 at a cost of $20,000 was erroneously debited to repairs expense and that the error is discovered after adjusting entries have been made as of December 31 but before the books have been closed. Assume further that the equipment has an estimated life of 10 years and that the company uses the straight-line method of depreciation. The correcting entry to be recorded as of December 31 may be determined as follows:

Entry Made			Entries That Should Have Been Made			Correcting Entries		
Repairs	20,000		Equipment........	20,000		Equipment........	20,000	
Accounts Pay.		20,000	Accounts Payable.		20,000	Repairs........		20,000
			Depr. Exp. — Equip.	2,000		Depr. Exp. — Equip.	2,000	
			Accum. Depr. — Equipment......		2,000	Accum. Depr. — Equipment......		2,000

In the foregoing illustration the error was corrected before the financial statements were prepared and the books were closed for the year. Had the error not been discovered and corrected, the effect on the income statement for the year and the balance sheet at December 31 would have been as follows:

(1) Income Statement — Overstatement of repairs expense, $20,000; understatement of depreciation expense, $2,000; net understatement of income, $18,000.
(2) Balance Sheet — Understatement of equipment, $20,000; understatement of accumulated depreciation, $2,000; net understatement of assets, $18,000; net understatement of retained earnings, $18,000.

When errors in revenues and expenses are not discovered until a later period, accountants are not in agreement as to how they should be corrected and reported in the financial statements. There are also two points of view regarding the treatment of extraordinary items of revenue and expense. The latter category includes such items as gains or losses from lawsuits and losses resulting from floods, earthquakes, or other catastrophes of a nonrecurring nature not covered by insurance. In the following brief discussion of the two views it should be borne in mind that the concern is only with *material* items. Corrections and extraordinary debits or credits that are relatively insignificant may be treated as current revenue or expense under either of the two views.

Current operating performance statement. An income statement in which the items reported are limited to those of a normally recurring nature may be referred to as a *current operating performance* statement. The principal argument for excluding the nonrecurring items is that the income statement should present what the corporation was able to earn under normal conditions for the year. It is only in this way that comparisons can be made with other years and with the income statements of other corporations. When this view is adopted, the nonrecurring items are carried directly to the retained earnings account.

Applying the foregoing to the correction of income of the earlier year for the Douglas Corporation, the entries would be:

Mar.	10	Equipment	20,000	
		Retained Earnings		20,000
	10	Retained Earnings	2,000	
		Accumulated Depreciation — Equipment		2,000

The entries of $20,000 and $2,000 in Retained Earnings would be reported on the retained earnings statement as a correction of income of past years, and the income statement for the year in which the correction was made would not be affected. The manner in which the correction is reported on the retained earnings statement is illustrated on page 432.

All-inclusive statement. An income statement that includes all revenue and expense items, regardless of their source, is referred to as an *all-inclusive* statement. The basic argument is that the income statement should report the full story of operating results; the complete series of annual income statements will then include the entire income from the date of organization. Significant items of a nonrecurring nature should be set forth separately in the statement. The reader is then able to determine what the net income would have been under normal conditions.

Applying this view to the correction for the Douglas Corporation, the entry would be:

Mar.	10	Equipment	20,000	
		Accumulated Depreciation — Equipment		2,000
		Correction of Income of Earlier Period		18,000

The credit of $18,000 would be reported in the income statement as an extraordinary credit. It is quite common to include a section for extraordinary items as the last section on the income statement to follow "Net income after income tax." The final figure on the all-inclusive income statement is labeled "Net income and extraordinary items."

It is important to note that both methods provide for disclosure of extraordinary items and do not "bury" such items in other accounts. The difference between the two methods lies in the manner in which this is accomplished.

Amortization and write-off of intangibles

In accounting usage, the term *intangible asset* is applied to certain long-lived legal rights and competitive advantages belonging to a business enterprise. Included are organization costs, goodwill, patents, copyrights, secret processes, leases, and similar items. A requisite to the recognition of an intangible asset in the accounts is that it be purchased. For example, if the total price paid for a going concern exceeds the fair value of the identifiable net assets, the excess is payment for goodwill and it should be recorded as such in the accounts of the purchaser. On the other hand, a firm that builds up goodwill through successful operations would not be justified in recording goodwill in its accounts.

Some intangible assets have a limited term of existence. For example, the exclusive right to an invention granted by a patent runs for 17 years. Copyrights and leases also expire within a definite number of years. Other intangibles, such as organization costs, goodwill, and secret processes, ordinarily have no limitations on their term of existence; at least the length of life cannot be ascertained at the time the asset is acquired.

Intangibles that have a limited life should be amortized by periodic pro rata charges to expense. If a change in circumstances indicates a shorter or longer life than originally estimated, the amount of the periodic charge should be altered accordingly. If it should become evident that an intangible asset is worthless, it should be written off. If the amount of the write-off is material, it should be reported separately in the retained earnings statement or as an extraordinary charge in the income statement.

Intangible assets with an unlimited life should be carried on the books during the entire life of the enterprise, except when altered circumstances render them worthless. In such a case they should be written off. Here, too, the manner in which the write-off is reported may follow either the current operating performance statement theory or the all-inclusive statement theory.

Despite the lack of theoretical justification, intangible assets are sometimes amortized gradually or written off completely without regard to loss in value. For example, organization costs are frequently written off during the early years of a corporation's life. Such a practice is defended on the grounds of conservatism. Until recently, deductions for organization costs were not permitted in determining net income subject to the federal income tax, except in the year of dissolution. The Internal Revenue Code now provides that certain specified organization costs may be deducted from income ratably over a period of five years or longer.

The unamortized balance of intangibles is generally listed in a separate section in the balance sheet headed "Intangible assets." The corporate balance sheet is discussed in more detail in Chapter 19.

Retained earnings statement

The retained earnings statement is a formal summary of the debits and the credits to the retained earnings accounts during a fiscal period. It is one of the principal statements included in published financial reports of corporations.

The retained earnings statement is divided into two major sections: (1) appropriated and (2) unappropriated. The first section is composed of an analysis of all appropriation accounts, beginning with the opening balance, listing the additions or the deductions during the period, and ending with the closing balance. The second section is composed of an analysis of the retained earnings account and is similar in form to the first section. The final figure on the statement is the total retained earnings as of the last day of the period; it corresponds to the amount reported in the balance sheet as of that date.

To illustrate the form of the retained earnings statement and the sources from which the information is obtained, the pertinent accounts of the Douglas Corporation and its retained earnings statement for the year 1965 are given below and on the following page.

RETAINED EARNINGS APPROPRIATED FOR PLANT EXPANSION Acct. No. 3202

Date		Items	Post. Ref.	Debit	Credit	Balance	
						Debit	Credit
1965							
Jan.	1	Balance	√				30,000
Dec.	31	Transfer from retained earnings account	J25		25,000		55,000

RETAINED EARNINGS — Acct. No. 3300

Date		Items	Post. Ref.	Debit	Credit	Balance Debit	Balance Credit
1965							
Jan.	1	Balance	√				95,300
Mar.	10	Overstatement of repair expense	J20		20,000		115,300
	10	Understatement of depreciation expense	J20	2,000			113,300
	20	Dividends	J21	9,875			103,425
June	19	Dividends	J21	9,875			93,550
Sept.	18	Dividends	J22	9,875			83,675
Dec.	18	Dividends	J22	17,875			65,800
	31	Organization costs	J23	4,000			61,800
	31	Net income after income tax	J24		100,000		161,800
	31	Appropriation for plant expansion	J25	25,000			136,800

Douglas Corporation
Retained Earnings Statement
For Year Ended December 31, 1965

Appropriated:			
Appropriated for plant expansion, balance January 1, 1965		$ 30,000	
Add appropriation in 1965 (see below)		25,000	
Retained earnings appropriated, December 31, 1965			$ 55,000
Unappropriated:			
Balance, January 1, 1965	$ 95,300		
Add: Net income for year after income tax	100,000		
Overstatement of repair expenses in 1964	20,000	$215,300	
Deduct: Cash dividends declared	$ 47,500		
Organization costs written off	4,000		
Understatement of depreciation expense in 1964	2,000		
Transfer to appropriation for plant expansion (see above)	25,000	78,500	
Retained earnings unappropriated, December 31, 1965			136,800
Total retained earnings, December 31, 1965			$191,800

Retained earnings statement

Retained earnings statements are frequently shorter and simpler than the one illustrated. If there are no appropriation accounts or income corrections to be reported, the increases and the decreases may be confined to current earnings and dividends. There are many possible variations in the form of the statement. It may also be appended to the income statement to form a combined statement of income and retained earnings, which is illustrated in Chapter 27. If there should be changes in paid-in capital during the period, they should be presented separately in a paid-in capital statement.

QUESTIONS

1. Ryan Corporation is given land as an inducement to locate in a particular community. (a) At what amount should the land be recorded in the accounts? (b) What account is credited to record such a transaction?

2. Accountants generally agree that plant assets should be reported in the balance sheet at original cost less accumulated depreciation. How can current values be communicated to the reader of the balance sheet?

3. What is the customary manner of presenting income tax in the income statement?

4. To what account is the balance in Expense and Revenue Summary for a corporation closed at the end of each fiscal period?

5. Appropriations of retained earnings may be (a) required by law, (b) required by contract, or (c) made at the discretion of the board of directors. Give an illustration of each type of appropriation.

6. Does a credit balance in Retained Earnings represent cash? Explain.

7. The board of directors of Hoffman Company votes to appropriate $150,000 of retained earnings for plant expansion. What is the effect of their action on (a) cash, (b) retained earnings, and (c) possible dividend declarations?

8. What are the three prerequisites to the declaration and the payment of a cash dividend?

9. The dates in connection with the declaration of a cash dividend are January 8, January 15, and January 31. Identify each date.

10. The Westlawn Corporation, with cumulative preferred stock and no-par common stock outstanding, has a substantial credit balance in the retained earnings account at the beginning of the current fiscal year. Net income for the current year after income tax is estimated at $50,000. The board of directors declares the regular $12,000 dividend on the preferred stock but takes no action on the common stock. Suggest reasons for passing the dividend on the common stock.

11. How should dividends in arrears on cumulative preferred stock be reported on the balance sheet?

12. State the effect of the following on assets, liabilities, and stockholders' equity: (a) declaration of a cash dividend, (b) payment of a cash dividend, (c) declaration of a stock dividend, (d) issuance of a stock dividend, (e) stock split-up.

13. The owner of 100 shares of Allied Corporation common stock receives a stock dividend of 10 shares. (a) What is the effect of the stock dividend on the book value of the stock per share? (b) Is the total book value of the 110 shares greater than, less than, or the same as the total book value of the 100 shares immediately before the dividend?

14. A corporation with 50,000 shares of no-par common stock issued, of which 2,000 shares are held as treasury stock, declares a cash dividend of $.50 a share. What is the total amount of the dividend?

15. A 10% stock dividend declared by the corporation in Question 14 would amount to what number of shares? Give two alternatives.

16. If a corporation with 1,500 shares of treasury stock has a stock split of 2 additional shares for each share issued, what will be the number of treasury shares after the split-up?

17. What is the purpose of a *quasi-reorganization?*

18. Contrast "current operating performance" and "all-inclusive" as terms applied to the income statement.

19. A building owned by the Hollaway Company was completely destroyed by a tornado. The building, which had cost $70,000 and had been depreciated in the amount of $30,000, was not covered by insurance. What entry would be made to record this occurrence (a) if the current operating performance view is adopted and (b) if the all-inclusive view is adopted?

20. (a) Name several examples of intangible assets. (b) Where does the unamortized cost of such assets appear in the balance sheet?

21. Into what two major sections is the retained earnings statement divided?

EXERCISES

1. The Ogden Company records its federal income tax at the close of each month. Give the entries, in general journal form, (a) to record an estimated income tax of $40,000 at the end of January, the first month of the fiscal year, and (b) to record the payment of $95,000 of estimated income tax on September 15.

2. The Renner Corporation purchases 1,000 shares of its own common stock at $60 for cash. The par is $50 and the book value before the purchase was $71. (a) Present the entries, in general journal form, (1) to record the purchase (treasury stock is recorded at cost) and (2) to provide for the appropriation of retained earnings. (b) One half of the treasury stock is sold at $66. Present the entries, in general journal form, (1) to record the sale and (2) to reduce the appropriation.

3. The dates in connection with a cash dividend of $60,000 on company stock are July 10, July 17, and August 1. Present the entries, in general journal form, required on each date.

4. The balance sheet of Horton, Inc. shows common stock (20,000 shares authorized), $100 par, $1,000,000; premium on common stock, $40,000; and retained earnings, $280,000. The board of directors declares a 10% stock dividend when the market price of the stock is $120 a share. (a) Present entries to record (1) the declaration of the dividend and (2) the issuance of the stock certificates. (b) Determine the book value per share (1) before the stock dividend and (2) after the stock dividend.

5. The board of directors of the Dexter Corporation decides to reduce the par of common shares from $100 to $25. This action will increase the number of outstanding shares to 800,000. The market price of the stock immediately before the stock split-up is $220 a share. (a) Determine the number of outstanding shares prior to the stock split-up. (b) Present the entries to record the stock split-up. (c) At approximately what price would a share of stock be expected to sell immediately after the stock split-up?

6. Prior to the closing of the accounts at July 31, the accountant discovered the following errors related to the current fiscal year. Present the entry to correct each error, assuming the use of the all-inclusive concept of net income.

(a) In recording a purchase on July 27 for which a note payable was given, Accounts Payable was credited for $4,000.
(b) A purchase of $250 of merchandise on account was debited to Office Supplies. The accounts have not been adjusted at July 31.
(c) Office equipment that had cost $6,000 and on which $3,500 of depreciation had accumulated at the time of sale was sold for $2,000. The transaction was recorded by a debit to Cash and a credit to Sales for $2,000.

7. The errors described below occurred during the fiscal year ending December 31. They are discovered in March of the following year. Present the correcting entries, assuming that the current operating performance concept is followed in preparing the income statement.

(a) A machine acquired on January 4 at a cost of $6,000 was debited to Purchases. No depreciation was recorded on Dec. 31. Use a 5-year life, $500 salvage value, and straight-line method of depreciation.
(b) Merchandise Inventory at Dec. 31 was overstated by $2,900.
(c) Accrued salaries of $2,200 were not recognized at Dec. 31.
(d) The $540 premium on a 3-year insurance policy acquired on July 1 was charged to Prepaid Insurance. No adjustment was made on Dec. 31.

8. The Allerton Corporation was organized on November 1 of the current year. Results of transactions affecting net income and retained earnings for the first complete year of operations are as follows:

Net income before income tax	$162,500
Income tax	71,500
Cash dividends declared	12,000
Appropriation of retained earnings for plant expansion	50,000

Prepare a retained earnings statement for the first fiscal year ended October 31.

PROBLEMS

18-1. Selected transactions completed by the Royer Corporation during the current fiscal year are as follows:

Jan. 11. Purchased 2,000 shares of own common stock at $22, recording the stock at cost. (Prior to the purchase there were 100,000 shares of $10 par common stock outstanding.)

Mar. 14. Paid $35,000, which represented one half of the income tax for the past year. Earlier accruals of income tax had been recorded correctly.

Apr. 10. Sold 1,000 shares of treasury stock at $26, receiving cash.

May 5. Declared a semiannual dividend of $1.50 on the 5,000 shares of preferred stock and a 30¢ dividend on the common stock to stockholders of record on May 20, payable on June 5.

June 5. Paid the dividends.

June 13. Paid remainder of income tax due for prior year, $35,000.

Sept. 18. Discovered that building construction costs of $20,000 incurred in the preceding fiscal year had been charged to the building maintenance expense account. The building has an estimated useful life of 25 years and the declining-balance method using twice the straight-line depreciation rate is used by the company. Construction was completed on July 1 of the preceding fiscal year. Correct through Retained Earnings.

Nov. 5. Declared semiannual dividends of $1.50 on the preferred stock and 30¢ on the common stock. In addition, a 5% common stock dividend was declared on the common stock outstanding. The fair market value of the common stock to be issued is estimated at $25.

Dec. 5. Paid the cash dividends and issued the certificates for the common stock dividend.

31. Recorded the estimated federal income tax for the year, $94,500.

31. The board of directors authorized the appropriation necessitated by the holdings of treasury stock.

Instructions: Record the above transactions in general journal form.

18-2. The retained earnings accounts of Sarver Implement Co. for the current fiscal year ended December 31 are as follows:

RETAINED EARNINGS APPROPRIATED FOR PLANT EXPANSION

DATE		ITEMS	POST. REF.	DEBIT	CREDIT	BALANCE DEBIT	BALANCE CREDIT
Jan.	1	Balance	√				130,000
Dec.	31	Transfer to retained earnings account	J50	50,000			80,000

RETAINED EARNINGS APPROPRIATED FOR BONDED INDEBTEDNESS

DATE		ITEMS	POST. REF.	DEBIT	CREDIT	BALANCE DEBIT	BALANCE CREDIT
Jan.	1	Balance	√				125,000
Dec.	31	Transfer from retained earnings account	J50		25,000		150,000

RETAINED EARNINGS

DATE		ITEMS	POST. REF.	DEBIT	CREDIT	BALANCE	
						DEBIT	CREDIT
Jan.	1	Balance	√				267,000
	10	Understatement of merchandise inventory at end of preceding year	J40		12,800		279,800
Mar.	12	Understatement of income tax of preceding year	J41	7,000			272,800
Oct.	18	Loss on sale of investments	J47	15,000			257,800
Nov.	30	Cash dividend	J48	50,000			207,800
	30	Stock dividend	J48	100,000			107,800
Dec.	31	Organization costs written off	J49	3,000			104,800
	31	Net income after income tax	J50		160,000		264,800
	31	Transfer from appropriation for plant expansion account	J50		50,000		314,800
	31	Transfer to appropriation for bonded indebtedness account	J50	25,000			289,800

Instructions: (1) Prepare a retained earnings statement for the fiscal year ended December 31.

(2) Which of the two views of net income does this company follow?

18-3. The stockholders' equity of J. C. Hall, Inc. on January 1 of the current fiscal year is as follows:

Common Stock, par $50 (20,000 shares authorized, 15,000 shares issued)	$750,000
Premium on Common Stock	225,000
Retained Earnings Appropriated for Plant Expansion	150,000
Retained Earnings Appropriated for Treasury Stock	70,000
Retained Earnings	300,000
Treasury Stock (1,000 shares, at cost)	70,000

The following selected transactions occurred during the year:

Jan. 12. Paid cash dividends of $1.50 per share on the common stock. The dividend had been properly recorded when declared on December 20 of the past fiscal year.

Feb. 1. Sold all of the treasury stock for $85,000 cash.

2. Issued 2,000 shares of common stock for $170,000 cash.

June 20. Declared a 4% stock dividend on common stock. The market price of the stock to be issued is $80 a share.

20. The board of directors authorized the write-off of patents with an unamortized cost of $60,000 as a direct charge to the retained earnings account. The patents were considered to be worthless as a result of patents on an improved product obtained by a competing business.

July 10. Issued the certificates for the dividend declared on June 20.

Oct. 6. Discovered that machinery purchased in the preceding year for $18,000 had been charged to Maintenance and Repairs. Depreciation of $3,600 was therefore omitted from the preceding year. Correct through Retained Earnings.

Dec. 1. Purchased 500 shares of treasury stock for $42,000.

20. Declared a $1.50 per share dividend on common stock.

20. The board of directors authorized the increase of the appropriation for plant expansion by $50,000.

20. Reduced the appropriation for treasury stock to $42,000.

31. Closed the credit balance of the expense and revenue summary account, $111,250.

Instructions: (1) Set up T accounts for the stockholders' equity accounts and enter the balances as of January 1.

(2) Prepare entries in general journal form to record the selected transactions and post to the stockholders' equity accounts. Set up additional stockholders' equity accounts as needed.

(3) Prepare the stockholders' equity section of the balance sheet as of December 31 of the current fiscal year.

(4) Prepare a retained earnings statement for the current fiscal year.

18-4. The following information was extracted from the records of Ridgeway, Inc. covering the fiscal year ended June 30, 1966:

Cost of merchandise sold	$520,000
Selling expenses	120,000
General expenses	93,000
Income tax	109,660
Sales	975,000
Retained earnings, July 1, 1965	414,000
Correction of income of earlier period — overstatement of depreciation	20,000
Fire loss	10,000
Retained earnings appropriated for contingencies, July 1, 1965	150,000
Cash dividends declared	40,000

Instructions: (1) Assuming the use of the current operating performance concept of net income, prepare an income statement and a retained earnings statement.

(2) Assuming the use of the all-inclusive concept of net income, prepare an income statement and a retained earnings statement.

18-5. The stockholders' equity section of the balance sheet of the Turner Corporation as of December 31, 1965, is given at the top of page 439. Included in the current assets section of the balance sheet were 1,000 shares of treasury stock at cost, $60,000.

Selected transactions occurring in 1966, together with related information, are as follows:

Feb. 20. Discovered the following errors and made necessary corrections through the retained earnings account:

(a) Discovered that a sales invoice for $9,000, dated December 29, 1965, was recorded as a sale on account on January 3, 1966. Payment was

Stockholders' equity

Paid-in capital:				
Common stock, $50 par (20,000 shares authorized, 18,000 shares issued)		$900,000		
Premium on common stock		54,000		
Total paid-in capital			$954,000	
Retained earnings:				
Appropriated:				
For contingencies	$50,000			
For treasury stock	60,000	$110,000		
Unappropriated		360,000		
Total retained earnings			470,000	
Total stockholders' equity				$1,424,000

received in January. The merchandise had been excluded from the inventory at December 31, 1965.

(b) New machinery with an estimated life of 10 years was purchased on January 4, 1965. The cost of freight and installation, amounting to $5,000, was charged to repairs expense. (Depreciation method used is declining-balance at twice the straight-line rate.)

(c) A December purchase invoice for $10,000 of merchandise was not recorded until January 3, 1966. The merchandise was on hand and included in the inventory at December 31, 1965.

(d) The 1965 charge for income tax was understated by $9,500. The additional tax has not been paid.

Mar. 12. Received land for a plant site valued at $25,000 from the Oakland Industrial Development Council as a donation.

June 30. Declared a cash dividend of $3 per share to stockholders of record on July 12, payable on July 21.

July 21. Paid the cash dividend.

Aug. 15. Issued 500 shares of treasury stock to officers as a salary bonus (Officers Salaries). Market price of the stock, $80.

Dec. 30. Declared a 5% stock dividend on the stock outstanding to stockholders of record on January 12, to be issued on January 21. The market value of the stock to be issued is $80.

Dec. 30. Reduced the treasury stock restriction on retained earnings to the appropriate amount.

Dec. 31. After closing all revenue and expense accounts, Expense and Revenue Summary has a credit balance of $150,000. Closed the expense and revenue summary account.

Instructions: (1) Set up T accounts for the accounts appearing in the stockholders' equity section of the balance sheet and for Treasury Stock and enter the balances as of January 1, 1966.

(2) Prepare entries in general journal form to record the transactions and other information, and post to the stockholders' equity accounts. Set up additional stockholders' equity accounts as needed.

(3) Prepare the stockholders' equity section of the balance sheet in good form as of December 31, 1966.

(4) Prepare a retained earnings statement for the year.

19.

Corporations—long-term obligations and investments

Financing corporations

Thus far in the discussion of corporations it has been assumed that the funds required for the enterprise are obtained by issuing stock or through the retention of earnings. Those purchasing stock acquire an ownership equity and expect to receive income on their investment in the form of dividends. It has been shown that the amount of dividends distributed depends upon earnings of the corporation and the dividend policies of the board of directors. The holders of preferred stock have a prior but usually a limited claim on earnings, and the holders of common stock have a residual but unlimited claim on earnings.

Because of the ease of transferring stock and the availability of earnings through dividends, corporations have generally found investors ready to exchange their money for shares of stock. Some corporations have acquired the property of competitors in exchange for shares of their own stock. The great business of investment banking and the huge volume of trading on the stock exchanges give evidence of the present-day interest in corporate stocks.

Corporations may obtain part of the funds needed for a long period of time by borrowing. They may borrow by selling bonds to many investors, or they may give long-term notes to a few investors or perhaps to a single investor such as an insurance company. In the following discussion reference is made to bonds; but, generally speaking, the accounting problems are the same if long-term notes are used.

When funds are borrowed through the issuance of bonds, there is a definite commitment to pay interest and to repay the principal at some future date. Those buying the bonds are creditors, and their claims for interest and for repayment of principal rank ahead of the claims of stockholders. Many financial institutions and nonprofit foundations are restricted by law or charter as to the proportion of their funds that may be invested in stocks. In addition, many individuals prefer to have greater certainty as to income (even though often a lesser amount) and greater safety of principal than stocks afford.

Many factors influence the incorporators or the board of directors in deciding upon the best means of obtaining funds. The subject will be limited here to a brief examination of the effect of different financing methods on the income of the corporation and its common stockholders. To illustrate, assume that three different plans for financing a $4,000,000 corporation are under consideration by its organizers. The three plans are as follows, assuming in each case that the securities will be issued at face value:

Plan 1.	Common stock	$4,000,000
Plan 2.	5% preferred stock	$2,000,000
	Common stock	$2,000,000
Plan 3.	4% bonds	$2,000,000
	5% preferred stock	$1,000,000
	Common stock	$1,000,000

The incorporators estimate that the enterprise will earn $600,000 annually, before considering interest on the bonds or income taxes, which are estimated at 50% of net income. The tabulation below indicates the amount of earnings that would be available to common stockholders under each of the three plans.

	PLAN 1	PLAN 2	PLAN 3
4% bonds			$2,000,000
5% preferred stock		$2,000,000	1,000,000
Common stock, $100 par	$4,000,000	2,000,000	1,000,000
Total	$4,000,000	$4,000,000	$4,000,000
Earnings before interest or income taxes	$ 600,000	$ 600,000	$ 600,000
Deduct: Interest on bonds			80,000
Balance	$ 600,000	$ 600,000	$ 520,000
Deduct: Income tax	300,000	300,000	260,000
Net income after income tax	$ 300,000	$ 300,000	$ 260,000
Dividends on preferred stock		100,000	50,000
Available for dividends on common stock	$ 300,000	$ 200,000	$ 210,000
Earnings per share on common stock	$ 7.50	$ 10.00	$ 21.00

According to Plan 1, the earnings per share on the common stock would be $7.50 per share. Under Plan 2, the effect of issuing 5% preferred stock for half of the capitalization results in $10 earnings per common share. The issuance of 4% bonds in Plan 3, with the remaining capitalization split between preferred and common, results in a return of $21 per share on common stock.

Obviously, under this set of conditions Plan 3 is the most attractive for common stockholders. If the total of assumed earnings increases beyond $600,000, the spread between the yield to common stockholders under Plan 1 and Plan 3 would become even greater. But if successively smaller amounts of earnings are assumed, the comparative attractiveness of Plan 2 and Plan 3 decreases. This is illustrated by the tabulation below, in which earnings, before deducting interest and income taxes, are assumed to be $200,000.

	PLAN 1	PLAN 2	PLAN 3
4% bonds			$2,000,000
5% preferred stock		$2,000,000	1,000,000
Common stock, $100 par	$4,000,000	2,000,000	1,000,000
Total	$4,000,000	$4,000,000	$4,000,000
Earnings before interest or income taxes	$ 200,000	$ 200,000	$ 200,000
Deduct: Interest on bonds			80,000
Balance	$ 200,000	$ 200,000	$ 120,000
Deduct: Income tax	100,000	100,000	60,000
Net income after income tax	$ 100,000	$ 100,000	$ 60,000
Dividends on preferred stock		100,000	50,000
Available for dividends on common stock	$ 100,000	—	$ 10,000
Earnings per share on common stock	$ 2.50	—	$ 1.00

The preceding analysis of financing methods concentrated on the effect of different plans on earnings per share to the common stockholder. Other factors must be considered in evaluating different methods of financing. For example, the issuance of bonds represents a fixed annual interest charge and an obligation that must be paid. On the other hand, a decision to finance by issuing only common stock will require a large investment by one stockholder or group of stockholders if they are to have control of the corporation.

Characteristics of bonds

When a corporation issues bonds, the total amount of the bond issue is divided into units, which may be of varying denominations. Ordinarily the principal of each bond, also referred to as the *face value*, is $1,000. The contract between the corporation and the bondholder is termed the *bond indenture*. The interest on bonds may be payable at annual, semiannual, or quarterly intervals. Most bonds provide for payment on a semiannual basis.

Registered bonds may be transferred from one owner to another only by proper endorsement on the certificate, and the issuing corporation maintains a record of the name and the address of each bondholder. Interest payments are made by check to the owner of record. Title to *bearer bonds*, which are also referred to as *coupon bonds*, is transferred by delivery. Interest coupons for the entire term of the bonds are attached to the bond certificate. The coupons are in the form of checks or drafts payable to bearer, and at each interest date the holder detaches the appropriate coupon and presents it at his bank for collection.

When all bonds of an issue mature at the same time, they may be called *term bonds*. If the maturities are spread over several dates, they are called *serial bonds*. For example, one tenth of an issue of $1,000,000, or $100,000, may mature eleven years from the issuance date, another $100,000 may mature twelve years from the issuance date, and so on until the final $100,000 matures at the end of the twentieth year. Bonds that may be exchanged for other securities under specified conditions are called *convertible bonds*. If the issuing corporation reserves the right to pay off the bonds before maturity, they are referred to as *callable bonds*.

A *secured bond* is one that gives the bondholder a claim on particular assets in the event that the issuing corporation fails to meet its obligations on the bonds. The properties mortgaged or pledged may be specific buildings and equipment, the entire plant, or stocks and bonds of other companies owned by the debtor corporation. Bonds issued on the basis of the general credit of the corporation are called *debenture bonds*.

Accounting for the issuance of bonds

The liability incurred by the issuance of bonds is recorded in the account Bonds Payable. If there is more than one bond issue, a separate account should be maintained for each issue. Bonds Payable are reported on the balance sheet as long-term or fixed liabilities. As the maturity date comes within one year of the balance sheet date, they should be transferred to the current liability classification if they are to be paid out of current assets. If they are to be paid with segregated funds or if they are to be replaced with another bond issue, they should remain in the noncurrent category and their disposition should be disclosed by an explanatory note. The listing in the balance sheet should include data as to security, interest rate, and due date.

All bonds of a particular issue are dated uniformly and the interest begins to accrue thereafter. If the bonds are issued at face value on this date, the transaction is recorded by a debit to Cash and a credit to Bonds Payable. Frequently a part or all of the bonds are sold some time after the interest has begun to accrue. In such cases the issuing corporation charges the purchaser for the interest accrued. This interest is then repaid to the purchaser, together with interest earned from the issuance date, at the time of the first regular interest payment. To illustrate, assume that 4½% bonds in the face amount of $100,000, dated January 1, are sold on March 1 at 100 plus accrued interest. Prices of bonds are stated in terms of percentage of face value; hence the price "100" indicates that the bonds are sold at face value. The entry to record the issuance of the bonds, in general journal form, is:

Mar. 1	Cash	100,750	
	Bonds Payable		100,000
	Interest Expense		750

The credit of $750 to the interest expense account is in reality interest payable. It is simpler, however, to credit the expense account so that when the interest is paid the entire amount of the payment may be debited to the expense account. The entry to record the semiannual interest payment on June 30, in general journal form, is:

June 30	Interest Expense	2,250	
	Cash		2,250

The debit balance of $1,500 ($2,250 – $750) in the interest expense account at June 30 represents the interest expense for the four months that the bonds have been outstanding.

Bonds sold at a premium. Bonds may be sold at a price above or below face value, depending upon the rate of interest offered and the general credit standing of the corporation. If a corporation offers a rate of interest that is higher than the market rate for similar securities, investors may be willing to pay a premium for the bonds. For example, assume that on January 1 a corporation issues $100,000 of 5%, 10-year bonds at 106, with interest payable annually on December 31. The entry for the transaction, in general journal form, is as follows:

Jan. 1	Cash	106,000	
	Bonds Payable		100,000
	Premium on Bonds Payable		6,000

The investors paid the premium because they were willing to lend money to the corporation at less than the contract rate of 5%. The premium represents an advance payment by the investors for the privilege of receiving interest in excess of the prevailing market rate.

The issuing corporation has incurred two liabilities: (1) to repay $100,000, the face amount of the bonds, in 10 years, and (2) to pay annual interest of $5,000 for 10 years. The $6,000 premium is not income to the corporation; rather it is an advance of interest collected from the bondholders that will be repaid to them over the life of the bonds. This may be demonstrated by determining the movement of cash related to the bond issue. As shown by the following tabulation, the excess of the cash paid during the 10-year period over the cash received from the sale of the bonds is $44,000. This amount represents the total interest expense for the 10-year period.

Cash to be paid:		
Face of the bonds	$100,000	
Interest — 10 payments of $5,000 each (5% of $100,000)	50,000	$150,000
Cash received:		
Face of the bonds	$100,000	
Premium on the bonds	6,000	106,000
Total interest expense for 10 years		$ 44,000
Interest expense per year		$ 4,400

The total interest expense for the life of the bonds is spread ratably over the 10 years by amortizing $^1/_{10}$ of the premium against interest expense each year. The entry to record the payment of interest, in general journal form, is:

Dec. 31	Interest Expense	5,000	
	Cash		5,000

Premium on the bonds is amortized by the following entry:

Dec. 31	Premium on Bonds Payable	600	
	Interest Expense		600

The debit of $5,000 to the expense account in the first entry is partially offset by the $600 credit to the expense account in the second entry, leaving a net interest expense of $4,400 for the year. At the time the bonds mature, the premium account will be completely written off.

Bonds sold at a discount. When the contract rate of interest on a bond issue is less than the prevailing market rate for comparable bonds, the bonds can be sold only at a discount. For example, assume that on January 1 a corporation issues 4%, 10-year bonds with a face value of $100,000. The prevailing rate of interest on similar securities being somewhat in excess of 4%, the bonds are sold at 96. The entry for the transaction, in general journal form, is:

Jan. 1	Cash	96,000	
	Discount on Bonds Payable	4,000	
	Bonds Payable		100,000

The bond discount is not an immediate loss or expense to the corporation. Rather, it represents a deferred charge to interest expense. The corporation has contracted to repay at maturity an amount greater than it received in cash. In return, however, it will pay interest at a lower rate than the prevailing one. The discount may be considered analogous to interest deducted in advance when a note is discounted.

The corporation contracts to pay: (1) $100,000, the face amount of the bonds, in 10 years, and (2) annual interest of $4,000 for 10 years. The total interest cost for the 10 years, as indicated in the tabulation below, will be $44,000, or $4,400 per year on a straight-line basis.

Cash to be paid:		
Face of the bonds	$100,000	
Interest—10 payments of $4,000 each (4% of $100,000)	40,000	$140,000
Cash received:		
Face of the bonds	$100,000	
Less discount on the bonds	4,000	96,000
Total interest expense for 10 years		$ 44,000
Interest expense per year		$ 4,400

The entry for the payment of the annual interest and the entry to amortize the discount, in general journal form, are:

Dec. 31	Interest Expense	4,000	
	Cash		4,000
31	Interest Expense	400	
	Discount on Bonds Payable		400

Over the life of the bonds the charges to the interest expense account will total $44,000, and the bond discount account will be in balance when the bonds fall due.

Another system of amortizing bond premium and discount, called the *compound-interest* method, yields a *uniform periodic rate* of interest on the carrying value of the bonds rather than an equal periodic amount of interest. *Carrying value* is the face value of the bonds plus the unamortized premium or minus the unamortized discount. The entries to record the periodic amortization by the compound-interest method are the same as those presented in the preceding illustrations, except that the amounts are different.

Extended illustration of accounting for bond premium

The two preceding illustrations were intentionally simplified in order to emphasize the basic principles. In both illustrations it was assumed that: (1) the bonds were sold on the issuance date, (2) the interest was payable annually, and (3) the interest payment date coincided with the last day of the fiscal year. In actual practice there is often interest accrued on the bonds at the time of sale, the interest is usually payable semi-annually, and neither of the interest payment dates may coincide with the end of the fiscal year. To illustrate the effect of these factors, assume that on April 1, 1965, 10-year, 6% bonds dated March 1, with a face value of $100,000, are sold to an insurance company for $105,950, plus accrued interest. The interest is payable on March 1 and September 1, and the corporation fiscal year ends on December 31. The entries, in general journal form, related to the bonds during the fiscal year in which they are issued, together with supporting data, are:

Sale of bonds

Premium on the bonds, $5,950. Interest accrued on $100,000 at 6% for one month (March 1 – April 1), $500.

Apr. 1	Cash	106,450	
	Bonds Payable		100,000
	Premium on Bonds Payable		5,950
	Interest Expense		500

Payment of semiannual interest

Interest for the six-month period March 1 to September 1, $3,000.

Sept. 1	Interest Expense	3,000	
	Cash		3,000

Adjusting entry for interest accrued at end of fiscal year

Interest accrued for the four-month period September 1 to December 31, $2,000.

Dec. 31	Interest Expense	2,000	
	Interest Payable		2,000

Amortization of bond premium at end of fiscal year

The bonds run 10 years or 120 months from March 1. They were not sold until April 1, however, so the corporation has the use of the borrowed funds for only 119 months. Time elapsed from April 1 to December 31 is 9 months. Therefore the amount of premium to be amortized is 9/119 × $5,950, or $450.

Dec. 31	Premium on Bonds Payable	450	
	Interest Expense		450

After the books are closed as of December 31, the entry accruing the bond interest should be reversed. The interest expense account for the year in which the bonds were issued and for the following fiscal year appears below. The entries for the remaining years will follow the

INTEREST EXPENSE

DATE		ITEMS	DEBIT	CREDIT	BALANCE DEBIT	BALANCE CREDIT
1965						
Apr.	1	Accrual, 1 mo.		500		500
Sept.	1	Cash payment, 6 mo.	3,000		2,500	
Dec.	31	Adjusting, 4 mo.	2,000		4,500	
	31	Premium amortization, 9 mo.		450	4,050	
	31	Closing, 9 mo.		4,050	——	——
1966						
Jan.	1	Reversing, 4 mo.		2,000		2,000
Mar.	1	Cash payment, 6 mo.	3,000		1,000	
Sept.	1	Cash payment, 6 mo.	3,000		4,000	
Dec.	31	Adjusting, 4 mo.	2,000		6,000	
	31	Premium amortization, 12 mo.		600	5,400	
	31	Closing, 12 mo.		5,400	——	——

pattern of the second year, except for the year in which the bonds are paid. It may be noted that the interest expense for the 9-month period, April 1 to December 31, is $4,050, which is three fourths of $5,400, the interest expense for the succeeding 12-month period.

Bond discount and bond premium on the balance sheet

The balance of the bond discount account is viewed as deferred interest that will be gradually added to interest expense over the life of the bonds. It is ordinarily reported in the balance sheet under the caption "Deferred expenses" or "Deferred charges," which is usually the last subheading of the asset section.

Premium on bonds is considered to be an advance of interest that is returned to bondholders as a part of the periodic interest payments. It is ordinarily reported in the balance sheet under the caption "Deferred credits," which is usually the last subheading of the liability section.

There is good theoretical justification for treating bond discount or premium as contra accounts related to the bonds payable account. For example, a $100,000 bond issue sold at 95 is reported, according to this view, as bonds payable of $100,000 less discount of $5,000, or a net liability of $95,000. As the discount is amortized, the net amount of the liability gradually increases until it reaches the face value of $100,000 at maturity. An objection to this approach is that the bond indenture agreement requires the payment of face value, and it is that amount for which the corporation is liable during the entire period that the bonds are outstanding.

Bond sinking fund

The bond indenture may provide that funds for the payment of bonds at maturity be accumulated over the life of the issue. The amounts set aside are kept separate from other assets in a special fund called a *sinking fund*. Cash deposited in the fund is ordinarily invested in income-producing securities. The periodic deposits plus the earnings on the investments should approximately equal the face amount of the bonds at maturity. Control over the fund may be exercised by the corporation or it may be in the hands of a *trustee*, which is usually a bank or trust company.

When cash is transferred to the sinking fund, an account called Sinking Fund Cash is debited and Cash is credited. The purchase of investments is recorded by a debit to Sinking Fund Investments and a credit to Sinking Fund Cash. As interest or dividends on the investments are received, the cash is debited to Sinking Fund Cash and Sinking Fund Income is credited.

To illustrate the accounting for a bond sinking fund, assume that the Arrow Corporation issues $100,000 of 10-year bonds dated January 1, with the provision that equal annual deposits be made in the bond sinking fund at the end of each of the 10 years. The fund is expected to be invested in securities that will yield approximately 3% per year. Reference to compound interest tables indicates that an annual deposit of approximately $8,725 is sufficient to provide a fund of $100,000 at the end of 10 years. Typical transactions and the related entries affecting a sinking fund are illustrated below in general journal form. It should be noted that they represent only a few of the numerous transactions that might occur during the 10-year period.

Deposit of cash in the fund

A deposit is made at the end of each of the 10 years.

Dec. 31	Sinking Fund Cash	8,725	
	Cash		8,725

Purchase of investments

The time of purchase and the amount invested at one time vary, depending upon market conditions and unit price of securities purchased.

Jan. 6	Sinking Fund Investments	8,700	
	Sinking Fund Cash		8,700

Receipt of income from investments

Interest and dividends are received at different times during the year. The amount earned per year increases as the fund increases. The entry below summarizes the receipt of income for the year on the securities purchased with the first deposit.

Dec. 31	Sinking Fund Cash	260	
	Sinking Fund Income		260

Sale of investments

Investments may be sold from time to time and the proceeds reinvested. Prior to maturity, all investments are converted into cash. The entry below records the sale of securities at the end of the tenth year.

Dec. 31	Sinking Fund Cash	88,900	
	Sinking Fund Investments		88,700
	Gain on Sale of Investments		200

Payment of bonds

The cash available in the fund at the end of the tenth year is assumed to have come from the following sources:

Proceeds from sales of investments (above)	$ 88,900
Income earned in tenth year	2,700
Last annual deposit	8,725
Total	$100,325

Dec. 31	Bonds Payable	100,000	
	Cash	325	
	Sinking Fund Cash		100,325

In the illustration on page 449 the amount of the fund exceeded the amount of the liability by $325. This excess was transferred to the regular cash account. If the fund had been less than the amount of the liability, for example $99,500, the regular cash account would have been drawn upon for the $500 deficiency.

Sinking Fund Income represents earnings of the corporation and is reported in the income statement as "Other Income." The cash and the securities comprising the sinking fund are classified in the balance sheet as "Investments." The investments section ordinarily appears immediately below the current assets section.

Restriction of dividends

The restriction of dividends during the life of a bond issue is another means of increasing the assurance that the obligation will be paid at maturity. Assuming that the Arrow Corporation in the preceding example is required by the indenture to appropriate $10,000 of retained earnings each year for the 10-year life of the bonds, the following entry would be made annually:

Dec. 31	Retained Earnings	10,000	
	Retained Earnings Appropriated for Bonded Indebtedness		10,000

As was indicated in the preceding chapter, an appropriation has no direct relationship to a sinking fund; each is independent of the other. When there is both a fund and an appropriation for the same purpose, the appropriation may be said to be *funded*.

Bond redemption

Callable bonds are redeemable by the issuing corporation within the period of time and at the price specified in the bond indenture. Ordinarily the call price is above face value. If the market rate of interest declines subsequent to issuance of the bonds, the corporation may sell new bonds at a lower interest rate and use the funds to redeem the original issue. The reduction of future interest expense is, of course, always an incentive to bond redemption. A corporation may also retire all or a portion of its bonds before maturity by purchasing them on the open market. Such action is particularly advisable if the bonds are selling at less than their carrying value, assuming that the corporation has available cash.

When a corporation retires bonds at a price below their carrying value, the corporation realizes a gain; if the price is in excess of carrying value, a loss is incurred. To illustrate redemption and retirement, assume that on June 30 the Barton Corporation has a bond issue of $100,000 outstanding, on which there is an unamortized premium of $4,000. The corporation has the option of calling the bonds at 105, which it exercises on this date. The entry to record the redemption, in general journal form, is:

June 30	Bonds Payable	100,000	
	Premium on Bonds Payable	4,000	
	Loss on Redemption of Bonds	1,000	
	Cash		105,000

If the bonds were not callable, the corporation might purchase a portion on the open market and retire them. Assuming that the corporation did buy $25,000 of bonds at 96 on June 30, the entry to record the retirement would be as follows, in general journal form:

June 30	Bonds Payable	25,000	
	Premium on Bonds Payable	1,000	
	Cash		24,000
	Gain on Retirement of Bonds		2,000

It should be noted that only the portion of the premium relating to the bonds retired is written off the books. The excess of the carrying value of the liability, $26,000, over the cash paid, $24,000, is recognized as a gain.

Investments in stocks and bonds

The issuance of stocks and bonds, the declaration and the payment of dividends, and other related transactions have thus far been discussed from the standpoint of the issuing corporation. Whenever a corporation records a transaction between itself and the owners of its stock or bonds, there is a reciprocal entry on the books of the investor. Investments in corporate securities may be made by individuals, partnerships, industrial corporations, financial corporations such as banks and life insurance companies, and other types of organizations. In this and the following sections of the chapter, attention will be given to some of the principles underlying the accounting for investments in stocks and bonds.

Corporate securities may be purchased directly from the issuing corporation or from other investors. Stocks and bonds may be *listed* on an organized exchange, or they may be *unlisted*, in which case they are said to be bought and sold *over the counter*. The services of a broker are usually employed in buying and selling both listed and unlisted securities. The record of transactions on stock exchanges is reported daily in the financial pages of newspapers. This record usually includes data on the volume of sales and the high, low, and closing prices for each security traded during the day. Prices for stocks are quoted in terms of fractional dollars, $^{1}/_{8}$ of a dollar being the usual minimum fraction. Some low-priced stocks are sold in lower fractions of a dollar, such as $^{1}/_{16}$ or $^{1}/_{32}$. A price of $40^{3}/_{8}$ per share means $40.375; a price of $40^{1}/_{2}$ means $40.50; and so on. As indicated earlier, prices for bonds are quoted as a percentage of face value; thus the price of a $1,000 bond quoted at $104^{1}/_{2}$ would be $1,045.

The cost of securities purchased includes not only the price paid but also other costs incident to the purchase, such as broker's commission and postage charges for delivery. When bonds are purchased between interest dates, the purchaser pays the seller the interest accrued from the last interest payment date to the date of purchase. The amount of the interest paid should be debited to Interest Income, as it is an offset against the amount that will be received at the next interest date. To illustrate, assume that a $1,000 bond is purchased at 102 plus brokerage fees of $5.30 and accrued interest of $10.20. The entry to record the transaction, in general journal form, is as follows:

April 2	Investment in Taylor Co. Bonds.	1,025.30	
	Interest Income.	10.20	
	Cash.		1,035.50

When stocks are purchased between dividend dates, there is no separate charge for the pro rata amount of the dividend. Dividends do not accrue from day to day, since they become an obligation of the issuing corporation only as they are declared by the directors. The price of stocks may be affected by the anticipated dividend as the usual declaration date approaches, but this anticipated dividend is only one of many factors that influence stock prices.

Temporary investments

A corporation may have on hand an amount of cash considerably in excess of its immediate requirements, but it may believe that this cash will be needed in operating the business, possibly within the coming year. Rather than allow this excess cash to lie idle until it is actually needed, the corporation may invest all or a portion of it in income-yielding securities. Such securities are known as *temporary investments* or *marketable securities.* These investments may actually be held by the corporation for several years, but they are still considered to be temporary if (1) they can be turned into cash readily at any time and (2) management intends to make them available for sale when the business needs additional cash in its normal operations.

Securities representing a temporary investment are classified in the balance sheet as current assets and are shown immediately below cash. They are usually valued at cost or at the lower of cost or market. If they are carried at cost, their market value at the balance sheet date may be disclosed by a footnote or a parenthetical statement.

Although temporary investments are often carried in the accounts at the lower of cost or market, minor declines in this market value need not be given recognition in the accounts. If their market value declines substantially below cost and there is evidence that the fluctuation is not temporary, the securities should be stated at market value. The reduction in value is treated as a loss of the period. If the same securities are still owned at subsequent balance sheet dates, adjustments are made only for the later declines in market price. If their market price has increased, the current market value should be disclosed parenthetically on the balance sheet.

Declines in the market value of securities are not recognized as losses for income tax purposes regardless of whether they are recorded in the accounts. When the securities are sold, the gain or the loss to be recognized for tax purposes is determined by comparing the proceeds from the sale with the original cost.

Long-term investments

Investments that are not intended as a ready source of cash in the normal operations of the business are known as *long-term investments*. A business may make long-term investments simply because it has cash that it cannot use in its normal operations; but a corporation is more likely to make long-term investments for other reasons.

It is not unusual for a corporation to purchase stocks or bonds as a means of establishing or maintaining business relations with the issuing company. Such investments are ordinarily held for an indefinitely long period and are not sold so long as the relationship remains satisfactory. Corporations may also acquire all or a substantial portion of the voting stock of another corporation in order to control its activities. Similarly, a corporation may organize a new corporation for the purpose of marketing a new product or for some other business reason, receiving stock in exchange for the assets transferred to the new corporation. Cash and securities in bond sinking funds are also considered long-term investments, as they are accumulated for the purpose of paying the bond liability.

Investments in long-term securities are recorded in the accounts at cost and are so shown on the balance sheet. Fluctuations in price subsequent to acquisition are ordinarily ignored except when there has been a permanent and material decline, in which case the recorded amount may be reduced or the facts may be disclosed by a parenthetical notation on the balance sheet. Long-term investments are listed in the balance sheet under the caption "Investments."

Income from investments in stocks

Cash dividends declared on stock owned either as temporary investments or as long-term investments may be recorded by a debit to Dividends Receivable and a credit to Dividend Income. The receivable account is then credited when the cash is received. For federal income tax purposes, however, dividends are not considered to be income until the cash is made available to the stockholder. For this reason a common practice is to ignore the receivable and to record the income when the cash is received. Although this is a deviation from accrual accounting, the practice ordinarily causes no material distortion of income when followed consistently.

A dividend in the form of additional shares of stock is ordinarily not income and hence no entry is necessary beyond a notation as to the additional number of shares now owned. The receipt of such a stock dividend does, however, affect the cost basis of each share of stock. For example, if a 25-share common stock dividend is received on 100 shares of common stock originally purchased for $4,500 ($45 per share), the unit cost basis of the 125 shares becomes $4,500 ÷ 125, or $36 per share.

Income from investments in bonds

Interest on bonds held as temporary investments is recorded in the same manner as interest on notes receivable. Interest received during a fiscal period is recorded as a debit to Cash and a credit to Interest Income. At the end of a fiscal period, an adjusting entry debiting Interest Receivable and crediting Interest Income is made for interest accrued. After the books are closed, the entry is reversed in order that all receipts of bond interest during the year may be credited to the interest income account.

When interest is recorded on temporary bond investments, the fact that these investments may have been purchased for more or less than their face value is ignored. But when the cost of bonds purchased for long-term investments is greater or less than the face value, the amount of the premium or the discount should be written off over the remaining life of the bonds in much the same manner in which the debtor corporation accounts for a premium or a discount on the original issuance of the bonds. To illustrate, assume that twenty $1,000, 5% bonds of the

Standard Corporation are purchased on July 1, 1965, at 105½ plus a brokerage fee of $55. Interest on the bonds is payable semiannually on April 1 and October 1 and the bonds are due 8¾ years from the date of purchase. Entries on the books of the purchaser at the time of purchase and for the remainder of the year would be as follows:

Transaction		Entry		
JULY 1, 1965:		Investment in Standard		
Purchase of bonds:		Corp. Bonds..........	21,155	
$20,000 face value at 105½...	$21,100	Interest Income......	250	
Brokerage...............	55	Cash.....................		21,405
Total cost..................	$21,155			
Accrued interest, $20,000 at 5% for 3 months, or $250.				
OCTOBER 1, 1965:		Cash................	500	
Receipt of semiannual interest; $20,000 at 5% for 6 months, or $500.		Interest Income.....		500
DECEMBER 31, 1965:				
(a) Interest accrued: $20,000 at 5% for 3 months, or $250.		Interest Receivable....	250	
		Interest Income.....		250
(b) Amortization of premium: $1,155 over 8¾ years, or $66 for 6 months.		Interest Income.......	66	
		Investment in Standard Corp. Bonds.....		66

The net effect of the four entries in the interest income account is a credit of $434, which represents interest at 5% for 6 months ($500) less amortization of premium for 6 months ($66). By following the foregoing procedures, the premium of $1,155 will be amortized against interest income over the life of the bonds, and the investment account will be reduced to $20,000 at the maturity date.

A similar procedure may be applied to bonds purchased at a price below face value. The amount of the discount is accumulated by periodic entries debiting the investment account and crediting Interest Income. It may be noted that when speculative bonds are purchased at a substantial discount, it would be imprudent to accumulate the discount because of the uncertainty of payment at maturity.

Sale of investments

When shares of stock that have been held as either temporary or long-term investments are sold, the cash account is debited for the proceeds (selling price less commission and other costs) and the investment account is credited for the cost of the shares sold. If there is a gain, it is credited to an account entitled Gain on Sale of Investments; if there is a loss, it is debited to an account entitled Loss on Sale of Investments.

A sale of bonds held as temporary investments is recorded in the same manner as a sale of stocks. A sale of bonds held as a long-term investment is also recorded in the same manner except when a premium or a discount has been amortized. If a premium or a discount has been amortized, the investment account is credited for the book value of the investment and not its original cost. The gain or the loss is then the difference between the book value and the amount received. For example, assume that the bonds of the Standard Corporation in the previous example are sold at 98 plus accrued interest on December 31, 1967. The entries, in general journal form, would be as follows:

Amortization of premium for year

Dec. 31	Interest Income	132	
	Investment in Standard Corp. Bonds		132

Sale of bonds and collection of accrued interest

Dec. 31	Cash	19,850	
	Loss on Sale of Investments	1,225	
	Interest Income		250
	Investment in Standard Corp. Bonds		20,825

In the foregoing entry the investment account was credited for the book value of the bonds sold, which was determined as follows:

Cost of bonds, July 1, 1965		$21,155
Deduct premium amortization: 1965	$ 66	
1966	132	
1967	132	330
Book value, December 31, 1967		$20,825

Corporation balance sheet

Several examples of the stockholders' equity section of corporation balance sheets have been presented in preceding chapters. An example of a complete balance sheet, illustrating other items peculiar to corporations, is presented on page 457.

There are innumerable variations in the form of corporation financial statements, as well as many alternatives in the terminology employed. A selection of statements taken from the annual reports of a number of corporations is presented in Appendix C.

Fieldcrest Corporation
Balance Sheet
December 31, 1965

Assets				
Current assets:				
Cash			$111,379	
Marketable securities, at cost (market price, $78,000)			70,000	
Accounts and notes receivable		$112,000		
Less allowance for doubtful accounts		2,000	110,000	
Inventories, at lower of cost or market			172,880	
Prepaid expenses			12,000	
Total current assets				$ 476,259
Investments:				
Bond sinking fund			$ 53,962	
Investment in affiliated company			140,000	
Total investments				193,962
	Cost	Accumulated Depreciation	Book Value	
Plant assets:				
Machinery and equipment	$600,000	$ 66,200	$533,800	
Buildings	220,000	79,955	140,045	
Land	50,000	—	50,000	
Total plant assets	$870,000	$146,155		723,845
Intangible assets:				
Goodwill			$100,000	
Organization costs			18,000	
Total intangible assets				118,000
Total assets				$1,512,066
Liabilities				
Current liabilities:				
Accounts payable			$ 58,710	
Income tax payable			90,500	
Dividends payable			18,000	
Accrued liabilities			7,400	
Total current liabilities				$ 174,610
Long-term liabilities:				
Debenture 5% bonds payable, due December 31, 1973				200,000
Deferred credit:				
Premium on bonds payable				5,600
Total liabilities				$ 380,210
Stockholders' equity				
Paid-in capital:				
Common stock, $20 par (50,000 shares authorized, 20,000 shares issued)		$400,000		
Premium on common stock		320,000		
Total paid-in capital			$720,000	
Retained earnings:				
Appropriated:				
For bonded indebtedness	$ 60,000			
For plant expansion	150,000	$210,000		
Unappropriated		201,856		
Total retained earnings			411,856	
Total stockholders' equity				1,131,856
Total liabilities and stockholders' equity				$1,512,066

Balance sheet for a corporation

QUESTIONS

1. Compare bonds with stocks as an investment in terms of potential amount of income and safety of principal.

2. Contrast the status of interest on bonds payable and cash dividends on stock in determining the income tax of corporations making such payments.

3. How are interest payments made to holders of (a) registered bonds and (b) bearer or coupon bonds?

4. Differentiate between term bonds and serial bonds.

5. Under what circumstances would Bonds Payable be reported in the balance sheet as a current liability?

6. If a corporation issues 5% bonds at a time when the market rate of interest on securities of this type is higher than 5%, is it likely that the bonds will be sold at face value, at a discount, or at a premium?

7. Under what caption would each of the following accounts be reported on the balance sheet: (a) Discount on Bonds Payable; (b) Premium on Bonds Payable; (c) Sinking Fund Investments; (d) Sinking Fund Cash; (e) Retained Earnings Appropriated for Bonded Indebtedness?

8. What is the purpose of a bond sinking fund?

9. What is the purpose of establishing an appropriation of retained earnings for bonded indebtedness?

10. What is the cost of the following securities, exclusive of commissions, etc.: (a) bonds with a face value of $10,000 purchased at 98½; (b) 100 shares of $50 par stock purchased at 90¾?

11. Is the interest accrued on bonds included in the quoted price?

12. Murray Corporation purchased $10,000 of Royse Company bonds at 102 plus accrued interest of $150. Brokerage commissions were $40. For what amount should the investment account be debited?

13. Are brokerage commissions on the sale of securities owned considered to be an expense of the period or a reduction in the sales proceeds?

14. A stockholder owning 100 shares of Hubbs Co. common stock acquired at a total cost of $4,400 receives a common stock dividend of 10 shares. (a) What is the unit cost basis of the 110 shares? (b) If the stockholder later sells 20 shares at 50, what is the gain or the loss?

EXERCISES

1. Two companies are financed as follows:

	Company X	Company Y
Bonds Payable, 5% (issued at face value).....	$ 200,000	$500,000
Preferred 6% Stock......................	300,000	500,000
Common Stock, $20 par..................	1,000,000	500,000

Income taxes are estimated at 50% of net income. Determine for each company the earnings per share of common stock, assuming the net income before bond interest and income taxes for each company to be (a) $85,000, (b) $125,000, and (c) $245,000.

2. The Freemont Corporation issued $100,000 of 10-year, 4% bonds at 95 on the first day of the fiscal year. On the same day, also the first day of its fiscal year, Melrose, Inc. issued $100,000 of 10-year, 5% bonds at 105.

(a) Present the entries, in general journal form, for the Freemont Corporation to record:
  (1) The sale of the bonds (the bonds were sold on the date of issue).
  (2) The payment of one year's interest at the end of the first fiscal year.
  (3) The amortization of the premium or the discount at the end of the first fiscal year.

(b) Present the entries for Melrose, Inc. to record the three transactions stated in (a).

(c) Determine the amount of the bond interest expense for the year for each company.

(d) What is the approximate effective rate of interest for such bonds?

3. The Walter Corporation issued $1,000,000 of 20-year bonds on the first day of the fiscal year. The bond indenture provides that a sinking fund be accumulated by 20 annual deposits, beginning at the end of the first year. The corporation expects to earn 5% on the fund and accordingly deposits $32,000 annually.

(a) Give the entry in general journal form to record the first deposit.

(b) Give the entry in general journal form to record the investment of the entire first deposit in securities.

(c) Assuming that the fund earns exactly 5%, give the summary entry in general journal form to record receipt of the income for the year following the first deposit.

4. The bond indenture for the Walter Corporation bonds (Exercise 3) also provides that dividends be restricted by equal annual appropriations of retained earnings, which are to total the face value of the bonds at maturity. Give the entry to record the appropriation at the end of the first year.

5. The Mayfair Corporation issued $2,000,000 of 20-year, 5% bonds dated April 1, 1965. Interest is payable semiannually on April 1 and October 1. Present in general journal form (a) all entries related to the bonds in 1965, assuming that the issue was sold on July 1 for $2,047,400 plus accrued interest to an underwriter (a firm employed to market the bond issue); (b) the reversing entry to be made on January 1, 1966, the first day of the fiscal year; and (c) the entry to be made on April 1, 1966, for the payment of interest.

6. Assuming that on April 1, 1968, the Mayfair Corporation (Exercise 5) purchases $200,000 of its outstanding bonds at 101 and retires them, give in general journal form the entries to record (a) the amortization of bond premium for the current year applicable to the bonds retired and (b) the purchase.

7. On May 5, Murphy Corporation acquired 100 shares of Allied Steel Co. common stock at 74¾ plus brokerage commission and postage charges of $27. On September 15, a cash dividend of $50 and a 10% stock dividend were received. On November 10, 50 shares were sold for 79 less brokerage commission and postage charges of $15. Present entries in general journal form to record (a) purchase of the stock, (b) receipt of the dividends, and (c) sale of the 50 shares.

8. The Bruin Corporation purchases $100,000 of 4% bonds of the Holliday Corporation at 96. The bonds are due 10 years from the date of purchase.

(a) Assuming that the bonds are classified as temporary investments, determine (1) the amount of the annual income, (2) the gain or the loss when the bonds are sold at 98½ exactly 3 years from the date purchased (no interest accrued), and (3) the total income from the bonds for the entire period held, including gain or loss on sale. (b) Assuming that the bonds are classified as long-term investments and the discount is amortized, make the three determinations required in (a).

PROBLEMS

19-1. The following transactions were completed by the Conrad Company:

1965
Mar. 31. Issued $1,000,000 of 20-year, 4½% bonds at 105. Interest is payable semiannually on March 31 and September 30.
Sept. 30. Paid the semiannual interest on the bonds.
Dec. 31. Recorded the adjusting entry for interest payable.
31. Recorded amortization of premium on bonds.
31. Closed the interest expense account.

1966
Jan. 1. Reversed the adjusting entry for interest payable.
Mar. 31. Paid the semiannual interest on the bonds.
Sept. 30. Paid the semiannual interest on the bonds.
Dec. 31. Recorded the adjusting entry for interest payable.
31. Recorded amortization of premium on bonds.
31. Closed the interest expense account.

Instructions: (1) Record the foregoing transactions in general journal form.
(2) State the amount of the interest expense in (a) 1965 and (b) 1966.
(3) What is the effective rate of interest expressed as a percentage of face value of the bonds?

19-2. During 1965 and 1966 Waldorf Industries, Inc. completed the following transactions relating to its $6,000,000 issue of 25-year, 5% bonds dated May 31, 1965. Interest is payable on May 31 and November 30. The corporation's fiscal year is the calendar year.

1965
July 15. Sold the bond issue for $5,880,600 plus accrued interest.
Nov. 30. Paid the semiannual interest on the bonds.
Dec. 31. Deposited $60,500 in a bond sinking fund.
31. Appropriated $110,000 of retained earnings for bonded indebtedness.
31. Recorded the adjusting entry for interest payable.
31. Recorded amortization of bond discount.
31. Closed the interest expense account.

1966
Jan. 1. Reversed the adjustment for interest payable.
10. Purchased various securities with sinking fund cash at a cost of $59,750.
May 31. Paid the semiannual interest on the bonds.
Nov. 30. Paid the semiannual interest on the bonds.
Dec. 31. Recorded the receipt of $2,220 of income on sinking fund securities, depositing the cash in the sinking fund.
31. Deposited $132,000 cash in the sinking fund.

Dec. 31. Appropriated $240,000 of retained earnings for bonded indebtedness.
31. Recorded the adjusting entry for interest payable.
31. Recorded amortization of bond discount.
31. Closed the interest expense account.

Instructions: (1) Record the foregoing transactions in general journal form.
(2) Prepare a columnar table, using the headings shown below, and present the information for each of the two years.

			Account Balances at End of Year				
					Sinking Fund		
Year	Bond Interest Expense for Year	Sinking Fund Income for Year	Bonds Payable	Discount on Bonds	Cash	Investments	Appropriation for B.I.

19-3. The following transactions relate to certain securities acquired by the Rochester Corporation:

1962
Apr. 1. Purchased $200,000 of Atlas Corporation 10-year, 6% coupon bonds dated February 1, 1962, directly from the issuing company for $205,900 plus accrued interest. Atlas is an important customer of the Rochester Corporation and it is expected that the bonds will be held as a long-term investment.
June 10. Purchased as a long-term investment 1,200 common shares of Waters, Inc. at 19½ plus commission and other costs of $360.
July 15. Received a semiannual dividend of $.60 per share on the Waters, Inc. stock.
Aug. 1. Deposited the coupons for semiannual interest on the Atlas Corporation bonds.
Dec. 31. Recorded the adjustment for interest receivable on the Atlas Corporation bonds.
31. Recorded the amortization of premium on the Atlas Corporation bonds.

(Assume that all intervening transactions and adjustments have been recorded properly, and that the amount of bonds and shares of stocks have not changed from December 31, 1962, to December 31, 1965.)

1966
Jan. 1. Reversed the adjustment for interest receivable.
Jan. 15. Received a semiannual dividend of $.60 per share and a 10% stock dividend on the Waters, Inc. stock.
Feb. 1. Deposited coupons for semiannual interest on the Atlas Corporation bonds.
July 1. Sold the Atlas Corporation bonds at 103½ plus accrued interest. The broker deducted $450 for commission and taxes, remitting the balance. The amortization of the premium for the year to date was also recorded.
July 15. Received the semiannual dividend of $.60 per share on the Waters, Inc. stock.
Nov. 1. Sold 200 shares of Waters, Inc. stock at 21. The broker deducted commission and other costs of $35, remitting the balance.

Instructions: Record the foregoing transactions in general journal form.

19-4. The rough draft of the balance sheet for the Sandwell Company as of June 30 of the current year, appearing below, is presented to you for review.

Sandwell Company
Balance Sheet
June 30, 19—

Assets			
Current assets:			
Cash		$172,500	
Marketable securities		95,000	
Treasury stock	$ 30,000		
Deduct reserve for treasury stock purchased	30,000	—	
Accounts receivable	$145,000		
Deduct accounts payable	90,000	55,000	
Inventories	$465,000		
Deduct reserve for possible price declines	60,000	405,000	
Discount on bonds payable		10,000	
Prepaid expenses		6,000	
Total current assets			$ 743,500
Plant assets:			
Machinery		$520,000	
Buildings	$350,000		
Deduct reserve for plant expansion	100,000	250,000	
Land		75,000	
Goodwill		50,000	
Investment in affiliated company		120,000	
Total plant assets			1,015,000
Total assets			$1,758,500
Liabilities			
Dividends payable		$ 48,000	
Accrued liabilities		18,000	
Bonds payable	$500,000		
Deduct bond sinking fund	156,000	344,000	
Total liabilities			$ 410,000
Stockholders' equity			
Paid-in capital:			
Common stock		$500,000	
Earnings and reserves:			
Premium on common stock	$ 90,000		
Reserve for doubtful accounts	15,000		
Reserve for depreciation — machinery	210,000		
Reserve for depreciation — buildings	170,000		
Reserve for income taxes	85,000		
Retained earnings	278,500	848,500	
Total stockholders' equity			1,348,500
Total liabilities and stockholders' equity			$1,758,500

During the course of your review and examination of the accounts and records, you assemble the following pertinent data:

(a) Marketable securities are stated at cost; the market price is $99,000.
(b) Treasury stock is composed of 600 shares purchased at $50 a share.
(c) Accounts receivable, machinery, buildings, land, goodwill, and investment in affiliated company are stated at cost. Provisions for doubtful accounts and depreciation have been recorded correctly in the usual manner.
(d) Inventories are stated at the lower of cost or market.
(e) Bonds payable (20-year) are due 12 years from the balance sheet date. They are secured by a first mortgage and bear 5% interest.
(f) The common stock is $20 par; 50,000 shares are authorized, 25,000 shares have been issued.
(g) The reserve for income taxes is the estimated liability for taxes on income of the current fiscal year ended June 30.

Instructions: Present a revised balance sheet in good order. Titles of items should be changed where appropriate.

19-5. The board of directors of Lynch Corporation is planning an expansion of plant facilities expected to cost $1,000,000. The board is undecided about the method of financing this expansion and has two plans under consideration:

Plan 1. Issue an additional 20,000 shares of no-par common stock at $50 per share.
Plan 2. Issue $1,000,000 of 20-year, 4% bonds at face value.

The condensed balance sheet of the Lynch Corporation at the end of the current fiscal year is presented below.

Lynch Corporation
Balance Sheet
December 31, 19—

Assets		Liabilities and Capital	
Current assets	$ 570,000	Current liabilities	$ 390,000
Plant assets	2,430,000	Common stock (40,000 shares issued)	2,100,000
		Retained earnings	510,000
Total assets	$3,000,000	Total liabilities and capital	$3,000,000

Net income has remained relatively constant over the past several years. The expansion program is expected to increase yearly net income before taxes (and before bond interest) from $280,000 to $420,000. Assume a tax rate of 50%.

Instructions: (1) Prepare a tabulation showing the expected earnings per share on common stock under each plan.

(2) List factors other than earnings per share that the board should consider in evaluating the two plans.

(3) Which plan offers the greater benefit to the present stockholders? Give reasons for your opinion.

19-6. The Milway Corporation issued $2,000,000 of 6% debenture bonds on March 1, 1965, at 98½. Interest is payable on March 1 and September 1. The bonds mature on March 1, 1975, but they may be called at 102 on any interest date after 4 years from the date of issue. The company's fiscal year ends on December 31. The following transactions and adjustments were selected from those relating to the bonds over the 10-year period.

1965
Mar. 1. Issued the bonds for cash.
Sept. 1. Paid semiannual interest.
Dec. 31. Recorded accrual of the interest.
31. Recorded amortization of the discount.
31. Closed the interest expense account.

1966
Jan. 1. Reversed the adjusting entry for accrued interest.
Mar. 1. Paid semiannual interest.
July 1. Recorded amortization of discount for the year related to bonds purchased. (See next transaction.)
1. Purchased $400,000 of bonds on the open market at 99 plus accrued interest and retired them.
Sept. 1. Paid semiannual interest.
Dec. 31. Recorded accrual of the interest.
31. Recorded amortization of the discount.
31. Closed the interest expense account.

(Assume that all intervening transactions and adjustments have been recorded properly, and that the number of bonds outstanding has not changed from January, 1967, to December, 1969.)

1970
Jan. 1. Reversed the December 31, 1969, adjusting entry for accrued interest.
Mar. 1. Paid semiannual interest.
1. Recorded amortization of discount for the year related to bonds called. (See next transaction.)
1. Called and retired $800,000 of the bonds.
Sept. 1. Paid semiannual interest.
Dec. 31. Recorded accrual of the interest.
Dec. 31. Recorded amortization of the discount.
31. Closed the interest expense account.

(Assume that all intervening transactions and adjustments have been recorded properly, and that the number of bonds outstanding has not changed from January, 1971, to December, 1974.)

1975
Jan. 1. Reversed the December 31, 1974, adjusting entry for accrued interest.
Mar. 1. Paid semiannual interest.
1. Recorded amortization of the discount.
1. Paid the bonds at maturity.
Dec. 31. Closed the interest expense account.

Instructions: Record the foregoing transactions in general journal form. (It is suggested that memorandum T accounts for Interest Expense, Discount on Bonds Payable, and Bonds Payable be maintained.)

PART EIGHT

Control accounting

20. Departments and branches

Accounting for departmental operations

Management of an enterprise that sells two or more distinct classes of services or commodities or that is divided into departments needs accounting reports to evaluate the various segments of the business. Such reports are needed by management not only to evaluate past operations of each department but also to control costs and to plan future operations. Departmental accounting is useful to service, merchandising, and manufacturing concerns. Although this chapter deals with merchandising businesses, the fundamental considerations are not affected by the type of operations.

Departmental accounting is more likely to be used by a large business than by a small one. Some degree of departmentalization may be employed by a small enterprise, however. For example, the owner of a one-man real estate and property insurance agency could account separately for real estate commissions and for insurance commissions. Analysis of the division of his time between the two activities and of his revenue and expenses by type of activity may indicate the desirability of devoting more time to one department and less to the other.

Departmental accounting for a large enterprise is likely to be both feasible and desirable. In a modern department store, for example, there are a number of distinct departments, each under the control of a departmental manager. A departmental breakdown for accounting and reporting helps place responsibility for the control of a department's operations upon departmental managers. It assists top management both in evaluating the relative operating efficiencies of individual departments and in planning future operations.

Accounting reports for departmental operations

Accounting reports for departmental operations are generally limited to income statements. Ordinarily they are of concern only to management and are not issued to stockholders or other outsiders. The degree to which departmental accounting may be adopted for a merchandising enterprise, therefore, varies with the desires of management. Analysis of operations by departments may end with the determination of gross profit on sales or it may extend through the determination of net income. An income statement that includes a departmental breakdown of revenue and expenses categorized by responsibility for the incurrence of costs has been widely used in recent years. The most common departmental income statements are described in the paragraphs that follow.

Gross profit by departments

For a merchandising enterprise, the gross profit on sales is one of the most significant figures in the income statement. Management directs its efforts toward obtaining a mix of sales that will maximize profits. Since the sales and the cost of merchandise sold are both, to a large extent, controlled by departmental management, the reporting of gross profit by departments is useful in cost analysis and control. By studying such reports, management may decide to change sales or purchases policies, curtail or expand operations, or shift personnel to achieve a higher gross profit for each department. Caution must be exercised in the use of such reports to insure that proposed changes affecting gross profit do not have an adverse effect on net income. For example, a change that increases gross profit but results in an even greater increase in operating expenses would decrease net income.

In order to determine gross profit on sales by departments, it is necessary to determine by departments each element entering into gross profit. There are two basic methods of doing this: (1) setting up departmental accounts and identifying each element by department at the time of the transaction, or (2) maintaining only one account for the element and then allocating it among the departments at the time the income statement is prepared. Ordinarily, the first method is used unless the time required in analyzing each transaction is too great. Allocation among departments at the end of a period is likely to yield less accurate results than the first method, but some degree of accuracy may be sacrificed to obtain a commensurate saving of time and expense.

The elements that must be departmentalized in order to determine gross profit by departments are merchandise inventory, purchases, sales, and the related cash discounts and returns and allowances. Depart-

York Company
Income Statement
For Year Ended December 31, 1965

	Department A			Department B			Total		
Revenue from sales:									
Sales		$280,000			$120,000			$400,000	
Less sales returns and allowances		7,600			3,100			10,700	
Net sales			$272,400			$116,900			$389,300
Cost of merchandise sold:									
Merchandise inventory, January 1, 1965		$ 40,300			$ 30,700			$ 71,000	
Purchases	$152,900			$ 87,300			$240,200		
Less purchases discount	2,800	150,100		1,300	86,000		4,100	236,100	
Merchandise available for sale		$190,400			$116,700			$307,100	
Less merchandise inventory, December 31, 1965		41,900			39,100			81,000	
Cost of merchandise sold			148,500			77,600			226,100
Gross profit on sales			$123,900			$ 39,300			$163,200
Operating expenses:									
Selling expenses								$ 54,700	
General expenses								53,900	
Total operating expenses									108,600
Net income from operations									$ 54,600
Other expense:									
Interest expense									1,200
Net income before income tax									$ 53,400
Income tax									19,132
Net income after income tax									$ 34,268

Income statement departmentalized through gross profit

mental accounts may be maintained for each element so that the entries may be classified by department at the time the transactions are recorded. This can be accomplished by providing special departmental columns in the appropriate journals. For example, in a furniture store that sells furniture and floor coverings, the sales journal may have a credit column for Furniture Sales and a credit column for Rug Sales. To facilitate the journalizing of departmental transactions, the supporting documents such as sales invoices, vouchers, and cash register readings must identify the department affected by each transaction. Postings to departmental accounts from the special journals follow the procedures described in earlier chapters.

An income statement showing gross profit by departments for the York Company, which has two sales departments, appears on page 467. For illustrative purposes, the operating expenses are shown in condensed form; ordinarily they would be listed in detail.

Net income by departments

Departmental reporting of income may be extended to various points, such as gross profit less selling expenses (gross selling profit), gross profit less all operating expenses (net operating income), net income before income tax, or net income after income tax. The underlying principle is the same for all degrees of departmentalization, namely, to assign to each department the portion of expense incurred for its benefit.

Some expenses may be easily identified with the department benefited. For example, if each salesperson is restricted to a particular sales department, the sales salaries may be assigned to the appropriate departmental salary accounts each time the payroll is prepared. On the other hand, the salaries of company officers, executives, and office personnel are not identifiable with a specific sales department and must therefore be allocated to the various sales departments on some equitable basis.

Many accountants prefer to apportion all expenses to departments only at the end of the accounting period. When this is done, there is no need for departmental expense accounts in the general ledger and fewer postings are required. The apportionments may be made on a work sheet, which serves as the basis for preparing the departmental income statement.

Apportionment of operating expenses

As was indicated in the preceding section, some operating expenses are directly identifiable with particular departments and some are not. When operating expenses are allocated, they should be apportioned to the respective departments as nearly as possible in accordance with the cost of services rendered to the departments. Determining the amount of an expense chargeable to each department is not always a simple matter. In the first place, it requires the exercise of judgment; and accountants of equal ability may well differ in their opinions as to the proper basis for apportionment. Second, the cost of collecting data for use in making an apportionment must be kept within reasonable bounds; consequently information that is readily available may be used even though it is not entirely satisfactory.

To illustrate the apportionment of operating expenses, assume that the York Company extends its departmentalization through net income from operations. The company's operating expenses for the calendar year and the methods used in apportioning them are presented in the paragraphs that follow.

Sales Salaries is apportioned to the two departments in accordance with the distributions shown in the payroll records. Of the $42,000 total in the account, $27,000 is chargeable to Department A and $15,000 is chargeable to Department B.

Advertising Expense, covering billboard advertising and newspaper advertising, is apportioned according to the amount of advertising incurred for each department. The billboard advertising totaling $2,000 emphasizes the name and the location of the company. This expense is allocated on the basis of sales, the assumption being that this basis represents a fair allocation of billboard advertising to each department. Analysis of the newspaper space costing $7,000 indicates that 65% of the space was devoted to Department A and 35% to Department B. The apportionment of the total advertising expense is indicated in the tabulation below.

	Total		Department A		Department B	
Sales — dollars	$400,000		$280,000		$120,000	
Sales — percent	100%		70%		30%	
Billboard advertising		$2,000		$1,400		$ 600
Newspaper space—percent	100%		65%		35%	
Newspaper advertising		7,000		4,550		2,450
Advertising expense		$9,000		$5,950		$3,050

Depreciation of Store Equipment is apportioned in accordance with the average cost of the equipment in each of the two departments. The computations for the apportionment of the depreciation expense are given on the following page.

	TOTAL	DEPARTMENT A	DEPARTMENT B
Cost of store equipment:			
January 1	$13,600	$ 8,800	$ 4,800
December 31	14,400	8,000	6,400
Total	$28,000	$16,800	$11,200
Average	$14,000	$ 8,400	$ 5,600
Percent	100%	60%	40%
Depreciation expense	$ 1,650	$ 990	$ 660

Officers' Salaries and *Office Salaries* are apportioned on the basis of the relative amount of time devoted to each department by the officers and by the office personnel. Obviously, this can be only an approximation. The number of sales transactions may have some bearing on the matter, as may billing and collection procedures and other factors such as promotional campaigns that might vary from period to period. Of the total officers' salaries of $26,000 and office salaries of $9,000, it is estimated that 60%, or $15,600 and $5,400 respectively, is chargeable to Department A and that 40%, or $10,400 and $3,600 respectively, is chargeable to Department B.

Rent Expense and *Heating and Lighting Expense* are usually apportioned on the basis of the floor space devoted to each department. In apportioning rent expense for a multistory building, differences in the value of the various floors and locations may be taken into account. For example, the space near the main entrance of a department store is more valuable than the same amount of floor space located far from the elevator on the sixth floor. For York Company, rent expense is apportioned on the basis of floor space used because there is no significant difference in the value of the floor areas used by each department. In allocating heating and lighting expense, it is assumed that the number of lights, their wattage, and the extent of use is uniform throughout the sales departments. If there are major variations and the total lighting expense is material, further analysis and separate apportionment may be advisable. The rent expense and the heating and lighting expense are apportioned as follows:

	TOTAL	DEPARTMENT A	DEPARTMENT B
Floor space, square feet	160,000	88,000	72,000
Percent	100%	55%	45%
Rent expense	$7,200	$3,960	$3,240
Heating and lighting expense	$2,400	$1,320	$1,080

Property Tax Expense and *Insurance Expense* are related primarily to the value of the merchandise inventory and the store equipment. Although there are differences between assessed value for tax purposes, value for insurance purposes, and cost, the latter is most readily available and is considered to be satisfactory as a basis for apportioning these expenses. The computation of the apportionment follows:

	TOTAL	DEPARTMENT A	DEPARTMENT B
Merchandise inventory:			
January 1	$ 71,000	$40,300	$30,700
December 31	81,000	41,900	39,100
Total	$152,000	$82,200	$69,800
Average	$ 76,000	$41,100	$34,900
Average cost of store equipment (computed previously)	14,000	8,400	5,600
Total	$ 90,000	$49,500	$40,500
Percent	100%	55%	45%
Property tax expense	$ 3,300	$ 1,815	$ 1,485
Insurance expense	1,900	1,045	855

Uncollectible Accounts Expense, *Miscellaneous Selling Expense*, and *Miscellaneous General Expense* may be apportioned on the basis of sales. The uncollectible accounts expense is assumed to vary with sales, while the miscellaneous selling and general expenses are apportioned on the basis of sales for lack of a better basis.

	TOTAL	DEPARTMENT A	DEPARTMENT B
Sales	$400,000	$280,000	$120,000
Percent	100%	70%	30%
Uncollectible accounts expense	$ 2,000	$ 1,400	$ 600
Miscellaneous selling expense	2,050	1,435	615
Miscellaneous general expense	2,100	1,470	630

An income statement presenting net income from operations by departments for York Company appears on page 472. The amounts for sales and cost of merchandise sold are presented in condensed form. Details could be reported, if desired, in the manner illustrated by the income statement on page 467.

Departmental margin approach to income reporting

Many accountants caution against the imprudent use of departmental income statements. They point out that the more the revenue and the expenses must be allocated to departments on an arbitrary basis, the less useful the statements become in evaluating past operations and in planning for the future. In addition, some accountants object to reporting net income by departments on the grounds that departments are not independent operating units but segments of one business and that therefore no single department of a business can earn a profit. For these reasons, accountants often prepare income statements that report the revenue and the expense in a manner that emphasizes the contribution each department makes to the expenses incurred on behalf of the busi-

York Company
Income Statement
For Year Ended December 31, 1965

	Department A			Department B			Total		
Net sales			$272,400			$116,900			$389,300
Cost of merchandise sold			148,500			77,600			226,100
Gross profit on sales			$123,900			$ 39,300			$163,200
Operating expenses:									
Selling expenses:									
Sales salaries	$ 27,000			$ 15,000			$ 42,000		
Advertising expense	5,950			3,050			9,000		
Depreciation expense — store equipment	990			660			1,650		
Miscellaneous selling expense	1,435			615			2,050		
Total selling expenses		$ 35,375			$ 19,325			$ 54,700	
General expenses:									
Officers' salaries	$ 15,600			$ 10,400			$ 26,000		
Office salaries	5,400			3,600			9,000		
Rent expense	3,960			3,240			7,200		
Property tax expense	1,815			1,485			3,300		
Heating and lighting expense	1,320			1,080			2,400		
Uncollectible accounts expense	1,400			600			2,000		
Insurance expense	1,045			855			1,900		
Miscellaneous general expense	1,470			630			2,100		
Total general expenses		32,010			21,890			53,900	
Total operating expenses			67,385			41,215			108,600
Net income (loss) from operations			$ 56,515			$ (1,915)			$ 54,600
Other expense:									
Interest expense									1,200
Net income before income tax									$ 53,400
Income tax									19,132
Net income after income tax									$ 34,268

Income statement departmentalized through net income from operations

ness as a whole. Income statements prepared in such a manner use the *departmental margin* or *contribution margin* approach to income reporting.

In preparing an income statement in the departmental margin format, the operating expenses are generally divided into two classes: (1) *direct expenses,* those expenses incurred for the benefit of and traceable to a specific department and thus generally subject to the control of the

York Company
Income Statement
For Year Ended December 31, 1965

	Department A		Department B		Total	
Net sales		$272,400		$116,900		$389,300
Cost of merchandise sold		148,500		77,600		226,100
Gross profit on sales		$123,900		$ 39,300		$163,200
Direct departmental expenses:						
Sales salaries	$27,000		$15,000		$42,000	
Advertising expense	4,550		2,450		7,000	
Property tax expense	1,815		1,485		3,300	
Uncollectible accounts expense	1,400		600		2,000	
Insurance expense	1,045		855		1,900	
Depreciation expense — store equipment	990		660		1,650	
Total direct departmental expenses		36,800		21,050		57,850
Departmental margin		$ 87,100		$ 18,250		$105,350
Indirect expenses:						
Officers' salaries					$26,000	
Office salaries					9,000	
Rent expense					7,200	
Heating and lighting expense					2,400	
Advertising expense					2,000	
Miscellaneous selling expense					2,050	
Miscellaneous general expense					2,100	
Total indirect expenses						50,750
Net income from operations						$ 54,600
Other expense:						
Interest expense						1,200
Net income before income tax						$ 53,400
Income tax						19,132
Net income after income tax						$ 34,268

Income statement departmentalized through departmental margin

department head; and (2) *indirect expenses*, those expenses incurred for the benefit of the business as a whole and not traceable to a specific department and consequently beyond the control of the department head. The direct expenses for each department are deducted from gross profit on sales, also determined for each department, in arriving at the *departmental margin.* The indirect expenses are not allocated to the departments but are deducted in total from the total departmental margin to determine the net income from operations.

Sales salaries for the York Company is a direct expense because it is directly traceable to a specific department. Officers' salaries for the York Company is an indirect expense because it benefits the entire company and cannot be traced to a specific department. Some operating expenses may have to be divided between the two categories. For example, the newspaper advertising portion of advertising expense for the York Company is directly related to each department. The billboard advertising, however, mentions only the name and the location of the company and is therefore an indirect expense. An income statement for the York Company prepared on the departmental margin basis appears on page 473.

The departmental margin income statement can be used advantageously in controlling expenses and maximizing net income. The manager of each sales department can be held strictly accountable for the expenses directly traceable to his department and hence subject to his control. A reduction in departmental gross profit or an increase in direct expenses of a department will have an adverse effect on the margin contributed to the enterprise by that department. Information on the current state of affairs is the first prerequisite to instituting remedial action.

The departmental margin income statement may also be useful to management in formulating fundamental plans for future operations. For example, this type of analysis can be employed when the advisability of discontinuing a particular operation or department is being considered. If a sales department yields a departmental margin, it generally should be retained even though the allocation of all of the operating expenses indicates a net loss for the department. This observation is based upon the assumption that the department in question represents a relatively minor segment of the enterprise. Its termination, therefore, would not cause any significant reduction in the volume of indirect expenses. If an enterprise occupying a rented three-story building is divided into twenty departments, each occupying about the same amount of space, the termination of the least thriving department would probably not cause any reduction in rent or other occupancy expenses. The space vacated would probably be absorbed by the remaining nineteen departments. On the other hand, if the enterprise were divided into three departments, each occupying approximately equal areas, the discontinuance of one could result in vacating an entire floor and consequently materially reduce occupancy expenses. When the departmental margin analysis is applied to problems of this type, consideration should be given to the organizational structure of the enterprise and to related proposals for the use of released space or productive capacity.

To illustrate the application of the departmental margin approach to long-range planning, assume that an enterprise with six departments has earned $70,000 before income tax during the past year, which is fairly typical of recent operations. Assume also that recent income statements, in which all operating expenses are allocated, indicate that Department 6 has been incurring losses, the net loss having amounted to $5,000 for the past year. Departmental margin analysis indicates that, in spite of the losses, Department 6 should not be discontinued unless there is sufficient assurance that a commensurate increase in the gross profit of other departments or a decrease in indirect expenses can be effected. The analysis, considerably condensed, may be presented in the following form:

Possible Effect of Discontinuance of Department 6

	Current Operations			Discontinuance of Department 6
	Department 6	Departments 1-5	Total	
Sales	$100,000	$900,000	$1,000,000	$900,000
Cost of merchandise sold	70,000	540,000	610,000	540,000
Gross profit on sales	$ 30,000	$360,000	$ 390,000	$360,000
Direct departmental expenses	20,000	210,000	230,000	210,000
Departmental margin	$ 10,000	$150,000	$ 160,000	$150,000
Indirect expenses			90,000	90,000
Net income before income tax			$ 70,000	$ 60,000

The analysis reveals a possible reduction of $10,000 in net income that would result from the discontinuance of Department 6. There are also other factors bearing on the matter that may need to be considered. For example, there may be problems regarding the displacement of sales personnel. It is also possible that customers attracted by the least profitable department may make substantial purchases in other departments, with the consequence that discontinuance of that department may adversely affect the sales of other departments.

The foregoing discussion of departmental income statements has suggested various ways in which income data may be made useful to management in making important policy decisions. It should be kept in mind that the format selected for the presentation of income data to management must be that which will be most useful under the circumstances for evaluating, controlling, and planning departmental operations.

Branch operations

Just as a firm may add a new department in an effort to increase its sales and income, it also may open new stores (branches) in different locations with the same objective in mind. Among the types of retail businesses in which branch operations were first successfully developed on a major scale were variety, grocery, and drug stores. There are a number of large corporations with hundreds or thousands of retail branches distributed over a large area. In addition to the national chain store organizations, there are many of a regional or local nature. The growth of suburban shopping centers in recent years has added materially to the number of firms, especially department stores, that have expanded through the opening of branches.

Although commonly associated with retailing, branch operations are also carried on by banking institutions, service organizations, and many types of manufacturing enterprises. Regardless of the nature of the business, each branch ordinarily has a branch manager. Within the framework of general policies set by top management, the branch manager may be given wide latitude in conducting the business of the branch. Data concerning the volume of business handled and the profitability of operations at each location are essential as a basis for decisions by the principal executives. It is also necessary to maintain a record of the various assets at the branch locations and of liabilities incurred by each branch.

The remainder of this chapter deals with the central office and the single branch of a merchandising business. The fundamental considerations are not materially affected, however, by a multiplicity of branches or by the particular type of business.

Systems for branch accounting

There are various systems of accounting for branch operations. The system may be highly centralized, with the accounting for the branch done at the home office. Or the system may be almost completely decentralized, with the branch responsible for the detailed accounting and only summary accounts carried by the home office for the branch. Or there may be some variation between these two extremes. Although there are many possible variations, two typical methods of branch accounting will be described.

Centralized system. The branch may prepare only the basic records of its transactions, such as sales invoices, time tickets for employees, and vouchers for liabilities incurred. Copies of all such documents are forwarded to the home office, where they are recorded in appropriate journals in the usual manner. When this system is used, the branch has no journals or ledgers. If the operating results of the branch are to be determined separately, which is normally the case, separate branch accounts for sales, cost of merchandise sold, and expenses must be maintained in the home office ledger. It is apparent that the principles of departmental accounting will apply in such cases, the branch being treated as a department.

One important result of centralizing the bookkeeping activities at one location may be substantial savings in office expense. There is also greater assurance of uniformity in accounting methods employed. On the other hand, there is some likelihood of delays and inaccuracies in submitting data to the home office, with the result that periodic reports on the operations of a branch may not be available when needed.

Decentralized system. When the accounting for branches is decentralized, each branch maintains its own accounting system with journals and ledgers. The account classification for assets, liabilities, revenue, and expenses in the branch books conforms to the classification employed by the home office. The accounting processes are comparable to those of an independent business, except that the branch does not have capital accounts. A special account entitled Home Office takes the place of the capital accounts. The process of preparing financial statements and adjusting and closing the books is substantially the same as for an independent enterprise. It is this system of branch accounting to which the remainder of the chapter will be devoted.

Underlying principles of decentralized branch accounting

When the branch has a ledger with a full complement of accounts, except capital accounts, it is apparent that there must be some tie-in between the branch ledger and the general ledger at the home office. The properties at the branch are a part of the assets of the entire enterprise, and liabilities incurred at the branch are similarly liabilities of the enterprise as a whole. Although the accounting system at the branch is much like that of an independent company, the fact remains that the branch is not a separate entity but only a segment of the business.

The tie-in between the home office and the branch is accomplished by the control-account-subsidiary-ledger technique, with an added modification that makes the branch ledger a self-contained unit. The basic features of the system are shown in the chart below. In the home office ledger, the account Branch #1 has a debit balance of $100,000. This balance represents the sum of the assets minus the sum of the liabilities recorded on the ledger at the branch. The various asset and liability accounts in the branch ledger are represented in the chart by one account for all assets ($120,000) and one account for all liabilities ($20,000). In order to make the branch ledger self-balancing, an account entitled Home Office is added. It has a credit balance of $100,000. The two accounts, Branch #1 in the home office books and Home Office in the branch books, have equal but opposite balances and are known as *reciprocal accounts.* The home office account in the branch ledger replaces the capital accounts that would be used if the branch were a separate entity. Actually, the account does represent the branch's portion of the entire capital of the home office.

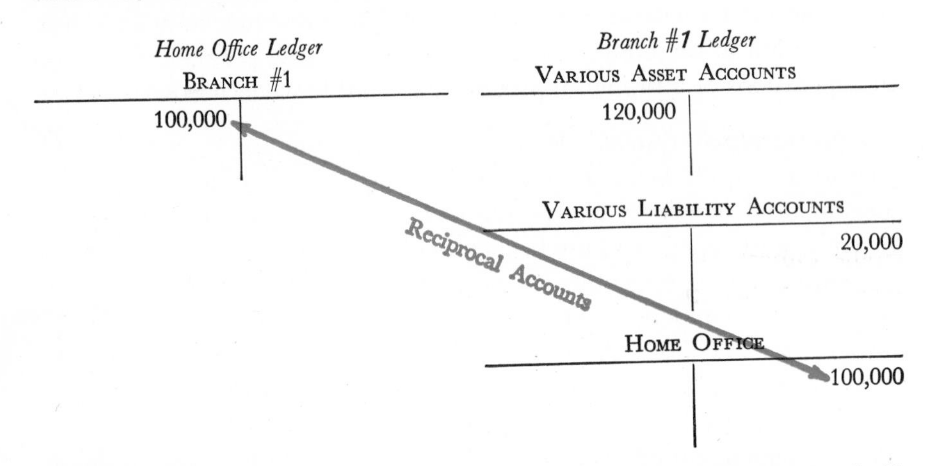

When the home office sends assets to the branch, it debits Branch #1 for the totals and credits the appropriate asset accounts. Upon receiving the assets, the branch debits the appropriate accounts and credits Home Office. To illustrate, assume that branch operations are begun by sending $10,000 in cash to the newly appointed branch manager. The entries in the two ledgers are presented in T accounts as follows:

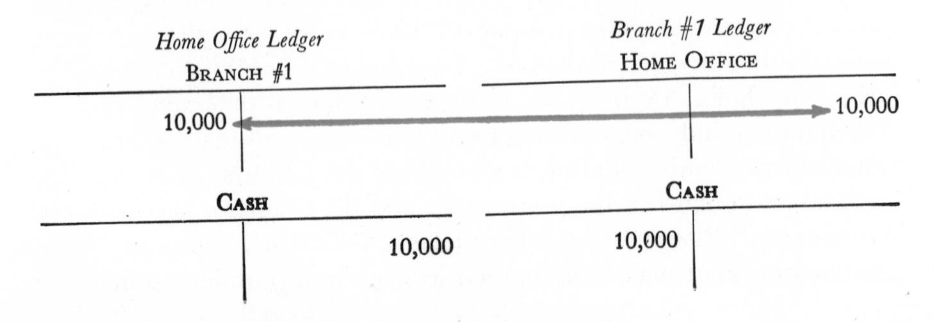

When the branch disburses the cash, it records the transactions as though it were an independent entity. For example, if the branch purchases office equipment for $4,000, paying cash, the transaction is recorded in the branch books by a debit to Office Equipment and a credit to Cash. No entry is required in the home office books because there is no change in the amount of the investment at the branch.

As the branch incurs expenses and earns revenue, the transactions are recorded in its books in the usual manner. Such transactions do affect the amount of the total investment of the home office at the branch, but recognition of the change is postponed until the books are closed at the end of the accounting period. At that time the expense and revenue summary account in the branch books is closed to the account Home Office. If operations have resulted in a net income, the account Home Office will be credited. In the home office books a net income at the branch is recorded by a debit to Branch #1 and a credit to Branch Net Income. For a net loss the entries would be just the reverse.

In a merchandising enterprise all or a substantial part of the stock in trade of the branch is usually supplied by the home office. A shipment of merchandise from the home office is recorded on the home office books by a debit to Branch #1 and a credit to Shipments to Branch #1. The branch records the transaction in its books by a debit to Shipments from Home Office and a credit to Home Office. It is evident from the T accounts below that the two shipments accounts are also reciprocal accounts.

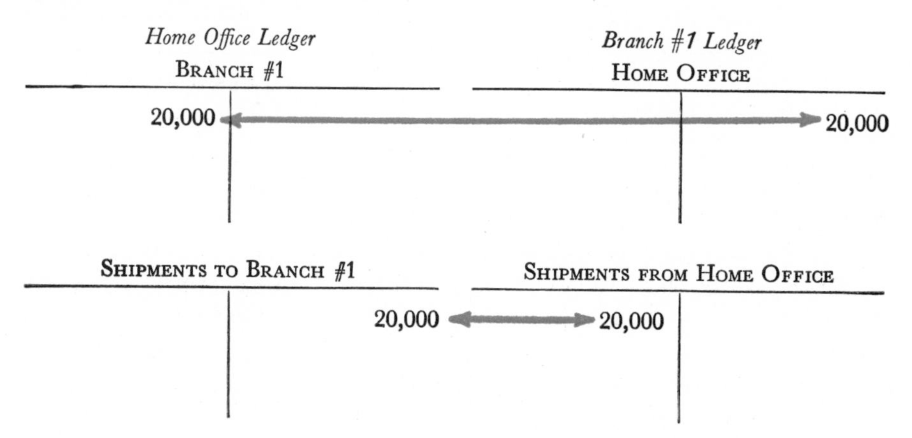

From the point of view of the home office, the account Shipments to Branch #1 is an unallocated reduction of its merchandise inventory and purchases accounts. From the standpoint of the branch, the account Shipments from Home Office is comparable to a purchases account. The final disposition of these accounts is described later in the chapter.

Illustration of decentralized branch accounting

A series of entries illustrating the underlying principles applicable to branch accounting on a decentralized basis is presented below. The illustration begins with the opening of a branch and continues with operations covering a complete accounting period. Typical transactions between the home office and the branch, and between the branch and outsiders, are considered. Transactions between the home office and outsiders are ignored unless they affect the branch. A summary of transactions, together with the entries on the home office books and the branch books, is presented below in general journal form.

Transactions	Home Office Books	Branch Books
(1) The home office established Branch #1, sending $10,000 in cash and $30,000 in merchandise.	Branch #1........40,000 Cash.......... 10,000 Shipments to Branch #1...... 30,000	Cash.............10,000 Shipments from Home Office......30,000 Home Office.... 40,000
(2) The branch purchased on account merchandise costing $10,000.		Purchases.........10,000 Accounts Pay... 10,000
(3) The branch sold merchandise for $16,000 in cash and for $8,000 on account.		Cash.............16,000 Accounts Rec...... 8,000 Sales........... 24,000
(4) The branch paid operating expenses amounting to $3,500.		Operating Exp.... 3,500 Cash........... 3,500
(5) The branch collected $6,000 on accounts receivable.		Cash............. 6,000 Accounts Rec... 6,000
(6) The branch paid $1,000 on accounts payable.		Accounts Pay...... 1,000 Cash........... 1,000
(7) The branch sent $20,000 in cash to the home office.	Cash.............20,000 Branch #1...... 20,000	Home Office......20,000 Cash........... 20,000

The entries to adjust and close the books of the branch at the end of the accounting period, together with the entries on the books of the home office to record the net income of the branch, are presented on the opposite page.

Adjusting & Closing	Home Office Books		Branch Books	
(a) To record the ending merchandise inventory of the branch.			Mdse. Inventory . . . 22,000 Expense and Revenue Summary . .	 22,000
(b) To close the sales account of the branch.			Sales . . . . 24,000 Expense and Revenue Summary . .	 24,000
(c) To close the cost and expense accounts of the branch.			Expense and Revenue Summary . . . . . 43,500 Shipments from Home Office . . . . Purchases . . . . Operating Exp. . .	 30,000 10,000 3,500
(d) To close the expense and revenue summary account on the books of the branch and to record the net income of the branch on the books of the home office.	Branch #1 . . . . 2,500 Branch Net Income	 2,500	Expense and Revenue Summary . . . . . 2,500 Home Office	 2,500

After the foregoing entries have been posted, the home office accounts affected and the branch ledger accounts appear as follows:

Home Office Ledger

CASH

(7)	20,000	(1)	10,000

Other cash transactions of the home office would also be recorded in the account above.

Branch Ledger

CASH

(1)	10,000	(4)	3,500
(3)	16,000	(6)	1,000
(5)	6,000	(7)	20,000
		Balance	7,500
	32,000		32,000
Balance	7,500		

ACCOUNTS RECEIVABLE

(3)	8,000	(5)	6,000
		Balance	2,000
	8,000		8,000
Balance	2,000		

Home Office Ledger	*Branch Ledger*

Branch Ledger — Merchandise Inventory

	Debit		Credit
(a)	22,000		

Branch Ledger — Accounts Payable

	Debit		Credit
(6)	1,000	(2)	10,000
Balance	9,000		
	10,000		10,000
		Balance	9,000

Home Office Ledger — Branch #1

	Debit		Credit
(1)	40,000	(7)	20,000
(d)	2,500	Balance	22,500
	42,500		42,500
Balance	22,500		

Branch Ledger — Home Office

	Debit		Credit
(7)	20,000	(1)	40,000
Balance	22,500	(d)	2,500
	42,500		42,500
		Balance	22,500

Home Office Ledger — Branch Net Income

	Debit		Credit
		(d)	2,500

Branch Net Income will be closed to the home office expense and revenue summary account.

Branch Ledger — Expense and Revenue Summary

	Debit		Credit
(c)	43,500	(a)	22,000
(d)	2,500	(b)	24,000
	46,000		46,000

Branch Ledger — Sales

	Debit		Credit
(b)	24,000	(3)	24,000

Home Office Ledger — Shipments to Branch #1

	Debit		Credit
		(1)	30,000

Shipments to Branch #1 is a deduction from purchases. It will be closed to the home office expense and revenue summary account.

Branch Ledger — Shipments from Home Office

	Debit		Credit
(1)	30,000	(c)	30,000

Home Office Ledger	Branch Ledger			
	PURCHASES			
	(2)	10,000	(c)	10,000
	OPERATING EXPENSES			
	(4)	3,500	(c)	3,500

Branch financial statements

Branch financial statements differ from those of a complete enterprise in two minor respects. In the income statement the shipments from the home office appear in the cost of merchandise sold section following purchases. In the balance sheet the account Home Office takes the place of the capital accounts. Actually it is not capital in the usual sense, but merely the balancing account. Statements for the branches are used only by management and are not published.

Combined statements for home office and branch

The income statement based on the home office ledger reports details of sales, cost of merchandise sold, expenses, and net income or loss from home office operations in the usual manner. The net income or loss of each branch is then listed, and the net operating results for the entire enterprise are reported. The assets section of the balance sheet prepared from the home office ledger will include the controlling accounts for the various branches. The nature and the amounts of the various assets and liabilities at the branch locations will not be disclosed. Such statements, together with financial statements for each individual branch, serve a useful purpose for management, but they are obviously unsuitable for presentation to stockholders and creditors.

Accordingly, it is necessary to combine the data on the income statements of the home office and the branches to form one overall income statement. The data on the balance sheets of the home office and of the various branches are also combined to form one balance sheet for the enterprise. The preparation of the combined statements is facilitated by the use of work sheets. The work sheets are similar in that each has a column for the home office account balances, a column for the account balances of each branch, a set of columns headed "Eliminations," and a final column to which the combined figures are extended.

The work sheet for the combined income statement of Taylor Corporation is presented on page 484. The account Shipments from Home

Office is canceled by a credit in the Eliminations column, and the account Shipments to Branch #1 is canceled by a debit in the Eliminations column. These eliminations are not recorded in either set of accounts, but they are necessary in the preparation of a combined statement that reports the home office and the branch as one operating unit. These two accounts are eliminated because they represent the shipment of goods within the company and not a sale to an outside party.

Taylor Corporation
Work Sheet for Combined Income Statement
For Month Ended March 31, 1965

	Home Office	Branch #1	Eliminations		Combined Income Statement
			Dr.	Cr.	
Sales	47,000	24,000			71,000
Cost of Merchandise Sold:					
Mdse. Inv., March 1	41,000				41,000
Purchases	52,000	10,000			62,000
	93,000				
Shipments from Home Office		30,000		30,000	
Less Shipments to Branch #1	30,000		30,000		
Mdse. Available for Sale	63,000	40,000			103,000
Less Mdse. Inv., March 31	35,000	22,000			57,000
Cost of Merchandise Sold	28,000	18,000			46,000
Gross Profit on Sales	19,000	6,000			25,000
Operating Expenses	10,500	3,500			14,000
Net Income from Operations	8,500	2,500	30,000	30,000	11,000

The income statement prepared from the data in the Combined Income Statement column of the work sheet is as follows:

Taylor Corporation
Income Statement
For Month Ended March 31, 1965

Sales		$71,000
Cost of merchandise sold:		
Merchandise inventory, March 1, 1965	$ 41,000	
Purchases	62,000	
Merchandise available for sale	$103,000	
Less merchandise inventory, March 31, 1965	57,000	
Cost of merchandise sold		46,000
Gross profit on sales		$25,000
Operating expenses		14,000
Net income from operations		$11,000

The work sheet for the combined balance sheet of Taylor Corporation appears below. The reciprocal account Branch #1 is canceled by a credit elimination, and the reciprocal account Home Office is canceled by a debit elimination.

Taylor Corporation
Work Sheet for Combined Balance Sheet
March 31, 1965

	Home Office	Branch #1	Eliminations Dr.	Eliminations Cr.	Combined Balance Sheet
Debit balances:					
Cash	53,000	7,500			60,500
Accounts Receivable	46,000	2,000			48,000
Merchandise Inventory	35,000	22,000			57,000
Prepaid Insurance	250				250
Branch #1	22,500			22,500	
Equipment	15,000				15,000
Total	171,750	31,500			180,750
Credit balances:					
Accumulated Depreciation	3,000				3,000
Accounts Payable	28,000	9,000			37,000
Home Office		22,500	22,500		
Common Stock	100,000				100,000
Retained Earnings	40,750				40,750
Total	171,750	31,500	22,500	22,500	180,750

The balance sheet prepared from the data in the Combined Balance Sheet column of the work sheet is as follows:

Taylor Corporation
Balance Sheet
March 31, 1965

Assets		
Cash		$ 60,500
Accounts receivable		48,000
Merchandise inventory		57,000
Prepaid insurance		250
Equipment	$15,000	
Less accumulated depreciation	3,000	12,000
Total assets		$177,750
Liabilities and capital		
Accounts payable		$ 37,000
Common stock	$100,000	
Retained earnings	40,750	140,750
Total liabilities and capital		$177,750

Shipments to branch billed at selling price

In the foregoing discussion and illustrations, the billing for merchandise shipped to the branch has been assumed to be at cost price. When all or most of the merchandise handled by the branch is supplied by the home office, it is not unusual for billings to be made at selling price. An advantage of this procedure is that it provides a convenient control over inventories at the branch. The branch merchandise inventory at the beginning of a period (at selling price), plus shipments during the period (at selling price), less sales for the period yields the ending inventory (at selling price). Comparison of the physical inventory taken at selling prices with the book amount discloses any discrepancies. A significant difference between the physical and the book inventories indicates a need for remedial action by the management.

When shipments to the branch are billed at selling prices, no gross profit on sales will be reported on the branch income statement. The merchandise inventory on the branch balance sheet will also be overstated by the amount of the markup included in the billed prices of the merchandise on hand. In combining the branch statements with the home office statements, it is necessary to convert the data back to cost by eliminating the markup from both the shipments accounts and the inventory accounts.

Analyses of operations

With the ever-increasing size and diversification of business units, the need for analysis of operations is likewise growing. It is necessary to account separately for the various segments that make up the larger unit. This accounting involves first an analysis of the accounts by departments or by branches, followed by a consolidation to show the unit as a whole.

In the large five-and-ten-cent store chains, for example, there is first a breakdown by commodities sold and second a breakdown by branches selling these commodities. For efficient administration of large mercantile establishments, it is necessary to have both departmental analysis and branch analysis. More and more attention is being directed to accounting for small units under a central administration.

QUESTIONS

1. Are departmental income statements ordinarily included in the published annual reports issued to stockholders and other parties outside the business enterprise?

2. As newly appointed general manager of a department store, you are studying the income statements presenting gross profit by departments in an attempt to adjust operations to achieve the highest possible gross profit for each department. (a) Suggest ways in which an income statement departmentalized through gross profit can be used in achieving this goal. (b) Suggest reasons why caution must be exercised in using such statements.

3. For each of the following types of expenses, select the allocation basis listed that is most appropriate for use in arriving at net income by departments:

Expense:	Basis of allocation:
(a) Sales salaries	(1) Physical space occupied
(b) Rent	(2) Departmental sales
(c) Property tax expense	(3) Cost of inventory and equipment
(d) Uncollectible accounts	(4) Time devoted to department

4. (a) Differentiate between a direct and an indirect operating expense. (b) Give two examples of each type of expense.

5. What term is applied to the dollar amount representing the excess of departmental gross profit over direct departmental expenses?

6. The Department Z income statement for the year just ended indicated operating expenses of $95,000 ($45,000 of which represented indirect expenses) and net operating loss of $25,000. The net operating income for all other departments of the enterprise for the same year was $125,000. It is estimated that the discontinuance of Department Z would not have affected the sales of the other departments nor have reduced the indirect expenses. Assuming the accuracy of these estimates, what would the net operating income of the enterprise have been if Department Z had been discontinued?

7. Where are the detailed accounting records maintained in a decentralized branch accounting system?

8. What are reciprocal accounts in branch accounting?

9. In the branch books, what is the name of the account that takes the place of the capital accounts common to separate accounting entities?

10. What accounts are debited and credited (a) to record the net income of the Westover Branch in the home office accounts and (b) to close the expense and revenue summary account in the accounts of the Westover Branch?

11. In the branch income statement, where does the amount of shipments from the home office appear?

12. In the Eliminations columns of the work sheet for a combined income statement for the home office and its Rosewood branch, what account is canceled against Shipments to Rosewood Branch?

13. In the Eliminations columns of the work sheet for a combined balance sheet for the home office and its Covington Branch, what account is canceled against Covington Branch?

14. After the books are closed, the asset accounts at a branch total $90,000; the contra asset accounts total $10,000; and liabilities to outsiders total $15,000. (a) What is the title of the remaining account in the branch ledger and what is the amount of its balance? (b) What is the title of the related account on the books of the home office and what is the amount of its balance? (c) Do these accounts appear in the combined balance sheet?

15. At the close of each accounting period Sommer, Inc. charges each of its branches with interest on the net investment in the branch. At the end of the current year the home office debited the branch accounts for various amounts and credited Interest Income for a total of $15,000. The branches make comparable entries, debiting Interest Expense and crediting Home Office. How should the interest income and the interest expense be handled on the work sheet for the combined income statement?

16. During the first year of operations of the Elm Street Branch, the home office shipped merchandise that had cost $180,000 to the branch. The branch was billed at $270,000, which was the selling price of the merchandise. Branch net sales for the year totaled $210,000 (all sales were at the billed price.) (a) What should be the amount of the branch ending physical inventory at billed prices? (b) Assuming that there are no inventory shortages at the branch, what is the cost of the closing inventory? (c) Which of the two amounts should be added to the home office inventory for presentation on the combined balance sheet? (d) How much gross profit will be reported on the branch income statement?

EXERCISES

1. Department A earned gross profit on sales of $60,000, which represented 20% of its net sales; Department B earned gross profit on sales of $32,000, which represented 16% of its net sales; Departments A, B, and C earned combined gross profit on sales of $127,500, which represented 17% of combined net sales. Determine the items indicated by X in the following tabulation:

	A	B	C	Total
Net sales....................	$ X	$ X	$ X	$ X
Gross profit on sales.........	60,000	32,000	X	127,500
Percent of net sales..........	20%	16%	X%	17%

2. Fallon Sports, Inc. conducts a retail sporting goods business in a two-story building. The departments and the floor space occupied by each are as follows:

Receiving and Storage —	Basement —	6,000 sq. ft.
Department A —	Basement —	4,000 sq. ft.
Department B —	First Floor —	5,000 sq. ft.
Department C —	First Floor —	5,000 sq. ft.
Department D —	Second Floor —	4,000 sq. ft.
Department E —	Second Floor —	4,000 sq. ft.
General Office —	Second Floor —	2,000 sq. ft.

The building is leased at an annual rent of $50,000, allocated to the floors as follows: basement, 20%; first floor, 50%; second floor, 30%. Determine the amount of rent to be apportioned to each department.

3. The Mead Store apportions depreciation of equipment on the basis of average cost of the equipment and apportions personal property taxes on the basis of the combined total of average cost of the equipment and average cost of the merchandise inventories. Depreciation of equipment amounted to $12,000 and personal property taxes amounted to $7,500 for the year. Determine the apportionment of the depreciation and the property taxes based on the following data:

Departments	Average Cost	
	Equipment	Inventories
Service		
X	$ 10,000	
Y	20,000	
Sales		
1	40,000	$ 60,000
2	50,000	100,000
3	80,000	140,000
Total	$200,000	$300,000

4. Universal Rug Co. maintains sales offices in several cities. The home office provides the sales manager at each office with a working fund of $10,000 with which to meet payrolls and to pay other office expenses. Give the entries, in general journal form, on the home office books to record the following:

(a) Established a $10,000 fund for Branch #7.
(b) Received a report from Branch #7 indicating the following payments: sales salaries, $5,000; office salaries, $1,100; rent, $1,300; advertising, $700; miscellaneous general expense, $50. Sent check to replenish the fund.

5. Give the entries, in general journal form, to record the following transactions on the books of the Dallas Branch. (This is not a complete list of transactions for the period).

May 1. The branch receives from the home office: cash, $2,000; store equipment, $2,500; merchandise at cost, $5,000.
8. The branch purchases merchandise on account from an outside firm, $3,000.
12. The branch sells merchandise as follows: on account, $5,000; for cash, $1,300.
16. The branch pays general operating expenses of $800.
22. The branch sends the home office cash of $1,000.
26. The branch receives merchandise at cost from the home office, $1,500.
31. The branch reports a net income of $1,100.

6. Present the entries, in general journal form, to record the transactions in Exercise 5 on the books of the home office.

7. The Richman Products Co. maintains accounts entitled Athens Branch and Wood River Branch. Each branch maintains an account entitled Home Office. The Athens Branch received instructions from the home office to ship to the Wood River Branch merchandise costing $1,000 that had been received from the home office. Give the general journal entry to record the transfer of the merchandise on the books of (a) the home office, (b) the Athens Branch, and (c) the Wood River Branch.

8. During the year, the home office shipped merchandise that had cost $600,000 to the branch. The branch was billed for $900,000, which was the selling price of the merchandise. No merchandise was purchased from any outside sources. Branch net sales for the period totaled $750,000. All sales were made at the billed price. Merchandise on hand at the beginning of the period totaled $100,000 at the billed price. Merchandise on hand at the end of the period as determined by physical count was $248,500 at the billed price. Determine the amount, at the billed price, of any discrepancy between the book amount and the physical count of inventory.

PROBLEMS

20-1. The Appliance Mart operates two sales departments: Department A for small household appliances and Department B for large household appliances. The following trial balance was taken on June 30 at the end of a fiscal year after all adjustments, including the adjustments for merchandise inventory, were recorded and posted:

Appliance Mart
Trial Balance
June 30, 19--

Cash	108,700	
Accounts Receivable	95,500	
Merchandise Inventory, Department A	27,500	
Merchandise Inventory, Department B	10,000	
Prepaid Insurance	2,600	
Supplies	250	
Store Equipment	53,100	
Accumulated Depreciation — Store Equipment		18,200
Accounts Payable		15,800
Income Tax Payable		35,620
Common Stock		150,000
Retained Earnings		25,900
Expense and Revenue Summary	30,500	37,500
Sales, Department A		585,000
Sales, Department B		195,000
Sales Returns and Allowances, Department A	15,200	
Sales Returns and Allowances, Department B	6,000	
Purchases, Department A	340,500	
Purchases, Department B	130,400	
Sales Salaries	87,600	
Advertising Expense	15,000	
Depreciation Expense — Store Equipment	12,500	
Miscellaneous Selling Expense	2,000	
Administrative Salaries	64,400	
Rent Expense	14,400	
Heating and Lighting Expense	3,600	
Insurance Expense	2,000	
Property Tax Expense	1,700	
Supplies Expense	400	

Miscellaneous General Expense	800	
Interest Expense	2,750	
Income Tax	35,620	
	1,063,020	1,063,020

Merchandise inventories at the beginning of the year were: Department A, $20,100; Department B, $10,400.

The bases to be used in apportioning expenses, together with other essential information, are as follows:

Sales salaries — Payroll records: Department A, $66,600; Department B, $21,000.
Advertising expense — Usage: Department A, $10,000; Department B, $5,000.
Depreciation expense — Average cost of equipment. Balances at beginning of year: Department A, $35,120; Department B, $14,980. Balances at end of year: Department A, $37,120; Department B, $15,980.
Administrative salaries — Department A, 75%; Department B, 25%.
Rent expense and heating and lighting expense — Floor space: Department A, 5,600 sq. ft.; Department B, 2,400 sq. ft.
Insurance expense and property tax expense — Average cost of equipment plus average cost of merchandise inventory.
Supplies expense — Requisitions: Department A, $300; Department B, $100.
Miscellaneous selling expense and miscellaneous general expense — Volume of gross sales.

Instructions: Prepare an income statement departmentalized through net income from operations.

20-2. The following data relating to revenue and expenses are obtained from the ledger of Stevens Rug Company on March 31, the end of the current fiscal year.

	Debit	Credit
Sales, Department 1		$200,000
Sales, Department 2		180,000
Cost of Merchandise Sold, Department 1	$140,000	
Cost of Merchandise Sold, Department 2	108,000	
Sales Salaries and Commissions	43,000	
Advertising Expense	4,900	
Depreciation Expense — Store Equipment	2,600	
Miscellaneous Selling Expense	1,650	
Officers' Salaries	22,500	
Office Salaries	8,900	
Rent Expense	7,500	
Uncollectible Accounts Expense	1,900	
Utilities Expense	2,800	
Insurance Expense	700	
Property Tax Expense	350	
Miscellaneous General Expense	1,100	
Interest Income		500
Income Tax	10,100	

Other essential data are:

Sales salaries and commissions — Salesmen are paid a basic salary plus 5% of sales. Basic salaries for Department 1, $14,000; Department 2, $10,000.
Advertising expense — All advertising expense was incurred for local newspaper advertising. Usages: Department 1, $2,400; Department 2, $2,500.
Depreciation expense — Average cost of store equipment: Department 1, $60,000; Department 2, $70,000.
Uncollectible accounts expense — Departmental managers are responsible for the granting of credit on the sales made by their respective departments. Uncollectible accounts expense is estimated at ½% of sales.
Insurance expense and property tax expense — Based on average cost of store equipment plus average cost of merchandise inventory. Average cost of merchandise inventory was $100,000 for Department 1 and $90,000 for Department 2.

Instructions: (1) Prepare an income statement departmentalized through departmental margin.
(2) Determine the rate of gross profit on sales for each department.
(3) Determine the rate of departmental margin to sales for each department.

20-3. Wiseman's Department Store has 18 departments. Those with the least sales volume are Department N, novelties, and Department P, phonograph records, which were established about a year ago on a trial basis. The board of directors feels that it is now time to give consideration to the retention or the termination of these two departments. The adjusted trial balance, severely condensed, as of May 31, the end of the first month of the current fiscal year, is presented below. May is considered to be a fairly typical month. The income tax accrual has no bearing on the problem and is excluded from consideration.

Wiseman's Department Store
Trial Balance
May 31, 19--

Current Assets	520,000	
Plant Assets	375,000	
Accumulated Depreciation — Plant Assets		170,000
Current Liabilities		178,000
Common Stock		400,000
Retained Earnings		122,300
Sales — Department N		6,100
Sales — Department P		20,100
Sales — Other Departments		460,200
Cost of Merchandise Sold — Department N	4,400	
Cost of Merchandise Sold — Department P	12,600	
Cost of Merchandise Sold — Other Departments	288,600	
Direct Expenses — Department N	3,700	
Direct Expenses — Department P	5,700	
Direct Expenses — Other Departments	82,500	
Indirect Expenses	63,200	
Interest Expense	1,000	
	1,356,700	1,356,700

Instructions: (1) Prepare an income statement departmentalized through departmental margin.

(2) What recommendations would you make about the retention of Departments N and P? Explain your reasoning.

20-4. Melbourne Products, Inc., of Los Angeles, opened a branch office in San Francisco on April 1 of the current year. Summaries of transactions, adjustments, and year-end closing for branch operations of the current year ended December 31 are described below:

(a) Received cash advance, $50,000, and merchandise (billed at cost), $150,000, from the home office.
(b) Purchased equipment for cash, $25,000.
(c) Purchased merchandise on account, $55,000.
(d) Sales on account, $150,000; cash sales, $30,000.
(e) Paid creditors on account, $47,500.
(f) Received cash from customers on account, $125,000.
(g) Paid operating expenses, $21,600 (all expenses are charged to Operating Expenses, a controlling account).
(h) Sent $75,000 cash to home office.
(i) Recorded accumulated depreciation, $550, and allowance for doubtful accounts, $350.
(j) Merchandise inventory at December 31, $65,000.
(k) Closed revenue and expense accounts.

Instructions: (1) Present, in general journal form, the entries on the branch books to record the foregoing. Post to the following T accounts: Cash, Accounts Receivable, Allowance for Doubtful Accounts, Merchandise Inventory, Equipment, Accumulated Depreciation, Accounts Payable, Home Office, Expense and Revenue Summary, Sales, Shipments from Home Office, Purchases, and Operating Expenses.

(2) Prepare an income statement for the period and a balance sheet as of December 31 for the branch.

(3) Present, in general journal form, the entries required on the home office books. Post to a T account entitled San Francisco Branch.

20-5. The adjusted trial balances of the home office of Foster, Incorporated and of its Denver branch as of August 31, the close of the current fiscal year, are given on the following page.

Instructions: (1) Prepare an income statement and a balance sheet for the branch.

(2) Prepare an income statement for the home office.

(3) Prepare the journal entry to record branch income on the home office books.

(4) Prepare a balance sheet for the home office, giving effect to the journal entry in (3).

(5) Prepare a work sheet for a combined income statement and a work sheet for a combined balance sheet.

(6) Prepare a combined income statement and a combined balance sheet.

	Home Office		Denver Branch	
	Dr.	Cr.	Dr.	Cr.
Cash	83,000		26,500	
Accounts Receivable	110,000		37,500	
Allowance for Doubtful Accounts		975		850
Merchandise Inventory	218,000		70,500	
Prepaid Expenses	900		400	
Denver Branch	121,950			
Equipment	30,000		10,000	
Accumulated Depreciation		22,000		1,700
Notes Payable		20,000		
Accounts Payable		48,500		3,600
Home Office				121,950
Common Stock		300,000		
Retained Earnings		74,375		
Expense and Revenue Summary	245,000	218,000	74,200	70,500
Sales		817,000		250,000
Shipments to Branch		130,000		
Purchases	670,000		25,000	
Shipments from Home Office			130,000	
Operating Expenses	152,000		74,500	
	1,630,850	1,630,850	448,600	448,600

20-6. The board of directors of Scott Corporation has tentatively decided to discontinue operating Department Q, which has incurred a net loss for several years. Condensed revenue and expense data for the most recent year ended June 30 are presented on the following page. Bases used in allocating operating expenses among departments are described below.

Expense	Basis
Sales commissions	Actual: 10% of net sales.
Advertising expense	Actual: all advertising consists of brochures distributed by the various departments advertising specific products.
Depreciation expense	Average cost of store equipment used.
Miscellaneous selling expense	Amount of net sales.
Administrative salaries	Each of the 12 departments was apportioned an equal share.
Rent expense	Floor space occupied.
Insurance and property taxes	Average cost of equipment used plus inventory on hand.
Utilities expense	Floor space occupied.
Miscellaneous general expense	Amount of net sales.

Instructions: Prepare a brief statement of your recommendation to the board, supported by such schedule(s) as you think will be helpful to them in reaching a decision.

Scott Corporation
Income Statement
For Year Ended June 30, 19—

	Department Q			Other Departments			Total		
Net sales			$ 71,600			$872,000			$943,600
Cost of merchandise sold			47,800			418,000			465,800
Gross profit on sales			$ 23,800			$454,000			$477,800
Operating expenses:									
Selling expenses:									
Sales commissions	$ 7,160			$ 87,200			$ 94,360		
Advertising expense	2,100			24,000			26,100		
Depreciation expense — store equipment	1,900			19,500			21,400		
Miscellaneous selling expense	1,790			21,800			23,590		
Total selling expenses		$ 12,950			$152,500			$165,450	
General expenses:									
Administrative salaries	$ 12,000			$132,000			$144,000		
Rent expense	3,000			37,500			40,500		
Insurance and property tax expense	2,500			26,000			28,500		
Utilities expense	2,000			25,000			27,000		
Miscellaneous general expense	1,432			17,440			18,872		
Total general expenses		20,932			237,940			258,872	
Total operating expenses			33,882			390,440			424,322
Net income (loss) from operations			$(10,082)			$ 63,560			$ 53,478
Other income:									
Dividend income									6,000
Net income before income tax									$ 59,478
Income tax									19,602
Net income after income tax									$ 39,876

21. Manufacturing and process costs

Manufacturing operations

Manufacturers employ labor and use machinery to convert materials into finished products. In thus changing the form of commodities, their activities differ from those of merchandisers. The automobile manufacturer, for example, converts steel plate and other materials into automobiles. The automobile retailer purchases the finished goods from the manufacturer and sells them without additional processing.

Accounting for a manufacturing business must provide for the accumulation of the accounting data for the transactions identified with manufacturing operations. Additional accounts are required. Additional subsidiary ledgers may be used to permit a division of labor within the accounting department and to help establish internal control over operations. Periodic reports to management and other interested parties must include data that will be useful in measuring the efficiency of manufacturing operations and in guiding future operations.

Balance sheet accounts for manufacturing businesses

Manufacturing companies carry on many of the functions of merchandising organizations, such as selling, administration, and financing. Many of the accounts of a manufacturing enterprise are therefore identical with those found in the ledger of a merchandising business. But there are some accounts that either are peculiar to manufacturing or are likely to be of greater significance in manufacturing than in merchandising operations.

Current assets. The merchandise inventory account appearing in the ledger of a merchandising business is replaced by three inventory accounts representing (1) goods in the state in which they are to be sold, (2) goods in the process of manufacture, and (3) goods in the state in which they were acquired. These inventories are called respectively *finished goods*, *work in process*, and *materials*. The balances in the inventory accounts may be presented in the balance sheet in the following manner:

Inventories:		
Finished goods	$300,000	
Work in process	55,000	
Materials	123,000	$478,000

The cost of finished goods and of work in process includes three categories of manufacturing costs: *direct materials*, *direct labor*, and *factory overhead*. Direct materials represent the delivered cost of the materials that enter directly into the finished product. Direct labor represents the wages of the workmen who convert the materials into a finished product. Factory overhead includes all of the remaining costs of operating the factory.

Plant assets. Because of the extensive use of machinery in manufacturing, the portion of total capital invested in plant assets by a manufacturing business tends to be larger than that invested by a trading concern. The number of items of machinery and equipment is usually sufficient to warrant the use of a subsidiary plant ledger.

The cost of tools and other portable equipment of small unit value is usually charged to a tools account rather than to a machinery or similarly titled account reserved for major items. Because of breakage, pilferage, and relatively short life, it is usually impracticable to apply depreciation methods to small tools. One common method of determining the cost expiration is to take a periodic inventory of the tools on hand, estimate their fair value based on original cost, and charge the remaining amount to Tools Expense. The same method may be used in accounting for dies, molds, patterns, and spare parts.

Enterprises engaged in extracting natural resources, such as metal ores or other minerals, also have appropriate accounts for recording the cost of the property and the allocation of such costs against periodic revenues. The portion of the cost of natural resources charged to expense is termed *depletion*. The amount of the periodic charge is based on the amount of the deposit removed in relation to the cost of the entire deposit. For example, if it is estimated that a mineral deposit contains 1,000,000 tons of ore of uniform grade and that the cost of the mineral rights is $400,000, the depletion is 40 cents per ton. Assuming that 70,000 tons were mined during a particular fiscal year, the depletion of $28,000 would be recorded by the following entry:

Depletion Expense	28,000	
Accumulated Depletion		28,000

The accumulated depletion account, like the accumulated depreciation account, is a contra asset account; it is presented in the balance sheet as a deduction from the cost of the mineral deposit. In determining income subject to the federal income tax, the amount of depletion allowed as a deduction from revenue is often greater than the amount based on cost. The Internal Revenue Code provides for a depletion deduction equal to a specified percent of revenues, the percent varying with the type of mineral. "Percentage depletion" is mentioned here only because references to it are frequently encountered in the financial press.

Intangible assets. Manufacturers may acquire exclusive rights to manufacture and sell products of a specified type or design. Such rights, called *patents,* are issued by the federal government to the inventor and continue in effect for 17 years. A manufacturing firm may develop new products in its own research department and obtain patents on them, or it may buy patent rights from others. When patents are purchased, the cost should be charged to a patents account. The cost should then be written off, or amortized, over the years of expected usefulness. This period may, of course, be less than the remaining legal life of the patent.

To illustrate, assume that an enterprise purchases a patent for $50,000 at the beginning of its fiscal year. The exclusive rights granted by the patent expire after 11 years, but they are expected to have value for only 5 years. The amortization for the year would be recorded as follows:

Patents Expense	10,000	
Patents		10,000

The unamortized balance of the patents account is reported in the balance sheet as an intangible asset.

The cost of obtaining patents from the government is usually nominal. The cost of the experimental work leading to the development of a new product may be substantial and in theory should be treated as an asset in the same manner as patent rights purchased from others. In practice, however, many research projects may be under way at the same time, costs may be incurred over a period of years, and the ultimate success or failure of the effort may be in doubt. In addition, research and development is a continuous process for many firms. Accordingly, some businesses view such research as a necessity if they are to remain competitive in their industry, and they treat their research and development costs as a part of current operating expense. To the extent that the amount of research costs incurred do not fluctuate greatly from year to year, the use of this method may not materially affect the amount of reported net income.

Exclusive rights to publish and sell literary, artistic, and musical compositions are called *copyrights*. They are issued by the federal government and extend for 28 years with the privilege of renewal for a like term. The costs assigned to a copyright include all costs of creating the work plus the cost of obtaining the copyright. A copyright that is purchased from another should be recorded at the price paid for it. Because of the uncertainty regarding the useful life of a copyright, it is usually amortized over a relatively short period of time.

Liabilities. Businesses that issue a warranty on their products may record the estimated amount of the liability that will have to be paid thereon in the future. Such items are frequently described as a "provision" or "reserve," but it is preferable to use the designation "Estimated Liability for Product Warranties."

Cost accounting systems

Principles and techniques of cost accounting have evolved gradually over the years. The two principal types of cost accounting systems are *process cost accounting* and *job order cost accounting.*

Under a process cost system, the costs are accumulated for each of the various departments or processes within the factory. The process system is best utilized by manufacturers of homogeneous units of product that are not distinguishable from each other during a continuous production process.

Job order cost systems provide for a separate record of the cost of each particular quantity of product that passes through the factory. It is best suited to industries that manufacture commodities to fill special orders from customers and to industries that produce heterogeneous lines of products for stock.

Each of the two systems is widely used, and a manufacturer may employ a process cost system for some of its products and a job order cost system for others.

Process cost systems

Companies manufacturing a homogeneous mass such as cement or flour do so on a continuous basis. The manufacturing costs incurred are accumulated for each manufacturing department or process. The cost elements are identified first with the separate processes and then with the physical output of these processes. For example, the cost of producing a ton of cement equals the sum of costs incurred in each separate process divided by the number of tons produced. Other industries that use process cost accounting include ink, paint, soap, and paper manufacturing.

Flow of costs in process cost systems

Perpetual inventory accounts for materials, work in process, and finished goods are requisites of a process cost accounting system. Each of these accounts is debited for all additions and is credited for all deductions. The balance of each account thus represents the inventory on hand.

All expenditures incidental to manufacturing move through the work in process account, the finished goods account, and eventually into the cost of goods sold account. The flow of costs through the perpetual inventory accounts is exemplified by the following diagram:

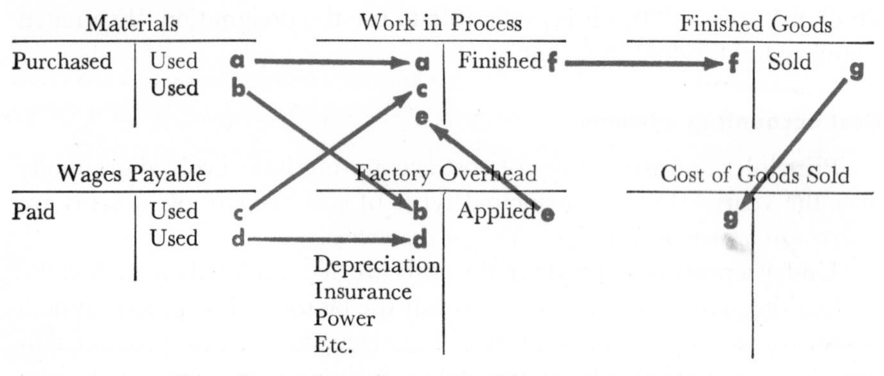

Flow of costs through perpetual inventory accounts

Materials used and factory labor used are classified as direct and indirect. When the materials and the factory labor are used directly in the process of manufacturing, they are charged to Work in Process (a and c in the diagram). When the materials and the factory labor used do not enter directly into the finished product, they are debited to Factory Overhead (b and d in the diagram). Examples of indirect materials are oils and greases, abrasives and polishes, cleaning supplies, gloves, molding sand, drilling soap, and brushes. Examples of indirect labor are salaries of supervisors, inspectors, material handlers, watchmen, and janitors. The appropriate amount of factory overhead costs, which include depreciation, insurance, power, taxes, and other indirect manufacturing costs as well as indirect materials and indirect labor, are transferred to Work in Process (e in the diagram). The costs of the goods finished are transferred from Work in Process to Finished Goods when they are finished (f in the diagram) and thence to Cost of Goods Sold when they are sold (g in the diagram).

The number of accounts presented in the flow chart was severely restricted. In practice, separate work in process accounts and factory overhead accounts are maintained for each department or *cost center* in the factory. There is ordinarily a separate account in a subsidiary ledger for each type of material used in manufacturing, controlled by the account Materials. Similarly, if numerous commodities are manufactured, an account for each type may be maintained in a subsidiary ledger, controlled by the account Finished Goods.

Cost and expense

Cost and expense are not mutually exclusive terms. Cost represents the amount of money expended or liability incurred for goods or services. Costs may be classified as *unexpired costs* or *expired costs*. Prepaid insurance is an unexpired cost, while insurance expense is an expired cost.

The term "expenses" is used in the broad sense to include all expired costs. It is also commonly used in a narrower sense to refer to the income statement categories of selling, general, and other expenses. The term "costs" is then restricted to items that become a part of the cost of product manufactured.

Service departments and process costs

In a factory with a number of processes, there may be one or more *service departments* that do not process the materials directly. They assist the processing departments in producing finished goods, and the costs that they incur must be charged to the processing departments. Service departments include such departments as the factory office, the power plant, and the maintenance and repair shop.

The services rendered by a service department give rise to internal transactions between that department and the processing departments that receive the benefit of the services. In these internal transactions the amount involved is the cost of the service rendered. The costs incurred by the service departments are periodically charged to the factory overhead accounts of the processing departments. The period usually chosen is a month, although a different period of time may be used.

For example, if the Power Department produced 300,000 kilowatt-hours during the month at a total cost of $6,000, the cost per kilowatt-hour is 2¢ ($6,000 ÷ 300,000). The factory overhead accounts for the departments that used the power are accordingly charged for power at the 2¢ rate. Assuming that during the month Department 1 used 100,000 kwh and Department 2 used 200,000 kwh, the accounts affected by the interdepartmental transfer of cost would appear as follows:

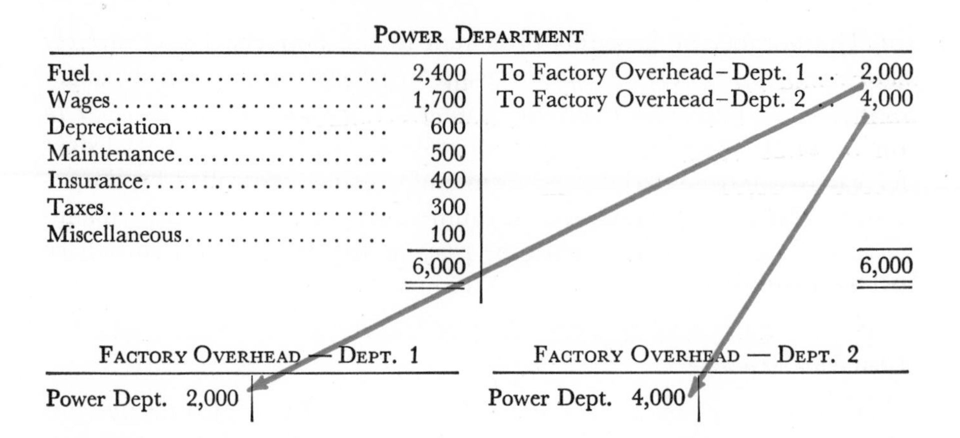

POWER DEPARTMENT

Fuel	2,400	To Factory Overhead–Dept. 1	2,000
Wages	1,700	To Factory Overhead–Dept. 2	4,000
Depreciation	600		
Maintenance	500		
Insurance	400		
Taxes	300		
Miscellaneous	100		
	6,000		6,000

FACTORY OVERHEAD — DEPT. 1

Power Dept. 2,000	

FACTORY OVERHEAD — DEPT. 2

Power Dept. 4,000	

Some service departments render services to other service departments. For example, the power department may supply electric current to light the factory office and to operate various bookkeeping and office machines. At the same time the factory office provides general supervision for the power department, maintains its payroll records, buys its fuel, and so on. In such cases the costs of the department rendering the greatest service to other service departments may be distributed first, ignoring the fact that it receives benefits from other service departments.

Processing costs

The cost of direct materials and direct labor incurred in each processing department is charged to the related work in process account. Each work in process account is also charged for its portion of the factory overhead. The costs incurred are summarized periodically, usually at the end of the month. The costs applicable to the output of each department during the month are then transferred to the next processing department or to Finished Goods, as the case may be. This flow of costs through a work in process account is illustrated below.

WORK IN PROCESS — DEPARTMENT 2

10,000 units at $1.20 from Dept. 1		12,000	To Dept. 3, 10,000 units	20,000
Direct labor	4,600		Cost per unit $\frac{\$20,000}{10,000} = \$2.00$	
Factory overhead	3,400	8,000		
		20,000		20,000

The debits to the above account may be grouped into two distinct categories: (1) direct materials cost, which in this case is composed of 10,000 units received from Department 1 at a total cost of $12,000, and (2) direct labor and factory overhead applicable to the process, which in this case totaled $8,000. This second group of costs is called the *processing cost*. In the illustration all of the 10,000 units were completed in Department 2 and passed on to Department 3. The unit cost of the product transferred to Department 3 is $2, which is composed of direct materials cost of $1.20 ($12,000 ÷ 10,000 units) and processing cost of $.80 ($8,000 ÷ 10,000 units). This cost of $2 per unit, the finished output of Department 2, is treated as direct materials cost in Department 3.

Factory overhead

Identifying factory overhead with a specific processing department is usually more difficult than identifying direct materials or direct labor with a specific processing department. For example, written requisition forms and time tickets may be employed as a record of direct materials and direct labor used by each processing department. Determining the portion of such factory overhead items as heat, depreciation, insurance, and salary of the factory superintendent used by each department is a more complex problem. The difficulty is complicated by a basic difference in the nature of the factory overhead costs. Some of them, such as insurance, remain constant or fixed regardless of the amount of goods produced, while others, such as power, vary closely with the volume of goods produced.

Factory overhead costs might be accumulated until the end of the fiscal period and then be apportioned to the various processing departments. Such a procedure is not especially difficult, although the accountant must exercise judgment in selecting the proper basis for apportionment. Such a procedure has, however, an important disadvantage in that management desires current cost data for the goods being produced and does not want to wait until the end of the period for this information. Therefore it is customary for businesses to employ estimated or *predetermined* factory overhead rates so that unit product costs may be computed at any time. Furthermore, when unit product costs are determined for relatively short periods of time, such as a month, the use of predetermined rates avoids fluctuations in unit overhead costs that result from monthly variations in the volume of production. For example, an enterprise may suspend factory operations for a two-week vacation period during which time the equipment is overhauled. If the curtailed output for that month were to be charged with the entire amount of overhead costs incurred, the resulting unit cost of the commodities produced would be unjustifiably exaggerated. The use of departmental overhead rates permits significant comparisons of unit product costs from month to month. In addition, management is better able to measure the efficiency of operations by comparing the amount of factory overhead incurred with the amount charged to processes.

Predetermined factory overhead rates. Factory overhead rates are determined by relating the estimated amount of factory overhead for each department for the forthcoming year to some common activity base, one that will equitably apply the factory overhead costs to the goods manufactured. The common bases include direct labor costs, direct labor hours, and machine hours. For example, if it is estimated that the total factory overhead costs for a particular department for the year will be $48,000 and that the total direct labor cost for that department will be $60,000, an overhead rate of 80% ($48,000 ÷ $60,000) may be applied to the direct labor cost incurred within the department during the year.

The actual factory overhead costs incurred are debited to the factory overhead accounts. The amounts of factory overhead costs applied to production are credited to the factory overhead accounts and debited to the work in process accounts. Assuming that the direct labor cost in Department 7 during a month is $5,000 and that the predetermined departmental overhead rate is 80%, the entry to apply factory overhead to production is as follows:

Work in Process — Department 7	4,000	
Factory Overhead — Department 7		4,000

Inevitably, factory overhead costs applied and factory overhead costs incurred during a particular period will differ. If the amount applied exceeds the actual costs, the factory overhead account will have a credit balance and the overhead is said to be *overapplied* or *overabsorbed;* if the amount applied is less than the actual costs, the account will have a debit balance and the overhead is said to be *underapplied* or *underabsorbed.* Both situations are illustrated in the account presented below.

FACTORY OVERHEAD — DEPARTMENT 7

DATE		ITEMS	DEBIT	CREDIT	BALANCE DEBIT	BALANCE CREDIT
May	1	Balance				300
	31	Costs incurred	4,510			
	31	Costs applied		4,000	210	

The $300 credit balance at the beginning of the month is an overapplied balance. During the month actual costs incurred amounted to $4,510 and factory overhead applied to work in process amounted to $4,000. The $210 debit balance at the end of the month is an underapplied balance.

Disposition of factory overhead balances. The balances in the factory overhead accounts are carried forward from month to month until the end of the year. The net amount of the balances is reported on interim balance sheets as either a deferred charge (net underapplied balance) or a deferred credit (net overapplied balance).

The nature of the balance in the factory overhead account for a particular department (underapplied or overapplied), as well as the amount, will fluctuate during the year. If there is a decided trend in either direction and the amount is substantial, the reason should be determined. If the variation is caused by alterations in manufacturing methods or by substantial changes in production goals, it may be advisable to revise the overhead rate. The accumulation of a large underapplied balance is more serious than a trend in the opposite direction and may indicate inefficiencies in production methods, excessive expenditures, or a combination of contributing factors.

Despite any corrective actions taken to avoid an underapplication or overapplication of factory overhead, the accounts will ordinarily have balances at the end of the fiscal year. Since the sum of the balances represent the underapplied or overapplied overhead applicable to the operations of the year just ended, it is not proper to report it in the year-end balance sheet as a deferred charge or a deferred credit to manufacturing costs of the following year.

There are two principal alternatives for disposing of the balances of factory overhead at the end of the year: (1) by allocation among work in process, finished goods, and cost of goods sold accounts on the basis of the total amounts of applied factory overhead included in those accounts at the end of the year or (2) by transfer of the balances to the cost of goods sold account. Theoretically only the first alternative is sound because it represents a correction of the estimated overhead rates and brings the accounts into agreement with the costs actually incurred. On the other hand, considerable time and expense may be required to make the allocation and to revise the unit costs of the work in process and finished goods inventories. Furthermore, in most manufacturing enterprises a very large proportion of the manufacturing costs for the year will have passed through the work in process and the finished goods accounts into the cost of goods sold account. Therefore, unless the amount of the underapplied or overapplied balance is substantial, it is satisfactory to transfer it to Cost of Goods Sold.

Inventories of partially processed materials

Preceding illustrations assumed that all materials entering a process were completely processed at the end of the accounting period. In such cases the determination of unit costs is quite simple. The total of direct materials, direct labor, and factory overhead charged to a department is divided by the number of units completed and passed on to the next department or to finished goods. Frequently, however, some partially processed materials remain in various stages of production in a department at the close of a period. When this is the case, the processing costs must be allocated between the units that have been completed and transferred to the next process and those that are only partially completed and remain within the department.

Materials may be placed in production at different stages of the manufacturing process. The stage at which materials are placed in production depends upon the nature of the product being manufactured. For some products it is necessary to have all materials on hand before any work commences. For other products, materials may be added to production in relatively the same proportion as processing costs are incurred. In still other situations, materials may enter the process at relatively few points, which may or may not be evenly spaced throughout the process.

In order to allocate the processing costs between the output completed and transferred and the inventory of goods within the process, it is necessary to determine (1) the number of *equivalent units* of production during the period and (2) the *processing cost per equivalent unit* for the same period. The equivalent units of production are the number of units that would have been produced if there had been no inventories within the process either at the beginning or the end of the period. For example, assume that there is no inventory of goods in process in a particular processing department at the beginning of the period, that 1,000 units of materials enter the process during the period, and that at the end of the period all of the units are 75% completed. The equivalent production in the processing department for the period would be 750 units (75% of 1,000). Assuming further that the processing costs incurred during the period totaled $15,000, the processing cost per equivalent unit would be $20 ($15,000 ÷ 750).

Ordinarily there is an inventory of partially processed units in the department at the beginning of the period, some units are completed during the period and transferred to the next department, and other units are partially processed and remain in the inventory at the end of the period. To illustrate the computation of equivalent units under such circumstances, the following data are assumed for Department 5 for the month of March:

Inventory within Department 5 on March 1:	600 units, ⅓ completed.
Completed in Department 5 and transferred to finished goods during March:	4,000 units, completed.
Inventory within Department 5 on March 31:	1,000 units, ⅗ completed.

The equivalent units of production in Department 5 for March may be determined as follows:

To process units in inventory on March 1:	600 units × 2/3......	400
To process units started and completed in March:	4,000 units − 600 units	3,400
To process units in inventory on March 31:	1,000 units × 2/5......	400
Equivalent units of production in March...........................		4,200

Continuing with the illustration, the next step is to allocate the costs incurred in Department 5 between the units completed during March and those remaining in process at the end of the month. If materials and processing costs were incurred uniformly throughout the month, the total costs of the process would be divided by 4,200 units to obtain the unit cost. On the other hand, if all materials were introduced at the beginning of the period, the full materials cost per unit must be assigned to the uncompleted units. The processing costs would then be allocated to the finished and the uncompleted units on the basis of equivalent units of production. The T account below is based on the latter assumption.

WORK IN PROCESS — DEPARTMENT 5

Process inventory, March 1:			Goods finished during March:	
600 units, 1/3 completed......		1,160	4,000 units..................	14,060
From Department 4:			Process inventory, March 31:	
4,400 units at $1...........		4,400	1,000 units, 2/5 completed.....	2,000
Direct labor............	6,000			
Factory overhead.......	4,500	10,500		
		16,060		16,060
Process inventory, April 1:				
1,000 units, 2/5 completed.....		2,000		

The processing costs incurred in Department 5 during March total $10,500. The equivalent units of production for March, determined above, is 4,200. The processing cost per equivalent unit is therefore $2.50 ($10,500 ÷ 4,200). Of the $16,060 debited to Department 5, $14,060 was transferred to Finished Goods and $2,000 remained in the account as work in process inventory. The calculation of the allocations to finished goods and to inventory is illustrated at the top of the following page.

Cost of production report

Periodically, generally monthly, a report is prepared for each processing department summarizing (1) the units for which the department is accountable and the disposition of these units and (2) the costs charged to the department and the allocation of these costs. This report, termed the *cost of production report*, may be used as the source of the computation of unit production costs and the allocation of the processing costs in the

GOODS FINISHED DURING MARCH

600 units:	Inventory on March 1, ⅓ completed	$1,160	
	Processing cost in March: 600 × ⅔, or 400 units at $2.50	1,000	
	Total		$ 2,160
	(Unit Cost: $2,160 ÷ 600 = $3.60)		
3,400 units:	Materials cost in March, at $1 per unit	$3,400	
	Processing cost in March: 3,400 at $2.50 per unit	8,500	
	Total		11,900
	(Unit Cost: $11,900 ÷ 3,400 = $3.50)		
4,000 units:	Goods finished during March		$14,060

PROCESS 5 INVENTORY ON MARCH 31

1,000 units:	Materials cost in March, at $1 per unit	$1,000	
	Processing cost in March: 1,000 × ⅖, or 400 at $2.50	1,000	
1,000 units:	Department 5 Inventory on March 31		$ 2,000

general ledger to the finished and the uncompleted units. More importantly, the report is used as a means of controlling costs. Each department head is held responsible for the units entering production and the costs incurred in his department. Any variations in unit product costs from one month to another are carefully scrutinized and the causes of significant variations are determined.

The cost of production report based on the data presented in the preceding section for Department 5 is illustrated on the opposite page.

By-products

If one of the products resulting from a process has little value in relation to the principal product, it is known as a *by-product*. The emergence of a by-product is only incidental to the manufacture of the principal product. All the costs incurred are therefore assigned to the process account in which the by-product emerges, and the value of the by-product is deducted to arrive at the cost of the principal product. The value of the by-product is considered to be its sales value reduced by any additional costs necessary to complete and sell it.

For example, if a by-product with an estimated value of $200 emerges in Department 4 during a cost period, that amount would be credited to Work in Process — Department 4 and debited to a finished goods account. The accounting for the sale of the by-product is comparable to that for the sale of the principal product. By-products may be leftover materials, such as sawdust and scraps of wood in a lumber mill; or they may be separated from the material at the beginning of production, as in the case of cottonseed from raw cotton.

Avery Manufacturing Company
Cost of Production Report — Department 5
For the Month Ended March 31, 19--

Quantities:		
Charged to production:		
In process, March 1		600
Received from Department 4		4,400
Total units to be accounted for		5,000
Units accounted for:		
Transferred to finished goods		4,000
In process, March 31		1,000
Total units accounted for		5,000
Costs:		
Charged to production:		
In process, March 1		$ 1,160
March costs:		
Materials from Department 4 ($1 per unit)		4,400
Processing costs:		
Direct labor	$ 6,000	
Factory overhead	4,500	
Total processing costs ($2.50 per unit)		10,500
Total costs to be accounted for		$16,060
Costs allocated as follows:		
Transferred to finished goods:		
600 units at $3.60	$ 2,160	
3,400 units at $3.50	11,900	
Total cost of finished goods		$14,060
In process, March 31:		
Materials (1,000 units at $1)	$ 1,000	
Processing costs (1,000 units × ⅖ × $2.50)	1,000	
Total cost of inventory in process, March 31		2,000
Total costs accounted for		$16,060
Computations:		
Equivalent units of production:		
To process units in inventory on March 1:		
600 units × ⅔		400
To process units started and completed in March:		
4,000 units − 600 units		3,400
To process units in inventory on March 31:		
1,000 units × ⅖		400
Equivalent units of production		4,200
Unit processing cost:		
$10,500 ÷ 4,200 = $2.50		

Cost of production report

Joint products

A manufacturing process may result in two or more products of significant value. In this situation the products are known conventionally as *joint products.* The distinction between a joint product and a by-product is merely one of relative market value. The description of a product may change from by-product to joint product if a new use is found for a product that was formerly of little value. The entire petrochemical industry, for example, is based on material that had very little value until a new use for it was developed.

In decisions involving production and sale of joint products or by-products, it is the total cost and the total revenue of the entire group of products that is relevant. There is nothing to be gained from an allocation of joint cost to individual products since one cannot be produced without the others. A decision to produce a joint product is effectively a decision to produce all of the products.

For one purpose, namely inventory valuation for periodic income statements, it is necessary to make an arbitrary allocation of joint cost among the joint products. One of the most common examples of joint products is the meat packing industry, where the cost of materials and processing must be allocated among a wide variety of end products. Another example is petroleum refining, with gasoline, naphtha, kerosene, and other products emerging from the processing of crude oil.

There are several different methods of allocating costs to joint products. The one that will be described here is the *market value* method. Its essential feature is the assignment of costs to the various products in accordance with their relative market (sales) values. To illustrate, it will be assumed that 10,000 units of Product X and 50,000 units of Product Y were produced at a total cost of $63,000. The market values of the two products and the allocation of the joint cost are presented below.

Joint Product	Units Produced	Total Cost	Sales Value Per Unit	Total Sales Value
X	10,000	$63,000	$3.00	$30,000
Y	50,000		1.20	60,000
Total sales value				$90,000

Allocation of total cost:

X $\frac{30,000}{90,000} \times \$63,000$	$21,000
Y $\frac{60,000}{90,000} \times \$63,000$	42,000

Unit cost:

X $21,000 ÷ 10,000 units	$2.10
Y $42,000 ÷ 50,000 units	.84

Inasmuch as joint products result from the same process, one cannot be manufactured without the other. The assignment of cost, then, cannot be based on actual expenditures because it is impossible to determine how much of the cost effort was directed to the manufacture of each product. By apportioning costs based on relative sales values, it is assumed that the cost of producing an item is proportional to its sales value.

Illustration of process cost accounting

To illustrate further the procedures described, the following facts are assumed: The Howell Manufacturing Company manufactures one principal product designated Product A. The manufacturing activity begins in Department 1, where all materials enter production. The materials remain in Department 1 for a relatively short time and there is ordinarily no inventory of work in process in that department at the end of the accounting period. A by-product, designated Product B, is also produced in Department 1. From Department 1 the materials comprising the principal product are transferred to Department 2. In Department 2 there are usually inventories at the end of the accounting period. Separate factory overhead accounts are maintained for Departments 1 and 2. Factory overhead is applied at 100% and 50% of direct labor cost respectively for Departments 1 and 2. There are two service departments, Maintenance and Power.

The trial balance of the general ledger on January 1, 1966, the first day of the fiscal year, is shown below.

Howell Manufacturing Company
Trial Balance
January 1, 1966

Cash	18,500	
Accounts Receivable	15,000	
Finished Goods — Product A (1,000 units at $11.50)	11,500	
Finished Goods — Product B (600 pounds at $.50)	300	
Work in Process — Department 2 (800 units, ½ completed)	7,800	
Materials	12,000	
Prepaid Expenses	2,150	
Plant Assets	310,000	
Accumulated Depreciation — Plant Assets		95,000
Accounts Payable		21,180
Wages Payable		1,400
Common Stock		200,000
Retained Earnings		59,670
	377,250	377,250

In order to reduce the illustrative entries to a manageable number and to avoid repetition, the transactions and the adjustments for the month of January are stated as summaries. In practice the transactions would be recorded from day to day in various journals. The descriptions of the transactions, followed in each case by the entry in general journal form, are presented below.

(a) Materials purchased and prepaid expenses incurred on account.

	Account	Debit	Credit
Entry:	Materials	33,500	
	Prepaid Expenses	1,100	
	Accounts Payable		34,600

(b) Materials requisitioned for use by the various factory departments.

	Account	Debit	Credit
Entry:	Maintenance Department	400	
	Power Department	2,000	
	Factory Overhead — Department 1	1,240	
	Factory Overhead — Department 2	900	
	Work in Process — Department 1	21,560	
	Materials		26,100

(c) Labor used by the various departments.

	Account	Debit	Credit
Entry:	Maintenance Department	1,200	
	Power Department	1,500	
	Factory Overhead — Department 1	950	
	Factory Overhead — Department 2	700	
	Work in Process — Department 1	6,640	
	Work in Process — Department 2	12,600	
	Wages Payable		23,590

(d) Expenses incurred on account by the various factory departments and by the sales and administrative divisions.

	Account	Debit	Credit
Entry:	Maintenance Department	200	
	Power Department	300	
	Factory Overhead — Department 1	600	
	Factory Overhead — Department 2	400	
	Selling Expenses	5,000	
	General Expenses	4,500	
	Accounts Payable		11,000

(e) Expiration of prepaid expenses chargeable to the various factory departments and to the sales and administrative divisions.

	Account	Debit	Credit
Entry:	Maintenance Department	100	
	Power Department	250	
	Factory Overhead — Department 1	450	
	Factory Overhead — Department 2	350	
	Selling Expenses	300	
	General Expenses	200	
	Prepaid Expenses		1,650

(f) Depreciation chargeable to the various factory departments and to the sales and administrative divisions.

	Account	Debit	Credit
Entry:	Maintenance Department	100	
	Power Department	350	
	Factory Overhead — Department 1	600	
	Factory Overhead — Department 2	900	
	Selling Expenses	200	
	General Expenses	100	
	Accumulated Depreciation — Plant Assets		2,250

(g) Distribution of Maintenance Department costs to other factory departments on the basis of maintenance services rendered.

Entry: Power Department	100	
Factory Overhead — Department 1	900	
Factory Overhead — Department 2	1,000	
Maintenance Department		2,000

(h) Distribution of Power Department costs to factory processing departments on the basis of kwh supplied.

Entry: Factory Overhead — Department 1	1,800	
Factory Overhead — Department 2	2,700	
Power Department		4,500

(i) Application of factory overhead costs to work in process accounts at predetermined rates of 100% and 50% of direct labor cost, respectively, for Departments 1 and 2. See transaction (c).

Entry: Work in Process — Department 1	6,640	
Work in Process — Department 2	6,300	
Factory Overhead — Department 1		6,640
Factory Overhead — Department 2		6,300

(j) Transfer of production costs from Department 1 to Department 2 and to Product B. 4,100 units were fully processed and 800 pounds of by-product B, valued at 50¢ per pound, were produced. There is no work in process remaining in Department 1 at the end of the month.

Allocation of total costs of $34,840 charged to Department 1:	
Product B, 800 × $.50	$ 400
Transferred to Department 2	34,440
Total costs	$34,840
Unit cost of product transferred to Department 2:	
$34,440 ÷ 4,100	$ 8.40

Entry: Finished Goods — Product B	400	
Work in Process — Department 2	34,440	
Work in Process — Department 1		34,840

(k) Transfer of production costs from Department 2 to Finished Goods. 4,000 units were completed, and the remaining 900 units were ⅔ completed at the end of the month.

Equivalent units of production:	
To process units in inventory on January 1:	
800 × ½	400
To process units started and completed in January:	
4,000 − 800	3,200
To process units in inventory on January 31:	
900 × ⅔	600
Equivalent units of production in January	4,200
Processing costs:	
Direct labor (c)	$12,600
Factory overhead (i)	6,300
Total processing costs	$18,900
Unit processing costs:	
$18,900 ÷ 4,200	$ 4.50

Allocation of costs of Department 2:		
Units started in December, completed in January:		
Inventory on January 1, 800 units ½ completed	$ 7,800	
Processing costs in January, 400 at $4.50	1,800	
Total ($9,600 ÷ 800 = $12 unit cost)		$ 9,600
Units started and completed in January:		
From Department 1, 3,200 units at $8.40	$26,880	
Processing costs, 3,200 at $4.50	14,400	
Total ($41,280 ÷ 3,200 = $12.90 unit cost)		41,280
Total transferred to Product A		$50,880
Units started in January, ⅔ completed:		
From Department 1, 900 units at $8.40	$ 7,560	
Processing costs, 600 at $4.50	2,700	
Total work in process — Department 2		10,260
Total costs charged to Department 2		$61,140

Entry: Finished Goods — Product A	50,880	
Work in Process — Department 2		50,880

(l) Cost of goods sold.

Product A, 3,800 units:		
1,000 units at $11.50	$11,500	
800 units at $12.00	9,600	
2,000 units at $12.90	25,800	
Total cost of Product A sold		$46,900
Product B, 1,000 pounds:		
1,000 pounds at $.50		500
Total cost of goods sold		$47,400

Entry: Cost of Goods Sold	47,400	
Finished Goods — Product A		46,900
Finished Goods — Product B		500

(m) Sales on account.

Entry: Accounts Receivable	71,100	
Sales		71,100

(n) Cash received on account.

Entry: Cash	70,000	
Accounts Receivable		70,000

(o) Cash disbursed.

Entry: Accounts Payable	50,000	
Wages Payable	22,000	
Cash		72,000

A chart of the flow of costs from the service and processing department accounts into the finished goods accounts and thence to the cost of goods sold account is illustrated on page 515. Entries in the accounts are identified by letters to facilitate comparison with the summary journal entries presented above.

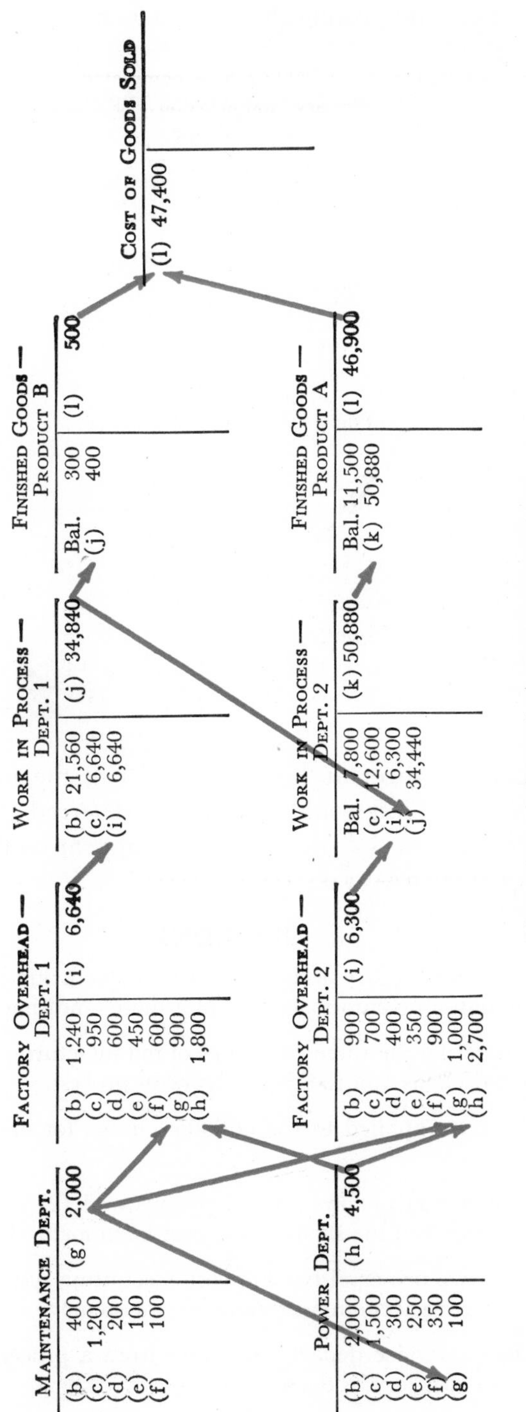

Flow of costs through process cost accounts

After recording and posting the foregoing entries, the trial balance of the ledger is as follows:

Howell Manufacturing Company
Trial Balance
January 31, 1966

Cash	16,500	
Accounts Receivable	16,100	
Finished Goods — Product A (1,200 units at $12.90)	15,480	
Finished Goods — Product B (400 pounds at $.50)	200	
Work in Process — Department 2 (900 units, ⅔ completed)	10,260	
Materials	19,400	
Prepaid Expenses	1,600	
Plant Assets	310,000	
Accumulated Depreciation — Plant Assets		97,250
Accounts Payable		16,780
Wages Payable		2,990
Common Stock		200,000
Retained Earnings		59,670
Sales		71,100
Cost of Goods Sold	47,400	
Factory Overhead — Department 1		100
Factory Overhead — Department 2	650	
Selling Expenses	5,500	
General Expenses	4,800	
	447,890	447,890

On the balance sheet at January 31, 1966, the net underapplied factory overhead of $550 would appear as a deferred charge. The balance in the cost of goods sold account would appear on the income statement as a deduction from sales.

QUESTIONS

1. Name the three inventory accounts of a manufacturing enterprise that replace the merchandise inventory account of a merchandising enterprise.

2. Name and describe the three categories of manufacturing costs included in the cost of finished goods and the cost of work in process.

3. What is the term applied to the periodic charge for ore removed from a mine?

4. (a) For what period of time are (1) patents and (2) copyrights granted? (b) Over what period of time should their cost be amortized?

5. (a) Name the two principal types of cost accounting systems. (b) How are the manufacturing costs accumulated under each system?

6. (a) How does a service department differ from a processing department? (b) Give examples of a service department.

7. If direct materials cost incurred is $8,000, direct labor cost incurred is $12,000, and factory overhead applied is $6,000, what is the processing cost?

8. Why do many manufacturing enterprises use predetermined factory overhead rates?

9. (a) How are predetermined factory overhead rates determined? (b) Name three common bases used in determining rates.

10. Factory employees in Department 3 of the Hayes Manufacturing Co. are paid widely varying wage rates. In such circumstances, would direct labor hours be a sounder basis than direct labor cost for applying factory overhead to the production of the department? Explain.

11. (a) What is (1) underapplied factory overhead and (2) overapplied factory overhead? (b) The factory overhead account for Department 4 has a debit balance. Was factory overhead underapplied or overapplied?

12. (a) What is meant by the term *equivalent units?* (b) If Department 1 had no work in process at the beginning of the period, 2,000 units entered the department during the period, and 500 units were 50% completed at the end of the period, what were the number of equivalent units of production for the period?

13. The information concerning production in Department 1 for June is presented below. All materials are placed in process at the beginning of production. Determine the number of units in work in process inventory at the end of the month.

Work in Process — Department 1

Process inventory, June 1:		Goods finished during June:	
800 units, ½ completed	1,980	3,000 units	11,890
Direct material, 2,700 units	2,430	Process inventory, June 30:	
Direct labor	6,100	_____ units, ⅘ completed	1,670
Factory overhead	3,050		
	13,560		13,560
Process inventory, July 1:			
_____ units, ⅘ completed	1,670		

14. (a) On interim balance sheets, where would the amount of (1) net underapplied factory overhead or (2) net overapplied factory overhead appear? (b) What disposition is made of the balances in the factory overhead accounts at the end of a fiscal year?

15. What is the most important purpose served by the cost of production report?

16. Distinguish between a by-product and a joint product.

17. Department 2 produces two products. How should the costs be allocated (a) if the products are joint products and (b) if one of the products is a by-product?

EXERCISES

1. Dixon Mining Company purchased land containing mineral deposits at a cost of $500,000, the estimated value of the land after exhaustion of the mineral deposit is $50,000, and the amount of recoverable mineral is estimated at 900,000 tons. Prepare the entry to record the removal of 72,000 tons.

2. The chief cost accountant for Mead Manufacturing, Inc. estimates total factory overhead cost for Department 1 for the year at $67,500 and total direct labor cost at $90,000. During January, actual direct labor cost totaled $8,400 and factory overhead cost incurred totaled $6,250. (a) What is the factory overhead rate based on direct labor cost? (b) Prepare the entry to apply factory overhead to production for January. (c) What is the balance of the account Factory Overhead — Department 1 at January 31? (d) Does the balance in (c) represent overapplied or underapplied factory overhead?

3. The charges to Work in Process — Department 1 for a period, together with information concerning production, are presented below. All materials are placed in process at the beginning of production.

Work in Process — Department 1

1,800 units, ⅔ completed	5,652	Product A, 5,500 units	22,252
Direct materials, 3,700 at $1	3,700		
Direct labor	5,150		
Factory overhead	7,750		
	22,252		22,252

Determine the following, presenting your computations: (a) equivalent units of production, (b) processing cost per equivalent unit, (c) total and unit cost of Product A started in prior period and completed in the current period, and (d) total and unit cost of Product A started and completed in the current period.

4. The debits to Work in Process — Department 2 of Stacy Company for the month of April of the current year, together with information concerning production, are presented below. All direct materials come from Department 1. The units completed include the 1,200 in process at the beginning of the period.

Work in Process — Department 2

1,200 units, ¼ completed	1,260	Product X, 6,200 units	—
From Dept. 1, 6,000 units	3,600	1,000 units, ½ completed	—
Direct labor	8,000		
Factory overhead	4,800		
	17,660		17,660
1,000 units, ½ completed	—		

Prepare a cost of production report.

5. The charges to Work in Process — Department 3, together with units of product completed during the period, are shown in the following account:

Work in Process — Department 3

From Department 2	4,500	By-product B, 1,000 units
Direct labor	4,600	Joint product X, 3,000 units
Factory overhead	6,900	Joint product Y, 1,500 units

The value of B is $.25 a unit; X sells at $4 a unit and Y sells at $6 a unit. There is no inventory of goods in process at either the beginning or the end of the period. Allocate the costs to the three products and determine the unit cost of each. Present your computations.

6. The Ronald Manufacturing Company produces its product by a continuous process involving five production departments. The records show that $12,200 of materials were issued to and $15,700 of factory labor incurred by Department 1 directly in the manufacture of the product; the factory overhead rate is 150% of direct labor cost; no work was in process in the department at the end of the period; and work in process at the beginning of the period totaled $3,900.

Prepare general journal entries to record: (a) the flow of costs into Department 1 during the period for (1) direct materials, (2) direct labor, and (3) factory overhead; (b) the transfer of production costs to Department 2.

PROBLEMS

21-1. On May 1, the Gifford Manufacturing Company had the following inventories:

Finished goods (400 units)	$16,000
Work in process	7,850
Materials	9,000

Departmental accounts are not maintained for work in process and factory overhead, nor are accounts maintained for service departments. Manufacturing operations for the month of May of the current fiscal year are summarized as follows:

(a) Materials purchased on account, $10,350.
(b) Materials requisitioned for use, $11,200, of which $10,700 was direct materials.
(c) Labor used, $9,150, of which $8,150 was used directly in the manufacture of the product.
(d) Factory overhead costs incurred on account: machinery repairs, $875; rent, $1,500; power and light, $650; and miscellaneous, $255.
(e) Expiration of prepaid insurance on machinery and equipment, $80.
(f) Depreciation of machinery and equipment, $320.
(g) Factory overhead applied to production, 60% of direct labor cost.
(h) Goods finished during month, $26,240 (640 units); work in process at end of month, $5,350.
(i) Sales on account (700 units), $47,500. (Use the first-in, first-out method in crediting the finished goods account.)

Instructions: Prepare entries in general journal form to record the foregoing operations.

21-2. Dodd Products manufactures Product M by a series of three processes, all direct materials being introduced in Department 1. From Department 1 the materials pass sequentially through Departments 2 and 3, emerging as finished Product M. All inventories are priced at cost by the first-in, first-out method.

The balances in the accounts Work in Process — Department 3 and Finished Goods were as follows on July 1:

Work in Process — Department 3	
Balance: 800 units, ¾ completed	$5,420
Finished Goods	
Balance: 600 units at $8 a unit	**4,800**

The following costs were charged to Work in Process — Department 3 during the month:

Materials transferred from Department 2: 6,800 units at $3.50	$23,800
Direct labor	18,040
Factory overhead	9,020

During the month of July, 6,400 units of M were completed. Inventories on July 31 were as follows:

Work in Process — Department 3: 1,200 units, ⅔ completed
Finished Goods: 1,100 units.

Instructions: (1) Determine the following, presenting the computations in good order: (a) equivalent units of production for Department 3; (b) unit processing cost for Department 3; (c) total and unit cost of Product M started in a prior period and finished in July; (d) total and unit cost of Product M started and finished in July; (e) total cost of goods transferred to finished goods; (f) work in process inventory, July 31; (g) cost of goods sold (indicate number of units and unit costs); (h) finished goods inventory, July 31.

(2) Set up T accounts for Work in Process — Department 3 and for Finished Goods. Record the balances at July 1 and the transactions for July in summary form; bring down the balances at July 31. Record the number of units and degree of completion, where appropriate, in the items sections of the accounts.

(3) Prepare a cost of production report for Department 3 for July.

21-3. The trial balance for Wilson Manufacturing Corporation at July 31, the end of the first month of the current fiscal year, is shown on the opposite page.

Instructions: (1) Prepare an income statement.

(2) Prepare a balance sheet.

21-4. The Wallace Company manufactures joint products X and Y. Materials are placed in production in Department 1 and after processing are transferred to Department 2, where more materials are added. The finished products emerge from Department 2. There are two service departments, Factory Office and Maintenance and Repair.

There were no inventories of work in process at either the beginning or the end of the period. Finished goods inventories at May 1 were as follows:

Finished Goods — Product X, 1,200 units	$7,200
Finished Goods — Product Y, 800 units	3,600

Transactions and other relevant data for the month of May in summary form are as follows:

(a) Materials purchased on account, $16,600.
(b) Prepaid expenses incurred on account, $1,100.
(c) Miscellaneous costs and expenses incurred on account: Department 1, $400; Department 2, $750; Factory Office, $350; Maintenance and Repair, $425; Selling Expenses, $3,950; and General Expenses, $1,610.
(d) Materials requisitioned for use, of which $5,600 entered directly into the products in Department 1 and $9,740 in Department 2: Department 1, $6,150; Department 2, $10,215; Maintenance and Repair, $775.

Wilson Manufacturing Corporation
Trial Balance
July 31, 19—

Account	Debit	Credit
Cash	52,300	
Accounts Receivable	97,700	
Allowance for Doubtful Accounts		6,100
Finished Goods — Product A	69,400	
Work in Process — Department 1	12,500	
Work in Process — Department 2	6,050	
Work in Process — Department 3	14,100	
Materials	44,100	
Office Supplies	2,650	
Prepaid Insurance	8,475	
Office Equipment	35,500	
Accumulated Depreciation — Office Equipment		16,700
Machinery and Equipment	192,400	
Accumulated Depreciation — Machinery and Equipment		91,200
Buildings	480,000	
Accumulated Depreciation — Buildings		235,350
Land	95,000	
Patents	15,000	
Accounts Payable		67,550
Wages Payable		10,200
Bonds Payable (due 1980)		200,000
Common Stock ($100 par)		300,000
Retained Earnings		175,995
Sales		242,810
Cost of Goods Sold	167,340	
Factory Overhead — Department 1		400
Factory Overhead — Department 2	200	
Factory Overhead — Department 3		980
Selling Expenses	33,850	
General Expenses	19,720	
Interest Expense	1,000	
	1,347,285	1,347,285

(e) Labor costs incurred, of which $7,300 and $3,500 were used directly in the manufacture of the products in Departments 1 and 2, respectively: Department 1, $8,200; Department 2, $4,200; Factory Office, $875; Maintenance and Repair, $1,630.

(f) Expiration of various prepaid expenses: Department 1, $150; Department 2, $125; Factory Office, $25; Maintenance and Repair, $75; Selling Expenses, $100; General Expenses, $75.

(g) Depreciation charged on plant assets: Department 1, $300; Department 2, $200; Factory Office, $50; Maintenance and Repair, $100; Selling Expenses, $125; General Expenses, $100.

(h) Factory Office costs allocated on the basis of man-hours worked: Department 1, 2,400 hours; Department 2, 1,000 hours; Maintenance and Repair, 600 hours.

(i) Maintenance and Repair costs allocated on the basis of services rendered: Department 1, 60%; Department 2, 40%.

(j) Factory overhead applied to production at the predetermined rates: 70% and 110% of direct labor cost, respectively, for Departments 1 and 2.
(k) Output of Department 1: 2,000 units.
(l) Output of Department 2: 4,000 units of Product X and 2,500 units of Product Y. Unit selling price is $8 for Product X and $6.40 for Product Y.
(m) Sales on account: 3,800 units of Product X at $8 and 2,000 units of Product Y at $6.40. Credits to the finished goods accounts are to be priced in accordance with the first-in, first-out method.
(n) Cash received on account, $41,500.
(o) Cash disbursements: on account, $20,000; wages $14,500.

Instructions: Prepare entries in general journal form to record the transactions. Include as an explanation for entry (l) the calculations for the allocation of the production costs for Department 2 to the joint products and as an explanation for entry (m) the units and the unit costs for each product sold.

21-5. The manufacturing operations of B. L. Golson are divided into three departments, through which the materials pass in sequential order from Department 1 through Department 3. The beginning inventory in Work in Process — Department 3 on March 1 and debits to the account during the month were as follows:

Balance, 2,000 units, ⅕ completed	$ 2,820
From Dept. 2, 8,700 units	10,440
Direct labor	9,500
Factory overhead	5,700

During March the 2,000 units in process on March 1 were completed, and of the 8,700 units entering the department, all were completed except 1,200 units, which were ⅓ completed.

Charges to Work in Process — Department 3 for the month of April were as follows:

From Dept. 2, 11,000 units	$13,750
Direct labor	9,635
Factory overhead	5,781

During April the units in process at the beginning of the month were completed, and of the 11,000 units entering the department, all were completed except 4,000 units, which were ⅖ completed.

Instructions: (1) Set up an account for Work in Process — Department 3. Record the balance as of March 1 and the debits and the credits to the account in March. Present computations for determination of (a) equivalent units of production, (b) unit processing cost, (c) cost of goods finished, differentiating between units started in the prior period and units started and finished in March, and (d) work in process inventory.

(2) Bring down the balance of the account as of April 1 and record the transactions for April. Present the computations listed in instruction (1).

(3) Determine the difference in unit cost between the product started and completed in March and the product started and completed in April. Determine also the amount of the difference attributable collectively to operations in Departments 1 and 2 and the amount attributable to operations in Department 3.

22. Job order costs

Job order and process costs distinguished

The process cost accounting system is best suited to manufacturing situations where the processes are continuous and the products are homogeneous. A job order cost accounting system is most appropriate where the product is made to customers' orders or specifications and the identity of each job or order is kept separate. A job order cost system is also appropriate when standard products are manufactured in batches rather than on a continuous basis. A job order cost system may be used to good advantage in such businesses as the construction industry, a custom shop producing made-to-order products, and machine shops where few jobs are identical.

Whether a process cost system or a job order cost system is used, costs for direct materials, direct labor, and factory overhead must be accumulated. With slight modifications, the accumulations for the process cost system also apply to the job order system. The most significant modification is that the job order cost system requires the identification of the individual jobs within the manufacturing processes and provides for a separate record of the costs applicable to each job. In factories with departmentalized operations, the costs are accumulated in factory overhead and work in process accounts maintained for each department. To simplify the discussions and illustrations of the job order system, a nondepartmentalized operation will be assumed in this chapter.

The discussion of the job order cost system directs considerable attention to the source documents that serve as the basis for the entries in the cost system and to the managerial uses of cost accounting in planning and controlling business operations. In many instances, methods and procedures described in terms of a job order cost system also apply to a process cost system. For example, in the discussion of accounting for materials cost in the job order cost system, the documents and the procedures for control over acquisition, storage, and issuance of materials also apply to the process cost system.

Materials

Procedures for procurement, control, and issuance of materials vary among businesses and production processes; yet there are fundamental procedures that apply to most manufacturing enterprises.

After engineering, design, and scheduling of the product for manufacture are completed, *purchases requisitions* are used to inform the purchasing department of the type and quantity of materials needed. The purchasing department requests delivery of the materials by issuing a *purchase order* to a supplier. After the goods have been received and inspected, the receiving department prepares a *receiving report* showing the quantity received and the condition of the materials. The quantity, the unit cost, and the total cost of the goods shipped as shown by the purchase invoice should be compared with the purchase order and the receiving report to make sure that the amount billed agrees with the materials ordered and received.

The amount of the purchase is entered in the voucher register or the purchases journal. From the book of original entry, the amount is posted as a part of the monthly total to the controlling account Materials in the general ledger. The subsidiary ledger for materials, which is called the *materials ledger*, contains a separate account for each type of material. Effective control over materials requires that the controlling account be kept by the accounting department and that the materials ledger be maintained by a person other than the custodian of the materials.

Information concerning quantity, unit cost, and total cost of materials received is entered in the materials ledger from the receiving reports or the purchases invoices. An account in the materials ledger is illustrated on the opposite page.

The accounts in the materials ledger are a constant reminder of the quantity of materials on hand. A comparison of the balance on hand with the predetermined reorder point, which appears in the upper right-hand corner of the materials ledger account, enables management to reorder materials systematically and to avoid interruption of production caused by lack of materials. A materials ordered column showing the quantity and the date of materials orders may be added to the materials ledger account illustrated above. This information is obtained by the *materials ledger clerk* from a copy of the purchase order. When the ordered

Material No. *23* Reorder Point *1,000*

Received			Issued			Balance			
Rec. Report No.	Quantity	Amount	Mat. Req. No.	Quantity	Amount	Date	Quantity	Amount	Unit Price
						19— Jan. 1	1,200	600 00	50
			672	500	250 00	4	700	350 00	50
196	3,000	1,620 00				8	700 3,000	350 00 1,620 00	50 54
			704	700 100	350 00 54 00	18	2,900	1,566 00	54

Materials ledger account

and the received columns are compared, the unfilled orders can be determined.

Materials are issued to the manufacturing departments on the basis of *materials requisitions* issued by the scheduling department or the manufacturing departments. A copy of the materials requisition must be presented to the *storekeeper* as authorization for the release of materials from the storeroom. Another copy of the materials requisition is sent to the materials ledger clerk for posting to the materials ledger. A summary of the materials requisitions issued during the month serves as the basis for recording the flow of materials into production. The flow of materials into production is illustrated by the following entry:

Work in Process	6,500	
Factory Overhead	420	
Materials		6,920

Since the materials requisition is the source document for charging the materials used to the specific job on which they were used, it must show the job order number.

The cost of the materials issued may be determined by the *first-in, first-out* method, the *last-in, first-out* method, or the *weighted-average* method. The fifo method was used in the illustration above. Of the 800 pounds of Material No. 23 issued in response to Materials Requisition No. 704, 700 pounds were priced at 50¢ and 100 pounds were priced at 54¢.

The perpetual inventory system for materials has three important advantages: (1) it provides for the prompt, accurate charging of materials to jobs and to factory overhead, (2) it serves as a check on the storekeeper, and (3) it avoids the necessity of a complete physical inventory of materials at one time, with the attendant interruption of production. Comparisons between a physical count of an item and the related materials ledger account can be made at any time, so that inventory-taking can be a continuous process spread throughout the year. After a physical count is taken, a report on inventory shortages and overages should be prepared. The storekeeper should then be required to explain any significant discrepancies.

Factory labor

A common method of accounting for factory labor uses *clock cards* as a means of recording the hours spent by employees in the factory. In order to charge each job order with the time and the cost of the direct labor incurred on the job and to charge factory overhead with the indirect labor cost, it is necessary to record labor costs on *time tickets*. Each time ticket provides space for recording the time the particular employee began work on a job, the time he ceased work on that job, the total time worked, the rate of pay, and the total cost. If a particular employee works on three different job orders during a day, the data will be recorded on three different time tickets. A similar report must be made for employees whose services are classified as indirect labor.

The total time reported on each employee's time tickets for a payroll period is compared with the time reported on his clock cards as an internal check on the accuracy of payroll disbursements. The time tickets are summarized at the end of each month or other time period, and Work in Process and Factory Overhead are charged for the appropriate amounts of the total labor costs incurred. The entry is completed by a credit to Wages Payable for the liability. The entry is illustrated as follows:

Work in Process	5,000	
Factory Overhead	1,100	
Wages Payable		6,100

Factory overhead

Although some manufacturers assign actual factory overhead costs to jobs, factory overhead is most often applied to jobs through use of a predetermined factory overhead rate. The use of a predetermined factory overhead rate assists management in pricing jobs. The costs of a job can be estimated by adding the costs for direct materials and direct labor based on past experience and by applying the factory overhead rate. This price determination is especially important for job order manufacturers because many of their products are manufactured to individual specifications. In addition, the use of a predetermined factory overhead rate permits determination of the total cost of a job shortly after the job is completed. Timely reporting enables management to make whatever adjustments seem necessary in pricing and manufacturing to achieve the best combination of revenue and expense on future jobs.

Amounts of factory overhead applied to work in process are summarized and recorded periodically. The following entry charges work in process with factory overhead at the predetermined rate of 80% of direct labor cost:

Work in Process	4,000	
Factory Overhead		4,000

Factory overhead is also applied to each job that is completed and each job that is in process at the end of the month.

Work in process

Costs incurred for the various jobs are debited to Work in Process. The charges to the account that were illustrated in the three preceding sections may be summarized as follows:

Direct Materials, $6,500 — Work in Process debited and Materials credited; data obtained from summary of materials requisitions.

Direct Labor, $5,000 — Work in Process debited and Wages Payable credited; data obtained from summary of time tickets.

Factory Overhead, $4,000 — Work in Process debited and Factory Overhead credited; data obtained by applying overhead rate to direct labor cost (80% of $5,000).

Ordinarily a number of jobs are in various stages of production at all times. The work in process account is a controlling account that contains summary information only. The details concerning the costs incurred on each job order are accumulated in a subsidiary ledger known as the *cost ledger*. Each account in the cost ledger, called a *job cost sheet*, has spaces for recording all direct materials and direct labor chargeable to the job and for the application of factory overhead at the predetermined rate. Postings to the job cost sheets are made from materials requisitions and time tickets or from summaries of these documents.

Upon completion of a job, the data on the related job cost sheet are summarized, the unit cost of the finished product is computed, and the sheet is removed from the cost ledger. A summary of the job cost sheets completed during the month provides the basis for an entry debiting Finished Goods and crediting Work in Process.

An illustrative work in process account and a summary of the four cost sheets in the related subsidiary ledger are presented on the next page.

WORK IN PROCESS

DATE		ITEMS	DEBIT	CREDIT	BALANCE DEBIT	BALANCE CREDIT
1966						
May	1	Balance			1,500	
	31	Direct materials	6,500		8,000	
	31	Direct labor	5,000		13,000	
	31	Factory overhead	4,000		17,000	
	31	Jobs completed		15,960	1,040	

COST LEDGER

Job No. 71 (Summary)

Balance	1,500
Direct Materials	1,000
Direct Labor	1,200
Factory Overhead	960
	4,660

Job No. 73 (Summary)

Direct Materials	3,000
Direct Labor	2,000
Factory Overhead	1,600
	6,600

Job No. 72 (Summary)

Direct Materials	2,000
Direct Labor	1,500
Factory Overhead	1,200
	4,700

Job No. 74 (Summary)

Direct Materials	500
Direct Labor	300
Factory Overhead	240
	1,040

The relationship between the work in process controlling account and the subsidiary cost ledger may be observed in the following tabulation of the data from the accounts illustrated above.

Work in Process (Controlling)		Cost Ledger (Subsidiary)	
Opening balance	$1,500 ↔	Opening balance	
		Job No. 71	$1,500
		Direct materials	
		Job No. 71	$1,000
Direct materials	$6,500 ↔	Job No. 72	2,000
		Job No. 73	3,000
		Job No. 74	500
			$6,500
		Direct labor	
		Job No. 71	$1,200
Direct labor	$5,000 ↔	Job No. 72	1,500
		Job No. 73	2,000
		Job No. 74	300
			$5,000

WORK IN PROCESS (Controlling)			COST LEDGER (Subsidiary)	
Factory overhead	$4,000	←→	Factory overhead	
			Job No. 71	$ 960
			Job No. 72	1,200
			Job No. 73	1,600
			Job No. 74	240
				$4,000
Jobs completed	$15,960	←→	Jobs completed	
			Job No. 71	$ 4,660
			Job No. 72	4,700
			Job No. 73	6,600
				$15,960
Closing balance	$ 1,040	←→	Closing balance	
			Job No. 74	$ 1,040

The data in the foregoing cost ledger were presented in summary fashion for illustrative purposes. A form of job cost sheet providing for the current accumulation of cost elements entering into a job order and for a summary at the time the job is completed is shown below for Job No. 72.

Job No. 72 Date May 7, 1966
Item 5,000 Type C Containers Date wanted May 23, 1966
For Stock Date completed May 21, 1966

Direct Materials		Direct Labor				Summary	
Mat. Req. No.	Amount	Time Summary No.	Amount	Time Summary No.	Amount	Items	Amount
434	400.00	2202	83.60	2248	22.50	Direct materials	2,000.00
438	500.00	2204	108.40	2250	87.30	Direct labor	1,500.00
441	700.00	2205	67.00	2253	55.40	Factory overhead (80% of direct labor cost)	1,200.00
464	400.00	2210	129.00				
		2211	98.30		1,500.00		
	2,000.00	2213	107.20				
		2216	110.00				
		2222	77.60				
		2224	217.40				
		2225	106.30			Total cost	4,700.00
		2231	53.20				
		2234	45.20				
		2237	70.00			No. of units finished	5,000
		2242	61.60			Cost per unit	.94

Job cost sheet

When Job No. 72 was completed, the direct materials costs and the direct labor costs were totaled and entered in the Summary column. Factory overhead was added at the predetermined rate of 80% of the direct labor cost, and the total cost of the job was determined. The total cost of the job, $4,700, divided by the number of units produced, 5,000, yielded a unit cost of 94 cents for the Type C Containers produced.

Upon the completion of Job No. 72, the job cost sheet was removed from the cost ledger and filed for future reference. At the end of the accounting period, the sum of the total costs on all cost sheets completed during the period is determined and the following entry is made:

Finished Goods	15,960	
Work in Process		15,960

The remaining balance in the work in process account then represents the total costs charged to the uncompleted job cost sheets.

Finished goods and cost of goods sold

The finished goods account is a controlling account. The related subsidiary ledger, which has an account for each kind of commodity produced, is called the *finished goods ledger* or *stock ledger*. Each account in the subsidiary finished goods ledger provides columns for recording the quantity and the cost of goods manufactured, the quantity and the cost of goods shipped, and the quantity, the total cost, and the unit cost of goods on hand. A finished goods account and an account in the finished goods ledger are illustrated on the opposite page.

Just as there are various methods of pricing materials entering into production, so also there are various methods of determining the cost of the finished goods sold. In the illustration the first-in, first-out method is used. The quantities shipped are posted to the finished goods ledger from a copy of the shipping order or other memorandum. The finished goods ledger clerk then records on the shipping order the unit price and the total amount of the commodity sold. A summary of the cost data on these shipping orders becomes the basis for the following entry:

Cost of Goods Sold	15,084	
Finished Goods		15,084

If goods are returned by a buyer and put back in stock, it is necessary to debit Finished Goods and credit Cost of Goods Sold for the cost.

Sales

For each sale of finished goods it is necessary to maintain a record of both the cost price and the selling price of the goods sold. As indicated above, the cost data may be recorded on the shipping orders. The sales

FINISHED GOODS

DATE		ITEMS	DEBIT	CREDIT	BALANCE DEBIT	BALANCE CREDIT
1966						
May	1	Balance			7,190	
	31	Job Nos. 71, 72, 73	15,960		23,150	
	31	Shipping Order Nos. 641–46		15,084	8,066	

Finished goods account in the general ledger

Item: *Type C Container*

Manufactured			Shipped			Balance				
Job Order No.	Quantity	Amount	Ship. Order No.	Quantity	Amount	Date		Quantity	Amount	Unit Price
						1966 May	1	2,000	1,960 00	98
			643	2,000	1,960 00		8	—	—	-
72	5,000	4,700 00					21	5,000	4,700 00	94
			646	2,000	1,880 00		23	3,000	2,820 00	94

An account in the finished goods ledger

journal may be expanded by the addition of a column for recording the total cost of the goods billed, the total of the column being posted at the end of the month as a debit to Cost of Goods Sold and a credit to Finished Goods. The total of the sales price column is posted at the end of the month as a debit to Accounts Receivable and a credit to Sales.

Summary illustration of job order cost accounting

To illustrate further the procedures described, the following facts are assumed: The Rockford Manufacturing Co. employs a job order cost accounting system. The trial balance of the general ledger on January 1, 1966, the first day of the fiscal year, is given on the following page.

Rockford Manufacturing Co.
Trial Balance
January 1, 1966

Cash	85,000	
Accounts Receivable	73,000	
Finished Goods	40,000	
Work in Process	20,000	
Materials	30,000	
Prepaid Expenses	2,000	
Plant Assets	850,000	
Accumulated Depreciation — Plant Assets		473,000
Accounts Payable		70,000
Wages Payable		15,000
Common Stock		500,000
Retained Earnings		42,000
	1,100,000	1,100,000

A summary of the transactions and the adjustments for the month of January, followed in each case by the related entry in general journal form, is presented below. In practice the transactions would be recorded from day to day in various journals.

(a) Materials purchased and prepaid expenses incurred on account.
Summary of receiving reports:

Material A	$ 20,000
Material B	17,000
Material C	12,000
Material D	13,000
Total	$ 62,000

Entry: Materials	62,000	
Prepaid Expenses	1,000	
Accounts Payable		63,000

(b) Materials requisitioned for use.
Summary of requisitions:

By Use

Job No. 1001	$12,000	
Job No. 1002	26,000	
Job No. 1003	22,000	$ 60,000
Factory Overhead		3,000
Total		$ 63,000

By Types

Material A	$ 16,000
Material B	18,000
Material C	15,000
Material D	14,000
Total	$ 63,000

Entry: Work in Process	60,000	
Factory Overhead	3,000	
Materials		63,000

(c) Factory labor used.
Summary of time tickets:

Job No. 1001	$60,000	
Job No. 1002	30,000	
Job No. 1003	10,000	$100,000
Factory Overhead		20,000
Total		$120,000

Entry: Work in Process	100,000	
Factory Overhead	20,000	
Wages Payable		120,000

(d) Costs and expenses incurred for factory overhead and by the sales and administrative divisions.

Entry: Factory Overhead	56,000	
Selling Expenses	25,000	
General Expenses	10,000	
Accounts Payable		91,000

(e) Expiration of prepaid expenses.

Entry: Factory Overhead	1,000	
Selling Expenses	100	
General Expenses	100	
Prepaid Expenses		1,200

(f) Depreciation chargeable to factory and to sales and administrative divisions.

Entry: Factory Overhead	7,000	
Selling Expenses	200	
General Expenses	100	
Accumulated Depreciation — Plant Assets		7,300

(g) Application of factory overhead costs to jobs at the rate of 90% of direct labor cost. See transaction (c).
Summary of factory overhead applied:

Job No. 1001 (90% of $60,000)	$ 54,000
Job No. 1002 (90% of $30,000)	27,000
Job No. 1003 (90% of $10,000)	9,000
Total	$ 90,000

Entry: Work in Process	90,000	
Factory Overhead		90,000

(h) Jobs completed.
Summary of completed cost sheets:

Job No. 1001	$146,000
Job No. 1002	83,000
Total	$229,000

Entry: Finished Goods	229,000	
Work in Process		229,000

(i) Sales on account and cost of goods sold.
Summary of sales invoices and shipping orders:

	Sales Price	Cost Price
Product X	$ 19,600	$ 15,000
Product Y	165,100	125,000
Product Z	105,300	80,000
Total	$290,000	$220,000

	Debit	Credit
Entry: Accounts Receivable	290,000	
Sales		290,000
Entry: Cost of Goods Sold	220,000	
Finished Goods		220,000

(j) Cash received and disbursed.

	Debit	Credit
Entry: Cash	300,000	
Accounts Receivable		300,000
Entry: Accounts Payable	190,000	
Wages Payable	125,000	
Cash		315,000

The flow of costs through the manufacturing accounts, together with summary details of the subsidiary ledgers, is illustrated on the opposite page. Entries in the accounts are identified by letters to facilitate comparisons with the summary journal entries presented above.

The trial balance taken from the general ledger of the Rockford Manufacturing Co. on January 31 is as follows:

Rockford Manufacturing Co.
Trial Balance
January 31, 1966

Cash	70,000	
Accounts Receivable	63,000	
Finished Goods	49,000	
Work in Process	41,000	
Materials	29,000	
Prepaid Expenses	1,800	
Plant Assets	850,000	
Accumulated Depreciation — Plant Assets		480,300
Accounts Payable		34,000
Wages Payable		10,000
Common Stock		500,000
Retained Earnings		42,000
Sales		290,000
Cost of Goods Sold	220,000	
Factory Overhead		3,000
Selling Expenses	25,300	
General Expenses	10,200	
	1,359,300	1,359,300

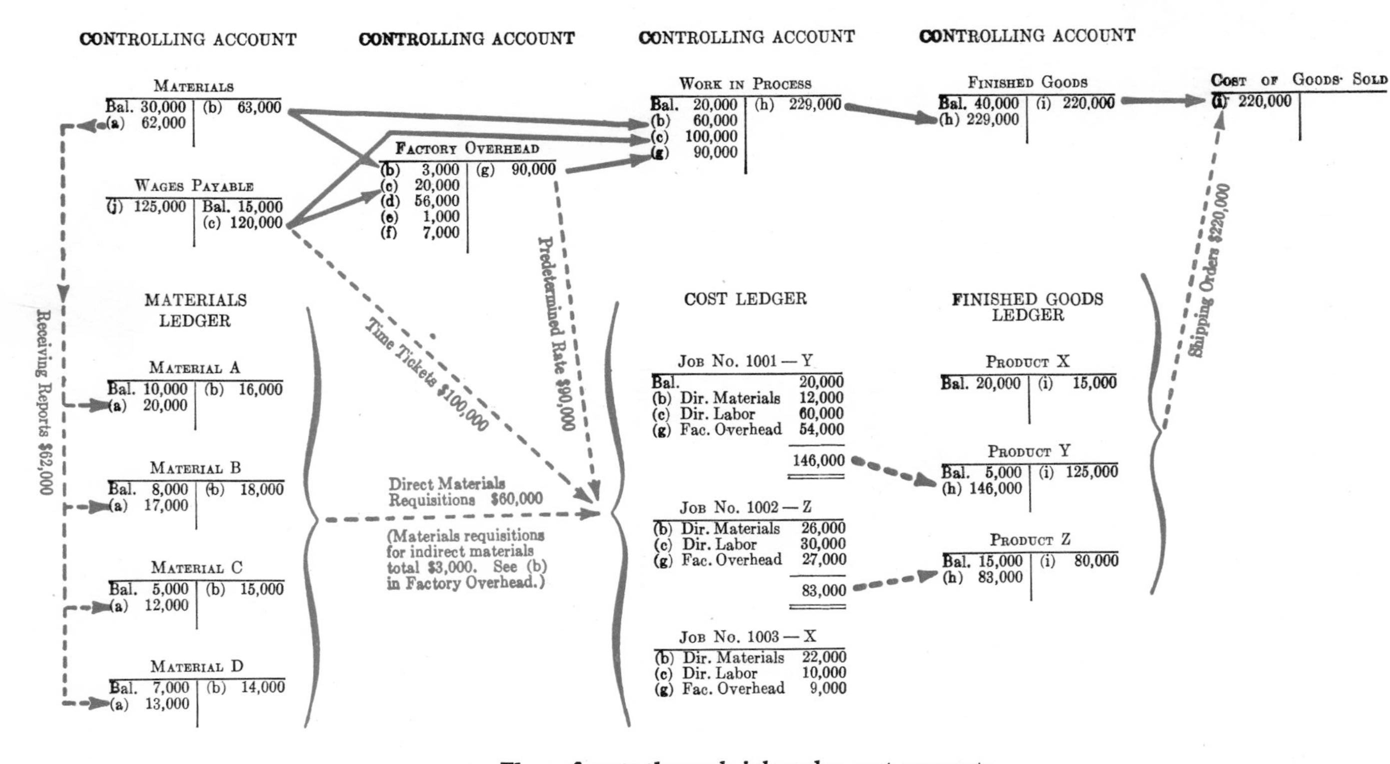

Flow of costs through job order cost accounts

The balances of the three inventory accounts, Materials, Work in Process, and Finished Goods, represent the respective inventories on January 31. Each account controls a subsidiary ledger. A comparison of the balances of the general ledger accounts with their respective subsidiary ledgers reveals the following:

Controlling Accounts		*Subsidiary Ledgers*		
Account	Balance	Account	Balance	
Materials	$29,000	Material A	$14,000	
		Material B	7,000	
		Material C	2,000	
		Material D	6,000	$29,000
Work in Process	$41,000	Job No. 1003		$41,000
Finished Goods	$49,000	Product X	$ 5,000	
		Product Y	26,000	
		Product Z	18,000	$49,000

The financial statements prepared from a job order cost system are similar to those prepared from a process cost system.

In order to simplify the illustration, only one work in process account and one factory overhead account have been used. Ordinarily a manufacturing business has several processing departments, each requiring separate work in process and factory overhead accounts. In the foregoing illustration, one predetermined rate was used in applying the factory overhead to jobs. In a factory with a number of processing departments, a single factory overhead rate may not provide accurate product costs and effective cost control. A single rate for the entire factory cannot give recognition to such factors as differences among departments in the nature of their operations and of relative amounts of factory overhead incurred. In such cases, each factory department should have its own overhead rate. For example, in a factory with twenty distinct operating departments, one department might have an overhead rate of 110% of direct labor cost, another a rate of $4 per direct labor hour, another a rate of $3.50 per machine hour, and so on.

Managerial uses of cost accounting

The principal purposes of cost accounting are to provide the data (1) to determine the cost of commodities manufactured and net operating income and (2) to assist management in planning and controlling operations in such a manner as to maximize profits. In the discussions and illustrations of process costs and job order costs, attention was directed to the role of source documents, the general ledger, and the journals in cost accounting. Interwoven into the discussion were references to the manner in which cost accounting can provide data useful to management in planning and controlling operations.

Regardless of the type of cost system employed, costs must be accumulated by department or cost center for effective control. Under the process cost system, a cost of production report is prepared for each department to inform management of the costs for which each department is accountable. Management must then keep these costs to a minimum. Supplementary reports prepared on a timely basis, such as daily reports for materials usage and direct labor usage, also assist in cost control.

Departmental responsibility for costs incurred under the job order system is fixed in much the same manner. The department heads are provided with reports of the costs for which they are accountable. In addition, the costs reported on the job cost sheets when compared with costs for similar jobs or estimated costs will reveal differences that should be investigated.

Periodic reports of gross profit by individual jobs or products are often prepared for use by management in evaluating past performance and determining future policies. Such reports indicate the jobs or the products that have been profitable and provide useful information for pricing future jobs or products. Other periodic reports, such as daily reports of spoilage, provide management with useful information in the control of costs.

Trend reports comparing cost data of the current period with those of earlier periods also assist management in the analysis of past operations and in the planning of future operations.

Many of the ways in which cost accounting can assist management in controlling and planning operations cannot be fully integrated with the general ledger and the journals that have been the focus of much of the discussion of the process cost and job order cost systems. For example, one of the most effective means of controlling costs is through the use of budgeting and standard costs, which often fall outside the general ledger. These concepts are discussed in the following chapter. In addition, subsequent chapters present other concepts, analyses, and reports that are useful to management in planning and controlling operations.

QUESTIONS

1. Which type of cost system, process or job order, would be best suited for the following: (a) printing shop, (b) oil refinery, (c) shipbuilder, and (d) automobile manufacturer? Give reasons for your answers.

2. Differentiate between a purchase requisition and a purchase order.

3. What is the materials ledger?

4. What document is the source for debiting the accounts in the materials ledger?

5. Name the form used to authorize the storekeeper to issue materials to a manufacturing department.

6. The beginning balance, a purchase, and an issuance to production of a particular type of material are described below in chronological sequence. What is (a) the cost of the materials issued to production and (b) the cost of the inventory after the issuance, determined by (1) the first-in, first-out method and (2) the last-in, first-out method?

Balance at beginning......	150 pounds @ $1.00 per pound......	$150
Purchase................	200 pounds @ $1.10 per pound......	$220
Issued to production......	100 pounds	

7. Discuss the advantages of a perpetual inventory system over a periodic system for materials.

8. If a perpetual inventory system is used, is it necessary to take a physical inventory? Discuss.

9. What purpose is served by (a) the clock card and (b) the time ticket?

10. Discuss how the predetermined factory overhead rate can be used in job order cost accounting to assist management in pricing jobs.

11. Describe the source of the data for debiting Work in Process for (a) direct materials, (b) direct labor, and (c) factory overhead.

12. What account is the controlling account for (a) the *cost ledger*, which contains the job cost sheets for the unfinished jobs, and (b) the *finished goods ledger* or *stock ledger*?

13. Name the form from which costs are posted to (a) the direct materials section of the job cost sheet and (b) the direct labor section of the job cost sheet.

14. In a factory with several departments, a separate factory overhead rate for each department is often used. Why is a single factory overhead rate often inadequate in such circumstances?

15. What are the principal purposes of cost accounting?

EXERCISES

1. Materials were received and issued during the month of October as follows:

Received

October	3	150 units @ $3.00..........	$450
	12	100 units @ 3.25..........	325
	25	100 units @ 3.10..........	310

		Issued
October	5	50 units
	17	100 units
	27	100 units

Determine the cost of each of the three issues using (a) the first-in, first-out method and (b) the last-in, first-out method.

2. Present the general journal entry to record the issuance of the materials represented by the following materials requisitions for the month:

Requisition No.	Description	Amount
372	Job No. 179	$5,250
373	Job No. 184	3,700
374	Job No. 180	4,525
375	General factory use	725
376	Job No. 182	2,470

3. A summary of the time tickets for the month of November follows:

Description of Work	Amount	Description of Work	Amount
Job No. 779	$1,460	Job No. 778	$1,120
Job No. 777	2,275	Job No. 780	630
Job No. 782	865	Indirect labor	1,040

Present the general journal entry to record the labor costs incurred.

4. The Davis Manufacturing Company applies factory overhead to jobs on the basis of direct labor hours. The factory overhead for the year is estimated at $90,000 and direct labor hours are estimated at 45,000 hours. (a) What is the factory overhead rate based on direct labor hours? (b) Prepare the general journal entry to apply factory overhead to production for January, during which 3,900 direct labor hours were worked. (c) If actual factory overhead incurred for January was $7,890, what was the balance of the factory overhead account on January 31? (d) Was factory overhead overapplied or underapplied on January 31?

5. The following account appears in the ledger after only part of the postings have been completed for the month of May:

Work in Process		
Balance, May 1	9,500	
Direct Materials	32,000	
Direct Labor	40,000	
Factory Overhead	36,000	

Jobs finished during the month are summarized below.

Job No. 107	$10,500
Job No. 109	27,750
Job No. 111	39,325
Job No. 112	22,175

(a) Prepare the general journal entry to record the jobs completed and (b) determine the cost of the unfinished jobs at the end of the month.

6. Mercer Industries, Inc. began business on July 1. Three jobs entered production during the month. Job No. 1 was completed and the other two jobs were still in process at the end of the month. The job cost sheets (No. 2 and No. 3 are incomplete) are presented below. In addition to the direct materials and the direct labor charged to the jobs, a total of $850 of indirect materials and $1,625 of indirect labor were used. Prepare entries in general journal form to record the following operations for the month:

(a) Issuance of materials.
(b) Use of factory labor.
(c) Application of factory overhead (the rate is based on direct labor cost).
(d) Completion of Job No. 1.

Job No. 1	
Direct Material	9,700
Direct Labor	4,900
Factory Overhead	2,450
Total	17,050

Job No. 2	
Direct Material	4,200
Direct Labor	2,600
Factory Overhead	

Job No. 3	
Direct Material	6,300
Direct Labor	3,500
Factory Overhead	

PROBLEMS

22-1. The Morton Manufacturing Corporation uses a job order cost system. The following data summarize the operations related to production for May, the first month of operations.

(a) Materials purchased on account, $30,000.
(b) Materials requisitioned and factory labor used:

	Materials	Factory Labor
Job No. 101	$3,250	$4,750
Job No. 102	2,700	3,880
Job No. 103	5,650	3,520
Job No. 104	4,400	5,200
Job No. 105	3,500	1,800
Job No. 106	1,750	900
For general factory use	950	1,850

(c) Factory overhead costs incurred on account, $17,200.
(d) Depreciation of machinery and equipment, $2,600.
(e) The factory overhead rate is 110% of direct labor cost.
(f) Jobs completed: Nos. 101, 103, 104, and 106.
(g) Job Nos. 101, 103, and 104 were shipped and customers were billed for $21,000, $21,500, and $25,000 respectively.

Instructions: (1) Prepare entries in general journal form to record the foregoing summarized operations.

(2) Set up T accounts for Work in Process and Finished Goods. Post to these accounts, using the identifying letters as dates. Bring down the end-of-the-month balances.

(3) Prepare a schedule of unfinished jobs to support the balance in the work in process account.

(4) Prepare a schedule of completed jobs on hand to support the balance in the finished goods account.

22-2. On April 30, the end of the fifth month of the current fiscal year, the following trial balance was taken from the general ledger of Dodson Manufacturing Company:

Dodson Manufacturing Company
Trial Balance
April 30, 19—

Cash	90,800	
Accounts Receivable	72,500	
Finished Goods	50,200	
Work in Process	14,000	
Materials	23,500	
Plant Assets	165,000	
Accumulated Depreciation — Plant Assets		80,000
Accounts Payable		42,500
Wages Payable		5,300
Capital Stock		150,000
Retained Earnings		78,950
Sales		425,000
Cost of Goods Sold	315,000	
Factory Overhead	1,250	
Selling and General Expenses	49,500	
	781,750	781,750

As of the same date, balances in the accounts of selected subsidiary ledgers are as follows:

Materials ledger:
Material A, $19,000; Material B, $4,200; Material C, $300

Cost ledger:
Job No. 601, $8,500; Job No. 602, $5,500

Finished goods ledger:
Commodity R, 1,000 units, $27,000; Commodity S, 800 units, $8,800; Commodity T, 2,400 units, $14,400

The transactions completed during May are summarized as follows:

(a) Materials were purchased on account as follows:

Material A	$16,000
Material B	18,400
Material C	2,800

(b) Materials were requisitioned from the storekeeper as follows:

Job No. 601, Material A, $5,500	$ 5,500
Job No. 602, Material A, $7,500; Material B, $5,950	13,450
Job No. 603, Material A, $9,800; Material B, $7,050	16,850
For general factory use; Material C	2,100

(c) Time tickets for the month were chargeable as follows:

Job No. 601	$14,000	Job No. 603	$12,600
Job No. 602	16,600	Indirect labor	4,500

(d) Various factory overhead charges of $25,400 were incurred on account.
(e) Depreciation on factory plant and equipment was recorded, $1,500.
(f) Factory overhead was applied to jobs at the rate of 75% of direct labor cost.
(g) Selling and general expenses incurred on account, $9,000.
(h) Jobs completed during the month: Job No. 601 produced 1,400 units of Commodity R; Job No. 602 produced 4,000 units of Commodity S.
(i) Total sales on account were $99,000. The goods sold were as follows (use first-in, first-out method): 1,100 units of Commodity R; 3,000 units of Commodity S; 1,000 units of Commodity T.
(j) Cash of $95,000 was received on accounts receivable.
(k) Factory payroll checks for $48,300 were issued.
(l) Payments on account were $67,000.

Instructions: (1) Open T accounts for the general ledger, the materials ledger, the cost ledger, and the finished goods ledger. Record directly in these accounts the balances listed on the trial balance, identifying them as "Bal." Record the quantities as well as the dollar amounts in the finished goods ledger.

(2) Prepare entries in general journal form to record the May transactions. After recording each transaction, post to the T accounts, using the identifying letters as dates. When posting to the finished goods ledger, record quantities as well as dollar amounts.

(3) Take a trial balance.

(4) Prove the subsidiary ledgers with the general ledger controlling accounts.

(5) Prepare an income statement for the six months ended May 31.

22-3. The trial balance of the Fleming Manufacturing Corporation at May 31 of the current year is presented below. The fiscal year ends on June 30.

Fleming Manufacturing Corporation
Trial Balance
May 31, 19—

Cash	116,700	
Accounts Receivable	76,200	
Allowance for Doubtful Accounts		2,100
Finished Goods	92,400	
Work in Process	26,100	
Materials	39,300	
Prepaid Insurance	4,160	
Factory Equipment	280,000	
Accumulated Depreciation — Factory Equipment		88,000
Office Equipment	19,200	
Accumulated Depreciation — Office Equipment		4,000
Accounts Payable		62,500
Income Tax Payable		26,200
Cash Dividends Payable		—
Wages Payable		1,900

Common Stock (no par, 5,000 shares)		300,000
Retained Earnings		127,760
Expense and Revenue Summary		—
Sales		520,000
Cost of Goods Sold	393,000	
Factory Overhead	1,550	
Selling Expenses	37,900	
General Expenses	19,750	
Income Tax	26,200	
	1,132,460	1,132,460

Transactions completed during June and adjustments required on June 30 are summarized as follows:

(a)	Purchased materials on account		$28,500
(b)	Incurred following costs and expenses on account:		
	Factory overhead	$11,700	
	Selling expenses	3,100	
	General expenses	1,950	16,750
(c)	Factory labor costs incurred:		
	Direct	$13,300	
	Indirect	2,300	15,600
(d)	Materials requisitioned for factory use:		
	Direct	$ 9,700	
	Indirect	500	10,200
(e)	Factory overhead at a predetermined rate: 140% of direct labor cost		
(f)	Cash disbursed:		
	Wages	$14,800	
	Accounts payable	60,200	75,000
(g)	Total cost of jobs completed		42,400
(h)	Sales, all on account:		
	Selling price		64,000
	Cost price		47,600
(i)	Cash received on account		62,400
(j)	Declared quarterly cash dividend of $1 per share.		
(k)	Depreciation charged:		
	Factory equipment		1,600
	Office equipment		240
(l)	Insurance expired:		
	Chargeable to factory	$ 240	
	Chargeable to selling expenses	60	
	Chargeable to general expenses	20	320
(m)	Uncollectible accounts receivable written off		640
(n)	Added to allowance for doubtful accounts based on credit department estimate: 1½% of sales for month		
(o)	Closed balance in Factory Overhead to Cost of Goods Sold.		
(p)	Recorded additional income tax		5,800

Instructions: (1) Open T accounts and record the initial balances indicated in the May 31 trial balance, identifying each as "Bal."

(2) Record the transactions and the adjustments directly in the accounts, using the identifying letters in place of dates.

(3) Record the necessary year-end closing entries directly in the accounts, using a capital "C" to designate these entries.

(4) Prepare an income statement for the year ended June 30.

(5) Prepare a balance sheet as of June 30.

22-4. Selected accounts for Harris Industries are presented below. For the purposes of this problem, some of the debits and credits have been omitted.

Materials

May 1 Balance	9,900	May 31 Requisitions	(A)
31 Purchases	12,200		

Work in Process

May 1 Balance	7,200	May 31 Goods finished	(D)
31 Direct materials	(B)		
31 Direct labor	21,000		
31 Factory overhead	(C)		

Finished Goods

May 1 Balance	12,400	May 31 Cost of goods sold	(F)
31 Goods finished	(E)		

Factory Overhead

May 1–31 Costs incurred	15,150	May 1 Balance	325
		31 Applied (70% of direct labor cost)	(G)

Cost of Goods Sold

May 31	(H)		

Inventories at May 31:

Finished goods	10,600
Work in process	8,400
Materials	6,500

Materials requisitions for May included $700 of materials issued for general factory use.

Instructions: (1) Determine the amounts represented by the letters (A) through (H), presenting your computations.

(2) Is factory overhead overapplied or underapplied at May 31? By how much?

23. Budgetary control and standard costs

Accounting aids to management

The basic functions of management are planning, coordination, and control. *Planning* is directed toward the establishment of desirable future objectives and the formation of an organizational structure to be followed in achieving them. *Coordination* consists of integrating individual and group effort with the overall objectives. *Control* results from the evaluation of individual and group effort in terms of the predetermined goals.

The effective discharge of these functions is essential to sound business management and successful operations. In a small sole proprietorship in which the owner personally supervises every phase of operations, the basic functions of management may be performed with little recourse to accounting data. In most companies, however, direct personal supervision by one individual is seldom possible and it is necessary to establish a chain of command from top management to division managers and department foremen. Under such circumstances, accounting becomes an indispensable tool of management. Accounting not only provides each level of management with relevant financial and operating data, but it also furnishes the basic facts required in planning, coordination, and control.

The accountant has at his disposal various techniques and procedures to obtain the data useful to management in making decisions regarding such matters as sales policies, production processes, purchasing procedures, and financing methods. The use of these techniques and procedures illustrates the point that accounting is not strictly a historical function, but that it is primarily a valuable tool for providing guidance to management.

Earlier chapters have described such accounting aids to management as internal control, financial statements, and process and job order cost accounting. This chapter will be devoted to two of the accounting tools most useful for the planning, coordination, and control of business operations — budgetary control and standard costs. Both of these accounting tools provides valuable data to the management of a business.

Nature and importance of cost control

Selling prices for many products are established by competition, and the profit potential of a firm depends to a large extent upon the control of costs. Effective cost control, by keeping operating costs within the limits set by the business plans, helps to insure efficient operations and maximum profits. Budgeting and standard costs facilitate cost control by signaling operating areas that may require investigation and changes to bring costs within acceptable limits.

Most of the preceding chapters concentrated on the determination of net income. One purpose of the determination of net income is to aid in the control of costs. The income statement, for example, reveals significant relationships between expired costs and revenues that enable management to determine the relative efficiency of departments and processes. The income determination procedures can assist in cost control by pointing out areas where steps should be taken to prevent the recurrence of excessive costs. Effective cost control, however, often extends beyond these methods. Cost control processes generally concentrate on preventive control by setting predetermined standards and keeping actual costs within these boundaries.

Individuals control business operations, and upon them rests the responsibility for the control of costs. For example, they decide upon the most efficient manufacturing processes, make the best use of materials and labor, and coordinate the entire manufacturing process. For effective cost control, those responsible for incurring the costs must be provided with the data necessary to keep the costs within acceptable limits. It is one of the functions of accounting, and more specifically of budgeting and standard costs, to make available to the responsible individuals the data that will lead to the most efficient utilization of the assets of the business.

Nature and objectives of budgeting

Budgeting consists of establishing specific future goals and periodically measuring results against the planned objectives. In this chapter, the business applications of budgeting will be stressed, but it is important to recognize that budgeting has wide applicability in other areas.

Budgeting, for example, plays an important role in operating a governmental agency, whether it be a small rural school district or the federal government. Budgeting is also an integral part of the operations of churches and charitable institutions and is often used by families and by individuals.

A *budget* is a formal written statement of management's plans for the future, expressed in financial terms. A budget charts the course of future action. Thus, it serves management in the same manner that the architect's blueprints assist the builder and the navigator's flight plan aids the pilot. A budget, like a blueprint and a flight plan, should contain sound, attainable objectives rather than mere wishful thinking.

In a business enterprise, budgeting embraces both accounting and management functions. It is a management function because it is an expression of management's plans. It is an accounting function because the plans are translated into financial terms by the accounting department, and subsequent comparisons of actual performance with the plans (budget) are made from accounting reports.

Budgeting and management

Probably no other instrument contributes more directly to effective management than a budget. Each of management's primary functions is directly served by budgeting. Planning is encouraged because careful study, investigation, and research must be undertaken to determine expected future operations if the budget is to contain sound, attainable goals. Advance planning, in turn, increases the reliance of management on fact finding in making decisions and lessens the role of hunches and intuition in managing a business enterprise.

Coordination is facilitated as each level of management participates in the preparation of the budget. In addition, a budget enables top management to explain its objectives to each stratum of management and to keep these goals before the entire organization. As a result, employees within a department are motivated to work as a team and the activities of each department are integrated with those of related departments. For example, production schedules can be developed in accordance with sales expectations, purchases of materials can be integrated with production and inventory requirements, and manpower requirements can be correlated with anticipated production and sales.

Although managerial planning and coordination are important, they must be accompanied by control. Budgeting contributes to effective management control through the preparation of frequent budget reports in which actual performance and budget objectives are compared and variations are revealed. The disclosure of variations enables management to focus attention on the areas that require immediate corrective action. Budget objectives also encourage efficiency and a reduction in costs and act as a deterrent to waste.

Budgeting procedures

Effective budgeting is dependent upon an organizational structure in which authority and responsibility are clearly defined. The establishment of definite responsibility is an essential requirement in budgeting, for without responsibility there can be no reliable basis of accountability. In order to obtain the maximum benefits of budgeting, accountability must parallel responsibility. This means that the accounting system should be designed in accordance with the division of responsibilities provided in the organizational structure of a company. For example, if primary responsibility for sales is vested in three divisional managers, the accounting system should provide for the accumulation of sales data by divisions.

The preparation of budgets is ordinarily assigned to a budget committee composed of the chief accounting officer or controller, the treasurer, the sales manager, the production manager, and perhaps others who have major functional responsibilities. The committee initially requests each supervisor or foreman to submit estimates for his area of operations. Requests for budget estimates should be extended to even the lowest level in the chain of accountability in order to enlist the cooperation of all strata of management and to avoid the resentment that may result from "know-it-all" planning by top management.

After the estimates have been received by the committee, they are reviewed and incorporated into a master plan. This process usually necessitates a revision of some of the estimates, and each supervisor is given an opportunity to defend his estimates and requests. The various budgets are then agreed upon and approved by the committee. Finally, the budgets are distributed and explained to each supervisor in the chain of accountability.

Periodically, budget reports are prepared to indicate the progress being made toward the planned objectives and to inform management of favorable and unfavorable results. Such reports may be prepared weekly, monthly, or annually depending upon the type of budget and the wishes of management. When monthly reports are used, cumulative data for the year to date are often included.

Sales budget

The sales budget represents the foundation of the entire planning program and the essential starting point in budgeting. Each of the other budgets is directly or indirectly related to the sales budget.

The sales budget may be expressed in terms of products, territories, or departments. Data for the sales budget are obtained from (1) an analysis of past sales performance, (2) a forecast of expected business conditions, and (3) market research. To illustrate the preparation of a sales budget, it is assumed that in 1965 the Linn Company sold 120,000 units of X at $6 each and 70,000 units of Y at $10 each. The forecast of general business conditions and market research indicates a 10% increase in the sales volume of X, no volume increase in Y, and an expected 10% price increase for each product in 1966. Based upon these expectations, the sales budget is as follows:

Linn Company
Sales Budget
For Year Ending December 31, 1966

Product	Sales Volume	Selling Price	Total Sales
X	132,000	$ 6.60	$ 871,200
Y	70,000	11.00	770,000
			$1,641,200

Production cost budget

The production cost budget sets forth the estimated cost of manufacturing the number of units that will be needed to meet expected sales and inventory requirements. The expected volume of production is determined by subtracting the number of units on hand at the beginning of the period from the sum of the units expected to be sold and the number of units desired in the inventory at the end of the period. In the Linn Company there are 22,000 units of X and 12,000 units of Y on hand at the beginning of the year, and desired ending inventories are 20,000 units of X and 15,000 units of Y. It will therefore be necessary to produce 130,000 units of X and 73,000 units of Y, as shown by the following tabulation:

	Units	
	Product X	Product Y
Expected sales volume	132,000	70,000
Desired ending inventory	20,000	15,000
Total	152,000	85,000
Less beginning inventory	22,000	12,000
Expected production	130,000	73,000

The production requirements must be carefully coordinated with the sales budget to assure that production and sales are kept in balance during the period. Ideally, there should be no idle productive capacity and neither excessive inventories nor inventories insufficient to fill sales orders.

After production volume requirements have been established, the budget for production costs is determined by multiplying the expected unit product cost of direct materials, direct labor, and factory overhead by the number of units that are to be produced. The unit cost of each product is derived from detailed budgets for each of the three basic cost elements. The summary of the unit cost budget for the Linn Company is presented below, followed by the production cost budget.

	Unit Cost	
Cost elements	Product X	Product Y
Direct materials	$1.00	$2.00
Direct labor	2.00	3.00
Factory overhead	1.50	2.25
Total	$4.50	$7.25

Linn Company
Production Cost Budget
For Year Ending December 31, 1966

Product	Quantity	Direct Materials	Direct Labor	Factory Overhead	Total Costs
X	130,000	$130,000	$260,000	$195,000	$ 585,000
Y	73,000	146,000	219,000	164,250	529,250
		$276,000	$479,000	$359,250	$1,114,250

In a merchandising business, a budget for commodities to be purchased would be used in place of a production cost budget.

Operating expense budget

The operating expense budget is an estimate of the expected selling expenses and general expenses. Some expenses, such as insurance and depreciation of buildings, may have to be allocated between selling expenses and general expenses. At the end of a budget period, the budgeted selling expenses and general expenses are compared with the actual expenses. All significant variations are analyzed to determine their cause and to find a remedy for unfavorable variations.

Estimated income statement

The estimated income statement indicates whether management's proposed operating program will yield a satisfactory net income. Much of the data required in the preparation of the estimated income statement is obtained from the sales, production cost, and operating expense budgets. If the results of the projected income statement are not satisfactory, the budgets should be reviewed and revised.

At the end of the period, the results should be compared with the projected figures. A budget report for the income statement of the Linn Company for 1966 showing this comparison is illustrated below.

Linn Company
Budget Report for Income Statement
For Year Ended December 31, 1966

	Budget	Actual	Over Under*
Sales	$1,641,200	$1,740,000	$ 98,800
Cost of goods sold:			
Finished goods inventory, Jan. 1, 1966	$ 172,000	$ 172,000	$ —
Cost of goods finished	1,114,250	1,250,750	136,500
Cost of goods available for sale	$1,286,250	$1,422,750	$136,500
Finished goods inventory, Dec. 31, 1966	198,750	206,250	7,500
Cost of goods sold	$1,087,500	$1,216,500	$129,000
Gross profit on sales	$ 553,700	$ 523,500	$ 30,200*
Operating expenses:			
Selling expenses:			
Sales salaries and commissions	$ 92,000	$ 95,200	$ 3,200
Advertising expense	64,500	69,500	5,000
Shipping expense	42,400	45,900	3,500
Traveling expense	24,700	23,750	950*
Miscellaneous selling expense	4,200	3,400	800*
Total selling expenses	$ 227,800	$ 237,750	$ 9,950
General expenses:			
Administrative and office salaries	$ 75,000	$ 73,000	$ 2,000*
Office supplies	14,500	12,500	2,000*
Depreciation — office equipment	12,000	12,500	500
Uncollectible accounts expense	8,200	9,400	1,200
Miscellaneous general expenses	6,700	7,450	750
Total general expenses	$ 116,400	$ 114,850	$ 1,550*
Total operating expenses	$ 344,200	$ 352,600	$ 8,400
Net income before income tax	$ 209,500	$ 170,900	$ 38,600*
Income tax	94,000	75,500	18,500*
Net income after income tax	$ 115,500	$ 95,400	$20,100*

All significant variations between the budget and the actual amounts should be analyzed to determine their cause. The budget report for the Linn Company reveals a favorable sales performance, but the cost of goods sold has exceeded budget estimates to such an extent that gross profit is $30,200 below planned objectives. An investigation should be made to determine the causes of the higher costs and to find means of possible corrective action. Further study of the variations indicates that actual operating expenses exceeded budget expectations. Investigation of the causes of this unfavorable variation should be directed primarily at the expenses that deviated materially from budgeted amounts.

In the foregoing example an estimated income statement for an entire year was employed. Similar budget reports are ordinarily prepared each month so that trends may be observed, estimates revised, and corrective measures taken.

Capital expenditures budget

Plant facilities must be replaced when they become inefficient, inadequate, or obsolete. In addition, forecasts of business activity may indicate a need for increases in productive capacity and hence for additional facilities. The capital expenditures budget is concerned with the acquisition of long-lived assets and the financing of such acquisitions.

Capital expenditures budgets ordinarily encompass a long period of time, often projecting from five to twenty years into the future. The anticipated expenditures for the immediate future must also be considered when other budgets are being prepared for the current period. For example, the acquisition of plant assets is likely to affect depreciation cost in the production cost budget, net income in the estimated income statement, and cash requirements in the cash budget.

Cash budget

An adequate amount of cash is essential to successful operations and to the fulfillment of management's future plans. A cash budget presents the cash balance at the beginning of a period, the estimated amount of receipts and disbursements for the period, and the expected cash balance at the end of the period. The period of time covered by a cash budget varies with the type of business and the company's cash position. When the supply of cash is critically short, a weekly or even a daily cash budget may be necessary. Ordinarily, however, twelve separate monthly budgets are prepared for the year.

In estimating cash receipts and cash disbursements, other budgets such as those for sales, production costs, operating expenses, and capital expenditures must be carefully studied. Consideration must also be given to dividend declarations, issuance of additional shares of capital stock, and other future plans of management that will affect cash. After cash receipts and cash disbursements have been estimated, a minimum cash balance is established that will be adequate to meet cash requirements. Separate monthly cash budgets for the first three months of a year are illustrated on the opposite page. Cash budgets are usually accompanied by detailed schedules of the major items summarized in the budgets.

Linn Company
Cash Budget
For Three Months Ending March 31, 1966

	January	February	March
Estimated cash receipts from:			
Cash sales	$ 48,000	$ 50,000	$ 53,000
Collections of accounts receivable	74,000	76,000	79,200
Other sources (issuance of securities, interest, etc.)	5,200	4,400	3,700
Total cash receipts	$127,200	$130,400	$135,900
Estimated cash disbursements for:			
Merchandise (production costs)	$ 74,250	$ 75,500	$ 77,500
Operating expenses	43,250	45,600	47,700
Capital expenditures	——	5,000	19,000
Other purposes (notes, interest, dividends, etc.)	5,000	3,500	9,000
Total cash disbursements	$122,500	$129,600	$153,200
Cash increase or decrease*	$ 4,700	$ 800	$ 17,300*
Cash balance at beginning of month	25,800	30,500	31,300
Cash balance at end of month	$ 30,500	$ 31,300	$ 14,000
Minimum cash balance	25,000	25,000	25,000
Excess or deficiency*	$ 5,500	$ 6,300	$ 11,000*

A cash budget contributes to more effective cash planning. Through a cash budget, management can anticipate the need for short-term loans and, by advance planning, may be able to obtain more favorable borrowing terms. Conversely, when the budget indicates periods of excess cash, such funds may be invested in readily marketable securities that will yield revenue. In the example above, borrowing would be necessary to meet cash requirements in March.

Estimated balance sheet

The estimated balance sheet can be prepared by utilizing much of the data accumulated in the other budgets and by reference to the balance sheet at the end of the preceding period. An estimated balance sheet projecting the expected financial position of an enterprise should be prepared at semiannual, quarterly, or even monthly intervals. Comparisons of the actual balance sheets with the projections may disclose trends and permit timely adjustments of operations. For example, the estimated balance sheet may disclose an unfavorable relationship that will adversely affect the company's credit rating and make the procurement of capital difficult. The disclosure of such a situation indicates a need for operating adjustments to avoid the occurrence of such an unfavorable relationship.

Flexible budgets

In the preceding sections of this chapter, fixed or static budgets were assumed. Under this type of budgeting, all estimates are based on one specific level of sales or production. Fixed budgets provide a satisfactory basis for evaluating performance when actual activity coincides with anticipated activity. Business is dynamic rather than static, however, and it is extremely difficult to estimate sales or production with pinpoint accuracy. Consequently, many companies use flexible budgets in measuring efficiency.

Flexible budgets consist of a series of separate budgets geared to different rates of activity. For example, production costs may be estimated at several possible levels of output and operating expenses may be budgeted at various amounts of sales. In preparing the budgets, careful consideration must be given to the effect of changes in volume on each item that is being budgeted.

Fixed expenses are generally defined as those expenses that remain constant in total regardless of changes in the volume of business activity. For example, depreciation of buildings, property taxes, property insurance, and salaries of executives tend to be independent of the level of operating activity. *Variable expenses* are generally defined as those expenses that vary in total as business activity changes. Expenses such as salesmen's commissions tend to vary directly with the volume of activity. If volume is halved, variable expenses will tend to be halved; if volume is doubled, variable expenses will tend to double.

A third category of expenses is referred to as *semivariable*. These expenses vary with volume of business activity but not in direct proportion. For example, one foreman is able to supervise the workers in his department up to a certain level of production. If additional workers are added to his department, the point is eventually reached where it is necessary to hire another foreman. It is usually desirable to break down semivariable expenses into fixed and variable elements.

A flexible budget for selling expenses is illustrated below. The first expense is variable, the next three are semivariable, and the last two are assumed to be fixed.

Flexible Selling Expense Budget

	Budget Allowances at Various Levels of Sales			
Expense Item	$700,000	$800,000	$900,000	$1,000,000
Salesmen's commissions	$ 35,000	$ 40,000	$ 45,000	$ 50,000
Advertising	21,000	21,500	22,000	22,500
Traveling	10,500	10,500	11,000	11,000
Miscellaneous	3,500	4,000	4,000	4,500
Depreciation — sales equipment	4,000	4,000	4,000	4,000
Insurance on sales equipment	2,000	2,000	2,000	2,000
Total selling expenses	$ 76,000	$ 82,000	$ 88,000	$ 94,000

In evaluating performance, results are compared with budget amounts that correspond to the level of activity actually achieved. If actual sales are $700,000, the actual selling expenses would be compared with the budget allowances in the first column; if actual sales are $900,000, the budget allowances in the third column would be used as the basis of comparison. Such comparisons provide a reliable basis for managerial control because the budgeted figures represent realistic and attainable goals. The flexible budget is also a significant motivating instrument because the individual who is being judged by the budget will know in advance the budget allowances at any given level of operations. Flexible budget reports are often prepared monthly to permit frequent review of operating performance.

Standard costs

The determination of the unit cost of products manufactured is fundamental to cost accounting. The process cost and the job order cost accounting systems described in the preceding chapters provide for the determination of *actual* or *historical* unit costs. The aim of both systems is to determine as accurately as possible the actual cost incurred in manufacturing the various commodities produced. The one deviation from actual cost is the use of estimated or predetermined factory overhead rates. One of the principal reasons for this departure from historical cost is to permit the determination of unit cost of product at frequent intervals.

Many industries and individual companies have extended the use of estimates to all manufacturing costs. Cost systems that employ scientifically determined estimates for direct materials, direct labor, and factory overhead are sometimes referred to as *standard cost systems*. The use of standards makes it possible to determine what a product should cost, what it actually did cost, and the cause of any differences between the actual cost and what the product should cost. Standard costs thus serve as a measuring stick for the determination of efficiency. If the standard cost of a product is $5 per unit and it is being currently produced at a cost of $5.50, the factors responsible for the excess cost may be found and remedial steps may be taken. As a result, employees become more cost-conscious and supervisors have a tool for controlling costs.

Standard costs may be used in either the job order type of production or the process type of production. For most effective control, standard costs should be used for each department or cost center in the factory. In many cases, however, standard costs are used in part of the factory and actual costs are used in other parts.

The establishment of standards requires an exhaustive study. Motion and time studies are made of each operation, and the work force is trained to use the most efficient methods. Direct materials and productive equipment are subjected to detailed study and tests in an effort to achieve maximum productivity at minimum cost. A wide variety of management skills are needed in setting standards. It requires the joint effort of accounting, engineering, personnel administration, and other managerial areas.

Relationship between budgets and standard costs

Both budgets and standard costs represent cost figures prepared in advance; both are useful tools in controlling costs.

Budgets present an overall plan of operations indicating expectations for a future period. They serve as yardsticks for measuring the effectiveness with which plans have been followed; they are used to point out departures from the plan of operations.

Standard costs are predetermined estimates of what costs ought to be rather than what they are expected to be. Standard cost systems stress the level to which costs can be reduced; they are goals that represent desired performance.

Variances from standards

Operating management's goal is the attainment of properly determined standards. If the standards are not attained, management wants to know the reason for the difference between actual costs and standard costs. These differences are referred to as *variances*. If actual cost incurred on a job is less than standard cost, the variance is favorable; if actual cost exceeds standard cost, the variance is unfavorable. When actual costs are compared with standard costs, only the "exceptions" or variances are reported to the individual responsible for cost control. This reporting by the "principle of exceptions" enables the one responsible for cost control to concentrate on the cause and the correction of the variances.

The total variance for a particular period or for a specific job is ordinarily a composite of a number of variances, some of which may be favorable and some unfavorable. There may be variances from standards in direct materials costs, in direct labor costs, and in factory overhead costs. The remainder of the chapter is devoted to the analysis of these variances. To simplify the discussion, it is assumed that only one kind of material is used and that only one processing department is maintained. Ordinarily a manufacturing business uses many kinds of materials and has several processing departments.

Direct materials variance

Two principal factors enter into the determination of standards for direct materials cost: (1) the quantity (usage) standard and (2) the price standard. Consequently, actual cost of direct materials may differ from standard because of *quantity variance*, *price variance*, or both. To illustrate, assume that the standard direct materials cost of producing 10,000 units of Product X and the direct materials cost actually incurred by Nelson Manufacturing Company during June were as follows:

Standard: 20,000 units at $.50	$10,000
Actual: 20,600 units at $.52	10,712

It is readily apparent that the unfavorable variance of $712 resulted in part from an excess usage of 600 units of direct materials and in part from an excess unit cost of $.02. The analysis of the variance is as follows:

Direct Materials Variance

	Units	Price	Amount	Variance
QUANTITY				
Actual	20,600 × Standard	$.50	$10,300	
Standard	20,000 × Standard	$.50	10,000	
Variance — unfavorable				$300
PRICE				
Actual	20,600 × Actual	$.52	$10,712	
Actual	20,600 × Standard	$.50	10,300	
Variance — unfavorable				412
DIRECT MATERIALS VARIANCE — unfavorable				$712

The physical quantity and the dollar amount of the quantity variance should be reported to the factory superintendent and other personnel responsible for production. The unit price and the total amount of the price variance should be reported to the purchasing department, which is responsible for controlling this variance.

Unfavorable variances are ordinarily but not invariably the result of the inefficiency of the department charged with responsibility. For example, if the excess usage of 600 units in the example above had been caused by maladjustment of equipment or other carelessness, it would be assignable to production personnel. On the other hand, if the waste was caused by inferior materials, the purchasing department should be held responsible. Similarly, the price variance may or may not be controllable by the purchasing department. If the materials could have been purchased from another supplier at the standard price, the variance was controllable. If the additional unit cost resulted from a market-wide price increase, the variance was not subject to control. The important point to note is that the possible causes of all variances should be carefully studied and the responsibility therefor assigned.

Direct labor variance

As in the case of direct materials, direct labor cost standards are divided into two parts: (1) the time (usage or efficiency) standard, and (2) the rate (price or wage) standard. If the actual direct labor hours spent producing a product differ from the standard hours, there is a *time variance*; if the wage rate paid differs from the standard rate, there is a *rate variance*. The standard cost and the actual cost of direct labor in the production of 10,000 units of Product X by Nelson Manufacturing Company during June are assumed to be as follows:

Standard:	8,000 hours at $2.00	$16,000
Actual:	7,900 hours at 2.10	16,590

The unfavorable direct labor variance of $590 is a composite of a favorable time variance and an unfavorable rate variance, as indicated below.

Direct Labor Variance

Hours	Rate	Amount	Variance
TIME			
Standard....8,000 × Standard	$2.00	$16,000	
Actual......7,900 × Standard	$2.00	15,800	
Variance — favorable			$200
RATE			
Actual......7,900 × Actual	$2.10	$16,590	
Actual......7,900 × Standard	$2.00	15,800	
Variance — unfavorable			790
DIRECT LABOR VARIANCE — unfavorable			$590

The control of direct labor cost is often in the hands of a production foreman. To assist the foreman in the control of direct labor costs, daily or weekly reports analyzing the cause of any direct labor variance are often prepared. A comparison of standard direct labor hours and actual direct labor hours will provide the basis for an investigation into the efficiency of direct labor (time variance). A comparison of the rates paid for direct labor with the standard rates highlights the efficiency of the foreman in selecting the proper grade of direct labor for production (rate variance).

Factory overhead variance

When standard costs are employed, factory overhead is applied to the commodities produced by use of a predetermined standard overhead rate. The standard rate is determined by dividing what the factory overhead costs should be by the standard amount of production activity, generally expressed in direct labor hours, direct labor cost, or machine hours. If direct labor hours are used as the base for determining the standard rate, factory overhead is applied to the commodities produced by multiplying the standard rate by the standard direct labor hours for producing the product.

In preceding chapters on process and job order cost accounting, a predetermined rate for factory overhead was used to apply factory overhead to processes and jobs. This predetermined factory overhead rate was based upon estimated total overhead and expected direct labor costs for the period. Factory overhead was then applied to product by multiplying this predetermined rate by the direct labor costs incurred.

The starting point in establishing standard overhead rates is the preparation of a detailed cost budget for factory overhead. This budget must take into consideration the changes in the individual items of factory overhead that occur as the volume of production changes. It is therefore desirable to prepare a flexible budget for the varying levels of production falling within the probable range of activity. The flexible budget and the standard overhead rate for Nelson Manufacturing Company for the month of June are presented below.

Nelson Manufacturing Company
Factory Overhead Budget
For Month Ending June 30, 1966

	Percent of Normal Productive Capacity			
	80%	90%	100%	110%
Direct labor hours	8,000	9,000	10,000	11,000
Standard production units	10,000	11,250	12,500	13,750
Budgeted factory overhead:				
Variable costs:				
Indirect factory wages	$ 6,400	$ 7,200	$ 8,000	$ 8,800
Power and light	2,800	3,150	3,500	3,850
Indirect materials	1,600	1,800	2,000	2,200
Maintenance	1,200	1,350	1,500	1,650
Total variable costs	$12,000	$13,500	$15,000	$16,500
Fixed costs:				
Supervisory salaries	$ 2,250	$ 2,250	$ 2,250	$ 2,250
Depreciation of plant and equipment	2,750	2,750	2,750	2,750
Insurance and property taxes	1,000	1,000	1,000	1,000
Total fixed costs	$ 6,000	$ 6,000	$ 6,000	$ 6,000
Total factory overhead	$18,000	$19,500	$21,000	$22,500
Factory overhead rate per direct labor hour ($21,000 ÷ 10,000)			$2.10	

To establish the standard unit cost of jobs or products, the budget for one particular level of capacity must be used in determining the standard factory overhead rate. Inasmuch as standards are used for purposes of planning and control, they should be based on operations at normal productive capacity. In the illustration the standard factory overhead rate of $2.10 per direct labor hour can be subdivided into $1.50 per hour for variable factory overhead ($15,000 ÷ 10,000 hours) and $.60 per hour for fixed factory overhead ($6,000 ÷ 10,000 hours).

Deviations from the standard factory overhead rate should be analyzed and the cause of the deviations should be reported to the appropriate management personnel. In practice, there are several methods of computing factory overhead variances. One common method is to analyze the variances into (1) *controllable variance* and (2) *volume variance.* To illustrate, assume that the standard cost and the actual cost of factory overhead in the production of 10,000 units of Product X by Nelson Manufacturing Company during June were as follows:

Standard:	8,000 hours at $2.10		$16,800
Actual:	Variable factory overhead	$12,300	
	Fixed factory overhead	6,000	18,300

The unfavorable factory overhead variance of $1,500 is composed of a controllable variance and a volume variance as indicated in the tabulation below.

Factory Overhead Variance

		Variance
CONTROLLABLE		
Actual factory overhead	$18,300	
Budgeted factory overhead for standard product produced	18,000	
Variance — unfavorable		$ 300
VOLUME		
Normal capacity hours	10,000	
Standard hours for product produced	8,000	
Normal capacity hours not utilized	2,000	
Multiplied by fixed overhead rate	X$.60	
Variance — unfavorable		1,200
FACTORY OVERHEAD VARIANCE — unfavorable		$1,500

Controllable variance. The controllable variance is the difference between the actual amount of factory overhead incurred and the amount of factory overhead budgeted for the level of production achieved during the period. The number of units produced by Nelson Manufacturing Company during June was 10,000, which represents 80% of normal capacity. According to the flexible budget on page 559, the factory overhead budgeted at this level of production is $18,000. The excess of the $18,300 of overhead costs actually incurred over the $18,000 budget yields the unfavorable controllable variance of $300.

The amount and the direction of the controllable variance indicate the efficiency in keeping the factory overhead costs within the limits established by the budget. Most of the controllable variance is related to the variable factory overhead items because generally there is little or no variation in the fixed factory overhead items. Therefore, responsibility for the control of this variance generally rests with the department foreman.

Volume variance. Inasmuch as fixed overhead costs are not affected by the volume of production, operation at any level below normal capacity of 10,000 hours will result in an unfavorable volume variance. The production achieved by Nelson Manufacturing Company in June was the equivalent of 8,000 standard direct labor hours. There were 2,000 hours not utilized, which is 20% of 10,000. The volume variance can be computed by multiplying the 2,000 idle hours by $.60, as illustrated on page 560, or the same result may be obtained by multiplying the total fixed costs of $6,000 by 20%.

The idle time may be due to such factors as the plant foreman's failure to maintain an even flow of work, machine breakdowns or repairs causing work stoppages, and the sales department's failure to obtain enough sales to keep the factory operating at full capacity. The accountant's job is to point out the cost of idle time. Management should then ascertain the causes of the idle time and should take corrective action. A volume variance caused by failure of the foreman to maintain an even flow of work, for example, can be corrected by the foreman in the short run. On the other hand, volume variances caused by lack of sales orders may be corrected only by adjusting plant capacity more closely to sales potential.

Reporting standard factory overhead variance. The most effective means of presenting standard factory overhead variance data is through a factory overhead variance report. Such a report can present both the controllable variance and the volume variance in a format that pinpoints the causes of the factory overhead variance and facilitates placing the responsibility for control. Such a report for Nelson Manufacturing Company is illustrated at the top of the following page.

The variance in many of the individual cost items can be subdivided into quantity and price variances, as was done with the variances in direct materials and direct labor. For example, the indirect factory wages variance may include both time and rate variances and the in-

Nelson Manufacturing Company
Standard Factory Overhead Variance Report
For Month Ended June 30, 1966

Normal production capacity for the month..............12,500 units or 10,000 hours
Actual production for the month......................10,000 units or 8,000 hours

	Budget	Actual	Variances Favorable	Variances Unfavorable
Variable costs:				
Indirect factory wages............	$ 6,400	$ 6,510		$ 110
Power and light..................	2,800	2,790	$10	
Indirect materials...............	1,600	1,800		200
Maintenance......................	1,200	1,200		
Total variable costs............	$12,000	$12,300		
Fixed costs:				
Supervisory salaries..............	$ 2,250	$ 2,250		
Depreciation of plant and equipment	2,750	2,750		
Insurance and property taxes.......	1,000	1,000		
Total fixed costs...............	$ 6,000	$ 6,000		
Total factory overhead..............	$18,000	$18,300		
Total controllable variances.........			$10	$ 310
				10
Net controllable variance — unfavorable				$ 300
Volume variance — unfavorable:				
Idle hours at the standard rate for fixed factory overhead — 2,000 x $.60				$1,200
Total factory overhead variance — unfavorable..........................				$1,500

direct materials variance may be composed of both a quantity variance and a price variance.

The foregoing brief introduction to analysis of factory overhead variance is suggestive of the many ramifications and complexities that may be encountered in actual practice. The rapid increase of automation in factory operations has been accompanied by increased attention to factory overhead costs. The use of predetermined standards, and the analysis of variances from such standards, provides management with the best possible means of establishing responsibility and controlling factory overhead costs.

Standards in the accounts

Although standard costs can be used purely for statistical purposes in evaluating actual performance, most accountants prefer to incorporate them into the accounts. Entering the standard cost figures in the accounts facilitates the bookkeeping as well as the reporting of actual and standard cost data.

One plan for incorporating standards into the accounts is to debit the work in process account for the actual costs for direct materials, direct labor, and factory overhead. This account is then credited at standard cost for the cost of goods transferred to the finished goods account. The work in process account for Nelson Manufacturing Company, assuming no beginning or ending work in process inventories for June, and the finished goods account are illustrated below.

Work in Process

1966			1966		
June 30	Direct materials (actual)	10,712	June 30	Finished goods (standard)	42,800
30	Direct labor (actual)	16,590	30	Balance (variances)	2,802
30	Factory overhead (actual)	18,300			
		45,602			45,602
July 1	Balance (variances)	2,802			

Finished Goods

1966					
June 1	Balance	39,800			
30	From work in process	42,800			

For effective control of production costs, variance reports should be prepared on a daily, weekly, or monthly basis indicating the particular costs that have varied from the standard. A report of variances for Nelson Manufacturing Company would isolate the direct materials, direct labor, and factory overhead elements of the $2,802 total variance. If there had been an inventory of work in process at the end of June, the balance remaining in the work in process account would have represented the sum of (1) the cost of the work still in process and (2) the variances attributable to the differences between actual and standard costs.

At the end of the fiscal period, the variances are closed to the cost of goods sold account. However, if the variances are material or if many of the goods manufactured are still on hand, the variances may be allocated to work in process, finished goods, and cost of goods sold on the basis of the amounts of the manufacturing costs in those balances at the end of the year.

Variances from standard costs are ordinarily not reported to stockholders and others outside the management group. However, it is customary to disclose the variances on income statements prepared for top management. The interim income statement for Nelson Manufacturing Company for the month of June is presented at the top of the following page.

Nelson Manufacturing Company
Income Statement
For Month Ended June 30, 1966

Sales		$77,900
Cost of goods sold — at standard		40,700
Gross profit on sales — at standard		$37,200
Less standard cost variances:		
Direct materials quantity variance — unfavorable	$ 300	
Direct materials price variance — unfavorable	412	
Direct labor time variance — favorable	(200)	
Direct labor rate variance — unfavorable	790	
Factory overhead controllable variance — unfavorable	300	
Factory overhead volume variance — unfavorable	1,200	2,802
Gross profit on sales		$34,398
Operating expenses:		
Selling expenses	$14,500	
General expenses	9,125	23,625
Net income		$10,773

QUESTIONS

1. Name the three basic functions of management.

2. Businessmen are often said to be "cost conscious." Discuss.

3. How do budgeting and standard costs aid in cost control?

4. Budgeting embraces both accounting and management functions. Explain.

5. How does a budget aid management in the discharge of its basic functions?

6. Why should requests for budget estimates be extended to even the lowest level in the chain of command?

7. (a) What purpose is served by an estimated income statement? (b) What purpose is served by a comparison of the income statement with the estimated income statement?

8. What is a capital expenditures budget?

9. Discuss the purpose of the cash budget.

10. (a) Distinguish between fixed and flexible budgets. (b) Why is the flexible budget more effective than the fixed budget in controlling expenses?

11. Which of the following costs incurred by a manufacturing enterprise tend to be fixed and which tend to be variable: (a) insurance on factory building; (b) property taxes on machinery; (c) cost of bronze gear entering into the final product; (d) electric power (purchased) to operate manufacturing machinery; (e) direct labor; (f) salary of factory superintendent; (g) cost of lighting the factory; (h) depreciation of factory building.

12. The Eastern Corporation uses flexible budgets. For each of the following variable operating expenses, indicate whether there has been a saving or an excess of expenditures, assuming actual sales were (a) $400,000, (b) $500,000.

Expense Item	Actual Amount	Budget Allowance Based on Sales
Advertising expense	$18,000	5.0%
Store supplies expense	6,200	1.5%
Uncollectible accounts expense	2,200	0.5%

13. What are the basic objectives in the use of standard costs?

14. (a) What are the two types of variances between actual cost and standard cost for direct materials? (b) Discuss some possible causes of these variances.

15. (a) What are the two types of variances between actual cost and standard cost for direct labor? (b) Who generally has control over the direct labor variance?

16. Describe the two variances between actual costs and standard costs for factory overhead.

17. Where do the variances for direct materials, direct labor, and factory overhead appear on interim income statements prepared for top management?

EXERCISES

1. The Hart Company manufactures two models of filing cabinets, A and B. Based on the following production data for the month of June of the current year, (a) determine the expected volume of production for each model and (b) prepare a production cost budget.

	A	B
Units on hand, 6/1	1,500	1,000
Desired inventory, 6/30	1,700	800
Expected sales volume	7,500	5,000
Unit costs:		
Direct materials	$10.00	$15.00
Direct labor	12.00	20.00
Factory overhead	9.60	16.00

2. The following estimated income statement was prepared for the Stevens Company from the sales, production cost, and operating expense budgets submitted in May of the current year:

Sales		$250,000
Cost of goods sold		165,000
Gross profit on sales		$ 85,000
Operating expenses:		
Selling expenses	$30,000	
General expenses	25,000	
Total operating expenses		55,000
Net income		$ 30,000

The actual operations for May produced the following results: sales, 10% over budget; cost of goods sold, 12% over budget; selling expenses, 15% over budget; general expenses, 5% over budget. Prepare a budget report showing the progress of the Stevens Company during the month of May.

3. Carter Company uses flexible budgets. Prepare a flexible selling expense budget for sales volumes of $400,000, $450,000 and $500,000 based upon the following data:

Salesmen's commissions	10% of sales
Advertising	\$20,500 for \$400,000 of sales 22,800 for 450,000 of sales 24,000 for 500,000 of sales
Travel	\$ 7,500 for \$400,000 of sales 8,250 for 450,000 of sales 8,700 for 500,000 of sales
Rent of building and equipment	\$ 7,500
Miscellaneous	\$ 9,000 plus 2% of sales

4. The following data relating to direct materials cost are taken from the records of Sullivan Manufacturing Company for the month of April of the current year:

Quantity of direct materials used	20,000 lbs.
Unit cost of direct materials	\$1.10 per lb.
Units of finished goods manufactured	9,500 units
Standard direct materials per unit of finished goods	2 lbs.
Direct materials quantity variance — unfavorable	\$1,000
Direct materials price variance — unfavorable	\$2,000

Determine the standard direct materials cost per unit of finished product, assuming that there was no inventory of work in process at either the beginning or the end of the month. Present your computations.

5. Standard costs and actual costs for direct materials, direct labor, and factory overhead incurred for the manufacture of 5,000 units of product were as follows:

	Standard Costs	Actual Costs
Direct materials	10,000 units at \$1.50	10,100 units at \$1.45
Direct labor	15,000 hours at \$2.50	15,300 hours at \$2.60
Factory overhead	\$2.00 per direct labor hour on normal capacity of 18,000 direct labor hours:	
	\$1.50 for variable overhead	\$22,800 variable
	.50 for fixed overhead	9,000 fixed

Determine (1) the quantity variance, price variance, and total direct materials variance; (2) the time variance, rate variance, and total direct labor variance; and (3) the controllable variance, volume variance, and total factory overhead variance.

6. The Hunter Manufacturing Company prepared the factory overhead budget for August of the current year shown at the top of the following page. It expected to operate at a normal capacity of 10,000 direct labor hours.

During August the plant was operated for 9,000 direct labor hours and the factory overhead costs incurred were: indirect factory wages, \$2,225; power and light, \$1,390; indirect materials, \$1,040; supervisory salaries, \$1,250; depreciation of plant and equipment, \$900; and insurance and property taxes, \$750.

Prepare a standard factory overhead variance report for August. To be useful for cost control, the budgeted amounts should be based on 9,000 direct labor hours.

Variable costs:		
Indirect factory wages	$2,500	
Power and light	1,500	
Indirect materials	1,100	
Total variable costs		$5,100
Fixed costs:		
Supervisory salaries	$1,250	
Depreciation of plant and equipment	900	
Insurance and property taxes	750	
Total fixed costs		2,900
Total factory overhead		$8,000

7. Prepare an income statement for presentation to top management from the following data taken from the records of Webster Manufacturing Company for the month of January, 1966:

Cost of goods sold (at standard)	$110,000
Direct materials quantity variance — unfavorable	750
Direct materials price variance — favorable	500
Direct labor time variance — unfavorable	1,250
Direct labor rate variance — unfavorable	400
Factory overhead controllable variance — favorable	300
Factory overhead volume variance — unfavorable	2,000
Selling expenses	27,000
General expenses	18,725
Sales	190,700

PROBLEMS

23-1. The Hayes Manufacturing Company prepared the following factory overhead budget for May:

Factory Overhead Budget

Direct labor hours — normal capacity		10,000
Direct labor hours — budgeted		8,000
Budgeted factory overhead:		
Variable costs:		
Indirect factory wages	$ 3,600	
Indirect materials	2,400	
Power and light	2,000	
Total variable costs	$ 8,000	
Fixed costs:		
Indirect factory wages	$ 4,800	
Supervisory salaries	4,200	
Depreciation of plant and equipment	2,900	
Insurance	1,700	
Power and light	1,500	
Property taxes	900	
Total fixed costs	$16,000	
Total factory overhead	$24,000	

Instructions: (1) Prepare a flexible budget for the month of June showing capacities of 8,000, 9,000, 10,000, and 11,000 direct labor hours and the determination of a standard factory overhead rate per direct labor hour.

(2) During June the following factory overhead costs were incurred when the plant was operated for 9,000 hours:

Indirect factory wages	$ 9,050
Supervisory salaries	4,200
Power and light	3,700
Depreciation of plant and equipment	2,900
Indirect materials	2,575
Insurance	1,700
Property taxes	900
Total overhead incurred	$25,025

Prepare a standard factory overhead variance report for June.

23-2. The estimated income statement of Dearborn, Inc. for 1966 is given below. The actual income statement for the month of January, 1966, is given on the opposite page.

Dearborn, Inc.
Estimated Income Statement
For Year Ending December 31, 1966

Sales			$800,000
Cost of merchandise sold:			
Merchandise inventory, January 1, 1966		$ 50,000	
Purchases		542,000	
Merchandise available for sale		$592,000	
Less merchandise inventory, December 31, 1966		72,000	
Cost of merchandise sold			520,000
Gross profit on sales			$280,000
Operating expenses:			
Selling expenses:			
Sales commissions	$80,000		
Delivery expense	16,000		
Advertising expense	18,760		
Depreciation — store equipment	6,240		
Store supplies expense	4,000		
Miscellaneous selling expense	1,500		
Total selling expenses		$126,500	
General expenses:			
Office and officers' salaries	$30,000		
Rent expense	22,800		
Uncollectible accounts expense	4,000		
Depreciation — office equipment	2,376		
Office supplies expense	1,800		
Miscellaneous general expense	924		
Total general expenses		61,900	
Total operating expenses			188,400
Net income before income tax			$ 91,600
Income tax (40%)			36,640
Net income after income tax			$ 54,960

In order to compare the actual results for January with the budgeted figures for the same month, it will be necessary to consider the following variations in the monthly breakdown of the annual budget estimates.

(a) Sales for January were estimated at 8% of annual sales. Expenses that were expected to vary proportionately with sales were: sales commissions, delivery expense, store supplies expense, and uncollectible accounts expense.
(b) The beginning inventory in the January budget was estimated at $50,000; the ending inventory at $52,000. The cost of merchandise sold and the gross profit on sales were computed at the same percentage of sales as in the annual budget, and purchases were budgeted at $43,600 for the month.
(c) Fixed expenses that were not expected to vary with sales were: miscellaneous selling expense, office and officers' salaries, rent expense, depreciation of store and office equipment, office supplies expense, and miscellaneous general expense. The advertising expense was budgeted for $1,200 in January.

Dearborn, Inc.
Income Statement
For Month Ended January 31, 1966

Sales			$69,400
Cost of merchandise sold:			
Merchandise inventory, January 1, 1966		$ 48,000	
Purchases		56,600	
Merchandise available for sale		$104,600	
Less merchandise inventory, January 31, 1966		53,700	
Cost of merchandise sold			50,900
Gross profit on sales			$18,500
Operating expenses:			
Selling expenses:			
Sales commissions	$6,940		
Delivery expense	1,400		
Advertising expense	1,200		
Depreciation — store equipment	520		
Store supplies expense	300		
Miscellaneous selling expense	110		
Total selling expenses		$ 10,470	
General expenses:			
Office and officers' salaries	$2,500		
Rent expense	1,900		
Uncollectible accounts expense	700		
Depreciation — office equipment	198		
Office supplies expense	150		
Miscellaneous general expense	60		
Total general expenses		5,508	
Total operating expenses			15,978
Net income before income tax			$ 2,522
Income tax (40%)			1,009
Net income after income tax			$ 1,513

Instructions: (1) Prepare a budget report for January, 1966.

(2) Which of the variations between budget and actual amounts would you analyze to determine the causes of the variations and to find means of possible corrective action?

23-3. The Corley Manufacturing Company maintains perpetual inventory accounts for materials, work in process, and finished goods. There was no inventory of work in process at the beginning or the end of the period. The records revealed the following data:

	Standard Cost Per Unit	
	Quantity	Price
Direct materials	4 lbs. @ $.50/lb.	$ 2.00
Direct labor	2 hours @ $2.50/hr.	5.00
Factory overhead	$1.75 per direct labor hour	3.50
		$10.50

The transactions relating to production completed during the first month of the current year are summarized as follows:

(a) Materials purchased on account, $26,400.

(b) Direct materials used, $20,196. This represented 39,600 pounds at $.51 per pound.

(c) Direct labor paid, $50,225. This represented 20,500 hours at $2.45 per hour. There were no accruals at either the beginning or the end of the period.

(d) Factory overhead incurred during the month included indirect labor, $18,400; depreciation on plant and equipment, $8,600; insurance, $800; and miscellaneous factory costs, $8,800. The indirect labor and miscellaneous factory costs were paid during the period, and the insurance represents an expiration of prepaid insurance. The fixed factory overhead incurred represented $14,700 of the total, while the variable factory overhead totaled $21,900.

(e) Goods finished during the period, 10,000 units.

Instructions: (1) Prepare journal entries to record the transactions, assuming that the work in process account is debited for actual production costs and credited with standard costs for goods finished.

(2) Prepare a T account for Work in Process and post to the account, using the identifying letters as dates.

(3) Prepare schedules of variance analyses for direct materials, direct labor, and factory overhead. Normal productive capacity for the plant is 21,000 direct labor hours.

(4) Total the amounts of the standard cost variances and compare this total with the balance of the work in process account.

23-4. The treasurer of Wilson Company wishes to prepare a monthly cash budget. He has the following budget information:

	January	February	March
Sales	$450,000	$500,000	$440,000
Production costs	300,000	334,000	296,000
Operating expenses	106,200	109,000	105,400
Capital expenditures	—	150,000	—

The company expects to sell about 40% of its merchandise for cash. Of sales on account, 90% are expected to be collected in full in the month following the sale and the remainder the next following month. Depreciation, insurance, and property taxes represent $10,000 of the estimated monthly production costs and $7,000 of the probable monthly operating expenses. Insurance and property taxes are paid in June and August, respectively. Of the remainder of the production costs and operating expenses, 75% are expected to be paid in the month in which they are incurred and the balance in the next month.

At the beginning of the current year, assets include cash, $65,500, accounts receivable, $246,500, and marketable securities, $100,000. The accounts receivable include $221,000 of December sales and $25,500 representing November sales. Liabilities on January 1 consisted of notes payable, $25,000, accounts payable, $89,600, and accrued liabilities, $27,700. The notes payable are non-interest-bearing and are due March 10. The other liabilities represent December production costs and selling and general expenses, respectively.

It is expected that $1,000 in interest will be received in January and $2,200 in dividends in February. The Wilson Company's regular quarterly dividend of $7,700 is expected to be declared in February and paid in March. Management desires to maintain a minimum cash balance of $60,000.

Instructions: (1) Prepare a monthly cash budget for January, February, and March.

(2) On the basis of the cash budget prepared in (1), do you have any advice for the treasurer in planning for the maintenance of a satisfactory cash balance?

23-5. The chief accountant for Baylor Manufacturing Company requests the sales manager to submit an estimate of sales and every other department head to submit estimates of expenses for the year 1966. It is assumed that inventories at the end of the year will be the same as those at the beginning of the year. The total of the manufacturing costs for the year are therefore assumed to be equal to the cost of goods sold. This information is presented in summary form below.

	Estimated Fixed Expenses	Estimated Variable Expenses (per unit sold)
Cost of goods sold:		
Direct materials	$ 0	$2.00
Direct labor	0	2.75
Factory overhead:		
Depreciation of plant and equipment	50,000	.00
Other factory overhead	80,000	1.25

	Estimated Fixed Expenses	Estimated Variable Expenses (per unit sold)
Selling expenses:		
Sales commissions	$17,500	$ .50
Advertising	20,000	.00
Miscellaneous selling expense	9,000	.25
General expenses:		
Office and officers' salaries	70,000	.15
Supplies	1,200	.05
Miscellaneous general expenses	8,000	.10

Selling price of the product is $13 per unit, and it is expected that the normal productive capacity output of 60,000 units will be sold.

The general ledger trial balance at January 1, 1966, is as follows:

Cash	$ 25,000	
Accounts Receivable	90,500	
Finished Goods	87,200	
Work in Process	38,100	
Materials	9,400	
Prepaid Expenses	2,300	
Plant and Equipment	400,000	
Accumulated Depreciation — Plant and Equipment		$190,000
Accounts Payable		43,500
Income Tax Payable		35,520
Common Stock		300,000
Retained Earnings		83,480
	$652,500	$652,500

The accounts receivable, prepaid expenses, and accounts payable balances at the end of the year are expected to be at about the same level as they were at the beginning of the year. The income tax rate for the year is expected to be 40%. The liability for income tax on January 1, 1966, will be paid during March. During July, $50,000 of dividends will be declared and paid.

Instructions: (1) Prepare an estimated income statement for 1966.

(2) Prepare an estimated balance sheet at December 31, 1966.

PART NINE

Decision-making

24. Income taxes and their effect on business decisions

Nature of income taxes

The base against which income taxes are assessed is net income, computed in accordance with statutes and administrative regulations of the governmental unit. Arbitrarily specified portions of net income, usually termed *exemptions*, may be excluded from the tax base as may income from particular sources, such as interest on certain governmental obligations. Economic entities against which a tax on annual income is levied include individuals, corporations, estates, and trusts. The federal government and approximately three fourths of the states levy an income tax. A few states permit enactment of an income tax by municipalities or other political subdivisions.

The amount of a taxpayer's liability is determined from information supplied by the taxpayer on forms that are referred to collectively as a *tax return*. Failure to keep adequate records does not relieve taxpayers from their tax obligation. If a taxpayer's records are incomplete or inaccurate, the statutes authorize the appropriate governmental agency to determine the amount of taxable income, using any evidence available. There may also be severe penalties, both civil and criminal, for willful failure to comply with the tax laws.

A characteristic common to taxes on net income, particularly those assessed against individuals, is the system of tax rates that provides for higher rates as the tax base increases. Because of this characteristic of successively higher rates applicable to successively higher segments of income, the income tax is sometimes called a *progressive* tax.

Relationship to accounting

Because of the intricacies of income determination, it is inevitable that accounting and income taxes should be closely interrelated. An understanding of any but the simplest aspects of income taxes is almost impossible without some knowledge of accounting concepts. In turn, the federal income tax has influenced accounting practices to a significant extent.

Examples of income tax procedures that are at variance with accounting principles have been cited in earlier chapters. Methods prescribed by statutes or regulations may nevertheless be adopted for financial reporting purposes if standards of materiality and consistency are not thereby violated. However, the net income of a business as determined for income tax purposes will ordinarily differ from the net income reported in the income statement. In such cases it is always possible to reconcile the two amounts by determining the quantitative effect of the variations in method.

One of the most important phases of income tax accounting deals with tax avoidance or minimization. It can be said without exaggeration that competent business management makes few decisions about material changes in operating procedures or about proposed new ventures without giving consideration to the tax consequences. In many situations there are two or more acceptable methods of measuring a particular segment of revenue or expense and the one selected may materially affect the amount of annual income tax. One of the examples considered in an earlier chapter was the effect of the fifo and lifo inventory methods on income during periods of rising price levels. The effect of various depreciation methods and of many other alternatives has also been demonstrated.

Before proceeding with further consideration of the impact of income taxes on business decisions, some familiarity with the structure of income taxes is essential.

Federal income tax system

The federal income tax, with which this chapter is concerned, dates from the ratification of the Sixteenth Amendment to the Constitution in 1913. At the present time all of the basic income tax laws are codified in Subtitle A of the Internal Revenue Code (IRC) of 1954, as amended. The executive office charged with general responsibility for interpreting and enforcing the statutes is the Treasury Department. Detailed regulations, explanations, and rulings are issued from time to time under authority of the Secretary of the Treasury, the Attorney General, and other governmental agencies. The branch of the Treasury Department concerned specifically with collection, enforcement, and the myriad details of income taxation is the Internal Revenue Service (IRS), headed by the Commissioner of Internal Revenue. Unresolved disputes between government and taxpayers may be taken to the federal courts for adjudication, usually beginning with the United States Tax Court. Over the years decisions on many important tax matters have been issued by the United States Supreme Court.

The income tax is not imposed upon business units as such, but upon taxable entities. Business enterprises organized as sole proprietorships are not taxable entities. The net income or the net loss of a sole proprietorship is reported by the owner as an individual, together with his income from other sources, his allowable deductions, and his exemptions. As was indicated in an earlier chapter, partnerships are ordinarily not taxable entities but are required to file an informational return.

Corporations engaged in business for profit are generally treated as distinct taxable entities. However, it is possible for two or more corporations with common ownership to join in filing a consolidated return. Notwithstanding the general rules, corporations that meet detailed specifications of the Internal Revenue Code may elect to be treated as partnerships and, conversely, it is possible for some partnerships and some sole proprietorships to elect to be taxed as though they were corporations.

Accounting methods

The Internal Revenue Code does not establish uniform methods of accounting for use by all taxpayers. To safeguard tax revenues, however, the Internal Revenue Service is given authority to prescribe accounting methods where those employed by a taxpayer fail to yield a fair determination of income. In general, taxpayers have the option of using either the cash basis or the accrual basis of determining income. Changes from one method to the other may be made only with official permission.

Cash basis. Individuals who do not own a business or professional enterprise ordinarily adopt the cash basis of determining net income. If the taxpayer's sources of income are restricted to salary, dividends, and interest, the difference between the results obtained by the cash basis and those obtained by the accrual basis are usually minor. The principal advantage of the cash basis is its simplicity.

The salaries reported to employees and to the Internal Revenue Service by businesses are the amounts paid rather than the amounts accrued. Payments of interest and dividends are similarly required to be reported by businesses in accordance with the cash method. Copies of such notifications, supplemented by check stubs, invoices, and other memorandums, frequently provide all of the information needed by an individual to determine his tax base.

Business and professional enterprises that sell services rather than commodities also customarily use the cash basis of determining net income. Amounts billed to customers or clients are not recorded as revenue until the cash is collected. No advance provision need be made in the ledger for doubtful receivables. Similarly, customers' accounts that do prove to be uncollectible do not require recognition in the ledger; they represent a reduction in anticipated revenue rather than an expense. Bills received for electricity, supplies, telephone, and other expenses are not recorded in the accounts until they are paid. The treatment of cash payments for long-lived business assets as current expense is, of course, not permissible. Depreciation expense may be claimed on buildings and equipment used for business purposes in the same manner as under the accrual basis, regardless of when payment is made. Similarly, when advance payments for insurance premiums or rentals on business property exceed a period of one year, the total cost must be prorated over the life of the contract.

Recognition of revenue in accordance with the cash method is not always contingent upon the actual receipt of cash. When revenue becomes available to the taxpayer without restrictions, it is said to be *constructively* received. For example, a check received late in December in payment of services performed in December represents December income even though the check is not cashed until the following January. Other examples of constructive receipt are matured bond interest coupons and interest credited to a savings account.

Accrual basis. For businesses in which production or trading in commodities is a material factor, purchases and sales must be accounted for on the accrual basis. Thus, revenues from sales must be reported as such in the year in which the goods are sold, regardless of when the cash is received. Similarly, the cost of commodities purchased must be reported in the year in which the liabilities are incurred, regardless of when payment is made. The usual adjustments must also be made for beginning and ending inventories in order to determine the cost of goods sold and the gross profit on sales. However, manufacturing and mercantile enterprises are not required to extend the accrual basis to all other phases of their operations. A considerable degree of hybridization of accounting methods is allowed, provided they are used consistently and the results are reasonable.

Methods of accounting in general, as well as many of the regulations affecting the determination of net business or professional income, are not affected by the legal nature or the organizational structure of the taxpayer. On the other hand, the tax base and the rate structure for individuals differ markedly from those applicable to corporations.

Tax base of individuals

The tax base to which the tax rates for individuals is applied is identified by the IRC as *taxable income.* The starting point in the computation is the determination of the amount of *gross income* to be reported. Amounts subtracted from gross income are divided into two principal categories. The first category is composed of expenses of operating a business or profession and certain other expenses that may be related to the earning of revenues. Subtraction of these *deductions* from gross income yields an intermediate balance identified as *adjusted gross income.* The second category is subdivided into (1) so-called *nonbusiness* expenses, (2) specified expenses that are primarily of a personal nature, and (3) arbitrary allowances known as *personal exemptions.* The foregoing steps in the computation may be outlined as follows:

Gross income		$11,600
Deductions (expenses related to business or specified revenue)		1,700
Adjusted gross income		$ 9,900
Deductions:		
Expenses (nonbusiness and personal)[1]	$1,080	
Personal exemption	600	1,680
Taxable income		$ 8,220

Gross income and filing requirements

Gross income is defined in Section 61(a) of the Internal Revenue Code as follows:

> Except as otherwise provided in this subtitle, gross income means all income from whatever source derived, including (but not limited to) the following items: (1) compensation for services, including fees, commissions, and similar items; (2) gross income derived from business; (3) gains derived from dealings in property; (4) interest; (5) rents; (6) royalties; (7) dividends; (8) alimony and separate maintenance payments; (9) annuities; (10) income from life insurance and endowment contracts; (11) pensions; (12) income from discharge of indebtedness; (13) distributive share of partnership gross income; (14) income in respect of a decedent; and (15) income from an interest in an estate or trust.

Statutory items of gross income are sometimes referred to as *taxable gross income* or *includable gross income;* items identified by the IRC as exceptions are frequently termed *nontaxable gross income* or *excludable gross income.*

Examples of common items of inclusions and exclusions of individuals are presented on page 578. They are illustrative only and should not be considered to be exhaustive lists.

Wholly excludable items of gross income, such as interest on state bonds, are not reported on the tax return. Partly excludable items, such

[1]Instead of itemizing these deductions, an alternative *standard deduction* may be elected. The alternative is described later in the chapter.

Includable in Gross Income of Individuals	Excludable from Gross Income of Individuals
Wages and other remuneration from employer.	Federal and state old-age pensions.
Tips and gratuities for services rendered.	State unemployment benefits.
Interest on United States obligations.	Value of property received as a gift.
Interest on commercial and industrial obligations.	Value of property received by bequest, devise, or inheritance.
Dividends on stock in excess of $100.	Dividends on stock of $100 or less.
Portion of pensions, annuities, and endowments representing income.	Life insurance proceeds received because of death of insured.
Rents and royalties.	Interest on obligations of a state or political subdivision.
Gross profit from a business.	Undergraduate scholarships for which no services are required.
Taxable gains from the sale of real estate, securities, and other property.	Portion of pensions, annuities, and endowments representing return of capital invested.
Distributive share of partnership income.	Compensation for injuries or for damages related to personal or family rights.
Income from an estate or trust.	Workmen's compensation insurance for sickness or injury.
Prizes won in contests.	Limited sick pay benefits.
Gains from wagering.	

as dividends on corporation stocks and annuity benefits, are reported in their entirety and the excludable portion is then deducted.

Partnerships and corporations organized for profit are required to file annual income tax returns regardless of the amount of their income. Individuals under 65 years of age as of the last day of the taxable year must file a return if their gross income for the year is $600 or more. Those who are 65 or older are required to file if their gross income is $1,200 or more.

Deductions from gross income

Business expenses and other expenses connected with earning certain types of revenue are deducted from gross income to yield adjusted gross income. The categories of such expenses that are of general applicability are described in the following paragraphs.

Business expenses other than as an employee. Ordinary and necessary expenses incurred by the taxpayer in the operation of his own unincorporated business or profession are deductible from gross income. The tax forms provide spaces for reporting sales, cost of goods sold, gross profit, salaries, taxes, depreciation, and other business expenses, and finally net income, which represents the adjusted gross income derived from the enterprise.

Business expenses of an employee. The types of expenses that an employee may deduct from salary and similar remuneration are carefully circumscribed by the statutes and regulations. The broad term "ordinary and necessary expense" used in the preceding paragraph does not apply to employees. The types of expenses that an employee may deduct from his remuneration in determining adjusted gross income are described in the following paragraphs. In each case it is assumed, of course, that the expense is directly related to the employment.

Outside salesmen's expenses. An outside salesman is an employee engaged principally in the solicitation of business for his employer at places other than the employer's place of business. The expenses incurred by such employees for transportation or travel are deductible in accordance with the rules stated below. In addition, expenses incurred for meals, telephone, secretarial help, split commissions on subcontracts, and other purposes related to their employment are also deductible from gross income.

Transportation and travel expenses. Expenses of transportation, meals, and lodging incurred by an employee while away from home *overnight* are deductible from gross income. When the required travel is local or the employee returns to his home at night, only the expenses of transportation are deductible. To illustrate, assume that an administrative employee with a salary of $20,000 for the taxable year had been required to make several trips away from home overnight, during which he spent a total of $800 for travel (transportation, meals, and lodging). His adjusted gross income from his salary would be $19,200. Had the travel not required absence from home overnight, only the amount spent for transportation would have been deductible.

Moving expenses. An employee who changes his place of residence in connection with beginning work in a new location may deduct the reasonable moving expenses incurred provided (1) that the distance between his old residence and the new place of employment is at least 20 miles greater than the distance between his old residence and his old place of employment, and (2) that he is a full-time employee in the new place of employment for at least 39 weeks during the 12-month period immediately following the move. Moving expenses include travel expenses of the employee and members of his household, as well as the cost of moving furnishings and personal effects.

Reimbursed expenses. All employment-related expenses for which an employee receives reimbursement from his employer are deductible from gross income. If the amount of the reimbursement and the expense incurred are exactly equal, they offset each other and have no effect on adjusted gross income. If the reimbursement exceeds the expense, the excess must be included in gross income. If the payments exceed the reimbursement, the excess is deductible from gross income only if the expense qualifies as one of the employee expenses described in the preceding paragraphs. For example, assume that an administrative employee (not an outside salesman) receives a salary of $15,000 and a customer-entertainment allowance of $800 during the taxable year. If his actual entertainment expenses amounted to $700, his adjusted gross income would be $15,100; if they amounted to $1,000, his adjusted gross income would be $15,000.

Expenses attributable to rents and royalties. Expenses that are directly connected with earning rent or royalty income are allowable as deductions from gross income. Expenses commonly incurred in connection with rental properties include depreciation, taxes, repairs, wages of custodian, and interest on indebtedness incurred to purchase property. For example, a taxpayer who received rent income of $1,800 for a one-family house during the taxable year and incurred related expenses of $960 would have adjusted gross income from rent of $840 ($1,800 − $960).

Losses from sale or exchange of property. Losses from the sale or the exchange of property are deductible from gross income provided the property was acquired or held for the production of income. Thus, losses from the sale of rental property or of investments in stocks and bonds are deductible; losses from the sale of the taxpayer's residence or of his family automobile are not deductible.

Adjusted gross income

Each category of expenses described in the preceding section is deducted from the amount of related gross income to yield adjusted gross income. If the adjusted gross income from a particular source is a negative amount, such as a net loss from business operations or from property rentals, it is deducted from the positive amounts in the other categories. The system of assembling data on each type of gross income and its related deductions is illustrated by the following summary for a hypothetical taxpayer:

Summary of Gross Income and Deductions		Adjusted Gross Income
Salary from employment	$12,600	
Deductions	700	$11,900
Rental income	$ 1,500	
Deductions	1,700	(200)
Dividends from corporation stocks	$ 820	
Exclusion	100	720
Interest on savings deposits		300
Total adjusted gross income		$12,720

Deductions from adjusted gross income

Certain specified expenditures and arbitrary allowances are deductible from adjusted gross income in arriving at taxable income, the base against which the tax rates are applied. These allowable deductions may be classified as follows:

(1) Expenses and other disbursements and losses.
 (a) Nonbusiness expenses.
 (b) Specified expenses, contributions, and losses of a personal nature that are wholly unrelated to income-producing activities.

(2) Personal exemptions.

The deductions from adjusted gross income that are of general applicability are described in the paragraphs that follow.

Nonbusiness expenses. The term applied to these deductions is somewhat inappropriate because the category is more closely related to gainful pursuits than to purely personal activities. Specifically, nonbusiness expenses are expenses attributable to the collection of income, the management of income-producing property, or the determination, collection, or refund of any tax, except expenses that qualify as deductions from *gross income.* Labor union dues and the cost of protective clothing are examples of expenses that may be deducted by an employee. The rental of a safe deposit box for the safekeeping of securities, payments to investment counselors, interest on money borrowed to purchase investments, and other expenses incurred by an individual in managing his own investments also qualify as nonbusiness expenses, as do fees paid for the preparation of a personal income tax return.

Charitable contributions. Contributions made by an individual to domestic corporations, foundations, or associations created exclusively for religious, charitable, scientific, literary, or educational purposes, or for the prevention of cruelty to children or animals, are deductible provided the organization is nonprofit and does not devote a substantial part of its activities to influencing legislation. Contributions to federal, state, or local governments, or to agencies thereof, and to organizations of war veterans are also deductible.

The total amount of the deduction for charitable contributions may in general not exceed 20% of adjusted gross income. However, there is an additional allowance of 10% of adjusted gross income for charitable contributions to organizations that are publicly supported, or to federal, state, or local governments for exclusively public purposes.

Contributions in excess of the combined 30% limitation may be carried forward for a period of 5 years and deducted in order of time as though they were paid in the later years.

Churches, Community Chests, the Salvation Army, and the American Red Cross are examples of publicly supported organizations to which the additional 10% allowance applies. Family foundations or other private organizations are ordinarily not publicly supported.

Interest expense. Interest expense of an entirely personal nature, such as on indebtedness incurred to buy a home, household appliances, or an automobile, is deductible. The deductibility of interest as a nonbusiness expense was mentioned above. It should also be noted that interest expense attributable to the operation of a business or to rents and royalties is deductible from gross income rather than from adjusted gross income.

Taxes. Some state and local taxes of a personal or nonbusiness nature are deductible from adjusted gross income. Federal excise taxes may qualify as deductions only when the expense to which they relate is deductible as a nonbusiness expense. For example, excise taxes on telephone services and on safe deposit box rentals are deductible as telephone expense and safe deposit box expense, respectively, if they were incurred in the production of income or maintenance of income-producing property. Federal income taxes and federal and state taxes incident to gifts or to transfers of property at death are never deductible from adjusted gross income. Taxes of general applicability are listed below, classified according to their status.

DEDUCTIBLE	NOT DEDUCTIBLE
State and Local	*State and Local*
Real estate taxes.	Gift, inheritance, and estate taxes.
Personal property taxes.	Auto licenses and drivers' licenses.
Income taxes.	Cigarette and tobacco taxes.
General sales taxes.	Alcoholic beverage taxes.
Gasoline taxes.	Admission taxes.
	Hunting and fishing licenses.
Federal	*Federal*
Federal excise taxes on items of deductible *nonbusiness* expense.	Gift and estate taxes.
	Employees FICA taxes.
	Income taxes.
	Excise taxes on *personal* expenditures.

Medical expenses. Medical and dental expenses paid by the taxpayer and not compensated for by insurance are deductible to the extent that they exceed 3% of adjusted gross income. Amounts paid for medicines and drugs may be included only to the extent that they exceed 1% of adjusted gross income. For example, if a taxpayer with an adjusted gross income of $9,000 paid $100 for medicines and $500 for other medical expenses during the year, he would be entitled to a medical expense deduction of $240, computed as follows:

Medical expense deduction:		
Medicines	$100	
Less 1% of adjusted gross income of $9,000	90	$ 10
Other medical expenses		500
Total		$510
Less 3% of adjusted gross income of $9,000		270
Amount deductible		$240

Neither the 1% limitation on medicines nor the 3% general limitation apply to medical expenses incurred by a taxpayer for his dependent mother or father who has attained 65 years of age by the end of the taxable year. Similarly, neither limitation applies to medical expenses of a taxpayer or his spouse if either has attained 65 years of age by the end of the taxable year.

The maximum amount that may be deducted for medical expenses ranges from $5,000 to $40,000, depending upon the type of return, the number of dependents, and whether or not the taxpayer is 65 or over and disabled.

Casualty and theft losses. Personal property losses in excess of $100 resulting from fire, storm, automobile accident or other casualty, or theft are deductible to the extent not compensated for by insurance. The $100 limitation applies to each occurrence rather than to total losses for the year. It should be noted that only a loss of taxpayer's own property is deductible; there is no deduction for payments to another person for property damage or personal injury caused by the taxpayer.

The loss sustained is the lesser of (1) the reduction in value of the property, and (2) the taxpayer's basis for the property, which is ordinarily its cost. The deductible amount is then determined by subtracting $100 and the insurance or other compensation received. To illustrate, assume that a taxpayer's summer residence, purchased several years ago for $10,000, was valued at $18,000 before a severe windstorm and was worth only $3,000 immediately after the storm, and that insurance proceeds amounted to $7,000. The casualty loss deduction would be $2,900, computed as follows:

Casualty loss deduction:			
Value of property before casualty			$18,000
Value of property after casualty			3,000
Reduction in value		(A)	$15,000
Basis (cost) of property		(B)	$10,000
Lesser of (A) and (B)			$10,000
Less: Insurance proceeds	$7,000		
Nondeductible loss	100		7,100
Amount deductible			$ 2,900

Care of dependent expenses. Widows, widowers, and certain married persons who, in order to earn a living, incur expenses for the care of dependents are allowed a limited deduction for such expenses. The expenses must be incurred for the care of a child or children under the age of 13, or other dependent, regardless of age, who is physically or mentally incapable of caring for himself. The maximum deduction is $600 a year if there is only one qualifying dependent or $900 if there are two or more qualifying dependents.

Married persons are allowed the deductions only if they combine their income and deductions in a single return, called a *joint return*. If their combined adjusted gross income exceeds $6,000, the amount of the allowable deduction is reduced to the extent of such excess. However, this limitation does not apply if the taxpayer husband is incapable of self-support because of mental or physical defects or if the taxpayer wife is institutionalized for at least 90 consecutive days during the year.

No deduction is permitted for amounts paid to a person whom the taxpayer is allowed to claim as a dependent. Thus, if a working widow pays her mother $500 during the year to take care of her children and the mother qualifies as a dependent, the $500 paid as care-of-dependent expense is not deductible.

Standard deduction. Instead of itemizing the expense deductions described in the preceding paragraphs, a taxpayer may elect to claim a so-called *standard deduction* from adjusted gross income. The maximum standard deduction is $1,000 for joint returns of husband and wife or for returns of single individuals; it is $500 for separate returns of married individuals.

There are alternative methods of computing the deduction: (1) the *10% standard* and (2) the *minimum standard*. The former is equal to 10% of the adjusted gross income; the latter, except for separate returns of married individuals, is equal to $200 plus $100 for each exemption. For separate returns of married taxpayers, it is $100 plus $100 for each exemption. To illustrate, assume that a husband and wife, each entitled to 1 exemption, with 3 dependent children, have combined adjusted gross income of $9,000. The 10% computation would yield $900 (10% of $9,000) and the minimum computation would yield $700 ($200 plus 5 exemptions at $100 each). Their standard deduction would therefore be $900. If we assume their adjusted gross income to be $6,000 instead of $9,000, the 10% computation would yield $600 (10% of $6,000) and the minimum would be unchanged at $700. In this case their standard deduction would be $700.

It is important to note that taxpayers should not elect the standard deduction unless it yields a greater amount than the sum of the actual deductions. It should also be borne in mind that the maximum of $1,000 applies only to the standard deduction; there is no limit on the total amount of actual deductions that may be claimed.

Personal exemptions. In addition to the allowable deductions from adjusted gross income described above, every individual taxpayer is entitled to at least one personal exemption of $600 for himself and an additional exemption of the same amount for each dependent.

In general, a dependent is a person who satisfies all of the following requirements: (1) is closely related to the taxpayer, (2) received over one half of his support from the taxpayer during the year, (3) had less than $600 of gross income during the year, and (4) if married, does not file a joint return with his or her spouse. However, the $600 limitation on gross income does not apply to a child of the taxpayer who is either under 19 years of age at the close of the taxable year or who has been a full-time student at an educational institution during each of five months of the year.

An additional personal exemption is allowed to a taxpayer who has attained the age of 65 years by the last day of the year, and another exemption if the taxpayer is blind. Thus, the number of exemptions for a taxpayer and his spouse, both of whom are at least 65 years of age and blind, is six. The extra exemptions for old age and blindness do not apply to a taxpayer's dependents.

Taxable income

The total amount of the deductions described in the preceding section is subtracted from an individual's adjusted gross income to yield *taxable income*, the base against which the tax rates are applied.

Income tax rate schedules

Simplified tax tables are provided for taxpayers with adjusted gross income of less than $5,000 who wish to elect the standard deduction. Taxpayers who itemize their deductions from adjusted gross income or who have adjusted gross income of $5,000 or more must compute the amount of their income tax liability by applying the appropriate tax rate schedule.

Single person. A portion of a tax rate schedule applicable to single taxpayers and married persons filing separate returns is given on page 586. The income tax on a single person with taxable income of $6,800 is computed as follows, applying this schedule:

Tax on $6,000	$1,130
Tax on $800 at 25%	200
Total tax	$1,330

SINGLE TAXPAYERS

If the taxable income is:		The tax is:		
Not over $500		14% of the taxable income		
Over	*But not over*			*of excess over*
$ 500	$ 1,000	$ 70	plus 15%	$ 500
1,000	1,500	145	plus 16%	1,000
1,500	2,000	225	plus 17%	1,500
2,000	4,000	310	plus 19%	2,000
4,000	6,000	690	plus 22%	4,000
6,000	8,000	1,130	plus 25%	6,000
8,000	10,000	1,630	plus 28%	8,000
10,000	12,000	2,190	plus 32%	10,000
12,000	14,000	2,830	plus 36%	12,000
14,000	16,000	3,550	plus 39%	14,000
16,000	18,000	4,330	plus 42%	16,000
18,000	20,000	5,170	plus 45%	18,000
20,000	22,000	6,070	plus 48%	20,000
22,000	26,000	7,030	plus 50%	22,000

The schedule of tax rates is frequently changed by Congress, but the progressive characteristic is a permanent feature of the income tax system.

Married person. Married persons may file separate returns and apply the tax schedule presented above or they may combine their income and deductions in a joint return and compute their tax by using a schedule designed specifically for such returns. The percentages are the same in both rate schedules, but the segment of income in each tax bracket of the joint return schedule is double the amount contained in the schedule applicable to separate returns. The effect of the joint return is to attribute half of the combined taxable income to each spouse. Marital status is determined as of the last day of the taxable year or at the date of death if one spouse dies during the year. A portion of a tax rate schedule applicable to joint returns is presented below.

MARRIED TAXPAYERS — JOINT RETURN

If the taxable income is:		The tax is:		
Not over $1,000		14% of the taxable income		
Over	*But not over*			*of excess over*
$ 1,000	$ 2,000	$ 140	plus 15%	$ 1,000
2,000	3,000	290	plus 16%	2,000
3,000	4,000	450	plus 17%	3,000
4,000	8,000	620	plus 19%	4,000
8,000	12,000	1,380	plus 22%	8,000
12,000	16,000	2,260	plus 25%	12,000
16,000	20,000	3,260	plus 28%	16,000
20,000	24,000	4,380	plus 32%	20,000
24,000	28,000	5,660	plus 36%	24,000
28,000	32,000	7,100	plus 39%	28,000
32,000	36,000	8,660	plus 42%	32,000
36,000	40,000	10,340	plus 45%	36,000
40,000	44,000	12,140	plus 48%	40,000
44,000	52,000	14,060	plus 50%	44,000

When both spouses have approximately the same amount of taxable income, their total tax liability will be much the same regardless of whether they file a joint return or separate returns. If the difference between their individual incomes is material, it is ordinarily, though not invariably, advantageous to file a joint return. The advantage tends to increase as the difference between the amounts of their individual incomes and/or the amount of the total combined income increases. To illustrate the possible advantages of a joint return, assume taxable income of husband and wife of $20,000 and $6,000 respectively. Their tax liability according to each of the two filing methods would be as follows:

Separate returns:	Husband — tax on taxable income of $20,000....	$6,070	
	Wife — tax on taxable income of $6,000........	1,130	$7,200
Joint return:	Tax on taxable income of $26,000............		6,380
	Tax saving from joint return................		$ 820

In spite of the foregoing, it is possible for the advantages of the joint return to be outweighed by the availability of greater deductions for medical expenses or certain specified losses when separate returns are filed. In doubtful cases the tax should be computed according to both filing methods and the method yielding the lower tax should be elected.

For the two years following the year in which a married person dies, the surviving spouse may continue to use the joint return rate schedule, provided the surviving spouse (1) maintains as his or her home a household in which a dependent son or daughter resides and (2) does not remarry.

Head of household. A third tax schedule giving approximately half of the split-income advantage of the joint return may be used by tax-

HEADS OF HOUSEHOLD

If the taxable income is: Not over $1,000 .... 14% of the taxable income

Over	*But not over*	*The tax is:*	*of excess over*
$ 1,000 —	$ 2,000	$ 140, plus 16% —	$ 1,000
2,000 —	4,000	300, plus 18% —	2,000
4,000 —	6,000	660, plus 20% —	4,000
6,000 —	8,000	1,060, plus 22% —	6,000
8,000 —	10,000	1,500, plus 25% —	8,000
10,000 —	12,000	2,000, plus 27% —	10,000
12,000 —	14,000	2,540, plus 31% —	12,000
14,000 —	16,000	3,160, plus 32% —	14,000
16,000 —	18,000	3,800, plus 35% —	16,000
18,000 —	20,000	4,500, plus 36% —	18,000
20,000 —	22,000	5,220, plus 40% —	20,000
22,000 —	24,000	6,020, plus 41% —	22,000
24,000 —	26,000	6,840, plus 43% —	24,000
26,000 —	28,000	7,700, plus 45% —	26,000

payers who qualify as a head of household. To qualify as a head of household, an individual must be unmarried at the close of the taxable year and must, in general, maintain as his home a household in which at least one of the following persons lives: (1) an unmarried son or daughter or one of their descendents, (2) a married son or daughter or one of their descendents who qualifies as a dependent of the taxpayer, or (3) any other close relative who qualifies as a dependent of the taxpayer. The head of household status may also be claimed by a taxpayer who maintains his dependent mother or father in a separate household.

Capital gains and losses

Gains and losses of individuals resulting from the sale or the exchange of certain types of assets, called *capital assets*, are accorded special treatment for income tax purposes. Capital assets most commonly bought by taxpayers are stocks and bonds. Under certain conditions, land, buildings, and equipment used in business may also be treated as capital assets.

Gains and losses from the sale or the exchange of capital assets are divided into two classes, based on the period of time the asset was held by the taxpayer. If the asset was held for 6 months or less, the gain or loss is *short-term;* if the asset was held for more than 6 months, the gain or loss is *long-term.* The aggregate of all short-term gains and losses during a taxable year is called a *net short-term capital gain* or a *net short-term capital loss.* The aggregate of all long-term gains and losses is identified as a *net long-term capital gain* or a *net long-term capital loss.*

After determining the net short-term and the net-long term results, the two amounts are combined to yield *net capital gain* or *net capital loss.* If there is a net capital loss, it can be deducted from gross income to the extent of $1,000 only; however, any excess may be carried forward and used in future years.

A net capital gain is reported as a part of gross income. To the extent that the net capital gain is composed of an excess of net long-term gain over net short-term loss (if any), the taxpayer is allowed to deduct 50% of such excess from gross income.

The application of these provisions may be demonstrated by the following three examples:

	A	B	C
Net short-term capital gain (loss)	($2,000)	$8,000	$3,000
Net long-term capital gain (loss)	8,000	(2,000)	3,000
Net capital gain — gross income	$6,000	$6,000	$6,000
Long-term capital gain deduction	3,000	—	1,500
Adjusted gross income from capital gain	$3,000	$6,000	$4,500

In addition to the long-term capital gain deduction allowed to individuals, the IRC limits the amount of tax on the taxable portion of the net long-term gain to a maximum of 50%. This ceiling limitation is of benefit only to taxpayers with sufficient taxable income to place them above the 50% tax bracket.

Payment of tax; filing returns

The income tax withheld from an employee's earnings by his employer represents current payments on account. An individual whose income is not subject to withholding, or only partially so, or an individual whose income is fairly large must estimate his income tax in advance and file a tax form known as a *Declaration of Estimated Income Tax*. The estimated tax for the year, after deducting the estimated amount to be withheld and any credit for overpayment from prior years, must also be paid currently, usually in four installments. Self-employed persons, taxpayers whose estimated income from salary exceeds certain minimum amounts, and persons with anticipated income from investments are required to follow this procedure.

Annual income tax returns must be filed within 3½ months following the end of the taxpayer's taxable year. Any balance due must accompany the return. If the return indicates an overpayment, the taxpayer may direct (1) that it be credited to his estimated tax for the following year, (2) that it be applied to the purchase of U.S. Savings Bonds, with the excess over the purchase price refunded, or (3) that the entire amount be refunded.

Determination of income tax of individuals

The method of assembling income tax data and determining the tax liability will be illustrated by the hypothetical case of Mr. and Mrs. James T. Clark, who file a joint return. Mr. Clark owns and operates a retail mercantile enterprise; Mrs. Clark owns a building with four apartments and is also employed as a part-time secretary. They are entitled to 2 exemptions for themselves and 2 additional exemptions for their dependent children. Sources and amounts of includable gross income, itemized deductions, exemptions, and other data are presented in condensed form on page 590. In practice, the data would be reported in considerably greater detail on the official tax form.

Corporation taxable income

Incorporated business enterprises are impersonal taxable entities. The expenses that corporations may deduct from gross income to arrive at taxable income are not subdivided into the separate categories of busi-

MR. AND MRS. JAMES T. CLARK
FEDERAL INCOME TAX STATEMENT

Gross income and deductions:			
Salary			$ 2,500
Dividends on corporation stocks:			
Owned by husband	$470		
Owned by wife	80	$ 550	
Exclusion ($100 for husband plus $80 for wife)		180	370
Rents:			
Gross income		$ 6,800	
Expenses		3,700	3,100
Business:			
Sales		$112,000	
Cost of merchandise sold		74,000	
Gross profit		$ 38,000	
Expenses		20,600	17,400
Capital gains and losses:			
Net long-term capital gain		$ 4,000	
Net short-term capital loss		1,000	
Net capital gain		$ 3,000	
Long-term capital gain deduction		1,500	1,500
Adjusted gross income			$24,870
Deductions and exemptions:			
Charitable contributions	$730		
Interest on residence mortgage	640		
Real estate taxes on residence	539		
State sales tax	220		
State gasoline tax	30		
Safe deposit box rental	11	$ 2,170	
Exemptions (4 × $600)		2,400	4,570
Taxable income			$20,300
Income tax:			
On $20,000		$ 4,380	
On 300 at 32%		96	$ 4,476
Payments:			
Tax withheld		$ 265	
Estimated tax payments		4,000	4,265
Balance due			$ 211

ness, nonbusiness, and personal. There are no standard deductions and no personal exemptions. The *taxable income* of a corporation is roughly comparable to the *adjusted gross income* of an unincorporated business enterprise. Three variations of broad applicability merit explanation.

Dividends received deduction. Dividends received on stock of other companies are includable in gross income in their entirety. However, a special deduction from gross income of 85% of the dividends received is ordinarily allowed. Certain small corporations may deduct 100% of dividends received.

Charitable contributions. Corporations may deduct charitable contributions as a business expense. The amount that may be deducted is limited to 5% of taxable income, computed without regard to the contributions and the special deductions for dividends received. Contributions in excess of the limitation may be carried forward and treated as contributions of the 5 succeeding years.

Capital gains and losses. Capital gains and losses are subdivided into short-term and long-term in the same manner applicable to individuals. The excess of the net long-term gain over the net short-term loss (if any) is subject to a maximum tax of 25%. A net capital loss for the year may be carried forward and deducted from capital gains for up to 5 years; no part of such a loss can be deducted from ordinary income.

Corporation income tax

The federal income tax on corporations is subdivided into a *normal tax* and a *surtax*. The normal tax is a percentage of taxable income and the surtax is a percentage of the amount by which taxable income exceeds $25,000.

The computation of corporate taxable income and income tax at rates currently in effect may be illustrated as follows:

Gross income (including dividends received of $6,000)	$100,000
Deductions (expenses)	40,000
Taxable income before special deduction	$ 60,000
Less special deduction for dividends received (85% × $6,000)	5,100
Taxable income	$ 54,900
Normal tax, 22% of $54,900	$ 12,078
Surtax, 26% of ($54,900 — $25,000)	7,774
Total income tax	$ 19,852

Minimizing income taxes

There are various means of minimizing or reducing federal income taxes, some of which are of broader applicability than others. Much depends upon the volume and the sources of a taxpayer's gross income, the nature of his expenses and other deductions, and the accounting methods employed. For example, an individual with relatively high income and a substantial amount of liquid assets may completely avoid income tax on a part of his income by investing in tax-exempt bonds of municipalities or other political subdivisions of a state. The yield on such investments is usually low, mainly because of the tax shelter provided. Nevertheless, if the tax rate applicable to the top segment of an individual's taxable income (called the *marginal* rate) is 60%, a tax-exempt yield of 3% is equivalent to a taxable yield of 7½%. Safe investments at the latter yield rate are not likely to be available.

The cash method of reporting frequently permits some tax savings by judicious timing of revenue and expense items. For example, near the end of a particular year in which taxable income is above average, a taxpayer may be able to shift additional taxable income to the succeeding year and thus avoid tax at a higher bracket than usual. It may be possible to postpone the receipt of gross income by delayed billings to clients, expenses of the period may be increased by payment of outstanding bills prior to the end of the year, and the timing of expenditures for such expenses as redecorating, repairs, and advertising may be readily subject to control.

Individuals whose principal source of income is salary may also have opportunities to save a modest amount by careful planning of payments for contributions, medical expenses, and other allowable deductions. For example, if a substantial amount of medical expense is incurred near the end of the year, it would be preferable to pay all such bills before the end of the year if by so doing the medical expense deduction and other itemized deductions will exceed the standard deduction. Conversely, if early payment would not yield a reduction in taxes for the current year, postponement of payment might be beneficial. The "bunching" of deductions for contributions to religious, charitable, educational, and similar organizations also affords opportunities for tax savings. Because of differences between the taxable year of the individual, which is usually the calendar year, and the fiscal year of the organizations, contributions for two successive fiscal years may be made in a single calendar year.

A closely related means of effecting a modest tax savings is the alternation between itemization of deductions and election of the standard deduction. To illustrate, assume that a married couple has average annual adjusted gross income of $12,000 and average annual deductions, exclusive of exemptions, of $900. By claiming the standard deduction of $1,000, they benefit to the extent of the tax on $100 computed at their marginal tax rate. If they were able to alternate $700 of their deductions from year to year, they would then be able to claim actual deductions of $1,600 ($900 + $700) in one year and the standard deduction of $1,000 in the alternate year. By this means a saving equivalent to the tax on $600 at the marginal rate could be effected.

The installment method of determining gross income from sales of merchandise was described in Chapter 14. This method of accounting may be adopted by business enterprises that sell on the installment plan. It may also be used, under certain conditions, for reporting the income from a sale of real estate or of personal property. In the case of real estate, the installment method may be used provided the payments received in the year of sale do not exceed 30% of the selling price. The amount of tax savings that may be accomplished by electing this option is affected by a number of variables; it may range from zero to a material amount. The point to note is the importance of advance planning when entering into a transaction of this type.

The timing of capital gains and losses is ordinarily subject to a high degree of control by the taxpayer because he is able to sell capital assets or to refrain from selling them as he chooses. Postponement of a sale by only a single day can result in a substantial tax saving. To illustrate, assume that an individual sells securities that he has held exactly six months, realizing a gain of $4,000. The gain would be classified as a short-term capital gain and taxed as ordinary income. Assuming a marginal rate of 60%, the tax on the $4,000 would be $2,400. On the other hand, if the individual holds the securities at least one additional day before selling them, the $4,000 gain (assuming no change in selling price) would qualify as a long-term capital gain, of which only half is subject to tax at a rate not higher than 50%. Thus, if the sale were postponed by at least one day, the tax would have been $1,000 instead of $2,400.

When an individual owns various lots of an identical security that were acquired at different dates and at different prices, it may also be possible to choose between realizing a gain and realizing a loss, and perhaps to a limited extent the amount desired to be realized. For example, a taxpayer who has realized gains from the sale of securities may wish to offset them, in whole or in part, by losses from the sale of other securities. If he owns three 100-share lots of a particular common stock purchased at $40, $50, and $60 a share respectively and the current price is $45, he may establish a gain of $500 or a loss of $500 or $1,500, as he chooses. Averaging of the cost of different lots is not permitted, and where the particular lot sold is not identifiable, the first-in, first-out method must be employed.

One of the most important considerations in selecting the form of organization to use in operating a business enterprise is the impact of the federal income tax. In a sole proprietorship the owner is taxed on the business income as it is earned. In a partnership the individual partners are taxed on their distributive shares of the business income in much the same manner as a sole proprietor. A corporation, on the other hand, is a taxable entity and must pay a tax on its income. The owners are required to pay an additional tax when corporate after-tax earnings are distributed as dividends. It might seem that this double taxation would outweigh any possible advantages of the corporate form for a family enterprise or other closely held business; however, this is not necessarily the case. For every business enterprise there are likely to be both advantages and disadvantages in each form of organization. Some of the factors that need to be considered are nature of the income, methods of financing the enterprise, present and expected future individual and corporation tax rates, salaries of the owners, amount of income earned by the owners from other sources, and dividend policies to be adopted. The best form of organization, from the standpoint of the federal income tax, can be determined only on an individual basis and then only by a careful detailed analysis.

Impact of income taxes generally

The foregoing description of the federal income tax system and discussion of tax minimization, together with explanations in other chapters, demonstrates the importance of income taxes to business enterprises. The most important factor influencing a business decision is often the federal income tax. Many accountants, in both private and public practice, devote their entire attention to tax planning for their employer or their clients. The statutes and the administrative regulations, which change frequently, must be studied continuously by anyone who engages in this phase of accounting.

QUESTIONS

1. Who initially determines the *taxable income* of a taxpayer?

2. Does the failure to maintain acceptable records qualify as a legitimate means of tax avoidance? Discuss.

3. A particular individual owns three unincorporated business enterprises, maintaining a separate accounting system for each. (a) Is a separate income tax return required for each enterprise? (b) May the owner elect to file a separate return and determine the tax on each enterprise separately?

4. (a) Are partnerships ordinarily subject to the federal income tax? (b) May partnerships ever elect to be taxed as a corporation?

5. The net income of an unincorporated business for the year was $25,000, determined in accordance with requirements of the Internal Revenue Code. The owner withdrew $15,000 from the business during the year, using $10,000 for living expenses and investing $5,000 in common stocks. What amount of income from the business must he include in his income tax return?

6. A taxpayer owns one fourth of the common stock of the Saratoga Corporation, which has only one class of stock. The corporation earned a net income of $200,000 for the year before federal income taxes of $90,000. The taxpayer received cash dividends of $16,000 on his stock during the year. What amount of income from the corporation must the taxpayer include in his income tax return?

7. What method of accounting is most commonly used by individuals in determining their taxable income?

8. Items of gross income earned by a taxpayer who reports for the calendar year by the cash method are described below. Which amounts should be reported in year A and which in year B, the following year?

(a) Bond interest of $100; coupons are payable on December 15 of year A and are deposited in the bank on January 25 of year B.
(b) Salary bonus of $1,500 for year A; check is dated and received on January 2 and deposited in the bank on January 5 of year B.
(c) Interest of $163 credited to a savings account on December 31 of year A; $50 is withdrawn on that date and the remaining $113, together with principal of $1,000, is withdrawn on July 10 of year B.
(d) Monthly rent of $200 for December of year A, due on December 1; payment is received from tenant on January 4, year B.

9. An architect who uses the cash basis of reporting income determines at the end of the year that a fee of $300 owed by a former client is uncollectible. Is the uncollectible account deductible from gross income as an expense in determining taxable income? Discuss.

10. Outline the procedure for determining the income tax base of an individual by arranging the following in proper sequence:

(a) Adjusted gross income.
(b) Personal exemption.
(c) Gross income.
(d) Expenses related to business or specified revenue.
(e) Taxable income.
(f) Nonbusiness and personal expenses.

11. Identify the following as (a) taxable gross income or (b) nontaxable gross income.

(1) Salary as member of a state legislature.
(2) Freshman scholarship received from a state university.
(3) U.S. Treasury notes received as an inheritance.
(4) Rent received from room rented to a student.
(5) Interest received on the U.S. Treasury notes acquired in (3) above.
(6) Cash received in repayment of a non-interest-bearing loan to a friend.
(7) Interest on municipal bonds.
(8) Federal old-age benefits.
(9) Salary as judge of a federal court.
(10) Compensation received for personal injuries.

12. Which of the following are required to file an income tax return?

(a) Unmarried man, 70 years old, with gross income of $1,100.
(b) Child actor, 10 years old, with gross income of $1,500.
(c) Married man, 45 years old, with gross income of $10,000.
(d) Wife of man in (c), 40 years old, with gross income of $200.
(e) College student, 20 years old, with gross income of $700, dependent on father for support.

13. Identify the following items as (a) deductible from gross income in determining adjusted gross income, (b) deductible from adjusted gross income in determining taxable income, or (c) not deductible. (Ignore any possible limitations on the amount of the deduction.)

(1) Fire damage to family residence, not covered by insurance.
(2) State automobile license tax (commuting between home and office).
(3) State gasoline tax (commuting between home and office).
(4) Property taxes on apartment building held as an investment.
(5) Contributions to a political campaign fund.
(6) Insurance on taxpayer's residence.
(7) Federal excise tax on commodities purchased for family use.
(8) State sales taxes on commodities purchased for family use.
(9) Loss incurred by physician on sale of investments.
(10) Federal excise tax on rental of safe deposit box used for safekeeping of stock certificates in (9).
(11) Local transportation expenses incurred by employee in collecting receivables owed to employer.
(12) Luncheon expenses incurred by employee described in (11).
(13) State inheritance tax.
(14) Interest on money borrowed for use in unincorporated business.
(15) Contributions to local Community Chest by owner of unincorporated business.

14. Indicate the amount of the standard deduction that can be claimed on each of the following tax returns, assuming that each is entitled to only one exemption for himself and that the married couples file a joint return:
(a) Single person, 2 dependents, adjusted gross income of $8,000.
(b) Married couple, 4 dependents, adjusted gross income of $6,900.
(c) Married couple, 1 dependent, adjusted gross income of $7,000.
(d) Married couple, no dependents, adjusted gross income of $15,000.

15. An acquaintance asks your advice about acting on an opportunity that will earn for him an additional $500 during the year but that will place him in a higher tax bracket. What would you advise?

16. An unmarried son of the taxpayer, 22 years of age, was a full-time student at a university until his graduation in August; his gross income for the year was $1,800. (a) What requirement must be met to enable the taxpayer to claim the son as a dependent? (b) If the son was married during the year, would there be an additional requirement? Discuss.

17. What is the holding period for short-term and long-term gains and losses from sales of capital assets?

18. If a taxpayer realizes gains on all sales of capital assets made during the year, why is it preferable that they be long-term gains rather than short-term gains?

19. What is the limitation on the deductibility of a net capital loss by individuals?

20. What terms are applied to the two corporation income tax rates?

EXERCISES

1. An employee (not an outside salesman) who received a salary of $12,000 during the year incurred the following unreimbursed expenses related to his employment: transportation, $350, and meals, $150, not away from home overnight; travel while away from home overnight, $600; and customer entertainment, $200. Determine his adjusted gross income from salary.

2. From the information given below, indicate whether the moving expenses incurred by employees A, B, and C are deductible, assuming in each case that they meet the employment requirements.

Distance between:	A	B	C
Old place of residence and old place of employment	10 mi.	30 mi.	5 mi.
Old place of employment and new place of employment	300	60	30
Old place of residence and new place of employment	290	45	25
New place of residence and old place of employment	295	50	40
New place of residence and new place of employment	5	20	10

3. Determine the adjusted gross income from salary of employees J, K, and L, assuming that none of them is an outside salesman and that no travel was involved.

	J	K	L
Salary	$10,000	$12,000	$9,000
Reimbursement from employer for entertainment expenses	800	900	600
Entertainment expenses incurred	700	1,100	600

4. Taxpayer husband and wife, each entitled to one exemption, with two dependent children, have adjusted gross income of $14,000. Payments for medicines totaled $192 and for other medical expenses totaled $812. (a) Determine the amount of their allowable deduction for medical expenses. (b) What is the maximum amount that they may deduct for charitable contributions? (c) What is the amount of their minimum standard deduction? (d) What is the maximum amount that they may claim as a standard deduction? (e) Assuming that they claim the standard deduction, determine their income tax, applying the appropriate schedule of rates appearing in this chapter.

5. Details of a single casualty loss sustained by each of three taxpayers, X, Y, and Z, are summarized below. Determine the amount of casualty loss deductible by each.

	X	Y	Z
Basis of property	$20,000	$15,000	$10,000
Value of property before casualty	18,000	20,000	15,000
Value of property after casualty	13,000	2,000	14,400
Insurance proceeds	3,000	10,500	0

6. Data related to the deduction for care-of-dependent expenses of three married taxpayers filing jointly are presented below. In all cases the expenses were extra expenses incurred in order that the taxpayers could earn a living. In all cases the children for whom the expenses were incurred were under 13 years of age and in no case was the husband incapable of self-support or the wife institutionalized. Determine the amount of the deductions.

	R	S	T
Number of children	3	1	2
Care-of-dependent expenses	$ 950	$ 850	$ 800
Adjusted gross income	$6,000	$6,250	$7,000

7. The capital gains and losses of an individual taxpayer during the year are listed below. Losses are identified by parentheses.

Short-term: $2,000, ($1,000), ($4,000).
Long-term: ($2,000), $6,000, $3,000.

Determine the following amounts: (a) net short-term capital gain or loss, (b) net long-term capital gain or loss, (c) net capital gain or loss, (d) long-term capital gain deduction, if any, and (e) adjusted gross income from capital gain or loss.

8. Taxpayer husband and wife, entitled to one exemption each and three additional exemptions for dependents, file a joint return. Other summary data related to their income tax return are as follows:

Includable gross income	$20,000
Allowable deductions from gross income	2,000
Allowable itemized deductions from adjusted gross income	910
Tax withheld	2,200
Estimated tax payments	400

Determine their (a) adjusted gross income, (b) taxable income, (c) total tax, using the appropriate schedule of rates appearing in this chapter, and (d) balance due.

PROBLEMS

24-1. John T. Chapman maintains a special bank account that he uses in connection with a small office building that he owns and for occasional payments of personal expenses. He uses the cash method of determining income. During the current taxable year ending December 31, he deposited $21,000 of rent receipts in the special account. In addition he deposited $200 received from a tenant for canceling the remaining three months of a lease that provided for a monthly rental of $200. The space vacated by the tenant remained unoccupied for the remaining two months of the year.

Disbursements from the special bank account during the current year are summarized as follows:

Wages of custodian (gross earnings $3,900)	
Paid to custodian	$3,386
Withheld for FICA tax and paid to IRS	156
Withheld for income tax and paid to IRS	358
Real estate tax	1,650
Payments of federal income tax of the preceding year	950
Payments of federal income tax applicable to the current year	3,000
Interest on mortgage note on land and office building	1,200
Installment payments of principal on mortgage note	1,600
Utilities expense	650
Air-conditioning units installed in three offices not previously air-conditioned	1,840
Repainting interior of two offices	174
Repairs to heating and plumbing equipment	261
FICA tax expense	156
Premium on a three-year insurance policy on the building, effective July 1	360
Community Chest, Salvation Army, and American Red Cross	650
Miscellaneous expenses incurred in earning rentals	413

In addition to the foregoing data, you determine from other records and the tax return for the preceding year that the allowable deduction for depreciation expense is $3,700 and that current expirations of insurance premiums paid in earlier years total $215.

Instructions: Prepare a statement of gross income from rents and the deductions from gross income that are allowable in determining adjusted gross income.

24-2. T. Harold Gibson, unmarried and entitled to one exemption for himself, is engaged in the practice of architecture. He qualifies as a head of household and is entitled to an exemption for his mother, age 68, who has no gross income.

Mr. Gibson uses the cash method of determining taxable income and he reports on the calendar-year basis. A summary of his record of cash receipts and disbursements for the current calendar year is presented below.

Receipts	
Professional fees	$38,150
Borrowed from bank (professional purposes)	3,000
Inheritance from uncle's estate	2,500
Dividends on corporation stocks	410

Disbursements	
Wages of draftsmen and typist:	
Taxes withheld and paid to IRS	$ 1,495
Paid to employees	9,855
Cost of new automobile (purchased January 4)	4,950
Office equipment (purchased at various times)	800
Payroll taxes	668
Fees to collaborating engineers	2,450
Office rent	2,700
Telephone expense (office)	264
Electricity (office)	192
Payment on loan from bank (see above)	2,000
Blueprint expense	465
Office supplies expense	75
Insurance on office equipment (3-year policy, dated January 1)	99
Interest on bank loan	140
Contributions to church, United Fund, and Red Cross	350
Payment on principal of mortgage note on home	1,200
Interest on mortgage note on home	700
Personal property tax on office equipment	50
Real property tax on home	520
State sales tax on purchases for personal use	160
State inheritance tax	75
Automobile operating expenses (gasoline, oil, insurance, etc.)	585
Purchase of 50 shares of Warren Corporation stock	1,850
Medical expenses for mother:	
Medicines	60
Other	378
Payments of estimated income tax for current year	2,800

The automobile was used ⅔ of the time for professional purposes. It is to be depreciated by the declining-balance method at twice the straight-line rate, assuming an estimated life of 3 years. Allocate ⅔ of the depreciation and other automobile expenses to professional purposes.

The cost of the office equipment owned at the beginning of the year was $2,600. None of the equipment was disposed of during the year. However, in addition to the disbursements of $800 for office equipment listed above, payment for a copying machine acquired in December at a cost of $300 is not due until January. Use a composite depreciation rate of 10%, based on the average.

Instructions: Determine Mr. Gibson's taxable income, income tax, and balance due, presenting the details in good order. Apply the appropriate schedule of tax rates appearing in this chapter.

24-3. The preliminary income statement of the Beehive Record Shop, a sole proprietorship, appearing below was prepared as of the close of the calendar year in which the business was established. You are engaged to review the business records, revise the accounting system to the extent necessary, and determine the adjusted gross income.

Sales		$87,642
Purchases		72,310
Gross profit on sales		$15,332
Operating expenses:		
Salaries	$11,630	
Rent	2,000	
Store equipment	4,400	
Insurance	360	
Utilities	443	
Fuel	370	
Advertising	565	
Taxes	424	
Donations	115	
Miscellaneous	358	20,665
Net loss		$ 5,333

You obtained the following information during the course of your examination:

(a) The preliminary income statement is in reality an accurate summary of cash receipts and disbursements. Sales to customers on account are evidenced only by duplicate sales tickets, and invoices for merchandise and other purchases that have not been paid are filed in an unpaid file until they are paid.

(b) Uncollected sales to customers on account at December 31 amount to $2,342.

(c) Unpaid invoices at December 31 for expenditures of the past year are summarized as follows:

Merchandise	$7,416
Utilities	47
Fuel	34

(d) The inventory of merchandise on hand at December 31 amounted to $15,431.

(e) Withdrawals of $4,800 by the proprietor were included in the amount reported as Salaries.

(f) The agreement with the two part-time salesclerks provides for a bonus equal to 1% of total sales for the year, payable in January. (Figure to nearest dollar).

(g) The rent for January of the following year ($200) was paid in December.

(h) The store equipment reported in the preliminary income statement was installed on April 2. It has an estimated life of 10 years and no residual value. Depreciation is to be claimed for 9 months, using the sum-of-the-years-digits method.

(i) A total of $195 of insurance premiums was unexpired at December 31.

(j) Taxes paid are composed of payroll taxes of $310 and personal federal income taxes of $114 for the preceding year. Accrued payroll taxes and property taxes on the equipment and inventory as of the end of the year total $320.

(k) Payments classified as Donations were contributions to charitable, religious, and educational organizations.

Instructions: Prepare a statement of adjusted gross income from the business for submission with the income tax return of T. R. Reynolds, the owner, employing the accrual method of accounting.

24-4. Henry B. Jordan is negotiating the sale of a parcel of unimproved real estate to Desert Homes, Inc., to become effective on January 1 of next year. The sales price of the property is $90,000, payable in 10 equal annual installments, with the first installment payable on the effective date of the sale. Interest of 5% per annum is to be paid on the remaining balance. The property, which was acquired by Jordan as an inheritance a number of years ago, has a cost basis of $10,000.

Exclusive of the gain on the sale of the land, which qualifies as a long-term capital gain, Mr. and Mrs. Jordan expect to have approximately $8,000 of ordinary taxable income (adjusted gross income less itemized deductions and exemptions) annually for the next 10 years. The $8,000 includes estimated gross income from the note and from reinvestment of the annual installment payments.

Instructions: (1) Assuming the accuracy of the estimate of future income and no changes in the Internal Revenue Code, determine the Jordans' total estimated federal income tax (joint return) for ten years, beginning with next year, based on (a) reporting the entire gain next year and (b) reporting the gain by the installment method. Apply the appropriate schedule of tax rates appearing in this chapter.

(2) What is the amount of federal income tax saved by electing the installment method?

(3) Could the installment method have been elected if the terms provided for a down payment of one third of the sales price?

24-5. Three married individuals, designated as A, B, and C, who are engaged in related types of businesses as sole proprietors, plan to combine their enterprises to form Dee Co. They have discussed the relative merits of the partnership and the corporation form of organization, exclusive of the effect of the federal income tax. You are engaged to assemble and analyze the relevant data and to determine the current income tax consequences to each of them of the two forms of organizations. The consolidation is planned to take effect as of January 1 of the coming year.

Each of the three is to be designated as an officer of the corporation, or alternatively is to be assigned managerial duties as a partner. In either event, each is to be paid an annual salary, which is to be treated as an operating expense of the enterprise. The agreed salaries and the capital investments to be made by each individual are stated below. Distribution of earnings in excess of salaries is to be made in accordance with the ratio of capital investment.

	Total	A	B	C
Salary	$ 40,000	$ 15,000	$ 10,000	$ 15,000
Capital investment	400,000	120,000	200,000	80,000

The annual net income of the three separate enterprises has typically totaled $80,000, with no allowances having been made for salaries of the owner-managers. It is anticipated that economies of operations and other advantages of combining the enterprises will increase the annual net income by $20,000 (total of $100,000 before salaries). In addition to their salaries, they plan to withdraw $10,000 of earnings annually, which are to be allocated to A, B, and C in accordance with their original investments. The remaining earnings are to be retained in the business for use in expanding operations.

The estimated ordinary adjusted gross income from sources other than Dee Co., for each individual and his wife, and other relevant data are listed below. The amount reported for each includes dividends on corporation stocks in excess of the allowable exclusion, and each files a joint return for the calendar year in accordance with the cash method.

	A	B	C
Ordinary adjusted gross income, exclusive of salary and profits of Dee Co	$2,000	$5,000	$30,000
Allowable deductions from adjusted gross income, including exemptions	3,000	4,000	7,000

Instructions: (1) Assuming that the Dee Co. is organized as a partnership and is so treated for income tax purposes: (a) Present an estimated capital statement for the partnership for the first complete year of operations. (b) Present a report of the estimated federal income tax of A, B, and C for the first complete year of business operations, applying the appropriate schedule of tax rates appearing in this chapter.

(2) Assuming that the Dee Co. is organized as a corporation and is so treated for income tax purposes: (a) Present a report of the estimated federal income tax of the corporation for the first complete year of operations, applying the corporation tax rates appearing in this chapter. (b) Present an estimated capital statement for the corporation for the first complete year of operations, allocating each increase and decrease to each of the three stockholders in the manner employed in instruction (1) (a). (c) Present a report of the estimated federal income tax of A, B, and C for the first complete year of business operations, applying the appropriate tax rates appearing in this chapter.

(3) Present a comparison of the estimated income tax effects of the two methods of organization on each of the three individuals. For purposes of this report, the corporation income tax should be allocated among the individuals.

24-6. In December of the current taxable year, ending on December 31, Mr. and Mrs. John B. Morrow engage you to prepare their income tax return and to advise them concerning other matters that may affect the amount of their tax liability. They are entitled to a total of 5 exemptions for themselves and their dependent children. They have been using the cash method of determining taxable income and expect to file a joint return.

Mr. Morrow is employed at a salary of $15,000 for the current year. He is assured of a salary increase of $150 per month for the following year, which will become effective in January. He has no deductions for travel or transportation. His dividend income is expected to amount to $900 for both the current and the following year. Mrs. Morrow's sole income is from dividends, which are expected to amount to $500 annually for both the current and the following year.

Both Mr. and Mrs. Morrow plan to sell one of the stocks in their respective investment portfolios in the near future. Based on current market prices, Mr. Morrow would incur a loss of $1,000 on the sale of A Company stock and Mrs. Morrow would realize a gain of $2,000 on the sale of B Company stock. In both cases the securities have been owned for several years and their market prices are quite stable at the present time.

Payments for the current year to date that may qualify as deductions from adjusted gross income are estimated as follows: charitable contributions, $30; interest on note payable, $300; property taxes on residence and investments, $200; deductible sales and gasoline taxes, $80; medicines and drugs, $40; other medical expenses, $350.

Unpaid pledges to their church and other charities for the current year total $570. They ordinarily pay such pledges in December; however, the fiscal years of the organizations end within the next calendar year. They contemplate making contributions of $700 for the year following the current taxable year. The payments made to date for interest and property taxes represent one half of the amounts due for the year; the remaining half is due late in December, but payment may be postponed until January without penalty or other disadvantage. The annual property taxes and the interest expense are expected to remain constant for the following year. Payments for deductible sales and gasoline taxes are expected to total $100 (including the $80 already paid) for the current year. It is reasonable to assume that a like amount will be spent during the following year. All medical expenses incurred during the current taxable year have been paid, except a surgeon's bill for $500 received in December. The additional amount of medical expenses that will be incurred and paid during the following year is estimated at $1,700, including $100 for medicines.

Instructions: (1) Advise Mr. and Mrs. Morrow concerning the contemplated sales of securities and the timing of deductions from adjusted gross income. Consideration is to be given only to the current taxable year and to the following taxable year; the Internal Revenue Code and regulations, as well as the taxpayers' exemptions, are assumed to remain unchanged during the period; and the estimates for the succeeding year are assumed to be accurate.

(2) Determine the estimated tax liability for Mr. and Mrs. Morrow for (a) the current taxable year and (b) the subsequent taxable year, assuming that they follow your advice and that the actual amount of income and deductions agree exactly with the estimates. Apply the appropriate schedule of tax rates appearing in this chapter. Present details in good order.

24-7. Mr. and Mrs. Paul M. Hunter, each of whom is entitled to one exemption, have 2 dependent children. The older child, 18 years of age, earned $900 during the year, and the younger child earned $120. Mr. Hunter also contributed more than half of the cost of supporting his mother, who received gross income of $675 during the year. During the current year ended December 31, Mr. Hunter realized a net long-term capital gain of $3,200 and Mrs. Hunter incurred a net short-term capital loss of $600. Other details of their receipts and disbursements during the year are presented below.

Receipts

Mr. Hunter:	
Salary as sales manager of Weldon Computer Co. (Earnings, $36,000. Withholdings: income tax $4,667; FICA tax, $216; stock purchases, $5,000.)	$26,117.00
Interest on bonds of City of Boulder	500.00
Dividends on corporation stocks	600.00
Mrs. Hunter:	
Withdrawals (not treated as salary) from Arden & Co., a partnership in which she is a partner (distributive share of the net income for the year, $6,500)	3,600.00
Rent from property owned	4,800.00
Insurance proceeds (death of father)	5,000.00
Dividends on corporation stocks	87.50
Interest on short-term U.S. Treasury bills	342.10

Disbursements

Mr. Hunter:	
Charitable contributions	764.00
Interest on mortgage on residence	660.60
Automobile license fees (family cars)	30.00
Real estate tax on residence	715.35
State sales tax on items purchased for personal or family use	223.40
State gasoline tax (family cars)	92.00
Federal gasoline tax (family cars)	60.00
Accident damages to family automobile not compensated by insurance	350.00
Payments of estimated income tax for current year	6,000.00
Mrs. Hunter:	
Rental property:	
Property taxes	465.00
Insurance (one-year policies)	95.00
Painting and repairs	782.50
Mortgage note payments:	
Principal	2,500.00
Interest	1,225.00
(Building was acquired several years ago at a cost of $50,000 and is being depreciated at the rate of 4%).	
Charitable contributions	192.00

Instructions: Determine Mr. and Mrs. Hunter's taxable income, income tax, and balance due, presenting the details in good order. It is your responsibility to determine whether they should file separate returns or a joint return. Apply the appropriate schedule of tax rates appearing in this chapter.

25. Cost relationships for management

Alternative concepts of cost

One of the primary objectives of accounting is the determination of net income. For this purpose costs are classified as either expenses or assets. To the extent that a cost contributes to the earning of current revenues, it is considered to be an expense. To the extent that it is expected to contribute in some measurable way to future revenues, it is considered to be an asset. This concept of cost has been explored in detail in earlier chapters; its applicability has also been implicit in discussions of budgeting, standard costs, and other control procedures.

Another important objective of accounting is to provide data that will be useful to management in analyzing and resolving current problems and making plans for the future. For any particular problem there is ordinarily a variety of alternative solutions, only one of which can be chosen. Much of the analysis entering into consideration of alternatives is concerned with costs and revenues. Relevant data on past costs and revenues may be available in the accounts, but relevant data regarding proposed new projects are not likely to be found there. In any case, the record of past events is frequently quite inadequate as the sole basis for a decision affecting the future.

As has been demonstrated earlier, budgeting and standard costs are two concepts useful both in controlling costs and in providing goals for future operations. However, for many decisions affecting the future, additional concepts of cost are needed, concepts that will be useful in separating relevant data from those which, for the problem at hand, may be ignored. The more important cost concepts and relationships and their application to decision-making are described in this chapter.

Historical cost and replacement cost

As used in a broad generic sense, the term "cost" means the amount of money or other property expended, or liability or other claim incurred, for goods or services purchased. References to the amount of property expended or liability incurred for goods or services may be expressed by the shorter phrase "cash or equivalent." One of the important factors in discussions of cost is time, which often necessitates the use of the modifying adjective "historical" or "replacement."

Historical cost is the cash or equivalent outlay for goods or services actually acquired. *Actual cost* is sometimes used to mean the same thing, particularly if comparisons are being made with estimates or standards. Historical costs are recorded in the ledgers and other basic accounting records; the expired portions are reported as expenses in the income statement and the unexpired portions are reported as assets in the balance sheet. Historical costs are relevant in the determination of periodic net income and current financial status. They may be of only slight consequence or entirely irrelevant, however, in planning for the future.

Replacement cost is the cost of replacing an asset at current market prices. In many planning situations the cost of replacing an asset is of greater significance than its historical cost. To illustrate, assume that an offer is received for goods to be manufactured at a specific price. Assume also that there is a sufficient quantity of unprocessed materials in stock that were acquired at a considerably higher cost than current market prices. In deciding whether to accept the offer, it is the replacement cost of the materials that is relevant. It might be advisable to accept the offer even though, on the basis of historical costs, a loss is likely to result.

Replacement cost analysis is useful in planning the replacement of worn-out or obsolete plant assets. New equipment to be acquired is rarely identical with the asset that it replaces. The cost of the replacement asset is likely to differ not only because of technological improvements and other changes in physical characteristics, but also because of changes in price levels. A variant of this type of analysis is to compare annual depreciation expense based on historical cost with depreciation based on estimated replacement cost. The difference between the two represents the estimated amount of net income that should be retained in order to maintain the productive capacity of the physical plant. For example, if depreciation expense recorded for the year is $130,000 and depreciation based on estimated replacement cost is $210,000, the board of directors should be informed of the $80,000 deficiency. If reported net income is $180,000, it may be prudent to consider no more than $100,000 as suitable for distribution as dividends to stockholders.

The significance of replacement cost, adjusted for depreciation, in the admission or the withdrawal of a partner was considered in an earlier chapter. Similar analyses play a significant role in negotiations for the purchase and the sale of a going business, in the merging of two separate enterprises, and in weighing the consequences of liquidating an enterprise. The values finally placed on plant assets in such situations are greatly influenced by the bargaining process, but consideration of replacement cost is often the starting point.

Variable costs and fixed costs

Variable costs are generally defined as those costs that tend to vary in total as business activity varies. *Fixed costs* are those costs that tend to remain relatively constant in total regardless of changes in the volume of business activity.

To classify costs as fixed or variable, certain assumptions must be made. Among these are the assumptions of relatively stable use of plant facilities and the continuance of managerial policies without great change. For example, if production is reduced from 100% to 95%, supervisory salaries probably will not be affected and hence would be considered a fixed cost. However, if production is reduced from 100% to 10%, supervisory salaries may be decreased materially. Under conditions of substantial change in the use of plant facilities, very few costs would be fixed. In addition, whether a cost is variable or fixed often depends on the policies and decisions of management. For example, if employees are hired on a daily or weekly basis, wages are a variable cost. On the other hand, if it is the management's policy to grant employees a guaranteed annual wage, wage costs are fixed up to the guaranteed minimum.

The distinction between variable costs and fixed costs is especially useful in the control of costs because variable costs are traceable to, and therefore controllable by, the department that incurs them. Such a breakdown of costs is also useful in production planning, product pricing, and other management functions.

Direct costing and absorption costing

Direct costing is a concept that considers the cost of products manufactured to be composed of only those costs that vary with production volume. Fixed factory overhead costs, which are excluded from product cost, are treated as an expense of the period in which they are incurred.

The variable manufacturing costs are composed of direct materials, direct labor, and variable factory overhead. Because of their close relationship to productive activity, the variable costs are sometimes called *activity costs.* The word "variable" is also frequently substituted for "direct" in referring to the basic concept, as in *variable costing.* Most of the fixed factory overhead costs are closely related to the passage of time. For example, depreciation of factory buildings and the cost of insurance and taxes on factory equipment accrue from day to day regardless of changes in the volume of production. Because of this characteristic, fixed costs are often referred to as *period costs* or *capacity costs.*

Absorption costing is the term applied to the older and more conventional concept described and illustrated in the chapters on process and job order cost accounting. This traditional concept regards both variable costs and fixed costs as integral parts of the total cost of products manufactured. Any distinctions that may be made between variable and fixed costs are for purposes of analysis only and have no effect on the accounts or the financial statements.

Direct costing and the financial statements

The use of direct costing necessitates very little change from the accounting procedures employed for absorption costing. The variable manufacturing costs are separated from the fixed factory overhead and are treated as part of the cost of the product. The fixed factory overhead is excluded from product cost and is closed directly to the expense and revenue summary account at the end of the period.

There are also variations from the usual format of the income statement and in the amount of net operating income reported. The differences may be illustrated by two statements prepared from the same basic data, which are as follows:

Inventories, production, and sales in units:	Units
Beginning inventory	none
Production	15,000
Sales	12,000
Ending inventory	3,000

Variable costs and expenses:	Amount	Per Unit
Manufacturing costs	$ 75,000	$5.00
Selling and general expenses	$ 12,000	$1.00
Fixed costs and expenses:		
Manufacturing costs	$ 30,000	$2.00
Selling and general expenses	$ 10,000	.83

The parenthetical notations in the condensed income statements presented on the following page are for explanatory purposes. In practice the expenses might be listed in greater detail and the explanatory notes would be omitted.

ABSORPTION COSTING INCOME STATEMENT

Sales (12,000 units @ $10)		$120,000
Cost of goods sold:		
Cost of goods manufactured (15,000 units @ $7)	$105,000	
Less ending inventory (3,000 units @ $7)	21,000	
Cost of goods sold		84,000
Gross profit on sales		$ 36,000
Selling and general expenses ($12,000 + $10,000)		22,000
Net income from operations		$ 14,000

DIRECT COSTING INCOME STATEMENT

Sales (12,000 units @ $10)		$120,000
Variable cost of goods sold:		
Variable cost of goods manufactured (15,000 units @ $5)	$ 75,000	
Less ending inventory (3,000 units @ $5)	15,000	
Variable cost of goods sold		60,000
Manufacturing margin		$ 60,000
Variable selling and general expenses (12,000 units @ $1)		12,000
Marginal income		$ 48,000
Fixed costs and expenses:		
Fixed manufacturing costs	$ 30,000	
Fixed selling and general expenses	10,000	40,000
Net income from operations		$ 8,000

Comparison of absorption costing and direct costing income statements

In the absorption costing income statement, both fixed and variable manufacturing costs are included in cost of goods sold, and the excess of sales over cost of goods sold is identified as gross profit on sales. In the direct costing income statement, only the variable manufacturing costs are included in cost of goods sold; the excess of sales over the variable cost of goods sold is termed *manufacturing margin*. Deduction of the variable selling and general expenses from manufacturing margin yields *marginal income*, which is the remaining amount of revenue available for fixed manufacturing costs, fixed expenses, and profit. The fixed costs and expenses are then deducted from marginal income to yield *net income* from operations.

When the level of inventory fluctuates from period to period, the net income reported under absorption costing differs from that reported under direct costing. The difference in net income arises because absorption costing, by including the fixed factory overhead as a part of the cost of the product produced, defers to another period that portion of the fixed factory overhead included in inventory on hand, whereas direct costing includes all the fixed factory overhead costs incurred during the period as expenses of the period. In a period in which the level of inventory increases, such as in the illustration above, the net income reported by absorption costing will be larger than the net income reported by direct costing. When inventory decreases, the reverse is true; that is, a smaller net income will be reported if absorption costing is used. Of course, if the inventory levels do not change from one period to the next, the net income reported by each method is identical.

The determination of the cost of inventories and of net income by the direct costing method is not acceptable for published financial statements[1] or, generally, for federal income tax purposes. When the accounts are maintained in accordance with direct costing principles, it is necessary to convert inventory amounts to conform to absorption costing methods before preparing statements for stockholders, creditors, or others outside the management group. Financial and operating data prepared in accordance with the direct costing concept are often useful to operating management in connection with cost control, in pricing products, and in many planning situations.

Direct costing as an aid in cost control

All costs are controllable by someone within the firm, but they are not all controllable at the same level of management. For example, a plant foreman has control over the excessive use of materials in his department, but he cannot control the cost of insurance on the building that houses his department. For a specific level of management, *controllable costs* are costs that it controls directly, and *uncontrollable costs* are costs that another level of management controls. This distinction, as applied to specific levels of management, is useful in fixing the responsibility for incurrence of costs and then for reporting the cost data to those responsible for cost control.

Variable manufacturing costs are subject to the control of the operating level of management on a current basis because they vary with changes in production. By including only the variable manufacturing costs in the cost of the product, direct costing provides a product cost figure that is subject to control by operating management. The fixed factory overhead costs are generally the responsibility of a higher echelon of management. When the fixed factory overhead costs are reported as a separate item in the direct costing income statement, they are easier to evaluate and control than when they are divided among units of product as is the case under absorption costing. Also, the variable selling and general expenses are reported separately from the fixed selling and general expenses under direct costing. Because the variable and fixed operat-

---

[1] *Accounting Research and Terminology Bulletins, Final Edition*, "No. 43, Restatement and Revision of Accounting Research Bulletins," 1961 (New York: American Institute of Certified Public Accountants), pp. 28–29.

ing expenses are often subject to the control of different levels of management, it is easier for the responsible party to evaluate and control them when they are reported in the direct costing format.

Direct costing as an aid in pricing

Many factors enter into the determination of the selling price of a product. One of these is the cost of making the product. Microeconomic theory deduces, from a set of restrictive assumptions, that income is maximized by expanding output to the volume where the revenue realized by the sale of the final unit (marginal revenue) is equaled by the cost of that unit (marginal cost). Since the exact information assumed in economic theory is rarely available, a firm can seldom make the precise adjustments in selling price that are necessary to maximize income. Nevertheless, the concepts of marginal revenue and marginal cost can be used in pricing decisions.

In the short run, the firm is committed to the existing capacity of its manufacturing facilities, and the pricing decision should be based upon making the best use of such capacity. Net income from the production and sale of a product is maximized in the short run if the revenue from the sale exceeds the variable costs and expenses of making and selling the product. Since the variable costs and expenses can be saved if a company does not produce the product, they set the lower limit to selling price. Any revenue above variable costs and expenses contributes toward covering fixed costs and expenses and providing net income. Under direct costing, data on these relevant costs and expenses are readily available.

In the long run, plant capacity can be increased or decreased, and if a firm is to remain in business the selling price of its product must be set at a figure that is expected to cover all costs and expenses. Hence, in setting pricing policy for the long run, cost information prepared on an absorption costing basis is needed.

In the final analysis, management must compare alternative pricing proposals and select the one that appears most advantageous. The accountant can assist management by presenting the anticipated results of various pricing plans covering both the short run and the long run.

Direct costing as an aid in production planning

Production planning has both short-run and long-run implications. In the short run, production is limited to existing capacity, and operating decisions must be made promptly before opportunities are lost. For example, a company manufacturing products with a seasonal demand may have an opportunity to obtain an off-season order that will not compete with regular products. The relevant factors for such a short-run decision are the revenues and the variable costs and expenses. If the revenues from the special order will provide marginal income, the order should be accepted because it will add to the company's net income.

In production planning, then, direct costing, by including only the variable costs in product cost and by separating the variable operating expenses from the fixed operating expenses, supplies the cost data in a format especially useful for short-run decision-making. For long-run planning, management must also consider the fixed costs and expenses.

Illustrative applications of direct costing

To control and plan operations, management needs information on the profitability of the various segments of its business, such as types of products, sales territories, and methods of distributing the products. Direct costing makes a significant contribution to management decision-making in providing data for effective profit planning in such areas. Two aspects of profit planning are (1) determination of the most profitable sales mix of a company's products and (2) determination of the contribution being made by each sales territory.

Sales mix studies. *Sales mix* is generally defined as the relative distribution of sales among the various products. Ordinarily some lines are more profitable than others, and management should concentrate its sales efforts on those products that will provide the maximum total net income. The marginal income and the amount of production facilities required to produce each product are two important factors for management to consider in selecting the products that should be emphasized in sales promotion. To illustrate, assume unit sales and cost data of a manufacturing enterprise to be as follows:

	Product A	Product B
Sales price	$6.00	$10.00
Less variable costs and expenses	4.50	8.00
Marginal income	$1.50	$ 2.00

Of the two products, Product B provides the larger contribution to the recovery of the fixed costs and expenses and the realization of net income. If both products require the same amount of production facilities, Product B obviously would be the product towards which sales efforts should be directed. However, if Product B requires twice as many production facilities as Product A — that is, if in order to increase the sales of Product B by one unit, 2 units of Product A would have to be given up

— Product A would be the more profitable product. Thus either 2 units of Product A (marginal income of $3) or 1 unit of Product B (marginal income of $2) could be produced from the same amount of production facilities. Obviously, a change in sales mix designed to increase sales of Product A would be desirable under such circumstances.

Sales mix studies are based on assumptions, such as the ability to sell one product in place of another and the ability to convert production facilities to accommodate manufacture of one product instead of another. Research relating to sales mix studies indicates that they often affect only small segments of a company's total operations. In such cases, changes in sales mix can often be made within the limits of existing capacity, and the presentation of cost and revenue data in the direct costing form is useful in achieving the most profitable sales mix.

Contribution of sales territories. An income statement presenting the marginal income by sales territories is often useful to management in appraising past performance and in directing operations. An income statement prepared in such a format is illustrated below in abbreviated form.

	Territory A	Territory B	Total
Sales.	$210,000	$335,000	$545,000
Less variable costs and expenses.	126,000	167,500	293,500
Marginal income.	$ 84,000	$167,500	$251,500
Less fixed costs and expenses.			198,000
Net income from operations.			$ 53,500

Income statement with marginal income by sales territories

In addition to sales volume and marginal income, the marginal income ratio for each territory is also of importance to management. For Territory A the ratio is 40% ($84,000 ÷ $210,000), and for Territory B it is 50% ($167,500 ÷ $335,000). The marginal income ratio helps management compare sales territories, evaluate performance, and direct operations towards more profitable activities.

Differential cost and revenue analysis

One of management's principal tasks is planning for future operations. Planning is chiefly decision-making. For some decisions, revenue and cost information drawn from the general ledger and other basic accounting records is very useful. For example, historical cost data in the absorption costing format are helpful in setting pricing policies for the long run, and historical cost data in the direct costing format are useful for pricing decisions affecting the short run. However, the revenue and cost data needed to evaluate courses of future operations or to choose among competing alternatives are often not available in the basic accounting records.

The relevant revenue and cost data in the analysis of future possibilities are the differentials for the alternatives under consideration. Accountants generally use the term "differential" to mean the differences in individual revenues and costs arising from a contemplated change in activity. The area of accounting concerned with the effect of alternatives on revenues and costs is called *differential analysis.*

Differential revenue is the additional revenue expected from a particular course of action as compared with an alternative. To illustrate, assume that an enterprise is considering the manufacture and sale of Product X as compared with the manufacture and sale of Product Y. Analysis of the market indicates probable monthly revenue of $50,000 from sales of Product X as compared with probable monthly revenue of $75,000 from sales of Product Y. The anticipated differential revenue from the latter course of action would be $25,000.

The amount of change in cost that is expected from a particular course of action compared with an alternative is *differential cost.* For example, if an increase in advertising expenditures from $100,000 to $150,000 is contemplated in hopes of adding additional revenue, the differential cost of the undertaking would be $50,000.

Accountants often use the term *sunk costs* to refer to costs already incurred that will not be affected by subsequent decisions. Because sunk costs cannot be changed, they should be ignored in differential analysis. For example, the remaining undepreciated cost of a plant asset is a sunk cost. If the plant asset is continued in use, the cost will be gradually charged against operating revenue as depreciation expense; if it is sold, the cost will be applied against the revenue from its sale. In either case, the undepreciated cost cannot be avoided by any current action and it should be ignored when future uses of the plant asset are being evaluated.

The principal advantage of differential analysis is its emphasis on relevant revenues and costs. The exclusion of irrelevant information from the mass of data related to alternate courses of action helps to focus attention, clarify issues, and save time.

It is usually necessary to consider both the differential revenues and the differential costs associated with alternative proposals. For example, assume that an enterprise has an item of manufacturing equipment that is no longer needed and has the option of selling or leasing it. The original cost of the equipment was $100,000, and accumulated depreciation to date totals $60,000. The equipment can be sold for $50,000 or it can be leased for a period of years for a total rental of $80,000 and then sold as scrap for a negligible amount. The estimated cost of repairs, insurance, and property taxes during the lease period is $17,500. The differential revenue from leasing the property will be $30,000 ($80,000 – $50,000) and the differential cost will be $17,500, yielding an estimated differential net income of $12,500 ($30,000 – $17,500). It should be noted that it was not necessary to consider the $40,000 book value ($100,000 – $60,000) of the equipment. As a sunk cost it was not relevant to the decision. The relevant revenues and costs are the alternative future revenues and costs. The validity of this analysis is proved by the following tabulation:

	Alternatives		
	Sell	Lease	
Proceeds from sale of equipment	$50,000		
Revenue from leasing equipment			$80,000
Book value of equipment	40,000		
Depreciation expense		$40,000	
Repairs, insurance, and property taxes		17,500	57,500
Net gain from sale	$10,000		
Net income from lease			$22,500

Net advantage from leasing equipment:
$22,500 – $10,000 = $12,500

The preceding illustration was simplified to emphasize the approach to differential analysis. Although other factors might be relevant in an actual situation, the approach to the analysis of the alternative courses of action would be similar to that illustrated. Two such factors, (1) the effect of income tax on each proposal and (2) the revenue from investing the funds generated by each proposal, deserve special mention.

An important factor influencing many business decisions is the federal income tax. In some cases, the tax savings offered by one alternative may be sufficient to offset the advantages of another course of action. One type of tax advantage can be illustrated by referring to the example described above. As noted in the preceding chapter, gains and losses resulting from the sale of plant assets are often afforded special treatment for income tax purposes. Hence, in the case cited above, the tax rate on the gain on the sale of the equipment may be substantially lower than the tax rate on the net income resulting from the rental of the property. Thus, before deciding between alternative courses of action, the effect of the income tax on each alternative should be determined.

If proposed courses of action would affect the receipt of cash, consideration should also be given to the revenue that would be earned by the investment of the cash. For example, in the foregoing illustration assume that revenue from investing the sale proceeds less the income tax allocable to the revenue is estimated at $10,000 and that the comparable net amount to be realized from investing the rental proceeds is estimated at $4,000, both computed for the period of the lease. If this should be the case, the differential income from leasing the property reported earlier would be decreased by $6,000 ($10,000 – $4,000).

Differential analyses can be used advantageously by management in arriving at decisions on a variety of alternatives, such as whether or not to obtain additional business through price cutting, whether to discontinue an unprofitable activity, whether to manufacture or purchase a needed part or machine, whether to introduce new products or abandon old products, and whether to expand or contract production capacity. The remainder of the chapter is devoted to the use of differential analysis in analyzing some of these alternatives.

Acceptance of business at a special price

In considering the advisability of accepting additional business at a special price, management must consider the differential revenue that would be provided and the differential costs that would be required. If the company is operating at full capacity, the additional production will increase both fixed and variable production costs; but if the normal production of the company is below full capacity, additional business may be undertaken without increasing fixed production costs. In the latter case, the variable costs will be the differential costs of the additional production and the only costs pertinent in making a decision to accept or reject the order. If the operating expenses are subject to change, these differential expenses must also be considered.

To illustrate, assume that a manufacturer normally produces 10,000 units a month for which he receives $10 per unit. At this level of operations, which is below full capacity, variable costs and expenses total $4 per unit and fixed costs and expenses amount to $2.50 per unit. The manufacturer has an offer from an exporter for 5,000 units at $6 per unit. Acceptance of the offer will not interfere with normal production or domestic pricing policies. A comparison of the selling price of $6 with the present total cost per unit of $6.50 would indicate that the offer should be rejected. However, the decision should not be based on total costs, because fixed costs will not increase if the special order is accepted. The pertinent costs are the differential costs, which in this case are the variable costs of $4 per unit. On this basis, a decision to accept the additional business would be indicated, because the selling price exceeds the differential costs by $2 per unit ($6 – $4) and, as indicated on the following page, a net income of $10,000 (5,000 × $2) would result.

	Normal Volume	Additional Volume	Total Volume
Sales: 10,000 at $10	$100,000		$100,000
5,000 at $ 6		$30,000	30,000
Total sales	$100,000	$30,000	$130,000
Variable costs and expenses: 10,000 at $4	40,000		40,000
5,000 at $4		20,000	20,000
Marginal income	$ 60,000	$10,000	$ 70,000
Fixed costs and expenses	25,000		25,000
Net income from operations	$ 35,000	$10,000	$ 45,000

In deciding whether to accept business at a special price, consideration should also be given to the effect of the decision on regular customers and principal market areas. This consideration was not pertinent in the above illustration because the goods were for foreign consumption. The problem is likely to be more complex when only domestic markets are involved. Clearly it would be inadvisable to increase sales volume in one territory by a price reduction if doing so would jeopardize sales in other areas. Also, a manufacturer must exercise care to avoid a violation of the Robinson-Patman Act, which prohibits price discrimination within the United States unless the difference in price can be justified by a difference in the cost of serving different customers.

Elimination of an unprofitable endeavor

If a department, branch, territory, or other segment of an enterprise is operating at a loss, management may be faced with the decision of whether or not to eliminate the unprofitable endeavor. It might be assumed that the net income of the enterprise as a whole will be increased by discontinuing the unsuccessful activity. Discontinuance of the losing venture will eliminate the variable costs and expenses of the activity. However, if the losing venture represents a relatively minor segment of the enterprise, the fixed costs and expenses such as depreciation, property taxes, and insurance will continue even though the operation is terminated. It is entirely possible in this situation for the total net income of a company to be reduced rather than increased by eliminating an unprofitable endeavor. The significant costs and expenses to be considered are the differential costs. To illustrate, an income statement for an average year is presented at the top of the following page. For purposes of this illustration it is assumed that the discontinuance of the losing venture, Product C, will not affect the fixed costs and expenses.

	Product			
	A	B	C	Total
Sales	$400,000	$500,000	$100,000	$1,000,000
Cost of goods sold:				
Variable costs	$200,000	$220,000	$ 60,000	$ 480,000
Fixed costs	80,000	120,000	20,000	220,000
Total cost of goods sold	$280,000	$340,000	$ 80,000	$ 700,000
Gross profit on sales	$120,000	$160,000	$ 20,000	$ 300,000
Operating expenses:				
Variable expenses	60,000	95,000	25,000	180,000
Fixed expenses	20,000	25,000	6,000	51,000
Total operating expenses	$ 80,000	$120,000	$ 31,000	$ 231,000
Net income (loss) from operations	$ 40,000	$ 40,000	$(11,000)	$ 69,000

The differential revenue associated with the discontinuance of Product C is $100,000 and the differential costs total $85,000 ($60,000 + $25,000). Thus if Product C were to be discontinued, the total net income of the business would be reduced by $15,000, the excess of the differential revenue over the differential costs. The effect of the discontinuance of Product C may be emphasized by preparing a special report for management. The possible format of such a report is illustrated below.

	Retain Product C		Eliminate Product C	
Sales		$1,000,000		$900,000
Cost of goods sold:				
Variable costs	$480,000		$420,000	
Fixed costs	220,000		220,000	
Total cost of goods sold		700,000		640,000
Gross profit on sales		$ 300,000		$260,000
Operating expenses:				
Variable expenses	$180,000		$155,000	
Fixed expenses	51,000		51,000	
Total operating expenses		231,000		206,000
Net income from operations		$ 69,000		$ 54,000

If the segment of the enterprise operating at a loss can be discontinued and the plant capacity reduced with a consequent savings in fixed costs and expenses, the differentials representing the savings in these fixed costs and expenses would be included in the differential analysis.

In decisions involving the elimination of an unprofitable endeavor, management must also consider such other factors as the effect of such a decision on employees and customers. If a segment of the business is discontinued, some employees may have to be discharged and others may have to be relocated and retrained. Also important is the possible loss of customers who may be attracted to the firm by that segment of the business.

Make or buy

A substantial element of manufacturing operations is often the assembly of numerous parts. Many of the large factory complexes of automobile manufacturers are specifically designated as assembly plants. Some of the components of the finished automobile, such as the motor, are produced by the automobile manufacturer, while other parts, such as tires, are often purchased from other manufacturers. Even in manufacturing the motors, such items as spark plugs, nuts and bolts, and other items may be acquired from suppliers in their finished state. When parts or components are purchased, it is generally because management has evaluated the question of "make or buy" and has concluded that a savings in cost results from buying the part rather than manufacturing it. However, "make or buy" options are likely to arise anew when a manufacturer has excess productive capacity with attendant unused equipment, space, and labor.

To illustrate this type of decision, assume that a manufacturer has been purchasing a particular part for $4.25 per unit. The enterprise is operating at 80% of plant capacity, and factory overhead is charged to production at the rate of 100% of direct labor cost. The cost of manufacturing the part, determined by absorption costing methods, is estimated at $5, which is composed of direct materials of $1, direct labor of $2, and factory overhead of $2 (100% of direct labor). At this cost, it would clearly be cheaper to buy the part at $4.25 per unit. However, to the extent that unused capacity could be used in manufacturing the part, there would be no increase in the total amount of fixed factory overhead costs; hence only the variable factory overhead costs need to be considered. Detailed analysis reveals that variable factory overhead costs such as power, lubricants, and maintenance will amount to approximately 50% of direct labor cost. Therefore, the estimated cost of making the part is $4 per unit, computed as follows:

Direct materials	$1.00
Direct labor	2.00
Variable factory overhead (50% of direct labor)	1.00
Total cost per unit	$4.00

A comparison of this cost per unit, which represents the differential cost of making the part, with the cost of buying the part, $4.25, indicates that it would be cheaper for the manufacturer to make the part.

In addition to a comparison of appropriate costs, there are other factors that management should consider in arriving at a decision to make or buy. For example, if normal production of the principal product is expected to reach 100% of plant capacity in the future, it may be physically impossible to manufacture the part without increasing plant capacity. The effect of the alternative courses of action on employees and on future business relations with the supplier, who may be providing other parts or materials that are essential to the production of the principal product, should also be studied.

Equipment replacement

During the useful life of an item of equipment, management may wish to investigate the desirability of retaining the existing asset or of replacing it with new equipment. In making the cost study, the accountant should consider only alternative future costs. The unexpired cost of the existing equipment is a sunk cost and is not relevant to the decision. The relevant costs are the expenditures required to purchase the new equipment and the expenditures required to operate the new equipment as compared with the expenditures required to operate the old equipment.

To illustrate, assume that the book value of several half-depreciated machines owned by an enterprise totals $100,000. They have an estimated remaining useful life of 5 years and no significant salvage value. A new machine that would serve in place of the several pieces of equipment has just been placed on the market. The cost of the machine is $250,000, its estimated useful life is 5 years, and its residual value is negligible. Analysis of the specifications of the new machine and of accompanying changes in manufacturing methods indicate an estimated annual reduction in variable manufacturing costs from $225,000 to $150,000. No other changes in the manufacturing costs or the operating expenses are expected.

In deciding whether or not to replace the machines, the $100,000 book value of the old machines is irrelevant. The fixed manufacturing costs and the operating expenses are also irrelevant for purposes of the decision because they are expected to remain unchanged.

The cost of the new machine is relevant because the expenditure can be avoided. The savings in variable manufacturing costs are also relevant to the problem. The relevant data bearing on this decision can be summarized in a manner similar to the following:

Reduction in variable manufacturing costs ($75,000 × 5 years)	$375,000
Less cost of new equipment	250,000
Additional net income expected from replacing equipment	$125,000

The validity of this analysis is proved by the following schedule presenting the abbreviated income statements for the 5 years under each of the two alternatives:

	Alternatives			
	Retain Old Equipment		Buy New Equipment	
Sales ($500,000 per year)		$2,500,000		$2,500,000
Costs and expenses:				
Variable manufacturing costs	$1,125,000		$750,000	
Depreciation of machinery	100,000		250,000	
Other manufacturing costs	550,000		550,000	
Operating expenses	200,000		200,000	
Loss on disposal of equipment			100,000	
Total costs and expenses		1,975,000		1,850,000
Net income from operations		$ 525,000		$ 650,000

This illustration could be complicated by other factors, such as failure of the remaining useful life of the old equipment and the life of the new equipment to coincide, or some improvement in the product resulting from the use of the new equipment. The impact of income taxes on each alternative must also be considered. Another factor that deserves mention is the importance of alternative uses for the outlay necessary to acquire the new equipment. If the $250,000 had not been used to purchase the new equipment but had been used for another purpose, what net income could have been realized from the alternative investment? This advantage foregone is termed an *opportunity cost*; that is, if the resources had not been used to acquire the new equipment, they could have been put to another use that would have provided income. This by-passed income represents an opportunity cost to the business that must be considered in deciding whether or not the equipment should be replaced. In the illustration above, unless an alternative investment of the $250,000 could have produced more than $125,000 in net income over the 5 years, a decision to purchase the new equipment seems advisable.

Interrelation of the alternate cost concepts

If cost data are to be used intelligently by management, it must be realized that no single cost figure can serve all the varied purposes for which cost information is needed. For one decision, one type of cost figure or a combination of cost classifications may be most useful; for another decision, another cost concept or an entirely different grouping of costs may be best. It is therefore imperative that the accountant recognize the limitations of a single concept of cost and be aware of the usefulness of various concepts of costs for different purposes. In this way, he can assist management in directing business operations by providing the relevant information for the decision at hand.

QUESTIONS

1. Why is one concept of cost often not sufficient for both income determination and managerial decision-making purposes?

2. (a) Differentiate between historical cost and replacement cost. (b) Why would replacement costs be more useful than historical costs in preparing a capital expenditures budget?

3. (a) Describe the concept of direct costing. (b) If the direct costing concept is followed, which of the following production costs would be included as part of the cost of the product: (1) insurance on plant, (2) direct materials, (3) foremen's salaries, (4) direct labor, (5) electricity purchased to operate machinery, and (6) property taxes on plant.

4. What is the basic difference between direct costing and absorption costing?

5. How are the fixed factory overhead (fixed manufacturing) costs reported on the direct costing income statement?

6. What does the term "manufacturing margin" that appears on the direct costing income statement signify?

7. How is marginal income determined on the direct costing income statement?

8. What types of costs and expenses are included in the fixed costs and expenses category on the income statement prepared on the basis of direct costing?

9. Is direct costing generally acceptable for use in (a) published financial statements and (b) federal income tax returns?

10. All costs of operating a business are controllable. What then is an uncontrollable cost?

11. Discuss how the use of financial data prepared on the basis of direct costing can assist management in the development of short-run pricing policies.

12. Explain the meaning of (a) differential revenue and (b) differential cost.

13. Acme Lumber, Incorporated currently sells its lumber as a rough cut for $60 per thousand board feet. The cost for processing this rough cut is $15 per thousand board feet. The company is contemplating processing the lumber into a machined form that can be sold for $72 per thousand board feet. The cost of this finishing process is $10 per thousand board feet, which would mean a total processing cost per thousand board feet of $25. What are the differential revenue and the differential cost to be considered in deciding whether or not to further process the rough cut lumber?

14. (a) What are sunk costs? (b) A company is contemplating replacing an old piece of equipment, which cost $10,000 and has accumulated depreciation to date of $6,000, with a new machine costing $22,000. What is the sunk cost in this situation?

15. Burr Company manufactures three products. The income statement for the current year is presented at the top of the following page.

	Product			
	X	Y	Z	Total
Sales	$70,000	$240,000	$370,000	$680,000
Less variable costs and expenses	50,000	145,000	200,000	395,000
Marginal income	$20,000	$ 95,000	$170,000	$285,000
Less fixed costs and expenses	25,000	90,000	135,000	250,000
Net income or (loss)	$(5,000)	$ 5,000	$ 35,000	$ 35,000

Management anticipates no significant change in the sales volume or the variable costs and expenses associated with the production and sale of Product X and proposes that it be dropped from the product line. If Product X is discontinued, the fixed costs and expenses will not be materially affected. Do you agree with management's proposal? Explain.

16. (a) What is opportunity cost? (b) The Eubank Company is currently earning 4% on $100,000 invested in marketable securities. It proposes to use the $100,000 to acquire plant facilities to manufacture a new product that is expected to add $9,000 to net income. What is the opportunity cost involved in the decision to produce the new product?

EXERCISES

1. The Gelvin Manufacturing Company is contemplating the purchase of the Hall Lumber Company. Hall Lumber Company has lumber on hand that cost $110,000 and is included in its accounts at that figure. Its replacement cost is $125,000. (a) At what figure should the inventory of lumber be included on the balance sheet of Hall Lumber Company? Briefly explain the reasoning behind your answer. (b) How much should Gelvin Manufacturing Company pay for the inventory if it purchases the Hall Lumber Company? Briefly explain the reasoning behind your answer.

2. On June 1, the Nobel Company began operations and operated at 100% of capacity during June. The following data summarizes the results for June:

Sales (25,000 units)		$115,000
Production costs (30,000 units):		
Direct materials	$ 60,000	
Direct labor	30,000	
Variable factory overhead	15,000	
Fixed factory overhead	9,900	114,900
Selling and general expenses:		
Variable selling and general expenses	$ 5,750	
Fixed selling and general expenses	3,700	9,450

(a) Prepare an income statement in accordance with the absorption costing concept. (b) Prepare an income statement in accordance with the direct costing concept. (c) What is the reason for the difference in the amount of net income reported in (a) and (b)?

3. Harris Company normally operates at 90% of productive capacity, producing 9,000 typewriters per month. The total manufacturing costs for a normal month are typically as follows:

Direct materials	$180,000
Direct labor	162,000
Variable factory overhead	72,000
Fixed factory overhead	90,000
Total production costs	$504,000

The company has been invited by a governmental agency to submit a bid for 1,000 typewriters to be delivered within a month. If the contract is obtained, it is anticipated that the additional activity will not interfere with normal production or increase the selling or general expenses. (a) What is the present unit product cost on an absorption costing basis? (b) What is the present unit product cost on a direct costing basis? (c) What is the unit cost below which the Harris Company should not go in bidding on the government contract? (d) Is a unit cost figure based on absorption costing or one based on direct costing more useful in arriving at a bid on this contract? Explain.

4. The Jamison Manufacturing Company has a plant capacity of 500,000 units, but production currently is 400,000 units. Fixed costs and expenses are $750,000 and variable costs and expenses are $5.50 per unit. The present selling price is $9 per unit. The company has an opportunity to sell 50,000 additional units at $7 per unit to a firm that plans to market the units under its own brand name. The additional business is not expected to affect the regular selling price or quantity of sales of Jamison Manufacturing Company. (a) Prepare a schedule presenting the net income for the present level of operations, the net income expected from the additional business, and the total net income if the additional business is accepted. Use a format that shows the marginal income for each volume. (b) Briefly explain the reason why the acceptance of this additional business will increase net income. (c) What is the minimum price per unit that would produce marginal income?

5. An income statement by product line for Busey Manufacturing, Inc. indicated a net loss for Product Y of $55,000. This net loss resulted from sales of $400,000, cost of goods sold of $320,000, and operating expenses of $135,000. It is estimated that 25% of cost of goods sold represents fixed factory overhead costs and that 50% of operating expenses is fixed. Since Product Y is but one of many products, the fixed costs and expenses will not be materially affected if the product is discontinued. (a) What is the dollar amount of (1) differential revenue and (2) differential cost associated with the retention of Product Y as compared with that for the discontinuance of the product? (b) Should Product Y be retained? Explain.

6. Barton, Inc. has been purchasing carrying cases for its portable typewriters at a delivered cost of $7 per unit. Currently Barton, Inc. is operating at 80% of capacity and factory overhead is charged to production at the rate of 150% of direct labor cost. The direct materials and direct labor costs per unit to produce comparable carrying cases are expected to be $3 and $2 respectively. If the carrying cases are made, fixed factory overhead costs will not increase and variable factory overhead costs associated with the manufacture of the cases are expected to be 70% of direct labor costs. (a) For purposes of this decision, what is the estimated cost of making the carrying cases? (b) On the basis of the data presented, would it be advisable to make or to continue buying the carrying cases?

7. The Bedford Company produces a product partly by hand and partly by machine. The machine, which originally cost $30,000, has a remaining life of 5 years, no present salvage value, and an undepreciated balance of $10,000. A proposal has been made to replace the present operation with a fully automatic machine costing $75,000. This machine has a useful life of 5 years and no significant scrap value. For use in evaluating the proposal, the accountant has accumulated the following additional data covering operations for the past year and yearly expected operations if the automatic machine is acquired. The volume of operations is not expected to change significantly over the next 5 years.

	Present Operations	Proposed Operations
Sales	$ 75,000	$ 75,000
Direct materials	22,000	22,000
Direct labor	19,600	—
Power and maintenance	3,700	5,100
Taxes, insurance, etc.	2,200	2,700
Selling and general expenses	10,000	10,000

(a) Prepare an income statement covering the 5 years, presenting (1) operations under present conditions and (2) operations under proposed conditions. (b) Prepare a brief report containing only the relevant data bearing on the decision. (c) Based only on the data presented, should the proposal be accepted? (d) Before a final decision is made, what are some other factors that should be considered?

8. Snell Company is considering leasing a building and purchasing the necessary equipment to operate a public warehouse. The project would be financed by selling $150,000 of 4% federal bonds due in 20 years. The bonds had been purchased at face value and are currently selling at face value. The following data have been assembled:

Cost of equipment	$150,000
Life of equipment	20 years
Estimated scrap value of equipment	$ 2,000
Yearly costs to operate the warehouse	$ 35,000
Yearly expected revenues — first 5 years	$ 40,000
— next 15 years	$ 50,000

(a) Prepare a differential analysis presenting the differential revenues and the differential costs associated with the proposed leasing compared with present conditions. (b) Based upon the results disclosed by the differential analysis, should the proposal be accepted? (c) If the proposal is accepted, what would be the net income from operation of the warehouse for the 20 years?

PROBLEMS

25-1. The Eddy Chemical Company refines Product X in batches of 50,000 gallons. This product sells for $.20 per gallon. The associated unit costs and expenses include:

	Costs Per Gallon		Costs Per Gallon
Direct materials	$.080	Fixed factory overhead	$.020
Direct labor	.030	Salesmen's commissions	.005
Variable factory overhead	.025	Fixed selling and general expenses	.015

The company is considering putting Product X through several additional processes to yield Products X and Y. Until recently, the company found such further processing unwise, but new processing methods have reopened this question. Existing facilities can be used for this processing; but since the additional processing requires an extra day and the plant is operating at full capacity for an eight-hour day, the processing would have to be performed at night. Additional costs of processing would be $1,500 per batch. In processing there would be an evaporation loss of 5%, with 45% of the processed material emerging as Product X and 50% as Product Y. Selling price of Product Y is $.30 per gallon. Sales commissions are a uniform percentage based on the sales price.

Instructions: (1) Prepare a schedule presenting the differential revenue and the differential costs per batch associated with the processing to produce Products X and Y compared with processing to produce Product X.

(2) Would you recommend the additional processing of Product X?

25-2. The Spencer Publishing Company purchased a printing press costing $75,000 on January 2, 1965. The company's manufacturing costs for a normal year exclusive of depreciation total $150,000, operating expenses are $80,000 yearly, and revenues total $290,000 yearly. The annual depreciation for this printing press is $15,000 based on a 5-year useful life and no residual value.

On January 2, 1966, a manufacturer placed on the market a new printing press that costs $100,000, has a 4-year life with no salvage value, and promises to reduce the Spencer Publishing Company's manufacturing costs, exclusive of depreciation, to $100,000 yearly. The old machine can be sold for only $10,000. Revenues and operating expenses will not be affected by the use of either press.

Instructions: (1) Prepare an estimated income statement for the period covering the four years 1966 through 1969 under both alternatives.

(2) Prepare a differential analysis comparing the proposed acquisition with operations using the present equipment. The analysis should indicate the additional net income or reduction in net income that would result over the 4-year period if the new press is acquired.

(3) What other factors should be considered before a final decision is reached?

25-3. The Porter Company is planning a one-month sales promotion campaign during which it expects to spend $100,000 on advertising and $75,000 on other promotional activities such as prizes for a contest and redeemable coupons. The company makes two products but has decided to direct all its promotion to just one of them. The data on the following page have been assembled to assist in selecting which product to promote.

Because the campaign would last only one month, no increase in facilities would be necessary to produce and sell the increased output. It is anticipated that 100,000 additional units of Product X or 80,000 additional units of Product Y could be sold without any change in the unit selling price.

Instructions: (1) Prepare a schedule presenting the additional revenue and additional costs and expenses anticipated from the promotion of (a) Product X and (b) Product Y.

	Product X		Product Y	
Unit selling price		$13.00		$15.00
Unit production costs:				
Direct materials	$ 3.00		$ 3.00	
Direct labor	3.00		2.50	
Fixed factory overhead	1.00		2.50	
Variable factory overhead	2.00		2.00	
Total unit production costs		9.00		10.00
Unit variable selling and general expenses		1.50		2.50
Unit fixed selling and general expenses		.50		1.50
Total unit costs and expenses		$11.00		$14.00
Net income per unit		$ 2.00		$ 1.00

(2) The president of the company decided to promote Product X. He reasoned that net income could be increased by $25,000 ($2 net income per unit times 100,000 units less promotion expenses of $175,000). He also reasoned that selecting Product Y would have decreased net income by $95,000 ($1 net income per unit times 80,000 units less promotion expenses of $175,000). Do you agree with his decision? Briefly explain why.

25-4. The Winslow Shirt Company manufactures three styles of shirts, X, Y, and Z. The income statement has consistently indicated a net loss for Style Z and management is considering three proposals: (1) continue Style Z, (2) discontinue Style Z and reduce total output accordingly, or (3) discontinue Style Z and conduct an advertising campaign to expand the sales of Style X so that the entire plant capacity can continue to be used. The sales, costs, and expenses have been relatively stable over the past few years and they are expected to remain so for the foreseeable future. The income statement for the past year is presented below.

	Style			
	X	Y	Z	Total
Sales	$400,000	$300,000	$100,000	$800,000
Cost of goods sold:				
Variable costs	$200,000	$160,000	$ 65,000	$425,000
Fixed costs	100,000	75,000	25,000	200,000
Total cost of goods sold	$300,000	$235,000	$ 90,000	$625,000
Gross profit on sales	$100,000	$ 65,000	$ 10,000	$175,000
Less selling and general expenses:				
Variable expenses	$ 40,000	$ 30,000	$ 10,000	$ 80,000
Fixed expenses	25,000	20,000	9,000	54,000
Total selling and general expenses	$ 65,000	$ 50,000	$ 19,000	$134,000
Net income or (loss)	$ 35,000	$ 15,000	$ (9,000)	$ 41,000

If Style Z is discontinued and production curtailed, the annual fixed production costs and fixed selling and general expenses could be reduced by $2,500 and $1,500 respectively. The third proposal calls for an expenditure of $10,000 yearly on advertising Style X with the expectation that sales of Style X will increase by 25% and the plant facilities left idle by abandoning Style Z will be used to manufacture the additional units of Style X.

Instructions: (1) Prepare an income statement in the direct costing format indicating the projected annual net income under each of the three proposals.

(2) Why would total net income be reduced below its present level if Proposal 2 is accepted?

(3) Why would total net income increase above its present level if Proposal 3 is accepted?

25-5. The Orr Company manufactures many products including Product A. The demand for Product A has dropped sharply because of recent competition from a superior product. The company's chemists are currently completing tests of new formulas. It is anticipated that the manufacture of a superior product can be started on August 1, one month hence. No change will be needed in the present production facilities to manufacture the new product because only the mixture of the various materials will be changed.

The controller has been asked by the president of the company for advice on whether to continue production during July or to suspend the manufacture of Product A until August 1. The controller has assembled the following data:

Orr Company
Income Statement — Product A
For Month Ended June 30, 19—

Sales (150,000 units)	$150,000
Less cost of goods sold	125,000
Gross profit on sales	$ 25,000
Less selling and general expenses	45,000
Net loss	$ 20,000

The production costs per unit based on a production of 150,000 units are:

Direct materials	$.20
Direct labor	.20
Variable factory overhead	.10
Fixed factory overhead	.33⅓

The selling and general expenses for the month ended June 30 are:

Variable selling and general expenses	$.20 per unit
Fixed selling and general expenses	$15,000

Sales for July are expected to drop about 30% below those of the preceding month. No significant changes are anticipated in the production costs or operating expenses. No extra costs will be incurred in shutting down the portion of the plant associated with Product A. The inventory at the beginning and end of July will be negligible.

Instructions: (1) Prepare an estimated income statement in absorption costing form for July for Product A, assuming that production continues during the month.

(2) Prepare an estimated income statement in direct costing form for July for Product A, assuming that production continues during the month.

(3) (a) What would the net loss arising from the activities associated with Product A be for July if the plant is temporarily shut down? (b) Does the absorption costing or the direct costing income statement make this figure most easily accessible?

(4) What should the controller's decision be? Explain.

26.

Special analyses and internal reports

Need for special analyses

A basic function of accounting is to provide the records and the procedures needed in reporting the results of the economic activities of an enterprise to all interested parties. One group making extensive use of accounting data is operating management. The manager of even a very small business needs factual data to assist him in making decisions. As the size and the complexity of businesses increase, the importance of accounting as a tool in directing operations becomes more apparent.

In assisting management, the accountant relies upon a variety of methods of analysis. The use of cost accounting and of cost relationships as they affect planning, coordinating, and controlling operations was described in preceding chapters. This chapter is devoted to additional analyses useful to management.

Cost-volume-profit relationships

Revenues and costs, and in turn net income, are affected by a great variety of internal and external conditions. Revenues are affected by such factors as the firm's pricing policies, the competitive conditions of the market, and the intensity of market demand for the product. Costs are affected by such factors as the nature of the product, the efficiency of operations, and the volume of production. Three factors affecting net income — selling price, volume, and costs — deserve special attention because they play an important part in management decision-making.

The determination of the selling price of a product is a complex matter that is often affected by forces partially or entirely beyond the control of management. Nevertheless, management must formulate pricing policies within the bounds permitted by the market place. Accounting can play an important role in the development of policy by supplying management with special reports on the relative profitability of its various products, the probable effects of contemplated changes in selling price, and other cost-volume-profit relationships.

The unit cost of producing a commodity ordinarily varies with the volume produced. An increase in volume of output within the reasonable limits of plant capacity is likely to result in a decrease in unit cost. Changes in the unit selling price of a product are ordinarily accompanied by changes in the volume of the product sold and in the total amount of revenue from its sale. If a decrease in selling price is followed by an increase in sales volume and an increase in total revenue, and if an increase in output reduces the unit cost of the product, a substantial increase in net income may be achieved.

Quantitative data relating to the effect on net income of changes in unit selling price, sales volume, production volume, production costs, and operating expenses enable management to improve the relationship among these variables. If a change in selling price appears to be desirable or, because of competitive pressure, unavoidable, the possible effect of the change on sales volume and product cost needs to be studied. Inquiry into the likely effect on net income of a promotional sales campaign is another example of special studies that may be undertaken.

A basic requisite of cost-volume-profit analysis is the subdivision of costs into two categories: (1) fixed and (2) variable. Direct costing procedures facilitate such analysis because direct costing requires that costs be so classified. If conventional absorption costing is employed, it is necessary as a preliminary step to divide the relevant cost data into fixed and variable categories. Some of the analyses employed in evaluating the interactions of selling price, sales volume, variable cost, fixed cost, and net income are illustrated in the pages that follow.

Break-even analysis

The point in the operations of an enterprise at which revenues and expired costs are exactly equal is called the *break-even point.* At this particular level of operations an enterprise will neither realize a net income nor incur a net loss. Break-even analysis can be applied to past periods, but it is most useful when applied to future periods as a guide to business planning, particularly if either an expansion or a curtailment of operations is anticipated. In such cases it is concerned with future prospects and future operations and hence relies upon estimates. Obviously the reliability of the analysis is greatly influenced by the accuracy of the estimates.

The break-even point can be computed by means of a mathematical formula or it can be ascertained from a graphic presentation of the relationship between revenue, costs, and volume of productive capacity. The basic data required in making the determination are estimates of (1) total fixed costs and expenses chargeable against revenue and (2) the total variable costs and expenses, stated as a percent of sales revenue. The formula for computing the break-even point is S = FC + VC, where S represents sales dollars, FC represents fixed costs and expenses stated in dollars, and VC represents variable costs and expenses stated as a percent of sales. To illustrate, assume that fixed costs and expenses are estimated at $120,000 and that variable costs and expenses are expected to equal 40% of sales. The break-even point is $200,000 of sales revenue, computed as follows:

$$\begin{aligned} S &= FC + VC \\ S &= \$120,000 + 40\%S \\ 60\%S &= \$120,000 \\ S &= \$200,000 \end{aligned}$$

Break-even analysis may also be employed in estimating the sales volume required to yield a specified amount of net income. The formula stated above can be modified for use in this computation by the addition at the end of the equation of the desired amount of net income (NI). For example, the sales volume required to yield net income of $60,000 for the enterprise assumed above would be $300,000, computed as follows:

$$\begin{aligned} S &= FC + VC + NI \\ S &= \$120,000 + 40\%S + \$60,000 \\ 60\%S &= \$180,000 \\ S &= \$300,000 \end{aligned}$$

A break-even chart, based on the foregoing data, is illustrated on page 632. It is constructed in the following manner:

(1) Percentages of productive capacity of the enterprise are spread along the horizontal axis, and dollar amounts representing operating data are spread along the vertical axis. The outside limits of the chart represent 100% of productive capacity and the maximum sales potential at that level of production.

(2) A diagonal line representing sales is drawn from the lower left corner to the upper right corner.

(3) A point representing fixed costs is plotted on the vertical axis at the left and a point representing total costs at maximum capacity is plotted at the right edge of the chart. A diagonal line representing total costs at various percentages of capacity is then drawn connecting these two points. In the illustration, the fixed costs are $120,000 and the total costs at maximum capacity amount to $280,000 ($120,000 plus variable costs of 40% of $400,000 or $160,000).

(4) Horizontal and vertical lines are drawn at the point of intersection of the sales and cost lines, which is the break-even point, and the areas representing net income and net loss are identified.

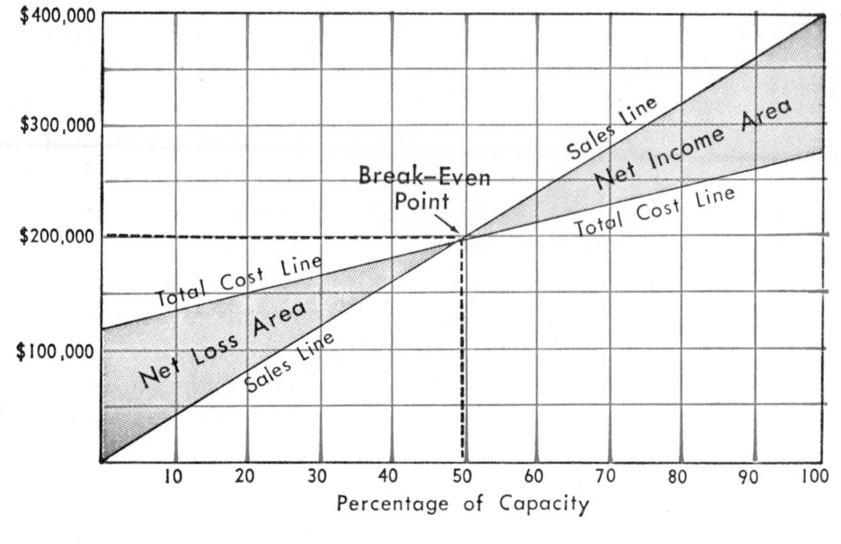

Break-even chart

Presentation of break-even analysis in the chart form is frequently preferred over the equation form. From such a chart the approximate net income or net loss associated with any given sales volume or percentage of capacity can be readily determined.

Relying as it does on rigid assumptions concerning the behavior of sales and costs, break-even analysis should be employed with caution. If the selling price of a product is increased or decreased or if the amount of costs and expenses changes, the analysis prepared prior to such action will no longer be valid. In addition, fixed costs may not remain constant for all levels of activity, and variable costs may not be uniformly variable at each level. For example, in the foregoing illustration it is quite possible that at 10% of capacity fixed costs would be less than $120,000 and variable costs would be more than 40% of sales. It should also be noted that a break-even chart for an enterprise selling two or more products must be based on a specified "product-mix." Changes in the mix would necessitate additional analysis and construction of a new chart. Recognition of the inherent assumptions and the limitations of break-even analysis is essential to the effective use of studies of this type in management planning.

Margin of safety

Business enterprises do not adopt the break-even point as their goal for future operations. Rather, they seek to achieve the largest possible volume of sales above the break-even point. The difference between the current sales revenue and the sales at the break-even point is called the *margin of safety*. It represents the possible decrease in sales revenue that may occur without there being a net loss, and it may be expressed either in terms of dollars or as a percentage of sales. For example, if the volume of sales is $250,000 and sales at the break-even point amount to $200,000, the margin of safety (MS) is $50,000 or 20% as indicated by the following computation:

$$MS = \frac{\text{Sales} - \text{Sales at Break-Even Point}}{\text{Sales}}$$

$$MS = \frac{\$250{,}000 - \$200{,}000}{\$250{,}000} = 20\%$$

The margin of safety is useful in evaluating past operations and as a guide to business planning. For example, if the margin of safety is low, management should carefully evaluate forecasts of future sales revenue because even a small decline in sales revenue will result in a net loss.

Profit-volume ratio

Another relationship between costs, volume, and profits that is especially useful in business planning because it gives an insight into the profit potential of a firm is the *profit-volume ratio*, sometimes referred to as the marginal income ratio. This ratio (PV) indicates the percentage of each sales dollar available to cover the fixed expenses and to provide a profit. For example, if the volume of sales is $250,000 and variable expenses amount to $150,000, the PV ratio is 40% as indicated by the following calculation:

$$PV = \frac{\text{Sales} - \text{Variable Expenses}}{\text{Sales}}$$

$$PV = \frac{\$250{,}000 - \$150{,}000}{\$250{,}000} = 40\%$$

The only variable factor reflected by the PV ratio is volume of sales. Therefore, in employing profit-volume analysis, factors other than sales volume, such as the amount of fixed expenses, the percentage of variable expenses to sales, and the unit sales price, are assumed to remain constant. If these factors are not constant, the effect of any change in these factors must be considered in applying profit-volume analysis.

The PV ratio permits the quick determination of the effect on profit of an increase or a decrease in sales volume. To illustrate, assume that the management of a firm with a PV ratio of 40% is evaluating the effect on profit of the addition of $25,000 in sales orders. Multiplying the PV ratio (40%) times the change in sales volume ($25,000) indicates an increase in net income of $10,000 if the additional orders are obtained.

The PV ratio is also useful in setting business policy. For example, if the PV ratio of a firm is large, a comparatively large increase in net income can be expected from an increase in sales volume. Conversely, a comparatively large decrease in net income can be expected from a decline in sales volume. A firm in such a position might decide to devote considerable effort to additional sales promotion because of the substantial change in net income that will result from changes in sales volume. On the other hand, a firm with a small PV ratio will probably want to devote considerable attention to reducing costs and expenses before concentrating large efforts on additional sales promotion.

Rate of return on assets

The percentage of net income to sales revenue is one of the traditional ratios employed in judging the effectiveness of business operations. But this measure has the important limitation of ignoring the magnitude of the investment employed in the process of earning the income. For example, assume that the annual sales and the net income of an enterprise for several years have approximated $1,000,000 and $100,000 respectively, yielding a ratio of 10%. If the magnitude of the assets employed had been $400,000, an evaluation of the ratio would be quite different from an evaluation based on assets of $2,000,000. Such disparities in the amount of assets committed to operations are revealed by the measure called the *rate of return on assets*, which is determined by the following formula:

$$\text{Rate of Return on Assets} = \frac{\text{Net Income}}{\text{Assets}}$$

In addition to employing the measure for an entire business, the rate of return on assets can be used as an indicator of the relative efficiency of individual assets or of the employment of assets by branches or departments. The only limiting factor is the necessity of identifying the amount of income attributable to the specific assets. This basic determination may be fairly difficult or it may be fairly simple, as in computing the rate of return on a group of stocks and bonds owned by an enterprise. For example, if the total cost of such investments is $100,000 and the dividends and the interest earned amount to $4,500, the rate of return on the assets is 4.5%. Even in a relatively clear-cut situation of this type, complicating elements may be introduced, such as allocation of administrative expense and income taxes to the earnings and the use of current market values of the securities instead of their original cost.

The rate of return on assets is often computed on a departmental basis for the purpose of measuring relative operating performance. For such computations the interest on borrowed funds and income taxes are ordinarily not taken into consideration. In evaluating a segment of a business, such nonoperating items as interest on borrowed funds should not be considered because the return on assets is basically a measure of the efficiency with which the assets have been used. The nonoperating items are not relevant to the evaluation of divisional management efficiency because such items are beyond the control of the division managers.

To illustrate, assume that the two operating divisions of a business have about the same volume of sales and approximately the same net income from operations. There is, however, a considerable difference between the amounts of assets employed by each. The significance of this disparity can be presented in the following manner:

	Division A	Division B
Sales	$400,000	$435,000
Operating expenses	350,000	380,000
Net income from operations	$ 50,000	$ 55,000
Ratio of net income to sales	12.5%	12.6%
Assets employed	$500,000	$300,000
Rate of return on assets	10%	18.3%

Information such as that presented in the above report would alert top management to the far greater effectiveness of Division B in the employment of assets. It would indicate the need for a careful study of the operating policies of the two divisions and the causes of the variation in rate of return on assets. The rate of return on assets can also be used as a control device by the establishment of a minimum rate of return and then by comparison of rates actually achieved with this minimum.

The rate of return on assets also assists in product pricing by making it possible to determine the price of new products that will be necessary to earn a certain rate of return on the assets employed. This ratio is also useful in profit-planning and in decision-making. For example, it aids management in evaluating proposed purchases of machinery and equipment and other capital expenditures. The use of the rate of return on assets in evaluating capital expenditure proposals is presented in the following section.

Analysis of proposed capital expenditures

With the accelerated growth of American industry in recent years, increasing attention has been given to accounting analyses designed to evaluate plans requiring substantial outlays for plant replacement, improvement, and expansion. Three types of analysis employed in evaluating proposals for major capital expenditures will be described.

Average rate of return. The expected *average rate of return* is a measure of the anticipated profitability of an investment in plant assets. The amount of the investment may be considered to be the original cost of the plant assets, or recognition may be given to the effect of depreciation on the amount of the investment. According to the latter view, the investment gradually declines from the original cost to the estimated residual value at the end of its useful life. Assuming straight-line depreciation and no residual value, the average investment is equal to one half of the original expenditure. The amount of net income expected to be earned from the investment is also stated as an annual average over the number of years the asset is to be used. The formula is as follows:

$$\text{Average Rate of Return} = \frac{\text{Average Net Income}}{\text{Average Investment}}$$

To illustrate, assume that management is considering the acquisition of a particular machine at a cost of $50,000, that it is expected to have a useful life of 4 years, and that its residual value will be negligible. Further, the use of the new item of equipment is expected to yield total net income of $20,000 during the 4 years. The expected average annual net income is therefore $5,000 ($20,000 ÷ 4) and the average investment is $25,000 ($50,000 ÷ 2). Accordingly, the expected average rate of return on the average investment is 20% ($5,000 ÷ $25,000). Comparison of this expected rate of return with the rate established by management as the minimum reward for the risks involved will indicate the comparative attractiveness of the proposed expenditure. If the foregoing analysis had been based on original cost of the equipment instead of the average investment, the rate of return would have been computed as 10% ($5,000 ÷ $50,000). It is readily apparent that reports on accounting analyses of this type should disclose the method employed.

A limitation of the use of average rate of return on average investment is that no consideration is given to the exact timing of the recovery of the cash outlay for the plant assets or to the timing of the net income. Funds derived from the recovery of the cost of a capital expenditure and from the net income that it has generated can be reinvested in other income-producing activities. Therefore a project that recovers a high proportion of its investment and yields high income early in its life is more desirable than a project with the same average rate of return but with lower recovery and income in the earlier years.

Cash payback period. The expected period of time that will elapse between the date of a capital expenditure and a complete recoupment in cash or equivalent is called the *cash payback period.* To simplify the analysis, the revenues and the out-of-pocket operating expenses expected to be associated with the operation of the plant assets are assumed to be entirely in the form of cash. The excess of the cash flowing in from revenue over the cash flowing out for expenses is termed *net cash flow.* The time required for the net cash flow to equal the initial outlay for the plant asset is the payback period.

For purposes of illustration, assume that the proposed expenditure for a plant asset with an 8-year life is $200,000 and that the annual net cash flow is expected to be $40,000. The estimated cash payback period for the expenditure is 5 years ($200,000 ÷ $40,000).

The cash payback concept is widely used by owners and managers in evaluating proposals for expansion and for investment in new projects. A relatively short payback period is desirable, because the sooner the recovery, the sooner the availability for reinvestment in other projects. In addition, there is likely to be less possibility of loss from changes in economic conditions and other unavoidable risks when the commitment is short-term. The cash payback concept is also of interest to bankers and other creditors who may be dependent upon net cash flow for the repayment of claims associated with the initial capital expenditure.

The principal limitation of the cash payback period as a basis for decisions is its lack of concern with the expected profitability of a proposal. A project with a very short payback period coupled with relatively poor profitability would be less desirable than one for which the investment was committed for a longer period but with satisfactory profitability.

Discounted cash flow. An expenditure for plant and equipment may be looked upon as the acquisition of a series of future net cash flows composed of two elements: (1) recovery of the initial expenditure and (2) net income. Both the absolute and the relative amounts of these two elements are obviously important. The period of time over which the net cash flows will be received is also important. Any specified amount of cash that is to be received at some date in the future is not the equivalent of the same amount of cash on hand at the present. This element of timing is given recognition in *discounted cash flow* analysis. The expected future net cash flows originating from proposed present capital expenditures are reduced to their present values.

The concept of present value of future payments was encountered in an earlier chapter in connection with discounting promissory notes.

Application of the concept to discounted cash flow analysis may be illustrated by computing the amount to be deposited at a given rate of interest that will yield a specified sum at a later date. If the rate of interest is 6% and the sum to be accumulated in one year is $1,000, the amount to be invested is $943.40 ($1,000 ÷ 1.06). If the funds were to be invested a year earlier, with the interest compounded at the end of the first year, the amount of the deposit would be $890.00 ($943.40 ÷ 1.06).

Instead of determining the present value of future sums by a series of divisions in the manner just illustrated, it is customary to find the present value of 1 from a table of present values and to multiply it by the amount of the future sum. A partial table is presented below. Multiplication of .890, the present value of $1 two years hence at 6%, by $1,000 yields the same amount that was determined by the two successive divisions in the preceding paragraph. The rounding of the values in the table at three decimal places would not be sufficiently accurate for some purposes, but any greater exactitude is not necessary for our analysis.

Present Value of 1 at Compound Interest

Years	6%	10%	15%	20%
1	.943	.909	.870	.833
2	.890	.826	.756	.694
3	.840	.751	.658	.579
4	.792	.683	.572	.482
5	.747	.621	.497	.402
6	.705	.564	.432	.335
7	.665	.513	.376	.279
8	.627	.467	.327	.233
9	.592	.424	.284	.194
10	.558	.386	.247	.162

The rate of return selected in any particular case is affected by the nature of the business enterprise and its relative profitability, the purpose of the capital expenditure, and other related factors. If the present value of the net cash flow expected from a proposed expenditure, at the selected rate, equals or exceeds the amount of the expenditure, the proposal is desirable. For purposes of illustration, assume a proposal for the acquisition of a $200,000 facility with an expected useful life of 5 years and a minimum desired rate of return of 10%. The anticipated net cash flow for each of the 5 years and the analysis of the proposal is given on the following page. The analysis indicates that the proposal is expected to recover the investment and provide more than the minimum rate of return.

Year	Present Value of 1 at 10%	Net Cash Flow	Present Value of Net Cash Flow
1	.909	$ 70,000	$ 63,630
2	.826	60,000	49,560
3	.751	50,000	37,550
4	.683	40,000	27,320
5	.621	40,000	24,840
Total		$260,000	$202,900
Amount to be invested			200,000
Excess present value			$ 2,900

Each of the three methods of analyzing proposals for capital expenditures has both advantages and limitations. It is often advisable to employ a combination of methods in evaluating the various economic aspects of major projects. It is obvious, of course, that estimates play a substantial role in all analyses of future expectations. Such factors as product pricing, improvements in products, availability and training of personnel, marketing procedures, and severity of competition must also be given consideration in arriving at decisions.

Operations research

Each of the various uses of accounting data in planning, coordinating, and controlling business operations that has been described has been concerned with a restricted number of objectives or variables. In recent years there has been developed a framework of analytical methods known as *operations research*, in which the skills of engineers, mathematicians, economists, accountants, and psychologists are combined in solving problems for business enterprises. Mathematical models encompassing a large number of interdependent variables are often employed.

One of the areas for which operations research is often utilized is inventory control. For each category of materials in the inventory it is important to know the ideal quantity to be purchased in a single order and the minimum and maximum quantities to be on hand at any time. Such factors as economies of large-scale buying, storage costs, work interruption due to shortages, and seasonal and cyclical variations in production schedules need to be considered. Much of the data required for analyses of this type is supplied by the accounting and finance divisions of the enterprise.

Nature and purpose of internal reports

The term *internal reports* may be applied to various schedules, statements, and summaries prepared for management by the accounting department. They are designed to facilitate the more effective discharge of management's responsibilities by providing detailed information about various phases of operations. In order to be of maximum usefulness, internal reports should be prepared in accordance with the following principles:

(1) The organizational structure and chain of responsibility of the enterprise should be observed.
(2) Irrelevant and immaterial data should be excluded.
(3) The data should be sufficiently accurate for the purpose.
(4) Terminology employed should be familiar to the reader.
(5) Comparative data should be used to develop significant trends and relationships.
(6) Reports should be timely.

The significance of the chain of responsibility in the preparation and the issuance of reports merits special consideration. The organization chart of an enterprise sets forth both the functional responsibilities and the various strata of management. There is considerable variation among companies in the titles employed and the number of levels of responsibility. The range is from the principal officers, who are the top executives, through vice presidents, division managers, and on down to department heads or factory foremen. Rarely will a single internal report be suitable for all levels of management because the duties and the responsibilities of each stratum differ from the others. For example, the principal executives establish the major goals and the overall operating plans and procedures. Internal reports prepared for their use will ordinarily cover a functional area of the enterprise and will be broad in scope. In contrast, factory foremen are responsible for the direct supervision of a specific group of employees in their day-to-day activities. The reports prepared for their guidance will contain much more detailed information about a narrower segment of the business. The frequency with which reports are issued and the period of time covered is also likely to vary in accordance with the management level for which they are prepared. Generally, those at the top need less frequent reports than those nearer the operating level.

Some internal reports are based entirely on the accounting records of past performance and are issued in accordance with an established time schedule. Other reports, particularly those dealing with alternative courses of action, may require investigation and research beyond the accounting records. They may also utilize estimates as well as factual data, and may be prepared once only.

Gross profit analysis

Gross profit on sales is frequently considered to be the most significant intermediate figure in the income statement. It is customary to determine its percentage relationship to sales and to make comparisons with prior periods. However, the mere knowledge of the percentages and the degree and direction of change from prior periods is insufficient; management needs information about the underlying factors. The procedures employed in developing such information is termed *gross profit analysis.*

Inasmuch as gross profit is the excess of sales over the cost of goods sold, it follows that a change in the amount of gross profit can be caused by an increase or a decrease in sales, by an increase or a decrease in the cost of goods sold, or by a combination of the two. Increases or decreases in sales or the cost of goods sold may in turn be attributable to a change in unit price, to a change in the number of units sold, or to a combination of both.

The various factors contributing to a change in sales or to a change in the cost of goods sold may be summarized as follows:

(1) *Price factor.* The effect of a change in unit price, assuming no change in number of units sold.

(2) *Quantity factor.* The effect of a change in number of units sold, assuming no change in price.

(3) *Price-quantity factor.* The effect of a change in unit price on a change in number of units sold.

The data presented below will be used as the basis for illustrating gross profit analysis and the form of the internal report. For the sake of simplicity, a single commodity will be assumed. The amount of detail entering into the analysis would be greater if a number of different commodities were sold, but the basic principles would not be affected.

	1966	1965	Increase Decrease*
Sales	$225,000	$200,000	$ 25,000
Cost of goods sold	162,500	140,000	22,500
Gross profit	$ 62,500	$ 60,000	$ 2,500
Units sold	125,000	100,000	25,000
Unit selling price	$1.80	$2.00	$.20*
Unit cost price	$1.30	$1.40	$.10*

The analysis of the data is presented at the top of the following page. This analysis indicates that although the quantity factor would have resulted in an increase of $50,000 in sales, the increase was partially offset by a $20,000 decrease in the price factor and a $5,000 decrease in the price-quantity factor. In addition, the quantity factor would have resulted in an increase of $35,000 in cost of goods sold had it not been partially offset by a $10,000 decrease in the price factor and a $2,500 decrease in the price-quantity factor.

Analysis of Increase in Gross Profit
For the Year 1966

Increase in sales attributed to:		
Decrease in unit sales price of $.20 on 100,000 units	$(20,000)	
Increase in sales volume of 25,000 units at $2.00	50,000	
Decrease in unit sales price of $.20 on increased sales volume of 25,000 units	(5,000)	
Increase in sales		$25,000
Increase in cost of goods sold attributed to:		
Decrease in unit cost price of $.10 on 100,000 units	$(10,000)	
Increase in sales volume of 25,000 units at $1.40	35,000	
Decrease in unit cost price of $.10 on increased sales volume of 25,000 units	(2,500)	
Increase in cost of goods sold		22,500
Increase in gross profit		$ 2,500

The data reported are useful in evaluating past performance and in planning for the future. For example, if the increased sales volume and the price reduction had not been accompanied by a reduction in unit cost, the gross profit would have decreased by $10,000 as indicated by the following analysis:

Increase in sales attributed to:		
Decrease in unit sales price	$(20,000)	
Increase in sales volume	50,000	
Decrease in unit sales price on increased sales volume	(5,000)	$25,000
Increase in cost of goods sold attributed to:		
Increase in sales volume		35,000
Decrease in gross profit resulting from decrease in unit sales price and increase in sales volume		$(10,000)

The actual increase in gross profit was made possible, therefore, by the ability of management to reduce the unit cost price. The effect of the reduction in cost price on the increase in gross profit was $12,500, as indicated by the following tabulation:

Decrease in cost of goods sold attributable to:	
Decrease in unit cost price	$10,000
Decrease in unit cost price on increased sales volume	2,500
Increase in gross profit resulting from a decrease in unit cost price	$12,500

The means by which the change in unit cost price was accomplished is also significant. If the reduction was attributable to the spreading of fixed overhead costs over the larger number of units produced, the decision to reduce the sales price in order to achieve a larger volume was probably wise. On the other hand, if the reduction in unit cost price was attributable to operating efficiencies disassociated from increased production, the reduction in sales price was unwise. This may be demonstrated by the following schedule. This schedule compares the operating results of 1966 with the results that would have been obtained if the 1965 sales volume and unit selling price had been maintained with the 1966 unit cost.

	Actual		Assumed	
Units sold	125,000		100,000	
Unit selling price	$1.80		$2.00	
Sales		$225,000		$200,000
Unit cost	$1.30		$1.30	
Cost of goods sold		162,500		130,000
Gross profit		$ 62,500		$ 70,000

If the reduction in unit cost had been achieved by a combination of the two means, the approximate effects of each could be determined by additional analyses.

The methods employed in gross profit analysis may also be extended, with some modifications, to the analysis of changes in selling and general expenses. When budgets and standard costs are employed, the determination of variances and their causes follow a somewhat similar pattern.

Efficiency reports

Efficiency reports reveal variations between actual performance and standards or budgets. The frequency of efficiency reports depends upon the nature of the item, the need for control, and the level at which control is to be effected. For example, department foremen and line supervisors should receive daily or weekly cost reports because they represent the focal point of control over manufacturing costs. Efficiency reports frequently result in management action. Accordingly, they should be received by management as soon as possible so that waste and inefficiency can be eliminated quickly. Efficiency reports include daily or weekly reports on material usage, direct labor, idle machine hours, and inventory shortages as well as monthly comparisons of actual performance with budget expectations.

The weekly scrap report presented on the following page is illustrative of an efficiency report prepared for a department foreman. Because scrap is unavoidable in many operations, a column for normal scrap loss is frequently provided in a scrap report. A report on material usage often accompanies a scrap report as the two are closely related.

Plating Department
Scrap Report
Week Ended March 20, 1966

Job No.	Units Spoiled		Dollar Loss			Remarks
	Actual	Normal	Actual	Normal	Abnormal	
1446	185	180	$ 18.50	$ 18.00	$ .50	
1727	320	160	64.00	32.00	32.00	Inexperienced employee
1938	540	400	162.00	120.00	42.00	Substandard materials
2046	135	100	27.00	20.00	7.00	Machine breakdown
			$271.50	$190.00	$81.50	

The scrap losses on Jobs 1727, 1938, and 2046 were excessive and the foreman should take corrective action to prevent their recurrence.

Trend reports

Trend reports contain data for more than one period or point of time and are useful to management in planning. From the data contained in the reports, significant trends and relationships can be observed. Such knowledge is helpful to management in continuing developments that are favorable and in correcting those that are unsatisfactory. A trend report of quarterly sales by territories prepared for the sales manager is shown below.

Sales Report
First Quarter, 1966–1965

Territory	1966	1965	Increase Decrease*
A	$225,000	$160,000	$ 65,000
B	310,000	335,000	25,000*
C	365,000	305,000	60,000
	$900,000	$800,000	$100,000

This report reveals that quarterly sales have increased in Territories A and C and have decreased in Territory B. The causes of these changes should be investigated by management. The report could also have revealed each territory's contribution to total quarterly sales through the use of percentages. For example, in 1965 Territory A sales accounted for 20% of total quarterly sales, whereas in 1966 they represented 25% of total quarterly sales.

Reports for special needs

Periodic reports provide the basis for most management decisions. However, users of the recurring reports may on occasion desire more detailed information on certain items in the periodic reports, or special problems may arise that require information not provided by the recurring reports. In such situations the accountant should prepare a *special report* containing the information needed. There is no prescribed format for special reports, except that each should be designed specifically for the user and for the specific purpose it is to serve.

Many of the differential cost analyses and use of the alternative cost concepts described in previous chapters may be classified as special reports. Reports of the losses caused by strikes, by fire, or by some other catastrophe and analyses of the tax effect of alternative courses of action are additional examples of special reports.

QUESTIONS

1. (a) What is the break-even point? (b) How can the break-even point be calculated?

2. (a) If fixed costs and expenses are $800,000 and variable costs and expenses are 50% of sales, what is the break-even point? (b) What sales are required to realize net income of $100,000 under the conditions described in (a)?

3. Both the Farris Company and the Bowen Company had the same sales, total costs and expenses, and net income for 1966, yet the Bowen Company had a lower break-even point than the Farris Company. Explain the reason for this difference in break-even points.

4. What is the advantage of presenting break-even analysis in the chart form over the equation form?

5. (a) What is meant by the term "margin of safety"? (b) If sales are $200,000, net income $20,000, and sales at the break-even point $160,000, what is the MS?

6. What ratio indicates the percentage of each sales dollar that is available to cover fixed costs and expenses and to provide a profit?

7. An examination of the accounting records of Wagner Company disclosed a high profit-volume ratio and production at a level below maximum capacity. Based on this information, suggest a likely means of improving net income. Explain.

8. What does the rate of return on assets measure?

9. (a) As used in analysis of proposed capital expenditures, what is the cash payback period? (b) Discuss the principal limitation of this method for evaluating capital expenditure proposals.

10. In evaluating capital expenditure proposals, what factor is taken into consideration by the cash payback period method that is ignored by the average rate of return method?

11. What is operations research?

12. Why is it important to take into consideration the chain of responsibility of the enterprise in preparing internal reports?

13. Discuss the three factors affecting both sales and cost of goods sold to which a change in gross profit can be attributed.

14. The gross profit of the Harper Company increased by $10,000 over the preceding year. Discuss possible unfavorable occurrences that might have accompanied the increase.

15. The analysis of increase in gross profit report for Wilson Company includes the effect an increase in quantity of goods sold has had on sales. How is this figure determined?

16. (a) What are trend reports? (b) How can management use such reports?

EXERCISES

1. Mueller Company anticipates for the coming year fixed costs and expenses of $90,000 and variable costs and expenses equal to 40% of sales.

(a) Compute the anticipated break-even point.
(b) Compute the sales required to realize net income of $60,000.
(c) Construct a break-even chart, assuming sales of $300,000 at full capacity.
(d) Determine the probable net income if sales total $225,000.

2. Taylor Company operated at full capacity in 1965. Fixed costs and expenses were $240,000, variable costs and expenses were 40% of sales, and sales totaled $500,000. Management proposes to expand plant capacity by 50%, which will increase fixed costs and expenses by $90,000 yearly but will not affect the ratio of variable costs and expenses to sales.

(a) Compute the net income under present conditions.
(b) Compute the break-even point under present and proposed conditions.
(c) Compute the sales necessary under proposed conditions to reach current net income.
(d) Compute the maximum net income under proposed conditions.

3. (a) On sales of $400,000 the break-even point is $300,000. What is the margin of safety (MS) expressed (1) in dollars and (2) as a percentage of sales?

(b) Fixed costs and expenses were $140,000, variable costs and expenses were 30% of sales, and the margin of safety (MS) was 20%. Determine the sales for the year.

4. (a) On sales of $275,000 the fixed costs and expenses are $125,000 and the variable costs and expenses are $110,000. What is the profit-volume (PV) ratio?

(b) If sales are $700,000, fixed costs and expenses are $350,000, and the profit-volume (PV) ratio is 60%, what is the net income?

5. Williams Company had for the past year sales of $540,000, a margin of safety (MS) of 20%, and a profit-volume ratio (PV) of 40%. Compute:

(a) The break-even point.
(b) The variable costs and expenses.
(c) The fixed costs and expenses.
(d) The net income.

6. For 1965 the Packard Company had sales of $2,400,000, fixed costs and expenses of $768,000, a margin of safety (MS) of 20%, and a profit-volume (PV) ratio of 40%. During 1966 the variable costs and expenses were 60% of sales, the fixed costs and expenses did not change from the previous year, and the MS was 25%.

(a) What was the net income for 1965?
(b) What was the break-even point for 1966?
(c) What was the amount of sales for 1966?
(d) What was the net income for 1966?

7. The Murray Manufacturing Company is considering the acquisition of machinery at a cost of $14,000. The machinery has an estimated life of 5 years and no salvage value. It is expected to provide yearly net income of $2,200 and yearly net cash flows of $5,000. The company's minimum desired rate of return for discounted cash flow analysis is 20%. Compute:

(a) The average rate of return on investment.
(b) The cash payback period.
(c) The excess or deficiency of present value over the amount invested as determined by the discounted cash flow method. Use the table on page 638.

8. The sales, net income, and asset investments of two companies in the same industry are as follows:

	Company X	Company Y
Sales	$300,000	$450,000
Net income	30,000	45,000
Assets	200,000	900,000

(a) What is the percentage of net income to sales for each company?
(b) What is the rate of return on assets for each company?
(c) As far as the data permit, comment on the relative performance of these two companies.

9. From the following data for the Hines Company, prepare an analysis of the increase in gross profit for the year 1966.

	1966		1965	
Sales	40,000 units @ $6	$240,000	35,000 units @ $6.25	$218,750
Cost of goods sold	40,000 units @ $4	160,000	35,000 units @ $4.10	143,500
Gross profit on sales		$ 80,000		$ 75,250

10. Cummins, Incorporated has three sales divisions: East, Midwest, and West. Quarterly sales reports are prepared for each of the division managers, indicating by salesman the sales for the quarter, the sales for the corresponding quarter last year, the dollar increase or decrease in quarterly sales, and the percentage change in quarterly sales. Cummins sells a stable product that is unaffected by seasonal fluctuations, and there has been no change in selling price during the past 15 months. Applicable sales data are presented below.

Salesmen	Division	Sales: First Quarter 1966	Sales: First Quarter 1965
Avery	East	$33,050	$32,100
Black	West	22,100	19,990
Doyle	East	28,500	26,500
Lewis	Midwest	31,900	30,600
Porter	East	22,300	23,700
Reed	Midwest	26,400	27,500
Roberts	West	27,600	26,200
Sawyer	West	22,200	24,750
Webb	Midwest	26,100	22,400

(a) Prepare a quarterly sales report for the East division manager. (Percentages may be rounded to the nearest full percent.)
(b) Which salesman in the East division showed the most favorable trend?

PROBLEMS

26-1. Davis Typewriter Manufacturing Company is considering the addition of a new product to its line. For 1965, production was at 90% of capacity, the assets employed were $6,000,000 (original cost), and the income statement showed a net operating income of $480,000 computed as follows:

Sales		$7,200,000
Less: Cost of goods sold	$3,790,000	
Selling expenses	1,975,000	
General expenses	955,000	6,720,000
Net operating income		$ 480,000

If the new product is added, market research indicates that 10,000 units can be sold in 1966 at an estimated selling price of $70 per unit. The idle capacity will be utilized to produce the product, but an additional $500,000 in plant assets will be required. The cost data per unit for the new product is as follows:

Direct materials	$22.50
Direct labor	17.00
Factory overhead (includes depreciation on additional investment)	12.75
Selling expenses	8.00
General expenses	4.25
	$64.50

Instructions: (1) Prepare an estimated income statement for 1966 for the new product.

(2) Prepare a schedule indicating the rate of return on assets under present conditions and for the new product. Use the original cost of the assets in your computation.

(3) Would you recommend addition of the new product? Would you require other data before you make your decision? If so, what data would you require?

26-2. Benson Company prepares weekly reports of idleness of direct labor employees for the plant superintendent. These reports classify the idle time by departments. Idle time data for the week ended May 14 of the current year are as follows:

Department	Standard Hours	Productive Hours	Idle Hours
A	2,000	1,800	200
B	1,600	1,408	192
C	1,000	930	70
D	1,200	1,200	—

The hourly direct labor rates are $2.50, $3.00, $2.70, and $3.50, respectively, for Departments A through D. The idleness was caused by a lack of sales orders in Department A, a shortage of materials in Department B, and a machine breakdown in Department C.

Instructions: Prepare an idle time report classified by departments for the week ended May 14 for the plant superintendent. Use the following columnar headings for the report:

	Production			Idle Time		
Dept.	Standard Hours	Actual Hours	Percentage of Standard	Hours	Cost of Idle Time	Remarks

26-3. The capital expenditures budget committee is considering two projects. The estimated net income and net cash flows from each project are presented below:

	Project I		Project II	
Year	Net Income	Net Cash Flow	Net Income	Net Cash Flow
1	$ 3,000	$ 8,000	$ 7,000	$12,000
2	3,000	8,000	7,000	12,000
3	4,000	9,000	5,000	10,000
4	5,000	10,000	4,000	9,000
5	6,000	11,000	2,000	7,000
6	6,000	11,000	2,000	7,000
	$27,000	$57,000	$27,000	$57,000

Each project requires an investment of $30,000 with no salvage value expected. The committee has selected a rate of 15% for purposes of the discounted cash flow analysis.

Instructions: (1) Compute:

(a) The average rate of return for each project, giving effect to depreciation on the investment.

(b) The excess or deficiency of present value over original cost as determined by the discounted cash flow method for each project. Use the present value table on page 638.

(2) Prepare a brief report for the budget committee advising it on the relative merits of the two projects.

26-4. Moore Company expects to maintain the same inventories at the end of 1966 as at the beginning of the year. The total of all production costs for the year is therefore assumed to be equal to the cost of goods sold. With this in mind, the various department heads were asked to submit estimates of the expenses for their departments during 1966. A summary report of these estimates is presented below.

	Estimated Fixed Expense	Estimated Variable Expense (per unit sold)
Production costs:		
Direct materials	$ 0	$1.75
Direct labor	0	2.25
Factory overhead	140,000	1.20
Selling expenses:		
Sales salaries and commissions	25,150	.20
Advertising	20,000	0
Travel	12,750	0
Miscellaneous selling expenses	7,100	.30
General expenses:		
Office and officers' salaries	82,000	.15
Supplies	3,000	.05
Miscellaneous general expenses	10,000	.10
	$300,000	$6.00

It is expected that 90,000 units will be sold at a selling price of $10 a unit. Capacity output is 100,000 units.

Instructions: (1) Determine the break-even point in (a) dollars of sales, (b) units, and (c) terms of capacity.

(2) Prepare an estimated income statement for 1966.

(3) Construct a break-even chart, indicating the break-even point in dollars of sales.

(4) What is the expected margin of safety (MS)?

(5) What is the expected profit-volume (PV) ratio?

26-5. Dempsey Company manufactures only one product. In 1965, the plant operated at full capacity. At a meeting of the board of directors on December 10, 1965, it was decided to raise the price of this product from its price of $3.50, which had prevailed for the past few years, to $4, effective January 1, 1966. Although the cost price was expected to rise about $.20 per unit in 1966 because of a wage increase, the increase in selling price was expected to cover this increase and also add to net operating income. The comparative income statements for 1965 and 1966 are presented below.

	1966		1965	
Sales		$360,000		$385,000
Cost of goods sold — variable	$117,000		$121,000	
fixed	99,000	216,000	99,000	220,000
Gross profit on sales		$144,000		$165,000
Operating expenses — variable	$ 63,500		$ 66,500	
fixed	48,500	112,000	48,500	115,000
Net operating income		$ 32,000		$ 50,000

Instructions: (1) Prepare an analysis of the decrease in gross profit for the year 1966.

(2) At a meeting of the board of directors on February 10, 1967, the president, after reading the report of the decrease in gross profit, made the following comments:

"It looks as if the increase in unit cost price was $.40 and not the anticipated $.20. Had these costs been controlled and kept within the bounds of those in 1965, except for the anticipated $.20 increase in direct labor cost, there would have been an $18,000 increase in cost of goods sold attributed to the increase in unit cost price instead of $36,000, and gross profit would have changed very little."

Do you agree with this analysis of the increase in unit cost price? Explain.

26-6. Kessler, Incorporated operated at full capacity during 1965. Its income statement appears below.

Sales		$900,000
Cost of goods sold		600,000
Gross profit		$300,000
Operating expenses:		
Selling expenses	$120,000	
General expenses	90,000	
Total operating expenses		210,000
Net operating income		$ 90,000

An analysis of costs and expenses reveals the following division of costs and expenses between fixed and variable:

	Fixed	Variable
Cost of goods sold	25%	75%
Selling expenses	40%	60%
General expenses	80%	20%

The management of Kessler, Incorporated is considering a plant expansion program that will permit an increase of $300,000 in yearly sales. The expansion will increase fixed costs and expenses by $100,000 but will not affect the relationship between sales and variable costs and expenses.

Instructions: (1) Determine for present capacity (a) the total fixed costs and expenses, and (b) the total variable costs and expenses.

(2) Determine the percentage of total variable costs and expenses to sales.

(3) Compute the break-even point under present conditions.

(4) Compute the break-even point under the proposed program.

(5) Determine the amount of sales that would be necessary under the proposed program to realize the $90,000 of net operating income that was earned in 1965.

(6) Determine the maximum net operating income possible with the expanded plant.

(7) If the proposal is accepted and sales remain at the 1965 level, what will the net operating income be for 1966?

(8) Based upon the data given, would you recommend accepting the proposal? Explain.

27.

Funds statements, consolidated statements, and other statements

Funds and funds flow

The term "fund" has a variety of meanings in accounting and financial usage. Its first use in this book was in connection with segregations of cash for a special purpose, as in "change fund" and "petty cash fund." Later the term was employed to designate a segregation of assets for use in liquidating bonds or other long-term obligations at maturity. The amount of actual cash in a fund of this type, called a "sinking fund," is ordinarily minor, the greatest portion being composed of time deposits, government obligations, and other income-producing securities. When used in the plural without a modifying adjective, "funds" may be a synonym for "cash," as in the phrase associated with dishonor of a check, "not sufficient funds."

Another and more technical usage of "funds," and the one with which we are concerned in this chapter, is related to the flow of current assets and current liabilities during a period of time. The excess of the current assets of an enterprise over its current liabilities at a particular moment of time, such as at a balance sheet date, is usually called *working capital* or *net current assets*. The major categories of assets and liabilities typically included in working capital are presented in the comparative schedule at the top of the following page, together with the amount of change in each item during the year. The data were taken from a comparative balance sheet, which was of course based on the general ledger. In practice there is considerable variation in the amount of detail presented. In the illustration, for example, cash and marketable securities could have been combined into a single amount, or the notes and other accounts included in "Receivables (net)" could have been listed as separate items.

	December 31		Increase
	1966	1965	Decrease*
Current assets:			
Cash	$ 30,000	$ 35,000	$ 5,000*
Marketable securities	60,000	40,000	20,000
Receivables (net)	100,000	115,000	15,000*
Inventories	350,000	295,000	55,000
Prepaid expenses	10,000	15,000	5,000*
Total	$550,000	$500,000	$50,000
Current liabilities:			
Notes payable	$ 25,000	$ 20,000	$ 5,000
Accounts payable	80,000	95,000	15,000*
Income tax payable	110,000	120,000	10,000*
Dividends payable	15,000	15,000	—
Total	$230,000	$250,000	$20,000*
Working capital (net current assets)	$320,000	$250,000	$70,000

At the end of 1965 the $500,000 in current assets exceeded the $250,000 of current liabilities by $250,000, which is identified as the amount of working capital at that date. By the end of 1966 the current assets had increased to $550,000 and the current liabilities had decreased to $230,000, yielding working capital of $320,000. The combined effect of the increase of $50,000 in current assets and the decrease of $20,000 in current liabilities was to increase working capital by $70,000.

During the period between balance sheet dates, the amounts of most current assets and of most current liabilities fluctuate continually. Prepaid expenses are used up, direct materials progress through work in process to finished goods, finished goods are sold to customers on account, and accounts receivable are collected in cash. Cash flowing in is used to prepay expenses, to pay wages and other current expenses, to purchase additional materials, and to liquidate notes payable, accounts payable, and other liabilities. An understanding of this continual interplay among the various current assets and current liabilities is essential to an understanding of working capital and analyses related to it. In the illustration, for example, the fact that the amount of dividends payable at both the beginning and the end of the period was $15,000 is not an indication that the account remained unchanged throughout the year. If dividends are paid quarterly, four separate liabilities would have been created and four would have been liquidated during the year. It may also be noted that the amount of working capital is neither increased nor decreased by any transaction that affects only (1) current assets, (2) current liabilities, or (3) both current assets and current liabilities. Finally, it should be observed that working capital cannot be identified with any specific assets or equities; it is a "net" concept. It is increased by an increase in current assets; it is decreased by an increase in current liabilities.

Flow of funds analysis

Information about changes in working capital is important to managers, owners, and creditors because the success of a business enterprise is often materially affected by the relationship between current assets and current liabilities. The financial statement designed to impart this information is variously termed *funds statement*, *statement of source and application of funds*, *statement of resources provided and applied*, and *statement of changes in working capital*. Because of its brevity, "funds statement" will be used for discussion purposes; but the formal statement will be identified by the more descriptive title "statement of source and application of funds."

Both the purpose and the nature of funds-flow analysis has changed over the years. Originally the information was assembled almost exclusively for the use of management. The more recent trend is to present a formal funds statement as a part of the annual financial report to stockholders. Although the funds statement is not as basic as the income statement or the balance sheet, its increasing importance is evidenced by a trend toward its inclusion in the opinions (certificates) rendered by independent public accountants.

Just as there are a variety of titles for the statement and many variations in the nature of funds-flow analysis, there continues to be a considerable amount of experimentation in the form of the funds statement. Attention will be confined here to a basic form that is widely accepted.

The funds statement is divided into two major sections. The funds flowing into an enterprise are presented first, classified as to source, followed by the second section detailing the various ways in which the funds have been used or applied. Ordinarily the total of the sources section will not be exactly equal to the total of the applications section. If the inflow (sources) exceeds the outflow (applications), the excess has increased working capital. When the reverse situation occurs and the outflow exceeds the amount of the inflow, the excess is the amount by which working capital has decreased. Accordingly, the difference between the total of the sources and the applications sections of the funds statement is identified as either an increase in working capital or a decrease in working capital. The details of this balancing amount are also frequently presented in a third and subsidiary section of the statement or in a separate supporting schedule.

The period of time encompassed by a funds statement may be as short as a single month or as long as the entire period of a company's existence. The time period assumed in the discussion and the illustrations that follow will be a fiscal year.

Much of the funds-flow data of an enterprise appears in the major financial statements. As noted earlier, the balances of the current asset and the current liability accounts at the beginning and the end of a year appear in the comparative balance sheet. Information regarding net income, dividends, and other transactions affecting stockholders' equity accounts may also be readily available in the income and retained earnings statements. However, information regarding some of the sources and some of the applications of funds is not obtainable from those financial statements. For example, the comparative balance sheet will not necessarily reveal the amount of funds provided by the issuance of bonds nor the amount of funds applied to the purchase of plant assets. It is therefore necessary to obtain some of the relevant data from the general ledger or the journals.

Although there are many possible transactions that affect funds, consideration will be given only to the most common sources and applications. Not all accounts in the ledger need to be examined for source and application data. Adequate information about current asset accounts and current liability accounts is available in the balance sheet. As a matter of convenience in discussion, the term "noncurrent" will be employed to refer generally to all other asset and liability accounts.

Source of funds

Transactions that bring working capital into an enterprise are sources of funds. It is not necessary to review the journals or source documents and classify every transaction that occurred during the year to determine these sources. It is also unnecessary to determine the individual effects of a number of transactions of a similar nature. For purposes of discussion, source of funds transactions may be categorized in accordance with their three principal effects on noncurrent accounts as (1) decreases in noncurrent assets, (2) increases in noncurrent liabilities, and (3) increases in stockholders' equity.

Decreases in noncurrent assets. The sale of long-term investments, equipment, buildings, land, patents, or other noncurrent assets represents sources of funds. However, the amount of funds provided by the sale of a noncurrent asset is not necessarily the same as the amount of the credit to the account. For example, if a patent with a book value of $20,000 was sold during the year for $50,000, the funds provided by the sale amounted to $50,000 but the patents account decreased by only $20,000. Similarly, if long-term investments carried in the ledger at $100,000 at the beginning of the year were sold for $75,000, the transaction was the source of funds amounting to $75,000, rather than $100,000.

Increases in noncurrent liabilities. The issuance of bonds or long-term notes is a common source of funds. For example, if a $500,000 issue of bonds is sold at 100 during the year, the amount of funds provided by the transaction would be indicated by the $500,000 increase in the bonds payable account. If the bonds were not issued at face value, the accompanying increase in a bond premium or bond discount account would also need to be given consideration. For example, if the issuance price had been 90, the funds provided would have been $450,000.

It was assumed in the example that the bonds were issued in exchange for cash. If they had been issued in exchange for noncurrent assets, such as land, building, or equipment, the working capital would not have been affected and, from a purely technical viewpoint, the transaction would not have needed to be reported in the funds statement. The effect of a transaction of this type is sufficiently significant, however, to justify a broadening of the funds concept. It would be preferable to treat the single transaction as though there had been two transactions: first, the issuance of the bonds as a source of funds; and second, the application of the funds for the acquisition of the property.

Increases in stockholders' equity. Often the most important and the most frequently recurring source of funds is profitable operations. Revenue from sales of commodities or services is accompanied by increases in working capital, and many of the expenses are accompanied by decreases in working capital. Inasmuch as the significant details of revenue and expenses are presented in the income statement, only the net effect needs to be reported in the funds statement. However, the final net income figure is not necessarily the sole measure of the net funds provided by operations. Such expenses as depreciation of plant assets and amortization of patents and such revenue as amortization of discount on investment in bonds affect noncurrent accounts rather than current accounts and hence have no effect on working capital. The net income reported in the income statement must therefore be adjusted upward or downward to determine the amount of funds provided by operations.

If capital stock is sold during the period, the amount of funds provided will not necessarily be equal to the increase in the capital stock account; consideration must also be given to accompanying debits or credits to other paid-in capital accounts. Issuance of a stock dividend affects only stockholders' equity accounts and has no effect on funds.

Application of funds

As in the case of fund sources, it is convenient to classify the applications of funds according to their effects on noncurrent accounts. The outflow or application of funds may be classified as (1) increases in noncurrent assets, (2) decreases in noncurrent liabilities, and (3) decreases in stockholders' equity.

Increases in noncurrent assets. Funds may be applied to the purchase of equipment, buildings, land, long-term investments, patents, or other noncurrent assets. However, the amount of funds used for such purposes is not necessarily indicated by the net increases in the related accounts. For example, if the debits to the equipment account for acquisitions during the year totaled $100,000 and the credits to the same account for disposals amounted to $25,000, the net change in the account would be $75,000. Such facts can be determined only by reviewing the details in the account.

Decreases in noncurrent liabilities. The liquidation of bonds or long-term notes represents an application of funds. The amount of funds applied would be indicated by the decrease in the balance of the liability account if the face value was paid at maturity. If the obligations were redeemed prior to maturity, it would be necessary to consider any unamortized premium or discount as well as any gain or loss on the transaction.

Decreases in stockholders' equity. Probably the most frequent application of funds in reduction of stockholders' equity results from the declaration of cash dividends. Funds may also be applied to the redemption of preferred stock or the purchase of treasury stock. Appropriations of retained earnings or other transfers among stockholders' equity accounts have no effect on funds.

Assembling data for the funds statement

Much of the information on funds flow is obtained by the accountant in the process of preparing the balance sheet, the income statement, and the retained earnings statement. Working papers for the preparation of the funds statement may be used but are not necessary. Because of their complexity and the tendency of their use to obscure the basic concepts of funds analysis, special working papers will not be employed in this book.

The following paragraphs illustrate the assembling of data for the funds statement of the Bowman Corporation. The information is obtained from (1) the company's comparative balance sheet and (2) the noncurrent asset and liability accounts and the stockholders' equity accounts in the ledger. The comparative balance sheet in simplified form appears on the following page. The ledger accounts are presented as the individual items are discussed. Descriptive notations inserted in the ledger accounts are to facilitate the explanations; in practice it might be necessary to refer back to the journals in order to ascertain the complete effect of some of the transactions.

Bowman Corporation
Comparative Balance Sheet
December 31, 1966 and 1965

	1966	1965	Increase Decrease*
Assets			
Cash	$ 48,000	$ 22,000	$26,000
Trade receivables (net)	68,000	65,000	3,000
Inventories	171,000	180,000	9,000*
Prepaid expenses	2,000	3,000	1,000*
Equipment	107,000	88,000	19,000
Accumulated depreciation — equipment	(41,000)	(40,000)	(1,000)
Building	100,000	100,000	—
Accumulated depreciation — building	(34,000)	(30,000)	(4,000)
Land	4,000	10,000	6,000*
Total assets	$425,000	$398,000	$27,000
Liabilities			
Accounts payable	$ 41,000	$ 31,000	$10,000
Dividends payable	5,000	3,000	2,000
Bonds payable	80,000	100,000	20,000*
Total liabilities	$126,000	$134,000	$ 8,000*
Stockholders' equity			
Common stock	$200,000	$200,000	—
Retained earnings	99,000	64,000	$35,000
Total stockholders' equity	$299,000	$264,000	$35,000
Total liabilities and stockholders' equity	$425,000	$398,000	$27,000

Comparative balance sheet

Inasmuch as only the noncurrent accounts reveal sources and applications of funds, it is not necessary to examine the current asset and current liability accounts. The first of the noncurrent accounts listed on the comparative balance sheet of the Bowman Corporation is Equipment.

Equipment. The comparative balance sheet indicates that the cost of equipment increased $19,000. The equipment account and the accumulated depreciation account illustrated on the opposite page reveal that the net change of $19,000 resulted from the discarding of equipment costing $8,000 and the buying of equipment for $27,000. The equipment discarded was fully depreciated and no salvage was realized; therefore, that transaction had no effect on working capital and no effect on the amount of net income reported. (Depreciation will be discussed in a later paragraph.) If items to be reported on the funds statement are being assembled in memorandum fashion, the following notation may be made:

Application of funds:
Purchase of equipment $27,000

EQUIPMENT

DATE		ITEMS	DEBIT	CREDIT	BALANCE	
					DEBIT	CREDIT
1966						
Jan.	1	Balance			88,000	
May	9	Discarded, no salvage		8,000		
July	7	Purchased	27,000		107,000	

ACCUMULATED DEPRECIATION — EQUIPMENT

DATE		ITEMS	DEBIT	CREDIT	BALANCE	
					DEBIT	CREDIT
1966.						
Jan.	1	Balance				40,000
May	9	Discarded, no salvage	8,000			
Dec.	31	Depreciation for year		9,000		41,000

Building. According to the comparative balance sheet, there were no changes in the cost of the building during the year. This is confirmed by examination of the ledger account. The building account is therefore not included in the data for the funds statement.

Land. The comparative balance sheet indicates a $6,000 decrease in land. The land account, however, reveals that land costing $6,000 was sold for $18,000. (The gain of $12,000 will be discussed in a later paragraph.) The notation is therefore as follows:

Source of funds:
Sale of land $18,000

LAND

DATE		ITEMS	DEBIT	CREDIT	BALANCE	
					DEBIT	CREDIT
1966						
Jan.	1	Balance			10,000	
Apr.	10	Sold for $18,000		6,000	4,000	

Bonds payable. Bonds payable, the next noncurrent item on the balance sheet, decreased $20,000. Examination of the bonds payable account, which appears at the top of the following page, indicates that bonds payable amounting to $20,000 were purchased at face value. The effect of the transaction on funds was:

Application of funds:
Retirement of bonds $20,000

BONDS PAYABLE

DATE		ITEMS	DEBIT	CREDIT	BALANCE	
					DEBIT	CREDIT
1966						
Jan.	1	Balance				100,000
June	30	Purchased at face value	20,000			80,000

Common stock. The comparative balance sheet and the ledger account Common Stock indicate that this account remained unchanged.

Retained earnings. According to the comparative balance sheet, the retained earnings account increased $35,000. Examination of the ledger account, which is reproduced below, reveals that the account was debited for cash dividends of $10,000. The effect of the declaration of cash dividends on funds was as follows:

Application of funds:
Declaration of cash dividends............ $10,000

Although the $45,000 credited to the retained earnings account may appear to be the measure of funds provided by net income, some adjustments are required. In the examination of the land account, it was observed that land was sold at a profit of $12,000. The $12,000 was included in the $18,000 to be reported as funds from this source and therefore must be excluded when the net income is considered as a source of funds. The net income exclusive of the gain on sale of land is therefore $33,000 ($45,000 – $12,000), which is a source of funds.

Depreciation of equipment and building, together with other expenses, was deducted from revenue in determining net income. The amount of depreciation expense on the equipment, as indicated by the accumulated depreciation account presented earlier, was $9,000. Depreciation expense on the building, as indicated by the increase in the accumulated depreciation account reported in the comparative balance sheet, was $4,000. These amounts, totaling $13,000, did not require the application of funds during the period and must therefore be added back to net income to determine the total funds provided by operations. The effect of operations on funds may be noted as follows:

Source of funds:
Operations:
Net income, exclusive of gain on sale of land... $33,000
Depreciation on equipment and building..... 13,000 $46,000

RETAINED EARNINGS

DATE		ITEMS	DEBIT	CREDIT	BALANCE	
					DEBIT	CREDIT
1966						
Jan.	1	Balance				64,000
June	30	Cash dividend	5,000			
Dec.	31	Cash dividend	5,000			
	31	Net income		45,000		99,000

Form of the funds statement

Although there are many possible variations in the form and the content of the funds statement, it is customary to present the source of funds first and to present net income as the first item in the section. The other data are generally listed in the order of importance as indicated by the magnitude of the amounts. It is also common practice to present comparative data for the preceding year or for a series of years. A funds statement for the Bowman Corporation is illustrated below.

Bowman Corporation
Statement of Source and Application of Funds
For Year Ended December 31, 1966

Source of funds:			
Operations:			
Net income, exclusive of gain on sale of land	$ 33,000		
Add expenses not requiring funds:			
Depreciation on equipment and building	13,000	$ 46,000	
Sale of land		18,000	$64,000
Application of funds:			
Purchase of equipment		$ 27,000	
Retirement of bonds		20,000	
Declaration of cash dividends		10,000	57,000
Increase in working capital			$ 7,000

Schedule of changes in working capital:

	December 31 1966	December 31 1965	Working Capital Increase or Decrease*
Cash	$ 48,000	$ 22,000	$26,000
Trade receivables (net)	68,000	65,000	3,000
Inventories	171,000	180,000	9,000*
Prepaid expenses	2,000	3,000	1,000*
Accounts payable	41,000	31,000	10,000*
Dividends payable	5,000	3,000	2,000*
Increase in working capital			$ 7,000

Funds statement

Changes in working capital. The difference between the totals of the source section and the application section of the funds statement is identified as the increase or the decrease in working capital. The statement may conclude with this final amount, or the change in working capital may be supported by a schedule such as that appearing in the illustration. The two amounts reported as the increase or the decrease in working capital must obviously agree. Data for the schedule of changes are easily obtained from the comparative balance sheet.

Flow of funds from operations

A relatively recent development in financial analysis is termed *flow of funds from operations* or *cash flow*. As an examination of the accompanying illustration will reveal, it is concerned only with net income and adjustments thereto for revenues and expenses that had no effect on working capital. The use of the term "cash flow" is inaccurate because cash is not the equivalent of working capital.

Sawyer Manufacturing Company
Statement of Flow of Funds from Operations
For Year Ended December 31, 1966

Net income per income statement		$177,714
Add expenses not requiring funds:		
Depreciation	$97,642	
Amortization of patents	30,000	127,642
		$305,356
Deduct revenues not providing funds:		
Amortization of discount on long-term investments		15,000
Flow of funds from operations		$290,356

Statement of flow of funds from operations

This type of analysis is useful to internal financial management in considering the possibility of retiring long-term debt, in planning the replacement of plant facilities, and in formulating dividend policies. When it is employed in reports to stockholders, however, it is very likely to be misunderstood. This is particularly so if the amount of funds flow from operations, which may be substantially greater than net income, is divided by the number of shares of stock and the resulting amount is referred to as the "cash flow," "cash earnings," or "cash throw-off" per share. The reader may erroneously believe that the so-called "cash earnings" is superior to net income as a measure of earning power.

Parent and subsidiary corporations

The history of business organization in this country is characterized by the expansion of operations and the combining of separate but complementary enterprises to form larger operating units. Major motivating influences on such growth and diversification are increased efficiency of large-scale operations, reduction of competition, and improvement in product, with resulting maximization of profits.

One of the organizational devices frequently employed in expanding operations is the ownership by one corporation of a controlling interest in one or more other corporations. The corporation owning all or a majority of the voting stock of another corporation is known as the *parent* company and the corporation that is controlled is known as the *subsidiary* company. A corporation that controls a number of subsidiaries and confines its activities primarily to their management is sometimes called a *holding* company. Although each corporation maintains its separate legal identity, the relationship between parent and subsidiary is somewhat like that between the home office of an enterprise and one of its branch offices. Two or more corporations closely related through stock ownership are sometimes referred to as *affiliated* companies.

The investment in the stock of a subsidiary company is reported on the parent company's balance sheet as a long-term investment, and its share of the subsidiary's earnings is reported on the parent's income statement. Earnings of the subsidiary retained by it increase the parent company's investment, and distributions of earnings through dividends decrease the investment. Other intercorporate transactions that may affect the financial statements of the parent include purchase of one company's bonds or notes by the other and the sale and purchase of commodities and services between them. Because of this close relationship, it is often considered desirable to combine the statements of the parent and the subsidiary to form composite reports on the financial condition and operations of the related companies. Such statements are referred to generally as *consolidated statements*; specifically the statement title is modified by adding the term "consolidated," as in *consolidated balance sheet* or *consolidated income statement.*

Basic principles of consolidation

The basic principles applicable to the consolidation of the statements of a parent corporation and its subsidiaries are similar to those described earlier for combining the statements of a home office and its branch offices. The ties of relationship between the separate corporations are evidenced by the reciprocal accounts appearing in their respective ledgers and financial statements. It is necessary to eliminate these reciprocals from the statements that are to be consolidated. The remaining items on the subsidiary's financial statement are then combined with the like items on the financial statement of the parent.

The complexity of the problems encountered in determining the eliminations varies greatly, being influenced by the manner in which the parent-subsidiary relationship was created, the extent of the parent corporation's ownership of the subsidiary, and the nature of their continuing transactions with each other. If the parent corporation creates the subsidiary, holds all of its stock, and does not buy commodities or services from or sell them to the subsidiary, their financial statements can be consolidated with a minimum of difficulty. On the other hand,

If the parent corporation acquires control of an already existing company by purchasing less than 100% of its stock and engages in profit-making activities with the subsidiary, the consolidation of their statements may present intricate problems. Only the underlying principles will be discussed here and only situations of widest applicability will be used in the illustrations.

Consolidated balance sheet

The stock of a subsidiary acquired by the parent is recorded in an investment account in the parent company's ledger. The reciprocal of the investment account in the subsidiary's ledger at the date of acquisition is the composite of all of its stockholders' equity accounts. Attention will first be directed to consolidating the balance sheets immediately after the relationship of parent and subsidiary has been established. The illustrative companies will be identified merely as Parent and Subsidiary.

Consolidation at time of acquisition. To facilitate explanations, the term "book value" will be used in referring to the composite amount of the subsidiary stockholders' equity accounts and the term "net assets" will be substituted for the specific assets (Cash, Accounts Receivable, etc.) and the specific liabilities (Accounts Payable, etc.) that appear on the respective balance sheets.

Wholly owned subsidiary acquired at cost equal to book value. Assume that Parent creates Subsidiary, transferring to it $100,000 of net assets and taking in exchange 1,000 shares of $100 par common stock of Subsidiary. The effect of the transaction on Parent is to replace net assets of $100,000 with a single item: Investment in Subsidiary, $100,000. This effect on the balance sheet of Parent, together with the balance sheet of Subsidiary prepared immediately after the transaction, is depicted below.

	Assets	Capital
Parent:		
Investment in Subsidiary, 1,000 shares	$100,000	
Subsidiary:		
Net assets	$100,000	
Common stock, 1,000 shares		$100,000

In consolidating the balance sheets of the two corporations, the reciprocal accounts Investment in Subsidiary and Common Stock are offset against each other, or eliminated. The net assets of $100,000 on the balance sheet of Subsidiary are then added to the comparable accounts appearing on the balance sheet of Parent, and the resulting statement is the consolidated balance sheet.

Wholly owned subsidiary acquired at cost above or below book value. Instead of organizing a subsidiary corporation to develop a new product or territory, a corporation may acquire an established business by purchasing the stock of an existing company. In such cases the cost of the stock to the parent company ordinarily differs from the book value of the stock. To illustrate, assume that Parent acquires all of the outstanding stock of Subsidiary, which is represented by 1,000 shares of $100 par common. The stock is purchased from the stockholders of Subsidiary at a total cost of $130,000, and the book value of the stock is $150,000. The situation immediately after the transaction may be presented as:

	Assets	Capital
Parent:		
Investment in Subsidiary, 1,000 shares	$130,000	
Subsidiary:		
Net assets	$150,000	
Common stock, 1,000 shares		$100,000
Retained earnings		50,000

It is readily apparent that the reciprocal items on the separate balance sheets are unequal by the amount of $20,000. If the reciprocal items are eliminated and are replaced on the consolidated balance sheet solely by the $150,000 of net assets of Subsidiary, the total assets reported will exceed the total equities by $20,000. Therefore, the balancing amount of $20,000 must be reported on the consolidated balance sheet, usually as the last item in the liabilities section. It is identified as "Excess of book value of subsidiary interest over cost." When the reverse of the relationship between cost and book value illustrated above occurs, the difference between the two accounts is described as "Excess of cost over book value of subsidiary interest." It is reported in the assets section of the consolidated balance sheet, frequently as the last item.

Partially owned subsidiary acquired at cost above or below book value. When one corporation seeks to achieve control over another by purchase of its stock, it is not necessary and often not feasible to acquire all of the stock. To illustrate, assume that Parent acquires 80% of the 1,000 shares of $100 par common stock of Subsidiary that have a book value of $190,000. The 800 shares are purchased from the stockholders of Subsidiary at a total cost of $180,000. The relevant data immediately after the acquisition of the stock is presented below.

	Assets	Capital
Parent:		
Investment in Subsidiary, 800 shares	$180,000	
Subsidiary:		
Net assets	$190,000	
Common stock, 1,000 shares		$100,000
Retained earnings		90,000

The explanation of the inequality of the reciprocal items is less apparent than in the preceding illustration. Inasmuch as Investment in Subsidiary on Parent's balance sheet is a claim to only 80% of Subsidiary, it is only that portion of the stockholders' equity accounts reported on Subsidiary's balance sheet that can be eliminated. The remaining 20% of the stock is owned by outsiders, commonly referred to as the *minority interest*, and must be reported on the consolidated balance sheet, frequently as the first item in the stockholders' equity section. The disposition of Subsidiary's common stock and retained earnings for purposes of the consolidated balance sheet is therefore as follows:

Total stockholders' equity of Subsidiary	$190,000	
Eliminate 80% owned by Parent	152,000	
Minority interest		$38,000

The difference between the amount paid by Parent for the stock of Subsidiary and the book value of the interest acquired is reported in the assets section of the consolidated balance sheet. Details are as follows:

Investment in Subsidiary	$180,000	
Eliminate 80% of Subsidiary's stockholders' equity	152,000	
Excess of cost over book value of subsidiary interest		$28,000

It should be noted that the $152,000 elimination against the capital of Subsidiary is exactly matched by the $152,000 elimination against the investment of Parent.

Consolidation subsequent to acquisition. The net income of a subsidiary corporation increases its net assets and its retained earnings account. The parent company may give formal recognition to its share of the subsidiary's earnings subsequent to acquisition by annually debiting the account Investment in Subsidiary and crediting Income of Subsidiary. The latter account is then closed as a part of the usual periodic summary, and the parent's retained earnings account is increased accordingly. When dividends are declared and paid by the subsidiary company, the parent company debits Cash and credits Investment in Subsidiary for the amount received.

In preparing consolidated balance sheets subsequent to acquisition, the amount eliminated from Investment in Subsidiary on the parent's balance sheet and from the stockholders' equity accounts on the subsidiary's balance sheet will change each year, keeping pace with the changes in the balance of the subsidiary's retained earnings. For example, if the parent owns 90% of the stock of its subsidiary, 90% of the subsidiary's stock and retained earnings accounts will be eliminated. The amount originally determined as the difference between the cost and the book value of the subsidiary interest will, of course, remain unchanged, but the amount of the minority interest will continue to be equal to 10% of the stockholders' equity accounts of the subsidiary.

Ordinarily the activities of a subsidiary company complement those of its parent; but even when this is not the case, it is likely that the two will engage in transactions with each other. Any intercompany receivables and payables reported on their individual balance sheets should be fully eliminated from the consolidated balance sheet. If commodities sold by either of the related companies to the other are still on hand at the balance sheet date, all or part of the gross profit realized by the selling company should also be eliminated from the consolidated balance sheet. These and other complex matters go beyond the scope of the discussion here; they are mentioned in order to indicate the many ramifications of transactions between affiliated companies.

Consolidated income statement and other statements

The consolidation of the income statement and other statements of affiliated companies usually presents fewer complexities than are encountered in balance sheet consolidations. The difference is largely because of the inherent nature of the statements. The balance sheet reports cumulative effects of all transactions from the very beginning of an enterprise to a current date, whereas the income statement, the retained earnings statement, and the funds statement are restricted to selected transactions only and are for a limited period of time, usually a year.

In consolidating the income statements of a parent and its wholly or partly owned subsidiary, the amount of sales, purchases, interest income, interest expense, management fee revenue, management fee expense, and all similar operating data resulting from intercompany transactions should be fully eliminated. It may also be necessary to eliminate intercompany gross profit from beginning and ending inventories in determining consolidated gross profit. The eliminations required in consolidating the retained earnings statement and any other statements are based largely on data assembled in consolidating the balance sheet and the income statement.

Alternative forms of principal financial statements[1]

Conventional forms of the principal financial statements have been described and illustrated in earlier chapters. There are many possible

[1]A selection of corporation financial statements, including examples of the alternative forms described in this section, is presented in Appendix C.

variations in terminology, amount of condensation, and general format of such statements. Several recent innovations in form are sufficiently important to warrant illustration and a brief discussion.

Financial position form of balance sheet. The *financial position* form of balance sheet emphasizes the working capital position of an enterprise by deducting current liabilities from current assets. The illustration below was severely condensed to focus attention on its principal features. Such condensation is not an essential characteristic of the form.

Electronic Products, Inc.
Statement of Financial Position
September 30, 1966

Current assets		$420,600
Deduct:		
Current liabilities		180,400
Working capital		$240,200
Add:		
Investments	$150,000	
Plant assets (net)	522,300	672,300
Total assets less current liabilities		$912,500
Deduct:		
Long-term liabilities		200,000
Net assets		$712,500
Stockholders' equity:		
Common stock		$400,000
Retained earnings		312,500
Total stockholders' equity		$712,500

Financial position form of balance sheet

In addition to the specific disclosure of the amount of working capital, the financial position form presents the amount of the excess of total assets over current liabilities and the amount of the excess of total assets over total liabilities. The balancing amounts in the statement are thus the net assets and the total stockholders' equity. The principal advantage claimed for the financial position form is its emphasis on working capital, which is a significant factor in judging financial stability. A major criticism is its failure to present the total of the assets and the total of the liabilities. Readers are also likely to be less familiar with it than with the conventional form.

Single-step form of income statement. The *single-step* form of income statement gets its name from the fact that the total of all expenses is deducted from the total of all revenues. This is in contrast to the conventional multiple-step form, which contains a series of deductions and intermediate profit and income figures before arriving at the final amount, net income after income tax. A single-step form, greatly condensed, is illustrated below.

Electronic Products, Inc.
Income Statement
For Year Ended September 30, 1966

Revenue:		
Sales		$940,000
Interest income		27,500
Total revenue		$967,500
Expenses:		
Cost of merchandise sold	$530,000	
Selling expenses	146,800	
General expenses	120,400	
Interest expense	10,500	
Income tax	70,200	
Total expenses		877,900
Net income		$ 89,600

Single-step form of income statement

The single-step form has the advantage of simplicity and also emphasizes the two major determinants of net income. All expenses rank equally as deductions from revenue in arriving at the net income of the enterprise. In a frequently used variant, however, income taxes and nonrecurring items are presented in a separate last section. The objection to the single-step form is that such relationships as gross profit to sales and net operating income to sales are not as readily determinable as in the multiple-step form.

Combined income and retained earnings statement. It is not unusual to add the analysis of retained earnings at the bottom of the income statement to form a *combined* income and retained earnings statement. The income statement portion of the combined statement may be presented either in multiple-step form or in single-step form as in the illustration at the top of the following page.

The combined statement form emphasizes net income as the connecting link between the income statement and the retained earnings portion of the stockholders' equity and thus facilitates understanding by the reader. A possible criticism of the combined statement is the fact that net income, a very significant figure, is buried in the body of the statement. If a portion of retained earnings is appropriated for various purposes, or if there have been other increases or decreases of an unusual nature, separate statements may be preferable.

Electronic Products, Inc.
Income and Retained Earnings Statement
For Year Ended September 30, 1966

Revenue:		
Sales		$940,000
Interest income		27,500
Total revenue		$967,500
Expenses:		
Cost of merchandise sold	$530,000	
Selling expenses	146,800	
General expenses	120,400	
Interest expense	10,500	
Income tax	70,200	
Total expenses		877,900
Net income		$ 89,600
Retained earnings, October 1, 1965		262,900
		$352,500
Less dividends		40,000
Retained earnings, September 30, 1966		$312,500

Combined income and retained earnings statement

QUESTIONS

1. When used in the singular form, *fund* may mean (a) cash or (b) a combination of cash and investments. Give an example of each usage.

2. What is meant by *funds* as the term is employed in the funds statement?

3. (a) What is meant by *working capital*? (b) Name another term, other than "funds," that has the same meaning.

4. State the effect of each of the following transactions, considered individually, on working capital:

(a) Borrowed $50,000 cash, issuing a 60-day interest-bearing note.
(b) Issued a $4,000, 30-day note to a creditor in temporary settlement of an account payable.
(c) Sold for $100 cash merchandise that had cost $70.
(d) Received $200 from a customer in payment of his account.
(e) Issued 5,000 shares of common stock for $10 a share, receiving cash.
(f) Purchased office equipment for $2,000 on account.

5. What is the effect on working capital of writing off $5,000 of uncollectible accounts against Allowance for Doubtful Accounts?

6. Give examples of (a) noncurrent asset accounts and (b) noncurrent liability accounts.

7. A corporation issued $1,000,000 of 20-year bonds for cash at 105. Was this a source or an application of funds and what was the amount?

8. Office equipment with a cost of $10,000 and accumulated depreciation of $9,500 was sold for $1,000 cash. (a) What was the gain or loss on the sale? (b) What was the effect of the transaction on working capital? (c) How would the transaction be reported in the funds statement?

9. The board of directors declared a cash dividend in December of the fiscal year ending December 31, payable on January 10. (a) What was the effect of the declaration on working capital? (b) Did the declaration represent a source or an application of funds? (c) Did the payment of the dividend in January affect working capital, and, if so, how?

10. (a) What is the effect on working capital of the declaration and issuance of a stock dividend? (b) Does it represent a source or an application of funds?

11. The income statement reports a net loss of $15,000. The only revenue or expense item not affecting funds was $7,000 of depreciation expense for the year. Will "operations" appear in the source section or the application section of the funds statement, and at what amount?

12. The Bowen Corporation wrote off $4,000 of organization costs to retained earnings. (a) What was the effect on working capital? (b) Would the write-off be reported in the funds statement?

13. Why is depreciation expense for the year added to reported net income in arriving at the amount of funds provided by operations?

14. Parent Corporation transferred $1,000,000 of assets to its newly created subsidiary, receiving shares of common stock in return. The effect of the transaction on the books of Subsidiary Corporation was as follows, expressed in the form of a general journal entry:

Assets.	1,000,000	
Common Stock, no-par.		800,000
Premium on Common Stock		200,000

Name the reciprocal items that would be eliminated in preparing a consolidated balance sheet immediately after the issuance of the stock to Parent Corporation.

15. Are entries ever made in the ledger of (a) the parent corporation or (b) the subsidiary corporation for the eliminations used in preparing the consolidated statements?

16. Assume that the amount paid by a parent corporation for the stock of a subsidiary is either more or less than the book value of the subsidiary interest.

(a) If the cost exceeds the book value:
   (1) Where will the amount be reported on the consolidated balance sheet?
   (2) How should the amount be described on the consolidated balance sheet?

(b) If the book value exceeds the cost:
   (1) Where will the amount be reported on the consolidated balance sheet?
   (2) How should the amount be described on the consolidated balance sheet?

17. If a parent corporation owns 90% of the outstanding stock of a subsidiary, (a) what is the term applied to the remaining 10% and (b) where is it reported on the consolidated balance sheet?

18. Does the amount reported on the consolidated balance sheet as the difference between the cost and the book value of the subsidiary interest vary from year to year in accordance with the amount of income earned and retained by the subsidiary? Explain.

19. At the end of the year, cash dividends payable of $50,000 appear on the balance sheet of a corporation that is 80% owned by another corporation. (a) What reciprocal item (title and amount) should appear on the balance sheet of the parent corporation as of the same date? (b) What, if any, is the amount of the elimination required in preparing a consolidated balance sheet? (c) Assuming that the parent corporation lists $200,000 of dividends payable on its balance sheet at the same date, what amount should be reported as dividends payable on the consolidated balance sheet?

20. Sales and purchases of commodities for resale by a parent corporation and its wholly owned subsidiary during the year were as follows:

	Parent	Subsidiary
Sales	$2,000,000	$500,000
Purchases	1,200,000	300,000

If 10% of the sales of the parent corporation were to its subsidiary, what eliminations should be made in preparing the consolidated income statement?

21. At the end of the year, a wholly owned subsidiary has an inventory of $100,000, all of which had been purchased from the parent corporation. (a) Assuming that the parent corporation's gross profit rate is 30%, what amount should be eliminated from the inventory in preparing the consolidated statements? (b) What other item on the consolidated balance sheet will be affected by the elimination?

22. What relationships between assets and liabilities are emphasized in the financial position form of balance sheet?

EXERCISES

1. On the basis of the following information taken from the comparative balance sheet of Morton Corporation, prepare the section of the funds statement devoted to changes in working capital.

	December 31	
	1966	1965
Cash	$ 30,000	$ 25,000
Accounts receivable (net)	47,000	54,000
Notes receivable (short term)	8,000	14,000
Inventories	139,000	143,000
Prepaid expenses	2,500	2,100
Accounts payable	30,500	33,900
Salaries payable	3,600	6,600

2. The net income, after income taxes, reported on the income statement of Robeson's, Incorporated for the current year was $90,700. Adjustments to be made to net income to determine the amount of funds provided by operations, as well as some other data used for the year-end adjusting entries, are described below. Prepare the source of funds provided by operations section of the funds statement.

(a) Depreciation expense, $24,500.
(b) Uncollectible accounts expense, $2,800.
(c) Amortization of patents, $3,500.
(d) Interest accrued on notes receivable, $400.
(e) Income tax payable, $70,300.
(f) Wages accrued but not paid, $1,900.

3. Details of the stockholders' equity accounts of Boulder Industrial Corporation for the current fiscal year are presented below. List the sources and the applications of funds (exclusive of net income), together with their respective amounts, revealed by the accounts.

COMMON STOCK, $10 PAR

DATE		ITEMS	DEBIT	CREDIT	BALANCE DEBIT	BALANCE CREDIT
19—						
Jan.	1	Balance, 20,000 shares				200,000
July	1	5,000 shares issued for cash		50,000		250,000
Dec.	31	2,500 share stock dividend		25,000		275,000

PREMIUM ON COMMON STOCK

DATE		ITEMS	DEBIT	CREDIT	BALANCE DEBIT	BALANCE CREDIT
19—						
Jan.	1	Balance				20,000
July	1	5,000 shares issued		25,000		45,000
Dec.	31	Stock dividend		20,000		65,000

RETAINED EARNINGS

DATE		ITEMS	DEBIT	CREDIT	BALANCE DEBIT	BALANCE CREDIT
19—						
Jan.	1	Balance				110,000
June	30	Cash dividend	10,000			100,000
Dec.	31	Cash dividend	12,500			87,500
	31	Stock dividend	45,000			42,500
	31	Organization costs	5,000			37,500
	31	Net income		122,500		160,000

4. On the basis of the following data for Jackson Company, prepare a funds statement, omitting the schedule of changes in working capital. Assume that no items of equipment were disposed of during the year, that the stock was issued for cash, and that the only entries in the retained earnings account were for net income of $25,000 and cash dividends of $20,000.

	June 30 1966	June 30 1965
Cash	$ 20,000	$ 25,000
Inventories	92,000	70,000
Equipment	130,000	100,000
Accumulated depreciation	(55,000)	(40,000)
Land	60,000	50,000
	$247,000	$205,000
Accounts payable	$ 42,000	$ 60,000
Common stock, $10 par	150,000	100,000
Premium on common stock	5,000	—
Retained earnings	50,000	45,000
	$247,000	$205,000

5. On the last day of the fiscal year, Price Company acquired 90% of the common stock of Sullivan Company for $480,000, at which time Sullivan Company reported the following on its balance sheet: assets, $740,000; liabilities, $180,000; common stock, $5 par, $400,000; retained earnings, $160,000.

(a) In preparing a consolidated balance sheet as of the date of acquisition, where and in what amounts will the following be reported:
  (1) Difference between cost and book value of subsidiary interest.
  (2) Minority interest.

(b) During the following year Price Company realized net income of $900,000, exclusive of the income of the subsidiary, and Sullivan Company realized net income of $200,000. In preparing a consolidated income statement for the year, in what amounts would the following be reported:
  (1) Minority interest's share of net income.
  (2) Consolidated net income.

6. On December 31 of the current year, Perry Company purchased 90% of the stock of Shaw Company. The data reported on their separate balance sheets immediately after the acquisition are reported below. Prepare a consolidated balance sheet as of that date, in report form, omitting captions for current assets, plant assets, etc.

Assets	Perry Company	Shaw Company
Cash	$ 37,000	$ 15,000
Accounts receivable (net)	53,000	35,000
Inventories	199,000	60,000
Investment in Shaw Company	240,000	—
Equipment (net)	440,000	170,000
	$969,000	$280,000
Liabilities and stockholders' equity		
Accounts payable	$ 90,000	$ 27,000
Common stock, $10 par	500,000	200,000
Retained earnings	379,000	53,000
	$969,000	$280,000

7. Summary financial data for the Tabor Corporation at December 31 of the current year are as follows: common stock, $300,000; current assets, $340,000; current liabilities, $135,000; investments, $70,000; long-term liabilities, $100,000; plant assets (net) $240,000; and retained earnings, $115,000. Prepare a financial position form of balance sheet.

8. Summary operating data for the R. D. Cooper Company during the current year ending December 31 are as follows: cost of goods sold, $355,000; general expenses, $82,000; income tax, $31,000; interest expense, $5,000; rent income, $16,000; sales, $620,000; and selling expenses, $115,000. Prepare a single-step income statement.

PROBLEMS

27-1. The comparative balance sheet of the Dexter Corporation at June 30, 1966 and 1965, appears below in condensed form.

	June 30	
Assets	1966	1965
Cash	$ 17,400	$ 28,400
Accounts receivable (net)	21,600	33,200
Merchandise inventory	99,100	104,000
Prepaid expenses	2,800	2,960
Plant assets	216,000	170,000
Accumulated depreciation — plant assets	(64,000)	(94,000)
	$292,900	$244,560
Liabilities and stockholders' equity		
Accounts payable	$ 46,900	$ 22,280
Mortgage note payable	—	50,000
Common stock, $10 par	210,000	140,000
Discount on common stock	(14,000)	—
Retained earnings	50,000	32,280
	$292,900	$244,560

Additional data obtained from the income statement and from an examination of the noncurrent asset, noncurrent liability, and stockholders' equity accounts in the ledger are as follows:

(a) Net income for the year, $30,320.
(b) Depreciation expense for the year, $10,000.
(c) Cash dividends declared during the year, $12,600.
(d) The mortgage note payable was due in 1970, but the terms permitted earlier payment without penalty.
(e) An addition to the building was constructed during the year at a cost of $86,000, and fully depreciated equipment costing $40,000 was discarded, no salvage being realized.
(f) During the year 7,000 shares of common stock were issued for cash at $8.

Instructions: (1) On the basis of the comparative balance sheet and the other information, assemble in memorandum form the data needed to prepare a funds statement for the year ended June 30, 1966.

(2) Prepare a statement of source and application of funds, including a schedule of changes in working capital.

27-2. Parker Corporation purchased 80% of the outstanding stock of Sloan Company for $500,000. Balance sheet data for the two corporations immediately after the transaction, which occurred on May 31 of the current year, are presented below. The interest receivable reported on Sloan Co. balance sheet is the accrual on the bond investment.

Assets	Parker Corp.	Sloan Co.
Cash and marketable securities	$ 117,000	$ 66,000
Accounts receivable	96,000	72,600
Allowance for doubtful accounts	(2,000)	(1,500)
Interest receivable	—	2,500
Inventories	475,500	168,300
Investment in Sloan Company stock, 48,000 shares	500,000	—
Investment in Parker Corporation bonds, face value	—	100,000
Equipment	984,900	332,600
Accumulated depreciation	(210,000)	(101,400)
	$1,961,400	$639,100
Liabilities and stockholders' equity		
Accounts payable	$ 186,400	$ 76,800
Income tax payable	95,600	45,300
Interest payable	12,500	—
Bonds payable (due in 1975)	500,000	—
Common stock, $10 par	800,000	—
Common stock, $5 par	—	300,000
Retained earnings	366,900	217,000
	$1,961,400	$639,100

Instructions: (1) Prepare in report form a detailed consolidated balance sheet as of May 31 of the current year.

(2) Assuming that Sloan Company earns net income of $100,000 and pays dividends of $30,000 during the ensuing year and that Parker Corporation records its share of the earnings and dividends, determine the following as of the end of the year:

(a) The amount at which the investment in Sloan Company will appear on Parker Corporation's balance sheet.

(b) The amount of the difference between the cost and the book value of the subsidiary interest owned by the parent corporation.

(c) The amount of the minority interest.

27-3. The balances in the accounts of Blanton's, Inc. after adjustment at October 31, the close of the current fiscal year, are as follows:

Accounts Payable		47,300
Accounts Receivable	52,300	
Accumulated Depreciation — Buildings		7,700
Accumulated Depreciation — Equipment		26,500
Allowance for Doubtful Accounts		2,600
Bond Sinking Fund	35,400	
Bonds Payable (due 1974)		80,000
Buildings	66,000	
Cash in Bank	37,500	
Common Stock, $5 par		200,000
Cost of Goods Sold	244,600	
Dividends Payable		5,000
Equipment	147,000	
General Expenses	33,960	
Income Tax	27,500	
Income Tax Payable		27,500
Interest Expense	3,500	
Interest Income		2,100
Inventories	162,200	
Land	35,000	
Prepaid Insurance	2,700	
Retained Earnings		96,560
Sales		389,800
Salaries Payable		1,500
Selling Expenses	38,900	
	886,560	886,560

Dividends debited to Retained Earnings during the year totaled $20,000; there were no other debits or credits to the account during the year.

Instructions: (1) Prepare a combined income and retained earnings statement using the single-step form.

(2) Prepare a detailed balance sheet in the financial position form.

27-4. The comparative balance sheet of Lahey, Inc. at December 31, 1966 and 1965, in condensed form, and the noncurrent asset accounts, the noncurrent liability accounts, and the stockholders' equity accounts for 1966 are as follows:

Assets	1966	1965
Cash	$ 63,650	$ 48,050
Accounts receivable (net)	89,220	67,610
Inventories	240,800	245,500
Prepaid expenses	6,750	5,850
Equipment	445,000	375,000
Accumulated depreciation — equipment	(82,000)	(72,000)
Buildings	380,750	240,750
Accumulated depreciation — buildings	(31,100)	(22,500)
Land	50,000	80,000
Goodwill	—	10,000
Discount on bonds payable	9,500	—
	$1,172,570	$978,260

Liabilities and stockholders' equity		
Accounts payable	$ 31,250	$ 88,700
Income tax payable	37,600	15,600
Bonds payable	200,000	—
Common stock	630,000	600,000
Premium on common stock	18,000	15,000
Retained earnings appropriated for contingencies	50,000	30,000
Retained earnings	205,720	228,960
	$1,172,570	$978,260

EQUIPMENT

Date		Items	Debit	Credit	Balance Debit	Balance Credit
1966						
Jan.	1	Balance			375,000	
Mar.	10	Discarded, no salvage		27,000		
Apr.	18	Purchased	52,000			
June	12	Purchased	16,000			
Nov.	26	Purchased	29,000		445,000	

ACCUMULATED DEPRECIATION — EQUIPMENT

Date		Items	Debit	Credit	Balance Debit	Balance Credit
1966						
Jan.	1	Balance				72,000
Mar.	10	Equipment discarded	27,000			
Dec.	31	Depreciation for year		37,000		82,000

BUILDINGS

Date		Items	Debit	Credit	Balance Debit	Balance Credit
1966						
Jan.	1	Balance			240,750	
Dec.	2	Purchased	140,000		380,750	

ACCUMULATED DEPRECIATION — BUILDINGS

Date		Items	Debit	Credit	Balance Debit	Balance Credit
1966						
Jan.	1	Balance				22,500
Dec.	31	Depreciation for year		8,600		31,100

LAND

Date		Items	Debit	Credit	Balance Debit	Balance Credit
1966						
Jan.	1	Balance			80,000	
July	24	Sold for $45,000		30,000	50,000	

GOODWILL

DATE		ITEMS	DEBIT	CREDIT	BALANCE	
					DEBIT	CREDIT
1966						
Jan.	1	Balance			10,000	
Dec.	31	Written off		10,000	—	—

DISCOUNT ON BONDS PAYABLE

DATE		ITEMS	DEBIT	CREDIT	BALANCE	
					DEBIT	CREDIT
1966						
July	1	Bonds issued	10,000		10,000	
Dec.	31	Amortization		500	9,500	

BONDS PAYABLE

DATE		ITEMS	DEBIT	CREDIT	BALANCE	
					DEBIT	CREDIT
1966						
July	1	Issued 10-year bonds		200,000		200,000

COMMON STOCK, $5 PAR

DATE		ITEMS	DEBIT	CREDIT	BALANCE	
					DEBIT	CREDIT
1966						
Jan.	1	Balance				600,000
Dec.	10	Stock dividend		30,000		630,000

PREMIUM ON COMMON STOCK

DATE		ITEMS	DEBIT	CREDIT	BALANCE	
					DEBIT	CREDIT
1966						
Jan.	1	Balance				15,000
Dec.	10	Stock dividend		3,000		18,000

RETAINED EARNINGS APPROPRIATED FOR CONTINGENCIES

DATE		ITEMS	DEBIT	CREDIT	BALANCE	
					DEBIT	CREDIT
1966						
Jan.	1	Balance				30,000
Dec.	31	Appropriation		20,000		50,000

RETAINED EARNINGS

DATE		ITEMS	DEBIT	CREDIT	BALANCE	
					DEBIT	CREDIT
1966						
Jan.	1	Balance				228,960
Apr.	1	Cash dividend	12,000			
Oct.	1	Cash dividend	12,000			
Dec.	10	Stock dividend	33,000			
	31	Goodwill	10,000			
	31	Appropriated	20,000			
	31	Net income		63,760		205,720

Instructions: (1) On the basis of the comparative balance sheet and the accounts of Lahey, Inc., assemble in memorandum form the data needed to prepare a funds statement for the year ended December 31, 1966. (Exclude from operating income the gain on the sale of land.)

(2) Prepare a statement of source and application of funds, including a schedule of changes in working capital.

27-5. Plaza Company acquired 18,000 of the 20,000 outstanding shares of stock of Savoy Corporation on November 30 four years ago for $145,080, at which time total capital of the latter was $220,000. Since the date of acquisition, Plaza Company has debited the investment account for its share of the subsidiary's earnings and has credited the account for dividends declared. Balance sheet data for the two corporations as of November 30 of the current year appear below. Savoy Corporation holds $50,000 of short-term notes of Plaza Company, on which there is accrued interest of $2,500. Savoy Corporation owes Plaza Co. $20,000 for a management advisory fee for the second half of the year. It has been recorded by both corporations in their respective accounts payable and accounts receivable accounts.

Assets	Plaza Co.	Savoy Corp.
Cash	$ 83,800	$ 64,000
Notes receivable	20,000	50,000
Accounts receivable	197,000	72,000
Interest receivable	1,200	2,500
Dividends receivable	9,000	—
Prepaid expenses	4,800	3,000
Inventories	218,600	165,000
Investment in Savoy Corp. stock, 18,000 shares.	310,500	—
Equipment	494,000	230,000
Accumulated depreciation	(162,000)	(73,000)
	$1,176,900	$513,500
Liabilities and stockholders' equity		
Notes payable	$ 60,000	—
Accounts payable	105,800	$ 61,300
Income tax payable	82,000	38,400
Dividends payable	25,000	10,000
Interest payable	3,000	—
Common stock, $50 par	500,000	—
Common stock, $10 par	—	200,000
Premium on common stock	—	50,000
Retained earnings	401,100	153,800
	$1,176,900	$513,500

Instructions: (1) Prepare in report form a detailed consolidated balance sheet as of November 30 of the current year.

(2) What was the amount of the excess of book value of the subsidiary interest over cost at the date of acquisition?

(3) What was the amount of the minority interest at the date of acquisition?

28.

Statement analysis

Need for analysis

The financial condition and the results of operations of business enterprises are of interest to various groups, including owners, managers, creditors, governmental agencies, employees, and prospective owners and creditors. The principal statements, together with supplementary statements and schedules, present much of the basic information needed to form opinions and to make decisions regarding the business.

Most of the items in these statements are of limited significance when considered individually. Users of financial statements often gain a clearer picture through studying relationships and comparisons between items. The selection and the preparation of analytical aids is a part of the work of the accountant.

It will be readily recognized that particular aspects of financial condition or of operations are of greater significance to some interested groups than to others. In general, the varying interests of all groups fall in three principal categories: (1) solvency, (2) profitability, and (3) stability.

Solvency refers to the company's ability to meet its debts as they come due. *Profitability* relates to the success that the firm has had in earning a return on the assets. The amount and the trend of these earnings and their relationship to the assets employed in the business are criteria of profitability. *Stability* is composed of several factors — a continued demand for a firm's merchandise or service, a reasonably stable relation between revenues and expenses, and sufficient net income to pay a regular dividend. It also requires a reasonable relationship among the balance sheet items and satisfactory use of the assets.

Earlier chapters have included references to several types of statement analysis. For example, break-even analysis, gross profit analysis, and the funds statement were all forms of analysis. In this chapter, additional types of financial analysis will be discussed.

Basic analytical procedures

The analytical measures obtained from statements are usually expressed as ratios or percentages. For example, the relationship of $150,000 to $100,000 ($150,000/$100,000 or $150,000:$100,000) may be expressed as 1.5, 1.5:1, or 150%.

Analytical procedures may be used to compare the amount of specific items on a current statement with the corresponding amounts on earlier statements. For example, in comparing cash of $150,000 on the current balance sheet with cash of $100,000 on the balance sheet of a year earlier, the current amount may be expressed as 1.5 or 150% of the earlier amount. The relationship may also be expressed in terms of change, that is, the increase of $50,000 may be stated as a 50% increase.

Analytical procedures are also widely used to show relationships of individual items to each other and of individual items to totals on a single statement. To illustrate, assume that included in the total of $1,000,000 of assets on a balance sheet, cash appears at $50,000 and inventories at $250,000. In relative terms, the cash balance is 5% of total assets and the inventories represent 25% of total assets. Individual items in the current asset group could also be related to total current assets. Assuming that the total of current assets in the example is $500,000, cash represents 10% of the total and inventories represent 50% of the total.

There is no standard rule governing the rounding of computed ratios and percentages. Ordinarily, however, there is no need to carry calculations beyond one decimal point; the ratio 2.46:1, for example, may well be stated as 2.5:1 and 14.33% may be stated as 14.3%.

It should be noted that increases or decreases in items may be expressed in percentage terms only when the base figure is positive. If the base figure is zero or a negative value, the amount of change cannot be expressed as a percentage. For example, if comparative balance sheets indicate no liability for notes payable on the first, or base, date and a liability of $10,000 on the later date, the increase of $10,000 cannot be stated as a percent of zero. Similarly, if a net loss of $10,000 in a particular year is followed by a net income of $5,000 in the succeeding year, the increase of $15,000 cannot be stated as a percent of the loss of the base year.

In the discussion and the illustrations of analytical procedures that follow, the basic significance of the various measures will be emphasized. It should be borne in mind that the ratios and the percentages developed are not ends in themselves; they are only guides to the evaluation of financial and operating data. Many other factors, such as trends in the industry, changes in price levels, and general economic conditions and prospects may also need consideration in arriving at sound conclusions.

Horizontal analysis

The percentage analysis of increases and decreases in corresponding items in comparative statements is sometimes referred to as *horizontal analysis.* It may be used in all the principal accounting statements and their supporting schedules. The amount of each item on the most recent statement is compared with the corresponding item on one or more earlier statements. The increase or the decrease in the amount of the item is then listed, together with the percent of increase or decrease. When the comparison is made between two statements, the earlier statement is used as the base. If the analysis includes three or more statements, there are two alternatives in the selection of the base: the earliest date or period may be used as the basis for comparing all subsequent dates or periods, or each statement may be compared with the immediately preceding statement. The two alternatives are illustrated below.

Base: Earliest Year

				Increase or Decrease*			
				1964–65		1964–66	
Item	1964	1965	1966	Amount	Percent	Amount	Percent
A	$100,000	$150,000	$200,000	$ 50,000	50%	$100,000	100%
B	100,000	200,000	150,000	100,000	100%	50,000	50%

Base: Preceding Year

				Increase or Decrease*			
				1964–65		1965–66	
Item	1964	1965	1966	Amount	Percent	Amount	Percent
A	$100,000	$150,000	$200,000	$ 50,000	50%	$ 50,000	33%
B	100,000	200,000	150,000	100,000	100%	50,000*	25%*

Comparison of the amounts in the last two columns of the first analysis with the amounts in the corresponding columns of the second analysis reveals the effect of the base year on the direction of change and the amount and percent of change.

A condensed comparative balance sheet for two years, with horizontal analysis, is presented at the top of the following page.

The significance of the various increases and decreases cannot be fully determined without additional information. Although total assets at the end of 1966 were $91,000 or 7.4% less than at the beginning of the year, liabilities were reduced by $133,000 or 30%, and capital in-

Dawson Company
Comparative Balance Sheet
December 31, 1966 and 1965

	1966	1965	Increase or Decrease* Amount	Percent
Assets				
Current assets..................	$ 550,000	$ 533,000	$ 17,000	3.2%
Long-term investments........	95,000	177,500	82,500*	46.5%*
Plant assets (net).............	444,500	470,000	25,500*	5.4%*
Intangible assets..............	50,000	50,000	—	
Total assets...................	$1,139,500	$1,230,500	$ 91,000*	7.4%*
Liabilities				
Current liabilities............	$ 210,000	$ 243,000	$ 33,000*	13.6%*
Long-term liabilities..........	100,000	200,000	100,000*	50.0%*
Total liabilities..............	$ 310,000	$ 443,000	$133,000*	30.0%*
Stockholders' equity				
Preferred 6% stock, $100 par. .	$ 150,000	$ 150,000	—	—
Common stock, $10 par.......	500,000	500,000	—	—
Retained earnings............	179,500	137,500	$ 42,000	30.5%
Total stockholders' equity.....	$ 829,500	$ 787,500	$ 42,000	5.3%
Total liab. & stockholders' equity	$1,139,500	$1,230,500	$ 91,000*	7.4%*

creased $42,000 or 5.3%. It would appear that the reduction of $100,000 in long-term liabilities was accomplished, for the most part, through the sale of long-term investments. A funds statement would, of course, provide more definite information about the changes in the composition of the balance sheet items.

The foregoing statement may be expanded to show the details of the various categories of assets and liabilities, or separate schedules may be prepared. Opinions differ as to which method presents the clearer picture. The form of supporting schedules is illustrated by the following comparative schedule of current assets with horizontal analysis:

Dawson Company
Comparative Schedule of Current Assets
December 31, 1966 and 1965

	1966	1965	Increase or Decrease* Amount	Percent
Cash.......................	$ 90,500	$ 51,000	$ 39,500	77.5%
Marketable securities..........	75,000	75,000	—	—
Accounts receivable (net)......	115,000	120,000	5,000*	4.2%*
Merchandise inventory........	264,000	283,000	19,000*	6.7%*
Prepaid expenses.............	5,500	4,000	1,500	37.5%
Total current assets..........	$550,000	$533,000	$ 17,000	3.2%

The changes in the composition of the current assets would appear to be favorable, particularly in view of the increase in sales shown on the income statement below. The reduction in accounts receivable may have come about through changes in credit terms or improved collection policies. Similarly, a reduction in the merchandise inventory during a period of increased sales probably indicates an improvement in management of inventory.

The comparative income statement and the comparative retained earnings statement for Dawson Company, with horizontal analysis, appear on this and the following page. Examination of the income statement reveals an increase of 24.8% in net sales. An increase in sales, considered alone, is not necessarily favorable. The increase in sales was accompanied by a somewhat greater percentage increase in the cost of merchandise sold, which indicates a narrowing of the gross profit margin. Selling expenses increased markedly and general expenses increased slightly, making an overall increase in operating expenses of 20.7% as contrasted with a 19.7% increase in gross profit.

Dawson Company
Comparative Income Statement
For Years Ended December 31, 1966 and 1965

	1966	1965	Increase or Decrease* Amount	Percent
Sales	$1,530,500	$1,234,000	$296,500	24.0%
Sales returns and allowances	32,500	34,000	1,500*	4.4%*
Net sales	$1,498,000	$1,200,000	$298,000	24.8%
Cost of merchandise sold	1,043,000	820,000	223,000	27.2%
Gross profit on sales	$ 455,000	$ 380,000	$ 75,000	19.7%
Selling expense	$ 191,000	$ 147,000	$ 44,000	29.9%
General expense	104,000	97,400	6,600	6.8%
Total operating expense	$ 295,000	$ 244,400	$ 50,600	20.7%
Net operating income	$ 160,000	$ 135,600	$ 24,400	18.0%
Other income	8,500	11,000	2,500*	22.7%*
	$ 168,500	$ 146,600	$ 21,900	14.9%
Other expense	6,000	12,000	6,000*	50.0%*
Net income before income tax	$ 162,500	$ 134,600	$ 27,900	20.7%
Income tax	71,500	58,100	13,400	23.1%
Net income after income tax	$ 91,000	$ 76,500	$ 14,500	19.0%

Dawson Company
Comparative Retained Earnings Statement
For Years Ended December 31, 1966 and 1965

	1966	1965	Increase or Decrease* Amount	Percent
Retained earnings, Jan. 1......	$ 137,500	$ 100,000	$ 37,500	37.5%
Net income for year..........	91,000	76,500	14,500	19.0%
Total......................	$ 228,500	$ 176,500	$ 52,000	29.5%
Dividends:				
On preferred stock.........	$ 9,000	$ 9,000	—	—
On common stock..........	40,000	30,000	$ 10,000	33.3%
Total....................	$ 49,000	$ 39,000	$ 10,000	25.6%
Retained earnings, Dec. 31.....	$ 179,500	$ 137,500	$ 42,000	30.5%

Obviously, the increase in net operating income and in the final net income figure is favorable. It would be erroneous for the management to conclude, however, that its operations were at maximum efficiency. A study of fixed and variable expenses and additional analysis and comparisons of individual expense accounts should be made.

The income statement illustrated is in condensed form. If desired, the statement may be expanded to include details of the cost of merchandise sold, selling expenses, general expenses, other income, and other expense. In general, the condensed statements ordinarily provide sufficient information for all interested groups except management. The comparative schedule of cost of merchandise sold presented below is illustrative.

Dawson Company
Comparative Schedule of Cost of Merchandise Sold
For Years Ended December 31, 1966 and 1965

	1966	1965	Increase or Decrease* Amount	Percent
Merchandise inventory, Jan. 1..	$ 283,000	$ 311,000	$ 28,000*	9.0%*
Purchases..................	1,024,000	792,000	232,000	29.3%
Merchandise available for sale..	$1,307,000	$1,103,000	$204,000	18.5%
Merchandise inventory, Dec. 31.	264,000	283,000	19,000*	6.7%*
Cost of merchandise sold.......	$1,043,000	$ 820,000	$223,000	27.2%

Vertical analysis

Percentage analysis may also be used to show the relationship of the component parts to the total in a single statement. This type of analysis is sometimes called *vertical analysis.* As in horizontal analysis, the statements may be prepared in either detailed or condensed form. In the latter case, additional details may be presented in supporting schedules. Although the analysis is confined within each individual statement, the significance of both the amounts and the percents is increased by preparing comparative statements. The condensed comparative balance sheet of Dawson Company, with vertical analysis, is presented below.

Dawson Company
Comparative Balance Sheet
December 31, 1966 and 1965

	1966		1965	
	Amount	Percent	Amount	Percent
Assets				
Current assets	$ 550,000	48.3%	$ 533,000	43.3%
Long-term investments	95,000	8.3	177,500	14.4
Plant assets (net)	444,500	39.0	470,000	38.2
Intangible assets	50,000	4.4	50,000	4.1
Total assets	$1,139,500	100.0%	$1,230,500	100.0%
Liabilities				
Current liabilities	$ 210,000	18.4%	$ 243,000	19.7%
Long-term liabilities	100,000	8.8	200,000	16.3
Total liabilities	$ 310,000	27.2%	$ 443,000	36.0%
Stockholders' equity				
Preferred 6% stock	$ 150,000	13.2%	$ 150,000	12.2%
Common stock	500,000	43.9	500,000	40.6
Retained earnings	179,500	15.7	137,500	11.2
Total stockholders' equity	$ 829,500	72.8%	$ 787,500	64.0%
Total liab. & stockholders' equity	$1,139,500	100.0%	$1,230,500	100.0%

Each asset item is stated as a percent of total assets, and each liability and capital item is stated as a percent of total liabilities and capital. The major relative changes in assets were in the current asset and long-term investment groups. In the lower half of the balance sheet, long-term liabilities and retained earnings showed the greatest relative change. Stockholders' equity increased from 64.0% at the close of 1965 to 72.8% at the close of 1966, with a corresponding decrease in the claims of creditors.

If supporting schedules are prepared for current assets and other groups, the percentage analysis may be based on either the total of the schedule or the balance sheet total.

In vertical analysis of the income statement, each item is stated as a percent of net sales. The condensed comparative income statement of Dawson Company, with vertical analysis, appears below. Care must be used in judging the significance of differences between percentages for the two years. For example, the decline in the gross profit rate from 31.7% in 1965 to 30.4% in 1966 is only 1.3%. In terms of dollars of potential gross profit, however, it represents a decline of approximately $19,000 (1.3% × $1,498,000). The slight increase in the percent of selling expense to net sales also indicates the desirability of additional analysis.

Dawson Company
Comparative Income Statement
For Years Ended December 31, 1966 and 1965

	1966		1965	
	Amount	Percent	Amount	Percent
Sales	$1,530,500	102.2%	$1,234,000	102.8%
Sales returns and allowances	32,500	2.2	34,000	2.8
Net sales	$1,498,000	100.0%	$1,200,000	100.0%
Cost of merchandise sold	1,043,000	69.6	820,000	68.3
Gross profit on sales	$ 455,000	30.4%	$ 380,000	31.7%
Selling expense	$ 191,000	12.8%	$ 147,000	12.3%
General expense	104,000	6.9	97,400	8.1
Total operating expense	$ 295,000	19.7%	$ 244,400	20.4%
Net operating income	$ 160,000	10.7%	$ 135,600	11.3%
Other income	8,500	.6	11,000	.9
	$ 168,500	11.3%	$ 146,600	12.2%
Other expense	6,000	.4	12,000	1.0
Net income before income tax	$ 162,500	10.9%	$ 134,600	11.2%
Income tax	71,500	4.8	58,100	4.8
Net income after income tax	$ 91,000	6.1%	$ 76,500	6.4%

Common-size statements

Horizontal and vertical analyses with both dollar and percentage figures are helpful in disclosing relationships and trends in financial condition and operations of individual enterprises. Vertical analysis with both dollar and percentage figures is also useful in comparing one company with another or with industry averages. Such comparisons may be facilitated by the use of statements containing percentage relationships only. Such statements are called *common-size statements* because all values are expressed in relative terms (percentages) instead of in absolute terms (dollars). In comparing one enterprise with another or with industry-wide averages, the relative differences revealed by the common-size statement are likely to be more significant than any absolute differences. Trade associations and financial information services publish summary financial and operating data by industry classifications. Comparison of these percentages with those of individual companies yields information that is less readily apparent from the consideration of dollar amounts.

An example of a common-size income statement for Dawson Company and Grant Corporation is given below.

Dawson Company and Grant Corporation
Condensed Common-Size Income Statement
For Year Ended December 31, 1966

	Dawson Company	Grant Corporation
Sales	102.2%	102.3%
Sales returns and allowances	2.2	2.3
Net sales	100.0%	100.0%
Cost of merchandise sold	69.6	70.0
Gross profit on sales	30.4%	30.0%
Selling expense	12.8%	11.5%
General expense	6.9	4.1
Total operating expense	19.7%	15.6%
Net operating income	10.7%	14.4%
Other income	.6	.6
	11.3%	15.0%
Other expense	.4	.5
Net income before income tax	10.9%	14.5%
Income tax	4.8	5.5
Net income after income tax	6.1%	9.0%

Scrutiny of the common-size income statement presented above reveals that the revenues and the expenses are very similar except for the selling and general expenses. The variance in these expenses is the main factor causing Dawson Company to have a lower percentage of net income than Grant Corporation.

Other analytical measures

In addition to the percentage analyses discussed above, there are a number of additional relationships that may be expressed in ratios and percentages. The items used in the measures are taken from the accounting statements of the current period and hence are a further development of vertical analysis. Comparison of the items with the corresponding measures of earlier periods constitutes an extension of horizontal analysis.

Some of the most significant and commonly used ratios will be discussed in the sections that follow. The examples will be based on the statements of Dawson Company that appear earlier in the chapter. In a few instances items are also taken from the company's statements for 1964.

Current position analysis

To be useful, ratios must express significant relationships. One such relationship is the expression of the company's ability to meet its currently maturing debts. This expression or analysis is referred to as *current position analysis*. This analysis is of particular interest to short-term creditors.

Current ratio. The relationship between current assets and current liabilities is called the *current ratio*. It may also be referred to as the *working capital ratio* or *bankers' ratio*. The ratio is computed by dividing the total of current assets by the total of current liabilities. Marketable securities, receivables, and inventories may decline in value and there is no certainty as to when they will be converted into cash. On the other hand, current liabilities must be paid at their face value and at specific dates. It is desirable, therefore, that current assets always be materially in excess of current liabilities.

The excess of current assets over current liabilities is also frequently used as an index of current financial condition. It is referred to as *working capital* or *net current assets*. The working capital and the current ratio of Dawson Company at December 31, 1966 and 1965, are shown below, together with the underlying data:

	1966	1965
Current assets	$550,000	$533,000
Current liabilities	210,000	243,000
Working capital	$340,000	$290,000
Current ratio	2.6:1	2.2:1

The current ratio is a more dependable indication of solvency than is working capital. To illustrate, assume that Scott Corporation lists current assets of $2,000,000 and current liabilities of $1,540,000 on its balance sheet for December 31, 1966. The working capital of the corporation is $460,000 and the current ratio is 1.3:1. In comparison with

Dawson Company, Scott Corporation has a larger amount of working capital ($460,000 compared to $340,000) but a lower current ratio (1.3:1 compared to 2.6:1). Considering these facts alone, a bank is more likely to grant short-term loans to Dawson Company than to Scott Corporation.

Acid-test ratio. The current ratio and the amount of working capital are two indicators of a company's ability to meet currently maturing obligations. However, these two measures do not take into account the distribution of the various items making up the current assets, a distribution that may be very significant. To illustrate, assume the following current position data for Albert Corporation and Bailey Company:

	Albert Corporation	Bailey Company
Current assets		
Cash	$ 200,000	$ 550,000
Marketable securities	100,000	100,000
Receivables (net)	200,000	200,000
Inventories	800,000	450,000
Total current assets	$1,300,000	$1,300,000
Current liabilities	650,000	650,000
Working capital	$ 650,000	$ 650,000
Current ratio	2:1	2:1

Both companies have a current ratio of 2 to 1 and working capital of $650,000. But the ability of the two companies respectively to meet their currently maturing debts is vastly different. Albert Corporation has a large portion of its current assets in inventories, which must be sold and the receivables collected before the current liabilities can be paid in full. A considerable amount of time may be required to convert these inventories into cash in the normal operating processes. Declines in market prices and a reduction in demand could also impair the ability to pay current liabilities. Bailey Company has almost enough cash on hand to meet its current liabilities.

A ratio that measures the "instant" debt-paying ability of a company is called the *acid-test ratio*. It is the ratio of the sum of cash, receivables, and marketable securities, which are sometimes called *quick assets*, to current liabilities. The computation of the acid-test ratio of Dawson Company is shown on the following page.

A thorough analysis of a firm's current position would include the determination of the amount of working capital, the current ratio, and the acid-test ratio. These ratios are most useful when viewed together and when compared with similar ratios for previous periods and with those of other firms in the industry.

	1966	1965
Quick assets		
Cash	$ 90,500	$ 51,000
Marketable securities	75,000	75,000
Receivables (net)	115,000	120,000
Total	$280,500	$246,000
Current liabilities	$210,000	$243,000
Acid-test ratio	1.3:1	1.0:1

Accounts receivable analysis

The composition of accounts receivable changes continually during business operations. Sales on account increase the total, and collections reduce the total. Firms that grant long credit terms tend to have relatively greater amounts tied up in accounts receivable than those granting short terms. Increases or decreases in the volume of sales also affect the amount of outstanding accounts.

Accounts receivable yield no revenue, hence it is desirable to keep the amount invested in them at a minimum. The cash made available by prompt collection of receivables may be employed to reduce the amount of bank loans and thus yield a saving of interest, to purchase merchandise in larger quantities at a lower price, to pay dividends, or for other purposes. Prompt collection also reduces the risk of loss from uncollectible accounts.

Accounts receivable turnover. The relationship between sales volume and accounts receivable may be stated as the *accounts receivable turnover.* It is computed by dividing net sales on account by the average accounts receivable. The average of the monthly balances of accounts receivable should be used in the computation, as it takes seasonal fluctuations into account. When such data are not available, it is necessary to use the average of the balances at the beginning and the end of the year. If there are trade notes receivable as well as accounts, the two should be combined.

The accounts receivable turnover of Dawson Company is computed below. All sales were made on account.

	1966	1965
Net sales on account	$1,498,000	$1,200,000
Accounts receivable (net):		
Beginning of year	$ 120,000	$ 140,000
End of year	115,000	120,000
Total	$ 235,000	$ 260,000
Average	$ 117,500	$ 130,000
Accounts receivable turnover	12.7	9.2

Number of days' sales in receivables. Another means of expressing the efficiency of the collection of receivables is the *number of day's sales in receivables.* This measure is determined by dividing the accounts receivable at the end of the year by the average daily sales (net sales on account divided by 365).

The determination of the number of days' sales in receivables for Dawson Company is illustrated below.

	1966	1965
Accounts receivable, end of year..................	$ 115,000	$ 120,000
Net sales on account..........................	$1,498,000	$1,200,000
Net sales on account ÷ 365 = average daily sales	$ 4,104	3,288
Accounts receivable, end of year ÷ average daily sales = number of days' sales in receivables....	28.0	36.5

The number of days' sales in receivables gives a rough measure of the length of time the accounts receivable have been outstanding. A comparison of this measure with the credit terms, with figures for comparable firms in the same industry, and with figures of Dawson Company for prior years will help reveal the efficiency in collecting receivables and the trends in the management of credit.

Aging schedule of accounts receivable. Analysis using data not found on the financial statements is often necessary as a complement to statement analysis before a conclusion can be reached regarding a particular situation. For example, neither the accounts receivable turnover nor the number of days' sales in receivables indicates the makeup of the total accounts receivable at the balance sheet date. This makeup can be indicated by presentation of an *aging schedule of accounts receivable.* Such a schedule for Dawson Company at the close of 1966 and 1965 is illustrated below.

	December 31, 1966		December 31, 1965	
	Amount	Percent	Amount	Percent
Not yet due...........................	$ 60,000	52.2%	$ 55,000	45.8%
Not more than 30 days overdue..........	27,500	23.9%	38,000	31.7%
31–60 days overdue.....................	10,770	9.4%	12,600	10.5%
61–180 days overdue....................	6,380	5.5%	7,170	6.0%
181–365 days overdue...................	3,450	3.0%	3,730	3.1%
More than one year overdue.............	6,900	6.0%	3,500	2.9%
Total..................................	$115,000	100.0%	$120,000	100.0%

Both the accounts receivable turnover and the number of days' sales in receivables for Dawson Company indicate an improved accounts receivable position at the end of 1966 as compared with 1965. The aging schedule likewise shows fewer receivables in all the overdue categories, except those receivables more than one year overdue. In this category the percentage of receivables has doubled, a situation that should be investigated to determine its cause and possible means for taking corrective action.

Merchandise inventory turnover

Most of the observations in the first two paragraphs on accounts receivable are also applicable to merchandise inventory. Inventories in excess of the needs of the business tie up funds that could be used in other ways to better advantage and may cause increases in the amount of insurance, property taxes, storage, and other expenses. There is also added risk of loss through price declines and deterioration or obsolescence of the merchandise.

The *merchandise inventory turnover* is computed by dividing the cost of merchandise sold by the average inventory. If monthly data are not available, it is necessary to use the average of the inventories at the beginning and the end of the year. Given monthly figures for purchases and sales, the interim monthly inventories can be estimated by the gross profit method described in Chapter 10.

The calculation of the merchandise inventory turnover for Dawson Company is presented below.

	1966	1965
Cost of merchandise sold	$1,043,000	$820,000
Merchandise inventory:		
Beginning of year	$ 283,000	$311,000
End of year	264,000	283,000
Total	$ 547,000	$594,000
Average	$ 273,500	$297,000
Merchandise inventory turnover	3.8	2.8

The improvement in the turnover resulted from an increase in the cost of merchandise sold, combined with a decrease in average inventory. The variation in types of merchandise is too great to permit any broad generalizations as to what constitutes a satisfactory turnover. For example, a firm selling food should have a higher turnover than one selling furniture or jewelry, and the perishable foods department of a supermarket should have a higher turnover than the soaps and cleaners department. However, for each business or each department within a business there is a reasonable turnover rate. A turnover below this rate means that the company or the department is incurring extra expenses such as those for administration and storage, increasing its risk of loss because of obsolescence and adverse price changes, and incurring interest charges in excess of those considered necessary or failing to free funds for other uses.

Ratio of stockholders' equity to liabilities

Claims against the total assets of an enterprise are divided into two basic groups, those of the creditors and those of the owners. The relationship between the total claims of the two groups provides an indication of the margin of safety of the creditors and the ability of the enterprise to withstand adverse business conditions. If the claims of the creditors are large in proportion to the equity of the stockholders, there are likely to be substantial charges for interest payments. If earnings decline to the point of inability to meet interest payments, control of the business may pass to the creditors.

The relationship between stockholder and creditor equity is shown in the vertical analysis of the balance sheet. For example, the balance sheet of Dawson Company presented on page 687 indicates that on December 31, 1966, stockholders' equity represented 72.8% and liabilities represented 27.2% of the sum of the liabilities and stockholders' equity (100.0%). Instead of expressing each item as a percent of the total, the relationship may be expressed as a ratio of one to the other, as illustrated below.

	1966	1965
Total stockholders' equity	$829,500	$787,500
Total liabilities	310,000	443,000
Ratio of stockholders' equity to liabilities	2.7:1	1.8:1

By reference to the balance sheet of Dawson Company it may be seen that the principal factor affecting the change in the ratio was the $100,000 reduction in long-term liabilities during 1966. The ratio at both dates indicates a substantial margin of safety for the creditors.

Ratio of plant assets to long-term liabilities

Long-term notes and bonds are frequently secured by mortgages on plant assets. The ratio of total plant assets to long-term liabilities provides a measure of the margin of safety of the noteholders or bondholders. It also gives an indication of the potential ability of the enterprise to borrow additional funds on a long-term basis.

The ratio of plant assets to long-term liabilities of Dawson Company is computed as follows:

	1966	1965
Plant assets (net)	$444,500	$470,000
Long-term liabilities	100,000	200,000
Ratio of plant assets to long-term liabilities	4.4:1	2.4:1

Ratio of net sales to assets

The ratio of net sales to assets is a measure of the effectiveness of the utilization of assets. Assume that two competing enterprises have equal amounts of assets but that the sales of one are double the amount of the sales of the other. Obviously, the former is making better use of its assets. In computing the ratio, any long-term investments should be excluded from total assets as they make no contribution to sales. The units of product sold may also be used in place of the dollar amount of sales, if sales can be stated in a common unit.

Assets used in determining the ratio may be the total at the end of the year, the average at the beginning and the end of the year, or the average of the monthly totals. The computation for Dawson Company is as follows:

	1966	1965
Net sales	$1,498,000	$1,200,000
Total assets (excluding long-term investments):		
Beginning of year	$1,053,000	$1,010,000
End of year	1,044,500	1,053,000
Total	$2,097,500	$2,063,000
Average	$1,048,750	$1,031,500
Ratio of net sales to assets	1.4:1	1.2:1

Rate earned on total assets

The rate earned on total assets is a measure of the productivity of the assets, without regard to the equity of creditors and stockholders in the assets. The rate is therefore not affected by differences in methods of financing an enterprise.

The rate earned on total assets is derived by adding interest expense to net income and dividing this sum by total assets. By adding interest expense to net income, the productivity of the assets is determined without considering the means of financing the acquisition of the assets. The computation of the rate earned by Dawson Company on total assets appears below:

	1966	1965
Net income after income tax	$ 91,000	$ 76,500
Plus interest expense	6,000	12,000
Total	$ 97,000	$ 88,500
Total assets:		
Beginning of year	$1,230,500	$1,187,500
End of year	1,139,500	1,230,500
Total	$2,370,000	$2,418,000
Average	$1,185,000	$1,209,000
Rate earned on total assets	8.2%	7.3%

As in other operating measures based on assets, an average of the assets by months is preferable. When such data are not available, the assets at the beginning or the end of the year, or the average of the two amounts, may be used.

It is sometimes considered preferable to determine the rate of net operating income (net income before nonoperating income, nonoperating expense, and income tax) to total assets. If nonoperating income is excluded from consideration, the investments yielding such income should be excluded from the assets. The use of net income before income tax eliminates the effect of changes in the tax structure on the rate of earnings. When considering published data on rates earned on assets, it is obviously important that the reader take note of the exact nature of the measure.

Rate earned on stockholders' equity

Another relative measure of earnings is obtained by dividing net income by the total stockholders' equity. In contrast to the rate earned on total assets, this measure emphasizes the income yield in relationship to the amount invested by the stockholders.

The amount of the total stockholders' equity varies throughout the year; additional stock may be issued, a class of stock may be retired, dividends may be paid, and net income accrues gradually. If monthly figures are not available, the average of the stockholders' equity at the beginning and the end of the year is used. The computation for Dawson Company follows:

	1966	1965
Net income after income tax	$ 91,000	$ 76,500
Stockholders' equity:		
Beginning of year	$ 787,500	$ 750,000
End of year	829,500	787,500
Total	$1,617,000	$1,537,500
Average	$ 808,500	$ 768,750
Rate earned on stockholders' equity	11.3%	10.0%

The rate earned on stockholders' equity may differ from the rate earned on total assets because funds may be provided by creditor interests as well as by stockholders. If the rate earned on the assets exceeds the rate of interest on borrowed funds, the excess is income for the benefit of the stockholders, and vice versa.

A comparison of the rate earned on stockholders' equity and the rate earned on total assets for Dawson Company for 1966 and 1965 indicates a favorable return to stockholders from the use of creditor funds. For

1966, for example, Dawson Company had a rate earned on total assets of 8.2% compared with a rate earned on stockholders' equity of 11.3%.

Equity ratio

A company may use borrowed funds when it expects to realize a return on the investment of the borrowed funds that will exceed the cost of borrowing them. However, no company should be so dependent on borrowed funds that it cannot survive adverse economic changes. The less a company uses borrowed funds, the better it is able to survive business situations where earnings on assets do not exceed the interest on debt. In addition, the more borrowed funds are used, the greater is the debt that must be paid if the company is not to be forced into liquidation.

A very useful measure of the financial strength of a company is the *equity ratio*. This ratio is determined by dividing the stockholders' equity by the total assets. This ratio indicates the percentage of the company's assets that is provided by the owners. Many financial analysts consider the current ratio and the equity ratio the two most important measures of financial strength. The current ratio indicates short-run solvency, and the equity ratio indicates long-run solvency.

Each business must decide upon a reasonable equity ratio, one that will permit it to make reasonable use of borrowed funds and still face the future without fear of insolvency caused by business recession. Generally, the more stable the business's earnings, the more borrowed funds can be used safely. Public utilities, for example, with their relatively stable earnings frequently have a lower equity ratio than do most manufacturing firms.

Data on the equity ratio for Dawson Company are as follows:

	1966	1965
Stockholders' equity	$ 829,500	$ 787,500
Total assets	1,139,500	1,230,500
Equity ratio	72.8%	64.0%

Rate earned on common stockholders' equity

When a corporation has both preferred and common stock outstanding, the holders of the common stock have the residual claim on earnings. The net income for the period, reduced by the preferred dividend requirements, may be stated as a percent of the average equity of the common stockholders.

Dawson Company has $150,000 of preferred 6% nonparticipating stock outstanding at both balance sheet dates, hence annual preferred dividends amount to $9,000. The common stockholders' equity is the total capital reduced by the par of the preferred stock ($150,000). The computation is as follows:

	1966	1965
Net income after income tax	$ 91,000	$ 76,500
Preferred dividends	9,000	9,000
Remainder — identified with common stock	$ 82,000	$ 67,500
Common stockholders' equity:		
Beginning of year	$ 637,500	$ 600,000
End of year	679,500	637,500
Total	$1,317,000	$1,237,500
Average	$ 658,500	$ 618,750
Rate earned on common stockholders' equity	12.5%	10.9%

The rate earned on common stockholders' equity may differ from the rate earned on total assets or the rate earned on stockholders' equity. As noted earlier, the difference between the rate on stockholders' equity and the rate earned on total assets is due to the use of borrowed funds. The rate earned on common stockholders' equity will differ from both of these rates if preferred shares are issued, because such shares have a claim on earnings prior to the common shares but secondary to the claim of creditors.

Earnings per share on common stock

One of the financial measures commonly determined is earnings per share on common stock. If there is only one class of stock, the earnings per share are determined by dividing net income by the number of shares outstanding at the end of the year. If there is both preferred and common stock outstanding, the net income must be reduced first by the amount necessary to meet the preferred dividend requirements.

Any unusual changes in the number of shares outstanding during the year, such as stock dividends or stock splits, should be disclosed in quoting earnings per share. Also, if net income includes material amounts of income or losses of a nonrecurring nature, the facts should be disclosed.

The computation of the earnings per share of common stock of Dawson Company is as follows:

	1966	1965
Net income after income tax	$91,000	$76,500
Preferred dividends	9,000	9,000
Remainder — identified with common stock	$82,000	$67,500
Shares of common stock outstanding	50,000	50,000
Earnings per share on common stock	$1.64	$1.35

Earnings per share is especially useful to the investor or prospective investor in weighing the merits of various investment opportunities. This ratio is one of the figures most commonly quoted in the financial press.

Use of financial analyses

The ratios, rates, and turnovers discussed and illustrated in the foregoing sections are representative of the many that can be developed. In analyzing the financial statements of a particular firm, some of them might well be omitted; others might be stated in a different manner; and additional measures might be developed. Dawson Company, used to illustrate financial statement analysis in this chapter, was a medium-sized merchandising firm. For firms of different sizes in other lines of business, additional measures might be more significant. For example, a public utility or a railroad normally has a large ratio of debt to assets, that is, it has a small equity ratio in comparison with that of a merchandising business. In such a situation, the number of times a firm's income covers its interest charges is a useful indication of the financial strength of the firm. This ratio indicates not only the firm's ability to meet its interest payments but the safety factor afforded the creditors, that is, the amount of decrease in income that can take place before interest payments cannot be covered by earnings. An illustration of the calculation of the number of times interest charges were earned for Central Gas and Electric appears below.

	1966	1965
Net income before income taxes	$ 900,000	$ 800,000
Add interest charges	300,000	250,000
Amount available to meet interest charges	$1,200,000	$1,050,000
Number of times interest charges earned	4	4.2

A similar calculation can be used to determine the *number of times dividends are earned.* Such ratios are commonly reported in the financial press for stocks that pay a regular dividend regardless of whether they are preferred or common.

Only those measures that assist in interpreting the statements and the relationships should be prepared. Furthermore, there is no magic in ratios; they are only an analytical tool. Thus, all ratios must be interpreted in light of the general economic environment at the time of the analysis, the conditions peculiar to the particular enterprise, and the conditions in the industry of which the enterprise is a part.

The ratios for a particular business are of most value when related to one another, when one firm's ratios are compared from one period to another, and when the firm's measurements are related to a norm or industry standard.

QUESTIONS

1. Sims Company and Laker, Inc. are both department stores. For the current year, they reported net income after income tax of $750,000 and $250,000 respectively. Is Sims Company a more profitable company than Laker, Inc.? Discuss.

2. Differentiate between horizontal analysis and vertical analysis of financial statements.

3. Illustrate (a) horizontal analysis and (b) vertical analysis, using the following data taken from a comparative balance sheet:

	Current Year	Preceding Year
Cash	$150,000	$120,000
Total current assets	600,000	400,000

4. What is the advantage of using comparative statements for financial analysis rather than statements for a single date or period?

5. What are common-size financial statements?

6. (a) Name three measures or ratios that are useful in the analysis of a firm's current position. (b) Why is the analysis of current position of particular interest to short-term creditors?

7. Company A and Company B have working capital of $100,000 and $50,000 respectively. Does this mean that Company A has a higher current ratio than Company B? Explain.

8. The working capital for Browning Company at December 31, 1966, exceeds the working capital at December 31, 1965, by $25,000 as reported below. Does this mean that the current position at the end of 1966 is stronger than at the end of 1965? Explain.

	1966	1965
Current assets:		
Cash, marketable securities, and accounts receivable	$ 75,000	$125,000
Merchandise inventory	225,000	125,000
Total current assets	$300,000	$250,000
Current liabilities	150,000	125,000
Working capital	$150,000	$125,000

9. Name three measures that are useful in the analysis of accounts receivable.

10. A company that grants terms of n/30 on all sales has an accounts receivable turnover for the year, based on monthly averages, of 5. Is this a satisfactory turnover? Discuss.

11. Why is it advantageous to have a high merchandise inventory turnover?

12. In comparing two dissimilar enterprises, such as a grocery chain and a manufacturer of automotive accessories, which measure is more appropriate as a basis for comparison, the rate of net income to sales or the rate of net income to stockholders' equity? Explain.

13. Explain how the rate earned on stockholders' equity can differ from the rate earned on common stockholders' equity for a particular company for the same period of time.

14. The net income after income tax of Deller, Inc. was $2 per common share in the latest year and $5 per common share for the preceding year. At the beginning of the latest year, the number of shares outstanding was doubled by a stock split. There were no other changes in the amount of stock outstanding. What were the earnings per share in the preceding year, adjusted to place them on a comparable basis with the latest year?

15. Favorable business conditions may bring about certain seemingly unfavorable ratios, and unfavorable business operations may result in apparently favorable ratios. For example, Champion Company has increased sales and net income substantially for the current year, yet the current ratio at the end of the year is lower than at the beginning of the year. Discuss some possible causes of the apparent weakening of the current position while sales and net income have increased substantially.

EXERCISES

1. Prepare an income statement in comparative form for the Baxter Company based upon the data presented below, presenting the increase or decrease in each item for 1966 both in dollars and in percentages.

	1966	1965
Sales	$720,000	$600,000
Cost of merchandise sold	506,000	440,000
Selling expense	70,200	60,000
General expense	33,000	30,000
Income tax	46,700	27,100

2. The following data were abstracted from the balance sheet of Herbert Bros.:

Cash	$ 92,000
Marketable securities	50,000
Accounts and notes receivable (net)	122,000
Merchandise inventory	273,500
Prepaid expenses	12,500
Accounts and notes payable (short term)	175,000
Accrued liabilities	45,000

(a) Determine (1) working capital, (2) current ratio, and (3) acid-test ratio. (Present figures used in your computations.)

(b) What conclusions can be drawn from this data as to the company's ability to meet its currently maturing debts?

3. The following data were taken from the financial statements for Bash and Redman, Inc.:

	1966	1965
Accounts receivable, end of year	$ 356,000	$ 214,000
Monthly average accounts receivable (net)	285,000	207,000
Net sales on account	1,720,000	1,450,000

Terms of all sales are 2/10, n/60.

(a) Determine for each year (1) the accounts receivable turnover and (2) the number of days' sales in receivables.

(b) What conclusions can be drawn from these data concerning the composition of accounts receivable?

4. The following data were abstracted from an income statement:

Sales	$320,000
Sales returns and allowances	6,400
Merchandise inventory, beginning of year	34,000
Merchandise inventory, end of year	32,000
Purchases (net)	201,840
Operating expenses	64,660
Income tax	15,100

Determine the following, presenting figures used in your computations: (a) rate of sales returns and allowances on net sales, (b) rate of gross profit on net sales, (c) rate of net income after income tax on net sales, (d) merchandise inventory turnover.

5. The data presented below were taken from the financial statements of Manning Company for the current fiscal year.

Plant assets (net)				$ 540,000
Liabilities:				
Current liabilities			$100,000	
Long-term liabilities			200,000	
Total liabilities				300,000
Stockholders' equity:				
Preferred 6% stock, $100 par, cumulative, nonparticipating (no change during year)			$100,000	
Common stock, $10 par (no change during year)			500,000	
Retained earnings:				
Balance, beginning of year	$227,800			
Net income after income tax	103,200	$331,000		
Preferred dividends	$ 6,000			
Common dividends	25,000	31,000		
Balance, end of year			300,000	
Total stockholders' equity				$ 900,000
Net sales				1,440,000
Interest expense				12,000

Determine the following, presenting figures used in your computations: (a) ratio of stockholders' equity to liabilities, (b) ratio of plant assets to long-term liabilities, (c) ratio of net sales to assets, (d) rate earned on total assets, (e) rate earned on stockholders' equity, (f) equity ratio, (g) rate earned on common stockholders' equity.

6. The net income reported on the income statement of Staley Implements, Inc. was $2,500,000. There were 500,000 shares of no-par common stock and 25,000 shares of $100 par 6% preferred stock outstanding throughout the year. The income statement included a gain on the sale of plant assets of $1,000,000 and a loss from a patent infringement suit of $500,000. What were the earnings per share on common stock (a) as reported and (b) after adjustment for nonrecurring charges and credits?

PROBLEMS

28-1. Data pertaining to Peterson Lumber Company's current position is presented below.

Cash	$ 95,000	Prepaid expenses	$ 10,000
Marketable securities	50,000	Accounts payable	150,000
Accounts and notes receivable (net)	155,000	Notes payable (short-term)	80,000
Merchandise inventory	190,000	Accrued liabilities	20,000

Instructions: (1) Compute (a) working capital, (b) current ratio, and (c) acid-test ratio.

(2) Consider each of the following transactions separately and assume that only that transaction affects the data given above.

(a) Purchased merchandise on account, $50,000.
(b) Paid notes payable, $80,000.
(c) Borrowed $100,000 from bank on a long-term note.
(d) Paid accounts payable, $75,000.
(e) Declared a cash dividend, $15,000.
(f) Received cash on account, $60,000.
(g) Purchased marketable securities, $25,000.
(h) Paid cash for office supplies, $1,000.
(i) Declared a common stock dividend on common stock, $10,000.
(j) Issued additional shares of stock for cash, $50,000.

State the effect of each transaction (increase, decrease, or no effect) on working capital, current ratio, and acid-test ratio. Use the following column headings for recording your answers:

	Effect on		
Item	Working Capital	Current Ratio	Acid-Test Ratio

28-2. Presented below for the current calendar year are revenue and expense data for Eastman Chemical Company and for the chemical industry. The Eastman Chemical Company data are expressed in dollars, while the chemical industry averages are expressed in percentages.

	Eastman Chemical Company	Chemical Industry Average
Sales	$3,267,200	102.0%
Sales returns and allowances	67,200	2.0%
Cost of merchandise sold	2,080,000	67.5%
Selling expense	451,200	12.2%
General expense	252,800	6.8%
Other income	28,800	1.0%
Other expense	25,600	.8%
Income tax	194,700	6.2%

Instructions: (1) Prepare a common-size income statement comparing the results of operations for Eastman Chemical Company with the industry average.

(2) As far as the data permit, comment on significant relationships revealed by the comparisons.

28-3. For 1966, Garber and Co. initiated an extensive sales promotion campaign that included the expenditure of an additional $50,000 on advertising. At the end of the year, John Garber, the president, is presented with the following condensed comparative income statement:

Garber and Co.
Comparative Income Statement
For Years Ended December 31, 1966 and 1965

	1966	1965
Sales	$950,000	$620,000
Sales returns and allowances	50,000	20,000
Net sales	$900,000	$600,000
Cost of merchandise sold	585,000	360,000
Gross profit on sales	$315,000	$240,000
Selling expense	$180,000	$ 90,000
General expense	72,000	60,000
Total operating expense	$252,000	$150,000
Net operating income	$ 63,000	$ 90,000
Other expense	3,600	3,000
Net income before income tax	$ 59,400	$ 87,000
Income tax	22,000	35,300
Net income after income tax	$ 37,400	$ 51,700

Instructions: (1) Prepare a comparative income statement for the two-year period, presenting an analysis of each item in relationship to net sales for each of the years.

(2) To the extent the data permit, comment on the significant relationships revealed by the vertical analysis prepared in (1).

28-4. The financial statements of Austin, Inc. for the current year are presented on pages 706 and 707.

Additional data taken from the balance sheet at December 31, 1965, are as follows:

Accounts receivable (net)	$ 220,000
Long-term investments	225,000
Total assets	2,900,000
Total stockholders' equity (preferred and common stock outstanding same as in 1966)	2,000,000

Instructions: Determine for 1966 the ratios, turnovers, and other measures listed below, presenting the figures used in your computations:

(1) Working capital.
(2) Current ratio.
(3) Acid-test ratio.
(4) Accounts receivable turnover.
(5) Number of days' sales in receivables.
(6) Merchandise inventory turnover.
(7) Ratio of stockholders' equity to liabilities.
(8) Ratio of plant assets to long-term liabilities.
(9) Ratio of net sales to assets.
(10) Rate earned on total assets.
(11) Rate earned on stockholders' equity.
(12) Equity ratio.
(13) Rate earned on common stockholders' equity.
(14) Earnings per share on common stock.

Austin, Inc.
Balance Sheet
December 31, 1966

Assets		
Current assets:		
Cash	$ 225,000	
Marketable securities	100,000	
Accounts receivable (net)	330,000	
Merchandise inventory	720,000	
Prepaid expenses	25,000	
Total current assets		$1,400,000
Long-term investments:		
Bond sinking fund		250,000
Plant assets:		
Equipment (net)	$ 650,000	
Buildings (net)	1,200,000	
Land	200,000	
Total plant assets		2,050,000
Total assets		$3,700,000
Liabilities		
Current liabilities:		
Accounts payable	$ 495,000	
Income tax payable	135,000	
Total current liabilities		$ 630,000
Long-term liabilities:		
Mortgage note payable, due 1986	$ 500,000	
Bonds payable, 5%, due 1977	500,000	
Total long-term liabilities		1,000,000
Total liabilities		$1,630,000
Stockholders' equity		
Preferred 5% stock, cumulative, nonparticipating, $100 par	$ 500,000	
Common stock, $50 par	1,000,000	
Retained earnings	570,000	
Total stockholders' equity		2,070,000
Total liabilities and stockholders' equity		$3,700,000

Austin, Inc.
Retained Earnings Statement
For Year Ended December 31, 1966

Retained earnings, January 1, 1966		$ 500,000
Net income for year		160,000
Total		$ 660,000
Dividends:		
On preferred stock	$ 25,000	
On common stock	65,000	90,000
Retained earnings, December 31, 1966		$ 570,000

Austin, Inc.
Income Statement
For Year Ended December 31, 1966

Sales	$3,490,000	
Sales returns and allowances	90,000	
Net sales		$3,400,000
Cost of merchandise sold:		
Merchandise inventory, January 1, 1966	$ 460,000	
Purchases (net)	2,670,000	
Merchandise available for sale	$3,130,000	
Merchandise inventory, December 31, 1966	720,000	
Cost of merchandise sold		2,410,000
Gross profit on sales		$ 990,000
Operating expenses:		
Selling expenses	$ 480,000	
General expenses	180,000	
Total operating expenses		660,000
Net operating income		$ 330,000
Other income		15,000
		$ 345,000
Other expense (interest)		50,000
Net income before income tax		$ 295,000
Income tax		135,000
Net income after income tax		$ 160,000

28-5. William McBride was considering making a substantial investment in Austin, Inc. The financial statements for 1966 for Austin, Inc. were given in Problem 28-4. As part of his evaluation of the company, Mr. McBride secured the financial statements presented below, which cover the prior year.

Austin, Inc.
Balance Sheet
December 31, 1965

Assets		*Liabilities*	
Current assets:		Current liabilities:	
Cash	$ 200,000	Accounts payable	$ 274,000
Marketable securities	100,000	Income tax payable	126,000
Accounts receivable (net)	220,000	Total current liabilities	$ 400,000
Merchandise inventory	460,000	Long-term liabilities:	
Prepaid expenses	20,000	Bonds pay., 5%, due 1977	$ 500,000
Total current assets	$1,000,000	Total liabilities	$ 900,000
Long-term investments:			
Bond sinking fund	$ 225,000	*Stockholders' equity*	
Plant assets:		Preferred 5% stock, cumulative, nonparticipating, $100 par	$ 500,000
Equipment (net)	$ 550,000		
Buildings (net)	900,000		
Land	200,000	Common stock, $50 par	1,000,000
Total plant assets	$1,650,000	Retained earnings	500,000
Intangible assets: Patents	$ 25,000	Total stockholders' equity	$2,000,000
Total assets	$2,900,000	Total liabilities and stockholders' equity	$2,900,000

Austin, Inc.
Income Statement
For Year Ended December 31, 1965

Sales	$2,980,000	
Sales returns and allowances	80,000	
Net sales		$2,900,000
Cost of merchandise sold:		
Merchandise inventory, January 1, 1965	$ 400,000	
Purchases (net)	2,035,000	
Merchandise available for sale	$2,435,000	
Merchandise inventory, December 31, 1965	460,000	
Cost of merchandise sold		1,975,000
Gross profit on sales		$ 925,000
Operating expenses:		
Selling expenses	$ 440,500	
General expenses	189,500	
Total operating expenses		630,000
Net operating income		$ 295,000
Other income		6,000
		$ 301,000
Other expense (interest)		25,000
Net income before income tax		$ 276,000
Income tax		126,000
Net income after income tax		$ 150,000

Austin, Inc.
Retained Earnings Statement
For Year Ended December 31, 1965

Retained earnings, January 1, 1965		$ 435,000
Net income for year		150,000
Total		$ 585,000
Dividends:		
On preferred stock	$ 25,000	
On common stock	60,000	85,000
Retained earnings, December 31, 1965		$ 500,000

Additional data taken from the balance sheet at December 31, 1964, are as follows:

Accounts receivable (net)	$ 180,000
Long-term investments	200,000
Total assets	2,925,000
Total stockholders' equity (preferred and common stock outstanding same as in 1965)	1,935,000

Instructions: Prepare a report for Mr. McBride based on an analysis of the financial statements for 1966 and 1965 and the related data. In preparing your report, include all ratios and other data that will be useful in arriving at a decision regarding the investment.

PART TEN

Appendixes

A. Automated data processing

Data processing methods

With pencil, paper, and sufficient time, one or more persons can process all the data needed by an enterprise. If the business requirements for data are few, manually kept records may serve reasonably well. But as businesses become larger and more complex, manual processing becomes excessively costly and time-consuming. The trend, therefore, is toward replacing manual effort with machines that reduce the cost and speed up the processing of business data.

Some of the more common machines are the typewriter, cash register, adding machine, calculator, and bookkeeping machine. The efficiency of the typewriter is frequently increased by merely using carbon paper. Cash registers can record and accumulate totals for credit sales, cash sales, sales taxes, and receipts on account. The use of adding machines and calculators speeds up processing and minimizes the annoyance and the expense caused by arithmetical errors. Conventional bookkeeping machines, which have movable carriages and keyboards similar to those of a typewriter and accumulating devices similar to adding machines, are commonly used in journalizing transactions and posting to ledger accounts. For example, both a customer's ledger account and the sales journal can be placed in the machine together so that sales transactions can be recorded in the sales journal and debits can be posted to the accounts receivable ledger simultaneously. The sales journal remains in the machine until all sales for the day are recorded and posted to customers' accounts. The total credit to Sales and debit to Accounts Receivable for the day and the cumulative total for the month and the year to date are then automatically recorded. Similar techniques are employed for recording cash received on account and posting the credits to the customers' accounts. Additional forms may also be inserted in the machine with the accounting records so that monthly statements can be prepared simultaneously with the recording of sales and cash receipts.

Although bookkeeping machines and other mechanical equipment speed up the accounting process and reduce the clerical costs of processing data, large enterprises need equipment that can process data even faster, cheaper, and more efficiently. This latent demand has led to the development of elaborate mechanical equipment and in more recent years to increasingly sophisticated electronic equipment.

The goal of efficient systems of data processing is to assemble the maximum amount of useful information at a minimum cost. The illustrations of data processing and related practice materials in this book have for the most part been based on manual methods, which for some enterprises may be the most efficient. However, the major emphasis has been on concepts and principles rather than on procedures. A background of basic principles and an understanding of the general framework of accounting are prerequisites to any meaningful consideration of automated data processing. *Automated data processing* (ADP) is the general term applied to the processing of data by mechanical and/or electronic equipment (sometimes referred to as "hardware") that operates with a minimum of manual intervention. When all of the equipment employed by a processing system operates electronically, it may be termed *electronic data processing* (EDP).

Nature of automated equipment

A wide variety of automated equipment is produced by numerous manufacturers. It is an area noted for rapid technological progress and continuous innovation. Any detailed cataloguing of the available equipment would be of little value for our purposes here. There are, however, some characteristics common to all automated systems that need to be understood at the outset.

It is customary to subdivide automated data processing systems generally into three major parts: (1) input, (2) processing, and (3) output. *Input* refers to the raw data introduced into the system. The tapes or other forms taken by the data in preparation for processing are called the *input media*. The *processing* portion of a system is concerned largely with the processing equipment that manipulates the data in the desired manner. The information emitted by the system is, of course, the *output*. The form taken by the various summary figures and reports is called the *output media*.

Automated data processing systems may employ various combinations of input media, processing equipment, and output media. Such variables as the nature and the volume of data to be processed, the significance of speed and operating costs, and the type of output desired will influence the type of installation. The relationship of input media, processing equipment, and output media is indicated by the diagram below.

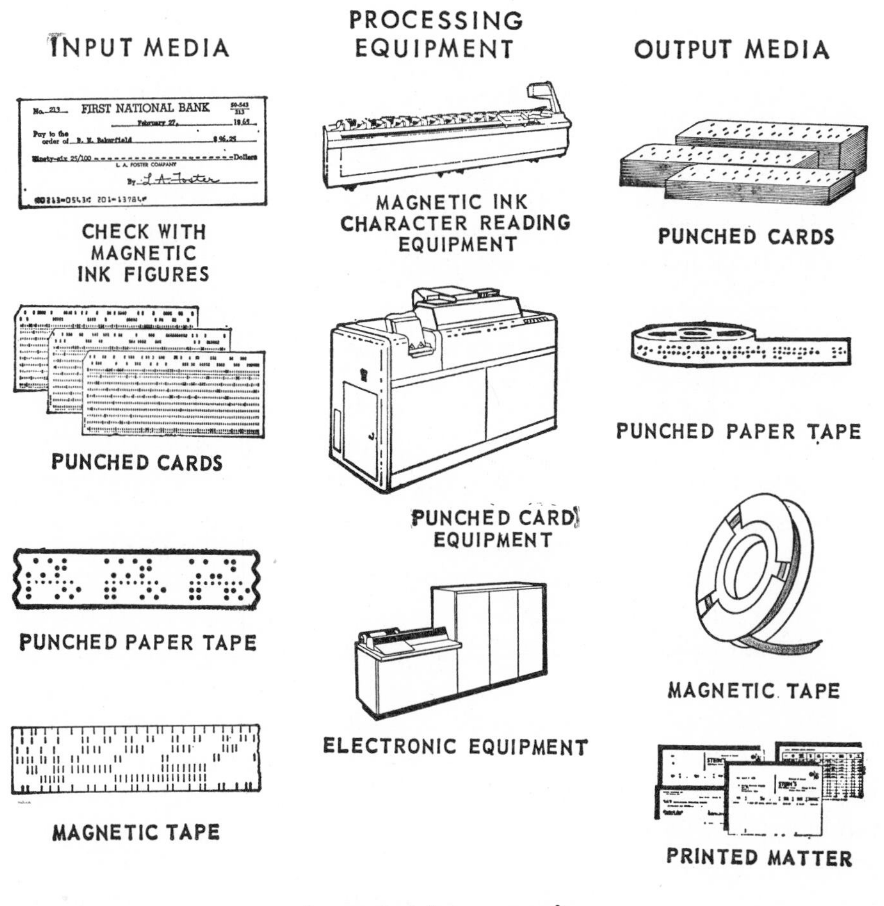

Automated data processing

Input media

Data to be processed automatically must be translated into special symbols and transcribed on a medium that can be read by the processing equipment. Much of the input is prepared from documents similar to those described in this book. For example, if automated equipment is employed in recording purchases transactions and maintaining the creditors' ledger, the input would be prepared from a copy of the purchase invoice.

Common input media include paper printed with magnetic ink, punched cards, punched paper tape, and magnetic tape. Magnetic ink is commonly used on check forms to facilitate sorting and processing of checks by banks.

Cards with punched holes that represent data may be used both as a basic business document and as input media for the processing equipment. For example, an expanding variety of enterprises, including public utilities, commonly prepare an invoice or a customer's statement of account in punched card form. A system of this type reduces clerical costs and transcribing errors.

A punched card that serves as a bill for a public utility is illustrated below. The customer is instructed to return the stub with his remittance. The returned stubs serve as the input media for the posting of credits to the customers' ledger and for accumulating the total of cash receipts.

Punched card used as a bill

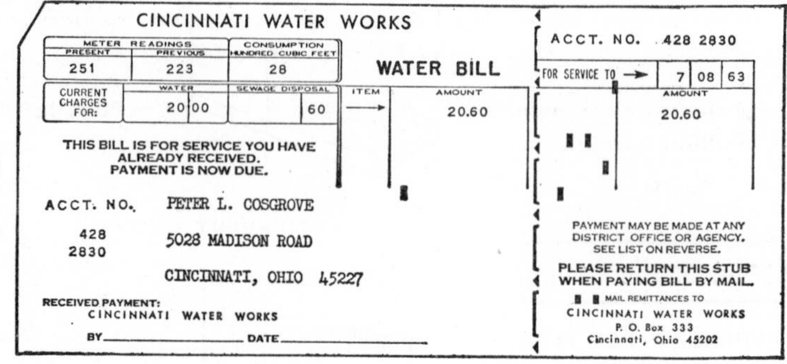

CINCINNATI WATER WORKS

METER READINGS		CONSUMPTION
PRESENT	PREVIOUS	HUNDRED CUBIC FEET
251	223	28

CURRENT CHARGES FOR:	WATER	SEWAGE DISPOSAL
	20 00	60

WATER BILL

ITEM	AMOUNT
⟶	20.60

THIS BILL IS FOR SERVICE YOU HAVE ALREADY RECEIVED. PAYMENT IS NOW DUE.

ACCT. NO. 428 2830

PETER L. COSGROVE
5028 MADISON ROAD
CINCINNATI, OHIO 45227

RECEIVED PAYMENT:
CINCINNATI WATER WORKS
BY __________ DATE __________

ACCT. NO. 428 2830

FOR SERVICE TO ⟶ 7 08 63

AMOUNT
20.60

PAYMENT MAY BE MADE AT ANY DISTRICT OFFICE OR AGENCY. SEE LIST ON REVERSE.

PLEASE RETURN THIS STUB WHEN PAYING BILL BY MAIL.

MAIL REMITTANCES TO
CINCINNATI WATER WORKS
P. O. Box 333
Cincinnati, Ohio 45202

Punched paper tape is used, but less widely than punched cards, as an input medium. It is also used for communication between machines. For example, memorandums for sales orders received by a branch office can be typed on a special typewriter that simultaneously transcribes the information in the form of holes in paper tape. The paper tape is used to activate a teletype machine that transmits the information to the home office, where a duplicate punched paper tape is produced. The duplicate tape is then introduced into a machine at the home office that issues instructions to the shipping department and eventually prepares the invoices and posts to the customers' accounts. Machines that can communicate with one another through a medium such as punched paper tape are called *common language* machines.

Magnetic tape, which is similar to the tape used with an ordinary tape recorder, is often preferred over both punched cards and punched paper tape because the processing equipment can sense the data more rapidly and the medium requires less storage space.

Processing equipment

Three of the most common types of processing equipment for automated systems are magnetic ink character reading equipment, punched card equipment, and electronic equipment.

Magnetic ink character reading equipment. Many banks use magnetic ink character reading equipment to process depositors' accounts. Although the extent to which the processing is automated varies, many banks print the depositor's identification number in magnetic ink on the check forms and the deposit forms issued to the depositor. When checks and deposits are presented to the bank, the amounts are also recorded in magnetic ink on the respective forms by special typewriters. The magnetic ink character reading equipment senses these magnetic ink markings and processes the checks and deposits automatically to the depositor's account. The preparation of statements for depositors at monthly or other specified intervals is also completely automatic. Although magnetic character reading equipment is widely used in banking, it has not been used to any great extent by other types of business enterprises.

Punched card equipment. Equipment that uses the punched card as its input medium was the first development for the mechanization of data processing on a large scale. The holes punched in the card represent a code that can be translated by the equipment. Each hole must therefore be placed with exactitude at the proper point in order to represent the specified input datum.

Punched card equipment usually consists of a series of machines, each of which performs a specific operation.

A *key punch* machine, which utilizes a keyboard similar to a typewriter, prepares the cards. Both alphabetical and arithmetical data are represented by the holes in the card. The same data can be printed across the top of the card simultaneously, thus facilitating reading of the card if the need arises.

A *sorter* can be set to sense the holes and to sort the cards by desired locations or combinations of locations, such as by number or in alphabetical order. A typical sorter can sort punched cards representing sales invoices, for example, into alphabetical order at the rate of 650 per minute.

A *reproducer* punches new cards by transcribing selected portions or all of the data from existing cards. A reproducer can also be used to convert marks made on a card with a special lead pencil into punched holes in the same card. This process, known as *mark sensing*, is used by some water utilities to facilitate the recording of water meter readings and in processing customers' bills. In such cases the meter reader uses a special pencil to record each meter reading on a card that was previously prepared automatically by the reproducer from cards punched (and printed) with the customer's name, address, and previous meter reading. The reproducer converts the manually recorded meter reading to punched holes, and the customer's statement is then automatically prepared by other machines.

A *collator* merges or matches two different batches of punched cards. For example, a stack of cards representing newly opened customers' accounts can be merged in alphabetical order with the group of cards representing previously existing accounts receivable.

A *calculator* performs the basic arithmetical operations of addition, subtraction, multiplication, and division and converts the answers to punched holes in the cards.

A *tabulator* accumulates and summarizes the data punched in the cards and prints such documents as invoices, payroll checks, and detailed or summary reports such as sales classified by product, territory, and salesmen. A typical tabulator prints about 150 lines per minute.

By combining the punched card equipment in the proper sequence, it is possible to process payrolls, sales, and purchases transactions; to journalize the transactions; to post to ledger accounts; to obtain trial balances; and to print checks, statements of account, withholding tax statements, financial statements, and other reports. Human intervention is required only in preparing the punched cards, instructing the equipment, and transferring the cards from one machine to another. "Instructing" the equipment often consists of the setting of dials or the wiring of control panels to achieve the proper flow and summarization of data.

Electronic equipment. Electronic equipment is actuated by the movement of electrical impulses through vacuum tubes and transistors. Some electronic equipment is hundreds of times faster than data processing equipment that functions mechanically. For example, electronic computers are available that can add two ten-digit numbers at a rate faster than 1/100,000 of a second. Electronic equipment also provides for an uninterrupted flow of processing from the input data at the beginning to the output data at the end.

Although punched cards and punched tape can be used as input media for electronic equipment, magnetic tape is more commonly used because the equipment can sense data from magnetic tape much more rapidly than from any other media. For example, some magnetic tape has an input speed approximately 100 times faster than that of punched cards.

The electronic equipment directs its own operations in accordance with a set of instructions called a *program*. Both the data to be processed and the program are internally stored in a part of the equipment that is commonly called the *memory unit*. The computer can then perform arithmetical computations, compare two sets of data, and store intermediate results as directed by the program. All of the equipment functions at incredibly high speeds.

Output media

Output commonly takes the form of punched cards, punched paper tape, magnetic tape, and printed matter. The form depends upon the use to be made of the end product of the processing. For example, if the end product is customers' statements of account, they can be automatically printed by high-speed printers at the rate of as many as 1,000 lines per minute. A magnetic tape or punched cards containing end-of-the-month balances might also be produced. The tape or the punched cards would be used along with a tape or punched cards containing sales and cash receipts data for the following month as input for processing customers' statements of account for the following month.

Applications of automated equipment

Although in recent years the processing of data has become highly automated for many businesses, the accounting principles and objectives have not changed. Financial statements remain the same, documents to evidence transactions are still essential, and principles of internal control and systems design discussed in this book are still applicable. The form of the accounting records may be somewhat different, and the sequence of processing may also be altered. The time required to process accounting data is materially reduced, and additional analyses and controls are made feasible by automated equipment.

The potential uses of automated equipment in accounting are innumerable. However, much of the equipment is quite costly, whether leased or purchased. Its use is therefore practical only where a mass of data needs to be processed on a continuous basis. In many cities the advantages of rapid and efficient processing of data are available to business enterprises at data processing centers. These centers process data on a fee basis. Several applications of automated equipment to accounting are described briefly in the paragraphs that follow.

Accounts receivable. A common method of processing accounts receivable is described in the following outline:

(1) A master card is prepared for each account receivable, holes being punched for the name, address, and any other desired information.
(2) A combination typewriter and card punch are used to prepare simultaneously conventional sales invoices and punched cards, the sales

invoices being sent to customers and the cards becoming the input media.

(3) The punched cards for sales are sorted alphabetically by customer and are merged with the customers' master accounts receivable cards.

(4) As remittances are received, punched cards are prepared, sorted, and merged with the other punched cards.

(5) At the end of the month, the punched cards in the customers' ledger are processed by a tabulator that prints the monthly statement of account. The cards representing sales and cash receipts are removed for storage. A card is then punched with the ending balance of each account and is merged with the master cards, ready for transactions of the following month.

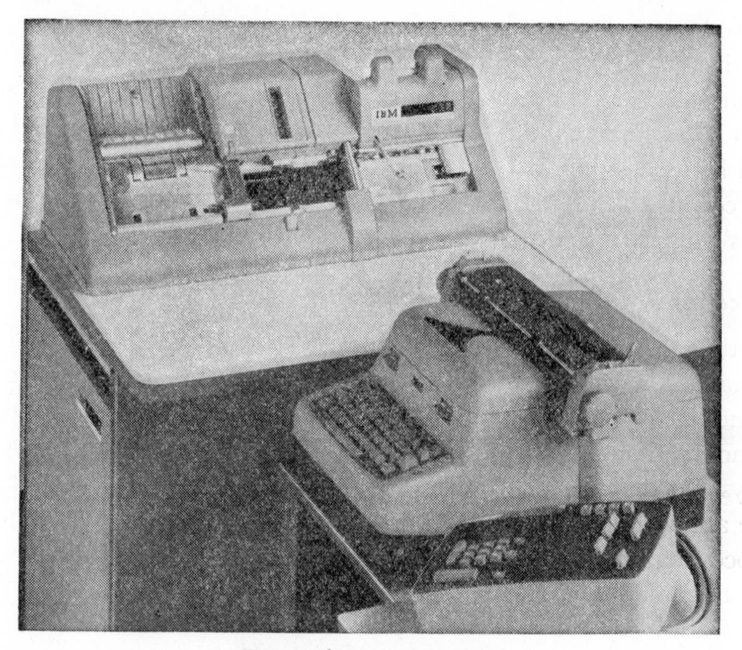

Typewriter card punch

Although the outline was confined to the processing of customers' accounts, it should be noted that the cards punched for sales and cash receipts can also be used in determining total sales and total cash receipts, in posting to perpetual inventory records, and in obtaining analyses of sales by product and territory.

Inventories. Perpetual inventories are readily adaptable to automated processing. Input data are composed of the descriptions, quantities, and unit costs of each commodity purchased or manufactured and of each commodity sold or entering into production. All computations are performed automatically, and a complete inventory listing or the details of a particular commodity can be obtained at any time desired.

The system can also be extended to improve management's control over quantities and thereby effect a minimization of investment and losses from obsolescence without curtailing sales. It is first necessary to determine the minimum quantity of each commodity to be stocked and the most efficient number to purchase or produce. When data on these factors are merged with the actual inventory data, the equipment can be programmed to prepare purchase requisitions or other memorandums to initiate production.

Payrolls. Payroll processing is commonly automated because many of the operations involved are routine and repetitive. For example, employees' hourly rates of pay usually remain constant for a number of pay periods, and the FICA tax and income tax withholding structures are revised only infrequently. Furthermore, the processing of the payroll for each employee follows identical procedures: computing the gross pay, the deductions, and the net pay; updating the employee's earnings record; recording the payroll in the payroll register; and preparing the payroll check.

Data for each employee for each pay period, such as social security number, rate of pay, and number of withholding exemptions, are punched into master cards. Other cards are used for recording the time worked during the current period and for the year-to-date earnings and withholdings. At the end of the pay period, the current earnings card and the year-to-date card are merged with the master card for each employee. The cards are then processed by the punched card calculator, and the employee's gross pay, deductions, and net pay are computed and the year-to-date card is brought up to date. The tabulator prints the payroll register and the payroll checks. This operation is illustrated by the diagram on the following page.

Integrated data processing

The use of automated equipment employing mechanical means is quite common in processing masses of relatively homogeneous financial data in such areas as accounts receivable, inventories, and payrolls. There are usually intermediate outputs before reaching the ultimate objectives, and human intervention is ordinarily required at various stages. Electronic equipment has made it possible to reduce the delays and the errors caused by such interruption of data flow.

The systematization of processing operations in such a manner as to eliminate retranscriptions of data and to minimize the rehandling and resorting of data from one stage to the next is termed *integrated data processing* (IDP). The term may be applied to a particular segment of the operations of an enterprise or to its entire operations. The processing

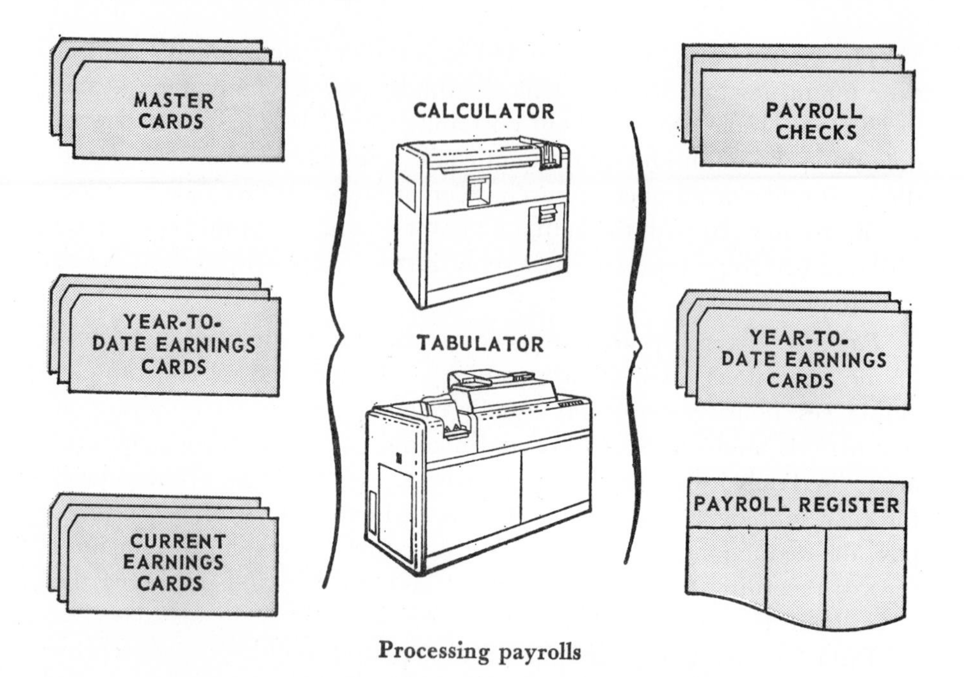

Processing payrolls

of data in an integrated manner requires an exacting coordination of all of the manual, mechanical, and electronic processing devices employed.

Highly sophisticated data processing systems usually employ electronic equipment (1) with a memory unit of large capacity and (2) with the capability of manipulating heterogeneous financial data in random order. Large memory capacity within the equipment permits continuous accumulation of processed data, comparisons with related data, issuance of the necessary instructions and documents, and restorage for further use. The remainder of this appendix is devoted to describing the principal features of a hypothetical integrated data processing system.

When a sales order is received from a customer, all of the pertinent data, such as name and address, quantity and description of the items ordered, and delivery instructions, are recorded on magnetic tape. This is the input for this part of the system. Acting upon instructions stored in the memory unit, the output unit prints the customer's name and address on a sales invoice and shipping order. The quantity and description data from the order are automatically transmitted to an electronic computer where comparisons are made with the perpetual inventory record, which is also contained in the memory unit. If the stock on hand is sufficient to fill the order, the description, quantity, and sales price are printed on the invoice, and the inventory record in the memory unit is adjusted for the quantity and the cost of the units sold. The inventory balance of the item is then compared with the reorder quantity, which is also automatically transmitted to the computer. If a reorder is indicated, a purchase requisition is printed automatically. The sales data and the cost of goods sold data for each transaction are accumulated and stored within the system, and their totals are automatically available at the end of the month.

If the quantity of a commodity on hand is not sufficient to fill the order, the lesser quantity and its sales price are recorded on the invoice, the inventory record is modified, and the sales data and the cost of goods sold data are added to the existing balances. In addition, the reason for shipping the smaller quantity is printed on the invoice and a "back order" is printed for the remaining quantity. Later, when the back-ordered goods become available, a sales invoice and a shipping order for the quantity necessary to complete the original order are automatically prepared.

This process is repeated for each item of a sales order. When the order for the last item has been processed, the total amount of the sale is printed on the invoice. The current accounts receivable balance and the credit limit, which are stored in the memory unit, are then transmitted to the computer. The total of the sales invoice is added to the customer's account balance, and the resulting balance is compared with the credit limit. If the comparison indicates adequate credit, the invoice and the shipping order are released. The computer performs all of the comparisons described above during the time the output unit is printing the sales invoice and the shipping order.

If inadequate credit is indicated, the invoice is routed to the credit department for approval. If the credit department approves the sale, the invoice and its shipping order are released. If the credit department does not approve the sale, sales cancellation data are entered into the system to cancel all of the original transaction data that were recorded.

The only visible records produced from a routine sales transaction are the sales invoice and the shipping order. The remainder of the transaction data, including the customer's record and the perpetual inventory record, is accumulated and stored within the memory unit until again needed.

When cash is received on account, the details are introduced into the system by means of magnetic tape. The balances of the individual customers' accounts are automatically revised and the cumulative totals of the general ledger accounts are brought up to date.

Details of purchases transactions, cash disbursements, and related data are processed automatically in a similar manner. The individual accounts with creditors are debited and credited, the inventory records are debited for materials or merchandise purchased, and the amounts of assets acquired and expenses incurred are automatically added to the preceding balances of the appropriate general ledger accounts. When a creditor's account is due for payment, the account balances affected by payment, including purchases discount, are revised and the output unit automatically prints a disbursement check ready for signature. Payrolls are also processed automatically, the output media being payroll checks.

If information is needed at any time about a specific item, such as the balance owed a particular creditor or the inventory of a particular commodity, it can be extracted from the system almost instantly. At the end of the month the general ledger accounts, the trial balance, and the financial statements are printed automatically. Whenever desired, the equipment can produce a printed list of the balances in any of the subsidiary ledgers, the individual withholding tax forms for employees, and analyses of sales and other data in the memory unit.

Standards and other budgetary controls can be integrated with the system in such a manner that budgeted data and actual data are compared automatically. Any significant variations between the two are emitted by the system in the form of printed variance reports. Historical data in the memory unit can also be analyzed and compared with other input data representing hypothetical future conditions. Output media in the form of reports on the effects of alternative courses of action aid management in making decisions.

The most advanced integrated data processing systems combine engineering and scientific tasks with the processing of financial data. For example, by introducing into the system all data on orders received, job specifications, quantities to be produced, materials required, production priorities, and other relevant factors, the system can be *programmed* to prepare the production orders for each department of the factory. If the results of production are also introduced, the system can monitor the manufacturing operations and prepare up-to-the-minute reports on the progress of production and deviations from the scheduled operations.

The foregoing brief descriptions demonstrate how automated equipment can be employed in achieving partial or total integration of data processing. Although highly sophisticated installations are not currently in operation on a wide scale, the potentialities of complete automation are virtually unlimited.

Automation has affected requirements for clerical personnel, and its continued development will undoubtedly further reduce the need for manual processing. The demand for accountants, on the other hand, continues to exceed the available supply, and the shortage is expected to continue into the foreseeable future.

B.

Alternative method of recording merchandise inventories

Difference in methods

The recording of adjusting entries for merchandise inventory at the end of the accounting period is described and illustrated in Chapter 7. The alternative method presented here classifies the entries for the beginning and the ending merchandise inventories as *closing* entries instead of *adjusting* entries. The difference in viewpoint has a minor effect on the work sheet, the sequence of entries in the journal, and the expense and revenue summary account in the ledger. It does not affect the overall results, nor does it alter the financial statements in any way.

Work sheet

The merchandise inventory at the beginning of the period is to be reported on the income statement as a part of the cost of merchandise sold. On the work sheet it is therefore extended from the Trial Balance Dr. column to the Income Statement Dr. column.

The inventory at the end of the period is to be reported on the balance sheet as an asset and on the income statement as a deduction from the cost of merchandise available for sale. The ending inventory is therefore entered on the work sheet as a debit in the Balance Sheet Dr. column and as a credit in the Income Statement Cr. column. Both the debit and the credit amounts are placed on the same line as that used for the beginning merchandise inventory.

All adjustments are recorded in the Adjustments columns of the work sheet in the same manner as was illustrated on pages 154 and 155 except that by this method no entries are required in the Adjustments columns for merchandise inventory. The balances are then extended to the In-

Bennett Electrical Supplies
Work Sheet
For Year Ended December 31, 1965

Account Titles	Trial Balance		Adjustments		Income Statement		Balance Sheet	
	Dr.	Cr.	Dr.	Cr.	Dr.	Cr.	Dr.	Cr.
Cash	9,675						9,675	
Accounts Receivable	8,900						8,900	
Merchandise Inventory	16,600				16,600	18,200	18,200	
Store Supplies	1,270			(a) 580			690	
Office Supplies	580			(b) 240			340	
Prepaid Insurance	1,520			(c) 716			804	
Store Equipment	12,000						12,000	
Accumulated Depr. — Store Equip.		4,700		(d) 1,000				5,700
Office Equipment	3,400						3,400	
Accumulated Depr. — Office Equip.		680		(e) 340				1,020
Building	28,000						28,000	
Accumulated Depr. — Building		3,500		(f) 700				4,200
Land	3,000						3,000	
Accounts Payable		9,270						9,270
Commissions Payable				(g) 564				564
Salaries Payable				(h) 212				212
Mortgage Payable		8,000						8,000
John Bennett, Capital		43,751						43,751
John Bennett, Drawing	12,000						12,000	
Sales		163,574				163,574		
Sales Returns and Allowances	3,150				3,150			
Sales Discount	1,314				1,314			
Purchases	103,920				103,920			
Purchases Returns and Allowances		2,640				2,640		
Purchases Discount		1,857				1,857		
Sales Salaries	14,510		(h) 152		14,662			
Sales Commissions	6,867		(g) 564		7,431			
Advertising Expense	2,580				2,580			
Depreciation Expense — Store Equip.			(d) 1,000		1,000			
Delivery Expense	963				963			
Store Supplies Expense			(a) 580		580			
Insurance Expense — Selling			(c) 420		420			
Miscellaneous Selling Expense	724				724			
Office Salaries	5,064		(h) 60		5,124			
Taxes Expense	1,762				1,762			
Depreciation Expense — Office Equip.			(e) 340		340			
Depreciation Expense — Building			(f) 700		700			
Office Supplies Expense			(b) 240		240			
Insurance Expense — General			(c) 296		296			
Miscellaneous General Expense	693				693			
Rent Income		1,000				1,000		
Interest Expense	480				480			
	238,972	238,972	4,352	4,352	162,979	187,271	97,009	72,717
Net Income					24,292			24,292
					187,271	187,271	97,009	97,009

Work sheet

come Statement and Balance Sheet columns, and the work sheet is completed. A work sheet employing this alternative procedure is illustrated on the preceding page. Observe that the totals of the Income Statement and Balance Sheet columns and the Net Income shown on this work sheet are the same as those on the work sheet on page 155.

Adjusting entries

The adjusting entries made from the alternative work sheet are illustrated below. They are exactly the same as those illustrated on page 164 except that adjustments for inventory are not made.

	Adjusting Entries			
31	Store Supplies Expense	616	580	
	Store Supplies	115		580
31	Office Supplies Expense	715	240	
	Office Supplies	116		240
31	Insurance Expense — Selling	617	420	
	Insurance Expense — General	716	296	
	Prepaid Insurance	117		716
31	Depreciation Expense — Store Equip.	614	1,000	
	Accumulated Depreciation — Store Equip.	122		1,000
31	Depreciation Expense — Office Equip.	713	340	
	Accumulated Depreciation — Office Equip.	124		340
31	Depreciation Expense — Building	714	700	
	Accumulated Depreciation — Building	126		700
31	Sales Commissions	612	564	
	Commissions Payable	212		564
31	Sales Salaries	611	152	
	Office Salaries	711	60	
	Salaries Payable	213		212

Adjusting entries

Closing entries

All items in the Income Statement Dr. column of the work sheet are closed in one compound entry to the debit of Expense and Revenue Summary. All items in the Income Statement Cr. column are closed in one compound entry to the credit of Expense and Revenue Summary. Expense and Revenue Summary and the drawing account are then closed to the capital account with the same entries as the last two illustrated on page 165. All of the closing entries for the alternative procedure are presented on page 724.

		Closing Entries			
1965					
Dec.	31	Expense and Revenue Summary	313	162,979	
		Merchandise Inventory	114		16,600
		Sales Returns and Allowances	412		3,150
		Sales Discount	413		1,314
		Purchases	511		103,920
		Sales Salaries	611		14,662
		Sales Commissions	612		7,431
		Advertising Expense	613		2,580
		Depreciation Expense — Store Equip.	614		1,000
		Delivery Expense	615		963
		Store Supplies Expense	616		580
		Insurance Expense — Selling	617		420
		Miscellaneous Selling Expense	618		724
		Office Salaries	711		5,124
		Taxes Expense	712		1,762
		Depreciation Expense — Office Equip.	713		340
		Depreciation Expense — Building	714		700
		Office Supplies Expense	715		240
		Insurance Expense — General	716		296
		Miscellaneous General Expense	717		693
		Interest Expense	911		480
	31	Merchandise Inventory	114	18,200	
		Sales	411	163,574	
		Purchases Returns and Allowances	512	2,640	
		Purchases Discount	513	1,857	
		Rent Income	812	1,000	
		Expense and Revenue Summary	313		187,271
	31	Expense and Revenue Summary	313	24,292	
		John Bennett, Capital	311		24,292
	31	John Bennett, Capital	311	12,000	
		John Bennett, Drawing	312		12,000

Closing entries

Expense and revenue summary account

The difference between the debit and the credit posted to the expense and revenue summary account from the compound closing entries represents the net income or the net loss for the period. The posting of the entry transferring the net income or the net loss to the capital account closes Expense and Revenue Summary. The account is illustrated below.

EXPENSE AND REVENUE SUMMARY Account No. 313

Date		Items	Post. Ref.	Debit	Credit	Balance Debit	Balance Credit
1965							
Dec.	31		J29	162,979		162,979	
	31		J29		187,271		24,292
	31		J29	24,292		—	—

Expense and revenue summary account

C.

Specimen corporation statements

Champion Papers Inc.
and Consolidated Subsidiaries

Statement of Consolidated Income

Years Ended December 31	1964	1963
Net Sales	$385,958,042	$364,436,114
Deduct:		
Cost of products sold	308,436,614	288,582,245
Selling, general, and administrative expenses	45,154,091	43,753,759
Total	353,590,705	332,336,004
Profit Attributable to Manufacturing and Selling Operations	32,367,337	32,100,110
Other Charges (Credits):		
Interest and debt expense	2,193,666	2,227,349
Interest received	(663,246)	(446,196)
Miscellaneous—net	(109,310)	86,658
Other charges—net	1,421,110	1,867,811
Income Before Income Taxes	30,946,227	30,232,299
Provision for Federal and State Income Taxes	14,150,000	15,200,000
Net Income for the Year	$ 16,796,227	$ 15,032,299

See notes to financial statements

Consolidated Balance Sheet

Assets

	Dec. 26, 1964	*Dec. 28, 1963*
Cash	$ 54,202,675	$ 50,679,173
Marketable securities, at cost	31,865,048	15,494,697
Receivables	14,100,982	11,802,767
Inventories (Note 1)	169,500,867	156,420,181
Store and general supplies	7,347,555	6,955,002
Prepaid and miscellaneous assets	5,975,325	5,245,647
TOTAL CURRENT ASSETS	282,992,452	246,597,467
Investment in unconsolidated subsidiary, at cost (Note 2)	778,459	2,758,337
Land, buildings and equipment, at cost or less	272,338,949	255,575,802
Less allowance for depreciation	(118,098,924)	(108,401,030)
Leaseholds and leasehold improvements, net	44,117,107	43,779,850
Excess cost of investment in subsidiaries over net assets acquired	13,286,339	11,921,764
TOTAL ASSETS	$495,414,382	$452,232,190

December 26, 1964 and December 28, 1963

Liabilities

	Dec. 26, 1964	Dec. 28, 1963
Accounts payable	$113,287,193	$ 93,504,610
Accrued expenses	44,846,084	41,045,394
Provision for federal taxes	20,024,247	16,507,026
Long-term indebtedness (Note 3)	1,711,000	1,591,268
TOTAL CURRENT LIABILITIES	179,868,524	152,648,298
Long-term indebtedness (Note 3)	41,234,292	42,973,704
Deferred federal income taxes	29,780,000	23,570,000
Deferred investment credit	2,091,000	2,350,000
Employees' benefit fund	7,159,013	5,885,217
Minority interest in subsidiary	42,757	212,556
CAPITAL		
Preferred capital stock:		
First preferred, par $100	24,000	24,700
Cumulative preferred, voting, par $50 (Notes 4, 5 and 6) Authorized: 750,000 shares Outstanding: Series A; 1964, 472,669 shares; 1963, 464,351 shares	23,633,450	23,217,550
Common capital stock, par $1 (Notes 5 and 6) Authorized: 18,000,000 shares Outstanding: 1964, 12,585,312 shares after deducting 252,199 shares in treasury at cost, $7,718,377; 1963, 12,633,546 shares after deducting 152,771 shares in treasury at cost, $4,404,937	53,740,986	56,205,003
Accumulated earnings (Note 3)	157,840,360	145,145,162
TOTAL CAPITAL	235,238,796	224,592,415
TOTAL LIABILITIES AND CAPITAL	$495,414,382	$452,232,190

INTERNATIONAL MINERALS & CHEMICAL CORPORATION

CONSOLIDATED FINANCIAL POSITION

ANNUAL REPORT 1964

IMC

At June 30	1964	1963
CURRENT ASSETS:		
Cash	$ 13,468,310	$ 3,774,621
Receivables (less allowances of $1,131,575 in 1964 and $738,688 in 1963)	53,090,921	41,343,860
Refundable federal income taxes		2,051,331
Inventories, at lower of cost (principally average cost) or market—		
Raw materials, in process and finished products	28,531,537	26,698,120
Operating materials and supplies	6,629,422	6,767,040
Total current assets	101,720,190	80,634,972
CURRENT LIABILITIES:		
Notes payable to banks		12,000,000
Accounts payable and accrued liabilities	23,277,902	15,179,411
Income taxes	1,913,289	671,278
Current maturity on long-term debt	162,343	115,673
Total current liabilities	25,353,534	27,966,362
WORKING CAPITAL	76,366,656	52,668,610
INVESTMENTS, AT COST:		
In affiliated domestic companies	3,085,597	1,244,707
In foreign companies	2,635,859	1,994,809
Other investments	3,072,993	2,007,715
	8,794,449	5,247,231
PROPERTY, PLANT AND EQUIPMENT, at cost less accumulated depreciation and depletion (Note 3)	138,108,882	124,303,079
PREPAID EXPENSES AND DEFERRED CHARGES	6,633,795	5,524,775
Total assets less current liabilities	229,903,782	187,743,695
Deduct:		
Long-term debt, less current maturity (Note 4)	80,472,336	64,556,959
Deferred federal income taxes	4,684,000	3,671,800
	85,156,336	68,228,759
NET ASSETS APPLICABLE TO SHAREHOLDERS' EQUITY	$144,747,446	$119,514,936
SHAREHOLDERS' EQUITY (Notes 4 and 5):		
Preferred stock	9,833,000	9,833,000
Common stock	15,517,090	14,038,365
Capital in excess of par value	50,869,248	36,618,638
Retained earnings	68,528,108	59,024,933
	$144,747,446	$119,514,936

(SEE NOTES TO FINANCIAL STATEMENTS)

General Electric

Consolidated Statement of Financial Position

	December 31	
	1963	1962
Cash on hand and in banks	$ 383,308,940	$ 81,861,808
Marketable securities (short-term investments readily convertible to cash)	237,809,454	263,939,952
Receivables* (money owed to the Company by customers, to be paid within a year)	698,274,792	716,040,558
Inventories (materials, and products being made or completed and ready for sale)	742,964,766	722,774,339
	2,062,357,952	1,784,616,657
Deduct: Collections from customers on contracts in progress and anticipated price adjustments on contracts	188,108,055	228,123,379
CURRENT ASSETS (cash, or items generally convertible to cash within a year)	**1,874,249,897**	**1,556,493,278**
Investments and advances* (mainly securities of wholly owned companies not consolidated, plus loans to them)	284,628,100	257,963,496
Plant and equipment less accumulated depreciation* (original cost of land, buildings and equipment—less estimated cost consumed by wear and obsolescence)	694,768,299	712,917,860
Other assets* (long-term receivables, special funds, etc.)	161,485,018	319,612,876
TOTAL ASSETS (items owned at the end of the year)	3,015,131,314	2,846,987,510
Notes payable by consolidated subsidiaries	150,000	50,000
Accounts payable* (money owed for materials and services supplied by others)	203,163,325	209,478,404
Dividends payable to share owners	49,197,136	44,399,899
Taxes accrued (taxes owed to local, state, Federal and Canadian governments)	260,119,319	252,418,277
Other costs and expenses accrued* (amounts to be paid for wages, interest, etc.)	313,836,712	279,393,028
CURRENT LIABILITIES (amounts generally due within the year ahead)	826,466,492	785,739,608
3½% debentures due May 1, 1976 (amount owed on long-term borrowings)	203,008,000	222,472,000
Other liabilities* (long-term payables, etc.)	86,417,398	61,550,493
Remainder of premium received from 1956 sales of debentures	687,314	785,622
Miscellaneous reserves (provision for future payment of costs incurred to date)	34,054,459	36,042,392
Minority share owners' interest in Canadian General Electric Company, Ltd.	18,907,834	18,074,474
TOTAL LIABILITIES, reserves and minority interest (amount owed at year end)	1,169,541,497	1,124,664,589
Excess of Assets over Liabilities, Reserves and Minority Interest——Ownership	$1,845,589,817	$1,722,322,921
This ownership (share owners' equity) is evidenced by:		
Common stock* (issued shares of stock, each with a par value of $5)	$ 452,435,485	$ 449,444,830
Amounts in excess of par value received for stock*	212,596,492	179,834,853
Earnings reinvested in the Company	1,180,557,840	1,093,043,238
TOTAL SHARE OWNERS' EQUITY	$1,845,589,817	$1,722,322,921

*Details shown on page 30

FORD MOTOR COMPANY AND CONSOLIDATED SUBSIDIARIES

Consolidated Balance

ASSETS	1963	1962
CURRENT ASSETS		
Cash	$ 167,737,468	$ 137,936,167
Marketable securities, at cost and accrued interest (approximates market)	907,591,042	819,104,348
Receivables	658,881,298	575,039,239
Inventories, at the lower of cost (principally first-in, first-out) or market	1,193,668,733	1,088,024,726
Prepaid expenses and other current assets	62,640,241	49,020,702
Total current assets	2,990,518,782	2,669,125,182
INVESTMENTS AND NONCURRENT RECEIVABLES		
Equities in net assets of unconsolidated subsidiaries	218,535,993	180,796,536
Other investments, at cost, and noncurrent receivables	44,400,779	29,753,195
Total investments and noncurrent receivables	262,936,772	210,549,731
PROPERTY, PLANT AND EQUIPMENT		
Property, plant and equipment, at cost	4,268,748,882	3,970,366,966
Less accumulated depreciation	1,988,431,574	1,830,203,960
Net property, plant and equipment	2,280,317,308	2,140,163,006
DEFERRED CHARGES	137,844,199	121,595,936
EXCESS OF COST OF INVESTMENTS IN CONSOLIDATED SUBSIDIARIES OVER EQUITIES IN NET ASSETS	277,164,933	275,040,587
Total assets	$5,948,781,994	$5,416,474,442

The accompanying notes are a part of the financial statements.

Sheets *DECEMBER 31, 1963 AND 1962*

LIABILITIES AND STOCKHOLDERS' EQUITY	1963	1962
CURRENT LIABILITIES		
Accounts payable and accrued liabilities	$1,266,574,587	$1,026,028,068
United States and foreign income taxes	422,479,693	430,256,577
Long term debt, payable within one year	12,497,080	11,591,098
Short term debt of consolidated subsidiaries	90,769,790	93,799,448
Total current liabilities	1,792,321,150	1,561,675,191
LONG TERM DEBT	208,647,526	233,132,398
OTHER LIABILITIES AND RESERVES		
Supplemental compensation awards, deferred installments	26,702,586	24,176,441
Supplemental compensation reserve, unawarded balance	49,683,675	49,140,092
Unrealized profits on sales to unconsolidated subsidiaries	10,600,000	7,600,000
Deferred investment credit	12,324,832	4,831,123
Reserve for foreign operations	48,100,000	36,500,000
Other	2,477,756	2,721,523
Total other liabilities and reserves	149,888,849	124,969,179
MINORITY INTERESTS IN NET ASSETS OF CONSOLIDATED SUBSIDIARIES	80,000,282	78,274,665
STOCKHOLDERS' EQUITY		
Capital stock, par value $2.50 per share, 1963—110,614,252 shares and 1962—110,312,256 shares	276,535,630	275,780,640
Capital account in excess of par value of stock	313,651,931	304,737,450
Earnings retained for use in the business	3,127,736,626	2,837,904,919
Total stockholders' equity	3,717,924,187	3,418,423,009
Total liabilities and stockholders' equity	$5,948,781,994	$5,416,474,442

LIBBEY-OWENS-FORD

BALANCE SHEET

December 31, 1963

ASSETS

Current Assets		
Cash		$ 20,032,096.28
U. S. Government securities, at cost and accrued interest (quoted market $28,463,000.00)		28,317,808.75
Trade receivables, less reserve of $2,100,000.00		16,475,505.13
Inventories, at the lower of cost or market:		
Raw materials	$ 5,017,266.51	
In-process and finished products	22,646,439.74	
Manufacturing supplies, and materials and supplies in transit	13,108,224.89	40,771,931.14
TOTAL CURRENT ASSETS		$105,597,341.30
Investment in Marketable Securities		
Common stock of Johns-Manville Corporation, at cost (quoted market $26,998,968.00)	$ 11,847,359.38	
Common stock of Nippon Sheet Glass Co., Ltd., at cost (quoted market $6,803,000.00)	2,437,260.87	
Common stock of Alside, Inc., at cost (quoted market $4,251,101.00)	3,499,990.00	17,784,610.25
Plant Improvement and Replacement Fund		
Cash	$ 6,179.11	
U. S. Government securities, at cost and accrued interest (quoted market $58,309,375.00)	58,036,078.19	
Other marketable securities, at cost and accrued interest (quoted market $1,813,357.00)	1,837,715.53	59,879,972.83
Plants and Properties—on the basis of cost		
Land, land improvements, buildings, machinery, and equipment	$245,172,902.57	
Less accumulated depreciation, and obsolescence	189,277,682.84	55,895,219.73
Other Assets		
Gas properties—equity at cost and accumulated net earnings	$ 2,678,555.11	
Miscellaneous securities, receivables, deposits, and advances	10,195,250.53	12,873,805.64
Patents and Licenses		1.00
Prepaid Expenses		3,093,359.59
		$255,124,310.34

ANNUAL REPORT

LOF GLASS

BALANCE SHEET

December 31, 1963

LIABILITIES AND SHAREHOLDERS' EQUITY

Current Liabilities		
Trade accounts payable		$ 6,024,153.13
Employes' compensation and amounts withheld therefrom for taxes, bond purchases, etc.		11,838,390.24
Taxes, other than federal taxes on income		3,553,913.77
Estimated federal taxes on income	$ 24,780,000.00	
Less U. S. Government tax notes	24,304,000.00	476,000.00
TOTAL CURRENT LIABILITIES		$ 21,892,457.14
Reserve for Rebuilding Furnaces		3,050,052.46
Shareholders' Equity		
Common Stock—par value $5.00 a share—Note A:		
Authorized—20,000,000 shares		
Outstanding—10,470,030 shares (after deducting 125,200 shares in treasury)	$ 52,350,150.00	
Additional paid-in capital	9,199,846.31	
Retained earnings employed in the business	168,631,804.43	230,181,800.74
		$255,124,310.34

See notes to financial statements.

SHELL OIL COMPANY *and Subsidiary Companies*

STATEMENT OF FINANCIAL CONDITION

Assets	DECEMBER 31, 1963	DECEMBER 31, 1962
CURRENT ASSETS		
Cash	$ 35,530,000	$ 37,105,000
Short term securities, at cost approximating market	202,889,000	87,497,000
Receivables and prepayments	328,265,000	311,966,000
Owing by affiliated companies	6,420,000	6,095,000
Inventories of oils and chemicals (Note 3)	203,329,000	202,611,000
Materials and supplies, at average cost or less	21,695,000	24,456,000
TOTAL CURRENT ASSETS	798,128,000	669,730,000
LONG TERM RECEIVABLES, OTHER INVESTMENTS, ETC., at cost	38,942,000	37,993,000
PROPERTIES, PLANT AND EQUIPMENT, at cost, less accumulated depreciation, depletion and amortization (Note 4)	1,301,733,000	1,281,377,000
	$2,138,803,000	$1,989,100,000

Liabilities and Shareholders' Investment	DECEMBER 31, 1963	DECEMBER 31, 1962
CURRENT LIABILITIES		
Payables, accruals, etc.	$ 224,453,000	$ 190,854,000
Income, operating and consumer taxes	129,213,000	99,223,000
Owing to affiliated companies	5,189,000	9,023,000
Long term debt due within one year (Note 5)	3,550,000	2,550,000
TOTAL CURRENT LIABILITIES	362,405,000	301,650,000
LONG TERM DEBT (Note 5)	273,219,000	283,123,000
SHAREHOLDERS' INVESTMENT		
Common stock, authorized 80,000,000 shares at $1.00 par value, issued 60,602,868 shares (1962—60,583,768 shares) at stated value (Note 6)	227,180,000	227,161,000
Amount in excess of common stock stated value (Note 6)	244,785,000	244,099,000
Retained earnings	1,035,465,000	934,271,000
	1,507,430,000	1,405,531,000
Less 107,100 shares (1962—36,200 shares) held in treasury, at cost	4,251,000	1,204,000
TOTAL SHAREHOLDERS' INVESTMENT	1,503,179,000	1,404,327,000
	$2,138,803,000	$1,989,100,000

WALGREEN CO. and Subsidiaries

Consolidated Statements of Income, Earned Surplus, and Source and Application of Funds

For the Years Ended September 30, 1964 and 1963

Income

	1964	1963
SALES AND OTHER INCOME:		
Net sales and other store income	$391,325,977	$366,748,036
Other income (net)	557,862	478,467
	391,883,839	367,226,503
COSTS AND DEDUCTIONS:		
Cost of sales	283,299,122	263,493,688
Selling, occupancy and administration	94,623,819	90,973,733
Contribution to Employees' Profit-Sharing Retirement Trust	1,473,264	1,336,003
Improvements to leased properties	210,435	289,721
Federal and state income taxes	5,150,000	5,105,000
	384,756,640	361,198,145
NET INCOME	$ 7,127,199	$ 6,028,358

Earned Surplus

	1964	1963
BALANCE, beginning of year	$ 33,961,272	$ 30,384,155
Net income	7,127,199	6,028,358
Cash dividends ($1.00 per share in 1964 and $.80 in 1963)	(3,082,821)	(2,451,241)
BALANCE, end of year	$ 38,005,650	$ 33,961,272

Source and Application of Funds

	1964	1963
SOURCE OF FUNDS:		
Net income	$ 7,127,199	$ 6,028,358
Depreciation	2,990,257	2,861,820
Deferred Federal income taxes	475,000	455,000
Notes payable to banks	2,000,000	2,000,000
Other sources	149,807	527,518
	$ 12,742,263	$ 11,872,696
APPLICATION OF FUNDS:		
Net additions to property and equipment	$ 4,299,360	$ 2,643,993
Cash dividends	3,082,821	2,451,241
Investment in affiliated and other companies	213,728	124,763
Increase in working capital	5,146,354	6,652,699
	$ 12,742,263	$ 11,872,696

The accompanying notes to consolidated financial statements are an integral part of the above statements.

ARMOUR AND COMPANY
CONSOLIDATED STATEMENT OF EARNINGS

and earnings employed in the business

	fifty-two weeks ended Oct. 31, 1964	fifty-two weeks ended Nov. 2, 1963
Income		
Sales, including service revenues	$1,887,025,580	$1,810,626,100
Other income	2,339,295	2,656,389
	1,889,364,875	1,813,282,489
Costs		
Cost of products, supplies and services	1,671,618,013	1,613,935,039
Selling and administrative expenses	129,480,276	124,421,579
Depreciation	15,408,088	13,840,407
Employe pension plans	9,680,574	8,694,816
Interest expense	7,666,772	6,620,903
Taxes (other than Federal income taxes)	17,013,722	16,180,149
Provision for Federal income taxes (note 2)	15,722,000	13,269,000
	1,866,589,445	1,796,961,893
Net earnings for the year	**22,775,430**	**16,320,596**
Earnings employed in the business (note 7)		
at beginning of the year	137,442,215	128,670,941
Dividends paid	(7,641,605)	(7,549,322)
at end of the year	$ 152,576,040	$ 137,442,215

(see Notes to financial statements)

OPINION OF INDEPENDENT ACCOUNTANTS

Chicago, January 4, 1965

To the Board of Directors and Stockholders of Armour and Company

In our opinion, the accompanying statements present fairly the consolidated financial position of Armour and Company and its consolidated subsidiaries at October 31, 1964 and the results of their operations for the fiscal year, in conformity with generally accepted accounting principles applied on a basis consistent with that of the preceding year. Our examination of these statements was made in accordance with generally accepted auditing standards and accordingly included such tests of the accounting records and such other auditing procedures as we considered necessary in the circumstances.

PRICE WATERHOUSE & CO.

International Shoe Company

CONSOLIDATED INCOME AND RETAINED EARNINGS

Years Ended November 30,	1964	1963
Sales and other income:		
Net sales	$345,448,310	$295,615,393
Income from rentals and services	277,330	297,471
Interest and other income	1,020,289	1,037,685
	346,745,929	296,950,549
Deductions:		
Cost of sales, selling, general and administrative expenses	324,965,454	277,804,495
Depreciation	4,475,788	4,053,318
Interest and amortization of expense on long-term debt	2,527,790	2,479,338
Other interest and sundry charges	380,319	311,462
	332,349,351	284,648,613
Income before Federal and Canadian income taxes	14,396,578	12,301,936
Federal and Canadian income taxes, estimated	5,517,629	6,527,786
	8,878,949	5,774,150
Proportion of net income of subsidiaries applicable to minority interests	438,159	281,037
NET INCOME FOR YEAR APPLICABLE TO CAPITAL STOCK OF COMPANY (note 6)	$ 8,440,790	$ 5,493,113
Retained earnings at beginning of year:		
International Shoe Company	$ 62,399,327	$ 60,910,523
P. N. Hirsch & Co., net of minority interests	4,520,552	—
	66,919,879	60,910,523
Net income for year applicable to capital stock of company	8,440,790	5,493,113
	75,360,669	66,403,636
Deduct:		
Dividends on common stock, $1.20 per share, both years	4,118,186	4,004,309
Charge arising from pooling of interests, less amount charged to capital in excess of stated amount	4,510,723	—
	8,628,909	4,004,309
RETAINED EARNINGS AT END OF YEAR	$ 66,731,760	$ 62,399,327

CONSOLIDATED CAPITAL IN EXCESS OF STATED AMOUNT

Years Ended November 30,	1964	1963
Balance at beginning of year:		
International Shoe Company	$ 991,316	$ 1,010,236
P. N. Hirsch & Co., net of minority interests	516,779	—
	1,508,095	1,010,236
Adjustments resulting from treasury stock transactions and issuance of stock under option plans	60,272	(18,920)
	1,568,367	991,316
Deduct excess of stated value of common stock and cost of treasury stock issued over par value of P. N. Hirsch & Co. stock, acquired under pooling of interests concept	6,005,381	—
Less balance charged to retained earnings	4,510,723	—
	1,494,658	—
CAPITAL IN EXCESS OF STATED AMOUNT AT END OF YEAR	$ 73,709	$ 991,316

See accompanying notes to financial statements.

MONSANTO CHEMICAL COMPANY AND SUBSIDIARIES

STATEMENT OF CONSOLIDATED INCOME

	1963	1962	Increase *Decrease*
	(In Thousands)		
Income:			
Net sales	$1,192,270	$1,063,195	$129,075
Other	13,470	11,731	1,739
	1,205,740	1,074,926	130,814
Deductions:			
Cost of goods sold	849,669	762,218	87,451
Selling, administrative and research expenses	176,109	151,724	24,385
Interest	15,750	15,422	328
Minority interests	1,700	1,600	100
Other	2,106	2,679	*573*
	1,045,334	933,643	111,691
Income Before Income Taxes	160,406	141,283	19,123
Provision for Income Taxes:			
Current	65,043	51,464	13,579
Deferred	12,373	11,451	922
	77,416	62,915	14,501
Net Income	$ 82,990	$ 78,368	$ 4,622

The above statement should be read in conjunction with pages 22 and 23 of this report.

STATEMENT OF CONSOLIDATED SURPLUS

YEAR ENDED FEBRUARY 29, 1964

EARNED SURPLUS (Retained Earnings)

Balance at beginning of year (including companies merged in 1963—$4,091,937.97)		$ 81,221,354.28
Net earnings for the year		14,711,602.65
		95,932,956.93
Deduct:		
Dividends paid on:		
4½% cumulative preferred stock	$ 344,722.97	
$4 convertible preference stock (including $178,751.16 paid by merged company prior to date of merger)	390,000.00	
Common stock, $1.40 a share	6,976,682.65	
	7,711,405.62	
Charge arising from mergers (see capital surplus)	7,380,290.55	15,091,696.17
Balance at end of year		$ 80,841,260.76

CAPITAL SURPLUS

Balance at beginning of year		$ 310,126.45
Excess of option price over stated value of 16,943 shares of common stock issued under stock option plan		392,586.00
		702,712.45
Deduct excess of stated value of preference stock and cost of treasury common shares issued in mergers over stated capital of merged companies	$ 8,083,003.00	
Less amount charged to earned surplus	7,380,290.55	702,712.45
Balance at end of year		$ -0-

See accompanying notes to consolidated financial statements

NORTH AMERICAN AVIATION, INC. AND SUBSIDIARIES

STATEMENT OF SOURCE AND APPLICATION OF CONSOLIDATED WORKING CAPITAL

YEAR ENDED SEPTEMBER 30	1964	1963
WORKING CAPITAL PROVIDED BY:		
Operations:		
Net income for the year	$49,334,000	$41,196,000
Add charges not requiring current use of working capital:		
Provision for depreciation and amortization	35.489,000	29,528,000
Other	330,000	410,000
Total	85,153,000	71,134,000
Proceeds from sale of capital stock to option holders	433,000	1,438,000
Total	85,586,000	72,572,000
WORKING CAPITAL APPLIED TO:		
Property additions	49,340,000	56,821,000
Dividends	20,205,000	16,801,000
Total	69,545,000	73,622,000
INCREASE (DECREASE) IN WORKING CAPITAL	$16,041,000	$ (1,050,000)
NOTE—The changes within working capital were as follows:		
Increases (decreases) in current assets:		
Cash	$ (9,220,000)	$ 6,792,000
Accounts receivable	(25,784,000)	(53,904,000)
Inventories (net)	(55,511,000)	29,168,000
Prepaid taxes, insurance, etc.	(700,000)	264,000
Decreases in current liabilities:		
Notes payable to banks	95,000,000	15,000,000
Other current liabilities	12,256,000	1,630,000
Total	$16,041,000	$ (1,050,000)

DEERE & COMPANY

Consolidated Working Capital

	1964	1963
Additions to Working Capital:		
Net income	$ 59,445,407	$ 48,370,468
Provision for depreciation	28,814,673	25,304,820
4½% debentures issued	50,000,000	—
Increase in long-term debt of foreign subsidiaries	3,690,704	406,365
Total additions	$141,950,784	$ 74,081,653
Deductions from Working Capital:		
Cash dividends	20,740,661	17,948,504
Additions to property and equipment less book value of property retired or sold	62,762,876	31,396,343
Increase (decrease) in investment in unconsolidated subsidiaries	(10,293,250)	6,341,017
Long-term debt purchased for retirement or transferred to current liabilities	15,100,000	2,435,000
Other	2,674,774	2,932,712
Total deductions	90,985,061	61,053,576
Net Increase	$ 50,965,723	$ 13,028,077

Working capital changed in amount and composition as shown below:

	1964	1963
Working Capital at Beginning of Year	$370,387,086	$357,359,009
Cash	+ 4,656,495	− 6,261,841
Receivables from John Deere Credit Company	−12,853,768	−11,333,948
Trade receivables—net	+72,619,406	+29,637,504
Inventories	+59,600,243	+13,980,354
Total current assets	+124,022,376	+26,022,069
Accrued taxes	+ 8,056,349	+ 5,421,910
Other current liabilities	+65,000,304	+ 7,572,082
Total current liabilities	+73,056,653	+12,993,992
Net change	+50,965,723	+13,028,077
Working Capital at End of Year	$421,352,809	$370,387,086

The B.F.Goodrich Company

AND CONSOLIDATED SUBSIDIARIES

Statement of Financial Position

AT DECEMBER 31, 1963 AND 1962

Assets

CURRENT ASSETS	1963	1962
Cash	$ 14,061,135	$ 24,813,887
Marketable securities, at cost (approximate market)	11,994,491	15,227,555
Accounts and notes receivable, less allowance for doubtful accounts	149,211,095	146,810,823
Inventories—Note B		
Finished products	132,724,404	126,359,715
In process	17,185,275	16,903,155
Raw materials and supplies	35,666,785	35,108,582
	$185,576,464	$178,371,452
Total Current Assets	$360,843,185	$365,223,717
INVESTMENTS		
Shares of Unconsolidated Subsidiary and Associate Companies, at cost—Note A	31,071,262	29,457,969
Other investments and advances	29,759,312	31,295,946
	$ 60,830,574	$ 60,753,915
PROPERTY		
Land, buildings, machinery, equipment and leasehold improvements, at cost	476,323,005	454,686,716
Accumulated allowances for depreciation and amortization	243,019,598	236,287,723
	$233,303,407	$218,398,993
DEFERRED CHARGES	3,391,125	3,335,762
TOTAL ASSETS	$658,368,291	$647,712,387

See notes to financial statements

THE B.F.GOODRICH COMPANY AND CONSOLIDATED SUBSIDIARIES

Liabilities and Shareholders' Equity

CURRENT LIABILITIES	1963	1962
Notes payable and bank loans—foreign	$ 5,442,161	$ 4,435,986
Accounts payable	41,332,082	39,610,782
Accrued expenses	36,992,808	32,070,736
Federal and foreign income taxes	13,176,637	16,217,753
Long-term debt payable within one year, less bonds purchased for sinking fund	1,048,069	1,004,791
Total Current Liabilities	$ 97,991,757	$ 93,340,048
LONG-TERM DEBT PAYABLE AFTER ONE YEAR		
Debentures—4⅝% maturing 1966 to 1985	60,000,000	60,000,000
First Mortgage Bonds—2¾% maturing in 1965, less bonds in treasury	14,944,000	16,575,000
Notes—3¼% maturing 1966 to 1977	19,000,000	19,000,000
Other—maturing 1965 to 1981	1,420,413	1,633,000
	$ 95,364,413	$ 97,208,000
RESERVES		
For purchase contracts, foreign losses, sales adjustments and other purposes	15,593,807	14,932,960
SHAREHOLDERS' EQUITY		
Common Stock—$10 par value:		
Authorized 10,000,000 shares, issued 9,165,441 shares (excludes 14,196 shares held by the Company)—Note C	91,654,410	91,655,550
Capital in excess of par value of shares—Note C	38,794,711	38,491,758
Income retained in the business—Note D:		
Appropriated for increased replacement cost of facilities	33,000,000	33,000,000
Unappropriated	285,969,193	279,084,071
	$318,969,193	$312,084,071
Total Shareholders' Equity	$449,418,314	$442,231,379
TOTAL LIABILITIES AND SHAREHOLDERS' EQUITY	$658,368,291	$647,712,387

THE B.F.GOODRICH COMPANY AND CONSOLIDATED SUBSIDIARIES

Statement of Income

YEAR ENDED DECEMBER 31

	AMOUNT		PERCENT OF SALES	
	1963	**1962**	**1963**	**1962**
NET SALES (discounts, transportation and excise tax deducted)	$828,838,513	$812,025,872	100.0	100.0
OTHER INCOME	5,413,395	4,464,730	.7	.5
TOTAL	$834,251,908	$816,490,602	100.7	100.5
COSTS AND EXPENSES				
Cost of products sold	601,556,688	592,548,907	72.6	73.0
Selling and general administrative expenses	146,832,311	141,570,821	17.7	17.4
Depreciation and leasehold amortization	31,637,246	27,953,245	3.8	3.4
Interest expense	4,711,635	4,390,866	.6	.6
	$784,737,880	$766,463,839	94.7	94.4
INCOME BEFORE TAXES ON INCOME	$ 49,514,028	$ 50,026,763	6.0	6.1
FEDERAL AND FOREIGN INCOME TAXES	22,463,000	23,693,000	2.7	2.9
NET INCOME	$ 27,051,028	$ 26,333,763	3.3	3.2
Net income per share of common stock outstanding at end of year	$2.95	$2.87		
Number of common shares	**9,165,441**	**9,165,555**		

Income Retained in the Business

YEAR ENDED DECEMBER 31

	1963	**1962**
UNAPPROPRIATED AT BEGINNING OF YEAR	$279,084,071	$272,913,526
NET INCOME	27,051,028	26,333,763
	$306,135,099	$299,247,289
CASH DIVIDENDS PAID ON COMMON STOCK $2.20 a share	20,165,906	20,163,218
UNAPPROPRIATED AT END OF YEAR	$285,969,193	$279,084,071
APPROPRIATED FOR INCREASED REPLACEMENT COST OF FACILITIES	33,000,000	33,000,000
INCOME RETAINED IN THE BUSINESS AT END OF YEAR	$318,969,193	$312,084,071

See notes to financial statements

D.

Alternate problems

The numbers assigned to the alternate problems in this appendix correspond to the numbers of the comparable problems presented at the end of the chapters, with the addition of the letter A. For example, Problem 1-2A in the appendix is the alternate for Problem 1-2 appearing at the end of Chapter 1. The working papers that are available for use with the text may be used either for the problems at the end of the chapters or for the alternate problems.

Chapter 1

1-2A. On January 1 of the current year the amount of George Fisher's capital in Colonial Co. was $36,730. During the year he made weekly cash withdrawals of $325 (total of $16,900). The amounts of the enterprise's assets and liabilities at December 31 of the current year and of its revenue and expense for the year ended on that date are listed below.

Accounts payable	$ 5,750	Insurance expense	$ 920
Accounts receivable	10,250	Land	3,400
Advertising expense	4,290	Miscellaneous expense	1,630
Building	42,000	Prepaid insurance	2,120
Accumulated depreciation — building	22,570	Sales	72,740
Cash	8,150	Salaries payable	310
Depreciation expense — building	1,045	Salary expense	27,835
Depreciation expense — equipment	1,490	Supplies	2,370
Equipment	18,750	Supplies expense	2,080
Accumulated depreciation — equipment	10,430	Taxes expense	3,490
		Taxes payable	830
		Utilities expense	2,640

Instructions: (1) Prepare an income statement for the current fiscal year ending December 31, exercising care to include each item of expense listed.

(2) Prepare a capital statement for the current fiscal year.

(3) Prepare a balance sheet as of December 31 of the current fiscal year.

1-3A. H. J. Barker operates a business known as Quality Dry Cleaners. The actual work of dry cleaning is done by another company at wholesale rates. The assets and the liabilities of the business on March 1 of the current year are as follows: Cash, $1,000; Accounts Receivable, $300; Supplies, $80; Equipment, $4,600; Accumulated Depreciation, $1,100; Accounts Payable, $640. His business transactions during March are summarized below.

(a) Paid rent for March, $200.
(b) Purchased supplies for cash, $70.
(c) Paid creditors on account, $480.
(d) Received $1,200 from cash customers for dry cleaning sales.
(e) Charged customers for dry cleaning sales on account, $600.
(f) Received $520 from customers on account.
(g) Received monthly invoice of $850 for dry cleaning expense (to be paid by April 10).
(h) Reimbursed a customer $20 for a garment lost by the cleaning company, which agreed to deduct the amount from the invoice received in transaction (g).
(i) Paid the following: wages expense, $155; truck expense, $60; utilities expense, $25; miscellaneous expense, $30.
(j) Purchased an item of equipment on account, $50.
(k) Paid personal expenses by checks drawn on the business, $360, and withdrew $100 in cash for personal use.
(l) Determined by taking an inventory that $15 of supplies had been used during the month.
(m) Estimated depreciation of equipment (including truck) for the month at $105.

Instructions: (1) State the assets, liabilities, and capital as of March 1 in equation form similar to that shown in this chapter.

(2) Record the transactions in tabular form, determining the new balances after each transaction. Identify increases and decreases in capital by appropriate notations.

(3) Prepare an income statement, a capital statement, and a balance sheet.

1-4A. On September 1 of the current year John Lee established a business enterprise. The transactions of the business for the four months ending on December 31 are summarized below.

(a) Deposited cash in a business bank account....		$10,000
(b) Purchased a going business operating under the name of Progressive Parcel Delivery.		
Assets acquired:		
Accounts receivable..................	$ 3,200	
Automobile supplies..................	720	
Office supplies......................	80	
Trucks...............................	11,000	$15,000
Liabilities assumed:		
Accounts payable.....................		2,000
Terms of payment to be made:		
Cash.................................	$ 5,000	
Four non-interest-bearing notes payable of $2,000 each, due at three-month intervals..............	8,000	$13,000

(c) Charged delivery service sales to customers on account	$12,500
(d) Purchased office supplies for cash	60
(e) Purchased automobile supplies on account	1,400
(f) Received cash from customers on account	12,000
(g) Paid creditors on account	1,300
(h) Paid first of the four notes payable	2,000
(i) Purchased automobile supplies on account	150
(j) Paid license taxes in advance	360
(k) Paid insurance premiums in advance	1,280
(l) Paid drivers' wages	4,200
(m) Paid rent expense	400
(n) Paid miscellaneous expense	70
(o) Paid utilities expense	80
(p) Paid repairs expense	230
(q) Paid to Lee as personal withdrawals	1,450
(r) Depreciation of trucks	750
(s) Automobile supplies used	1,200
(t) Office supplies used	35
(u) Insurance expired	275
(v) Taxes expired	90

Instructions: (1) List the following captions in a single line at the top of a sheet turned sideways.

Cash + **Accounts Receivable** + **Automobile Supplies** + **Office Supplies** + **Prepaid Insurance** + **Prepaid Taxes** + **Trucks**

− **Accumulated Depreciation** = **Notes Payable** + **Accounts Payable** + **John Lee, Capital** **Capital Notations**

(2) Record Lee's original investment and the remaining transactions in the appropriate columns, identifying each by letter. Indicate increases by + and decreases by −. *Do not determine the new balances of the items after each transaction.* In the space for capital notations, identify each revenue and expense item and withdrawals by the owner.

(3) Insert the final balances in each column and determine that the equation is in balance at December 31, the end of the period.

(4) Prepare the following: (a) income statement for the four months, (b) capital statement for the four months, (c) balance sheet as of December 31. (The name of the business was not changed.)

Chapter 2

2-2A. The accounts in the ledger of Thomas Blair, M.D., are listed below, together with their balances as of October 1 of the current year: Cash, $3,900; Accounts Receivable, $6,500; Supplies, $200; Prepaid Insurance, $360; Equipment, $11,000; Accounts Payable, $1,250; Thomas Blair, Capital, $20,710; Thomas Blair, Drawing; Professional Fees; Salary Expense; Rent Expense; Laboratory Expense; Utilities Expense; Miscellaneous Expense.

Transactions completed during October were as follows:

(a) Paid office rent for October, $550.
(b) Purchased supplies on account, $90.
(c) Purchased equipment on account, $1,800.

(d) Received cash on account from patients, $3,200.
(e) Sold X-ray film to another doctor at cost, as an accommodation, receiving cash, $35.
(f) Returned part of equipment purchased in (c), $75.
(g) Paid cash for renewal of property insurance policy, $220.
(h) Paid salaries of receptionist and nurses, $1,550.
(i) Paid cash to creditors on account, $1,650.
(j) Received cash in payment of services rendered to patients during October, $2,800.
(k) Paid water expense, $26.
(l) Paid gas and electricity expense, $143.
(m) Paid cash from business bank account for personal expenses, $1,025.
(n) Paid invoice for laboratory analyses, $155.
(o) Recorded fees charged to customers on account for services rendered in October, $1,950.
(p) Paid miscellaneous expenses, $95.
(q) Discovered that a fee of $55 was erroneously charged to a patient in (o).
(r) Paid telephone expense, $41.

Instructions: (1) Set up a ledger of T accounts and record the balances as of October 1. Identify the balances by writing "Bal." to the left of the amount.

(2) Record the transactions for October. Identify each debit and each credit by the letter designating the transaction.

(3) Prepare a trial balance as of October 31 of the current year.

(4) Assuming that the total of supplies expense, insurance expense, and depreciation expense for the month of October is determined to be $325:

(a) What is the amount of the net income for the month?
(b) What is the capital as of October 31?

2-4A. The following transactions were completed by James R. Hill during September of the current year:

(a) Deposited $18,500 cash in a bank account for use in acquiring and operating Highland Drive-In Theatre.
(b) Purchased the Highland Drive-In Theatre for $25,500, allocated as follows: equipment, $7,000; buildings, $11,000; land, $7,500. Paid $12,500 in cash and gave a mortgage note for the remainder.
(c) Paid for September billboard and newspaper advertising, $425.
(d) Paid premiums for property and casualty insurance policies, $1,156.
(e) Purchased supplies, $250, and equipment, $900, on account.
(f) Paid miscellaneous expenses, $43.
(g) Cash receipts from admissions for the week, $2,017.
(h) Paid miscellaneous expense, $65.
(i) Cash receipts from admissions for the week, $2,100.
(j) Paid semimonthly wages, $1,750.
(k) Returned portion of equipment purchased in (e) to the supplier, receiving full credit for its cost, $175.
(l) Entered into a contract for the operation of the refreshment stand at a rental of 8% of the concessionaire's sales, with a minimum of $300 a month, payable in advance. Received cash of $150 as the advance payment for the period September 16, the effective date of the contract, to September 30.
(m) Purchased supplies for cash, $22.
(n) Cash receipts from admissions for the week, $1,890.

(o) Paid cash to creditors on account, $525.
(p) Paid electricity and water bills, $172.
(q) Cash receipts from admissions for remainder of the month, $2,420.
(r) Paid semimonthly wages, $1,750.
(s) Paid for advertising leaflets for September, $35.
(t) Paid creditors on account, $145.
(u) Recorded invoice of $1,950 for rental of film for September. Payment is due on October 10.
(v) Withdrew cash for personal use, $650.
(w) Recorded amount due from concessionaire, based on his report of sales of $2,100 for the second half of September. Payment is not due until October 6.

Instructions: (1) Record the transactions in the following T accounts, identifying each debit and credit by letter: Cash; Accounts Receivable; Prepaid Insurance; Supplies; Equipment; Buildings; Land; Accounts Payable; Mortgage Note Payable; James R. Hill, Capital; James R. Hill, Drawing; Admissions Income; Concession Income; Wages Expense; Film Rental Expense; Advertising Expense; Electricity & Water Expense; Miscellaneous Expense.

(2) Prepare a trial balance as of September 30 of the current year.

Chapter 3

3-2A. The ledger of Ward Electric Service includes the accounts listed below. The amounts shown for the asset, liability, and capital accounts are the balances as of August 1 of the current year.

Acct. No.	*Account Title*	*Balance*	*Acct. No.*	*Account Title*	*Balance*
11	Cash	$1,454.20	22	Accounts Payable.	$ 426.10
12	Supplies	649.00	31	T. L. Ward, Capital . .	4,746.10
13	Prepaid Insurance. . . .	68.40	32	T. L. Ward, Drawing .	——
14	Prepaid Rent.	——	41	Service Sales.	——
16	Equipment.	4,924.60	51	Wages Expense.	——
17	Accumulated Depr . . .	1,924.00	52	Utilities Expense	——
21	Notes Payable	——	53	Advertising Expense. . .	——
			58	Miscellaneous Exp. . . .	——

The transactions completed by the business during August were as follows:

Aug. 2. Paid rent for three months, beginning August 1, $405.
3. Purchased supplies for cash, $88.70.
4. Paid premium on property insurance, $39.
6. Recorded cash sales for the week, $407.90.
11. Purchased equipment for $1,200, paying $480 cash and giving a note payable for the balance.
12. Paid cash for advertising, $25.
13. Paid biweekly wages, $390.
13. Recorded cash sales for the week, $391.10.
14. Purchased supplies on account, $99.90.
16. Owner withdrew cash for personal use, $200.
17. Paid cash for repairs to equipment, $28.80.
18. Returned supplies purchased on the 14th for credit, $13.30.
20. Recorded cash sales for the week, $501.10.
24. Paid creditors on account, $227.40.

Aug. 26. Paid miscellaneous expenses, $25.90.
27. Recorded cash sales for the week, $401.80.
27. Paid biweekly wages, $395.
30. Owner withdrew cash for personal use, $225.
31. Paid electricity and gas expenses for the month, $45.50.
31. Recorded cash sales for the remainder of the month, $155.40.
31. Paid water expense for the month, $8.50.

Instructions: (1) Open all accounts listed above.

(2) Record the balances in the accounts under the date of Aug. 1, write "Balance" in the Items column, and place a check mark in the posting reference column.

(3) Record the transactions for August in a four-column journal similar to the one illustrated on page 64.

(4) Total and rule the journal. Prove the equality of debits and credits.

(5) Post to the ledger.

(6) Take a trial balance of the ledger.

(7) How many additional postings would have been required if a two-column journal had been used instead of a four-column journal?

3-3A. The selected transactions and errors described below relate to the accounts of Valley Services Co. during the current fiscal year:

June 16. I. W. Thompson established the business with the investment of $6,000 in cash and $1,200 in equipment, on which there was an unpaid balance of $500. The account payable is to be recorded on the books of the enterprise.

July 1. Acquired land and a building to be used as an office at a contract price of $15,000, of which $1,500 was allocated to the land. The property was encumbered by a mortgage of $10,000. Paid the seller $5,000 in cash and agreed to assume the responsibility for paying the mortgage note.

July 18. Discovered that $45 of supplies returned to the supplier for credit had been journalized and posted as a debit to Accounts Receivable and a credit to Equipment.

Aug. 1. Discovered that a withdrawal of $500 by the owner had been charged to Salary Expense.

Aug. 12. Paid $1,224 as payment on a note payable ($1,200) and interest expense ($24).

Aug. 25. Discovered that cash of $240, received from a customer on account, had been journalized and posted as a debit to Accounts Receivable and a credit to Commissions Earned.

Sept. 10. Discovered that a cash payment of $27 for prepaid insurance had been journalized and posted as a debit to Miscellaneous Expense of $72 and a credit to Cash of $72.

Dec. 9. Paid the installment due on the mortgage note, $375, and interest expense, $125.

Instructions: Journalize the transactions and the corrections in a two-column journal. When there are more than two items in an entry, present the entry in compound form.

3-4A. Robert Conlon owns and manages Conlon Realty, which acts as an agent in buying, selling, renting, and managing real estate. The account balances at the end of April and the transactions for May of the current year are presented below.

		Dr.	*Cr.*
11	Cash	1,742	
12	Accounts Receivable	4,624	
13	Prepaid Insurance	297	
14	Office Supplies	85	
16	Automobile	4,800	
17	Accumulated Depreciation — Automobile		2,700
18	Office Equipment	3,160	
19	Accumulated Depreciation — Office Equipment		965
21	Accounts Payable		148
31	Robert Conlon, Capital		5,607
32	Robert Conlon, Drawing	4,000	
41	Revenue from Fees		24,912
51	Salary and Commission Expense	13,200	
52	Rent Expense	1,200	
53	Advertising Expense	765	
54	Automobile Expense	283	
59	Miscellaneous Expense	176	

May 1. Paid rent for month, $300.
2. Paid premium on automobile insurance, $185.
2. Purchased office supplies on account, $96.
10. Received cash from clients on account, $2,592.
15. Paid salaries and commissions, $1,732.
15. Recorded revenue earned and billed to clients during first half of month, $2,650.
16. Purchased office equipment on account, $405.
19. Returned for credit office equipment purchased on May 16, $75.
20. Received cash from clients on account, $3,248.
23. Paid advertising expense, $126.
27. Paid creditors on account, $622.
28. Paid automobile expenses, $92.
29. Paid miscellaneous expenses, $187.
30. Conlon withdrew cash for personal use, $750.
31. Discovered that the $96 amount stated and journalized for the transaction of May 2 should have been $69.
31. Recorded revenue earned and billed to clients during second half of month, $2,447.
31. Paid salaries and commissions, $1,695.

Instructions: (1) Open an account in the ledger for each item for which an account balance is given.

(2) Record the balance in each account under the date of May 1, write the word "Balance" in the Items column, and place a check mark in the posting reference column.

(3) Record the transactions for May in a two-column journal.

(4) Post to the ledger.

(5) An error is discovered in billing the fees for the second half of the month. The correct amount is $2,474 instead of $2,447. Journalize the correcting entry and post.

(6) Take a trial balance of the ledger.

(7) What is the nature of the balance in Accounts Payable?

Chapter 4

4-1A. The trial balance of Belmont Laundromat at December 31, the end of the current fiscal year, and data needed for year-end adjustments are presented below.

Belmont Laundromat
Trial Balance
December 31, 19—

Cash	825	
Laundry Supplies	1,011	
Prepaid Insurance	312	
Laundry Equipment	9,800	
Accumulated Depreciation		3,400
Accounts Payable		155
Don Ford, Capital		3,495
Don Ford, Drawing	3,000	
Laundry Revenue		12,520
Wages Expense	2,950	
Rent Expense	820	
Utilities Expense	510	
Miscellaneous Expense	342	
	19,570	19,570

Adjustment data:

(a) Laundry supplies on hand at December 31	$169
(b) Insurance expired during the year	129
(c) Depreciation for the year	780
(d) Wages accrued at December 31	32

Instructions: (1) Record the trial balance on a ten-column work sheet.

(2) Complete the work sheet.

(3) Prepare an income statement, a capital statement (no additional investments were made during the year), and a balance sheet in report form.

(4) Record the adjusting entries in a two-column journal.

(5) Record the closing entries in a two-column journal.

(6) Compute the following:
- (a) Percent of net income to revenue.
- (b) Percent of net income to the capital balance at the beginning of the year.

4-2A. As of September 30, the end of the current fiscal year, the accountant for Allen Company prepared a trial balance, journalized and posted the adjusting entries, prepared an adjusted trial balance, prepared the statements, and completed the other procedures required at the end of the accounting cycle. The two trial balances as of September 30, one before adjustments and the other after adjustments, are presented on the following page.

Instructions: (1) Present the eight journal entries that were required to adjust the accounts at September 30. None of the accounts was affected by more than one adjusting entry.

(2) Present the journal entries that were required to close the books at September 30.

(3) Prepare a capital statement for the fiscal year ended September 30. There were no additional investments during the year.

Allen Company
Trial Balance
September 30, 19—

	Unadjusted		Adjusted	
Cash	2,750		2,750	
Supplies	3,050		550	
Prepaid Rent	4,700		1,550	
Prepaid Insurance	600		450	
Automobiles	6,750		6,750	
Accumulated Depreciation — Automobiles		1,500		3,000
Equipment	4,800		4,800	
Accumulated Depreciation — Equipment		480		960
Accounts Payable		560		640
Salaries Payable		—		170
Taxes Payable		—		30
Ben Allen, Capital		6,085		6,085
Ben Allen, Drawing	9,900		9,900	
Service Fees Earned		42,250		42,250
Salaries Expense	16,700		16,870	
Rent Expense	—		3,150	
Supplies Expense	—		2,500	
Depreciation Expense — Automobiles	—		1,500	
Utilities Expense	950		1,030	
Depreciation Expense — Equipment	—		480	
Taxes Expense	210		240	
Insurance Expense	—		150	
Miscellaneous Expense	465		465	
	50,875	50,875	53,135	53,135

If the working papers correlating with this textbook are not used, omit Problem 4-3A.

4-3A. The ledger of Quality Home Repairs as of October 31, the end of the first month of its current fiscal year, is presented in the working papers. The books had been closed on September 30.

Instructions: (1) Prepare a trial balance of the ledger, listing only the accounts with balances, on a ten-column work sheet.

(2) Complete the ten-column work sheet. Data for the adjustments are as follows:

Supplies on hand at October 31	$431.20
Insurance expired during the month	23.50
Truck depreciation for the month	195.50
Equipment depreciation for the month	59.00
Salaries accrued at October 31	193.50

(3) Prepare an income statement, a capital statement, and a balance sheet.

(4) Record the adjusting entries in a two-column journal and post.

(5) Record the closing entries in a two-column journal and post.

(6) Rule the closed accounts and balance and rule the remaining accounts that contain more than one entry.

(7) Prepare a post-closing trial balance.

Chapter 5

If the working papers correlating with the textbook are not used, omit Problem 5-2A.

5-2A. Three journals, the accounts receivable ledger, and portions of the general ledger of Clifton Company are presented in the working papers. Sales invoices and credit memorandums were entered in the journals by an assistant. Terms of sales on account are 2/10, n/30, FOB shipping point. Transactions in which cash was received during May of the current year are as follows:

May 1. Received cash for sale of store supplies at cost, as an accommodation, $9.
2. Received cash from Evans & Ford, Inc. in payment of April 22 invoice, less discount, $931.

Post transactions of May 2, 3, and 4 to customers' accounts.

6. Received cash for a note receivable due today, $400.
9. Received cash from J. K. McDonald Corp. in payment of April 9 invoice, $1,400; no discount.
10. Received cash for return of defective equipment purchased for cash in April, $525

Post transactions of May 9, 10, 12, and 15 to customers' accounts.

16. Cash sales for first half of May, $7,984.
17. Received cash for note receivable due today, $1,200.
20. Received cash from Evans & Ford, Inc. in payment of balance due on May 10 invoice, less discount, $1,029.
22. Received cash from J. K. McDonald Corp. in payment of May 12 invoice, less discount, $539.

Post transactions of May 18, 20, 22, 23, 24, 25 and 26 to customers' accounts.

28. Received cash from Evans & Ford, Inc. in payment of May 18 invoice, less discount, $196.
29. Received cash from Henry R. Wilson in payment of April 28 invoice, no discount.
30. Received cash from Paul Black & Co. in partial payment of May 3 invoice, $350; no discount.
31. Cash sales for second half of May, $6,533.

Post transactions of May 28, 29 and 30 to customers' accounts.

Instructions: (1) Record the cash receipts for May and post all three journals to the customers' accounts, in date sequence, at the points indicated in the narrative of transactions.

(2) Post the appropriate individual transactions to the general ledger.

(3) Add the columns of the sales journal and the cash receipts journal and post the appropriate totals to the general ledger. Insert the balance of each account after the last posting.

(4) Prepare a schedule of accounts receivable and compare the total with the balance of the controlling account.

5-3A. Transactions related to sales and cash receipts completed by J. R. Gilbert Co. during June of the current year are described below. The terms of all sales on account are 2/10, n/30, FOB destination.

June 2. Sold merchandise on account to Draper Corp., Invoice No. 204, $1,759.
3. Sold merchandise on account to S. T. Wheeler Co., Invoice No. 205, $1,322.
5. Additional cash investment made by the owner, J. R. Gilbert, $2,000.
6. Issued to S. T. Wheeler Co. a credit memorandum for merchandise damaged in shipment, $22.
9. Sold merchandise on account to Martin & Martin, Inc., Invoice No. 206, $2,300.
11. Received cash refund for a premium overcharge on property insurance, $32.
12. Issued to Martin & Martin, Inc. a credit memorandum for merchandise returned, $50.
13. Received cash from S. T. Wheeler Co. in payment of the balance due on the June 3 invoice, less discount.
14. Sold merchandise on account to S. T. Wheeler Co., Invoice No. 207, $1,150.
15. Cash sales for June 1 to 15, $6,628.
19. Received cash from Martin & Martin, Inc. in payment of the balance due on the June 9 invoice, less discount.
20. Sold merchandise on account to Draper Corp., Invoice No. 208, $1,908.
24. Received cash from S. T. Wheeler Co. in payment of the balance due on the June 14 invoice, less discount.
26. Sold merchandise on account to Draper Corp., Invoice No. 209, $2,478.
28. Received cash for a note receivable due today, $350.
30. Received cash from Draper Corp. in payment of the June 2 invoice; no discount.
30. Cash sales for June 16 to 30, $7,792.

Instructions: (1) Open the following accounts in the general ledger.

111 Cash
112 Notes Receivable
113 Accounts Receivable
117 Prepaid Insurance
311 J. R. Gilbert, Capital
411 Sales
412 Sales Returns and Allowances
413 Sales Discount

(2) Open the following accounts in the accounts receivable ledger: Draper Corp.; Martin & Martin, Inc.; S. T. Wheeler Co.

(3) Record the transactions for the month in a sales journal similar to the one illustrated on page 106, a cash receipts journal similar to the one illustrated on page 114, and a two-column general journal. All postings to the *accounts receivable ledger* should be made immediately after journalizing each entry affecting a customer's account.

(4) Post the appropriate individual transactions to the *general ledger*.

(5) Add the columns of the sales journal and the cash receipts journal and post the appropriate totals to the general ledger. The balances of the accounts need not be determined except for Accounts Receivable.

(6) Determine whether the subsidiary ledger is in agreement with the controlling account.

5-4A. Transactions related to sales and cash receipts completed by A. J. Becker Company during January of the current year are described below. The terms of all sales on account are 1/10, n/30, FOB shipping point. All delivery charges are prepaid and charged to the customer.

Jan. 2. Issued Invoice No. 676 to H. T. Vance Co., $1,350; delivery, $32; total, $1,382.
4. Received cash from Zimmer & Tobin for the balance owed on January 1, less discount.
5. Received cash from J. M. Jacobs for the balance owed on January 1, less discount.
7. Issued Invoice No. 677 to Arden Co., $800; delivery, $21; total, $821.
Post all journals to the accounts receivable ledger.
8. Received cash from Arden Co. for the balance owed on January 1, no discount.
9. Issued Credit Memo No. 26 to H. T. Vance Co., $50.
10. Issued Invoice No. 678 to J. M. Jacobs, $700; delivery, $19; total, $719.
12. Received cash from H. T. Vance Co. in payment of the balance due on the January 2 invoice, less discount.
13. Issued Invoice No. 679 to Zimmer & Tobin, $1,958; delivery, $46; total, $2,004.
14. Received cash in payment of note receivable, $1,250.
Post all journals to the accounts receivable ledger.
15. Issued Credit Memo No. 27 to Zimmer & Tobin, $58.
16. Recorded cash sales for first half of the month, $5,295.
16. Issued Invoice No. 680 to J. M. Jacobs, $2,018; delivery, $48; total, $2,066.
17. Received cash from Arden Co. in payment of the January 7 invoice, less discount.
20. Received cash from J. M. Jacobs in payment of the January 10 invoice, less discount.
23. Received cash refund for return of office supplies, $17.
23. Issued Credit Memo No. 28 to J. M. Jacobs, $18.
Post all journals to the accounts receivable ledger.
25. Issued Invoice No. 681 to Arden Co., $1,275; delivery, $29; total, $1,304.
26. Received cash from J. M. Jacobs in payment of the balance due on the January 16 invoice, less discount.
29. Issued Invoice No. 682 to H. T. Vance Co., $2,150; delivery, $52; total, $2,202.
31. Recorded cash sales for the second half of the month, $5,523.
Post all journals to the accounts receivable ledger.

Instructions: (1) Open the following accounts in the general ledger, inserting the balances indicated, as of January 1:

111 Cash	$2,964	411 Sales	______
112 Notes Receivable	2,400	412 Sales Returns and Allow.	______
113 Accounts Receivable	3,557	413 Sales Discount	______
115 Office Supplies	195	615 Delivery Expense	______

(2) Open the following accounts in the accounts receivable ledger, inserting the balances indicated, as of January 1: Arden Co., $982, including a delivery charge of $32; J. M. Jacobs, $1,845, including a delivery charge of $45; H. T. Vance Co.; Zimmer & Tobin, $730, including a delivery charge of $30. Make a notation of the amount of the delivery charges in the Items column of each account.

(3) Record the transactions for the month in a sales journal similar to the one illustrated on page 120, a sales returns and allowances journal similar to the one illustrated on page 111, and a cash receipts journal similar to the one illustrated on page 114. Post to the accounts receivable ledger at the points indicated in the narrative of transactions.

(4) Add the columns of the journals and post the appropriate individual entries and totals to the general ledger. Insert the account balances after the last posting.

(5) Determine that the subsidiary ledger is in agreement with the controlling account.

Chapter 6

6-2A. Clermont Men's Wear was established in July of the current year. Transactions related to purchases, returns and allowances, and cash payments during the remainder of the month are described below.

July 16. Purchased store equipment on account from Taylor Supply Co., $5,400.
16. Purchased merchandise on account from Worthmore Clothes, Inc., $2,920.
17. Issued Check No. 1 in payment of rent for July, $250.
17. Issued Check No. 2 in payment of office supplies, $84, and store supplies, $43.
17. Purchased merchandise on account from Lee & Co., $1,900.
18. Purchased merchandise on account from Barron Clothing Co., $1,248.
19. Received a credit memorandum from Worthmore Clothes, Inc., for returned merchandise, $120.

Post the journals to the accounts payable ledger.

24. Issued Check No. 3 to Worthmore Clothes, Inc., in payment of balance owed, less 2% discount.
24. Issued Check No. 4 to a cash customer for merchandise returned, $25.
25. Received a credit memorandum from Barron Clothing Co. for defective merchandise, $48.
25. Purchased merchandise on account from Worthmore Clothes, Inc., $2,200.
26. Issued Check No. 5 to Taylor Supply Co. in payment of invoice of $5,400.
26. Issued Check No. 6 to Lee & Co. in payment of invoice of $1,900, less 3% discount.

Post the journals to the accounts payable ledger.

29. Issued Check No. 7 to Barron Clothing Co. in payment of the invoice of $1,248 less the credit of $48.
30. Purchased the following from Taylor Supply Co. on account: store supplies, $44; office supplies, $43; office equipment, $700.
30. Purchased merchandise on account from Barron Clothing Co., $1,875.
31. Issued Check No. 8 in payment of transportation charges on merchandise purchased, $156.
31. Issued Check No. 9 in payment of sales salaries, $720.

Post the journals to the accounts payable ledger.

Instructions: (1) Open the following accounts in the general ledger, using the account numbers indicated.

111 Cash	412 Sales Returns and Allowances
116 Store Supplies	511 Purchases
117 Office Supplies	512 Purchases Returns and Allow.
121 Store Equipment	513 Purchases Discount
122 Office Equipment	611 Sales Salaries
211 Accounts Payable	712 Rent Expense

(2) Open the following accounts in the accounts payable ledger: Barron Clothing Co.; Lee & Co.; Taylor Supply Co.; Worthmore Clothes, Inc.

(3) Record the transactions for July, using a purchases journal similar to the one illustrated on pages 130 and 131, a purchases returns and allowances journal similar to the one illustrated on page 136, and a cash payments journal similar to the one illustrated on page 138. Post to the *accounts payable ledger* at the points indicated in the narrative of transactions.

(4) Post the appropriate individual entries to the *general ledger.*

(5) Add the columns of the purchases journal, the purchases returns and allowances journal, and the cash payments journal, and post the appropriate totals to the general ledger.

(6) Prepare a schedule of accounts payable.

If the working papers correlating with the textbook are not used, omit Problem 6-3A.

6-3A. Husky Novelty Co. uses carbon copies of its sales invoices as a sales journal, posting to the accounts receivable ledger directly from the invoices. At the end of the month the invoices are totaled and the appropriate entry is recorded in the general journal. Purchases on account are handled in a similar manner, the invoices being used as a purchases journal. Sales and purchases on account during March of the current year were as follows:

Sales

Mar.	4. No. 719 John Payne Corp.	$1,900
	6. No. 720 Frank Gordon	650
	10. No. 721 Lewis Abbott & Co.	1,150
	16. No. 722 Lewis Abbott & Co.	2,166
	17. No. 723 Wilson & Young	3,271
	22. No. 724 Frank Gordon	850

Purchases

Mar.	2. Eaton & Co.: store supplies, $120; office supplies, $32	$ 152
	3. Martin Corp., merchandise	2,675
	11. Hill-Burns, Inc., merchandise	1,750
	18. Eaton & Co., store supplies	94
	24. E. V. Richards, store equipment	1,175
	29. Hill-Burns, Inc., merchandise	1,264
	31. Trenton Manufacturing Co., merchandise	865

Other transactions completed during the month were recorded in a 4-column general journal, a cash receipts journal, and a cash payments journal, all of which are presented in the working papers. The subsidiary ledgers and the general ledger accounts affected by transactions of the month are also presented in the working papers.

Instructions: (1) Summarize the sales invoices and the purchases invoices listed above and record the appropriate entries in the 4-column general journal.

(2) Post all items affecting the *subsidiary* ledgers, in the following order: sales invoices, purchases invoices, general journal, cash receipts journal, cash payments journal. When postings are made daily, which is the usual practice, the entries in customers' and creditors' accounts will appear in chronological order. The fact that in this problem postings to some of the accounts will not be in perfect date sequence is immaterial.

(3) Post all items recorded in the Sundry Accounts Dr. and Sundry Accounts Cr. columns of the journals, in the following order: general journal, cash receipts journal, cash payments journal.

(4) Add the columns of the general journal and post the appropriate columnar totals of each journal, following the same sequence as in instruction (3).

(5) Prepare a trial balance.

(6) (a) What is the sum of the balances in the accounts receivable ledger?
(b) What is the sum of the balances in the accounts payable ledger?

6-4A. The transactions completed by Kent's during June, the first month of the current fiscal year, were as follows:

June 1. Issued Check No. 593 for June rent, $400.
2. Purchased merchandise on account from Price-Spencer Corp., $2,350.
3. Purchased equipment on account from Collins Supply Co., $1,350.
3. Issued Invoice No. 815 to Sanders Corp., $940.
4. Received credit memorandum from Price-Spencer Corp. for merchandise returned to them, $150.
5. Received check for $1,552 from Bryant & Ross in payment of $1,600 invoice, less discount.
8. Issued Invoice No. 816 to Zeller & Co., $1,450.
8. Issued Check No. 594 in payment of miscellaneous selling expense, $175.
9. Issued Check No. 595 for $3,069 to Allen Manufacturing Co. in payment of $3,100 balance less 1% discount.
9. Received check from Norman Corp. on account, $850; no discount.
10. Issued Check No. 596 to G. W. Ludlow & Co. in payment of invoice of $810; no discount.

Post all journals to the accounts receivable ledger and the accounts payable ledger.

10. Received check from Sanders Corp. on account, $690; no discount.
11. Issued Check No. 597 to Wade Co. in payment of account, $1,450; no discount.
14. Issued Invoice No. 817 to Bryant & Ross, $2,740.
15. Issued Check No. 598 for $2,156 to Price-Spencer Corp. in payment of $2,200 balance less 2% discount.
15. Issued Check No. 599 for $610 for cash purchase of merchandise.
15. Issued Check No. 600 in payment of miscellaneous general expense, $196.
15. Cash sales for June 1–15, $5,499.
17. Purchased merchandise on account from G. W. Ludlow & Co., $2,270.
17. Issued credit memorandum to Bryant & Ross for damaged merchandise, $140.
18. Received check for return of merchandise that was originally purchased for cash, $21.

June 22. Purchased the following on account from Collins Supply Co.: store supplies, $40; office supplies, $45.

22. Issued Check No. 601 in payment of advertising expense, $505.

Post all journals to the accounts receivable ledger and the accounts payable ledger.

23. Issued Invoice No. 818 to Norman Corp., $1,117.
24. Purchased the following on account from Allen Manufacturing Co.: merchandise, $1,040; store supplies, $22.
25. Issued Invoice No. 819 to Zeller & Co., $1,510.
26. Issued Check No. 602 to Collins Supply Co. in payment of account, $1,350; no discount.
29. Issued Check No. 603 to Roy Kent as a personal withdrawal, $800.
29. Received check for $2,522 from Bryant & Ross in payment of $2,600 balance less discount.
30. Issued Check No. 604 for monthly salaries as follows: sales salaries, $950; office salaries, $275.
30. Cash sales for June 16–30, $4,942.
30. Issued Check No. 605 for transportation on commodities purchased during the month as follows: merchandise, $86; equipment, $39.

Post all journals to the accounts receivable ledger and the accounts payable ledger.

Instructions: (1) Open the following accounts in the general ledger, entering the balances indicated as of June 1:

111	Cash	$ 7,240	411	Sales
113	Accounts Receivable	3,140	412	Sales Returns and Allow.
114	Merchandise Inventory	23,220	413	Sales Discount
115	Store Supplies	390	511	Purchases
116	Office Supplies	188	512	Purchases Discount
117	Prepaid Insurance	577	611	Sales Salaries
121	Equipment	14,718	612	Advertising Expense
121.1	Accumulated Depreciation	7,139	619	Miscellaneous Selling Exp.
211	Accounts Payable	5,360	711	Office Salaries
311	Roy Kent, Capital	36,974	712	Rent Expense
312	Roy Kent, Drawing		719	Miscellaneous General Exp.

(2) Open the following accounts in the accounts receivable ledger, entering the balances as of June 1 in the balance columns: Bryant & Ross, $1,600; Norman Corp., $850; Sanders Corp., $690; Zeller & Co.

(3) Open the following accounts in the accounts payable ledger, entering the balances as of June 1 in the balance columns: Allen Manufacturing Co., $3,100; Collins Supply Co.; G. W. Ludlow & Co., $810; Price-Spencer Corp.; Wade Co., $1,450.

(4) Record the transactions for June using a sales journal (as on page 106), a purchases journal (as on pages 130 and 131), a cash receipts journal (as on page 114), a cash payments journal (as on page 138), and a 2-column general journal. The terms of all sales on account are FOB shipping point, 3/15, n/60. Post to the subsidiary ledgers at the points indicated in the narrative of transactions.

(5) Post the appropriate individual entries to the *general ledger.*

(6) Add the columns of the special journals and post the appropriate totals to the general ledger.

(7) Prepare a trial balance.

(8) Prepare a schedule of accounts receivable and a schedule of accounts payable.

Chapter 7

7-1A. The accounts in the ledger of the Robinson Company, with the balances on December 31, the end of the current fiscal year, are as follows:

Cash	$ 3,450	Sales	$146,000
Accounts Receivable	8,920	Purchases	93,500
Merchandise Inventory	23,600	Sales Salaries	16,250
Store Supplies	680	Advertising Expense	1,750
Prepaid Insurance	1,900	Delivery Expense	1,450
Store Equipment	13,600	Depreciation Expense — Store Equipment	——
Accum. Depreciation — Store Equipment	2,800	Store Supplies Expense	——
Accounts Payable	5,600	Rent Expense	6,200
Salaries Payable	——	Insurance Expense	——
Floyd Robinson, Capital	28,630	Misc. General Expense	2,050
Floyd Robinson, Drawing	9,500	Loss on Disposal of Equipment	180
Expense and Revenue Summary	——		

The data needed for year-end adjustments on December 31 are as follows:

Merchandise inventory on December 31	$25,500
Store supplies inventory on December 31	280
Insurance expired during the year	550
Depreciation of the current year	1,250
Accrued salaries on December 31	240

Instructions: (1) Prepare an eight-column work sheet for the fiscal year ended December 31, listing all of the accounts in the order given.

(2) Prepare an income statement (Exhibit A).

(3) Prepare a capital statement (Exhibit C). There were no additional investments during the year.

(4) Prepare a balance sheet (Exhibit B).

(5) Compute the following:
- (a) Percent of net income from operations to net sales.
- (b) Percent of net income to the capital balance at the beginning of the year.

If the working papers correlating with this textbook are not used, omit Problem 7-2A.

7-2A. R. D. Scott owns and operates Scott Appliances. The general ledger balances at the beginning of the twelfth month and the journals for the twelfth month of the current fiscal year are presented in the working papers.

Instructions: (1) Post the appropriate individual items and the totals of the journals to the general ledger accounts. The balances need not be determined until the posting is completed. An assistant has posted entries to the subsidiary ledgers.

(2) Take a trial balance at December 31 on an eight-column work sheet, listing all of the accounts in the ledger.

(3) Complete the work sheet. Adjustment data are:

Merchandise inventory at December 31	$15,230.00
Prepaid insurance at December 31	895.00
Supplies on hand at December 31	173.00

Depreciation for the current year on:

Store equipment	745.00
Office equipment	140.00
Accrued taxes at December 31	191.50

(4) Prepare an income statement, a capital statement, and a balance sheet. There were no additional investments of capital by the owner during the year.

(5) Journalize the adjusting entries and post to the ledger.

(6) Journalize the closing entries and post to the ledger, indicating closed accounts by inserting a line in both balance columns.

(7) Prepare a post-closing trial balance.

(8) Journalize the reversing entry or entries as of January 1 and post to the ledger.

7-3A. A portion of the work sheet of Morgan Wholesale Co. for the current year ending December 31 is presented below.

Account Titles	Income Statement		Balance Sheet	
	Dr.	Cr.	Dr.	Cr.
Cash			27,500	
Accounts Receivable			43,300	
Merchandise Inventory			49,500	
Supplies			1,540	
Prepaid Rent			440	
Prepaid Insurance			1,420	
Store Equipment			13,600	
Accumulated Depr. — Store Equipment				5,100
Office Equipment			4,500	
Accumulated Depr. — Office Equipment				1,750
Accounts Payable				27,600
Sales Salaries Payable				630
Mortgage Note Payable				17,000
Jerome Morgan, Capital				68,700
Jerome Morgan, Drawing			9,500	
Expense and Revenue Summary	45,600	49,500		
Sales		296,750		
Sales Returns and Allowances	8,750			
Purchases	209,900			
Purchases Discount		2,550		
Sales Salaries	17,800			
Delivery Expense	12,500			
Supplies Expense	2,400			
Depreciation Expense — Store Equipment	1,320			
Miscellaneous Selling Expense	500			
Office Salaries	11,000			
Rent Expense	5,280			
Insurance Expense	2,520			
Depreciation Expense — Office Equipment	430			
Miscellaneous General Expense	410			
Interest Income		130		
	318,410	348,930	151,300	120,780

Instructions: (1) Journalize the adjusting entries to be recorded on the books of Morgan Wholesale Co., based on the partial work sheet presented above. The only accounts affected by more than one adjusting entry were Merchandise Inventory and Expense and Revenue Summary. The balance in Prepaid Rent after adjustment represents the remainder of the prepayment of thirteen months' rent in January of the year just ended.

(2) Determine:

(a) The amount of net income for the year.

(b) The amount of the owner's capital at the end of the year.

7-6A. On January 31 of the current fiscal year the following errors were discovered in the books of Nelson's Hardware.

(a) Merchandise inventory at the end of the preceding year was understated $2,500.

(b) Purchases returns and allowances totaling $570 in December of the preceding year were erroneously recorded as credits to Sales.

(c) The adjusting entry for prepaid insurance at the end of the preceding year transferred $460 to the expense account. The amount should have been $640.

(d) Land purchased for $3,000 in December for use as a site for Nelson's new home was charged to Land.

(e) No provision was made at the end of the preceding year for accrued office salaries payable, $480.

(f) An addition to the building last year at a cost of $4,000 was erroneously debited to Repairs Expense. As a result the building depreciation for the year was understated by $200.

Instructions: (1) Journalize the necessary correcting entries.

(2) Open a general ledger account for Marshall Nelson, Capital, and enter a balance of $28,600 as of January 1 of the current year in the account. Post the applicable portions of the correcting entries to the account.

(3) As of December 31 of the current year, journalize the entries to close the expense and revenue summary account (credit balance, $18,350) and the drawing account (debit balance, $9,700).

(4) Post the closing entries to the capital account; extend the balance after the last posting.

(5) Prepare a capital statement for the current year.

Chapter 8

8-2A. The following were selected from among the transactions completed by Robert E. Hamilton & Co. during the current year:

Jan. 4. Sold merchandise on account to Benham & Gray, $720.

8. Accepted a 30-day, 5% note for $720 from Benham & Gray on account.

Feb. 7. Received from Benham & Gray the amount due on the note of January 8, $723.

10. Sold merchandise on account to Kilby Corp., $700, charging an additional $25 for prepaid transportation costs.

Feb. 20. Received from Kilby Corp. the amount due on the invoice of February 10, less 2% discount.
Mar. 24. Loaned $450 cash to John Baxter, a customer, receiving a 30-day, 6% note.
Apr. 23. Received interest of $2.25 from John Baxter and a new 30-day, 6% note, as a renewal of the loan.
May 23. Received from John Baxter the amount due on his note, $452.25.
July 6. Sold merchandise on account to J. T. Clifford, Inc., $1,800.
Aug. 5. Accepted a 60-day, 7% note for $1,800 from J. T. Clifford, Inc. on account.
25. Discounted the note from J. T. Clifford, Inc. at the Red River Bank at 6%, receiving proceeds of $1,808.86.
Oct. 4. Received notice from Red River Bank that J. T. Clifford, Inc. had dishonored its note. Paid the bank the amount of the face of the note, $1,800, interest of $21, and a protest fee of $4.50.
24. Received from J. T. Clifford, Inc. the amount owed on the dishonored note, plus additional interest of $7.10.

Instructions: Record the transactions in general journal form, using a two-column general journal.

8-3A. The following were selected from among the transactions completed by Huron Co. during the current fiscal year.

Mar. 1. Purchased merchandise on account from Casper, Inc., $900.
8. Sold merchandise on account to W. H. Weaver, invoice No. 424, $480.
12. Discounted a 90-day, non-interest-bearing note payable for $4,500 at National Bank of Huron; discount rate 6%.
18. Received cash from W. H. Weaver for the invoice of March 8, less 2% discount.
31. Sold merchandise on account to T. L. Sherman, invoice No. 457, $810.
31. Issued a 90-day, 5% note for $900 to Casper, Inc. on account.
Apr. 8. Sold merchandise on account to Warroad Co., invoice No. 472, $1,300.
15. Purchased merchandise on account from Weston Bros., $600.
25. Issued check No. 789 to Weston Bros. for the amount due on the purchase of April 15, less 2% discount.
30. Received from T. L. Sherman on account a 60-day, 5% note for $810, dated April 30.
May 4. Sold merchandise on account to Shanks Co., invoice No. 580, $720.
8. Received from Warroad Co. on account a 1-month, 6% note for $1,300, dated May 8.
20. Discounted T. L. Sherman's $810 note, dated April 30, at Michigan National Bank, discount rate 6%.
June 7. Received from Shanks Co. on account a 30-day, 5% note for $720, dated June 7.
7. Received cash from Warroad Co. for the amount owed on the note dated May 8.
10. Issued check No. 856 to National Bank of Huron for the amount due on the note dated March 12.
29. Received notice from Michigan National Bank that T. L. Sherman had dishonored his note dated April 30. Issued check No. 896 in payment of the amount due; no protest fee.

June 29. Issued check No. 897 to Casper, Inc. in payment of the note dated March 31.
July 7. Shanks Co. dishonored its note dated June 7. Charged the dishonored note to their account.
14. Received cash from T. L. Sherman for the principal and interest on his dishonored note, plus additional interest at 8% on the total amount from June 29.

Instructions: Record the transactions, using the following journals: sales journal (as illustrated on page 106); purchases journal (with only one money column, headed Purchases Dr. and Accts. Pay. Cr.); cash receipts journal (as illustrated on page 184); cash payments journal (as illustrated on page 184); two-column general journal.

8-4A. The following transactions were completed by G. E. Follmer Co. during the current fiscal year:

Mar. 7. Received from Angola Steel Co. a 90-day, non-interest-bearing note for $6,000, dated March 6, on account.
11. Issued to Leland & Son a 2-month, 5% note for $4,500, on account.
Apr. 11. Discounted at LaGrange Trust Co. at 6% the note received from Angola Steel Co., dated March 6.
May 11. Issued check No. 528 to Leland & Son in payment of the note issued on March 11.
14. Discounted a 60-day, non-interest-bearing note payable for $7,200 at LaGrange Trust Co.; discount rate, 7%.
June 6. Received from Federal Supply Co. a 60-day, 7% note for $2,000, dated June 4, on account.
15. Purchased land for a building site from Willow Vale Co. for $29,500, issuing check No. 564 for $4,500 and a 5% mortgage note for the balance. The contract provides for payments of $2,500 of principal plus accrued interest at intervals of six months.
July 1. Discounted at the LaGrange Trust Co. at 6% the note received from Federal Supply Co., dated June 4.
13. Issued check No. 588 to LaGrange Trust Co. for the amount due on the note payable issued on May 14.
Aug. 4. Received notice from the LaGrange Trust Co. that Federal Supply Co. had dishonored the note due on August 3. Issued check No. 633 for the amount due on the note, plus a protest fee of $5.
11. Received from Crosstown Plaza a 90-day, 6% note for $750, dated August 10, on account.
Oct. 2. Received from Federal Supply Co. the amount due on the note dishonored on August 3, including interest at 6% from August 3 to October 2 on the maturity value of the note plus protest fee.
Nov. 9. Crosstown Plaza dishonored its note dated August 11. Charged the dishonored note to their account.
Dec. 15. Issued check No. 749 for principal and interest due on mortgage note.

Instructions: Record the transactions, using the following journals: cash receipts journal (as illustrated on page 187); cash payments journal (as illustrated on page 187, except for an additional column for Sundry Accounts Cr.); two-column general journal.

Chapter 9

9-1A. The accounts listed below appear in the ledger of Beltrami Realty at December 31, the end of the current fiscal year. None of the year-end adjustments has been recorded.

113 Interest Receivable	$ ——	313 Expense and Revenue Sum.	$ ——
114 Supplies	690	411 Rental Income	125,700
115 Prepaid Insurance	1,800	511 Salary and Com. Expense	27,300
116 Prepaid Advertising	——	513 Advertising Expense	4,350
117 Prepaid Interest	——	514 Insurance Expense	——
213 Salaries and Commissions Payable	——	515 Supplies Expense	——
215 Unearned Rent	——	611 Interest Income	570
		711 Interest Expense	780

The following information relating to adjustments at December 31 was obtained from physical inventories, supplementary records, and other sources:

(a) Interest accrued on notes receivable at December 31, $127.
(b) Inventory of supplies at December 31, $130.
(c) The insurance record indicates that $1,335 of insurance is unexpired at December 31.
(d) Of a prepayment of $600 for advertising space in a local newspaper, 40% has been used and the remainder will be used in the following year.
(e) A short-term non-interest-bearing note payable was discounted at a bank in December. The amount of the total discount of $220 applicable to December is $70.
(f) Salaries and commissions accrued at December 31, $1,865.
(g) Rent collected in advance that will not be earned until the following year, $5,920.

Instructions: (1) Open the accounts listed and record the balances as of December 31.

(2) Journalize the adjusting entries and post to the appropriate accounts after each entry. Identify the postings by writing "Adjusting" in the items columns.

(3) Prepare a compound journal entry to close the revenue accounts and another compound entry to close the expense accounts.

(4) Post the closing entries. Identify the postings by writing "Closing" in the items columns.

(5) Prepare the reversing journal entries that should be made on January 1 and post to the appropriate accounts. Write "Reversing" in the items columns.

9-2A. Sharp Co. closes its books annually on December 31. All relevant data regarding notes payable and interest from November 1 through February 17 of the following year are presented below. (All notes are dated as of the day they are issued.)

Nov. 5. Issued a $9,000, 6%, 90-day note on account.
25. Issued a $4,500, 6%, 60-day note on account.
Dec. 7. Borrowed $7,000 from Citizens National Bank, issuing a 6%, 60-day note.
14. Paid principal, $4,000, and interest, $80, on note payable due today.
31. Recorded an adjusting entry for the interest accrued on the notes dated November 5, November 25, and December 7. There are no other notes outstanding on this date.

Dec. 31. Recorded the entry to close the interest expense account.
Jan. 1. Recorded a reversing entry for the accrued interest.
18. Issued a $5,000, 6%, 30-day note on account.
24. Paid $4,545 on the note issued on November 25.
Feb. 3. Paid $9,135 on the note issued on November 5.
5. Paid $7,070 on the note issued on December 7.
17. Paid $5,025 on the note issued on January 18.

Instructions: (1) Open accounts for Interest Payable (Acct. No. 214) and Interest Expense (Acct. No. 711), and record a debit balance of $542 in the latter account as of November 1 of the current year.

(2) Present entries, in general journal form, to record the transactions and other data above, posting to the two accounts after each entry affecting them.

(3) If the reversing entry were not made as of January 1, how would the four interest payments subsequent to that date be recorded? Arrange your answers in this form:

Note (face amount)	Dr. Interest Payable	Dr. Interest Expense

If the working papers correlating with the textbook are not used omit Problem 9-4A.

9-4A. The J. T. Parker Company prepares interim financial statements at the end of each month and closes its books annually on December 31. Their income statement for the two-month period, January and February of the current year, is presented in the working papers. In addition, the trial balance of the ledger as of one month later is presented on an eight-column work sheet in the working papers. Data needed for adjusting entries at March 31, the end of the three-month period, are as follows:

(a) Estimated merchandise inventory at March 31, $79,824.
(b) Insurance expired during the three-month period:
Allocable as selling expense, $195.
Allocable as general expense, $85.
(c) Estimated inventory of store supplies at March 31, $260.
(d) Included in notes payable is a $10,000, 90-day non-interest bearing note discounted at Merchants Bank and Trust Co. on March 1. The $150 discount was debited to interest expense.
(e) Depreciation for the three-month period of:
Store equipment, $420.
Office equipment, $105.
(f) Estimated property tax of $120 a month was accrued for January and February. The tax statement, which was received in March, indicates a liability of $1,560 for the calendar year.
(g) Salaries accrued at March 31:
Sales salaries, $300.
Office salaries, $60.
(h) Included in notes payable is a $2,000, 6%, 6-month note dated December 1 of the preceding year. (Accrue interest for 4 months.)

Instructions: (1) Complete the eight-column work sheet for the three-month period ended March 31 of the current year.

(2) Prepare an income statement for the three-month period, using the last three-column group of the nine-column form in the working papers.

(3) Prepare an income statement for the month of March, using the middle three-column group of the nine-column form in the working papers.

(4) Prepare a capital statement for the three-month period. There were no additional investments during the period.

(5) Prepare a balance sheet as of March 31.

9-5A. The Hoosier Co. prepares interim statements at the end of each month and closes its books annually on December 31. Property taxes are assessed for fiscal years beginning on July 1 and ending on June 30. Selected transactions and property tax allocations for the period July 1 to December 31 of one year and of January 1 to June 30 of the following year are presented below.

July 31. Property tax allocation for July based on estimated property tax of $4,800 for the taxing authority's fiscal year beginning July 1.
Oct. 31. Property tax allocation for October, based on tax statement dated October 20 indicating a tax assessment of $4,704.
Nov. 2. Paid first half of tax assessment, $2,352.
30. Property tax allocation for November.
Dec. 31. Property tax allocation for December.
Jan. 31. Property tax allocation for January.
Apr. 4. Paid second half of tax assessment, $2,352.
30. Property tax allocation for April.
June 30. Property tax allocation for June.

Instructions: Present, in general journal form, the entries to record the selected tax allocations and payments, assuming in all cases that appropriate entries have been recorded in the books for all intervening months.

9-7A. Selected accounts from the ledger of Lewisburg Co., with the account balances before and after adjustment, at the close of the fiscal year are:

	Unadjusted Balance	Adjusted Balance
Interest Receivable	$ —	$ 80
Supplies	1,250	450
Prepaid Insurance	1,410	1,020
Prepaid Property Tax	300	—
Prepaid Interest	—	95
Accumulated Depreciation — Equipment	2,700	3,125
Wages Payable	—	250
Interest Payable	—	65
Unearned Rent	—	810
Rent Income	9,100	8,290
Wages Expense	24,650	24,900
Depreciation Expense — Equipment	—	425
Supplies Expense	—	800
Property Tax Expense	1,300	1,600
Insurance Expense	—	390
Interest Income	460	540
Interest Expense	300	270

Instructions: (1) Journalize the adjusting entries that were posted to the ledger at the close of the fiscal year.

(2) Insert the letter "R" in the date column opposite each adjusting entry that should be reversed as of the first day of the following fiscal year.

Chapter 10

10-1A. The following transactions, adjusting entries, and closing entries related to doubtful accounts were completed during the current fiscal year ending December 31:

Feb. 7. Received $225 from Walter P. Fry in payment of his account, which was written off in the preceding year.
Apr. 19. Wrote off the account of Hunt & Co., $315.
May 16. Received 10% of the $750 balance owed by Dye & Edwards and wrote off the remainder as uncollectible.
July 27. Wrote off the account of A. J. Perkins, Inc., $175.
Aug. 28. Received $120 from James A. Gordon in payment of his account, which was written off in the preceding year.
Nov. 15. Wrote off the following accounts as uncollectible (compound entry): Willard Davis, $310; D. W. Frank & Co., $420; Reid & Tyler, $180.
Dec. 31. On the basis of an analysis of the accounts receivable, Allowance for Doubtful Accounts is to be adjusted to a balance of $2,175.
Dec. 31. Recorded the entry to close the appropriate account to Expense and Revenue Summary.

Instructions: (1) Open the following accounts, recording the credit balance indicated as of January 1:

114.1 Allowance for Doubtful Accounts.................... $1,950
313 Expense and Revenue Summary.................... —
718 Uncollectible Accounts Expense.................... —

(2) Record in general journal form the transactions, adjusting entries, and closing entries described above, and post to the three accounts, extending the balance after each entry.

(3) The accounts receivable account has a debit balance of $93,750 at December 31. What is the expected realizable value of the accounts receivable at that date?

(4) Assuming that, instead of basing the provision for uncollectible accounts on an analysis of receivables, the adjusting entry on December 31 had been based on an estimated loss of ¾ of 1% of net sales for the year of $280,000, determine the following:

(a) Uncollectible accounts expense for the year.
(b) Balance in Allowance for Doubtful Accounts after the adjustment of December 31.
(c) Expected realizable value of the accounts receivable on December 31.

10-2A. Details regarding the inventory at January 1, purchases during the year, and the inventory count at December 31 for Mansfield Appliance are as follows:

Model	Inventory Jan. 1	1st Purchase	2nd Purchase	3rd Purchase	Inventory Count Dec. 31
118	6 at $ 47	5 at $ 51	9 at $ 51	8 at $ 54	9
120	7 at 347	6 at 352	5 at 359	——	4
217	6 at 129	5 at 135	4 at 144	——	6
218	2 at 282	4 at 294	9 at 294	4 at 300	5
430	7 at 104	8 at 109	5 at 114	6 at 115	8
709	4 at 98	8 at 101	4 at 103	5 at 106	3
872	5 at 250	6 at 250	7 at 259	5 at 265	7

Instructions: (1) Determine the cost of the inventory on December 31 by the first-in, first-out method. Present data in columnar form, using the columnar headings indicated below. If more than one unit cost is applied to the inventory of a particular model, use a separate line for each.

Model	Quantity	Unit Cost	Total Cost

(2) Determine the cost of the inventory on December 31 by the last-in, first-out method, following the same procedures prescribed in instruction (1).

(3) Determine the cost of the inventory on December 31 by the weighted average method, using the same columnar headings as in instruction (1).

10-3A. Data needed to estimate the merchandise inventory by the retail method and the gross profit method are presented below.

	Cost	Retail
(a) Retail method:		
Merchandise inventory, January 1	$192,700	$308,320
Transactions during January and February:		
Purchases	225,734	363,680
Purchases discounts	1,794	
Sales		326,300
Sales returns and allowances		3,700
(b) Gross profit method:		
Merchandise inventory, September 1	$175,300	
Transactions during September:		
Purchases	194,700	
Purchases discounts	3,500	
Sales		$285,700
Sales returns and allowances		7,900
Estimated gross profit rate		41%

Instructions: (1) Determine the estimated cost of the inventory on February 28 in (a), presenting details of the computation.

(2) Determine the estimated cost of the inventory on September 30 in (b), presenting details of the computation.

If the working papers correlating with the textbook are not used, omit Problem 10-4A.

10-4A. Data on the physical inventory of Ward & Co. as of December 31 of the current year are presented in the working papers. The quantity of each commodity on hand has been determined and recorded on the inventory sheet; unit prices obtained from current price quotations and other sources have also been recorded on the sheet. The inventory is to be priced at the lower of cost or market, with cost being determined by the first-in, first-out method. The quantity of each commodity purchased and the unit cost for the last two purchases are summarized at the top of the opposite page.

Instructions: Record the relevant unit cost data on the inventory sheet and complete the pricing of the inventory. When there are two different unit costs applicable to a commodity, rule out the quantity shown on the inventory sheet and substitute the number to which the most recent cost applies. Record the quantity and the unit cost of the remaining portion of the inventory on the following line.

Description	Most recent purchase Quantity	Most recent purchase Unit Cost	Next most recent purchase Quantity	Next most recent purchase Unit Cost
1821A	15	$ 52	10	$ 51
326LM	90	26	95	24
1931M	100	88	40	86
WD190	70	16	100	15
SL911	400	11	200	10
942VW	20	38	30	37
1839B	100	17	75	15
XXX86	200	6	125	5
555FS	150	12	85	11
FC566	80	76	110	75
CS999	73	20	125	19
OPL14	30	209	40	198
E3B1Y	250	13	175	14
JG796	8	245	17	238
MJ630	225	6	485	5
BC042	325	5	128	4
AAA40	57	52	94	51
653ND	600	10	450	9

10-5A. The following preliminary income statement was prepared before the books were adjusted or closed at the end of the year:

Milford Sales Co.
Income Statement
For Year Ended December 31, 19—

Sales (net)		$213,780
Cost of merchandise sold:		
Merchandise inventory, January 1, 19—	$ 39,760	
Purchases (net)	149,175	
Merchandise available for sale	$188,935	
Less: Merchandise inventory, December 31, 19—	42,170	
Cost of merchandise sold		146,765
Gross profit on sales		$ 67,015
Operating expenses		48,325
Net income		$ 18,690

The following errors were discovered by the independent accountant retained to conduct the annual audit:

(a) A number of errors were discovered in pricing inventory items, in extending amounts, and in footing inventory sheets. The net effect of the corrections, exclusive of those described below, was to decrease by $2,850 the amount stated as the ending inventory on the income statement.
(b) A sales invoice for $1,500, dated December 31, had not been recorded. The merchandise was shipped on December 31, FOB shipping point, and its cost, $920, was not included in the ending inventory.
(c) A sales order for $1,350, dated December 31, had been recorded as a sale but the merchandise was not shipped until January 3. The cost of the merchandise ($1,020) was not included in the ending inventory.

(d) A purchase invoice for merchandise of $525, dated December 31, had been correctly recorded but the merchandise was in transit on December 31 and had not been included in the ending inventory. Title had passed to Milford Sales Co.

(e) A purchase invoice for merchandise of $975, dated December 29, was not received until after December 31 and had not been recorded. The merchandise had arrived, however, and was properly included in the ending inventory.

(f) An item of equipment, received on December 31, was included in the ending merchandise inventory at its cost, $830. The invoice had been recorded correctly.

Instructions: (1) Journalize any entries necessary to correct accounts in the general ledger, inserting the identifying letters in the date column. All purchases and sales were made on account. (An assistant will make the necessary corrections to the subsidiary ledgers.)

(2) Enter the reported ending inventory of $42,170 in a T account and record the necessary corrections based on the audit, identifying each item by letter.

(3) Prepare a revised income statement.

Chapter 11

11-1A. The following expenditures and receipts are related to land, land improvements, and buildings acquired for use in a business enterprise. The receipts are identified by an asterisk.

(a) Cost of land and building for a plant site	$ 50,000
(b) Delinquent real estate taxes on property, assumed by purchaser	1,750
(c) Cost of razing and removing the building	2,500
(d) Cost of land fill and grading the land	1,800
(e) Architect's fee for plans and supervision	24,000
(f) Premium on 1-year insurance policy during construction	4,200
(g) Fee paid to attorney for title search	500
(h) Paid to building contractor for new building	480,000
(i) Cost of paving parking lot to be used by employees and customers	1,200
(j) Cost of underground water lines	750
(k) Money borrowed to pay building contractor	320,000*
(l) Cost of fences	1,350
(m) Real estate taxes accrued during period of construction	1,800
(n) Interest accrued on building loan during period of construction	21,000
(o) Special assessment for installation of sewers, paid to city	800
(p) Proceeds from sale of salvage materials from old building	900*
(q) Cost of repairing windstorm damage during construction	3,100
(r) Proceeds from insurance company for windstorm damage	3,000*
(s) Refund of premium on insurance policy (f) canceled after 11 months	275*
	$270,575

Instructions: (a) Assign each expenditure and receipt (indicate receipts by an asterisk) to Land, Land Improvements, Building, or "Other Accounts." Identify each item by letter and list the amounts in columnar form, as follows:

Item	Land	Land Improvements	Building	Other Accounts

(b) Total the amount columns.

11-2A. An item of new equipment acquired at a cost of $65,000 at the beginning of a fiscal year has an estimated life of 5 years and an estimated trade-in value of $5,000. The manager requested information regarding the effect of alternative methods on the amount of the annual depreciation expense.

Upon the basis of the data presented to the manager in accordance with Instruction 1, the sum-of-the-years-digits method was elected. At the beginning of the fourth year the equipment was traded in for similar equipment priced at $75,000. The trade-in allowance on the old equipment was $12,000 and a note payable was issued for the balance.

Instructions: (1) Determine the annual depreciation for each of the estimated 5 years of use and the book value of the equipment at the end of each year by (a) the straight-line method, (b) the declining-balance method (at twice the straight-line rate), and (c) the sum-of-the-years-digits method. The following columnar headings are suggested for each schedule:

Year	Depreciation Expense	Book Value End of Year

(2) Present the debits and the credits required to record the trade-in transaction at the beginning of the fourth year, (a) recognizing gain or loss on the disposal and (b) postponing recognition of gain or loss on the disposal.

If the working papers correlating with the textbook are not used, omit Problem 11-3A.

11-3A. Leader Printing Co. maintains a subsidiary equipment ledger for the printing equipment and accumulated depreciation accounts in the general ledger. A small portion of the subsidiary ledger, the two controlling accounts, and a general journal are presented in the working papers. The company computes depreciation on each individual item of equipment. Transactions and adjusting entries affecting the printing equipment are described below.

1965

Sept. 7. Purchased a power cutter (Zephyr model, Serial No. 58432) from Anderson Typograph Co. on account for $5,184. The estimated life of the asset is 8 years, it is expected to have no residual value, and the straight-line method of depreciation is to be used. (This is the only transaction of the year that directly affected the printing equipment account.)

Dec. 31. Entered depreciation for the year in subsidiary accounts 125-64 to 66, and inserted the new balances. (It is assumed that an assistant enters the depreciation and the new balances in accounts 125-1 to 63.)

31. Recorded the annual depreciation on printing equipment. The depreciation for the year entered in subsidiary accounts 125-1 to 63 totals $18,732, to which must be added the depreciation entered on accounts 125-64 to 66.

1966
May 3. Purchased a Model A10 rotary press from Kistler Press, Inc., priced at $28,750, giving the Model 21 flatbed press (Acct. No. 125-64) in exchange plus $10,000 cash and a series of twelve $1,000 notes payable, maturing at 6-month intervals. (Record depreciation to date in 1966 on item traded in; gain or loss on the disposal is not to be recognized.)

Instructions: (1) Record the transaction of September 7 in general journal form. Post to the printing equipment account in the general ledger and to Account 125-66 in the subsidiary ledger.

(2) Make the entries required on December 31 and post to the accumulated depreciation — printing equipment account in the general ledger.

(3) Make the entries in general journal form required by the purchase of printing equipment on May 3. Post to the printing equipment account and to the accumulated depreciation — printing equipment account.

(4) Assuming that the rotary press purchased on May 3 has an estimated residual value of $6,000 and an estimated life of 10 years, determine the depreciation on this press by the declining-balance method, at twice the straight-line rate, for the fiscal years ending December 31, (a) 1966 and (b) 1967.

11-4A. The following transactions, adjusting entries, and closing entries were completed by Early American Furniture Co. during a three-year period. All are related to the use of delivery equipment.

1965
June 10. Purchased a used delivery truck for $2,400, paying cash.
14. Paid garage $160 for new tires and $212 for extensive repairs to the truck.
Oct. 16. Paid garage $42 for miscellaneous repairs to the motor.
Dec. 31. Recorded depreciation on the truck for the fiscal year. The estimated life of the truck is 2 years, with a trade-in value of $300. The straight-line method of depreciation is used.
Dec. 31. Closed the appropriate accounts to Expense and Revenue Summary.

1966
Sept. 28. Traded in the used truck on a new truck priced at $4,908, receiving a trade-in allowance of $800 and paying the balance in cash. (Record depreciation to date in 1966; gain or loss on exchange is not to be recognized.)
Oct. 19. Paid garage $29 for repairs to the truck.
Dec. 31. Recorded depreciation on the truck. It has an estimated trade-in value of $900 and an estimated life of 4 years. The declining-balance method (twice the straight-line rate) of depreciation is used.
31. Closed the appropriate accounts to Expense and Revenue Summary.

1967
May 23. Purchased a new truck for $4,752, paying cash.
Aug. 25. Sold the truck purchased in 1966 for $2,500 cash. (Record depreciation).
Dec. 31. Recorded depreciation on the remaining truck. It has an estimated trade-in value of $600 and an estimated life of 4 years. The declining-balance method (twice the straight-line rate) of depreciation is used.
31. Closed the appropriate accounts to Expense and Revenue Summary.

Instructions: (1) Open the following accounts in the ledger:

121 Delivery Equipment	614 Depreciation Expense — Delivery Equipment
121.1 Accumulated Depreciation — Delivery Equipment	615 Truck Repair Expense
	912 Loss on Disposal of Plant Assets

(2) Record the transactions and the adjusting and closing entries in general journal form. Post to the accounts and extend the balances after each entry.

11-6A. The trial balance of Gem Markets at December 31, the end of the current fiscal year, before adjustments, is as follows:

Cash	32,615	
Merchandise Inventory	116,830	
Prepaid Expenses	7,707	
Delivery Equipment	20,485	
Accumulated Depreciation — Delivery Equipment		7,860
Store Equipment	36,220	
Accumulated Depreciation — Store Equipment		18,960
Office Equipment	5,950	
Accumulated Depreciation — Office Equipment		3,436
Buildings	94,800	
Accumulated Depreciation — Buildings		35,950
Land	6,000	
Notes Payable (short term)		25,000
Accounts Payable		37,910
L. J. Harper, Capital		138,666
L. J. Harper, Drawing	13,200	
Sales (net)		964,110
Purchases (net)	791,270	
Operating Expenses (control account)	106,095	
Gain on Disposal of Plant Assets		510
Interest Expense	810	
Loss on Disposal of Plant Assets	420	
	1,232,402	1,232,402

Data needed for year-end adjustments:

(a) Merchandise inventory at December 31, $135,817.

(b) Insurance and other prepaid operating expenses expired during the year, $2,370.

(c) Depreciation is computed by the straight-line method on the average of the beginning and ending balances of the plant asset accounts. Beginning balances and average rates are as follows:
- Delivery equipment, $16,395, 25%.
- Store equipment, $32,004, 12½%.
- Office equipment, $6,130, 10%.
- Buildings, $94,800, 2½%.

(d) Accrued liabilities at the end of the year, $2,110, of which $650 is for interest on the notes and $1,460 is for wages and other operating expenses.

Instructions: (1) Prepare an income statement for the current year.

(2) Prepare a balance sheet in report form, presenting the plant assets in the manner illustrated in this chapter.

Chapter 12

12-1A. The cash in bank account for Cowen Company at October 31 of the current year indicated a balance of $3,639.95 after both the cash receipts journal and the check register for October had been posted. The bank statement indicated a balance of $5,101.10 on October 31. Comparison of the bank statement and the accompanying canceled checks and memorandums with the records revealed the following reconciling items:

(a) A deposit of $610.20 representing receipts of October 31 had been placed in the bank's night depository at the close of business on October 31. The deposit did not appear on the bank statement.
(b) Checks outstanding totaled $1,830.50.
(c) A check for $450 returned with the statement had been recorded in the check register as $540. The check was a payment to Williams Company on account for the purchase of machinery and equipment.
(d) A check for $150 drawn by Cohen Company had been erroneously charged by the bank to Cowen Company's account.
(e) The bank had collected for Cowen Company $306 on a note left for collection. The face of the note was $300.
(f) Bank service charges for October amounted to $5.15.

Instructions: (1) Prepare a bank reconciliation.
(2) Journalize the necessary entries. The books have not been closed.

12-2A. Daly and Sons, Inc. has the following vouchers in its unpaid voucher file at June 30 of the current year:

Due Date	Voucher No.	Creditor	Date of Invoice	Amount	Terms
July 6	801	Blum, Inc.	June 26	$500	1/10, n/30
July 13	795	Carter Bros.	June 13	410	n/30

The vouchers prepared and the checks issued during the month of July are presented below.

Vouchers

Date	Voucher No.	Payee	Amount	Terms	Distribution
July 1	805	Hicks Sales Co.	$ 190	Cash	Store supplies
1	806	Petty Cash	50	—	Petty cash
7	807	Cox Bros.	1,400	2/10, n/30	Purchases
9	808	Alvis Co.	350	n/30	Office equipment
12	809	Lynn Office Supply	90	cash	Office supplies
15	810	Penn Co.	2,300	2/10, n/30	Purchases
19	811	Knox Motors	4,400	cash	Delivery equip.
20	812	First National Bank	1,020	—	Notes pay., $1,000 Interest exp., $20
23	813	News Gazette	200	n/30	Advertising exp.
26	814	Stark Supply	3,500	2/10, n/30	Purchases
28	815	S&W Sales	400	cash	Store supplies
30	816	Sanders Co.	75	cash	Office supplies
30	817	Petty cash	41	—	Store supplies, $8 Delivery exp., $10 Misc. sell. exp., $9 Misc. gen. exp., $14

Checks

Date	Check No.	Payee	Voucher Paid	Amount
July 1	940	Hicks Sales Co.	No. 805	$ 190
1	941	Petty cash	806	50
6	942	Blum, Inc.	801	495
12	943	Lynn Office Supply	809	90
13	944	Carter Bros.	795	410
17	945	Cox Bros.	807	1,372
19	946	Knox Motors	811	4,400
20	947	First National Bank	812	1,020
28	948	S&W Sales	815	400
30	949	Sanders Co.	816	75
30	950	Petty cash	817	41

Instructions: (1) Set up a four-column account for Accounts Payable, Account No. 212, and record the balance of $910 as of July 1.

(2) Record the July vouchers in a voucher register similar to the one illustrated in this chapter, with the following amount columns: Accounts Payable Cr., Purchases Dr., Store Supplies Dr., Office Supplies Dr., and Sundry Accounts Dr. Purchases invoices are recorded at the gross amount.

(3) Record the July checks in a check register similar to the one illustrated in this chapter, but omit the Bank Deposits and Balance columns. As each check is recorded in the check register, the check number should be inserted in the appropriate place in the Check No. column of the voucher register. Assume that appropriate notations are made in the Paid column of the voucher register when the June vouchers are paid.

(4) Total and rule the registers and post to the accounts payable account.

(5) Prepare a schedule of unpaid vouchers.

If the working papers correlating with the textbook are not used, omit Problem 12-3A.

12-3A. Portions of the following accounting records of D. L. Mason Co. are presented in the working papers:

Voucher Register
Check Register
General Journal
Insurance Register
Notes Payable Register

General ledger accounts:
Prepaid Insurance
Notes Payable
Accounts Payable

Expenditures, cash disbursements, and other selected transactions completed during the period March 25–31 of the current year are described below.

Mar. 25. Recorded Voucher No. 647 payable to Harlem and Co. for merchandise, $2,900, 2/10, n/30. (Purchases invoices are recorded at the gross amount.)

26. Issued Check No. 907 to Hayes Bros. in payment of Voucher No. 629 for $5,900, less cash discount of 1%.

26. Recorded Voucher No. 648 payable to Hamilton Insurance Co. for the following insurance policy, dated today: No. 1726X, automobiles, 1 year, $1,128.

26. Issued Check No. 908 in payment of Voucher No. 648.

Mar. 27. Recorded Voucher No. 649 payable to Merchants State Bank for note payable (No. 34), $10,000.
27. Issued Check No. 909 in payment of Voucher No. 649.
28. Issued a 90-day, 6% note, dated today (No. 36) to Lang and Son in settlement of Voucher No. 619, $3,400. The note is payable at American National Bank.
28. Recorded Voucher No. 650 payable to Ajax Fire Insurance Co. for the following insurance policy, dated today: No. 947BR, merchandise & equipment, $50,000, 3 years, $666.72.
28. Issued Check No. 910 in payment of Voucher No. 650.
29. Recorded Voucher 651 payable to Kettering Times for advertising, $170.
30. Recorded Voucher No. 652 payable to Olson Corporation for merchandise, $3,200, 2/10, n/30.
30. Recorded Voucher No. 653 payable to R. L. Eaton Co. for note payable (No. 33), $3,000 and interest, $30.
30. Issued Check No. 911 in payment of Voucher No. 653.
31. Issued Check No. 912 to Harris & Co. in payment of Voucher No. 642 for $2,000 less cash discount of 2%.
31. Recorded Voucher No. 654 payable to Petty Cash for $172.10 distributed as follows: Store Supplies, $32.10; Advertising Expense, $9.50; Delivery Expense, $16.20; Miscellaneous Selling Expense, $57.70; Miscellaneous General Expense, $56.60.
31. Issued Check No. 913 in payment of Voucher No. 654.

After the journals are posted at the end of the month, the cash in bank account has a debit balance of $16,306.22.

The bank statement indicates a March 31 balance of $22,042.44. Comparison of paid checks returned by the bank with the check register reveals that Nos. 910, 911, and 912 are outstanding. Check 858 for $175, which appeared on the February reconciliation as outstanding, is still outstanding. A debit memorandum accompanying the bank statement indicates a charge of $95.50 for a check drawn by Harold Burt, a customer, which was returned because of insufficient funds.

Instructions: (1) Record the transactions for March 25–31 in the appropriate journals. Immediately after recording a transaction, post individual items, where appropriate, to the three general ledger accounts given.

(2) Make the necessary notations in the notes payable register and the insurance register, rounding insurance expirations to the nearest month.

(3) Total and rule the voucher register and the check register, and post totals to the accounts payable account.

(4) Complete the schedule of unpaid vouchers. (Compare the total with the balance of the accounts payable account as of March 31.)

(5) Prepare a bank reconciliation and journalize any necessary entries.

(6) Total the Expired Premium column for March in the insurance register, journalize the adjusting entry, and post to the prepaid insurance account. (Determine the balance of prepaid insurance as of March 31 from the columns in the insurance register and compare it with the balance of the prepaid insurance account as of the same date.)

(7) Determine the amount of interest accrued as of March 31 on notes payable (No. 32 and No. 36). (Assume 28 days in February.)

(8) Determine the amount of interest prepaid as of March 31 on notes payable (No. 35). (The non-interest-bearing note was discounted by the bank.)

12-5A. Baskin and Trier makes all disbursements by check in conjunction with a voucher system and deposits receipts in a night depository after banking hours each Wednesday and Friday. The data necessary for reconciling the bank statement as of April 30 of the current year are presented below.

Balance in the cash in bank account as of April 1.	$4,917.70
Total of Cash in Bank Dr. column in cash receipts journal for April	5,771.19
Total of Cash in Bank Cr. column in check register for April . .	5,236.65

The firm's records indicated the following deposits during April:

Date	Amount	Date	Amount	Date	Amount
April 2	$417.25	April 14	$849.89	April 23	$390.95
7	931.69	16	476.22	28	972.22
9	520.85	21	756.60	30	455.52

The check register indicated that the following checks were issued during April:

Check No.	Amount	Check No.	Amount	Check No.	Amount
784	$347.77	791	$320.31	798	$167.26
785	261.12	792	277.17	799	85.20
786	89.94	793	95.14	800	300.50
787	713.40	794	176.65	801	117.26
788	417.73	795	377.15	802	189.89
789	105.16	796	217.10	803	461.12
790	Void	797	24.00	804	492.78

Data appearing on the bank statement for April and the memos and checks accompanying the bank statement are as follows:

Balance, April 1	$5,031.02

Deposits reported on the bank statement:

Date	Amount	Date	Amount	Date	Amount
April 1	$695.25	April 10	$520.85	April 22	$756.60
3	417.25	15	849.89	24	390.95
8	931.69	17	476.22	29	972.22

Checks rearranged in numerical order:

Check No.	Amount	Check No.	Amount	Check No.	Amount
780	$265.17	788	$417.73	796	$217.10
782	195.33	789	105.16	797	24.00
783	307.92	791	320.31	799	85.20
784	347.77	792	277.17	800	30.50
785	261.12	793	95.14	802	189.89
786	89.94	794	176.65	804	492.78
787	713.40	795	377.15		

Bank memorandums:

Date	Description	Amount
April 9.	Bank debit memo for check returned because of insufficient funds	$ 54.50
17.	Bank credit memo for note collected:	
	Principal	200.00
	Interest	6.00
30.	Bank debit memo for service charges	2.20
Balance, April 30		$6,201.81

The bank reconciliation as of March 31 of the current year was as follows:

Baskin and Trier
Bank Reconciliation
March 31, 19—

Balance per bank statement			$5,031.02
Add: Deposit of March 31, not recorded by bank			695.25
			$5,726.27
Deduct: Outstanding checks			
	No. 606	$ 40.15	
	780	265.17	
	782	195.33	
	783	307.92	808.57
Adjusted balance			$4,917.70
Balance per books			$4,920.05
Deduct: Service charges			2.35
Adjusted balance			$4,917.70

Instructions: (1) Prepare a bank reconciliation as of April 30. If errors in recording deposits or checks are discovered, assume that the errors were made by the company.

(2) Journalize the necessary entries. The books have not been closed.

(3) What is the amount of Cash in Bank that would appear on the balance sheet at April 30?

Chapter 13

13-1A. The Northern School Supply has nine employees. They are paid on an hourly basis, receiving time-and-one-half pay for all hours worked in excess of 40 a week. The record of time worked for the week ended Saturday, July 25, of the current year, together with other relevant information, is summarized at the top of the opposite page.

In addition to withholdings for income tax, FICA tax, and bond purchases, $10 is to be withheld from I for partial payment of his account receivable.

A, B, and H are office employees; the others are salesmen. The following tax rates and limitations are assumed: FICA, 4% on maximum of $5,400; state unemployment (employer only), 1.8% on maximum of $3,000; federal unemployment, .4% on maximum of $3,000.

Name	Total Hours	Hourly Rate	Income Tax Withheld	Bond Deductions	Cumulative Earnings, July 18
A	44	$2.40	$12.20	$3.00	$2,984
B	40	2.10	10.10	1.75	2,636
C	35	3.00	7.90	2.50	3,720
D	39	2.80	9.70	1.00	3,555
E	45	2.70	14.30		2,890
F	42	3.70	18.10	5.00	4,660
G	46	3.90	20.10	4.00	5,325
H	40	2.20	8.90		2,910
I	41	2.90	15.40	1.50	3,415

Instructions: (1) Prepare the payroll register for the week, using a form like the one illustrated on pages 312 and 313 of the textbook.

(2) Journalize the entry to record the payroll for the week.

(3) The company uses a voucher system and pays by regular check. Give the necessary entries in *general journal form* to record the payroll voucher and the issuance of the checks.

(4) Complete the payroll register by inserting the check numbers, beginning with No. 651.

(5) Journalize the entry to record the employer's payroll taxes for the week.

13-2A. The following accounts, with the balances indicated, appear in the ledger of Reliable Sales Co. on December 1 of the current year:

214	Salaries Payable	——
215.1	FICA Tax Payable	$ 296.40
215.2	Employees Income Tax Payable	843.70
215.3	State Unemployment Tax Payable	97.64
215.4	Federal Unemployment Tax Payable	223.38
216.1	Bond Deductions Payable	327.50
216.2	Medical Insurance Payable	425.00
611	Sales Salary Expense	86,420.60
711	Officers Salary Expense	31,900.00
712	Office Salary Expense	8,420.40
719	Payroll Tax Expense	4,318.24

The following transactions relating to payroll, payroll deductions, and payroll taxes occurred during December:

Dec. 1. Prepared Voucher No. 714, payable to Citizens Bank, for $187.50 to purchase U.S. Savings Bonds for employees.

2. Issued Check No. 892 in payment of Voucher No. 714.

14. Prepared Voucher No. 740, payable to Citizens Bank, for the amount of employees income tax and FICA tax due on December 15.

14. Issued Check No. 916 in payment of Voucher No. 740.

14. Prepared a general journal entry to record the biweekly payroll for the period ending yesterday. A summary of the payroll record follows:
Deductions: FICA tax, $71.60; income taxes withheld, $523.20; bond deductions, $80.75; medical insurance deductions, $75.00
Salary distribution: sales, $4,050; officers, $1,530; office, $500.
Net amount: $5,329.45.

Dec. 14. Prepared Voucher No. 761, payable to Payroll Bank Account, for the net amount of the biweekly payroll.
14. Issued Check No. 922 in payment of Voucher No. 761.
16. Prepared Voucher No. 765, payable to United Insurance Co., for $425, the semiannual premium on group medical insurance policy.
17. Issued Check No. 926 in payment of Voucher No. 765.
28. Prepared a general journal entry to record the biweekly payroll for the period ending yesterday. A summary of the payroll record follows: Deductions: FICA tax, $69.20; income taxes withheld, $518.40; bond deductions, $83.25.
Salary distribution: sales, $4,075; officers, $1,530; office, $500.
Net amount: $5,434.15.
28. Prepared Voucher No. 783 payable to Payroll Bank Account, for the net amount of the biweekly payroll.
28. Issued Check No. 943 in payment of Voucher No. 783.
29. Prepared Voucher No. 784, payable to Citizens Bank, for $150 to purchase U.S. Savings Bonds for employees.
30. Issued Check No. 946 in payment of Voucher No. 784.
31. Prepared a general journal entry to record the employer's payroll taxes on earnings paid in December. Taxable earnings for the two payrolls, according to the payroll records, are as follows: subject to FICA tax, $3,520; subject to unemployment compensation tax, $1,155. Assume the following tax rates: FICA, 4%; state unemployment, 1.8%; federal unemployment, .4%.

Instructions: (1) Open the accounts listed and enter the account balances as of December 1.

(2) Record the transactions, using a voucher register, a check register, and a general journal. The only amount columns needed in the voucher register are Accounts Payable Cr. and Sundry Accounts Dr. (subdivided into Account, Post. Ref., and Amount). The only amount columns needed in the check register are Accounts Payable Dr. and Cash in Bank Cr. After each entry, post to the accounts opened in the ledger and extend the new balances to the appropriate balance column.

(3) Journalize the adjusting entry on December 31 to record salaries for the incomplete payroll period. Salaries accrued are as follows: sales salaries, $415; officers salaries, $150; office salaries, $45. Post to the accounts.

(4) Journalize the entry to close the salary expense and payroll tax expense accounts to Expense and Revenue Summary and post to the accounts.

(5) Journalize the entry on January 1 to reverse the adjustment of December 31 and post to the accounts.

13-3A. The state statutes require that retailers collect a sales tax of 3% on all sales to consumers except on certain items, such as seeds and fertilizers, and on sales to governmental units, such as public schools, cities, and counties. In the event that the amount collected is less than 3% of taxable sales, the deficiency must be borne by the retailer. Payments for each calendar quarter are payable by the end of the month following the quarter.

The balances in certain accounts of H. T. Herron & Sons as of March 31, after adjustments were made for the additional tax liability for the first quarter, and as of June 30 of the current fiscal year are presented below. The company closes its books on December 31.

	March 31	June 30
Sales Tax Payable	$ 3,776.89	$ 3,988.83
Sales	132,576.50	274,287.20
Sales Returns and Allowances	1,983.50	4,329.40
Sales Tax Expense	14.85	14.85

Supplementary records indicate that sales for the period April 1 through June 30 included nontaxable sales of $6,375.25 and that returns and allowances on nontaxable sales for the same period amounted to $482.95.

Instructions: (1) Determine the amount of the liability for sales tax for the second quarter of the year, presenting your figures in good order.

(2) Present the entry as of June 30 to record the additional liability for sales taxes for the second quarter.

(3) Present the entry on July 31, in general journal form, to record payment of the sales tax liability for the second quarter.

(4) On the basis of the ledger information presented above, determine the amount of the net taxable sales for the *first* quarter of the year.

13-4A. The following information relative to the payroll for the week ended December 30 of the current year was abstracted from the payroll register and other records of Vester Furnace Co.:

Salaries:

Sales salaries	$37,600
Warehouse salaries	7,600
Office salaries	9,100
	$54,300

Deductions:

Income tax withheld	$4,630
U.S. Savings Bonds	715
Group insurance	240
FICA tax withheld is assumed to total the same amount as the employer's tax.	

Tax rates assumed:

FICA, 4%.
State unemployment (employer only), 2.0%.
Federal unemployment, .4%.

Instructions: (1) Assuming that the payroll for the last week of the year is to be paid on December 31, present the following entries:

(a) December 30, to record the payroll. Of the total payroll for the last week of the year, $14,100 is subject to FICA tax and $3,380 is subject to unemployment compensation taxes.
(b) December 30, to record the employer's payroll taxes on the payroll to be paid on December 31.

(2) Assuming that the payroll for the last week of the year is to be paid on January 2 of the following fiscal year, present the following entries:

(a) December 31, to record the payroll.
(b) January 2, to record the employer's payroll taxes on the payroll to be paid on January 2.

Chapter 14

14-1A. During its first three years of operation, Gordon Bros. determined the cost of the merchandise inventory at the end of the period by the last-in, first-out method, depreciation expense by the straight-line method, and uncollectible accounts expense by the direct write-off method. The amounts of net income reported and the amounts of the foregoing items for each of the three years were as follows:

	First Year	Second Year	Third Year
Net income reported	$35,000	$45,000	$60,000
Ending merchandise inventory	50,000	65,000	75,000
Depreciation expense	8,000	8,500	9,500
Uncollectible accounts expense	700	2,500	5,000

The firm is considering the possibility of changing to the following methods in determining net income for the fourth and subsequent years: first-in, first-out inventory, declining-balance depreciation at twice the straight-line rate, and provision for doubtful accounts through the use of an allowance account. In order to consider the probable future effect of these changes on the determination of the net income, the management requests that net income of the past three years be recomputed on the basis of the proposed methods. The inventory, depreciation, and uncollectible accounts expense for the past three years, computed in accordance with the proposed methods, are as follows:

	First Year	Second Year	Third Year
Ending merchandise inventory	$47,000	$60,000	$71,000
Depreciation expense	16,000	14,500	13,500
Uncollectible accounts expense	2,200	3,900	4,500

Instructions: Recompute the net income for each of the three years, presenting the figures in an orderly manner.

14-3A. The A. D. Dauton Construction Company began the construction of two office buildings during 1965. One building was completed in 1966 and the other in 1967. The contract prices, estimated total costs, and costs incurred are as follows:

Building	Contract Price	Estimated Costs	1965 Costs	1966 Costs	1967 Costs
#1	$10,000,000	$8,000,000	$4,000,000	$4,100,000	——
#2	7,500,000	6,400,000	640,000	1,280,000	$4,525,000

Instructions: Determine the amount of revenue and the net income to be recognized for the following years: 1965, 1966, 1967. Assume that the recognition of revenue is to be spread over the life of the contract. Present computations in good order.

14-5A. The income statement and the balance sheet prepared from the unadjusted accounts of Crossroads Gift Shop at the close of the first year of operations are presented at the top of the opposite page.

Crossroads Gift Shop
Income Statement
For Year Ended December 31, 19—

Sales		$80,000
Purchases		69,000
Gross profit on sales		$11,000
Operating expenses:		
Salary expense	$10,000	
Rent expense	4,550	
Utilities expense	850	
Miscellaneous expense	2,100	
Total operating expenses		17,500
Net loss		$ 6,500

Crossroads Gift Shop
Balance Sheet
December 31, 19—

Cash	$ 3,500
Equipment	5,000
T. S. Perkins, Capital	$ 8,500

Perkins has maintained the accounting records. The only transactions recorded have been those in which cash was received or disbursed. The accounts have not been closed for the year. Because of the large net loss reported by the income statement, Perkins is considering discontinuing operations. Before making a decision, he asks you to review the accounting methods employed and, if material errors are found, to prepare revised statements. The following information is elicited during the course of the review:

(a) The business was established on January 2 by an investment of $15,000 in cash by the owner.
(b) The equipment listed on the balance sheet at $5,000 was purchased for cash on January 4. Equipment purchased July 1 for $1,000 in cash was debited to Purchases. Equipment purchased on December 29 for $1,500, for which a 60-day non-interest-bearing note was issued, was not recorded.
(c) Depreciation on equipment has not been recorded. The equipment is estimated to have a useful life of 10 years and a salvage value of 10% of its original cost. (Use straight-line method.)
(d) Accounts receivable from customers at December 31 total $6,500.
(e) Uncollectible accounts are estimated at $400.
(f) A total of $4,000 is owed to merchandise creditors on account at December 31.
(g) The merchandise inventory at December 31, as nearly as can be determined, has a cost of $17,500.
(h) Insurance premiums of $600 were charged to miscellaneous expense during the year. The unexpired portion at December 31 is $250.
(i) Supplies of $750 purchased during the year were debited to Purchases. An estimated $275 of supplies were on hand at December 31.
(j) Rent Expense includes an advance payment of $350 for the month of January in the subsequent year.
(k) Salaries owed but not paid on December 31 total $200.

(l) The classification of expenses as "selling" and "general" is not considered to be sufficiently important to justify the cost of the analysis.
(m) The proprietor made no additional investments or withdrawals during the year.

Instructions: (1) On the basis of the financial statements presented above, prepare an unadjusted trial balance as of December 31 of the current year on an eight-column work sheet.

(2) Record the adjustments and the corrections in the Adjustments columns and complete the work sheet.

(3) Prepare an income statement, a capital statement, and a balance sheet.

(4) On the basis of your financial statements, evaluate the effectiveness of the first year of operations.

Chapter 15

15-1A. On April 1 of the current year William Carr and John Desmond form a partnership.

Carr is to invest certain business assets at valuations to be agreed upon, is to transfer business liabilities, and is to contribute sufficient cash to bring his total capital to $25,000. Details regarding the book values of the business assets and liabilities, and the agreed valuations, follow:

	Carr's Ledger Balance	Agreed Valuation
Accounts Receivable	$ 7,000	$ 7,000
Allowance for Doubtful Accounts	500	750
Merchandise Inventory	14,800	14,000
Store Equipment	5,000	2,800
Accumulated Depreciation — Store Equipment	2,600	
Office Equipment	2,500	950
Accumulated Depreciation — Office Equipment	1,300	
Accounts Payable	6,000	6,000

Desmond agrees to invest merchandise inventory priced at $5,000 and $10,000 in cash.

The articles of copartnership include the following provisions regarding the division of net income: interest on original investment at 6%, salary allowances of $5,000 and $8,000 respectively, and the remainder equally.

Instructions: (1) Give the entries, in general journal form, to record the investments of Carr and Desmond on the partnership books.

(2) Prepare a balance sheet as of April 1, the date of formation of the partnership.

(3) After adjustments and the closing of revenue and expense accounts at March 31, the end of the first full year of operations, the expense and revenue summary account has a credit balance of $18,200 and the drawing accounts have debit balances of $4,500 (Carr) and $8,400 (Desmond). Present the journal entries to close the expense and revenue summary account and the drawing accounts as of March 31.

15-2A. R. D. Reese and H. L. Scott have agreed to form a partnership. Reese is to invest $30,000 and is to devote full time to the business. Scott is to invest $50,000 and is to devote one half of his time to the business. The following plans for the division of income are under consideration:

(a) Equal division.
(b) In the ratio of original investments.
(c) In the ratio of time devoted to the business.
(d) Interest of 5% on original investments and the remainder equally.
(e) Interest of 5% on original investments, salaries of $10,000 to Reese and $5,000 to Scott, and the remainder equally.
(f) Plan (e), except that Reese is also to be allowed a bonus equal to 10% of the amount by which net income exceeds the salary allowances.

Instructions: Determine the division of income under each of the following assumptions: net income of $48,000 and net income of $12,000. Present the data in tabular form, using the following columnar headings:

	$48,000		$12,000	
Plan	Reese	Scott	Reese	Scott

15-5A. Downs, Evans, and Fern decide to discontinue business operations as of July 31 and to liquidate their enterprise. The firm's post-closing trial balance at that date appears below.

(4, 5)

Downs, Evans, and Fern
Post-Closing Trial Balance
July 31, 19—

Cash	9,500	
Accounts Receivable	6,300	
Allowance for Doubtful Accounts		900
Merchandise Inventory	24,000	
Prepaid Insurance	600	
Supplies	800	
Equipment	10,000	
Accumulated Depreciation — Equipment		5,200
Building	40,000	
Accumulated Depreciation — Building		16,000
Land	8,000	
Accounts Payable		8,700
Mortgage Note Payable		15,000
H. E. Downs, Capital		22,500
A. C. Evans, Capital		20,900
R. K. Fern, Capital		10,000
	99,200	99,200

The partners share net income and losses in the ratio 2:2:1. The realization and liquidation transactions are summarized as follows:

(a) Collected $5,500 of accounts receivable; the remainder are worthless.
(b) Realized $450 cash from cancellation of the insurance policies.
(c) Sold the supplies for $550
(d) Sold the merchandise for $21,500.

(e) Sold the land and buildings for $35,000, purchaser paying $20,000 cash and assuming the mortgage note. The mortgage holder released the partners from further liability.
(f) Sold the equipment for $3,500 cash.
(g) Paid miscellaneous expenses in connection with the sale of the assets, $400. (Debit Loss and Gain on Realization.)
(h) Distributed the loss on realization to the partners' capital accounts.
(i) Paid the accounts payable in full.
(j) Distributed remaining cash to the partners.

Instructions: (1) Set up T accounts for Cash, Loss and Gain on Realization, and the capital accounts.

(2) Record the July 31 balances in the T accounts.

(3) Present entries, in general journal form, to record the liquidation; post to the T accounts as appropriate; rule the accounts.

(4) Assuming a net loss on realization of $45,000, prepare a complete summary of the liquidation in the form shown in the chapter. No entries are required.

(5) Assuming a net loss on realization of $52,000, prepare a complete summary of the liquidation in the form shown in the chapter. No entries are required.

Chapter 16

16-1A. The net income or loss of A. B. James, Inc. for a period of eight years is shown in the table below. During the entire period the corporation had outstanding 2,000 shares of cumulative 6% preferred stock, par $100, and 25,000 shares of common stock, par $20. At the end of each year the board of directors (1) applied earnings to offset any accumulated deficit, (2) declared a partial or full dividend on the preferred stock to the extent of the available current or accumulated earnings, and (3) distributed one half of any remaining balance of current earnings as a dividend on the common stock.

		Preferred Dividend		Common	Increase or	Retained
					Decrease* in	Earnings
	Net Income		Total	Dividend	Retained	(Deficit*)
Year	or Loss*	Declared	Arrears	Declared	Earnings	Balance
Balance			$12,000			$4,500*
1960	$10,500					
1961	50,000					
1962	37,000					
1963	7,000					
1964	14,500*					
1965	9,000					
1966	34,000					
1967	62,000					

Instructions: (1) Indicate the disposition of the net income or loss for each year by completing the schedule presented above. Use an asterisk to denote deductions and negative items.

(2) Determine the total dividends per share declared on each class of stock.

16-3A. Selected data from the balance sheets of six corporations, identified by letter, are presented below:

A. Total assets, $1,245,000; total liabilities, $345,900; common stock outstanding, 30,000 shares, $25 par.

B. Common stock, $50	$1,500,000
Retained earnings	90,000
C. Preferred 6% stock, noncumulative, nonparticipating, $100 par	$ 500,000
Common stock, $20	1,000,000
Retained earnings	522,500
D. Preferred 6% stock, noncumulative, nonparticipating $100 par	$ 600,000
Common stock, $10	960,000
Deficit	119,040

Preferred stock has prior claim to assets upon dissolution.

E. Preferred 5% stock, cumulative, nonparticipating $50 par	$ 300,000
Common stock, $25 par	1,000,000
Retained earnings	50,000

Dividends on preferred stock are in arrears for 2 years. Preferred stock is entitled to unpaid cumulative dividends upon dissolution to the extent of retained earnings.

F. Preferred 6% stock, cumulative, nonparticipating, $100 par	$ 500,000
Common stock, $50 par	1,200,000
Retained earnings	54,600

Dividends on preferred stock are in arrears for 3½ years. Preferred stock is entitled to unpaid cumulative dividends upon dissolution, regardless of the availability of retained earnings.

Instructions: Determine for each corporation the book value per share of each class of stock, presenting the total capital allocated to the class and the number of shares outstanding.

16-4A. The Decatur Transfer Company was organized by Clark, Jamison, and Roberts. The charter authorized 20,000 shares of common stock with a par of $10. The following transactions were completed during August of the current year, the first month of operations:

(a) Issued to Clark 100 shares of stock for promotional services connected with organizing the corporation.
(b) Sold 2,000 shares of stock at par to Roberts for cash.
(c) Paid an attorney $700 for legal fees connected with organizing the corporation.
(d) Purchased land and a building from Jamison. The building has a 6%, 22-year mortgage of $18,000 and there is accrued interest of $450 on the mortgage note at the time of the purchase. It is agreed that the land is to be priced at $7,500 and the building at $32,000, and that Jamison is to accept stock at par for his equity. The corporation agreed to assume responsibility for paying the mortgage note and the accrued interest.
(e) Paid Clark $250 cash to reimburse him for the incorporation fees that he had remitted with the charter application.
(f) Purchased equipment from Clark for $25,000. Clark accepted a 6-month non-interest-bearing note for $5,000 and 2,000 shares of stock for the equipment.
(g) Paid contractor $4,000 cash for constructing addition to building.

(h) Purchased additional equipment for $5,000 cash.
(i) Paid advertising expenses of $900.
(j) Paid semiannual interest on the mortgage note.
(k) Paid various expenses of $1,350.
(l) Received $2,750 for services rendered.
(m) Recorded depreciation charges of $50 and $200 on buildings and equipment respectively.

Instructions: (1) Record the corporation's transactions in general journal form.

(2) Assuming that there were no additional transactions and no accruals, prepare a balance sheet for the corporation as of August 31. Omit subcaptions for current assets, current liabilities, etc.

Chapter 17

17-1A. The following accounts and their balances appear in the ledger of the J. S. Kimball Company on January 1 of the current year:

Common Stock Subscriptions Receivable	——
Preferred 7% Stock, par $100, noncumulative, non-participating (10,000 shares authorized and issued)	$1,000,000
Premium on Preferred Stock	30,000
Common Stock, no par (500,000 shares authorized, 250,000 shares issued)	2,900,000
Common Stock Subscribed	——
Retained Earnings	1,145,000

At a meeting of the board of directors early in the fiscal year, it was decided to issue additional common stock for the purpose of redeeming the preferred stock. To carry out this plan, the following transactions were completed during the year:

Feb. 20. Holders of the common stock were issued rights to subscribe to additional shares at $20 a share, at the rate of 1/5 share for each share held. (No entry.)

April 1. Subscriptions, together with a down payment of 50% of the subscription price, were received for 80% of the shares for which rights were issued.

July 1. Collected the remainder due from all subscribers to common stock and issued the stock certificates.

15. Issued 10,000 shares of common stock at $22, receiving cash.

31. In accordance with contract provisions of the preferred stock, the 10,000 shares were redeemed at $105 and retired.

Dec. 31. After closing all revenue and expense accounts for the year, Expense and Revenue Summary has a credit balance of $225,000. Close Expense and Revenue Summary.

Instructions: (1) Set up T accounts for the accounts listed and record the balances as of January 1.

(2) Record the foregoing transactions in general journal form and post to the selected accounts in the ledger.

(3) Prepare the stockholders' equity section of the balance sheet as of December 31.

(4) Determine the book value per share of common stock as of December 31.

17-3A. Mason Construction Company was organized on March 1 of the current year with an authorization of 2,000 shares of $100 par 6% preferred stock and 30,000 shares of $10 par common stock. Transactions completed during March and April are summarized as follows:

Mar. 10. Received subscriptions to 10,000 shares of common stock at par.
10. Received cash for 50% of the subscription price from all common stock subscribers.
12. Paid cash for organization costs of $1,000 and issued 250 shares of common stock to the promoters at par in payment for their services.
15. Received subscriptions for 1,000 shares of preferred stock at $102.
15. Received cash for 25% of the subscription price from all preferred stock subscribers.
17. Purchased construction materials for cash, $40,000.
24. Issued 1,000 shares of preferred stock for equipment valued at $55,000, a building valued at $38,000, and land valued at $9,000.

Apr. 10. Received cash for 50% of the subscription price from March 10 subscribers to 9,000 shares of common stock and issued the certificates.
10. Received cash for 25% of the subscription price from March 10 subscribers to 1,000 shares of common stock.
15. Received cash for 25% of subscription price from preferred stock subscribers of March 15.
23. Purchased additional equipment for cash, $30,000.
30. Received subscriptions to 5,000 shares of common stock at $11.
30. Received cash for 50% of the subscription price from all April 30 subscribers to common stock.
30. Received the balance due from the March 10 subscribers to 1,000 shares of common stock and issued the certificates.

Instructions: (1) Set up T accounts for the following accounts:

101 Cash
113 Preferred Stock Subscriptions Receivable
114 Common Stock Subscriptions Receivable
122 Construction Materials
133 Equipment
135 Buildings
137 Land
141 Organization Costs
301 Preferred Stock
302 Preferred Stock Subscribed
304 Premium on Preferred Stock
311 Common Stock
312 Common Stock Subscribed
314 Premium on Common Stock

(2) Record the transactions in general journal form and post to the general ledger accounts.

(3) Assuming that no other transactions occurred during the period, prepare a balance sheet as of April 30.

17-4A. The capital and related accounts appearing in the ledger of Downing Paper Products Corporation on January 1 of the current year are listed below.

Common Stock Subscriptions Receivable	$ 750,000
Preferred 5% Stock, par $100 (50,000 shares authorized and 40,000 shares issued)	4,000,000
Premium on Preferred 5% Stock	80,000
Preferred 7% Stock, par $100 (20,000 shares authorized and issued)	2,000,000
Premium on Preferred 7% Stock	20,000
Common Stock, par $10 (1,000,000 shares authorized; 600.000 shares issued)	6,000,000

Common Stock Subscribed (100,000 shares)	$1,000,000
Premium on Common Stock	2,400,000
Retained Earnings	4,750,000

During the year the corporation completed a number of transactions affecting the capital structure. They are summarized below.

(a) Received balance due on common stock subscribed and issued the certificates.
(b) Issued 50,000 shares of common stock at $16, receiving cash.
(c) Called the preferred 7% stock for redemption and retirement, paying the redemption price of $104.
(d) Purchased 30,000 shares of treasury common stock for $450,000.
(e) Received subscriptions to 10,000 shares of preferred 5% stock at $103, collecting 50% of the subscription price.
(f) Sold 15,000 shares of treasury common stock for $240,000.
(g) Received balance due from subscribers to preferred 5% stock and issued the certificates.
(h) Sold 5,000 shares of treasury common stock for $85,000.

Instructions: (1) Prepare entries in general journal form to record the transactions listed above. (Use of T accounts for the capital and related accounts is suggested for accumulating balances needed to record particular transactions and for use in remainder of problem.)

(2) Prepare the stockholders' equity section of the balance sheet as of December 31. Net income for the year amounted to $810,500. Dividends charged to Retained Earnings during the year totaled $520,000.

Chapter 18

18-1A. Selected transactions completed by Martin Brothers, Inc. during the current fiscal year are as follows:

Jan. 5. Declared a semiannual dividend of $1.25 on the 10,000 shares of preferred stock and a 40¢ dividend on the common stock to stockholders of record on January 20, payable on February 5. (At this date there are 50,000 shares of $20 par common stock outstanding.)
26. Purchased 1,000 shares of own common stock at $32, recording the stock at cost.
Feb. 5. Paid the dividends declared on January 5.
Mar. 13. Paid $47,500, which represented one half of the income tax for the past year. Earlier accruals of income tax had been recorded correctly.
May 20. Sold 500 shares of treasury stock at $35, receiving cash.
June 14. Paid remainder of income tax due for prior year, $47,500.
July 5. Declared semiannual dividends of $1.25 on the preferred stock and 40¢ on the common stock. In addition, a 5% common stock dividend was declared on the common stock outstanding. The fair market value of the common stock to be issued is estimated at $35.
Aug. 5. Paid the cash dividends and issued the certificates for the common stock dividend.
Oct. 22. Discovered that building construction costs of $40,000 incurred in the preceding fiscal year had been charged to the building maintenance expense account. The building has an estimated useful life of 40 years with no salvage value. The straight-line method of depreciation is

used by the company. Construction was completed on July 1 of the preceding fiscal year. Correct through Retained Earnings.

Dec. 31. Recorded the estimated federal income tax for the year, $89,700.

31. The board of directors authorized the appropriation necessitated by the holdings of treasury stock.

Instructions: Record the above transactions in general journal form.

18-3A. The stockholders' equity of Columbia Company, Inc. on January 1 of the current fiscal year is as follows:

Common Stock, par $25 (50,000 shares authorized, 25,000 shares issued)	$625,000
Premium on Common Stock	180,000
Retained Earnings Appropriated for Plant Expansion	100,000
Retained Earnings Appropriated for Treasury Stock	35,000
Retained Earnings	250,000
Treasury Stock (1,000 shares, at cost)	35,000

The following selected transactions occurred during the year:

Jan. 7. Sold all of the treasury stock for $37,000 in cash.

15. Paid cash dividends of $.75 per share on 24,000 shares of common stock to stockholders of record on December 30. The dividend had been properly recorded when declared on December 10 of the past fiscal year.

Mar. 2. Issued 2,000 shares of common stock at $38, receiving cash.

June 10. Declared a 4% stock dividend on common stock. The market price of the stock to be issued is $40 a share.

10. The board of directors authorized the write-off of patents with an unamortized cost of $22,500 as a direct charge to the retained earnings account. The patents were considered to be worthless as a result of patents on an improved product obtained by a competing business.

July 15. Issued the certificates for the dividend declared on June 10.

Sept. 4. Discovered that machinery purchased in the preceding year for $15,000 had been charged to Maintenance and Repairs. Depreciation of $2,250 was therefore omitted from the preceding year. Correct through Retained Earnings.

Oct. 1. Purchased 500 shares of treasury stock for $20,000.

Dec. 10. Declared a $.75 per share dividend on common stock.

10. The board of directors authorized the increase of the appropriation for plant expansion by $25,000.

10. Reduced the appropriation for treasury stock to $20,000.

31. Closed the credit balance of the expense and revenue summary account, $88,375.

Instructions: (1) Set up T accounts for the stockholders' equity accounts and enter the balances as of January 1.

(2) Prepare entries in general journal form to record the selected transactions and post to the stockholders' equity accounts. Set up additional stockholder equity accounts as needed.

(3) Prepare the stockholders' equity section of the balance sheet as of December 31 of the current fiscal year.

(4) Prepare a retained earnings statement for the current fiscal year.

18-4A. The following information was extracted from the records of Moore Sporting Goods, Inc., covering the fiscal year ended December 31, 1966:

Sales	$845,000
Cost of merchandise sold	480,000
Retained earnings, January 1, 1966	377,700
Retained earnings appropriated for contingencies, January 1, 1966	100,000
Selling expenses	97,500
Income tax	87,100
General expenses	72,400
Cash dividends declared	30,000
Correction of income of earlier period — understatement of depreciation	15,000
Fire loss	13,000

Instructions: (1) Assuming the use of the current operating performance concept of net income, prepare an income statement and a retained earnings statement.

(2) Assuming the use of the all-inclusive concept of net income, prepare an income statement and a retained earnings statement.

Chapter 19

19-2A. During 1965 and 1966 Murphy Tea Company completed the following transactions relating to its $10,000,000 issue of 20-year, 4% bonds dated April 1, 1965. Interest is payable on September 30 and March 31. The corporation's fiscal year is the calendar year.

1965
July 1. Sold the bond issue for $9,786,700 plus accrued interest.
Sept. 30. Paid the semiannual interest on the bonds.
Dec. 31. Deposited $182,000 in a bond sinking fund.
31. Appropriated $375,000 of retained earnings for bonded indebtedness.
31. Recorded the adjusting entry for interest payable.
31. Recorded amortization of bond discount.
31. Closed the interest expense account.

1966
Jan. 1. Reversed the adjustment for interest payable.
12. Purchased various securities with sinking fund cash at a cost of $179,900.
Mar. 31. Paid the semiannual interest on the bonds.
Sept. 30. Paid the semiannual interest on the bonds.
Dec. 31. Recorded the receipt of $6,640 of income on sinking fund securities, depositing the cash in the sinking fund.
31. Deposited $312,000 cash in the sinking fund.
31. Appropriated $500,000 of retained earnings for bonded indebtedness.
31. Recorded the adjusting entry for interest payable.
31. Recorded amortization of bond discount.
31. Closed the interest expense account.

Instructions: (1) Record the foregoing transactions in general journal form.

(2) Prepare a columnar table, using the headings shown at the top of the opposite page, and present the information for each of the two years.

Year	Bond Interest Expense for Year	Sinking Fund Income for Year	Account Balances at End of Year					
			Bonds Payable	Discount on Bonds	Sinking Fund		Appropriation for B.I.
					Cash	Investments	

19-3A. The following transactions relate to certain securities acquired by the Chandler Corporation:

1962

May 1. Purchased $200,000 of Parker Co. 10-year, 6% coupon bonds dated April 1, 1962, directly from the issuing company for $188,100 plus accrued interest. Parker Co. is an important customer of the Chandler Corporation and it is expected that the bonds will be held as a long-term investment.

Aug. 20. Purchased as a long-term investment 900 common shares of Edwards, Inc. at 39½ plus commission and other costs of $360.

Sept. 20. Received a semiannual dividend of $1 per share on the Edwards, Inc. stock.

Oct. 1. Deposited coupons for semiannual interest on the Parker Co. bonds.

Dec. 31. Recorded the adjustment for interest receivable on the Parker Co. bonds.

31. Recorded the amortization of discount on the Parker Co. bonds.

(Assume that all intervening transactions and adjustments have been recorded properly, and that the amount of bonds and shares of stocks have not changed from December 31, 1962, to December 31, 1965.)

1966

Jan. 1. Reversed the adjustment for interest receivable.

Mar. 20. Received a semiannual dividend of $1 per share on the Edwards, Inc. stock.

April 1. Deposited coupons for semiannual interest on the Parker Co. bonds.

June 1. Sold the Parker Co. bonds at 99½ plus accrued interest. The broker deducted $390 for commission and taxes, remitting the balance. The amortization of the discount for the year to date was also recorded.

Sept. 20. Received the semiannual dividend of $1 per share and a 5% stock dividend on the Edwards, Inc. stock.

Dec. 1. Sold 300 shares of Edwards, Inc. stock at 35. The broker deducted commission and other costs of $125, remitting the balance.

Instructions: Record the foregoing transactions in general journal form.

19-5A. The board of directors of Garner Company is planning an expansion of plant facilities expected to cost $1,000,000. The board is undecided about the method of financing this expansion and has two plans under consideration:

Plan 1. Issue $1,000,000 of 20-year, 5% bonds at face value.

Plan 2. Issue an additional 40,000 shares of no-par common stock at $25 per share.

The condensed balance sheet of the Garner Company at the end of the current fiscal year is presented on the following page.

Net income has remained relatively constant over the past several years. The expansion program is expected to increase yearly net income before taxes (and before bond interest) from $270,000 to $420,000. Assume a tax rate of 50%.

Garner Company
Balance Sheet
December 31, 19—

Assets		Liabilities and Capital	
Current assets..........	$ 790,000	Current liabilities........	$ 480,000
Plant assets............	3,210,000	Common stock (100,000 shares issued).........	2,800,000
		Retained earnings.......	720,000
Total assets............	$4,000,000	Total liabilities and capital	$4,000,000

Instructions: (1) Prepare a tabulation showing the expected earnings per share on common stock under each plan.

(2) List factors other than earnings per share that the board should consider in evaluating the two plans.

(3) Which plan offers the greater benefit to the present stockholders? Give reasons for your opinion.

Chapter 20

20-1A. Colberts operates two sales departments: Department A composed of men's clothing, and Department B composed of women's clothing. The trial balance on the following page was taken on December 31 at the end of a fiscal year after all adjustments, including the adjustments for merchandise inventory, were recorded and posted.

Merchandise inventories at the beginning of the year were: Department A, $29,000; Department B, $14,900.

The bases to be used in apportioning expenses, together with other essential information, are as follows:

Sales salaries — Payroll records: Department A, $13,400; Department B, $11,200.
Advertising expense — Usage: Department A, $4,200; Department B, $4,000.
Depreciation expense — Average cost of equipment. Balances at beginning of year:
Department A, $21,100; Department B, $18,300. Balances at end of year: Department A, $22,100; Department B, $18,500.
Administrative salaries — Department A, 55%; Department B, 45%
Rent expense and heating and lighting expense — Floor space: Department A, 5,600 sq. ft.; Department B, 4,400 sq. ft.
Property tax expense and insurance expense — Average cost of equipment plus average cost of merchandise inventory.
Supplies expense — Requisitions: Department A, $300; Department B, $250.
Miscellaneous selling expense and miscellaneous general expense — Volume of gross sales.

Instructions: Prepare an income statement departmentalized through net income from operations.

Colberts
Trial Balance
December 31, 19—

Account	Debit	Credit
Cash	47,500	
Accounts Receivable	51,250	
Merchandise Inventory, Department A	33,400	
Merchandise Inventory, Department B	18,700	
Prepaid Insurance	2,200	
Supplies	800	
Store Equipment	40,600	
Accumulated Depreciation — Store Equipment		9,600
Accounts Payable		14,125
Income Tax Payable		21,990
Common Stock		100,000
Retained Earnings		11,375
Expense and Revenue Summary	43,900	52,100
Sales, Department A		192,600
Sales, Department B		128,400
Sales Returns and Allowances, Department A	4,920	
Sales Returns and Allowances, Department B	5,530	
Purchases, Department A	122,440	
Purchases, Department B	70,910	
Sales Salaries	24,600	
Advertising Expense	8,200	
Depreciation Expense —Store Equipment	1,200	
Miscellaneous Selling Expense	750	
Administrative Salaries	17,800	
Rent Expense	7,200	
Heating and Lighting Expense	2,400	
Property Tax Expense	1,400	
Insurance Expense	900	
Supplies Expense	550	
Miscellaneous General Expense	800	
Interest Expense	250	
Income Tax	21,990	
	530,190	530,190

20-3A. Mead's Department Store has 20 departments. Those with the least sales volume are Department F, fabrics, and Department P, paperback books, which were established about two years ago on a trial basis. The board of directors feels that it is now time to give consideration to the retention or the termination of these two departments. The adjusted trial balance, severely condensed, as of July 31, the end of the first month of the current fiscal year, is presented on page 798. July is considered to be a fairly typical month. The income tax accrual has no bearing on the problem and is excluded from consideration.

Instructions: (1) Prepare an income statement departmentalized through departmental margin.

(2) What recommendations would you make about the retention of Departments F and P? Explain your reasoning.

Mead's Department Store
Trial Balance
July 31, 19—

Current Assets	410,000	
Plant Assets	385,000	
Accumulated Depreciation — Plant Assets		105,000
Current Liabilities		122,500
Common Stock		400,000
Retained Earnings		139,800
Sales — Department F		6,500
Sales — Department P		12,900
Sales — Other Departments		440,300
Cost of Merchandise Sold — Department F	3,700	
Cost of Merchandise Sold — Department P	10,200	
Cost of Merchandise Sold — Other Departments	269,200	
Direct Expenses — Department F	1,600	
Direct Expense — Department P	3,900	
Direct Expenses — Other Departments	87,200	
Indirect Expenses	56,900	
Interest Income		700
	1,227,700	1,227,700

20-4A. Erhardt's, of Springfield, opened a branch in the Westgate Shopping Center on July 1 of the current year. Summaries of transactions, adjustments, and year-end closing for branch operations of the current year ended December 31 are described below:

(a) Received cash advance, $60,000, and merchandise (billed at cost), $100,000, from the home office.
(b) Purchased equipment for cash, $40,000.
(c) Purchased merchandise on account, $65,000.
(d) Sales on account, $100,000; cash sales, $40,000.
(e) Paid operating expenses, $23,750 (all expenses are charged to Operating Expenses, a controlling account).
(f) Paid creditors on account, $59,000.
(g) Received cash from customers on account, $80,000.
(h) Sent $25,000 cash to home office.
(i) Recorded accumulated depreciation, $1,000, and allowance for doubtful accounts, $550.
(j) Merchandise inventory at December 31, $62,500.
(k) Closed revenue and expense accounts.

Instructions: (1) Present, in general journal form, the entries on the branch books to record the foregoing. Post to the following T accounts: Cash, Accounts Receivable, Allowance for Doubtful Accounts, Merchandise Inventory, Equipment, Accumulated Depreciation, Accounts Payable, Home Office, Expense and Revenue Summary, Sales, Shipments from Home Office, Purchases, and Operating Expenses.

(2) Prepare an income statement for the period and a balance sheet as of December 31 for the branch.

(3) Present, in general journal form, the entries required on the home office books. Post to a T account entitled Westgate Branch.

Chapter 21

21-1A. On December 1, the Shuman Manufacturing Company had the following inventories:

Finished goods (600 units)	$18,000
Work in process	6,250
Materials	8,750

Departmental accounts are not maintained for work in process and factory overhead, nor are accounts maintained for service departments. Manufacturing operations for the month of December of the current fiscal year are summarized as follows:

(a) Materials purchased on account, $12,300.
(b) Labor used, $9,200, of which $8,300 was used directly in the manufacture of the product.
(c) Materials requisitioned for use, $11,750, of which $11,300 was direct materials.
(d) Factory overhead costs incurred on account: rent, $1,350; power and light, $470; machinery maintenance and repairs, $375; and miscellaneous, $230.
(e) Depreciation of machinery, $260.
(f) Expiration of prepaid insurance on machinery, $65.
(g) Factory overhead applied to production, 50% of direct labor cost.
(h) Goods finished during month, $24,400 (800 units); work in process at end of month, $5,600.
(i) Sales on account (900 units), $49,500. (Use the first-in, first-out method in crediting the finished goods account.)

Instructions: Prepare entries in general journal form to record the foregoing operations.

21-2A. Windal Products, Inc. manufactures Product D by a series of three processes, all direct materials being introduced in Department 1. From Department 1 the materials pass sequentially through Departments 2 and 3, emerging as finished Product D. All inventories are priced at cost by the first-in, first-out method.

The balances in the accounts Work in Process — Department 3 and Finished Goods were as follows on May 1:

Work in Process — Department 3	
Balance: 500 units, ½ completed	$ 2,050
Finished Goods	
Balance: 600 units at $5.70 a unit	3,420

The following costs were charged to Work in Process — Department 3 during the month:

Materials transferred from Department 2: 5,500 units at $2.50	$13,750
Direct labor	11,100
Factory overhead	5,550

During the month of May, 5,200 units of D were completed. Inventories on May 31 were as follows:

Work in Process — Department 3: 800 units, ¾ completed
Finished Goods: 1,000 units

Instructions: (1) Determine the following, presenting the computations in good order: (a) equivalent units of production for Department 3; (b) unit processing cost for Department 3; (c) total and unit cost of Product D started in a prior period and finished in May; (d) total and unit cost of Product D started and finished in May; (e) total cost of goods transferred to finished goods; (f) work in process inventory, May 31; (g) cost of goods sold (indicate number of units and unit costs); (h) finished goods inventory, May 31.

(2) Set up T accounts for Work in Process — Department 3 and for Finished Goods. Record the balances at May 1 and the transactions for May in summary form; bring down the balances at May 31. Record the number of units and degree of completion, where appropriate, in the items section of the accounts.

(3) Prepare a cost of production report for Department 3 for May.

21-4A. Fisher Products manufactures joint products A and B. Materials are placed in production in Department 1 and after processing are transferred to Department 2, where more materials are added. The finished products emerge from Department 2. There are two service departments, Factory Office and Maintenance and Repair.

There were no inventories of work in process at either the beginning or the end of the period. Finished goods inventories at July 1 were as follows:

Finished Goods — Product A, 900 units..................	$ 3,690
Finished Goods — Product B, 500 units..................	2,450

Transactions and other relevant data for the month of July in summary form are as follows:

(a) Materials purchased on account, $13,400.
(b) Prepaid expenses incurred on account, $900.
(c) Miscellaneous costs and expenses incurred on account: Department 1, $350; Department 2, $600; Factory Office, $275; Maintenance and Repair, $325; Selling Expenses, $3,200; and General Expenses, $1,470.
(d) Materials requisitioned for use, of which $4,400 entered directly into the products in Department 1 and $7,080 in Department 2: Department 1, $4,850; Department 2, $7,630; Maintenance and Repair, $600.
(e) Labor costs incurred, of which $4,000 and $7,200 were used directly in the manufacture of the products in Departments 1 and 2, respectively: Department 1, $4,250; Department 2, $7,600; Factory Office, $825; Maintenance and Repair, $1,400.
(f) Depreciation charged on plant assets: Department 1, $300; Department 2, $450; Factory Office, $75; Maintenance and Repair, $75; Selling Expenses, $125; General Expenses, $80.
(g) Expiration of various prepaid expenses: Department 1, $100; Department 2, $125; Factory Office, $25; Maintenance and Repair, $50; Selling Expenses, $100; General Expenses, $60.
(h) Factory Office costs allocated on the basis of man-hours worked: Department 1, 2,000 hours; Department 2, 1,500 hours; Maintenance and Repair, 500 hours.
(i) Maintenance and Repair costs allocated on the basis of services rendered: Department 1, 40%; Department 2, 60%.
(j) Factory overhead applied to production at the predetermined rates: 75% and 60% of direct labor cost, respectively, for Departments 1 and 2.

(k) Output of Department 1: 3,000 units.
(l) Output of Department 2: 2,500 units of Product A and 4,000 units of Product B. Unit selling price is $7.20 for Product A and $9 for Product B.
(m) Sales on account: 2,600 units of Product A at $7.20 and 3,500 units of Product B at $9. Credits to the finished goods accounts are to be priced in accordance with the first-in, first-out method.
(n) Cash received on account, $50,100.
(o) Cash disbursements: on account, $21,500; wages $14,200.

Instructions: Prepare entries in general journal form to record the transactions. Include as an explanation for entry (l) the calculations for the allocation of the production costs for Department 2 to the joint products and as an explanation for entry (m) the units and the unit costs for each product sold.

Chapter 22

22-1A. The Andrews Manufacturing Company uses a job order cost system. The following data summarize the operations related to production for August, the first month of operations.

(a) Materials purchased on account, $28,000.
(b) Materials requisitioned and factory labor used:

	Materials	Factory Labor
Job No. 101	$2,700	$5,350
Job No. 102	2,450	4,775
Job No. 103	4,300	6,325
Job No. 104	4,550	6,700
Job No. 105	2,650	3,050
Job No. 106	1,900	2,500
For general factory use	750	1,200

(c) Factory overhead costs incurred on account, $13,800.
(d) Depreciation of machinery and equipment, $2,000.
(e) The factory overhead rate is 60% of direct labor cost.
(f) Jobs completed: Nos. 101, 102, 104, and 106.
(g) Job Nos. 101, 102, and 106 were shipped and customers were billed for $16,500, $15,000, and $9,250 respectively.

Instructions: (1) Prepare entries in general journal form to record the foregoing summarized operations.

(2) Set up T accounts for Work in Process and Finished Goods. Post to these accounts, using the identifying letters as dates. Bring down the end-of-the-month balances.

(3) Prepare a schedule of unfinished jobs to support the balance in the work in process account.

(4) Prepare a schedule of completed jobs on hand to support the balance in the finished goods account.

22-4A. Selected accounts for Thomas Products are presented below. For the purposes of this problem, some of the debits and credits have been omitted.

Materials

July 1	Balance	5,400	July 31 Requisitions	19,600
31	Purchases	(A)		

Work in Process

July 1	Balance	6,400	July 31 Goods finished	(D)
31	Direct materials	(B)		
31	Direct labor	18,000		
31	Factory overhead	(C)		

Finished Goods

July 1	Balance	12,400	July 31 Cost of goods sold	(F)
31	Goods finished	(E)		

Factory Overhead

July 1	Balance	250	July 31 Applied (80% of direct labor cost)	(G)
31	Costs incurred	14,300		

Cost of Goods Sold

July 31		(H)		

Inventories at July 31:

Finished goods	$11,200
Work in process	6,700
Materials	4,900

Materials requisitions for July included $700 of materials issued for general factory use.

Instructions: (1) Determine the amounts represented by the letters (A) through (H), presenting your computations.

(2) Is factory overhead overapplied or underapplied at July 31? By how much?

Chapter 23

23-1A. J. D. Roberts, Inc. prepared the following factory overhead budget for July:

Factory Overhead Budget

Direct labor hours — normal capacity		20,000
Direct labor hours — budgeted		18,000
Budgeted factory overhead:		
Variable costs:		
Indirect factory wages	$ 7,200	
Power and light	1,800	
Indirect materials	1,440	
Total variable costs	$10,440	

Fixed costs:	
Indirect factory wages	$ 5,750
Supervisory salaries	5,200
Depreciation of plant and equipment	2,750
Power and light	1,300
Property taxes	1,100
Insurance	900
Total fixed costs	$17,000
Total factory overhead	$27,440

Instructions: (1) Prepare a flexible budget for the month of August showing capacities of 16,000, 18,000, 20,000, and 22,000 direct labor hours and the determination of a standard factory overhead rate per direct labor hour.

(2) During August the following factory overhead costs were incurred when the plant was operated for 16,000 hours:

Indirect factory wages	$12,300
Supervisory salaries	5,200
Power and light	2,850
Depreciation of plant and equipment	2,750
Indirect materials	1,350
Property taxes	1,100
Insurance	900
Total overhead incurred	$26,450

Prepare a standard factory overhead variance report for August.

23-3A. The Cuthbert Manufacturing Company maintains perpetual inventory accounts for materials, work in process, and finished goods. There was no inventory of work in process at the beginning or the end of the period. The records revealed the following data:

	Standard Cost per Unit	
	Quantity	Price
Direct materials	3 pounds @ $2 per pound	$ 6.00
Direct labor	2 hours @ $3 per hour	6.00
Factory overhead	$1.80 per direct labor hour	3.60
		$15.60

The transactions completed during the first month of the current period relating to production are summarized as follows:

(a) Materials purchased on account, $154,000.
(b) Direct materials used, $142,350. This represented 73,000 pounds at $1.95 per pound.
(c) Direct labor paid, $148,490. This represented 47,900 hours at $3.10 per hour. There were no accruals at either the beginning or the end of the period.
(d) Factory overhead incurred during the month included indirect labor, $40,600; depreciation on plant and equipment, $16,400; power and light, $11,500; insurance, $1,500; and miscellaneous factory costs, $17,500. The indirect labor, power and light, and miscellaneous factory

costs were paid during the period, and the insurance represents an expiration of prepaid insurance. The fixed factory overhead incurred represented $40,000 of the total, while the variable factory overhead totaled $47,500.

(e) Goods finished during the period, 24,000 units.

Instructions: (1) Prepare entries in general journal form to record the transactions, assuming that the work in process account is debited for actual production costs and credited with standard costs for goods finished.

(2) Prepare a T account for Work in Process and post to the account, using the identifying letters as dates.

(3) Prepare schedules of variance analyses for direct materials, direct labor, and factory overhead. Normal productive capacity for the plant is 50,000 direct labor hours.

(4) Total the amounts of the standard cost variances and compare this total with the balance of the work in process account.

23-4A. The treasurer of McGregor and Company instructs you to prepare a monthly cash budget for the next three months. He presents you with the following budget information:

	April	May	June
Sales	$700,000	$800,000	$750,000
Production costs	499,000	565,000	532,000
Operating expenses	161,000	171,500	166,400
Capital expenditures	50,000	——	150,000

The company expects to sell about 30% of its merchandise for cash. Of sales on account, 80% are expected to be collected in full in the month following the sale and the remainder the next following month. Depreciation, insurance, and property taxes represent $19,000 of the estimated monthly production costs and $5,000 of the probable monthly operating expenses. Insurance and property taxes are paid in January and July, respectively. Of the remainder of the production costs and operating expenses, two thirds are expected to be paid in the month in which they are incurred and the balance in the next month.

On April 1, assets include cash, $179,300, accounts receivable, $510,000, and marketable securities, $100,000. The accounts receivable include $420,000 of March sales and $90,000 representing February sales. Liabilities on April 1 consist of notes payable, $50,000, accounts payable, $175,000, and accrued liabilities, $64,500. The notes payable are noninterest-bearing and are due June 10. The other liabilities represent March production costs and selling and general expenses, respectively.

It is expected that $1,500 in dividends will be received in April. McGregor and Company's regular quarterly dividend of $6,500 is expected to be declared in April and paid in May. Management desires to maintain a minimum cash balance of $100,000.

Instructions: (1) Prepare a monthly cash budget for April, May, and June.

(2) On the basis of the cash budget prepared in (1), do you have any advice for the treasurer in planning for the maintenance of a satisfactory cash balance?

Chapter 24

24-1A. Ralph H. Burgess maintains a special bank account that he uses in connection with a small apartment building that he owns and for occasional payments of personal expenses. He uses the cash method of determining income. During the current taxable year ending December 31, he deposited $23,400 of rent receipts in the special account, including $600 applicable to January of the following year.

Disbursements from the special bank account during the current year are summarized as follows:

Wages of custodian and repairman (gross earnings $5,200):	
Paid to employee	$4,524
Withheld for FICA tax and paid to IRS	208
Withheld for income tax and paid to IRS	468
Real estate tax	1,720
Payment of federal income tax of the preceding year	937
Payment of federal income tax applicable to the current year	2,700
Interest on mortgage note on land and apartment building	1,400
Installment payments of principal on mortgage note	2,000
Utilities expense	610
Air conditioning units installed in 2 apartments not previously air conditioned	1,200
Redecorating three apartments	590
Miscellaneous repairs	416
Payroll tax expense	338
Premium on a five-year insurance policy on the building, effective March 1	330
United Appeal, American Red Cross, and Salvation Army	520
Miscellaneous expenses incurred in earning rentals	392

In addition to the foregoing data, you determine from other records and the tax return for the preceding year that the allowable deduction for depreciation expense is $4,100 and that current expirations of insurance premiums paid in earlier years total $232.

Instructions: Prepare a statement of gross income from rents and the deductions from gross income that are allowable in determining adjusted gross income.

24-2A. Robert L. Warner, unmarried and entitled to one exemption for himself, is engaged in the practice of architecture. He is the sole support of his father, who is 79 years of age and has no gross income.

Mr. Warner uses the cash method of determining taxable income and reports on the calendar-year basis. A summary of his record of cash receipts and disbursements for the current calendar year is presented below.

Receipts

Professional fees	$49,620
Borrowed from bank (professional purposes)	2,500
Inheritance from uncle's estate	5,000
Dividends on corporation stocks	460

Disbursements

Cost of new automobile (purchased January 3)	$ 5,200
Office equipment	900
Wages of draftsmen and typist:	
Taxes withheld and paid to IRS	2,029
Paid to employees	11,671
Payroll taxes	822
Fees to collaborating engineers	2,720
Office rent	2,400
Telephone expense (office)	340
Electricity (office)	216
Payment on loan from bank (see above)	1,500
Blueprint expense	537
Office supplies expense	163
Insurance on office equipment (3-year policy, dated Jan. 1)	120
Interest on bank loan	105
Charitable contributions	2,325
Payment on principal of mortgage note on home	960
Interest on mortgage note on home	610
Personal property tax on office equipment	45
Real estate tax on home	538
State sales tax on purchases for personal use	212
State inheritance tax	150
Automobile operating expenses (gasoline, oil, insurance, etc.)	620
Purchase of 50 shares of Cameron Corporation stock	1,750
Medical expenses for father: Medicines	155
Other	412
Payments of estimated income tax for current year	5,000

The automobile was used ¾ of the time for professional purposes. It is to be depreciated by the declining-balance method at twice the straight-line rate, assuming an estimated life of 4 years. Allocate ¾ of the depreciation and other automobile expenses to professional purposes.

The cost of the office equipment owned at the beginning of the year was $2,100. Office equipment was purchased on account during the year at a total cost of $1,300. The $900 listed above in the disbursements were payments on account. None of the equipment was disposed of during the year. Use a composite depreciation rate of 10%, based on the average.

Instructions: Determine Mr. Warner's taxable income, income tax, and balance due, presenting the details in good order. Use the schedule of tax rates applicable to heads of household appearing in this chapter.

24-4A. J. Philip Parker is negotiating the sale of a parcel of unimproved land to Emerald Development Co., to become effective on January 1 of next year. The sales price of the property is $100,000, payable in 10 equal annual installments, with the first installment payable on the effective date of the sale. Interest of 5% per annum is to be paid on the remaining balance. The property, which was acquired by Parker as an inheritance a number of years ago, has a cost basis of $15,000.

Exclusive of the gain on the sale of the land, which qualifies as a long-term capital gain, Mr. and Mrs. Parker expect to have approximately $8,500 of ordinary taxable income (adjusted gross income less itemized deductions and exemptions) annually for the next 10 years. The $8,500 includes estimated gross income from the note and from reinvestment of the annual installment payments.

Instructions: (1) Assuming the accuracy of the estimate of future income and no changes in the Internal Revenue Code, determine the Parkers' total estimated federal income tax (joint return) for ten years, beginning with next year, based on (a) reporting the entire gain next year and (b) reporting the gain by the installment method.

(2) What is the amount of federal income tax saved by electing the installment method?

(3) Could the installment method have been elected if the terms of sale provided for a down payment of $35,000?

24-6A. In December of the current taxable year, which ends on December 31, Mr. and Mrs. Harold D. Stoner engage you to prepare their income tax return for the year and to advise them concerning other matters that may affect the amount of their tax liability. They are entitled to a total of 5 exemptions for themselves and their dependent children. They have been using the cash method of determining taxable income and expect to file a joint return.

Mr. Stoner is employed at a salary of $18,000 for the current year. He is assured of a salary increase of $300 per month for the following year, to become effective as of January 1. He has no deductions for travel or transportation. His dividend income is expected to amount to $800 for the current year and $1,000 for the following year. Mrs. Stoner's sole income is from dividends, which are expected to amount to $600 annually for both the current and the following year.

Both Mr. and Mrs. Stoner plan to sell one of the stocks in their respective investment portfolios in the near future. Based on current market prices, Mrs. Stoner would realize a gain of $2,000 on the sale of A Company stock and Mr. Stoner would incur a loss of $1,000 on the sale of B Company stock. In both cases the securities have been owned for several years and their market prices are quite stable at the present time.

Payments for the current year to date that may qualify as deductions from adjusted gross income are estimated as follows: charitable contributions, $35; interest on note payable, $200; property taxes on residence and investments, $250; deductible sales and gasoline taxes, $90; medicines and drugs, $40; other medical expenses, $350.

Unpaid pledges to their church and other charities for the current year total $460. They ordinarily pay such pledges in December; however, the fiscal years of the organizations end within the next calendar year. They contemplate making contributions of $600 for the year following the current taxable year. The payments made to date for interest and for property taxes represent one half of the respective liabilities for the year; the remaining balances are due late in December but payment may be postponed until January without penalty or other disadvantage. The annual property taxes and the interest expense are expected to remain constant for the following year. Payments for deductible sales and gasoline taxes are expected to total $100 (including the $90 already paid) for the current year. It is reasonable to assume that a like amount will be spent during the following year. All medical expenses incurred during the current taxable year have been paid except for a surgeon's fee of $700 incurred in December. The only known medical expenses for the following year will be for hospitalization and health insurance, which will total $300.

Instructions: (1) Advise Mr. and Mrs. Stoner concerning the contemplated sales of securities and the timing of deductions from adjusted gross income. Consideration is to be given only to the current taxable year and to the following taxable year; the Internal Revenue Code and regulations, as well as the taxpayers' exemptions, are assumed to remain unchanged during the period; and the estimates for the succeeding year are assumed to be accurate.

(2) Determine the estimated tax liability for Mr. and Mrs. Stoner for (a) the current taxable year and (b) the subsequent taxable year, assuming that they follow your advice and that the actual amount of income and deductions agree exactly with the estimates. Apply the appropriate schedule of tax rates appearing in this chapter. Present details in good order.

Chapter 25

25-1A. The Owens Refining Company refines Product R in batches of 100,000 gallons. This product sells for $.20 per gallon. The associated unit costs and expenses include:

	Costs Per Gallon
Direct materials	$.075
Direct labor	.025
Variable factory overhead	.025
Fixed factory overhead	.020
Salesmen's commissions	.010
Fixed selling and general expenses	.010
	$.165

The company is considering putting Product R through several additional processes to yield Products R and S. Until recently, the company considered such further processing to be unwise, but new methods have now been developed. Existing facilities could be used for the additional processing; but inasmuch as additional machine time would be required and the plant is operating at full eight-hour day capacity, the processing would have to be performed at night. Additional costs of processing would be $3,800 per batch and there would be an evaporation loss of 10%, with 40% of the processed material evolving as Product R and 50% as Product S. Selling price of Product S is $.35 per gallon. Sales commissions are a uniform percentage based on the sales price.

Instructions: (1) Prepare a schedule presenting the differential revenue and the differential costs per batch associated with the processing to produce Products R and S compared with processing to produce Product R only.

(2) What is your recommendation?

25-2A. Palmer Printing, Inc. purchased a printing press costing $120,000 on January 2, 1964. The company's manufacturing costs for a normal year, exclusive of depreciation, total $200,000, operating expenses are $100,000 yearly, and revenues total $400,000 yearly. The annual depreciation for this printing press is $20,000 based on a 6-year useful life and no residual value.

On January 3, 1966, a manufacturer placed on the market a new printing press that costs $200,000, has a 4-year life with no salvage value, and promises to reduce the manufacturing costs of Palmer Printing, Inc., exclusive of depreciation, to $125,000 yearly. The old machine can be sold for $15,000. Revenues and operating expenses will not be affected by the use of either press.

Instructions: (1) Prepare an estimated income statement for the period covering the four years 1966 through 1969 under both alternatives.

(2) Prepare a differential analysis comparing the proposed acquisition with operations using the present equipment. The analysis should indicate the additional net income or reduction in net income that would result over the 4-year period if the new press is acquired.

(3) What other factors should be considered before a final decision is reached?

25-4A. The Hawkins Company manufactures three styles of folding chairs, A, B, and C. The income statement has consistently indicated a net loss for Style A and management is considering three proposals: (1) continue Style A, (2) discontinue Style A and reduce output accordingly, or (3) discontinue Style A and conduct an advertising campaign to expand the sales of Style C so that the entire plant capacity can continue to be used. Sales, costs, and expenses have been relatively stable over the past few years and are expected to remain so for the foreseeable future. The income statement for the past year is:

	Style			
	A	B	C	Total
Sales	$150,000	$300,000	$500,000	$950,000
Cost of goods sold:				
Variable costs	$ 95,000	$160,000	$270,000	$525,000
Fixed costs	35,000	70,000	115,000	220,000
Total cost of goods sold	$130,000	$230,000	$385,000	$745,000
Gross profit on sales	$ 20,000	$ 70,000	$115,000	$205,000
Less selling and general expenses:				
Variable expenses	$ 18,000	$ 36,000	$ 60,000	$114,000
Fixed expenses	12,000	18,000	20,000	50,000
Total selling and general expenses	$ 30,000	$ 54,000	$ 80,000	$164,000
Net income (loss)	$(10,000)	$ 16,000	$ 35,000	$ 41,000

If Style A is discontinued and production curtailed, the annual fixed production costs and fixed selling and general expenses could be reduced by $10,000 and $3,500 respectively. It is anticipated that an additional yearly expenditure of $12,000 for advertising Style C would yield an increase of 30% in its sales volume; also that the increased production of Style C would make use of the plant facilities released by the discontinuance of Style A.

Instructions: (1) Prepare an income statement in the direct costing format indicating the projected annual net income under each of the three proposals.

(2) Why would total net income be reduced below its present level if Proposal 2 is accepted?

(3) Why would total net income increase above its present level if Proposal 3 is accepted?

25-5A. Product P is one of the numerous products manufactured by the Kent Corporation. The demand for Product P has dropped sharply because of recent competition from a superior product. The company's chemists are currently completing tests of various new formulas and it is anticipated that the manufacture of a superior product can be started on May 1, one month hence. No changes will be needed in the present production facilities to manufacture the new product because only the mixture of the various materials will be changed.

The controller has been asked by the president of the company for advice on whether to continue production during April or to suspend the manufacture of Product P until May 1. The controller has assembled the following pertinent data:

Kent Corporation
Income Statement — Product P
For Month Ended March 31, 19—

Sales (100,000 units)	$200,000
Less cost of goods sold	160,000
Gross profit on sales	$ 40,000
Less selling and general expenses	65,000
Net loss	$ 25,000

The production costs per unit based on a production of 100,000 units are:

Direct materials	$.60
Direct labor	.50
Variable factory overhead	.20
Fixed factory overhead	.30

The selling and general expenses for the month ended March 31 are:

Variable selling and general expenses	$.40 per unit
Fixed selling and general expenses	$25,000

Sales for April are expected to drop about 25% below those of the preceding month. No significant changes are anticipated in the production costs or operating expenses. No extra costs will be incurred in shutting down the portion of the plant associated with Product P. The quantity of inventory at the beginning and end of April is negligible.

Instructions: (1) Prepare an estimated income statement in absorption costing form for April for Product P, assuming that production continues during the month.

(2) Prepare an estimated income statement in direct costing form for April for Product P, assuming that production continues during the month.

(3) (a) Determine the estimated amount of the net loss arising from the activities associated with Product P for April if production is temporarily suspended. (b) From which of the estimated income statements, (1) or (2), can this amount be more readily determined?

(4) What should the controller advise? Give reasons.

Chapter 26

26-1A. The Cox Manufacturing Company is considering the addition of a new product to its line. For 1965, production was at 80% of capacity, the assets employed were $5,000,000 (original cost), and the income statement indicated a net operating income of $450,000 computed as follows:

Sales		$5,500,000
Less: Cost of goods sold	$3,450,000	
Selling expenses	1,025,000	
General expenses	575,000	5,050,000
Net operating income		$ 450,000

If the new product is added, market research indicates that 20,000 units can be sold in 1966 at an estimated selling price of $40 per unit. The idle capacity will be utilized to produce the product, but an additional $500,000 in plant assets will be required. The cost data per unit for the new product is as follows:

Direct materials	$12.50
Direct labor	10.00
Factory overhead (includes depreciation on additional investment in plant assets)	8.50
Selling expenses	4.25
General expenses	1.75
	$37.00

Instructions: (1) Prepare an estimated income statement for 1966 for the new product.

(2) Prepare a schedule indicating the rate of return on assets under present conditions and for the new product. Use the original cost of the assets in your computation.

(3) Would you recommend addition of the new product? Would you require other data before you make your decision? If so, what data would you require?

26-3A. The capital expenditures budget committee is considering two projects. The estimated net income and net cash flows from each project are presented below:

	Project A		Project B	
Year	Net Income	Net Cash Flow	Net Income	Net Cash Flow
1	$ 7,000	$13,000	$ 4,000	$10,000
2	6,000	12,000	4,000	10,000
3	5,000	11,000	5,000	11,000
4	3,500	9,500	6,000	12,000
5	3,500	9,500	6,000	12,000
	$25,000	$55,000	$25,000	$55,000

Each project requires an investment of $30,000 with no salvage value expected. The committee has selected a rate of 20% for purposes of the discounted cash flow analysis.

Instructions: (1) Compute:

(a) The average rate of return for each project, giving effect to depreciation on the amount of the investment.

(b) The excess or deficiency of present value over original cost as determined by the discounted cash flow method for each project. Use the present value table on page 638.

(2) Prepare a brief report for the budget committee advising it on the relative merits of the two projects.

26-4A. Stanton Company expects to maintain the same inventories at the end of 1966 as at the beginning of the year. The total of all production costs for the year is therefore assumed to be equal to the cost of goods sold. With this in mind, the various department heads were asked to submit estimates of the expenses for their departments during 1966. A summary report of these estimates is presented below.

	Estimated Fixed Expense	Estimated Variable Expense (per unit sold)
Production costs:		
Direct materials	$ 0	$1.20
Direct labor	0	.90
Factory overhead	140,000	.60
Selling expenses:		
Sales salaries and commissions	50,500	.12
Advertising	45,150	0
Travel	15,250	0
Miscellaneous selling expenses	10,100	.20
General expenses:		
Office and officers' salaries	79,800	.05
Supplies	4,200	.03
Miscellaneous general expenses	15,000	.10
	$360,000	$3.20

It is expected that 80,000 units will be sold at a selling price of $8 a unit. Capacity output is 100,000 units.

Instructions: (1) Determine the break-even point in (a) dollars of sales, (b) units, and (c) terms of capacity.

(2) Prepare an estimated income statement for 1966.

(3) Construct a break-even chart, indicating the break-even point in dollars of sales.

(4) What is the expected margin of safety (MS)?

(5) What is the expected profit-volume (PV) ratio?

26-6A. Bolger Company operated at full capacity during 1965. Its income statement for 1965 is as follows:

Sales		$800,000
Cost of goods sold		525,000
Gross profit		$275,000
Operating expenses:		
Selling expenses	$100,000	
General expenses	50,000	
Total operating expenses		$150,000
Net operating income		$125,000

An analysis of costs and expenses reveals the following division of costs and expenses between fixed and variable:

	Fixed	Variable
Cost of goods sold	40%	60%
Selling expenses	30%	70%
General expenses	70%	30%

The management of Bolger Company is considering a plant expansion program that will permit an increase of $200,000 in yearly sales. The expansion will increase fixed costs and expenses by $60,000 but will not affect the relationship between sales and variable costs and expenses.

Instructions: (1) Determine for present capacity (a) the total fixed costs and expenses and (b) the total variable costs and expenses.

(2) Determine the percentage of total variable costs and expenses to sales.

(3) Compute the break-even point under present conditions.

(4) Compute the break-even point under the proposed program.

(5) Determine the amount of sales that would be necessary under the proposed program to realize the $125,000 of net operating income that was earned in 1965.

(6) Determine the maximum net operating income possible with the expanded plant.

(7) If the proposal is accepted and sales remain at the 1965 level, what will the net operating income be for 1966?

(8) Based upon the data given, would you recommend accepting the proposal? Explain.

Chapter 27

27-1A. The comparative balance sheet of the Sisley Corporation at September 30, 1966 and 1965, in condensed form is as follows:

	September 30	
Assets	1966	1965
Cash	$ 27,350	$ 36,250
Accounts receivable (net)	50,530	44,600
Merchandise inventory	125,500	108,200
Prepaid expenses	3,310	3,170
Plant assets	197,000	163,000
Accumulated depreciation — plant assets	(48,000)	(86,000)
	$355,690	$269,220

Liabilities and stockholders' equity		
Accounts payable	$ 38,650	$ 46,900
Mortgage note payable (due 1974)	45,000	—
Common stock, $25 par	200,000	175,000
Premium on common stock	11,000	10,000
Retained earnings	61,040	37,320
	$355,690	$269,220

Additional data obtained from the income statement and from an examination of the noncurrent asset, noncurrent liability, and stockholders' equity accounts in the ledger are as follows:

(a) Net income for the year, $32,470.
(b) Depreciation expense for the year, $12,000.
(c) Cash dividends declared during the year, $8,750.
(d) During the year 1,000 shares of common stock were issued for cash at $26.
(e) Equipment was purchased during the year at a cost of $84,000, and a fully depreciated building costing $50,000 was razed, no salvage being realized.

Instructions: (1) On the basis of the comparative balance sheet and the other information, assemble in memorandum form the data needed to prepare a funds statement for the year ended September 30, 1966.

(2) Prepare a statement of source and application of funds, including a schedule of changes in working capital.

27-2A. Paxton Corporation purchased 90% of the outstanding stock of Sarver Company for $450,000. Balance sheet data for the two corporations immediately after the transaction, which occurred on April 30 of the current year, are presented below. The interest receivable reported on Sarver Co. balance sheet is the accrual on the bond investment.

Assets	Paxton Corp.	Sarver Co.
Cash and marketable securities	$ 113,500	$ 83,000
Accounts receivable	92,550	67,300
Allowance for doubtful accounts	(1,800)	(1,100)
Interest receivable	—	1,500
Inventories	465,300	147,400
Investment in Sarver Company stock, 45,000 shares	450,000	—
Investment in Paxton Corporation bonds, face value	—	75,000
Equipment	948,700	308,900
Accumulated depreciation	(197,650)	(98,250)
	$1,870,600	$583,750

Liabilities and stockholders' equity		
Accounts payable	$ 153,100	$ 87,250
Income tax payable	88,700	36,500
Interest payable	8,000	—
Bonds payable (due in 1975)	400,000	—
Common stock, $10 par	850,000	—
Common stock, $5 par	—	250,000
Retained earnings	370,800	210,000
	$1,870,600	$583,750

Instructions: (1) Prepare in report form a detailed consolidated balance sheet as of April 30 of the current year.

(2) Assuming that Sarver Co. earns net income of $90,000 and pays dividends of $25,000 during the ensuing year and that Paxton Corporation records its share of the earnings and dividends, determine the following as of the end of the year:

(a) The amount at which the investment in Sarver Co. will appear on Paxton Corporation's balance sheet.
(b) The amount of the difference between the cost and the book value of the subsidiary interest owned by the parent corporation.
(c) The amount of the minority interest.

Chapter 28

28-1A. Data pertaining to the current position of C. H. Dixon and Company is presented below.

Cash	$140,000
Marketable securities	50,000
Accounts and notes receivable (net)	170,000
Merchandise inventory	183,000
Prepaid expenses	9,000
Accounts payable	155,000
Notes payable (short term)	60,000
Accrued liabilities	25,000

Instructions: (1) Compute (a) working capital, (b) current ratio, and (c) acid-test ratio.

(2) Consider each of the following transactions separately and assume that only that transaction affects the data given above.

(a) Paid notes payable, $60,000.
(b) Paid accounts payable, $75,000.
(c) Purchased merchandise on account, $100,000.
(d) Received cash on account, $80,000.
(e) Declared a cash dividend, $20,000.
(f) Declared a common stock dividend on common stock, $10,000.
(g) Borrowed $100,000 from bank on a long-term note.
(h) Issued additional shares of stock for cash, $70,000.
(i) Paid cash for store supplies, $1,000.
(j) Sold marketable securities, $25,000.

State the effect of each transaction (increase, decrease, or no effect) on working capital, current ratio, and acid-test ratio. Use the following column headings for recording your answers:

	Effect on		
Item	Working Capital	Current Ratio	Acid-Test Ratio

28-2A. Presented below for the current calendar year are revenue and expense data for Portland Chemical Company and for the chemical industry. The Portland Chemical Company data are expressed in dollars, while the chemical industry averages are expressed in percentages or a common size.

	Portland Chemical Company	Chemical Industry Average
Sales	$4,585,500	102.0%
Sales returns and allowances	85,500	2.0%
Cost of merchandise sold	3,105,000	67.5%
Selling expenses	458,500	12.2%
General expenses	256,600	6.8%
Other income	40,000	1.0%
Other expense	40,900	.8%
Income tax	319,400	6.2%

Instructions: (1) Prepare a common-size income statement comparing the results of operations for Portland Chemical Company with the industry average.

(2) As far as the data permit, comment on significant relationships revealed by the comparisons.

Index

I

J

K

L

M

N

O

P

Q

R

S

Stanley Szkoda